PARTNERSHIP TAXATION

OBJECTIVE

ROBERT R. WOOTTON
Professor of Practice
Northwestern Pritzker School of Law

Exam Pro®

WEST
ACADEMIC
PUBLISHING

The publisher is not engaged in rendering legal or other professional advice, and this publication is not a substitute for the advice of an attorney. If you require legal or other expert advice, you should seek the services of a competent attorney or other professional.

Exam Pro Series is a trademark registered in the U.S. Patent and Trademark Office.

© 2016 LEG, Inc. d/b/a West Academic
    444 Cedar Street, Suite 700
    St. Paul, MN 55101
    1-877-888-1330

West, West Academic Publishing, and West Academic are trademarks of West Publishing Corporation, used under license.

Printed in the United States of America

ISBN: 978-1-63459-494-3

To Philip,
who gave me a chance

About This Book

The world doesn't need another textbook on partnership taxation. The current offerings range from two towering treatises to a Nutshell written by a leading expert in the field. In between, there are many excellent volumes focused on the needs of students to learn and practitioners to, well, practice. So why did I write another one? Last semester, I finished teaching my twenty-fifth course on partnership taxation. This book isn't a celebration of that event, but it is a reflection on it. Students in every one of those courses have asked me where they can find a book that contains problems like the ones we do in class, with answers so they can see if they're getting it right. I've always answered that there is no such book and I've always wondered why not. The problem method is used in most partnership tax courses to teach the subject and in most partnership tax exams to test students' mastery of the material. A book of problems with complete answers would seem to be not only a perfect supplement to the course material during the semester, but an ideal way for students to prepare for the final exam. So here it is. In this book, there are 366 questions (it's a leap year). They are mainly multiple-choice, with full explanations of the correct (and incorrect) answers.

The book begins with an extensive "reading period," which breaks down partnership tax into 56 topics, arranged into 10 chapters. You can read it straight through if you want to, but you'll probably jump around, either to review the material that you just covered in class or to bone up for an exam. Clear, explanatory titles and extensive cross-references should help you find your way. Unless you are already confident in your understanding of partnership accounting, I recommend that you spend some time with the material at the beginning of Chapter 2, which introduces the simple accounting concepts that underlie all of partnership tax. Mastering these concepts will enhance your understanding—enjoyment, even—of the material in your partnership tax course. It will also improve your grade.

Each topic begins with an introductory essay, which may be a couple paragraphs or several pages in length. I wrote these essays mainly to introduce the study problems that follow and to make it easier for you to tackle them. You will not be able to answer all of the study problems based on the essays alone, but they should get you going in the right direction. Also, in my experience, as a student and as a teacher, it sometimes helps just to hear a difficult topic explained in different words. The words in these essays are drawn from lectures that students have found helpful in the past.

It is unlikely that you will cover all of the topics in this book in your partnership tax course. That's okay—just skip what you don't need. In each chapter, the topics are arranged in order of increasing difficulty. The practice questions in each topic are similarly arranged. Every practice question has a complete answer in the back of the book.

The "final exam" portion of the book includes nine sample exams of 10 questions each. Most of the questions come from exams that I have given in my basic or advanced partnership tax courses at Northwestern Pritzker School of Law. As with the study topics, the exams are arranged roughly in order of increasing difficulty. Complete answers are in the back.

Although the cover proclaims that this is a book on "partnership taxation," its sole focus is US federal income taxation in the domestic context. It mentions other US federal taxes—estate, gift and excise—only in passing and ignores completely the state and local tax consequences of operating a business as a partnership or limited liability company. It does not cover the procedural issues that arise in partnership audits. There is also little attention paid to the application of US federal income tax principles to international partnerships, although this is a subject becoming more important by the day. I console myself with the thought that most law school courses on partnership tax are similarly limited in scope.

I want to thank Larry Zelenak, Bill Golden and Chris Worek for their help in making this book come true. The remaining errors aren't their fault. When you catch one, or if you think of another way to improve this book, please let me know.

ROBERT R. WOOTTON
Chicago
May 2016
r-wootton@law.northwestern.edu

Table of Contents

PART 2. FINAL EXAMS

PARTNERSHIP TAXATION

OBJECTIVE

PART 1
READING PERIOD

CHAPTER 1
ENTITY STATUS

1.1   IS THERE AN ENTITY?

This is the first question to ask in any analysis under the "check the box" regulations. Treas. Reg. §§ 301.7701–1, –2 and –3. An affirmative answer is often assumed so that we can get on to more "interesting" questions. Sometimes, however, this question can be altogether too interesting on its own, and the existence or nonexistence of an entity can make a significant difference in the taxation of the players. Hard cases must be decided based on all the facts and circumstances. As you study the Questions below, ask yourself whether the parties are (1) co-owners of property, (2) engaged in a business, (3) for profit—the three indicia of the existence of an entity. In recent times, the third of these has risen to prominence in some tax-shelter cases, which have stressed that an entity cannot exist unless the parties in good faith and acting with a business purpose intended to join together in the present conduct of an enterprise—the so-called *"Culbertson* test." *Commissioner v. Culbertson*, 337 U.S. 733 (1949).

1.1.1   For the past two years, Ma and Pa Winkelvoss and their five adult children have been buying state lottery tickets, three each week for a dollar apiece. They do not keep close track of who pays for the tickets, but, over time, each of the seven of them have bought about the same number. Ma always keeps the family tickets in a glass jar in the kitchen. They talk sometimes about what each of them will do with the money if their numbers come up. One day, they do: one of their tickets pays $7 million. After consulting with a lawyer and tax accountant, the Winkelvoss family writes a simple partnership agreement, memorializing that the tickets purchased were for the benefit of the family rather than the individual who purchased each particular ticket and declaring that winnings are to be divided 25% to each of Ma and Pa and 10% to each of the kids. The Winkelvoss Family Partnership claims its prize from the state prior to the end of the year of the drawing. The IRS can prove that Ma bought the winning ticket and seeks to tax her alone on the jackpot. Does the IRS succeed?

a)   The IRS succeeds: a partnership cannot exist without a written agreement. This agreement was written after the winning ticket was drawn and is ineffective to shift the income away from Ma.

b)   The IRS succeeds: the purported partnership had no business purpose and carried on no trade, business, financial operation or venture.

c) The IRS loses: the partnership was a simple investment partnership and the written agreement memorialized an earlier oral agreement.

d) The IRS succeeds, but ultimately loses: the oral agreement must be construed to require equal sharing of the winnings among the family members and, to the extent that the written agreement is to the contrary, it is null and void. Each of the seven family members is taxed on $1 million of winnings.

1.1.2   Lyle is a real estate developer. He enters into an agreement with a local real estate investor, ACRE, Inc., pursuant to which Lyle will locate a suitable property for ACRE to develop and will manage the development for a payment equal to a share of the profits from the development, not to be less than 20%. The agreement is styled as a "Joint Venture Agreement," but Lyle's payment is referred to as "salary" and the joint venture does not maintain books of account, bank accounts or an office separate from ACRE. ACRE titles the property and enters into all necessary contracts in its own name. ACRE sells the property for a handsome profit and pays 20% of the profit to Lyle. How should Lyle treat this payment for federal tax purposes?

a) Lyle is an employee or independent contractor of ACRE, so he should report the payment as ordinary compensation income.

b) The arrangement between Lyle and ACRE is a partnership, in which Lyle holds a profits interest that was not taxable on receipt. If the partnership recognizes capital gain on the sale, Lyle's 20% profit share should retain that character in his hands.

c) The arrangement between Lyle and ACRE is a joint venture, not a partnership, because Lyle made no capital contribution. As a joint venturer, Lyle must recognize ordinary income on his profit share.

d) The arrangement between Lyle and ACRE is a partnership, in which Lyle holds a capital interest. Lyle recognized ordinary income on receipt of his capital interest, which was taxable as ordinary income in an amount equal to its value at that time. If the partnership recognizes capital gain on the sale, Lyle's 20% profit share should retain that character in his hands.

1.1.3   Debra owns an event-planning service that she operates as a sole proprietor out of a rented storefront property. She wishes to exit the business in order to become a full-time agent for professional athletes. Her view of the value of the business, however, exceeds any of the cash offers she has received. Reluctantly, she strikes a deal with AM Enterprises, Inc. pursuant to which it will take control of the business for a cash payment of $400,000 and an agreement to pay Debra 20% of net profits of the business for five years. AM will be responsible for the day-to-day operation of the business, but during Debra's payout period AM cannot discontinue any significant portion of the business or make any capital expenditure in excess of $50,000 without Debra's written consent. During the payout period Debra will remain as a consultant to the business in order to make nonbinding recommendations regarding any aspect of AM's strategy or operations. What is the best characterization of this arrangement for federal tax purposes?

a) Debra and AM are partners in the event-planning business, with percentage interests of 20% and 80%, respectively. Debra reports the $400,000 cash payment as proceeds of a "disguised sale" of the event-planning business to the partnership and her share of profits as ordinary income.

b) Debra is an independent contractor providing services to AM's event-planning business. Debra reports the $400,000 cash payment as proceeds of sale to AM and her share of profits as ordinary income.

c) Debra has sold her event-planning business to AM for current and deferred payments, all of which (other than interest imputed on deferred payments) she should report as proceeds of sale.

d) For the next five years, Debra should be treated as the continuing owner of the event-planning business, but is entitled to deduct from its taxable profits any amounts that she pays to AM under the agreement.

1.1.4   Guy Rudier, a successful dealer in fine art, has an opportunity to purchase an original Rodin bronze casting. This would make a magnificent long-term investment, Guy believes, but he also would not turn down the opportunity to sell the casting to the right buyer. Prior to moving forward with the purchase, he contacts Rupert Bagwell, a lawyer in town, about the possibility of financing the purchase jointly. Guy proposes a simple, written joint venture agreement for the purchase, holding and possible resale of this single piece. Although Guy will handle all of the negotiations surrounding the purchase and, should it occur, the sale of the sculpture, he will do so in the name of the venture. Guy will supply 99% of the capital and will be allocated 99% of all of the venture's income, gain and loss. Rupert agrees enthusiastically, delighted to own even a small share of a historically significant work of art. The Rupert Rudier Venture (as it says on the venture's letterhead, mailbox and bank account) closes the purchase and, as fate would have it, resells the sculpture 18 months later to an out-of-town collector who learned of its existence in a trade magazine. Rupert is crestfallen—his share of the profit is small and his brush with fame all too short. Guy is as surprised as Rupert that the sculpture sold so quickly, because the venture never advertised it for sale or even showed it in public. But Guy is more pleased than Rupert with his share of the profit, which is handsome. How should Guy's profit from the venture be taxed?

a) Long-term capital gain. The Rupert Rudier Venture is a partnership for tax purposes and held the Rodin sculpture as a capital asset.

b) Ordinary income. The Rupert Rudier Venture is a partnership for tax purposes and held the Rodin sculpture as inventory.

c) Ordinary income. The Rupert Rudier Venture is a sham, which must be ignored for tax purposes. Guy should be treated as entering into this transaction for his own account as an art dealer.

d) Ordinary income. Although the Rupert Rudier Venture is not a sham, it cannot be respected as an entity for tax purposes. The parties did not in good faith and acting with a business purpose intend to join together in the present conduct of an enterprise. Guy's profit share must therefore be taxed as it would be had he entered into the purchase and sale as an individual.

1.2   IS THE ENTITY AN ELIGIBLE BUSINESS ENTITY?

Once you have established the existence of an entity for federal income tax purposes, you have done most of the hard work required to determine whether its tax treatment can be elected by "checking the box." But you are not quite finished. Only "qualified entities" may elect their tax classification. This limitation is intended to exclude entities whose tax status is provided for explicitly elsewhere, like trusts. In order to be a qualified entity, an entity must first be a "business entity." So, the triage consists of three steps: (1) entity? (2) business entity? (3) qualified entity? The first of these steps is nuanced and judgmental; the latter two steps are more mechanical. Test your understanding of the latter two steps with these Questions.

———————

1.2.1   Which of the following arrangements is a "business entity" within the meaning of Treas. Reg. § 301.7701–2(a)? Mark all that apply.

a)   Real estate investment trust

b)   Delaware business corporation

c)   Pennsylvania limited liability company

d)   Publicly traded partnership

1.2.2   Which of the following arrangements is an "eligible entity" within the meaning of Treas. Reg. § 301.7701–3(a)? Mark all that apply.

a)   Real estate investment trust

b)   Delaware business corporation

c)   Pennsylvania limited liability company

d)   Publicly traded partnership

1.2.3   Which of the following arrangements is an "eligible entity" within the meaning of Treas. Reg. § 301.7701–3(a)? Mark all that apply.

a)   French Societe Anonyme

b)   Regulated investment company (RIC)

c)   Single-member limited liability company

d) Insurance company

1.2.4 Which of the following arrangements is an "eligible entity" within the meaning of Treas. Reg. § 301.7701–3(a)? Mark all that apply.

a) Nova Scotia Unlimited Liability Company

b) Delaware business trust

c) Austrian GmbH

d) Federally chartered bank (*i.e.,* national bank)

1.2.5 **Before you answer this Question, read Rev. Rul. 92–105, 1992–2 C.B. 204.** Which of the following arrangements is an "eligible entity" within the meaning of Treas. Reg. § 301.7701–3(a)? Mark all that apply.

a) Delaware statutory trust established to hold title to property, with no power to vary its investment

b) New York limited liability partnership

c) Korean Chusik Hoesa

d) Illinois land trust, in which the beneficiary has the exclusive right to manage the property and to receive the earnings and proceeds therefrom

1.3 THE CTB ELECTION AND THE DEFAULT RULES

Under the "check the box" regulations, an eligible entity with more than one owner can elect to be treated as a partnership or as a corporation for federal income tax purposes. An eligible entity with only one owner can elect to be disregarded or to be treated as a corporation. It is crucial for you to know the default rules, because they control the characterization of an eligible entity that fails or chooses not to file an election. In such circumstances, a domestic (US) entity is treated as a partnership if it has more than one owner and as a disregarded entity if it has a single owner. Treas. Reg. § 301.7701–3(b)(1). A foreign (non-US) entity with more than one owner is treated as a corporation if the governing law provides limited liability to all of its owners. It is treated as a partnership if any owner does not have limited liability under the governing law. A foreign entity with a sole owner is treated as a corporation if the governing law provides limited liability to its owner and as a disregarded entity if it does not. Treas. Reg. § 301.7701–3(b)(2). These default classifications can all be changed by affirmative elections. The classification of an entity can affect not only its own federal income tax treatment, but also the classification and tax treatment of other entities, as illustrated in the following Questions.

1.3.1 Topco, Inc., a Delaware business corporation traded on the New York Stock Exchange, owns all of the outstanding stock of Subco, Ltd, a private company formed under the laws of the United Kingdom. UK law provides limited liability to all of Subco's shareholders. Subco, in turn, owns 75% of the shares of Opco BV, a Dutch private company. Topco owns the remaining 25% of the shares of Opco. Under Dutch law, all of Opco's shareholders have limited liability. Assuming that no elections are made regarding the tax status of any of these entities, what is Opco for federal income tax purposes?

    a)   A corporation

    b)   A partnership

    c)   A branch of Topco

    d)   A branch of Subco

1.3.2   Same facts as Question 1.3.1, except that the charter of Opco provides, as allowed by Dutch law, that Subco but not Topco is liable for the debts of Opco. What is the classification of Opco for federal income tax purposes, assuming no contrary election?

    a)   A corporation

    b)   A partnership

    c)   A branch of Topco

    d)   A branch of Subco

1.3.3   Same facts as Question 1.3.1, except that Subco and Opco are both Delaware limited liability companies. What is the default classification of Opco for federal income tax purposes?

    a)   A corporation

    b)   A partnership

    c)   A branch of Topco

    d)   A branch of Subco

1.3.4   X is a limited liability company owned entirely by individual A. If X files no contrary election, X will not be liable for which of the following? (Mark all that apply.)

    a)   Federal income tax

    b)   Federal employment tax

    c)   Federal excise tax

    d)   All of the above

1.3.5   Individual A forms LLC, a domestic limited liability company, which timely elects to be treated as a corporation for federal income tax purposes as of the date of its formation. Four years later, when A is still LLC's sole owner, LLC files an election to be treated in accordance with its default classification as a disregarded entity. What is the effect of this election?

    a)   No effect, because LLC was not entitled to elect to be treated as other than a disregarded entity on formation.

b) No effect, because LLC is not entitled to change its initial election for a period of 60 months.

c) X becomes a disregarded entity as of the date specified in the new election; neither LLC nor A recognizes any gain or loss.

d) X becomes a disregarded entity as of the date specified in the new election; both LLC and A recognize any gain or loss that exists as of the date of this change in classification.

1.4 ELECTING OUT OF PARTNERSHIP STATUS

Since 1954, section 761(a) has permitted certain organizations to elect out of the application of Subchapter K—essentially, to declare that, while they could be partnerships for federal income tax purposes, they desire to be taxed as co-ownerships instead. While this election has its place—it can, for example, permit co-owners to dispose of their individual interests in like-kind exchanges under section 1031, which would not be permitted if they were partners—it suggests a discomfort with partnership taxation that seems a little old-fashioned. Generally speaking, the tax rules that apply to partnerships are more flexible and seldom less favorable than those that apply to co-ownerships. Indeed, in some common cases the availability of Subchapter K is all that stands between the parties and a tax nightmare.

1.4.1 Bryce Hardware Company is an Illinois general partnership formed by three unrelated individuals to operate a retail hardware store. Its default classification is partnership and it has not filed any election to the contrary. Bryce, however, files an election with its first federal income tax return to be excluded from the application of all of Subchapter K of the Internal Revenue Code. Is this election effective?

a) No, because the owners cannot compute their income without the use of inventories maintained by the entity.

b) No, because the entity is engaged in the active conduct of a business.

c) No, because the owners have not reserved the right to take or dispose of their respective shares of the entity's assets.

d) No, for all of the above reasons.

1.4.2 The Goethe Street Club is a bridge club whose members occasionally pool some extra money in order to purchase, in the name of the club, a favored stock. Everyone makes his or her own decisions about each purchase, and the club maintains good records regarding each member's share of each security owned, which any member may withdraw on reasonable notice to the club secretary. On the advice of a tax accountant, the club files an election in proper form to be excluded from the application of all of Subchapter K of the Internal Revenue Code. What is the effect of this election?

a)   The election is disregarded, because the club is not an entity for federal income tax purposes and is thus not entitled to file the election.

b)   The election is effective, but probably unnecessary.

c)   The election is not effective, because the members of the club determine their income by reference to (*i.e.*, as shares of) the income of the club.

d)   The election is not effective, because even the club's sporadic investment activities constitute an active business, which disqualifies the election.

1.4.3   K Street Investment Club is an "investing partnership" within the meaning of Treas. Reg. § 1.761–2 that has validly elected to be excluded from all of Subchapter K. Although mostly for fun, K Street has enjoyed considerable success with its investments, most of which are substantially appreciated. Ron Dahl wants to join the club and offers to contribute some appreciated stock that he owns in exchange for a 10% interest. If Ron goes ahead with this transaction:

a)   The transaction will be tax-free to Ron and to the existing members of the club.

b)   The admission of Ron to the club will cause it to be treated as a partnership with a required December 31 tax year.

c)   Ron and the existing members will all recognize gain.

d)   The admission of Ron to the club will automatically revoke its election and cause it to be treated as an association taxable as a corporation.

CHAPTER 2
TRANSFERS OF MONEY OR PROPERTY TO A PARTNERSHIP

2.1 THE GENERAL RULE OF NONRECOGNITION

When a partnership is formed, each partner in effect exchanges a portion of the property she contributes to the partnership for a portion of each of the properties contributed by others. Except in the unusual case where every partner contributes identical assets, this transaction changes the economic position of the partners by diversifying their holdings. So, for example, when Betty contributes Blackacre and Whitney contributes Whiteacre to an equal partnership, each exchanges ownership of half of the contributed property for half of the other property. Such an exchange is plainly a realization event for federal income tax purposes. Is gain or loss recognized?

Not usually. Instead of viewing this transaction as an exchange of partial interests in the properties (an aggregate approach), the tax law views the partnership as an entity to which Betty and Whitney contribute their properties. This change in perspective does not guarantee nonrecognition—each partner's exchange of contributed property for a partnership interest is a realization event on which gain or loss could be recognized. Under section 721(a), however, the exchange of property for a partnership interest is generally tax-deferred. This result is self-executing—there is no requirement that taxpayers affirmatively claim the benefit of section 721(a). Thus, if a partnership exists, the partners are not taxed on its formation—even if they are blissfully unaware that they have even formed a partnership.

So where in this genial world do problems lurk? In co-ownerships that are not partnerships and partnerships that do not have the protection of section 721(a). There are three situations to watch out for:

✓ *Not an entity*. Section 721(a) only applies to contributions to a partnership. If the Blackacre/Whiteacre co-ownership described above did not constitute an entity for tax purposes, Betty and Whitney would not have the benefit of section 721(a).

✓ *Election out*. If Betty and Whitney's business arrangement did constitute an entity, and they elected out of the application of Subchapter K under section 761(a), they would lose (perhaps unwittingly) the shelter of section 721(a).

✓   *Section 721(b) investment partnership.* If the partnership were an "investment partnership" within the meaning of section 721(b), the protection of section 721(a) would be denied.

2.1.1   **If you have not done so already, read section 721(b), section 351(e)(1) and the Treasury regulations thereunder before answering this and the following Questions.** Alice, Bernice and Chloe form an investment partnership by contributing the following items of property:

	Contribution	Value	Tax Basis
Alice	1,000 shares of closely held Alice Corp.	$60,000	$ 1,000
Bernice	100 shares of Google common stock	$60,000	$51,000
Chloe	2,000 shares of Wells Fargo common stock	$60,000	$66,000

What gain or loss, if any, does each of them recognize on this transaction?

a)   Alice, $0; Bernice, $0; Chloe, $0

b)   Alice, $59,000 gain; Bernice, $9,000 gain; Chloe, $6,000 loss

c)   Alice, $59,000 gain; Bernice, $9,000 gain; Chloe, $0

d)   Cannot tell based on the facts given.

2.1.2   Arthur, Barry and Chad form an investment partnership by contributing the following items of property:

	Contribution	Value	Tax Basis
Arthur	10 acres of farmland	$60,000	$ 1,000
Barry	100 shares of Google common stock	$60,000	$51,000
Chad	2,000 shares of Wells Fargo common stock	$60,000	$66,000

What gain or loss, if any, does each of them recognize on this transaction?

a)   Arthur, $0; Barry, $0; Chad, $0

b)   Arthur, $59,000 gain; Barry, $9,000 gain; Chad, $6,000 loss

c)   Arthur, $59,000 gain; Barry, $9,000 gain; Chad, $0

d)   Cannot tell based on the facts given.

2.1.3   Al, Ben and Charlie form an investment partnership by contributing the following items of property:

	Contribution	Value	Tax Basis
Al	Cash	$60,000	N/A
Ben	100 shares of Google common stock	$60,000	$51,000
Charlie	2,000 shares of Wells Fargo common stock	$60,000	$66,000

What gain or loss, if any, does each of them recognize on this transaction?

a)   Al, $0; Ben, $0; Charlie, $0

b)   Al, $0; Ben, $9,000 gain; Charlie, $6,000 loss

c)   Al, $0; Ben, $9,000 gain; Charlie, $0

d)   Cannot tell based on the facts given.

2.2   INSIDE AND OUTSIDE BASIS AND HOLDING PERIODS

Basis is an important concept throughout the tax law, never more so than in partnership tax. The mechanisms that set and adjust a partner's basis in her partnership interest ("outside basis") and a partnership's basis in its assets ("inside basis") are fundamental to achieving the goal of Subchapter K to tax all income earned through a partnership once and only once. During this Reading Period, we will approach this grand edifice one small step at a time. This Topic 2.2 reviews the fundamental rules for basis and holding periods as a prelude to the study of partnership balance sheets in the following three Topics. Later on, Chapter 5 revisits this subject in a more thorough manner, with an eye toward understanding why the rules are what they are. Finally, Topics 9.1 and 9.2 conclude our study of basis in the context of distributions.

The concepts of "inside" and "outside" basis would be unnecessary if the partnership were not treated as an entity for tax purposes. In a pure "aggregate" model, in which each co-owner is considered to own her proportionate share of the property directly and to earn directly her share of the income derived from the co-owned property, there would be only one basis, that being the basis of the owner in her share of the property. Once the notion of an entity is introduced, however, the partner is no longer considered to be the direct owner of the property, but instead the owner of an interest in an entity. The entity, in turn, owns the property. Logically, we must determine the basis of each owner in the thing owned.

Inside basis and holding periods

Under section 723, the basis of a partnership in contributed property is the basis of such property in the hands of the contributor at the time of the contribution, if the fair market value of such property is at least equal to its basis. This is termed a "transferred basis" by section 7701(a)(43) and is more often referred to as a "carryover basis."

At least to the extent that the contributed property is a capital asset or section 1231 property in the hands of the partnership, it will care about the holding period of the property. Under section 1223(2), because the partnership's basis in the contributed property is determined "in whole or in part" by reference to that of the contributing partner, the partnership is entitled to include ("tack") the contributor's holding period in determining the period for which it has held contributed property. This is so regardless of whether such property was a capital asset or section 1231 property in the contributor's hands.

There are two special rules that can complicate this simple picture. First, if the contributed property is worth less than its adjusted basis in the contributor's hands (so-called "built-in loss property"), the partnership's basis (at least as to all noncontributing partners) is capped at fair market value under section 704(c)(1)(C). This issue is discussed in more detail in Topic 6.6. Second, the partnership's basis in its property is increased by any gain recognized by the contributor under the investment partnership rules of section 721(b). In the latter case, the partnership can tack the contributor's holding period for the contributed property, because its basis is determined "in part" by the contributor's basis. In the former case, it presumably cannot (at least as to all noncontributing partners). *See* Rev. Rul. 70–6, 1970–1 C.B. 172.

Outside basis and holding periods

Under section 722, the basis of an interest in a partnership acquired by a contribution of property, including money, includes the amount of money and contributor's basis in such property at the time of contribution. Section 7701(a)(44) calls this an "exchanged basis." Section 704(c)(1)(C) does not interfere with the operation of this rule. Section 721(b) does. The partner's outside basis is increased by any gain she recognizes under section 721(b), mirroring the increase in inside basis.

Section 741 provides that the gain or loss recognized on the sale of a partnership interest is capital gain or loss, with an exception (discussed in Topic 6.3) for partnerships that hold so-called "section 751 assets." Therefore, a partner will almost always care about her holding period for the partnership interest. Under section 1223(1), a contributing partner is entitled to determine the holding period for her partnership interest by including her holding period for the contributed property, so long as she held such property as a capital asset or as section 1231 property.

Section 752 also affects a partner's outside basis, by including therein the partner's share of the partnership's liabilities. More particularly, section

752(a) treats an increase in a partner's share of partnership liabilities as a contribution of money to the partnership, thereby increasing the partner's outside basis. Section 752(b) treats a decrease in a partner's share of partnership liabilities as a distribution of money to the partner, thereby decreasing the partner's outside basis. These are extraordinarily important provisions, both practically and from a theoretical perspective. They are covered in more detail in Topics 2.4, 2.5, 5.3 and 5.4.

2.2.1   Aubrey contributes land worth $100,000 and $50,000 in cash to the Strong Will Manufacturing Company in exchange for a 10% interest as a general partner and a 25% interest as a limited partner. She has held the land as a capital asset for over a year and it has an adjusted basis in her hands of $75,000. Immediately following this contribution, her general partnership interest is worth $50,000 and her limited partnership interest is worth $100,000. For federal income tax purposes, what does Aubrey own?

  a)   A partnership interest with a single basis of $125,000. Her holding period for 2/3 of this interest is long-term and her holding period for 1/3 of this interest is short-term

  b)   Two partnership interests, one with a basis of $75,000 and a long-term holding period and one with a basis of $50,000 and a short-term holding period

  c)   A partnership interest with a single basis of $125,000. Her holding period for 3/5 of this interest is long-term and her holding period for 2/5 of this interest is short-term

  d)   Two partnership interests, one with a basis of $100,000 and a long-term holding period and one with a basis of $50,000 and a short-term holding period

2.2.2   In order to promote his business, Grayson, an artist, agrees to go into partnership with Grace, a gallery owner. The assets that Grayson will contribute to the new partnership on January 2, 2017 are as follows:

Asset	Acquired (or Created)	Adjusted Basis	Fair Market Value
Studio (purchased for $45,000)	May 30, 2002	$30,000	$ 45,000
Grayson's paintings	After Jan. 1, 2016	1,000	25,000
Grayson's paintings	Prior to 2016	1,500	35,000
Amounts due from sale of paintings during 2016	After Jan. 1, 2016	0	15,000
Artist's supplies	Prior to 2016	5,000	5,000
Total		$37,500	$125,000

As of the date of the partnership's formation, what is Grayson's holding period for his partnership interest?

a)   Long-term

b)   Short-term as to 32%; long-term as to 68%

c)   Short-term as to 20%; long-term as to 80%

d)   Short-term as to 64%; long-term as to 36%

2.3   ACCOUNTING FOR CONTRIBUTIONS OF MONEY OR PROPERTY ON PARTNERSHIP FORMATION

Okay, time for a pep talk. Many law students, like many other human beings, are not entirely comfortable with numbers. In much the same way that many mice are not entirely comfortable with cats. On the first day of partnership tax class, I tell my students that partnership tax law is numbers masquerading as words. They don't like to hear that, but it does prepare them for what is to come. The good news is that the alternative is much, much worse. The partnership tax law prior to 1954 was largely made by judges attempting to apply common-law principles of partnership law to ascertain tax consequences. The results of their well-intentioned efforts were inconsistent, economically irrational and tended to be based on essentially meaningless distinctions. It was a mess. The folks who remade the partnership tax law in the early 1950s were—you guessed it—accountants and lawyers with training in accounting. The result of their intervention was a system of taxation that largely, if not entirely, makes sense.

What does all this have to do with you? If you want to be any good at partnership tax, you must learn to construct and manipulate partnership balance sheets. Many Treasury regulations use balance sheets to lay out the facts and illustrate the solutions to partnership tax problems. The entire system for determining whether special allocations have "substantial economic effect" and therefore are respected for tax purposes is based on capital accounting. There are provisions in Subchapter K—section 734(b) comes to mind—that simply cannot be understood without an appreciation for the accounting concepts that lie at their core.

Relax—you don't have to learn very much and it's not very hard. There is no need to rush out and enroll in an accounting course (unless you want to). SEC rules on financial accounting will never come up. You will not learn how to compute the cost of goods sold. You will not even need to know how to prepare a profit and loss statement. Just simple balance sheets. Your reward will be an understanding of and facility with partnership tax that may surprise you.

Just as with our study of basis, we will take this one step at a time. The first task is to prepare an "opening" balance sheet, which reflects a partnership's assets, liabilities and capital at the moment of its creation. As you work through the Questions, keep in mind some basic principles:

✓ Assets = Liabilities + Capital. The total of a partnership's assets equals the total of its liabilities plus capital. If your opening balance sheet does not reflect this accounting identity, it is wrong. (Maddeningly, partnership distributions can sometimes disturb this result, but that's for another day.)

✓ Partnerships often keep two sets of books that are both relevant to tax reporting. These are generally referred to as the "book" accounts and the "tax" accounts.

✓ The book accounts reflect the partners' economic stakes in the partnership. The book accounts record the book values of the partnership's assets and the partners' book capital accounts. The book value of a contributed asset is its fair market value on the date of contribution. A partner's opening book capital account equals the amount of money and the fair market value of any property that she contributes to the partnership. Treas. Reg. § 1.704–1(b)(2)(iv) provides detailed rules for adjusting the book capital accounts.

✓ Do not make the mistake of thinking that the book accounts are determined by the rules of GAAP or financial accounting. If a partnership is subject to these rules, it will actually keep *three* sets of books.

✓ The tax accounts record the adjusted basis of each of the partnership's assets and the "tax capital" of each of the partners. Nowhere in the Treasury regulations is there a definition of tax capital or a guide to determining it. In a partnership with no liabilities, a partner's tax capital is her share of the inside basis of the partnership's properties. On formation, it is generally the amount of money and the adjusted basis of the property contributed by that partner. Contributions of built-in loss assets require special handling, as explored in Question 2.3.3.

✓ Tax capital is very similar but not identical to "previously taxed capital" as defined in Treas. Reg. § 1.743-1(d). This concept is discussed in Topic 6.5.

In the following Questions, and frequently in the balance sheets in the Reading Period and the Final Exams, a column is included to show the fair market values of the partnership's assets. These columns are for illustrative purposes only and are not part of the actual balance sheet of the partnership.

2.3.1   Addison and Benchley form a general partnership. Addison contributes $50,000 in cash and Benchley contributes land, purchased for $25,000, which is still worth exactly that amount. Complete the partnership's opening balance sheet.

Assets				Liabilities		
	(1) Tax	**(2)** Book	**(3)** FMV		**(4)** Tax	**(5)** Book
Cash	$	$	$50,000	[None]	$ 0	$ 0
Land			25,000			
				Capital		
				Addison		
				Benchley		
Total Assets	$	$	$75,000	Total Liabilities and Capital	$	$

2.3.2   Aaliyah, Blake and Carbury form a limited partnership to engage in a manufacturing business. Aaliyah, who will be the general partner, contributes a small plant, worth $220,000, on land that is worth $140,000. Aaliyah paid $300,000 for these assets two years ago, allocating $110,000 to the purchase of the land. She has not been entitled to depreciate the plant in the meantime. In exchange for interests as limited partners, Blake and Carbury contribute, respectively, cash of $120,000 and newly purchased manufacturing equipment with a value and basis of $60,000. Complete the partnership's opening balance sheet.

Assets				Liabilities		
	(1) Tax	**(2)** Book	**(3)** FMV		**(4)** Tax	**(5)** Book
Cash	$	$	$120,000	[None]	$ 0	$ 0
Equipment			60,000			
Plant			220,000	**Capital**		
Land			140,000	Aaliyah		
				Blake		
				Carbury		
Total Assets	$	$	$540,000	Total Liabilities and Capital	$	$

2.3.3   Aiden, Brooklyn and Caleb form an investment partnership. Aiden contributes $200,000 in cash; Brooklyn, land worth $200,000, purchased for $150,000; and Caleb, publicly traded stock worth $200,000, purchased for $250,000. Complete the partnership's opening balance sheet.

Assets				Liabilities	
(1) **Tax**	**(2)** **Book**	**(3)** **FMV**		**(4)** **Tax**	**(5)** **Book**
Cash $	$	$200,000	[None]	$ 0	$ 0
Land		200,000			
Stock		200,000	**Capital**		
			Aiden		
			Brooklyn		
			Caleb		
Total Assets $	$	$600,000	**Total Liabilities and Capital** $		$

2.4   ACCOUNTING FOR PARTNERSHIP LIABILITIES

The Treasury regulations provide detailed rules for the treatment of liabilities in determining the book capital accounts of partners. Treas. Reg. §§ 1.704–1(b)(2)(iv)(*b*) and (*c*). Students often find these rules confusing and try to learn them by rote or just ignore them altogether. The rudimentary principles of partnership accounting introduced in Topic 2.3 can help you do better than that.

The most basic rule is that partnership liabilities are not included in the partners' capital accounts (book or tax). Why is that? Think about the effect of a partnership liability on the balance sheet. Say, for example, a partnership borrows $1,000 and puts the money in its bank account. Assets of the partnership increase by $1,000 (the money in the bank). Liabilities also increase by $1,000 (reflecting the borrowed amount). If any portion of the liability also appeared in the capital accounts, the partnership's balance sheet would not balance—the accounting identity would be broken, because Assets ≠ Liabilities + Capital.

Continuing the example, assume that this partnership has two partners. When the partnership borrows $1,000, each partner's share of partnership liabilities may well increase by $500, under rules that we will study in Chapter 5. Section 752(a) tells us that such an increase is to be considered as a contribution of $500 of cash to the partnership. Ordinarily, you would think that this would increase each partner's capital account by $500. Don't fall for it. This rule of section 752(a) applies to outside basis, not to capital accounts. When the partnership puts the $1,000 of borrowed funds into the bank, its basis in its assets increases by $1,000. Section 752(a) ensures that the partners' aggregate outside basis also increases by $1,000.

A parallel analysis applies to the rule of section 752(b), which provides that a decrease in a partner's share of the partnership's liabilities is considered to be a distribution of cash from the partnership to the partner. Without these rules, inside basis would not equal outside basis. Later in the Reading Period, Chapter 5 makes the case that preserving the equality of aggregate inside basis and aggregate outside basis is critical to the proper operation of the partnership tax system.

There are two situations described in the Treasury regulations where liabilities do seem to enter into the determination of capital accounts. The first is when the partnership assumes an individual liability of a partner or, conversely, when a partner assumes a liability of the partnership. The Treasury regulations provide that for capital-account purposes the former situation is treated as a distribution of money (reducing the partner's capital account) and the latter is treated as a contribution of money (increasing the partner's capital account). The rationale for these rules again flows directly from the effect that these transactions have on the balance sheet. When the partnership assumes a partner's liability, it increases its liabilities without increasing its assets. In order to maintain the accounting identity, the partner's capital must go down. Conversely, when a partnership's liability is assumed by a partner, the partnership decreases its liabilities without any change in its assets, and capital must increase.

What is the effect of these assumptions of liability on outside basis? When a partnership assumes a $2,000 liability of one of its partners, there is no change in the inside basis of its assets, yet as we have seen the partner's capital is reduced by the amount of the liability assumed. All else being equal, this would cause aggregate outside basis to be less than aggregate inside basis by $2,000. Section 752(a) restores basis equality by providing that, for purposes of computing the partners' outside bases, they are collectively considered to have contributed $2,000 cash to the partnership, in accordance with their respective shares of the assumed liability.

In the case that a partner assumes a $2,000 partnership liability, there is again no change in the inside basis of the partnership's assets, but the assuming partner's capital increases by $2,000. Section 752(b) prevents an inequality from arising between inside and outside basis by providing that, for purposes of computing the partners' outside bases, they are collectively considered to have been distributed $2,000 cash from the partnership, in accordance with their respective shares of the partnership liability which now has been assumed.

Now, finally, you are in a position to uncover the dirty little secret lurking in sections 752(a) and 752(b). Each of these provisions describes two circumstances that increase or decrease a partner's outside basis. Only one of the two affects the capital accounts. This is absolutely mystifying if you do not understand balance sheets, but simple if you do.

Lastly, the Treasury regulations provide that a partner who contributes property that is encumbered by a liability must take the liability into account in determining her capital account—specifically, by netting it against the value of the contributed asset. This, too, is the only approach that would work from an accounting perspective. Upon such a contribution, the book value of the partnership's assets increases by the fair market value of the contributed property, while its liabilities increase by the amount of the liability assumed. The net increase, if any, must be reflected in the capital accounts. We will consider this transaction in more detail in Topic 2.5.

The following Questions change the presentation of the balance sheets from that used in Topic 2.3 to accommodate the addition of a column for outside basis. No values are provided for the partner's interests in the partnership. It is conventional to assume that the value of each partner's interest in the partnership equals that partner's share of the net value of the partnership's assets. Though easy, this assumption is dubious. For example, discounts in the value of a minority partnership interest for lack of control or marketability can cause the value of the interest to be significantly less than the value of its proportionate share of net assets—a proposition that lies at the heart of inter-generational wealth transfers accomplished via family partnerships.

2.4.1 The Strawberry Shamrock Landscape Company, organized as a limited liability company which is taxed as a partnership, has the following balance sheet, expanded to show the value of partnership assets:

Assets				
	Tax	**Book**	**FMV**	
Cash	$ 20,000	$ 20,000	$ 20,000	
Receivables	0	0	30,000	
Plant & Equipment	340,000	340,000	340,000	
Total Assets	$360,000	$360,000	$390,000	
Liabilities				
[None]	$0	$0	$0	
Capital				**Outside Basis**
Aaron	120,000	120,000		$120,000
Butch	120,000	120,000		120,000
Cassidy	120,000	120,000		120,000
Total Liabilities and Capital	$360,000	$360,000		$360,000

Anticipating the start of another successful planting season, the company borrows $150,000, with which it purchases new trucks from Wally's Chevy. How does this affect its balance sheet? How does it affect the partners' outside bases?

Assets			
	Tax	**Book**	**FMV**
Cash	$	$	$ 20,000
Receivables			30,000
Plant & Equipment			490,000
Total Assets	$	$	$ 540,000
Liabilities			
Bank Debt	$ 150,000	$ 150,000	$ 150,000

Capital				Outside Basis
Aaron				$
Butch				
Cassidy				
Total Liabilities and Capital	$	$		$

2.4.2   Across town, Wally's Chevy LLC, a limited liability company taxed as a partnership, is swimming in debt. To lighten its debt load, the company sells off a piece of land that it was holding to expand its used car lot. It recognizes no gain or loss on the land sale and uses the $360,000 proceeds to pay down its bank debt. Prior to these transactions, its balance sheet looked like this:

Assets			
	Tax	**Book**	**FMV**
Cash	$ 6,000	$ 6,000	$ 6,000
Receivables	150,000	150,000	150,000
Inventory	870,000	870,000	870,000
Showroom	290,000	290,000	290,000
Investment Land	360,000	360,000	360,000
Total Assets	$1,676,000	$1,676,000	$1,676,000
Liabilities			
Bank Debt	$940,000	$940,000	$ 940,000

Capital			**Outside Basis**
Alison	184,000	184,000	$ 419,000
Bailey	184,000	184,000	419,000
Wally	368,000	368,000	838,000
Total Liabilities and Capital	$1,676,000	$1,676,000	$1,676,000

How do these transactions affect the balance sheet? Outside basis?

Assets			
	Tax	**Book**	**FMV**
Cash	$	$	$ 6,000
Receivables			150,000
Inventory			870,000
Showroom			290,000
Investment Land			0
Total Assets	$	$	$1,316,000

Liabilities			
Bank Debt	$580,000	$580,000	$ 580,000

Capital				**Outside Basis**
Alison				$
Bailey				
Wally				
Total Liabilities and Capital	$	$		$

2.4.3   In the facts of Question 2.4.2, assume that the company does not sell land to pay down debt, but instead Wally approaches the bank to discuss taking over responsibility for a portion of the company's $940,000 loan. These discussions result in a novation agreement, whereby the bank releases the company from $360,000 of the original debt and enters into a new loan agreement under which Wally is the sole obligor. The company remains bound by the original terms of the loan agreement with respect to $580,000 of the debt. What is the effect of this workout on the company's balance sheet? What effect does it have on the partners' outside bases?

Assets			
	Tax	**Book**	**FMV**
Cash	$	$	$ 6,000
Receivables			150,000
Inventory			870,000
Showroom			290,000
Investment Land			360,000
Total Assets	$	$	$1,676,000

Liabilities			
Bank Debt	$580,000	$580,000	$ 580,000

Capital				**Outside Basis**
Alison				$
Bailey				
Wally				
Total Liabilities and Capital	$	$		$

2.4.4   Consider once again the facts of Question 2.4.2. Wally wants the company to keep its land, but also needs to reassure Alison and Bailey, his partners and best sales people, regarding the financial condition of the company. He enters into a written assumption agreement with them, in which he agrees to pay up to $360,000 of the company's bank debt, in the event and to the extent that the company is unable to do so. How does this agreement affect the company's balance sheet and the partners' outside bases?

Assets			
	Tax	**Book**	**FMV**
Cash	$	$	$ 6,000
Receivables			150,000
Inventory			870,000
Showroom			290,000
Investment Land			360,000
Total Assets	$	$	$1,676,000

Liabilities			
Bank Debt	$940,000	$940,000	$ 940,000

Capital				**Outside Basis**
Alison				$
Bailey				
Wally				
Total Liabilities and Capital	$	$		$

2.5   ACCOUNTING FOR CONTRIBUTIONS OF PROPERTY WITH LIABILITIES

In one sense, this Topic is a straightforward application of the capital-accounting and basis rules that we have reviewed in the last two Topics. In another, it is a tax disaster waiting to happen—the only way a taxpayer can manage to recognize gain and pay tax by contributing property to a partnership without actually receiving cash or property to show for it. A blunder here can cost a tax practitioner her client, or her job.

Let's start with the rule of Treas. Reg. § 1.704–1(b)(2)(iv)(b) that a partner who contributes property subject to indebtedness takes a book capital account that is equal to the excess of the fair market value of the property over the amount of the debt. Although the regulations do not rule out the possibility that this amount may be negative, that is unlikely. *See* Treas. Reg. § 1.704–1(b)(2)(iv)(*d*) (last sentence). But consider the contributing partner's tax capital. Applying the same approach used to determine book capital, the contributing partner's tax capital equals the excess of the adjusted basis of the contributed property over the amount of the debt. This number can be negative, and it happens all the time.

Many investors in properties like real estate use borrowing to withdraw the appreciation from their properties without paying current tax. Say, for example, Alan purchases a small commercial building for $1 million. Over the next ten years, its value increases to $3 million while allowable tax depreciation reduces its adjusted basis to $750,000. Alan finds a bank that will lend him $2.5 million against the building—returning all of his original investment and $1.5 million of the building's appreciation without his incurring any tax liability. If, more than two years later, Alan contributes this building to a partnership subject to the debt, his book capital account will equal the excess of the building's value over the debt—$500,000, if the building has not appreciated further. His tax capital, however, will be a negative $1.75 million.

Alan takes a tax basis in his partnership interest of $750,000 as a result of the contribution (section 722) and then receives a deemed distribution of cash of $2.5 million as a result of the partnership's assumption of his individual liability (section 752(b)). Although we will not review the tax rules for partnership distributions until Chapter 9, it may come as no surprise to you that this deemed distribution, standing alone, would cause Alan to recognize a gain of $1.75 million—the full amount of his negative tax capital. Said differently, Alan would recognize gain to the extent that the deemed cash distribution ($2.5 million) exceeds his outside basis prior to the distribution ($750,000).

This is, however, only half the story. In his role as a partner, Alan may well be allocated a share of the $2.5 million liability after the partnership has assumed it from him. Section 752(a) credits Alan with a cash contribution equal to his share of that liability, which increases Alan's outside basis (although not his tax capital). Every dollar of the debt that is allocated to Alan therefore reduces by a dollar the amount of gain he recognizes on his contribution of the encumbered building, because it increases by a dollar his outside basis. If he can be allocated at least $1.75 million of the debt, he is home free, at least for now. Treas. Reg. § 1.752–1(f) explicitly provides that the amount of the liability that the partnership assumes from Alan (a deemed cash distribution under section 752(b)) and the amount of his share of the partnership's liability (a deemed cash contribution under section 752(a)) must be netted together in determining the tax consequences of this transaction to Alan.

Thus the mantra, which I believe some partnership investors actually have engraved in stone above their fireplaces, *"Debt Covers My Negative Capital."* Not quite *"Home Sweet Home,"* but a tax advisor can relate. If Alan starts with negative tax capital, he must have a liability share equal to at least that amount in order to keep his outside basis at least equal to zero and thus avoid gain recognition.

In Chapter 5, we will review the rules for determining partners' shares of partnership liabilities. The examples that follow assume that all partners share partnership liabilities according to their percentage interests in the partnership. That is a reasonable assumption for recourse liabilities. It is flat wrong for nonrecourse liabilities, the allocation mechanism for which contains a built-in rule meant to minimize this problem. *See* Topic 5.4. In Topic 2.7, we will review a type of transaction known as a "disguised sale." None of the Questions below involves a disguised sale, because in each case the debt encumbering the contributed property is incurred more than two years before the date of the contribution. As we will see, the tax treatment of these transactions would be quite different if they were characterized as disguised sales.

2.5.1   Alan and Bethany form a general partnership. Bethany contributes $400,000 cash. Alan contributes a building with a value of $800,000 and adjusted tax basis of $500,000. The building is subject to a $400,000 recourse mortgage debt incurred four years earlier. Alan is personally liable to repay this debt to the extent that the value of the building is insufficient to satisfy it. The lender agrees to the assumption of the debt by the partnership and releases Alan. The partnership agreement and applicable tax law provide that Alan and Bethany share partnership liabilities in accordance with their respective percentage interests. What is the opening balance sheet of the partnership? What are the tax consequences to Alan and Bethany?

Assets			
	Tax	**Book**	**FMV**
Cash	$	$	$ 400,000
Building			800,000
Total Assets	$	$	$1,200,000

Liabilities			
Mortgage Debt	$ 400,000	$ 400,000	$ 400,000

Capital				**Outside Basis**
Alan				$
Bethany				
Total Liabilities and Capital	$	$		$

2.5.2   Same as Question 2.5.1, except that the amount of the recourse mortgage debt is $700,000. What is the opening balance sheet of the partnership?

Assets			
	Tax	**Book**	**FMV**
Cash	$	$	$ 400,000
Building			800,000
Total Assets	$	$	$1,200,000
Liabilities			
Mortgage Debt	$ 700,000	$ 700,000	$ 700,000
Capital			**Outside Basis**
Alan				$
Bethany				
Total Liabilities and Capital	$	$		$

2.5.3   Same as Question 2.5.2, except that on the day it is formed the partnership borrows $300,000 from the brokerage firm where it deposits Bethany's cash contribution. What is the opening balance sheet now?

Assets			
	Tax	**Book**	**FMV**
Cash	$	$	$ 700,000
Building			800,000
Total Assets	$	$	$1,500,000
Liabilities			
Mortgage Debt	$ 700,000	$ 700,000	$ 700,000
Brokerage Debt	300,000	300,000	300,000
Capital			**Outside Basis**
Alan				$
Bethany				
Total Liabilities and Capital	$	$		$

2.5.4   Same as Question 2.5.2, except that, rather than contributing cash to the partnership, Bethany replicates Alan by contributing land worth $800,000 with an adjusted basis of $500,000, subject to a recourse mortgage debt of $700,000 (incurred more than two years earlier) that is assumed by the partnership.

Assets			
	Tax	**Book**	**FMV**
Land	$	$	$ 800,000
Building			800,000
Total Assets	$	$	$1,600,000
Liabilities			
Mortgage Debt	$ 700,000	$ 700,000	$ 700,000
Mortgage Debt	700,000	700,000	700,000
Capital			**Outside Basis**
Alan			$
Bethany			
Total Liabilities and Capital	$	$	$

2.6   ACCOUNTING FOR SUBSEQUENT CONTRIBUTIONS OF MONEY OR PROPERTY: REVALUATIONS

It is often thought that revaluations are a creation of tax law, and without the Treasury regulations under section 704, there would be no such thing. Nothing could be further from the truth. Consider the following simple situation. Years ago, Peter, Paul and Mary formed a partnership, Puff Unlimited, with cash contributions of $10,000 each. The partnership built a small workshop to make string and sealing wax and other fancy stuff. The workshop prospered and the partnership is now worth $90,000. Jackie Paper, who believes he has found a new market for the output of the workshop, offers to contribute $30,000 cash to the partnership in exchange for a 25% interest.

What effect should this transaction have on the balance sheet of the partnership? Obviously, Jackie will get a $30,000 capital account to reflect the value of his contribution. If the capital accounts of the other partners are not adjusted, Jackie, who has bargained for a 25% partnership interest, will have more than 25% of the partnership's capital. Say, unrealistically, that

Peter, Paul and Mary's capital accounts are all at their initial levels, so that the entire appreciation in the value of the partnership is unrealized. In that case, Jackie's initial capital account ($30,000) would be equal to the capital accounts of all the other partners combined. This is not the deal that Peter, Paul and Mary thought they made.

How can they protect themselves? One way is to "revalue" the original partners' capital accounts to reflect the full fair market value of the workshop immediately before Jackie joins the partnership. This revaluation has the effect of "capturing" the full existing appreciation in the workshop in the capital accounts of the original partners. They will each have a book capital account of $30,000, equal to Jackie's. As we will see in Topic 8.5, the tax consequence of the revaluation is that the original partners will have to pay tax on this appreciation when it is realized by the partnership. They are, in effect, agreeing to accept responsibility for the tax on the existing appreciation in the workshop in exchange for having capital accounts that reflect the full value of the workshop. If their tax rate is anything less than 100%, this is a good trade.

What is a revaluation? You will often hear that a partnership has "revalued its capital accounts." This is shorthand. In a revaluation, the partnership adjusts (*i.e.*, increases and/or decreases) the book values of its assets to fair market value and allocates the resulting book gains and/or losses to the partners in accordance with the provisions of the partnership agreement and applicable law. This allocation changes the amounts of the book capital accounts. Revaluations never, ever change the adjusted tax bases of any of the partnership's assets or the tax capital of any of the partners. Therefore, revaluations can and usually do create or increase disparities between the book values of the assets and their adjusted tax bases (and corresponding disparities between the partners' tax capital and book capital).

Does a revaluation always involve all of the partnership's assets? No. Conceptually, there two different kinds of revaluations, both very common. The first is a revaluation of all of the assets (a "general revaluation"). It occurs in the circumstances described in Treas. Reg. § 1.704–1(b)(2)(iv)(*f*)(5) —and not otherwise. A partnership cannot undertake a general revaluation every time the value of its assets change, for the reasons discussed below. Two common circumstances where general revaluations are permitted are the contribution to or distribution by the partnership of money or property in exchange for an interest in the partnership. Notice that pro-rata distributions are not occasions for a general revaluation, because they do not change the interest of any partner in the partnership.

The other type of revaluation is very different and results from the manner in which book capital accounts are kept. Just as a contribution of property causes the book capital account of the contributing partner to increase by the fair market value of the contributed property, distributions of property decrease the book capital account of the distributee-partner by the fair market value of the distributed property. Capital accounts, however, are not routinely adjusted to reflect the fair market value of the partnership's property. In order for a property distribution not to have a disproportionate effect on the capital account of the distributee, it is necessary that the book value of the distributed asset be adjusted to fair market value and that the resulting book gain or loss be allocated to the partners immediately prior to the distribution. Treas. Reg. § 1.704–1(b)(2)(iv)(*e*). This revaluation (a "distributed-property revaluation") affects *only* the book value of the distributed property and must occur (*i.e.*, it is mandatory) whenever property is distributed—even in a pro-rata distribution.

Are general revaluations mandatory? A general revaluation is (1) prohibited except in the specifically enumerated circumstances in which it is allowed; (2) elective, not mandatory, in most of those circumstances; and (3) required, by current count, in two such circumstances. In order to accomplish a general revaluation, a partnership must know the fair market value of all of its assets. The Treasury regulations generally limit the circumstances in which a general revaluation is permitted to those where there is likely to be arm's-length negotiation by which the partnership can establish (and the IRS can audit) those valuations.

Although general revaluations are normally elective, the Treasury regulations contain a stern warning that partnerships that do not utilize them may be in for tax trouble. Treas. Reg. § 1.704–1(b)(2)(*f*) (flush language). The idea behind the government's skepticism is that, as illustrated in the case of Peter, Paul and Mary, revaluations generally make economic sense, either for the existing partners (if the assets are appreciated) or the new partner (if the assets are depreciated). Therefore, when they do not occur, some value is probably being transferred from one group to the other, and the government wants to know why. The cited regulation reserves the right to recharacterize the value transferred as compensation, a gift or otherwise as may be appropriate.

Currently, general revaluations are required on the exercise of a so-called "noncompensatory option." *See* Topic 2.8. Proposed regulations would require general revaluations in the event of a non-pro-rata distribution of money or property by a partnership that holds so-called "section 751 assets" after the distribution. Prop. Treas. Reg. §§ 1.704–1(b)(2)(iv)(*f*) and 1.751–1(b)(2)(iv). *See* Topic 9.6. Because many partnerships fit this description, the finalization of these proposed regulations would help cement the role of general revaluations in partnership tax accounting.

———

2.6.1   The Alpha Centauri Security Company, a limited liability company taxed as a partnership, has the following balance sheet (expanded to show asset values):

Assets				Liabilities		
	Tax	Book	FMV		Tax	Book
Cash	$ 40,000	$ 40,000	$ 40,000	Bank Debt	$200,000	$200,000
Equipment	160,000	160,000	130,000			
Plant	340,000	340,000	400,000	**Capital**		
Land	120,000	220,000	420,000	Adama	180,000	280,000
				Baltar	140,000	140,000
				Cally	140,000	140,000
Total Assets	$660,000	$760,000	$990,000	**Total Liabilities and Capital**	$660,000	$760,000

Under the partnership agreement, Adama has a 50% interest in profits and losses and the other two partners have percentage interests of 25% each. Dualla, a newcomer, offers to contribute $395,000 cash for a 33% interest. Assuming that the partnership undertakes a general revaluation in connection with this transaction, show the balance sheet both immediately before and immediately after Dualla's contribution.

Assets				Liabilities		
	Tax	Book	FMV		Tax	Book
Cash	$	$	$ 40,000	Bank Debt	$ 200,000	$ 200,000
Equipment			130,000			
Plant			400,000	**Capital**		
Land			420,000	Adama		
				Baltar		
				Cally		
Total Assets	$	$	$990,000	**Total Liabilities and Capital**	$	$

Assets				Liabilities		
	Tax	Book	FMV		Tax	Book
Cash	$	$	$ 435,000	Bank Debt	$200,000	$200,000
Equipment			130,000			
Plant			400,000	**Capital**		
Land			420,000	Adama		
				Baltar		
				Cally		
				Dualla		
Total Assets	$	$	$1,385,000	**Total Liabilities and Capital**	$	$

2.7 PROVIDING MONEY OR PROPERTY WITHOUT PARTNER RISK: SECTION 707

In the examples considered so far, the partners have contributed money or property in exchange for what might be termed common equity interests—interests that share in all profits and losses of the partnership. Sometimes, life is not that simple. In addition to, or instead of, common equity, a transferor of money or property to a partnership may receive interests in the entity's income or assets in a variety that is bounded only by the limits of imagination. Some of the more common interests include: (1) a fixed lump-sum or stream of cash payments; (2) an interest in the partnership that offers a fixed annual cash return, irrespective of the income of the partnership; (3) an interest in the partnership that receives a priority distribution of cash, matched, if possible, by a priority allocation of partnership income or gain; and (4) hybrid interests, consisting of common equity and any of the foregoing other interests in any conceivable mix.

Section 721(a) applies to a transfer of money or property to a partnership only if it is a "contribution" to the partnership "in exchange for an interest in the partnership." One place to start, then, is to decide whether the transferor in any given case is making such an exchange. Oft-quoted legislative history can help make this determination:

> Congress was mindful that to be considered partners for tax purposes, persons must, among other things, pool their assets and labor for the joint production of profit. To the extent that a partner's profit from a transaction is assured without regard to the success or failure of the joint undertaking, there is not the requisite joint profit motive, and the partner is acting as a third party.

STAFF OF THE JOINT COMMITTEE ON TAXATION, 98TH CONG., 2D SESS., GENERAL EXPLANATION OF THE REVENUE PROVISIONS OF THE DEFICIT

REDUCTION ACT OF 1984 at 226 (Comm. Print 1984). If the transferor is acting as a third party, section 707(a)(1) requires that her transfer be taxed not as a contribution under section 721(a) but instead as a transaction between the partnership and one who is not a partner. For example, a transfer of property in exchange for cash or an installment note is a sale of the property for tax purposes. If the partner retains ownership of the property, however, the partnership's payments might better be characterized as rent. If the asset transferred to the partnership is money, the transaction is likely a loan. The proper characterization depends on the particular facts of the transaction. *See* Treas. Reg. § 1.707–1(a).

In the right circumstances, it is entirely possible for a transfer of money or property in exchange for a fixed return to qualify as a "contribution . . . in exchange for an interest in the partnership." Suppose, for example, Amelia transfers property worth $1,000 in exchange for a partnership interest with respect to which the partnership is required to pay her $50 per year, whether or not the partnership earns that amount of income. Aside from the return of her $1,000 book capital account at some future date, this annual payment is all Amelia ever expects to receive from the partnership. Section 707(c), providing the tax treatment of "guaranteed payments," deals with just such an interest and clearly treats it as the interest of a partner. The distinction between Amelia's interest and an installment note treated as part of a sale transaction under section 707(a)(1) may seem paper-thin, but it is really just the distinction between equity and debt (which, admittedly, can seem paper-thin sometimes). One who transfers property in exchange for a partnership debt instrument has sold the property under section 707(a)(1); one who transfers property in exchange for partnership equity (even preferred equity) earning a guaranteed payment has made a capital contribution. The distinguishing feature between the two transactions is that the holder of preferred equity bears more entrepreneurial risk than the holder of a debt instrument, because the equity holder does not have the rights of a creditor and must wait to be paid until the creditors have been paid. This quantum of risk qualifies the holder of preferred equity as a partner for tax purposes.

Guaranteed payments for capital are usually stated as a fixed annual rate of return. Under section 707(c) and Treas. Reg. § 1.707–1(c), they are taxed as ordinary income to the recipient and are deductible by the partnership to the extent not required to be capitalized. (Because the partnership interest with respect to which the guaranteed payment is made is equity, not debt, the partnership's deduction is taken under section 162 (business expense), not section 163 (interest).) Making a guaranteed payment to a partner does not reduce her capital account, because a guaranteed payment is not a partnership distribution. To see this, apply what you already know about partnership accounting. When the partnership makes a guaranteed payment, its assets are reduced by the amount of the payment. The deduction allowed to the partnership reduces the partners' capital by a like amount. Any further reduction in capital (as would be required if the guaranteed payment were treated as a distribution) would violate the accounting identity. (In the unlikely event that the guaranteed payment must be capitalized, there is no net change in the assets of the partnership and no change in its capital.) *See* Treas. Reg. § 1.704–1(b)(2)(iv)(*o*).

Closely related to guaranteed payments are preferred returns, which are preferential distributions of partnership cash flow matched, to the extent available, by allocations of income or gain. The holder of a partnership interest with a preferred return bears more entrepreneurial risk than the holder of a comparable partnership interest providing for a guaranteed payment. To see this, imagine that the partnership never has any income. The assets of the partnership will be available to pay both a guaranteed payment and preferred return. Such payments, however, will reduce and ultimately liquidate the interest with the preferred return, but not the interest with the guaranteed payment, which will remain unreduced. Thus, the holder of the preferred return depends to a greater extent on the economic performance of the partnership. For this reason, a partnership interest bearing a preferred return is even more clearly equity than one yielding only a guaranteed payment.

Disguised sales

Among hybrid transactions, the most notorious is the so-called "disguised sale." In simplest form, it is a transfer of appreciated property to a partnership in exchange for one of the forms of equity (common or preferred) discussed above, plus cash or a note. In this simple version, the sale is not very disguised. Before turning to more subtle variations, however, it is useful to consider what is at stake. Suppose the property that Amelia transfers to the partnership is worth $1,000 but has an adjusted basis of only $600. If the partnership pays her $400 in a transaction that is treated as a distribution, Amelia will recognize no gain. Under section 731(a), she is entitled to apply her entire outside basis ($600) against the cash distribution before recognizing the first dollar of gain. But this result is only available if the $400 payment to Amelia is treated as a distribution, separate from her contribution of the property to the partnership.

If the relationship between the contribution and the distribution is taken into account, another model for taxation may suggest itself. If Amelia had transferred her property to a controlled corporation in exchange for stock and $400 of cash "boot," she would have recognized $400 of gain. Under section 351(b), the transferor must recognize the entire amount of the boot, up to the amount of the gain in the transferred property. The difference between these two treatments is, of course, basis recovery. The partnership rule in section 731(a) allows partners to apply their basis first against cash or other taxable property, minimizing the gain recognized on distributions. The corporate rule in section 351(b) forces shareholders to apply their basis last, maximizing recognized gain.

When Congress added section 707(a)(2)(B) in 1984, codifying the tax treatment of disguised sales, it chose a middle course. When the transfer of property by a partner and the transfer of money or property by the partnership are sufficiently related, they are treated together as a sale of all or a portion of the partner's property. This treatment is neither basis-first nor basis-last. Instead, it allocates basis in proportion to the amount of the property sold. In Amelia's case, for example, the $400 payment represents 40% of the value of the property transferred. Thus, in the disguised sale, she has sold 40% of the property and is entitled to apply 40% of her basis, recognizing $160 of gain ($400 amount realized—$240 basis). She has contributed the remaining 60% of the property to the partnership with the remaining 60% of her basis. The contributed property is worth $600 (60% of $1,000), so Amelia takes a book capital account of $600. Her remaining basis is $360 (60% of $600), so her initial outside basis in the partnership is $360 under section 722.

Disguised sales are seldom as easy to spot as Amelia's. In particular, the partnership's payment to her may be deferred by months or years and there may be no explicit contractual agreement obligating the partnership to make the payment. Alternatively, she may receive a partnership interest otherwise qualifying as equity, but with a "self-liquidating" feature. For example, the partnership could issue preferred equity with a fixed annual payment that is large enough to redeem the position in a short period of time. Treas. Reg. § 1.707–3 contains rules intended to draw a relatively bright line between transactions that are treated as disguised sales and those that are not. The touchstone is whether the deferred payment is subject in a meaningful way to the entrepreneurial risk of the partnership's operations. The regulation contains a listing of factors to help make this determination. In order to make outcomes more predictable, it establishes rebuttable presumptions that transfers within two years are a sale and transfers outside of that period are not. Treas. Reg. §§ 1.707–3(c), –3(d). Although these presumptions are a starting point, do not make the mistake of thinking that all distributions within two years following a contribution must be treated as the proceeds of a disguised sale. Distributions that will be funded, if at all, by appreciation in the value of a partnership's assets seldom indicate the existence of a disguised sale. Additionally, Treas. Reg. § 1.707–4 contains explicit exceptions for certain distributions, including guaranteed payments and preferred returns.

If the transfer of money or property to Amelia takes place other than on the same day as her contribution, the disguised sale is called "non-simultaneous." The bookkeeping for a non-simultaneous disguised sale is messy. The sale is treated as taking place on the date that the partnership becomes the owner of the property for tax purposes—generally, the date of contribution. Because the partnership's payment for the property is deferred, the sale is an installment sale, pursuant to which the partner recognizes gain as payments are received. Interest must imputed, unless it is provided for in the transaction, which would be unusual. Worse, the balance sheet for the year of the contribution must be restated retroactively to reflect the partnership's liability to make installment payments and corresponding adjustments to inside basis and partner capital. *See* Treas. Reg. §§ 1.707–3(a)(2), –3(f) example (2).

The disguised-sale rules would be porous indeed if they failed to cover "distributions" that take the form of borrowings against the value of appreciated property prior to the time that it is contributed to a partnership. Such a transaction can have much the same effect as a cash distribution made following the contribution of unencumbered property. Treas. Reg. § 1.707–5 fills this gap. The distinction to bear in mind in this case is between a "qualified liability," which can never be treated as part of the consideration for a disguised sale, and a liability that is not a "qualified liability." (Oddly, the Treasury regulations never call that sort of liability a "nonqualified liability," but everyone else does.) A liability incurred more than two years before the contribution (or agreement to contribute, if earlier) is qualified. Period. Treas. Reg. § 1.707–5(a)(6). A liability incurred later than that is presumed to be nonqualified, although the taxpayer can rebut this presumption. Treas. Reg. § 1.707–5(a)(7). There are other kinds of qualified liabilities as well, such as those that were incurred to improve the contributed property or incurred in the ordinary course of the business in which the contributed property was held (so long, in the latter case, as all property material to such business is contributed). Treas. Reg. § 1.707–5(a)(6).

If a disguised sale involves the partnership's assumption of a nonqualified liability, a portion of the liability is treated as consideration in the disguised sale. What portion? It is the excess of the amount of the liability assumed by the partnership from the contributor (which you learned in Topics 2.4 and 2.5 is treated as a deemed distribution of cash to the contributor under section 752(b)) over the contributor's share of that liability after its assumption by the partnership (which you learned is treated as a deemed contribution of cash by the contributor under section 752(a)). In Topics 5.3 and 5.4, we will review the rules for allocating partnership liabilities to partners. Those same rules apply here, with one exception: for purposes of the disguised-sale rules, the contributing partner's share of a nonrecourse liability is determined by treating the entire liability as an "excess nonrecourse liability" under Treas. Reg. § 1.752–3(a)(3). Don't expect that to make sense now, but come back to it after you have studied Topic 5.4.

2.7.1   Jacob is tired of trying to make a go of it on his small farm and he has lots of unpaid bills. He contacts Sunbelt Farms, a large local farm operating as a general partnership, to arrange a deal. Sunbelt readily agrees to a $2 million valuation on Jacob's acreage, in exchange for which it offers Jacob a general partnership interest. Sunbelt also accedes to Jacob's request to transfer $500,000 into his bank account at closing. Jacob's adjusted basis in his acreage is $200,000. What gain, if any, does Jacob recognize on his transaction with Sunbelt?

a) $0

b) $300,000

c) $450,000

d) $500,000

2.7.2   In Question 2.7.1, what is Sunbelt's basis in Jacob's land?

a) $200,000

b) $450,000

c) $650,000

d) $700,000

2.7.3   Stevie Rider owns cycling equipment valued at $90,000 with an adjusted tax basis of $24,000. She borrows $60,000 on a recourse basis and 30 days thereafter contributes the equipment to All Sports Unlimited, a general partnership, in exchange for a 25% interest. In connection with this contribution, All Sports assumes Stevie's debt and the lender releases her from personal responsibility. Under the All Sports partnership agreement and applicable tax law, Stevie is allocated a 25% share, or $15,000, of the liability. What income or gain, if any, does Stevie recognize on the contribution?

a) $0

b) $21,000

c) $27,000

d) $33,000

2.7.4   Same facts as Question 2.7.1, except that Sunbelt borrows the $500,000 it pays to Jacob. Under the Sunbelt partnership agreement and applicable tax law, Jacob is allocated 25%, or $125,000, of this liability. What gain, if any, does Jacob recognize on this transaction?

a) $175,000

b) $337,500

c) $375,000

d) $450,000

2.7.5   Cody owns an old rodeo arena near Cheyenne, valued at $450,000, in which he has an adjusted basis of $250,000. He borrows $300,000 from a local bank on a recourse basis and uses the borrowed funds to fix the old place up. When he is done, the refurbished arena is worth $1 million. The place attracts so much attention that Cody receives a proposal to use it for the steer wrestling competition at the annual Frontier Days event. After some negotiation, Cody contributes the arena for a 20% interest in Frontier Days LLC, a limited liability company treated as a partnership for tax purposes. His initial capital account is $700,000 and the bank releases him from individual responsibility on the debt. Under the Frontier Days partnership agreement and applicable tax law, Cody is allocated a 20% share of partnership liabilities. All of these events happen in the same calendar year. What gain, if any, does Cody recognize on his transaction with Frontier Days?

a) $0

b) $108,000

    c) $168,000

    d) $180,000

2.7.6   Eli is a one-third owner of an automobile repair business, ACE Garage LLC, a limited liability company taxed as a partnership. He owns an adjoining toolshop, which he agrees to let the partnership use for a ten-year period, during which time ACE will make preferred distributions to Eli equal to 5% of its gross income. Eli and his partners will continue to receive their regular one-third shares of the partnership's profit, calculated after taking the preferred distributions to Eli into account. At the end of ten years, ACE will have the option to purchase Eli's toolshop at its then fair market value. For federal income tax purposes, what is the best characterization of ACE's preferred distributions to Eli?

    a)   Rent

    b)   Proceeds from Eli's disguised sale of the toolshop

    c)   Distributive share of partnership income

    d)   Guaranteed payments for the use of capital

2.7.7   Isaac is in the business of subdividing and selling undeveloped real estate. He contributes a subdivided lot worth $35,000 with an adjusted basis in his hands of zero to Genessee Land Company, a partnership. A year later, Genessee makes a cash distribution of $10,000 to Isaac. Genessee has no liabilities and operates during the period in question at a small loss. Setting aside any difficulties in doing so, why might the IRS claim that these two transactions are parts of a disguised sale? (Circle all that apply.)

    a)   Timing of gain recognized

    b)   Character of gain recognized

    c)   Amount of gain recognized

    d)   No good reason

2.8 NONCOMPENSATORY OPTIONS

A "noncompensatory option" is an option issued by a partnership other than an option issued in connection with the performance of services. Treas. Reg. § 1.721–2(f). An "option" is a contractual right to acquire an interest in the issuing partnership. Treas. Reg. § 1.721–2(g)(1). A partnership may issue a noncompensatory option as a stand-alone instrument, bundle it with a debt instrument to form convertible debt or issue it as a warrant as part of an investment unit that includes debt.

There are several events in the life of a noncompensatory option that may have tax consequences, including (1) issuance, (2) exercise and (3) lapse. The tax issues include:

    ✓   *Does the partnership recognize income or gain when it receives money or other property as the "premium" paid for the issuance of the option?* No. *See* Rev. Rul. 78–182, 1978–1 C.B. 265; Rev. Rul. 58–234, 1958–1 C.B. 279.

✓ *If the option holder pays the premium in property (rather than money), does section 721 apply?* No. The option holder recognizes whatever gain or loss may be inherent in the transferred property. The partnership takes such property with a fair market value basis. Treas. Reg. §§ 1.721–2(b)(1), –2(h), example.

✓ *Is the option holder a partner?* Maybe. It depends on the terms of the option and the premium paid. Two sets of rules must be consulted to answer this question. The first is Treas. Reg. § 1.761–3. The second is general federal tax principles. *See* Treas. Reg. § 1.761–3(a)(2). An option that is reasonably certain to be exercised is trouble under both. *See* Treas. Reg. § 1.761–3(d). Under the regulations (but not under general tax principles), however, an option will not be characterized as an interest in the partnership unless doing so creates a strong likelihood of a substantial increase in the aggregate tax liabilities of the partners and the option holder. Treas. Reg. § 1.761–3(a)(1)(ii).

✓ *Does section 721 apply to the exercise of a noncompensatory option?* Yes. Neither the partnership nor the exercising option holder recognizes gain or loss. This result applies whether the exercise price is paid in cash or in property. Treas. Reg. § 1.721–2(a)(1). It does not apply to the extent that the exercise price is satisfied with the partnership's obligation for unpaid rent, royalties or interest. Treas. Reg. § 1.721–2(a)(2).

✓ *What are the tax consequences if a noncompensatory option lapses without being exercised?* The option holder recognizes a capital loss equal to the amount of the option premium, either long-term or short-term, depending on the period the option was held. The partnership recognizes a short-term capital gain. *See* section 1234.

Treasury regulations finalized in 2013 covered some of these issues, which are reviewed in the Questions below. They also established new rules for partnership revaluations in connection with the issuance and exercise of noncompensatory options. That aspect of the 2013 regulations is reserved for discussion until Topic 8.6.

———————

2.8.1 In 2017, Lillian pays Speedee Messenger Services LLC, a limited liability company taxed as a partnership, $10,000 in cash for an option to acquire a 10% membership interest for a payment of $100,000 in cash or property any time in the next three years. In 2019, Lillian exercises this option by transferring Apple common stock worth $100,000 in which she has a basis of $20,000. How much gain do Lillian and Speedee recognize on these transactions and when?

a) Lillian, $0; Speedee, $0

b) Lillian, $80,000 in 2019; Speedee, $0

c) Lillian, $0; Speedee, $10,000 in 2017

d) Lillian, $80,000 in 2019; Speedee, $10,000 in 2017 and $100,000 in 2019

2.8.2   In 2017, Lillian transfers to Speedee Messenger Services LLC $10,000 worth of Apple common stock in which she has an adjusted basis of $2,000 for an option to acquire a 10% membership interest by paying $100,000 in cash or property any time in the next three years. In 2019, Lillian exercises this option by transferring $100,000 in cash to the partnership. How much gain do Lillian and Speedee recognize on these transactions and when?

a) Lillian, $0; Speedee, $0

b) Lillian, $8,000 in 2017; Speedee, $0

c) Lillian, $0; Speedee, $10,000 in 2017

d) Lillian, $8,000 in 2017; Speedee, $10,000 in 2017 and $100,000 in 2019

2.8.3   *Read section 1234 prior to answering this Question.* Same facts as Question 2.8.1, except that Lillian never exercises the option and it lapses unexercised in 2020. How much gain or loss do Lillian and Speedee recognize on these transactions and when?

a) Lillian, $0; Speedee, $0

b) Lillian, $10,000 ordinary loss in 2020; Speedee, $10,000 ordinary income in 2020

c) Lillian, $10,000 long-term capital loss in 2020; Speedee, $10,000 short-term capital gain in 2020

d) Lillian, $10,000 long-term capital loss in 2020; Speedee, $10,000 long-term capital gain in 2020

2.8.4   High Tension Massage LLC, a limited liability company that is treated as a partnership for tax purposes, is a successful business in Boulder looking to expand. On January 1, 2017, Devon loans the partnership $80,000 to cover the initial cost of opening in two new locations. The loan bears annual interest at 3% and is due in five years. The terms of the loan provide that Devon has the option to convert it into a 25% membership interest at any time prior to maturity. Two years into the expansion, High Tension has experienced a surge of new business, and Devon is confident of its future prospects. He decides to convert his debt. Suppose that there is $4,000 of accrued but unpaid interest on Devon's convertible debt at the time that he converts it, and that High Tension settles this obligation by issuing him an additional membership interest worth $4,000. What are the federal income tax consequences of this portion of the transaction?

a) No income, loss or deduction to either party

b) Devon recognizes no income under section 721(a), but High Tension can claim a deduction of $4,000 for interest paid.

c) Devon has interest income of $4,000 and High Tension has an interest expense deduction of $4,000.

d) Devon has interest income of $4,000; High Tension has a $4,000 interest expense deduction and, in addition, recognizes gain or loss on the deemed sale of an undivided interest in $4,000 worth of its assets.

CHAPTER 3
PERFORMING SERVICES
FOR A PARTNERSHIP

3.1   THE GENERAL RULE OF RECOGNITION

The "general" rule for the receipt of a partnership interest in exchange for services provided to the partnership is that the fair market value of the interest is taxable as ordinary compensation income to the service provider. There are exceptions and they are important.

First, if a service provider receives no interest in the current capital of a partnership, she is not taxable on receipt of an interest in its future profits. This is the well-known distinction between a "capital interest" and a "profits interest" (also called a "carried interest" because the capital of the other partners "carries" or supports this one). You can tell whether a partner has a capital interest through a simple thought experiment. Imagine that the partnership sells all of its assets for cash equal to their fair market value, allocates the gains and losses from the sale to its partners, pays off all of its liabilities and liquidates by distributing its remaining cash to the partners in accordance with their capital accounts. Would the partner get anything? If so, she has a capital interest. If not, she has only a profits interest.

This thought experiment can be extended to the valuation of any partnership interest. This is the so-called "liquidation-value approach" to valuation and the IRS heartily endorses it in this context. A profits interest is an interest with a value of zero using the liquidation-value approach; a capital interest is an interest with a value greater than zero.

There have been several explanations offered over the years for why a profits interest is not taxable on receipt. The most compelling is that a profits interest is often very difficult to value. This rationale underlies the IRS' thoughtful treatment of this issue in General Counsel Memorandum 36,346 (July 25, 1977), as well as two significant Revenue Procedures on this topic. Rev. Proc. 2001–43, 2001–2 C.B. 191; Rev. Proc. 93–27, 1993–2 C.B. 343.

Second, a service provider may be offered a capital interest that she will be required to forfeit if she does not continue to provide services for an agreed period. This so-called "substantial risk of forfeiture" postpones taxation until her capital interest "vests." It is discussed in Topic 3.4.

Third, a service provider may receive an option to acquire a capital interest. If the exercise price is substantial, so that exercise is not a foregone conclusion, this should not be treated as a partnership interest and the service provider will not be subject to tax unless and until the option is exercised.

Finally, there are many other payment arrangements that a service provider (whether or not a partner) may have with a partnership that do not involve the receipt of a partnership interest (or an additional interest) at all. These are reviewed in Topic 3.5.

For its part, the partnership delivering a capital interest for services provided or to be provided has these principal concerns:

- ✓ *Is there a deduction?* The short answer is yes, if a payment by the partnership of the same amount of cash would be deductible.

- ✓ *What is the amount of the deduction?* It equals the amount of income recognized by the service provider, which is the fair market value of the capital interest. Determining this value is often easier said than done. The IRS has long allowed it to be established using the liquidation-value approach described in the thought experiment above. Treasury regulations proposed in 2005 would, if finalized, continue that policy. Prop. Treas. Reg. § 1.83–3(*l*).

- ✓ *Who gets the deduction?* The entire deduction is allocated to the partners other than the service provider. This result is harder than it should be to find in current Treasury regulations. It would be clarified by Prop. Treas. Reg. § 1.706–4(e)(2)(x), which would classify this deduction as an "extraordinary item" incurred immediately before the transfer of the partnership interest to the service provider. *See* Topic 6.1.

- ✓ *Does the partnership recognize gain or loss on the deemed sale of an undivided interest in its assets?* Despite commentary to the contrary, no decided case or ruling requires a partnership to recognize gain or loss on the issuance of a capital interest to a partner providing services to the partnership. The 2005 proposed regulations would, if finalized, confirm this result. Prop. Treas. Reg. § 1.721–1(b)(2)(i). This result does not extend to partners who transfer their partnership interests to someone who has provided services not to the partnership, but to the partners personally. *See* *McDougal v Commissioner*, 62 T.C. 720 (1974).

3.1.1   Box Manufacturing Company LLC, a limited liability company taxed as a partnership, is a nationally known maker of cardboard packaging materials. Its general manager has recently resigned to go to work for a competitor. Box recruits Beatrice Benchley to be its new manager. Beatrice is well represented and the negotiations are long and arduous. The final deal promises her an annual cash salary of $350,000, in addition to a 2% interest in the company transferred to her, no strings attached, as a "signing bonus." Looking to avoid a repeat of what happened with its prior manager, Box insists on a noncompete agreement, whereby Beatrice agrees not to provide services to any Box competitor during the term of her employment and for three years thereafter. Box executives are troubled to have been forced to transfer an equity interest worth $600,000 to a new hire. On the other hand,

Beatrice's agreement not to compete makes her much more likely to stay with Box and for that reason it is worth, they believe, half a year's salary, $175,000. What is Beatrice's compensation income for her first year of employment and what is the company's deduction?

a) Income, $950,000; Deduction, $350,000

b) Income, $950,000; Deduction, $1,125,000

c) Income, $775,000; Deduction, $775,000

d) Income, $950,000; Deduction, $775,000

3.1.2 406 West Madison LP is a limited partnership formed for the sole purpose of developing a small commercial building at that address. After raising $1 million in equity, the general partner approaches James Peal, a local contractor, with a proposal to act as the construction manager of the project in exchange for a 10% interest in the partnership that can reasonably be expected to be worth between $750,000 and $1,500,000 when the building is successfully completed and sold. If James accepts this offer, what is his compensation income that year and what is the partnership's deduction?

a) Income, $100,000; Deduction, $0

b) Income, $100,000; Deduction, $100,000

c) Income, $1,500,000; Deduction, $1,500,000

d) Income, $1,500,000; Deduction, $0

3.1.3 Same facts as Question 3.1.2, except that 406 West Madison LP grants James a 10% interest in the profits, if any, of the development after all expenses. Because this interest has no ownership of partnership capital at the time of the grant, its value is lower by that amount. Consequently, it can reasonably be expected to be worth between $650,000 and $1,400,000 when the building is successfully completed and sold. What is James' compensation income in the year of the grant?

a) $0

b) $100,000

c) $650,000

d) $1,400,000

3.1.4 Alternatively, in the facts of Question 3.1.2, assume that 406 West Madison LP grants James an option to acquire at any time during the development phase the same 10% interest for a payment of $100,000. Development proceeds successfully and when James exercises his option the interest he receives is worth $1,250,000. What is James' compensation income in the year the option is granted and in the year it is exercised?

a) Grant, $0; Exercise, $0

b) Grant, $100,000; Exercise, $0

c) Grant, $0; Exercise, $1,150,000

d)   Grant, $0; Exercise, $1,250,000

3.1.5   Sam Kwak operates a small and successful accounting service through a wholly owned limited liability company treated as a disregarded entity for tax purposes. For the past year, he has been using the services of Myra Birchenhalter, a young CPA, to help him get through the busy season. Sam has not yet paid Myra, hinting vaguely that he has a better idea in mind. Although Sam could easily afford to pay Myra in cash, he believes he can conserve cash for the expansion of his business by paying Myra for her services with a 25% interest in his company. He comes to you for a second opinion on this plan. What do you say?

a)   Genius! Paying Myra this way will be tax-free to her, thus assuring a very loyal new partner.

b)   Not a bad plan, but if you paid Myra in cash, you could deduct the payment against your business income, which would save you more than it would cost her because you are in a higher tax bracket.

c)   Any way you do this, Myra is going to have income and you will have a deduction of equal amount, so it really does not matter whether you give her cash or a 25% interest. Might as well save the cash.

d)   Not your best idea, Sam. Pay Myra in cash and have her reinvest in the business for a 25% interest.

3.2   ACCOUNTING FOR CONTRIBUTIONS OF SERVICES

As you might imagine, the accounting for issuance of a capital interest in a partnership in exchange for services is different than the accounting for issuance of such an interest in exchange for cash or property, because it must take into account recognition of compensation income by the service provider and either deduction or capitalization by the partnership. The issuance of a profits interest requires different accounting adjustments, mainly to ensure that it really is a profits interest.

3.2.1   Adair, Blair and Claire agree to form a partnership. Adair contributes property worth $180,000 with an adjusted basis of $120,000. Blair contributes $180,000 cash. Claire will manage the business and be an equal, one-third partner. Complete the opening balance sheet of this partnership, which takes into account compensation income and deduction. Assume that the value of Claire's interest is $120,000. Values of the partnership's assets are included for your reference.

Assets				Liabilities		
	Tax	**Book**	**FMV**		**Tax**	**Book**
Cash	$	$	$180,000	[None]	$ 0	$ 0
Property			180,000			
				Capital		
				Adair		
				Blair		
				Claire		
Total Assets	$	$	$360,000	**Total Liabilities and Capital**	$	$

3.2.2.   How would this balance sheet be different if Claire agreed to a covenant not to compete that is worth $60,000?

Assets				Liabilities		
	Tax	**Book**	**FMV**		**Tax**	**Book**
Cash	$	$	$180,000	[None]	$ 0	$ 0
Property			180,000			
				Capital		
				Adair		
				Blair		
				Claire		
Total Assets	$	$	$360,000	**Total Liabilities and Capital**	$	$

3.2.3   How would the balance sheet be different if the partnership instead offered Claire a one-third interest in future profits? Assume the value of her interest is determined using the liquidation-value approach.

Assets				Liabilities		
	Tax	**Book**	**FMV**		**Tax**	**Book**
Cash	$	$	$180,000	[None]	$ 0	$ 0
Property			180,000			
				Capital		
				Adair		
				Blair		
				Claire		
Total Assets	$	$	$360,000	**Total Liabilities and Capital**	$	$

3.2.4   In Question 3.2.3, the parties decide not to use the liquidation-value approach, but instead to value Claire's interest at $40,000, by reference to a Black-Scholes pricing model or other valuation methodology. What effect does this have on the balance sheet? How does this decision affect the parties' economic positions?

Assets				Liabilities		
	Tax	**Book**	**FMV**		**Tax**	**Book**
Cash	$	$	$180,000	[None]	$ 0	$ 0
Property			180,000			
				Capital		
				Adair		
				Blair		
				Claire		
Total Assets	$	$	$360,000	**Total Liabilities and Capital**	$	$

3.2.5   Suncoast LLC, a limited liability company taxed as a partnership, owns and operates a solar-thermal power plant in California. It has substantial assets and capital, but its plant has always run below expectations. Dr. Rupert Bork is a world-renowned electrical engineer who has had success in improving the performance of facilities like this. The members of Suncoast, both regulated utilities, are not interested in transferring any current ownership to Dr. Bork, but are willing to grant him a 5% profits interest in exchange for his services. The current balance sheet of Suncoast is shown below. What modifications are required to reflect the issuance of a 5% profits interest to Dr. Bork?

Assets (000s)				Liabilities (000s)		
	Tax	**Book**	**FMV**		**Tax**	**Book**
Cash	$ 500	$ 500	$ 500	Bank Debt	$ 60,000	$ 60,000
Plant & Equipment	114,500	114,600	117,000			
Land	5,000	5,000	12,500	**Capital (000s)**		
				CEG, Inc.	30,000	30,000
				Datalon, Inc.	30,000	30,000
Total Assets	$ 120,000	$ 120,000	$130,000	**Total Liabilities and Capital**	$120,000	$120,000

Assets (000s)				Liabilities (000s)		
	Tax	**Book**	**FMV**		**Tax**	**Book**
Cash	$	$	$ 500	Bank Debt	$ 60,000	$ 60,000
Plant & Equipment			117,000			
Land			12,500	**Capital (000s)**		
				CEG, Inc.		
				Datalon, Inc.		
Total Assets	$	$	$130,000	**Total Liabilities and Capital**	$	$

3.3   CONTRIBUTIONS OF SERVICE-FLAVORED PROPERTY

Contributions of services to a partnership and contributions of property lie on opposite sides of the Grand Canyon of taxation, one being entirely taxable and the other entirely tax-free. Yet the value of almost all property (a possible exception being undeveloped land) embodies some enhancement from the application of personal efforts. No particular problems arise if the efforts have been expended by persons unrelated to the partnership—the fact that the construction of an office building required the work of hundreds of construction workers does not make the completed building any less "property" in the hands of its owner, and she can contribute it to a partnership confident of having the protection of section 721. But what if the personal efforts are those of the owner herself? Does this cause the item in question not to be "property"?

Many battles have been fought over this issue, but not many since 1984. Two entirely unrelated developments in that year changed the terms of the argument, and the stakes in winning or losing it, for both taxpayers and the government. In 1984, the long-running *Stafford* litigation finally came to an end with the issuance of the fourth opinion by a Federal court in that case. *United States v. Stafford*, 727 F.2d 1043 (11th Cir. 1984). The opinion of the Eleventh Circuit Court of Appeals adopted a broad definition of the term "property" for purposes of section 721, concluding that even a letter of intent of questionable enforceability could qualify. This mirrored the liberal definition of property adopted by the Court of Claims about a decade earlier in the section 351 context. *E.I. DuPont de Nemours & Co. v. United States*, 471 F.2d 1211 (Ct. Cl. 1973) (non-exclusive patent license is property for purposes of section 351). These judicial developments have largely deprived government litigators of the killer argument that a contract, option or other writing that embodies the personal efforts of the contributor does not protect the contributor from current taxation because it is not property.

This does not, however, leave government litigators speechless. Instead, it shifts the terms of the argument from the *existence* of property to its *value*. Suppose, for example, that a real estate developer contributes to a partnership a contract that she has negotiated with a third party to acquire a development parcel. She receives in exchange a general partner's interest worth $400,000. If she can sustain a $400,000 valuation for the contract, she will pay no tax on the contribution. If the contract is worth less than that, however, she will pay tax on the difference as compensation income.

Additionally, where the contributed property is an unrealized receivable or other right to income, the government may argue that the contributing partner ought to be taxed on the unrealized amount under assignment-of-income principles.

Both of these arguments, however, became less important with the second of the 1984 developments, which was to make mandatory the application of section 704(c) and to expand its scope to cover contributions of income items, such as unrealized receivables. Continuing the earlier example, assume that the developer successfully establishes a $400,000 valuation for the acquisition contract. The built-in gain on the contract ($400,000, unless the developer has an investment in the contract that gives her basis) will be taxed to the developer when realized by the partnership. Thus, by winning the valuation argument, the developer can defer her income and quite possibly convert it to capital gain, but she cannot escape it altogether. In the case of assigned accounts receivable, the income will likely retain its ordinary character when received by the partnership. The possibility that the partnership might convert the income realized from selling a contributed receivable into capital gain was foreclosed by section 724(a), not coincidently also added to the statute in 1984.

3.3.1   For the past six months, Ann Turk has been working as a contract tax lawyer for Winken, Blinken & Nod LLP. Based on her submitted hours, the firm owes her $45,000. Ann contributes this account receivable to the partnership in exchange for a newly minted partnership interest and a picture of her taken with the firm's chairman, suitable for framing. Her opening capital account balance is $45,000. What are the tax consequences to Ann and the firm?

    a)   The transaction is tax-free to both Ann and Winken under section 721(a), assuming the picture has no monetary value.

    b)   Ann recognizes $45,000 of compensation income and Winken has an equal deduction.

    c)   Ann recognizes no gain under section 721(a); Winken has cancellation of debt income equal to $45,000.

    d)   Same as (c), except that Winken also has a $45,000 deduction, offsetting its cancellation of debt income.

3.3.2   In the facts of Question 3.3.1, assume that Ann has been working for a different firm, TaxesЯUs LLP, and the receivable she holds is owed to her by that firm. She receives an offer to join Winken as a capital partner. As a condition of its offer, Winken requires Ann to turn over to the firm any fees she receives for work performed for others. Ann dutifully assigns her Taxes receivable to Winken. As before, her opening capital account balance is $45,000. In due course, Taxes pays Winken the $45,000. What are the tax consequences to Ann and to Winken?

    a)   Ann recognizes $45,000 of compensation income and Winken has an equal deduction.

    b)   Winken has $45,000 of ordinary income, which it can allocate among its partners (including Ann) according to its partnership agreement, assuming such allocation has substantial economic effect.

    c)   Ann recognizes $45,000 of compensation income; Winken has no income or deduction.

    d)   Ann recognizes $45,000 of compensation income and can write off the $45,000 balance in her capital account, creating an offsetting deduction; Winken has no income or deduction.

3.3.3   Dickie is a talent agent of sorts who represents a number of animal acts (a talking horse and a mind-reading goose are two of his headliners). Big Top LLC, a limited liability company taxed as a partnership, operates circuses throughout the United States. Big Top contacts Dickie with a proposal to bring him on as a 10% partner in exchange for exclusive access to his top acts and his promotional services in the markets where he works. Dickie accepts this offer and, in anticipation of becoming a partner, he negotiates exclusivity agreements with managers of each of his animal acts in the name of and on behalf of the partnership. He pays the managers a total of $70,000 of his own money for entering into these agreements. Dickie is a good negotiator: the contracts, as negotiated, are worth $200,000 to Big Top. Dickie's 10% interest in Big Top is worth $450,000 when he receives it. What is the amount of compensation income Dickie recognizes in this transaction?

a) $0

b) $250,000

c) $380,000

d) $450,000

3.3.4 Hunter is a developer working in Scranton, Pennsylvania, who is interested in revitalizing the Steamtown shopping mall. To that end, she has acquired for $120,000 a vacant lot adjacent to the mall and negotiated a deal with a major hotel chain to operate an upscale property if she will build a hotel to their specifications on the lot she owns. She negotiates agreements for a construction loan from a local bank and mezzanine financing from a government agency, contingent on her raising at least $20 million of equity financing to move the project forward. She spends $60,000 on the organizational costs of a new limited partnership formed to raise money for the development project. After receiving commitments for $25 million from limited partners, she contributes her lot (value $180,000), the hotel agreement (value $40,000) and the financing commitments (value $80,000) to the limited partnership in exchange for an interest as the sole general partner with an initial book capital account of $500,000. Shortly after collecting the first capital call from the limited partners, the partnership pays Hunter $60,000 to reimburse her out-of-pocket costs. This payment does not affect Hunter's book capital account, because all parties treat it as an expense reimbursement, rather than a distribution. All of these transactions occur within the same tax year. What income or gain does Hunter recognize?

a) $140,000 compensation income; $0 gain on disguised sale

b) $200,000 compensation income; $0 gain on disguised sale

c) $140,000 compensation income; $30,000 gain on disguised sale

d) $200,000 compensation income; $30,000 gain on disguised sale

3.4 SUBSTANTIAL RISK OF FORFEITURE AND THE SECTION 83(b) ELECTION

When you think about it, giving a capital interest to a brand-new service partner is a little crazy. Before she even shows up for work on day one, she owns a piece of the partnership. Worse, she owns a piece of the partnership if she does not show up for work on day one. A partnership that has any degree of bargaining power will therefore seek to restrict access to the capital of the partnership until the service provider has proven her mettle. One very common approach is to issue the service provider a profits interest. As reviewed in Topic 3.1, a profits interest has no immediate right to any of the capital of the partnership.

Another approach is to issue the service provider a capital interest, but to condition her right to keep it on her continuing to work for the partnership for a prescribed period of time. For example, a partnership might provide that one-third of the service partner's interest is hers to keep after she completes her first year of service, another one-third interest after the second year, and the remainder after three years. This is known as the "vesting schedule" of the partner's interest—in this case, a three-year graduated, or "graded," schedule. If the partnership provides that all of a service provider's interest vests at the same time, the interest is subject to "cliff vesting."

Sometimes, a partnership combines these two approaches, by issuing a profits interest that is subject to a vesting schedule. A service partner who gets one of these—and indeed any recipient of a partnership interest with a vesting schedule—must reach agreement with the partnership regarding the cash distributions it will make to her and her obligation, if any, to return such amounts if she ultimately forfeits her interest.

As reviewed in Topic 3.1, the profits interest is a very tax-efficient way to compensate a service provider. The service provider is not taxable on receipt of a profits interest, but instead pays tax if and when profits are allocated to her. How does a capital interest with a vesting schedule compare?

Under Treas. Reg. § 1.83–1(a), a service provider is not taxable on a transferred capital interest until it is "substantially vested," which occurs when the interest is not subject to a "substantial risk of forfeiture" or when the service provider can transfer the interest to a third party free of such risk, whichever is earlier. Treas. Reg. § 1.83–3(b). Generally, a substantial risk of forfeiture exists if the service provider's rights to the interest are conditioned upon the future performance (or refraining from performance) of substantial services. Treas. Reg. § 1.83–3(c)(1).

Accordingly, a service provider who receives a capital interest subject to a vesting schedule does not pay tax on it until it vests. At that time, however, the service provider recognizes ordinary income equal to the value of the interest at the time of vesting, not its value at the time of the grant. This can substantially increase the service provider's tax bill, as explored in the Questions below. A service provider in this position should always consider making an election under section 83(b) to report compensation income at the time of the grant, as if the risk of forfeiture did not exist.

The status of the holder of a nonvested partnership interest as a partner for tax purposes is somewhat unclear under current law. In principle, such an individual should not be treated as a partner until vesting occurs or a section 83(b) election is made, as would be clarified by Treasury regulations proposed in 2005. Prop. Treas. Reg. § 1.761–1(b). Following this approach, any cash distributions to a non-electing holder of a nonvested interest should be treated as cash compensation for services rendered. On the other hand, a well-known Revenue Procedure, dealing with nonvested profits interests, seems to indicate that partnerships may treat holders of such interests as partners if they choose. Rev. Proc. 2001–43, 2001–2 C.B. 191. This Revenue

Procedure is widely interpreted, however, as a taxpayer-friendly effort by the IRS to deem section 83(b) elections to have been made, whether or not the appropriate election forms were actually filed, if the parties consistently behave as if they were.

The making of a section 83(b) election, however, is not without its risks. Let's say that, despite her best intentions, a service provider who has made an election quits before vesting and thus forfeits her entire partnership interest. Section 83(b)(1) (last sentence) and Treas. Reg. § 1.83–2(a) limit her loss on the forfeiture to the amount that she paid for the interest, which in many cases will be nothing. For this purpose, the amount paid does not include the income the service provider took into account by reason of making the section 83(b) election, nor does it include any amount of income or gain that the partnership has allocated to her as a partner during the period prior to the forfeiture. The 2005 proposed regulations would institute "forfeiture allocations" partially (but incompletely) to address the latter issue, but such allocations are not permitted under current law (*i.e.*, prior to the finalization of the proposed regulations). Prop. Treas. Reg. § 1.704–1(b)(4)(xii).

3.4.1   In Question 3.1.2, 406 West Madison LP is a limited partnership developing a small commercial building. Its initial total capital is $1 million. James is offered a 10% capital interest in the partnership in exchange for his services as construction manager for the project. Assume that the partnership's proposal to James includes two-year cliff vesting, meaning that James will forfeit his interest unless he works for the partnership for at least two years. On the vesting date, the development is complete and James' 10% interest is worth $1,250,000. What is James' compensation income in the year of the grant and in the year of vesting?

a)   Grant, $0; Vesting, $0

b)   Grant, $100,000; Vesting, $0

c)   Grant, $100,000; Vesting, $1,150,000

d)   Grant, $0; Vesting, $1,250,000

3.4.2   How do the results of Question 3.4.1 change if James timely makes an election under section 83(b)?

a)   Grant, $0; Vesting, $0

b)   Grant, $100,000; Vesting, $0

c)   Grant, $100,000; Vesting, $1,150,000

d)   Grant, $0; Vesting, $1,250,000

3.4.3   Assume, solely for purposes of this Question, that the partnership is not required to capitalize any portion of the compensation it pays to James. What is the effect of James' section 83(b) election on the partnership's deduction?

a)   No effect: because James is a partner rather than an employee, the partnership is not allowed a deduction.

b) No effect: the partnership is allowed to deduct the value of James' capital interest on grant, whether or not he makes an election.

c) No effect: the partnership is allowed to deduct the value of James' capital interest on vesting, whether or not he makes an election.

d) Big effect: the partnership's deduction is allowed only at the time(s) and in the amount(s) that James reports compensation income.

3.4.4 James makes a timely section 83(b) election in the year of the grant and a year later receives an offer from a big developer group that he simply cannot refuse. He leaves 406 West Madison LP and forfeits his interest. During his time as a partner, he has been allocated a loss of $32,000 and received no cash distributions. What is his allowable tax loss on the forfeiture?

a) $0

b) ($32,000)

c) $32,000

d) $100,000

3.4.5 In Question 3.1.3, 406 West Madison LP grants James a 10% profits interest. This partnership interest can reasonably be expected to be worth between $650,000 and $1,400,000 when the building is finished and ready for sale. Assume now that the partnership's proposal to James includes two-year cliff vesting. On the vesting date, the development is complete and James' 10% interest is worth $1,150,000. What is James' compensation income in the year of the grant and in the year of vesting if James makes no section 83(b) election and the partnership does not treat him as a partner during the vesting period?

a) Grant, $0; Vesting, $0

b) Grant, $0; Vesting, $650,000

c) Grant, $0; Vesting, $1,150,000

d) Grant, $0; Vesting, $1,400,000

3.4.6 How do the results of Question 3.4.5 change if James timely makes an election under section 83(b)?

a) Grant, $0; Vesting, $0

b) Grant, $100,000; Vesting, $0

c) Grant, $100,000; Vesting, $1,150,000

d) Grant, $0; Vesting, $1,150,000

3.4.7 For the past several years, Caroline Owens has been working as a business broker, assisting buyers and sellers of small and mid-sized businesses. Her deal-making prowess lands her an offer to join Mid-American Capital LP, a private-equity fund that has been the buyer of her client's businesses on several occasions in the past. She is offered a 4% profits interest with a four-year graded vesting schedule, 1% per year, in exchange for her services to Mid-American. Each 1% share can be expected to generate about $100,000 of capital gains annually and a modest amount of ordinary income. She asks you whether she should make a section 83(b) election. What do you say?

a) Yes. Are you free for lunch?

b) Yes, but the value that you will have to report as current compensation income as a result of the election is likely to be quite high.

c) Yes, you have nothing to lose, and the ability to report capital gains rather than ordinary income during the vesting period is valuable.

d) Yes, but be careful when you negotiate your rights to distributions during the vesting period.

3.4.8   Roy receives a one-third capital interest in the SDT Partnership, which is in the business of manufacturing and selling cellphones, headsets and other electronic gadgets. Roy invests no money in the partnership and receives his interest entirely for his promise to perform services for the SDT Partnership. Roy will have to forfeit his partnership interest if he leaves SDT for any reason within three years. What considerations should Roy have in mind as he thinks about whether to make a section 83(b) election? (Mark all that apply.)

a) Roy must report the value of his capital interest as compensation income in the year he makes the election.

b) Roy cannot claim a tax loss with respect to the amount he reports as income by reason of making the election.

c) Making an election will allow Roy to claim his share of the partnership's operating profits as capital gains.

d) Making an election will allow Roy to report as capital gain his share of any appreciation in the partnership's capital assets and section 1231 property accrued during the vesting period, if and when recognized by the partnership.

3.5   PROVIDING SERVICES WITHOUT PARTNER RISK: SECTION 707

This Topic is the bookend to Topic 2.7 (contributions without partner risk). Here, as there, the function of section 707 is to distinguish transactions between a partnership and a partner from transactions between a partnership and one acting other than in her capacity as a partner. You may be puzzled as to why this distinction is important (or even necessary) in the context of services. In the case of property contributions, the application of section 707 can make the difference between a taxable and a non-taxable transaction. In contrast, one who provides services to a partnership is always taxed. If she provides services in the capacity of a partner, she is taxed immediately on the value of any capital interest she receives in exchange for the services. Additionally, she will be taxed over time on the profits allocated to her with respect to any capital or profits interest she receives. If, on the other hand, she provides services other than in the capacity of a partner, she will be taxed on any property or money she receives from the partnership as fee income. So what's the big deal?

The function of section 707(a) in the services context is three-fold. First, it is intended to prevent end-runs around the requirement that partnerships capitalize their expenditures, just like other taxpayers. Second, it attempts to prevent persons who are not acting in their capacity as partners from taking their compensation in the form of capital gains or other tax-favored income. Third, in a limited number of cases, it may preserve an accurate characterization of the income paid for services rendered in a non-partner capacity for purposes of ancillary tax provisions.

Enforcing capitalization. Assume that 406 West Madison LP from Question 3.1.2 wants to engage an architect to design its small commercial building and is willing to pay her $50,000. If the architect is not a partner, she will be classified as an independent contractor. Whether the partnership pays her in cash or in property, the architect will have ordinary income and the partnership will be required to capitalize her fee into the cost of the building. If the architect happens also to be a partner of 406 West Madison LP because she made a capital contribution, section 707(a)(1) requires that the tax treatment of her $50,000 fee for architectural services not be affected by this additional relationship. To this extent, she is considered as acting in a non-partner capacity, even though she remains a partner for other purposes. The architect has $50,000 of ordinary income as an independent contractor and the partnership a $50,000 capitalizable cost.

What if the partnership allocates to the architect the first $50,000 of the gross rental income from the building, rather than paying her a fee? An allocation of income to one partner has the effect of a deduction to the other partners by reducing the amount of partnership income remaining to be allocated to them. Thus, if this arrangement is respected, it will reduce the income of the other partners of 406 West Madison LP by $50,000, which is the equivalent of a $50,000 deduction, without changing the tax treatment of the architect at all.

Section 707(a)(2)(A) was enacted in 1984 to deal with situations like this. The legislative history, which is extensive, indicates that the architect's status as a partner should be determined largely by the degree of entrepreneurial risk she is bearing:

> The first, and generally the most important, factor is whether the payment is subject to an appreciable risk as to amount. Partners extract the profits of the partnership with reference to the business success of the venture, while third parties generally receive payments which are not subject to this risk. Thus, an allocation and distribution provided for a service partner under the partnership agreement which subjects the partner to significant entrepreneurial risk as to both the amount and the fact of payment generally should be recognized as a distributive share

and a partnership distribution, while an allocation and distribution provided to a service partner under the partnership agreement which involve limited risk as to amount and payment should generally be treated as a fee under section 707(a). Examples of allocations that limit a partner's risk include both "capped" allocations of partnership income (*i.e.*, percentage or fixed dollar amount allocations subject to an annual maximum amount when the parties could reasonably expect the cap to apply in most years) and allocations for a fixed number of years under which the income that will go to the partner is reasonably certain.

STAFF OF THE JOINT COMMITTEE ON TAXATION, 98TH CONG., 2D SESS., GENERAL EXPLANATION OF THE REVENUE PROVISIONS OF THE DEFICIT REDUCTION ACT OF 1984 at 227-28 (Comm. Print 1984).

Proposed Treasury regulations under section 707(a)(2)(A) follow this legislative history, identifying lack of entrepreneurial risk as a sufficient factor by itself to conclude that an arrangement between a partnership and a partner is a disguised payment for services. Prop. Treas. Reg. § 1.707–2(c). The proposed regulations identify facts and circumstances that, if present, create a presumption that an arrangement lacks entrepreneurial risk. In addition to those mentioned in the legislative history quoted above, the proposed regulations include allocations of gross (rather than net) income. An allocation of net income is not above suspicion, however, if the arrangement is designed to assure that sufficient net profits are highly likely to be available to make the allocation to the service provider—for example, allocations of net profits from specific transactions or accounting periods that do not depend on the long-term future success of the enterprise. The proposed regulations, promulgated in July 2015, have not been finalized as of this writing.

Preventing character conversions. The second function of section 707(a) in the services context is to prevent character conversion by or on behalf of the service provider. Continuing the example, assume that 406 West Madison LP proposes to compensate the architect by allocating to her the first $50,000 of capital gain recognized by the partnership on the sale of the completed building. If successful, this will cause the architect to receive her compensation for personal services in the form of tax-favored capital gain, rather than as ordinary income. The other partners, of course, will recognize their "deduction" as reduced capital gain on sale, but that may be fine with them, since most or all of the profit realized by 406 West Madison LP is likely to be taxed as capital gain in any event. The issue is whether the partnership has given the architect a profits interest, which under current law does accomplish this character conversion, or a contract for personal services, which does not. The measuring stick for deciding this issue is the degree of entrepreneurial risk the architect has assumed. In making this determination, the proposed regulations would take into account facts and circumstances bearing on the likelihood that the partnership will recognize sufficient capital gain to make this allocation.

Application of provisions outside of Subchapter K. The final function, or effect, of section 707(a) in the services context is to treat compensation paid by a partnership for services rendered by a partner acting in a non-partner capacity consistently with compensation paid to one who is not a partner. For example, payments by a partnership to an independent contractor for services rendered are subject to self-employment tax. Under section 1402(a)(13), however, self-employment tax does not apply to a limited partner's share of partnership income. Thus the architect in the preceding example could avoid paying self-employment tax on her $50,000 compensation if she were a limited partner and could establish that she received her fee as a distributive share of partnership profits. Where it applies, section 707(a) prevents this result by treating the architect's compensation as an amount paid to an independent contractor.

Congress seems less enthusiastic about this third function of section 707(a) and it has always been limited in scope. Indeed, the 1954 legislative history of what is now section 707(a)(1) cautions that it may not be "appropriate" to treat a partner receiving a section 707(a) payment as a stranger to the partnership for purposes of applying other provisions of the internal revenue laws—thus inviting a section-by-section analysis of this question. H.R. Rep. No. 83–2543, 83d Cong., 2d Sess. 59 (1954). The seeming partner who, upon application of section 707(a), turns out not to be a partner at all is an easy case. There is no reason that payments to such a person should not be treated as payments to an employee or independent contractor for all purposes of the Internal Revenue Code. The service provider who, subsequent to the application of section 707(a), remains a partner is a tougher case. One might think, for instance, that a partner receiving a section 707(a) payment could be either an independent contractor or an employee, depending on the degree of direction and control exercised by the partnership. The IRS, however, has historically taken the position that a partner cannot also be classified as an employee for tax purposes. Rev. Rul. 69–184, 1969–1 C.B. 256. The Fifth Circuit disagreed with this position in *Armstrong v. Phinney*, 394 F.2d 661 (5th Cir. 1968), holding that a partner can also be an employee for purposes of applying section 119 (exclusion for meals and lodging furnished for the convenience of the employer).

Distinguishing section 707(a) payments from guaranteed payments under section 707(c). In Topic 2.7, we studied section 707(c) in relation to guaranteed payments for the use of capital provided by a partner. Section 707(c) also applies to guaranteed payments for services provided by a partner. As in the case of guaranteed payments for the use of capital, payments for services are not treated as guaranteed payments unless they are determined "without regard to the income of the partnership." Guaranteed payments for services are taxed as ordinary income to the service provider and are deductible by the partnership under section 162, except to the extent that capitalization is required.

Two questions come to mind: How does one distinguish a payment for services governed by section 707(c) from a payment for services governed by section 707(a)? And what difference does it make?

The answer to the first question is that guaranteed payments under section 707(c) are made to compensate a service provider acting in her capacity as a partner, whereas section 707(a) payments are compensation for services provided by a partner not acting in her capacity as such. As a practical matter, guaranteed payments are made to persons who are working *in the business* of the partnership, whereas section 707(a) payments are made to persons who are working *for the business* of the partnership. In other words, a partner earns a guaranteed payment by working as part of the business of the partnership, whereas a partner earns a section 707(a) payment by working in an independent business that provides services to the partnership. *Compare* Rev. Rul. 81–300, 1981–2 C.B. 143 (guaranteed payments to general partner for services provided as manager of partnership's business), *with* Rev. Rul. 81–301, 1981–2 C.B. 144 (section 707(a) payments to general partner acting as investment advisor to partnership).

This is not an entirely satisfying distinction, of course, and it is sometimes difficult to tell the difference between the two types of payments. Indeed, the 1984 legislative history of section 707(a)(2)(A) indicates that, following the enactment of that section, the payments described in Rev. Rul. 81–300 should be treated as section 707(a) payments, although that ruling treats them as guaranteed payments under section 707(c). STAFF OF THE JOINT COMMITTEE ON TAXATION, 98TH CONG., 2D SESS., GENERAL EXPLANATION OF THE REVENUE PROVISIONS OF THE DEFICIT REDUCTION ACT OF 1984 at 231 (Comm. Print 1984). Consistent with this change in approach, the IRS declared Rev. Rul. 81–300 obsolete as of July 23, 2015. Over the long haul, it seems likely that section 707(a) will devour section 707(c) and the latter section may even be repealed. In the meantime, subtle differences between the two will remain.

The most significant difference is timing. The service provider takes a section 707(a) payment into account when received or accrued, according to her regular method of tax accounting. A section 707(c) guaranteed payment, by contrast, is included in the service provider's income under section 706(a) in the taxable year within or with which ends the taxable year of the partnership in which it deducts or capitalizes the payment. Treas. Reg. § 1.707–1(c).

Another difference is the application of tax provisions outside of Subchapter K. The language of section 707(c) expressly limits its coverage to sections 61, 162(a) and 263. This suggests (and one might have thought requires) that a guaranteed payment must be treated as a partner's distributive share of partnership income in determining the application of all other tax provisions. Nevertheless, there are situations in which partner status is disregarded in determining the peripheral tax consequences of a guaranteed payment. The Tax Court has held, for example, that section 911 (exclusion for foreign earned income) can apply to guaranteed payments for services. *Miller v. Commissioner*, 52 T.C. 752 (1969). There is no similar authority for section 707(a) payments, although if this question were to arise in that context, the answer should be the same.

3.5.1 Samantha Struthers is a tax lawyer at Reigeluth, Barnes & Noble LLP ("RB&N"). She is paid a "salary" of $190,000 per year in addition to a 5% share of the profits of the firm after deduction of all expenses, including her salary. For the year 2017, Samantha receives her salary and an allocation of $300,000 of net profit, which she is allowed to withdraw from her capital account after the closing of the partnership's books in February 2018. Both Samantha and the partnership use the cash method. What is the amount and character of Samantha's 2017 income?

   a) Wages of $190,000, reportable on Form W–2; distributive profit share of $300,000, reportable on Schedule K-1

   b) Guaranteed payment of $190,000 and distributive profit share of $300,000, both reportable on Schedule K-1

   c) Wages of $490,000, reportable on Form W–2

   d) Guaranteed payment of $190,000, reportable on Schedule K-1; taxation of distributive profit share of $300,000 not reportable in 2017, but deferred until receipt in 2018

3.5.2 *Before answering this Question, read section 106, which excludes from the gross income of an "employee" the coverage provided by an "employer" under an accident or health plan.* RB&N pays $19,000 of premiums to cover Samantha under the firm's group health plan. Assuming that the partnership does not treat this amount as a distribution to Samantha, how does it affect her 2017 income from the partnership?

   a) Wages increase by $19,000

   b) No change to wage income

   c) Guaranteed payment increases by $19,000

   d) No change to guaranteed payment

3.5.3 Samantha is "senior counsel" at RB&N. The terms of her engagement with the firm are spelled out in the partnership agreement, which she signs. She is entitled to attend all meetings of the partners (even the ones in Hawaii), but she cannot vote and has no participation in firm profits. Instead, she receives a "draw" equal to $150,000 per year plus $300 for every hour she bills in excess of 1,000. The firm exercises direction and control over Samantha's activities sufficient to meet the common-law standard for an employee. In 2017, Samantha receives $225,000 in cash and the firm pays $19,000 of premiums to cover her under the health plan. What is the amount and character of Samantha's 2017 income?

   a) Wages of $225,000, reportable on Form W–2

   b) Wages of $244,000, reportable on Form W–2

   c) Guaranteed payment of $225,000, reportable on Schedule K-1

   d) Guaranteed payment of $244,000, reportable on Schedule K-1

3.5.4   Buffalo Pratt is the best salesman in the world. Through his company, Pratt Marketing LLC, he makes his services available, at a cost, to a wide market. Pratt Marketing is hired by Mid-American Pipeline LP ("MAP"), a limited partnership that owns and operates an interstate gas pipeline. MAP desires to sell units of partnership interest to the public in order to raise the equity capital needed for a substantial expansion of its business. If it is successful, MAP units will be traded on the New York Stock Exchange and MAP will qualify for treatment as a partnership under section 7704. Enter Pratt Marketing. Buffalo and his company put together investor presentations throughout the United States and Canada for the purpose of creating interest for the initial public offering of MAP units. Buffalo's normal fee for this amount of work would be $450,000, but he agrees instead to become a special limited partner of MAP with a priority allocation of 0.5% of the gross income from operating the existing pipeline for a period of three years. Buffalo is not quite sure why MAP offered this deal, but he is happy to take it. He estimates his share of the partnership's gross income will be at least $150,000 per year, probably closer to $200,000, and he can withdraw his share in cash as soon as the books are closed each year. Buffalo is never wrong about these things. What are the tax consequences of this arrangement to Pratt Marketing and to MAP?

a)   Pratt Marketing will receive a distributive share of partnership income.

b)   Pratt Marketing will receive guaranteed payments which MAP may deduct.

c)   Pratt Marketing will receive guaranteed payments which MAP may not deduct.

d)   Pratt Marketing will receive section 707(a) payments which MAP may not deduct.

CHAPTER 4
PARTNERSHIP INCOME, GAINS, LOSSES AND DEDUCTIONS

4.1 COMPUTING PARTNERSHIP INCOME, GAINS, LOSSES AND DEDUCTIONS

It is often said—nay, it is always said—that Subchapter K is an amalgam of entity and aggregate concepts. This means that the partnership tax laws sometimes reach results consistent with treating a partnership as an entity separate from the partners and other times reach results consistent with treating the partners as the owners of undivided interests in the partnership's assets. So, does this mean that a partnership is treated as an entity for some purposes and as an aggregate for others? No, it does not. Under Subchapter K, a partnership is *always* an entity. There are provisions in Subchapter K that seek to replicate aggregate treatment, of course, and we review them in this Reading Period. But these provisions *never* disregard the existence of the partnership as an entity (although regulatory anti-abuse rules or judicial doctrines may disregard the existence of the partnership entirely). Instead, in a very selective manner, certain provisions replicate the tax results that would be achieved if the partners owned undivided interests in the partnership's assets. They produce, in other words, aggregate results in an entity world.

Nowhere is this clearer than in the provisions of the Internal Revenue Code providing for the computation of partnership income, gains, losses, deductions and credits and the allocation of these items to the partners. Under section 703, a partnership computes its taxable income as a separate entity pretty much like an individual. In this process, section 702(b) determines the character of the partnership's items. The language of this section is singularly unhelpful and might even suggest (particularly when read late at night) that the existence of the partnership should be disregarded for this purpose. That is not the intended meaning, as confirmed by the examples in Treas. Reg. § 1.702–1(b). Instead, the partnership is treated as an entity in whose hands partnership income is characterized, and that character passes through to the partners in accordance with their distributive shares. Thus, for example, gain on sale of an asset that the partnership holds as a capital asset is capital gain to the partnership and to the partners, despite the fact that the asset might have been inventory in the hands of any particular partner and would have produced ordinary income if sold by that partner. As we will see in Chapter 7, there are certain "safeguards" in the Internal Revenue Code (namely, sections 724 and 735) that are intended to prevent abuse of this general rule.

Because section 701 provides that the partners, not the partnership, are liable for tax on the partnership's income, there needs to be a mechanism for divvying up the partnership's income among the partners. This is, of course, the subject of section 704, covered in Topic 4.3. Section 702(a) adds the somewhat mechanical but important rule that each partner must take her share of partnership items into account separately (rather than in the aggregate) if doing so affects the partner's tax liability. Continuing the earlier example, a partnership realizing capital gain must state it separately on the Schedules K-1 delivered to the partners, and the partners must report it, as capital gain, on their individual tax returns. Section 702(a) lists several specific items subject to this treatment and section 702(a)(7) and Treas. Reg. § 1.702–1(a)(8)(ii) provide a general rule requiring similar treatment for unlisted items.

4.1.1 *Please review sections 163(h), 179(b)(8) and 1231(a) before answering this Question.* In 2016, Yellow Sunflour Bakery LLC, a limited liability company taxed as a partnership, downsized by selling its location on Baker Street, although its original shop on Howell Street has continued to perform well. When it closes its books for the year, the partnership has the following items: (1) income (gross receipts less cost of goods sold) from the bakery business, (2) salaries, (3) depreciation on the Howell Street location for a full year and on the Baker Street location for part of the year, (4) section 179 expense for depreciable business property placed in service in 2016, (5) interest on the Howell Street mortgage, and (6) section 1231 loss on the sale of Baker Street. Under section 702(a), how should Yellow Sunflour report these items to its partners?

a) Section 179 expense (item 4), mortgage interest (item 5), section 1231 loss (item 6) and ordinary business income (item 1 less items 2 and 3)

b) Section 179 expense (item 4), section 1231 loss (item 6) and ordinary business income (item 1 less items 2, 3 and 5)

c) Section 1231 loss (item 6) and ordinary business income (item 1 less items 2, 3, 4 and 5)

d) Ordinary business expense (item 1 less all other items)

4.1.2 Scythe Investments LP, a calendar-year limited partnership, holds a diversified portfolio of publicly traded stocks and bonds. Jack Gutentag buys a 1% interest from the partnership with a cash contribution on October 1, the date of the partnership's regular quarterly opening. On December 15, Scythe sells several stock positions, netting a healthy long-term capital gain. Under the partnership agreement and section 704(c), Jack's share of this gain is limited to his share of the appreciation in the closed-out stock positions since October 1. This amount is $37,000. Under section 702, what does Scythe allocate to Jack for the year?

a) Short-term capital gain of $9,250

b)   Short-term capital gain of $37,000

c)   Long-term capital gain of $9,250

d)   Long-term capital gain of $37,000

4.1.3   Abe Claussen, a successful lawyer, is approached by an old law-school classmate, Mort Schimsky, with an idea that seems to mix profit with social awareness. Since graduation, Mort has worked in the inner city in legal aid, food distribution and, more recently, running a housing agency. He has come up with a plan to renovate old townhouses and sell them to residents willing to stay in the neighborhood to promote community development. Mort asks Abe for a $100,000 investment and Abe, thoroughly impressed, gives him $200,000. Mort proves to be an able real estate developer, arranging bank financing, acquiring, renovating and selling nine townhouses in the first year. The total profit is $90,000, which Mort and Abe have a handshake agreement to split equally. At year-end, however, they decide to recommit the money (Abe's original $200,000 investment plus the $90,000 profit) to redeveloping more properties the following year. What are the tax consequences to Abe from the first year's activities?

a)   No taxable income or loss

b) $5,000 capital loss

c) $45,000 capital gain

d) $45,000 ordinary income

4.2   REQUIRED TAXABLE YEARS

Section 706(b) limits the ability of a partnership to select a taxable year of its own choosing. The need for this limitation grows out of the way that a partnership's taxable income, gains, losses and deductions flow through to its partners. Section 706(a) provides that a partner's taxable income for a taxable year includes partnership items for any partnership taxable year ending with or within the partner's taxable year. In everyday language, the partnership's income or loss flows through to its partners at the end of the partnership's taxable year. This presents no problem if the partnership and all of its partners share the same taxable year, because in that case, the partnership's income or loss flows through to all of the partners on the last day of their respective taxable years and is taken into account by them for the same year in which it was earned by the partnership.

A problem can arise, however, if the taxable year of the partnership is "mismatched" from that of its partners. In that case, some of the partnership's income or loss will be taken into account, not in the partner's taxable year in which it was earned, but in the following taxable year. The purpose of section 706(b) is to limit this "deferral."

To understand section 706(b), you need to know how to measure the amount of the deferral achieved by any particular choice of partnership taxable year. A thought experiment will help. Imagine that a partnership could flow through its income to the partners at the end of every day, rather than only at the end of its taxable year. In that case, of course, there would be no deferral, because the income earned on, say, November 1 would flow through to all of the partners on November 1. Same for November 2 and for every other day of the year. The taxable year of the partnership would be irrelevant. This is your baseline for measuring deferral.

Now return to the real world where partnership income flows through at year-end. Suppose that Partnership A has a taxable year ending October 31 and all of its partners have calendar taxable years. In the partnership's year beginning November 1, the income that it earns in November and December will not flow through to the partners until October 31 of the following year, when it will be included in their income. Compared to the baseline of daily flow-through, taxation of the income from these two months will be deferred for a year. Somewhat confusingly, Partnership A's taxable year is said to offer two months of deferral to each of the partners. What it really offers is 12 months of deferral (from the partners' year ending 12/31/01 until the partners' year ending 12/31/02) of two months of income (that earned by the partnership from 11/1/01 through 12/31/01).

Suppose now that Partnership B chooses a taxable year ending January 31. In the partnership's year beginning February 1, the income that it earns for the next 11 months (February through December) will not flow through to the partners until the following year. Compared to the baseline of daily flow-through, the taxation of the income from 11 months will be deferred for a year. Accordingly, Partnership B's taxable year is said to offer 11 months of deferral to all partners.

FIGURE 4.2

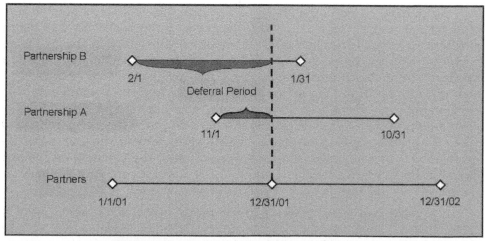

Income earned by the partnership during the "deferral period" is not included in the partners' taxable income until the year after it is earned.

Section 706(b) attempts to limit deferral, but with an eye toward simplicity. Its restraint is evident in the "waterfall" of section 706(b)(1)(B), which allows most partnerships to determine their required taxable year without ever calculating a deferral period. It is evident also in section

706(b)(4), which limits the frequency of changes in the required taxable year. And it is evident in section 706(b)(1)(C), which allows a partnership to have any taxable year for which it can establish a good business purpose.

Nevertheless, the concept of the deferral period is necessary to determine the required taxable year of any partnership that has neither a majority interest taxable year nor a single taxable year for all principal partners. The statute seems to require a calendar taxable year in such a case, but this has been replaced by the taxable year with "least aggregate deferral" under Treas. Reg. § 1.706–1(b)(3). In addition, section 444, which permits an election of a taxable year other than the required year, employs the concept of the deferral period as a way to measure the deferral achieved by the elected year as compared to the required year. For a new partnership, this deferral period cannot exceed three months. For a partnership that has already established a taxable year, however, the deferral period of the elected year cannot exceed the lesser of three months or the deferral period of the taxable year that is being changed.

4.2.1   InSight LLC, a limited liability company taxed as a partnership, is a joint marketing venture, 80% owned by many small companies and individuals who operate retail photography stores. None of these members has as much as a five percent interest in InSight and their taxable years end in September, October, November and December in roughly equal proportions. The managing member of Insight, holding the remaining 20% interest, is a Delaware business corporation with a taxable year ending March 31. What is the required taxable year of this partnership?

a)   March

b)   December

c)   Any of September, October, November or December

d)   Any of March, September, October, November or December

4.2.2   Corp X and Corp Y have taxable years ending on the last days of March and October, respectively. They wish to form a limited liability company, taxed as a partnership, in which they have equal membership interests. What is the required taxable year of this partnership?

a)   March

b)   October

c)   December

d)   March or October

4.2.3   Corp Q, Corp R and Corp S form a limited liability company taxed as a partnership. Q has a 42% interest and a taxable year ending October 31. R has a 42% interest and a taxable year ending June 30. S has a 16% interest and has adopted the calendar year as its taxable year. What is the required taxable year of this partnership?

a)   October

b)   December

c)   June

d)   Any of the above

4.2.4   *Take a quick look at Rev. Rul. 87–57, 1987–2 C.B. 117, before answering this Question.* The Cheese Factory LLC, taxed as a partnership, produces a delectable Wisconsin cheddar. Production begins in March for a selling season that runs from the summer through the Christmas holiday season. The company then shuts down for the months of January and February, to begin again in March. Currently, the company has a calendar taxable year, as do all of its members. The company desires to change its taxable year-end, in part because this would allow the outside accountants to complete their work outside of their busy season and the company would receive a reduced charge. Under these circumstances, and assuming that the Company is willing to make any required payments under section 7519, what is an acceptable taxable year for the Cheese Factory?

a)   September, October, November or December

b)   February

c)   December

d)   All of the above

4.3   ALLOCATING PARTNERSHIP INCOME, GAINS, LOSSES AND DEDUCTIONS: SUBSTANTIAL ECONOMIC EFFECT

Students often refer to this Topic as the study of special allocations. Humor me—I think it is better to begin the study of the allocation system of Subchapter K with "unspecial allocations." Imagine, for example, a partnership agreement that provides that each partner will be allocated a share of all partnership income and loss equal to the share of the partnership's capital which that partner has contributed. A partner contributing 10% of the partnership's aggregate capital gets 10% of the partnership's income and loss; 20% of the capital gets the partner 20% of the partnership's income and loss; and so on. These shares are stable, but they are not static. They will change whenever the partner's share of capital changes, which will occur every time that partner or another partner contributes or receives a distribution of capital.

Actually, you needn't have much imagination to picture such a partnership. They are everywhere. Described as partnerships with "straight-up allocations" or as "partnerships by shares," arrangements like this resemble corporations except that they do not pay income tax. They are appealing to folks who are comfortable with the use of a corporation to conduct business. For example, two unrelated corporations seeking to form a joint venture are likely to choose a limited liability company as the vehicle for the venture. Like a corporation, an LLC offers limited liability to all participants and it can be managed by a board of directors and officers like a corporation. All that is missing is the income taxes. In many such ventures, special allocations are viewed as an unnecessary complication, because the venturers are completely comfortable with proportional interests in capital, profits and losses—just as they would have if the venture entity were a corporation.

Another common example of this simple economic relationship is the S corporation. In this case, straight-up allocations are mandated by section 1366(a)(1), which requires that each shareholder must take into account her "pro rata share" of the S corporation's items of income, gain, loss, deduction and credit. This treatment of S corporations and their shareholders has not stopped more than four million corporations from electing to be treated in this fashion. The reason is that the avoidance of corporate-level tax is incentive enough to make the election, without the added benefit (or nuisance) of special allocations.

So why not prohibit special allocations in Subchapter K as well? Before answering that question, we need to be clear about what "prohibit" would mean in this context. One possible meaning is to prohibit partners from making any economic deal other than one that is pro-rata. While a possible meaning, this is an impossible suggestion. A partnership agreement is, at root, a contract, and the partners are free to make whatever deal they want regarding the sharing of profits and losses. Outlawing all but pro-rata partnerships would be a task far beyond the Internal Revenue Code. Even if a grand conclave of state legislatures convened to make the necessary changes to state laws, what would be the point? Any legislated prohibition on special allocations could almost certainly be avoided by breaking a partnership agreement into several separate contracts, each providing for permitted allocations or payments. More importantly, such a prohibition, if successful, would curtail the ability of entrepreneurs to make economically flexible arrangements that provide returns to capital and labor in such amounts and at such times as needed to promote the productive use of those resources.

A second, more feasible, approach might be to tax all partnerships as pro-rata, whether they are or not. While more feasible than the first idea, this one is no more sensible. In every case that the partnership agreement provided for special allocations, this approach would cause at least one partner to be taxed on partnership profit that, according to the partnership agreement, belonged to a different partner. Or to one partner enjoying the tax benefit of a partnership loss that was borne by a different partner.

So we really have no choice but to refine our objective. What is wrong with special allocations? Nothing at all, if the tax allocations match the economic allocations provided in the partnership agreement. Indeed, on grounds of economic efficiency alone, special allocations like this should be encouraged. The troublesome case is special allocations that are divorced from the economics of the partnership agreement and serve only to avoid taxes. Congress and the tax administrators have the unenviable task of identifying this sort of special allocation. Before 1976, section 704(b) explicitly required this identification, by refusing to recognize an allocation for tax purposes if "the principal purpose" of the allocation was tax avoidance or evasion. This standard was elaborated in Treasury regulations that required consideration of all the facts and circumstances in making this determination.

The section 704 that we study today is the result of the efforts of Congress in 1976 and of the Treasury Department and the IRS in the following years to refine this standard and make it more predictable. It is an essentially permissive standard. Under section 704(a), items of partnership income, gain, loss, deduction and credit, determined under the rules of sections 702 and 703 that we reviewed in Topic 4.1, are allocated among the partners as the partnership agreement provides. If the partnership agreement is silent or the allocations it provides do not possess "substantial economic effect," then section 704(b) requires allocation in accordance with each partner's respective "interest in the partnership."

Substantial economic effect. Three little words. Have ever three words created such anxiety, such emotion, such tears, such gnashing of teeth and cursing of Fate? Well, maybe. Back here in the world of partnership tax, however, you have less to fear than you thought. First, and most important, the scheme for determining economic effect depends on capital accounting, a subject that you have already begun to master. Second, so implemented, the process for determining economic effect is really quite mechanical, once you get used to it. And finally, the substantiality test, though also intended to be mechanical, confounds everyone with its complex, multi-layered structure, including at least one federal judge. You are in good company.

Economic effect

Under the gargantuan and indispensable Treasury regulations implementing section 704(b)(2), establishing that an allocation has substantial economic effect is a two-part process. First, the allocation must have economic effect. Second, the economic effect of the allocation must be substantial. By now, you should know the three requirements for meeting the safe harbor for economic effect established by Treas. Reg. § 1.704–1(b)(2)(ii): (1) the partnership must maintain proper capital accounts; (2) those accounts must govern liquidating distributions to partners; and (3) a partner having a negative balance in her capital account following the liquidation of her interest must be unconditionally obligated to restore (pay back to the partnership) that deficit in a timely fashion. Together, these three requirements are intended to ensure that, in the words of the regulation, "in the event there is an economic benefit or economic burden that corresponds to an allocation, the partner to whom the allocation is made must receive such economic benefit or bear such economic burden." Treas. Reg. § 1.704–1(b)(2)(ii)(a).

Assume, for example, that Anita contributes $1,000 to the capital of a general partnership. The partnership thereafter incurs a $600 loss, which it allocates entirely to Anita. This allocation reduces Anita's capital account by $600, the amount of the loss. Assume that the partnership never recovers this loss by generating income or through appreciation in the value of its property and, sometime later, it liquidates. Upon the liquidation of her interest, Anita receives only $400, the remaining balance in her capital account. In this case, the $600 loss did indeed turn out to have an economic burden, and Anita has borne this burden through a $600 reduction in the cash she receives on liquidation.

If the partnership's loss were $1,200 instead of $600, the allocation of all $1,200 to Anita would reduce her capital account to a negative $200. On liquidation, she would receive nothing from the partnership. If that were the end of it, however, she would not bear the economic burden of the last $200 of the loss. The requirement that she restore the $200 deficit balance in her capital account increases her real, economic loss to $1,200, the amount of the loss allocated to her.

What if Anita refuses to assume any deficit-restoration obligation? Assuming the partnership has no debt, this limits her commitment to the partnership to the amount of her invested capital. In this case, the so-called "alternate test" for economic effect would permit the partnership to allocate up to $1,000 of losses and deductions to Anita—that is to say, an amount sufficient to reduce the balance in her capital account to zero. There are three conditions. First, the partnership must maintain proper capital accounts and they must govern liquidating distributions. These are the first and second requirements of the general safe harbor, discussed above. Second, in determining Anita's capital-account balance for this purpose, the partnership must reduce her capital account by adjustments (other than allocations of losses or deductions) that are reasonably expected to reduce her capital account in the future. These adjustments are listed in Treas. Reg. §§ 1.704–1(b)(2)(ii)(*d*)(*4*), (*5*) and (*6*). Finally, the partnership agreement must contain a "qualified income offset," under which income and gain will be allocated to Anita if, despite the foregoing precautions, she winds up with a negative capital account in the future. The amount allocated under this backstop provision will be only the amount needed to return Anita's capital account to zero. Treas. Reg. § 1.704–1(b)(2)(ii)(*d*).

The qualified income offset is widely, and wildly, misunderstood. The most common mistake is to think that it kicks in whenever a partner's capital account falls below zero and can therefore justify allocations which create deficit balances in the capital accounts of partners who have no deficit-restoration obligation. No, no, no. No. The QIO, as it is known by its close friends, is in fact extraordinarily limited in scope. It only creates allocations of income and gain if a partner *unexpectedly* receives one of the adjustments to her capital account listed in Treas. Reg. §§ 1.704–1(b)(2)(ii)(*d*)(*4*), (*5*) and (*6*). Why unexpectedly? Because such adjustments, if they are expected, should already have reduced the partner's capital account for the purpose of determining how much, if any, loss and deduction the partnership can allocate to her under the alternate test. And what are these adjustments? They consist of ways that a partner's capital account can be reduced, other than through an allocation of losses or deductions. The most common is distributions that exceed expected income.

A related misunderstanding is to think that the alternate test itself allows losses and deductions to be allocated to Anita without limit, as though she had an unlimited deficit-restoration obligation. Under the alternate test, Anita cannot be allocated any more losses than the amount that would reduce her capital account, adjusted as aforesaid, to zero. If Anita agreed to restore the deficit balance in her capital account up to a limited dollar amount, the alternate test would permit the partnership to allocate losses and deductions to Anita up to the point that the deficit balance in her capital account equaled that dollar amount. But no more.

Bear in mind that all allocations under section 704(b) are allocations of so-called "book" income and loss. Later in the Reading Period, Topic 8.1 explores the distinction between book income and taxable income in some depth. Briefly, a partnership's book income is determined in the same manner as its taxable income, substituting the book values of the partnership's assets for their adjusted bases. Treas. Reg. § 1.704–1(b)(2)(iv)(*g*)(*3*). Given that these two measures of a partnership's assets are not always equal, it should come as no surprise that the income or loss of a partnership computed for book purposes is not always the same as its taxable income or loss. Section 704(b) and its test of substantial economic effect are concerned solely with the allocation of book income or loss. Consistently, the capital accounts referred to in the section 704(b) regulations are the partners' book capital accounts, which, if properly maintained, will be adjusted by the amounts of allocated book income or loss, not taxable income or loss. Treas. Reg. §§ 1.704–1(b)(2)(iv)(*d*)(*3*), –1(b)(4)(i).

To the extent that a partnership's taxable income matches its book income, section 704(b) governs the allocation of such taxable income. Thus, for example, all of the income or loss of a partnership that has no book-tax difference in any of its assets will be allocated under section 704(b), there being no difference at all between the book income or loss and the taxable income or loss of that partnership. The taxable income or loss of a partnership that is not matched by book income or loss does not have economic effect, because it is not reflected in the capital accounts. It must be allocated under the principles of section 704(c). *See* Topic 8.2.

Substantiality

As a means of testing the economic impact on a partner of an allocation of profit or loss, capital accounting has two glaring weaknesses. First, capital accounts are maintained on a pre-tax basis, not an after-tax basis. A $1.00 increase in a partner's capital account can be achieved by a contribution of $1.00 in cash or an allocation of $1.00 of ordinary income, capital gain or tax-exempt income. A $1.00 decrease in a partner's capital account follows from a distribution of $1.00 in cash to the partner or from an allocation of $1.00 of ordinary loss (say, depreciation), capital loss or nondeductible expense. From an after-tax perspective, however, these are quite different. For example, a partner in the 35% tax bracket would likely say that a $1.00 capital contribution cost her $1.00; an allocation of ordinary income, 35 cents; an allocation of capital gain, 20 cents; an allocation of tax-exempt income, nothing.

Second, capital accounts do not bear interest. In terms of the effect on the balances in the capital accounts, $1.00 of income allocated today is identical to $1.00 of income allocated ten years from now. Yet the partner who receives the earlier allocation must pay tax on it now, while the tax liability of the partner receiving the later allocation is deferred for ten years. Nevertheless, properly maintained capital accounts need not—in fact, cannot—take this timing difference into account. The partner receiving the earlier allocation of income gets no credit for having done so.

In the real world, of course, time value matters to partners and they make their investment decisions on an after-tax basis. By ignoring these two factors, capital accounting fails to reflect the "real" economic impact of partnership allocations on the partners who receive them. This paves the way for partnerships to act, at best, as powerful financing tools and, at worst, as vehicles for tax abuse.

To illustrate, imagine a general partnership, 720 West Oakdale Partners, formed to acquire, manage and ultimately sell a small commercial property at that address. Anita and Benjamin are the two partners. Each contributes $200,000 to fund the acquisition, the partnership borrows $600,000 on a recourse basis and acquires the building for $1 million. Assume for simplicity that the property operates at breakeven except for depreciation, which is about $25,600 per year (ignoring depreciation conventions). Because Anita pays tax in the 35% bracket and Benjamin has no taxable income due to losses from other projects, they decide to allocate all of the depreciation to Anita and to allocate the first gain on sale of the project to her to the extent of the previously allocated depreciation. Each partner has an unlimited obligation to restore any deficit balance in his or her capital account. The partnership sells the building ten years later for the amount of its original investment, $1 million. Alas, the entire project turns out to be a wash.

But not for Anita. Over the first nine years of this investment, the partnership allocates about $230,400 in depreciation to her ($25,600 per year for nine years), producing tax savings (at 35%) of about $80,640. If Anita invests her tax savings at 5%, she will earn about $18,160 over these nine years, bringing her after-tax benefit from the allocation of depreciation to $98,800 ($80,640 plus $18,160). In the tenth year, she receives an allocation of $230,400 of gain to offset the prior allocation of depreciation. This gain is not subject to recapture, but is taxed as section 1250 capital gain at a 25% rate. Anita's tax on this gain (at 25%) is $57,600. At the end of the project, Anita is ahead about $41,200 ($98,800 less $57,600) on an after-tax basis. Her entire return is attributable to her tax savings. As a tax-neutral party, Benjamin is not worse off as a result of Anita's gain, although he may be wishing that he had figured out a way to get a piece of her action. All the partnership's allocations satisfy the safe harbor for economic effect.

Is this abusive? The job of the substantiality test is to answer that question. It explicitly takes into account the after-tax, present-value effects of special allocations, thus addressing the weaknesses of the economic-effect test. It does this, however, in a complex and perplexing manner. Before delving into some of its mysteries, a general appraisal may be helpful. The substantiality test is a highly articulated anti-abuse rule. It does not apply to many cases because it was not intended to apply to many cases. In particular, it was never intended to shut down the role of partnerships as financing vehicles for projects with entrepreneurial risk, even if that means transferring tax benefits to "sweeten the pot" for investors. On the other hand, an investor who is offered a virtually riskless return premised on tax benefits has reason to worry. She may not be a partner at all. Even if she is, the promised allocation may be disallowed under the substantiality test.

Layers. One of the most frustrating aspects of the substantiality test of Treas. Reg. § 1.704–1(b)(2)(iii) is that, like Dante's *Inferno,* it has many levels. The substantiality test is actually four separate tests and four independent presumptions. The tests are:

✓   *The pre-tax-effect test.* The economic effect of an allocation is substantial if there is a reasonable possibility that the allocation will affect substantially the dollar amounts to be received by the partners from the partnership, independent of tax consequences.

✓   *The overall-tax-effect test.* The economic effect of an allocation is not substantial if (1) the after-tax economic consequences of at least one partner may, in present value terms, be enhanced compared to such consequences if the allocation were not contained in the partnership agreement and (2) there is a strong likelihood that the after-tax economic consequences of no partner will, in present value terms, be substantially diminished compared to such consequences if the allocation were not contained in the partnership agreement.

✓   *The shifting test.* The economic effect of an allocation in a single partnership taxable year is not substantial if there is a strong likelihood that (1) the net increases and decreases that will be recorded in the partners' respective capital accounts for such taxable year will not differ substantially from the net increases and decreases that would be recorded if the allocations were not contained in the partnership agreement and (2) the total tax liability of the partners will be less than if the allocations were not contained in the partnership agreement.

✓   *The transitory test.* The economic effect of "original allocations" and "offsetting allocations" over more than one partnership taxable year is not substantial if there is a strong likelihood that (1) the net increases and decreases that will be recorded in the partners' respective capital accounts for the taxable years to which the allocations relate will not differ substantially from the net increases and decreases that would be recorded if the allocations were not contained in the partnership agreement and (2) the total tax liability of the partners will be less than if the allocations were not contained in the partnership agreement.

Under all of these tests, whether there is a "strong likelihood" is tested as of the date that the special allocations become part of the partnership agreement—typically, but not always, the date of the partnership's formation.

It is unclear whether the pre-tax-effect test is actually a test at all. Better said, it is unclear whether this test is an exclusive identification of all allocations whose economic effect is substantial. If so, then the economic effect of any allocation that is not described by the test is by definition not substantial. On the other hand, the pre-tax-effect test could be viewed as non-exclusive, so that, even if an allocation is not described by the test, its economic effect may nevertheless be substantial. As written, the pre-tax-effect test certainly sounds exclusive. It admits that certain allocations it identifies as substantial may be found insubstantial under other tests, but it does not admit that there is any other way for an allocation to be substantial, other than to satisfy its requirement.

The counterargument—and it is a good one—is that this interpretation of the pre-tax-effect test would render both the shifting test and the transitory test unnecessary. Look at the statements of these two tests above. Clause (1) of both tests is essentially the pre-tax-effect test with "not" added. Therefore, the economic effect of any allocation described in clause (1) of either of these tests would not be substantial under the pre-tax-effect test, if it were interpreted as the exclusive definition of substantiality. There would be no reason to go on to clause (2) and, indeed, no reason ever to apply the shifting test or the transitory test at all.

This counterargument is convincing to me. You will have the opportunity to cast your own vote in Questions 4.3.7 and 4.3.9 below.

The pre-tax-effect test (if it is a test), the overall-tax-effect test and either the shifting test or the transitory test (but not both) apply in every case. If the economic effect of the allocation under review is determined to be insubstantial under any of the applicable tests, the allocation does not have substantial economic effect. In other words, you must "pass" all applicable tests; if you "fail" any one, the allocation is no good. (Hereafter, the terms "pass" and "satisfy" are used interchangeably, as are the terms "fail" and "violate.")

The presumptions incorporated into the substantiality test are:

✓ *Value-equals-basis.* The value of partnership property equals its adjusted basis (or its book value, in the case of properties with a book-tax disparity) and adjustments to the adjusted basis (or book value) are matched by corresponding changes in the property's value. This is a conclusive presumption, not rebuttable.

✓ *Five-year.* If there is a strong likelihood that the offsetting allocations will not, in large part, be made within five years of the original allocations (determined on a first-in, first-out basis), certain substantiality tests are deemed "passed."

✓ *Strong likelihood of shifting effect.* If it turns out that parts (1) and (2) of the shifting test are met, there was a strong likelihood that they would be met and thus the allocation is a shifting allocation. This presumption may be rebutted by the taxpayer.

✓ *Strong likelihood of transitory effect.* If it turns out that parts (1) and (2) of the transitory test are met, there was a strong likelihood that they would be met and thus the original allocations and the offsetting allocations are transitory allocations. This presumption may be rebutted by the taxpayer.

✓ The value-equals-basis presumption applies for purposes of all tests (although its usefulness in the shifting test is hard to see). The five-year presumption applies for purposes of the transitory test. It is unclear whether it also applies to the overall-tax-effect test. The two strong-likelihood presumptions apply only for purposes of their respective tests.

Entrepreneurial risk. The strongest support for the idea that the substantiality test is not intended to interfere with ordinary business arrangements is provided by the probability standards built into the tests. The overall-tax-effect, shifting and transitory tests all require a "strong likelihood" that the designated events will come to pass. This is well beyond 50%—more in the 80% to 90% range. In other words, if there is a one-in-five chance that, say, income will not be available in the future to charge back a loss, or that income will not be available in a later year to balance an earlier allocation of income to a different partner, then substantiality is not an issue. The same is true under the pre-tax-effect test (if you believe it is an independent test), which requires only a "reasonable possibility" that the allocations will effect substantially the dollars a partner receives from the partnership. This point cannot be overstressed: most regular business operations entail sufficient risk to take substantiality out of the picture. A prudent taxpayer will contemporaneously document the risk so as to be prepared to rebut the strong-likelihood presumptions should that become necessary.

Documentation of risk is unnecessary where depreciation is specially allocated, subject to a chargeback of gain on the sale of the depreciated asset. The value-equals-basis presumption represents a policy judgment to allow special allocations of depreciation, even if there is a strong likelihood (or a certainty) that a chargeback of gain on sale will take place. This answers the outstanding question: Anita is in the clear.

The five-year presumption reflects a similar attitude toward entrepreneurial risk. If a chargeback is strongly likely not to occur within five years, there is an increased risk that it will not happen at all. As illustrated in Question 4.3.10 below, figuring out whether the five-year presumption applies in any given case can be tricky.

The baseline. All of the substantiality tests require, explicitly or implicitly, a comparison between the after-tax results achieved by the special allocations with those that would have been achieved had the special allocations not been contained in the partnership agreement. One must therefore have a baseline for comparison. Seldom, if ever, will the parties negotiate a full set of allocation provisions, memorialize them in a draft and then set to work incorporating special allocations. Instead, the special allocations will appear in the earliest drafts of the partnership agreement. If the parties have not produced a baseline by their own efforts, where is one to look? In the first *Castle Harbor* decision, the District Court concluded that any baseline other than the allocations found in the partnership agreement would be "made out of whole cloth" and thus unacceptable. It followed that the special allocations and the baseline allocations were the same in that case. The court held that the overall-tax-effect test did not cause the economic effect of the special allocations to lack substantiality, over the government's protest that the court's approach rendered the test a dead letter. *TIFD III-E, Inc. v. United States*, 342 F. Supp. 2d 94 (D. Conn. 2004), *rev'd and remanded*, 459 F.3d 220 (2d Cir. 2006), *on remand*, 660 F. Supp. 2d 367 (D. Conn. 2009), *rev'd*, 666 F.3d 836 (2d Cir. 2012).

The Treasury regulations have since been amended to provide that the baseline allocations are determined in accordance with the partners' respective interests in the partnership, *disregarding the allocations being tested*. Treas. Reg. § 1.704–1(b)(2)(iii)(*a*) (last sentence). It remains to be seen whether the next judge will do any better with this standard. There is cause for concern. The baseline is, by its very nature, hypothetical. And, like the concept of a partner's interest in the partnership, it is ill-defined and unpredictable. It is also unavoidably at the heart of the substantiality analysis in the Treasury regulations. The next judge, and the one after that, might find it too unwieldly for deciding real cases.

Comparing the tests. For tax planners, the process of designing a special allocation has two parts. First, allocate income and loss so as to minimize the aggregate tax liability of the partners. Second, divide up the tax savings. The shifting and transitory tests are written from this perspective. They do not care how the tax savings are divided, just that they are there in the aggregate. The overall-tax-effect test is different. It looks partner-by-partner. In order to violate this test, there must be a strong likelihood that not a single partner will be substantially worse off as a result of the special allocations.

Each of the tests has its shortcomings. Astonishingly, the transitory test does not incorporate a present-value component. In determining the aggregate tax liability of the partners, we are apparently supposed to add up the tax liabilities of all of the partners for all of the years without discounting later liabilities back to present value. Under this approach, barring changes in tax rates, Anita's tax liability from receiving an allocation of $25,600 of depreciation in year one and a chargeback of $25,600 income in year ten is exactly the same as her tax liability from receiving an allocation of $25,600 income in year one and an allocation of $25,600 of depreciation in year ten, which in turn is exactly the same as receiving neither allocation. This cannot have been the intention of the drafters, but this drafting error has survived for decades without correction. There is no reported court case applying the transitory test.

The overall-tax-effect test presents a different sort of difficulty. Imagine a real-estate developer like Benjamin, except that he pays a low rate of tax rather than none at all. Call him Ishmael. If Ish agrees to a special allocation of losses or deductions to another partner who, like Anita, pays tax at a higher rate, Ish will most certainly be worse off from this allocation, which suggests that the overall-tax-effect test is not violated. There are a number of reasons, however, that Ish might be willing to make this deal, including: (1) to get a larger share of gain on sale; (2) to obtain a carried interest (or a larger carried interest) for his services; (3) to obtain a developer's fee (or a larger fee); or (4) to be able to do the deal at all. Although nothing is certain, it seems likely that (1) and (2) should be taken into account as part of the special allocations that are subject to the test. It seems equally likely that (4) should not be. Item (3) is commonplace, but may be outside of the scope of the test as written. On the other hand, an example suggests that a payment in exchange for tax benefits that takes the form of interest accruals on a partner's capital account is within the scope of the substantiality analysis. Treas. Reg. § 1.704–1(b)(5), example (9).

Partner's interests

In the event that an allocation provided by the partnership agreement does not have substantial economic effect, section 704(b)(2) requires that the affected items of income, gain, loss, deduction or credit be re-allocated in accordance with the partners' respective interests in the partnership. Treas. Reg. § 1.704–1(b)(3)(i) says that this requires allocation in accordance with the manner that the partners have agreed to share the economic benefits and burdens corresponding to the items in question and suggests that we look at all the facts and circumstances to figure that out. Although this is not a very satisfying standard, it is hard to think of a better one, given the purpose of section 704(b) to match tax with economics.

It is tempting to think that we should build a hypothetical partnership by shares, in which every partner's percentage interest in every item of income or loss equals her percentage interest in capital. In some simple partnerships this may indeed be the right answer. But the regulations explicitly disclaim this notion, stating that a partner's interest in any particular item may be different than her "overall interest" in the partnership.

It is hard to appreciate that statement until you read Treas. Reg. § 1.704–1(b)(3)(iii), the so-called "comparative-liquidation" test. This test allows a partnership that complies with the capital-accounting requirements of the safe harbor for economic effect to determine the partners' interests in an allocated item by making the allocation called for by the partnership agreement and then gauging the economic effect of the allocation by comparing its effect on the amounts of the distributions that would be received by the partners if the partnership sold all of its assets for their book values and liquidated in two scenarios: (1) at the end of the taxable year in which the allocation is made, and (2) at the end of the prior taxable year. This rule, when available, can preserve a special allocation that has fallen through the cracks of the safe harbor. More generally, it is useful in understanding and applying the concept of a partner's interest to more complex partnership arrangements. The operation of the comparative-liquidation test is illustrated in Questions 4.3.2 and 4.3.4 below.

Targeted allocations

Most courses on partnership tax do not cover targeted allocations. The main reason, I suppose, is that you can't do everything. Another reason is that targeted allocations are a drafting technique, not new or different law. They rely entirely on the tests for substantial economic effect contained in the Treasury regulations. The government has thus far resolutely resisted, or ignored, practitioners' calls for explicit rules related to targeted allocations.

The impetus for targeted allocations is the desire to be sure that the amount of cash that will be distributed to each partner matches the business deal. In traditional drafting, those amounts are determined by the positive balances in the capital accounts, which are in turn determined by the allocations of profits and losses. If there is an error in the allocations (in the sense that they do not comport with the business deal), the cash will be wrong, although the allocations will be respected for tax purposes.

Targeted allocations change the consequences of error. In a partnership agreement utilizing targeted allocations, cash distributions are not made in accordance with the positive capital-account balances, but instead according to the provisions in the distribution section of the partnership agreement. These are drafted to track the business deal exactly. Each year, profit and loss are allocated so as to establish balances in the capital accounts that equal the amounts that the distribution provisions would require to be distributed if the partnership were to sell all of its assets at book value and liquidate at year-end. If the allocations are unable to reach their capital-account "targets," the distribution of cash is unaffected, but the allocations may not be respected for tax purposes.

Many clients would rather risk tax allocations than cash, and targeted allocations are very common. For the tax professional, the challenge is never to run short of items to allocate, so that the capital accounts can always hit the targeted levels. It is not the same process as writing traditional allocations, but it is related. If writing traditional allocations is like shaving in a mirror, writing targeted allocations is like shaving in a mirror that is pointed at a mirror that is pointed at your face.

4.3.1   Aiden, Brayden and Caden form a general partnership with cash contributions of $25,000, $25,000 and $50,000, respectively. The partnership agreement provides for the maintenance of proper capital accounts, which will govern liquidating distributions. Each partner has an unconditional obligation to restore any deficit balance in his capital account upon liquidation. The partnership borrows $500,000 on a recourse basis and acquires an apartment building for $500,000, keeping a $100,000 cash reserve. For the next three years, the partnership operates the apartment building at an annual loss of $20,000, not including depreciation, which is an additional $20,000 per year (ignoring depreciation conventions). The partnership agreement provides that all items of income, gain, loss, deduction and credit will be allocated 25% to each of Aiden and Brayden and 50% to Caden, except for depreciation, which will be allocated entirely to Caden. At the end of three years, what are the cumulative amounts of operating loss and depreciation properly allocated to the three partners?

    a)   Aiden, $15,000; Brayden, $15,000; Caden, $90,000

    b)   Aiden, $25,000; Brayden, $25,000; Caden, $70,000

    c)   Aiden, $30,000; Brayden, $30,000; Caden, $60,000

    d)   Aiden, $35,000; Brayden, $35,000; Caden, $50,000

4.3.2   The facts are the same as Question 4.3.1, except that the partnership agreement provides that the obligation of the partners to restore deficits in their capital accounts is limited to the amounts needed to satisfy creditors and therefore excludes amounts needed for the partnership to repay the positive balances, if any, in the capital accounts of its partners. Governing state law permits this limitation. The partnership agreement includes a qualified income offset. At the end of three years, what are the cumulative amounts properly allocated to the three partners?

    a)   Aiden, $15,000; Brayden, $15,000; Caden, $90,000

    b)   Aiden, $25,000; Brayden, $25,000; Caden, $70,000

    c)   Aiden, $30,000; Brayden, $30,000; Caden, $60,000

    d)   Aiden, $35,000; Brayden, $35,000; Caden, $50,000

4.3.3   The facts are the same as Question 4.3.1, except that the partnership is now a limited partnership. Aiden and Brayden are the general partners and Caden is the sole limited partner. The partnership agreement provides that Caden has no obligation to restore any deficit in his capital account and that the obligations of Aiden and Brayden are limited to the amounts needed to satisfy creditors. State law permits these limitations. The partnership agreement contains a qualified income offset. At the end of three years, what are the cumulative amounts properly allocated to the three partners?

    a)   Aiden, $15,000; Brayden, $15,000; Caden, $90,000

    b)   Aiden, $25,000; Brayden, $25,000; Caden, $70,000

    c)   Aiden, $30,000; Brayden, $30,000; Caden, $60,000

    d)   Aiden, $35,000; Brayden, $35,000; Caden, $50,000

4.3.4   The facts are the same as Question 4.3.3, except that the hapless drafter of the limited partnership agreement forgot the qualified income offset. At the end of three years, what are the cumulative amounts properly allocated to the three partners?

    a)   Aiden, $15,000; Brayden, $15,000; Caden, $90,000

    b)   Aiden, $25,000; Brayden, $25,000; Caden, $70,000

    c)   Aiden, $30,000; Brayden, $30,000; Caden, $60,000

    d)   Aiden, $35,000; Brayden, $35,000; Caden, $50,000

    4.3.5   The facts are the same as Question 4.3.1, except that the partnership maintains no capital accounts and the partnership agreement contains no deficit-restoration obligation. The partnership agreement provides that all items of income, gain, loss, deduction and credit will be allocated 25% to each of Aiden and Brayden and 50% to Caden. At the end of three years, what are the cumulative amounts properly allocated to the three partners?

    a)   Aiden, $30,000; Brayden, $30,000; Caden, $60,000

    b)   Aiden, $35,000; Brayden, $35,000; Caden, $50,000

    c)   Aiden, $40,000; Brayden, $40,000; Caden, $40,000

    d)   There is no unique answer.

    4.3.6   After the close of its taxable year, when all items of partnership profit and loss are known, the Arcadia Investment Partnership amends its partnership agreement to provide that Gabriel, a 10% partner who prior to amendment was entitled to $700 of municipal bond interest and $700 of fully taxable interest, will receive $1,400 of municipal bond interest and that Peter, also a 10% partner with the same pre-amendment entitlements, will receive $1,400 of taxable interest. Gabriel and Peter are in the 35% and 15% tax brackets, respectively. Assuming that these special allocations satisfy the safe harbor for economic effect, is that effect substantial?

    a)   No, because they do not satisfy the shifting test

    b)   No, because they do not satisfy the overall-tax-effect test

    c)   No, because they do not satisfy the transitory test

    d)   Yes, because they satisfy all applicable tests

    4.3.7   The facts are the same as Question 4.3.6, except that Gabriel and Peter are in exactly the same tax position. Is the economic effect of these special allocations substantial?

    a)   No, because they do not satisfy the shifting test

    b)   No, because they do not satisfy the overall-tax-effect test

    c)   No, because they do not satisfy the pre-tax-effect test

    d)   Yes, because they satisfy all applicable tests

    4.3.8   The Arcadia Investment Partnership, always a creative bunch, identifies two of its partners who are in substantially different tax positions. To the low-bracket partner, who otherwise would be entitled to 20% of all items of income, gain and loss, it allocates 40% of its taxable interest income for a period of three years, at which point the allocation falls to 0% for three years and then reverts to 20% thereafter. To the high-bracket partner, also ordinarily entitled to 20% of all items, it allocates no taxable interest income for a period of three years, then 40% for three years, and then 20%

thereafter. There are no other changes to the partnership agreement, other than provisions designed to prevent either partner from liquidating any portion of that partner's interest during the period that these special allocations are in effect. Assuming that the allocations have economic effect, is that effect substantial?

a) No, because they do not satisfy the shifting test

b) No, because they do not satisfy the overall-tax-effect test

c) No, because they do not satisfy the transitory test

d) Yes, because they satisfy all applicable tests

4.3.9   The facts are the same as Question 4.3.8, except that Arcadia's taxable interest income is generated by a single large bond issued by a creditworthy corporation. There is a strong likelihood that Arcadia will receive the same amount of interest on this bond every year for the next decade and that, due to a change in its investment mandate, Arcadia will not acquire any other source of taxable interest income. In these circumstances, is the economic effect of the special allocations of this income substantial?

a) No, because they do not satisfy the transitory test

b) No, because they do not satisfy the overall-tax-effect test

c) No, because they do not satisfy the pre-tax-effect test

d) Yes, because they satisfy all applicable tests

4.3.10   Cloudeez LLC, a limited liability company treated as a partnership for tax purposes, is in the business of renting high-cost network servers to private enterprises. Typically, it enters into a 15-year contract with a customer and then acquires the servers needed to fulfill that contract. Cloudeez elects to depreciate the equipment for tax purposes on a straight-line basis over five years. Looking to expand its business, Cloudeez attracts a significant new equity investment from Bianca McCarthy by offering her a special allocation of 99% of the depreciation on the equipment financed by her capital contribution, to be followed by a chargeback of an equal amount of leasing income commencing at the end of the depreciation period. Given the nature of Cloudeez's business, this income chargeback is strongly likely to occur ratably over the last 10 years of the 15-year contract period. Assuming that these allocations have economic effect, is that effect substantial?

a) Yes, because the value-equals-basis presumption applies

b) Yes, because the five-year presumption applies

c) No, because neither presumption applies and the transitory test is not satisfied

d) No, because the five-year presumption applies, but it does not cover the overall-tax-effect test, which is not satisfied in this case

4.3.11   *Review Treas. Reg. § 1.1245–1(e)(2)(i) before answering this Question.* Cliffhangers LLC, a limited liability company taxed as a partnership, owns a depreciable asset with a recomputed basis (within the meaning of section 1245(a)(2)(A)) of $48,000 and an adjusted basis of $22,000. Mikayla has been allocated all of the depreciation on this asset. The operating agreement allocates gain on sale of the asset equally between Mikayla and Miles and does not mention depreciation recapture. If Cliffhangers sells the asset for its fair market value of $60,000, how will depreciation recapture be allocated between Mikayla and Miles?

   a)   Mikayla, $26,000; Miles, $0

   b)   Mikayla, $19,000; Miles, $7,000

   c)   Mikayla, $19,000; Miles, $19,000

   d)   Mikayla, $13,000; Miles, $13,000

4.4 ALLOCATING NONRECOURSE DEDUCTIONS

You may have noticed that in all previous examples in which the partnership borrowed money, the debt was recourse debt, meaning that one or more of the partners was personally obligated to repay it. Whether a partnership loss is funded by a partner's capital contribution or by debt that a partner is personally obligated to repay, if the loss has an economic burden, the partner will bear it. For this reason, the same allocation standard—substantial economic effect—applies to losses and deductions funded from either source.

If, on the other hand, a partnership loss is funded by partnership debt for which no partner has personal responsibility (the definition of nonrecourse debt in this context), the economic burden associated with the loss will be borne by the lender, not by any partner. An allocation of such a loss to a partner will not, by definition, have economic effect. One response might be to prevent this sort of loss from being allocated to the partners at all, but instead to suspend it at the entity level for application against any future income or gains the entity might generate. The loss would not be treated this way, however, if the debt were incurred by an individual directly or by a group of individuals acting as co-owners, and such treatment would not advance the general purpose of Subchapter K to achieve the same results as aggregate ownership.

Granting, then, that losses and deductions attributable to nonrecourse debt are to be allocated to some partner or partners, how should that allocation be made? As in the case of losses and deductions funded by capital or recourse debt, section 704(a) generally lets the partners decide. No matter what allocation is provided in the partnership agreement, however, it cannot have substantial economic effect. So in order to be respected for tax purposes, it must be in accordance with the partners' respective interests in the partnership. Treas. Reg. § 1.704–2(e) provides a four-part safe harbor that, if satisfied, causes allocations of nonrecourse deductions to be deemed to be in accordance with the partners' interests. We will return to it shortly.

The implicit ordering rules

To many students, the most obvious example of a deduction attributable to nonrecourse debt is the interest on a nonrecourse borrowing. Sadly, this is not even close to right. Attribution, in the sense used here, means determining the source of the funds that generate the deduction, not the use to which the funds are put or the reason for expending them. Knowing this, however, gets you nowhere, because there are too many possible answers. Because money is fungible, you might, for example, conclude that every partnership expense is funded in the same proportions by the partnership's capital, recourse borrowing and nonrecourse borrowing. Or you might use a tracing approach. Or perhaps a vintage-asset approach.

You will look in vain in the Treasury regulations for explicit guidance on which of these approaches to use. Indeed, as you look you will see only references to a mysterious new concept called "minimum gain." The relationship between this concept and the answer you are seeking is not intuitive for most people. But, in fact, it *is* the answer.

Through use of the concept of minimum gain, the Treasury regulations incorporate two implicit ordering rules. The first is a "tracing" rule: amounts borrowed on a nonrecourse basis are deemed to be used exclusively to acquire the property that secures the debt. For example, if a partnership with capital of $100,000 borrows $100,000 on a nonrecourse basis and buys property for $150,000 which it pledges to secure the repayment of the nonrecourse debt, the partnership will be deemed to have used all $100,000 of the nonrecourse borrowing to acquire the property, plus $50,000 of capital, rather than, say, $75,000 of borrowed funds and $75,000 of capital. This "tracing" rule does not apply to amounts borrowed in circumstances where the property securing the debt is neither acquired nor improved—for instance, when a partnership takes out a second mortgage on an appreciated property to "cash out" some of its value. Other, more specialized tracing rules step in then, as explained below.

The second ordering rule in the Treasury regulations is a "stacking" rule: the equity investment in an asset securing a nonrecourse debt is consumed first, before the investment represented by the nonrecourse debt. This rule is needed to determine the timing and amount of the deductions funded by the nonrecourse debt.

With these two ordering rules in mind, we can consider a simple hypothetical case, based on Treas. Reg. § 1.704–2(m), example (1). Partnership AB is a limited partnership in which A is the general partner with a 10% interest and B is the limited partner with a 90% interest. A and B contribute $2,000 and $18,000, respectively, to the partnership, which borrows $90,000 on a nonrecourse basis and acquires a building for $100,000. The partnership mortgages the building to secure repayment of the loan. The building produces gross rental income of $10,000 per year which, after operating expenses of $2,000 and interest of $6,000, yields net income before depreciation of $2,000 annually. Depreciation is (unrealistically) $10,000 per year.

The opening balance sheet of Partnership AB is as follows:

FIGURE 4.4.1

Assets			Liabilities		
	Tax	Book		Tax	Book
Cash	$ 10,000	$ 10,000	Bank Debt	$ 90,000	$ 90,000
Building	100,000	100,000			
			Capital		
			A	2,000	2,000
			B	18,000	18,000
Total Assets	$110,000	$110,000	**Total Liabilities and Capital**	$110,000	$110,000

Under the "tracing" rule, all of the nonrecourse borrowing is deemed to be invested in the building, the property that secures the nonrecourse loan. This means that none of the nonrecourse borrowing is deemed to fund any portion of the partnership's interest or operating expense. Under the "stacking" rule, the entire amount of the first year's depreciation on the building is deemed to be funded by the partnership's $10,000 equity in the building. Accordingly, there are no deductions attributable to nonrecourse debt—i.e., no nonrecourse deductions—in the first year.

Nonrecourse deductions

The Treasury regulations never speak of these ordering rules. Instead, they employ different, more economical language. In the words of the Treasury regulations, the amount of Partnership AB's nonrecourse deductions in its first year equals the net increase in "partnership minimum gain" for that year. Treas. Reg. § 1.704–2(c). Partnership minimum gain is the amount of gain that Partnership AB would realize if it disposed of the building for no consideration other than full satisfaction of the nonrecourse liability. Treas. Reg. § 1.704–2(d)(1). At the end of the first year, Partnership AB would realize no gain on such a disposition, because the amount realized ($90,000, the amount of the nonrecourse debt) would equal the adjusted basis of the building ($100,000 reduced by $10,000 depreciation). Thus, there is no increase in partnership minimum gain for the year and there are no nonrecourse deductions.

At the end of the first year, Partnership AB's balance sheet is as follows:

FIGURE 4.4.2

Assets			Liabilities		
	Tax	Book		Tax	Book
Cash	$ 12,000	$ 12,000	Bank Debt	$ 90,000	$ 90,000
Building	90,000	90,000			
			Capital		
			A	1,200	1,200
			B	10,800	10,800
Total Assets	$102,000	$102,000	Total Liabilities and Capital	$102,000	$102,000

The $2,000 addition to cash reflects the partnership's net income of $2,000 before depreciation, and the partners' capital accounts have been reduced by their respective shares of the partnership's $8,000 loss after depreciation. At the end of year 2, partnership minimum gain is $10,000 ($90,000 amount realized less $80,000 adjusted basis in the building). The increase in partnership minimum gain for year 2 is $10,000 and thus the partnership has $10,000 of nonrecourse deductions for that year. Note that this exceeds (by $2,000) the net tax loss of the partnership for year 2. The partnership's items of income and expense other than nonrecourse deductions produce net income of $2,000. At the end of year 2, Partnership AB's balance sheet is as follows:

FIGURE 4.4.3

Assets			Liabilities		
	Tax	Book		Tax	Book
Cash	$ 14,000	$ 14,000	Bank Debt	$ 90,000	$ 90,000
Building	80,000	80,000			
			Capital		
			A	400	400
			B	3,600	3,600
Total Assets	$ 94,000	$ 94,000	Total Liabilities and Capital	$ 94,000	$ 94,000

Notice that nonrecourse deductions have been allocated to the partners, despite the fact that both have positive capital accounts. Nonrecourse deductions appear when the equity in the *property* disappears (which is another way of saying when minimum gain appears), not necessarily when the equity in the *partnership* disappears.

Under Treas. Reg. § 1.704–2(g)(1), A and B each have a share of the partnership minimum gain from year 2, equal to the cumulative nonrecourse deductions that have been allocated to them. Accordingly, A has a share of $1,000 (10% of $10,000) and B has a share of $9,000 (90% of $10,000).

Assume now that the value of the building increases to $140,000. At the end of year 3, the partnership borrows an additional $20,000 on a second mortgage and distributes this amount, $2,000 to A and $18,000 to B, returning to them their original capital contributions. Otherwise, year 3 is a carbon copy of year 2. At the end of year 3, Partnership AB's balance sheet is as follows:

FIGURE 4.4.4

Assets			Liabilities		
	Tax	Book		Tax	Book
Cash	$ 16,000	$ 16,000	Bank Debt	$110,000	$110,000
Building	70,000	70,000			
			Capital		
			A	(2,400)	(2,400)
			B	(21,600)	(21,600)
Total Assets	$ 86,000	$ 86,000	**Total Liabilities and Capital**	$ 86,000	$ 86,000

The increase in partnership minimum gain for year 3 is $30,000, $10,000 attributable to depreciation and $20,000 attributable to the new borrowing. Ordinarily, you would expect this to mean that Partnership AB has $30,000 of nonrecourse deductions for year 3. Here, however, a special rule applies. Under Treas. Reg. § 1.704–2(c), the amount of the nonrecourse deductions is the increase in partnership minimum gain *less* the distributions made during the year of the proceeds of a nonrecourse borrowing that are allocable to an increase in partnership minimum gain. The amount of the nonrecourse deductions for year 3 is thus only $10,000. This special rule loosens the "tracing" rule discussed earlier. There is no increase in the adjusted basis of the building, so it is self-evident that the proceeds of the new nonrecourse borrowing cannot be traced there. The Treasury regulations instead require them to be traced to the distributions that were funded by the new borrowing.

A's and B's shares of partnership minimum gain include the distributions made to them. At the end of year 3, Partnership AB has partnership minimum gain of $40,000. A's share is $4,000, which consists of A's allocable share of nonrecourse deductions ($1,000 for each of years 2 and 3) plus A's distribution ($2,000). B's share is $36,000, which consists of B's share of nonrecourse deductions ($18,000) plus B's distribution ($18,000). Treas. Reg. § 1.704–2(g)(1).

What if Partnership AB borrows the additional $20,000 but does not distribute it prior to the end of year 3? In that case, the increase in partnership minimum gain for year 3 still appears to be $30,000 and, with no distributions, it appears that there are $30,000 in nonrecourse deductions. Trouble is, Partnership AB only has a total of $18,000 of deductions for the year, $10,000 depreciation, $6,000 interest expense and $2,000 operating expense. In this rather unusual situation, the Treasury regulations again modify the "tracing" rule, treating the proceeds of the new nonrecourse borrowing as the funding source for all $18,000 of the partnership's deductions. Thus, the amount of nonrecourse deductions for year 3 is $18,000. The increase in partnership minimum gain for year 3 is capped at $18,000. The remaining increase of $12,000 is carried over and treated as an increase in partnership minimum gain for year 4. Treas. Reg. §§ 1.704–2(j)(1)(ii), (iii).

Allocating nonrecourse deductions

Once we have determined the amount of nonrecourse deductions for the year, how do we allocate them? The answer, suggested earlier, is any way the partners choose, as long as the chosen allocation can be deemed to be in accordance with the partners' interests in the partnership. It is perilous to try to figure this out for oneself. Happily, the Treasury regulations provide a safe harbor that takes most of the worry, if not the work, out of answering this question. Read the four-part safe harbor in Treas. Reg. § 1.704–2(e). Of these four, two deserve separate discussion.

Minimum gain chargeback. Under Treas. Reg. § 1.704–2(e)(3), a partnership relying on the safe harbor must include a "minimum gain chargeback" in its partnership agreement. This means that, if the amount of partnership minimum gain decreases for the year, each partner must be allocated items of partnership income and gain equal to the partner's share of that decrease. The most obvious such decrease occurs when the property securing the nonrecourse debt is sold, in a normal sale or in a foreclosure sale. On such a sale, the partnership will realize at least the amount of the minimum gain attributable to that property—that is why it is called "minimum" gain. With the minimum gain chargeback requirement, the IRS is assured that the nonrecourse deductions allocated to each partner will be matched by allocations of income or gain, no later than the date of the disposition of the property.

The chargeback can also occur when the partnership minimum gain attributable to a property decreases for any other reason—for example, the repayment of all or a portion of the nonrecourse debt or a capital improvement to the property that increases its adjusted basis. There is an exception for decreases attributable to a partner's capital contribution. Treas. Reg. § 1.704–2(f)(3). Similarly, there is an exception when nonrecourse debt is converted to recourse debt with respect to which the partner bears the economic risk of loss. Treas. Reg. § 1.704–2(f)(2). The rationale for both of these exceptions is that the capital contribution or the recourse borrowing, had it occurred at the outset, would have funded the deductions and caused them to have economic effect.

Significant item consistency test. Under Treas. Reg. § 1.704–2(e)(2), nonrecourse deductions must be allocated "in a manner that is reasonably consistent with allocations that have substantial economic effect of some other significant partnership item attributable to the property securing the nonrecourse liabilities." This long-winded standard, referred to by tax lawyers as the "significant item consistency" test, constrains the allocations of nonrecourse deductions to be at least in the same neighborhood as the allocations provided in the partnership agreement for losses and deductions funded by partner capital or recourse loans. It seems to be motivated by the government's concern that the minimum gain chargeback, by itself, does not sufficiently regulate tax-motivated special allocations of nonrecourse deductions, because the required minimum gain chargeback may occur far in the future and may have a different character than the original deduction. In this sense, the significant item consistency test seems akin to a substantiality test. Like the substantiality test, it is subject to uncertainty in interpretation and application.

In any situation in which property is properly reflected on the books of the partnership with a book value different than its tax basis, all of the determinations of partnership minimum gain and nonrecourse deductions are made with reference to the property's book value. This parallels the rule for section 704(b) allocations generally.

Partner nonrecourse deductions

Finally, assume that A, the general partner in the previous example, personally guarantees the repayment of $30,000 of the partnership's debt. In this case, one-third of the partnership's debt is not nonrecourse, in the sense that we have been using this term, because A is in fact personally liable for repayment. On the other hand, if the lender's only recourse in the event of default is to foreclose on the building, the debt is still nonrecourse under Treas. Reg. § 1.1001–2 from the perspective of the partnership, which will include the amount of the liability as amount realized on transfer of the building in satisfaction of the debt.

The Treasury regulations deal with this situation by dividing the debt into two pieces. The portion not guaranteed by A is simply nonrecourse debt, governed by the rules we have just reviewed. The portion of the debt that A has guaranteed is called "partner nonrecourse debt." The tax system for nonrecourse debt is duplicated for partner nonrecourse debt. Thus, there is "partner nonrecourse debt minimum gain," which is the excess, if any, of the principal amount of the nonrecourse debt subject to the guarantee ($30,000) over the portion of the adjusted basis of the building that is allocable to the partner nonrecourse debt. Although this allocation can be tricky, if we assume that A guarantees the repayment of one-third of each dollar of the partnership's debt, the allocable portion of the adjusted basis of the building is one-third. *See* Treas. Reg. §§ 1.704–2(d)(2), –2(m), example (1)(vii). An increase in partner nonrecourse debt minimum gain (absent distributions) begets "partner nonrecourse deductions," all of which must be allocated to A, who bears the economic risk of loss with respect to those deductions. Treas. Reg. § 1.704–2(i)(1).

Applying this system to Partnership AB at the beginning of year 2 (Figure 4.4.2), the partnership has nonrecourse debt of $60,000 (the nonguaranteed portion of $90,000) and partner nonrecourse debt of $30,000. The adjusted basis of the building at the beginning of year 2 is $90,000. It is allocated $60,000 to the nonrecourse debt and $30,000 to the partner nonrecourse debt, yielding partnership minimum gain and partner nonrecourse debt minimum gain that both equal zero. At the end of year 2 (Figure 4.4.3), the adjusted basis of the building is $80,000, allocated $53,333 and $26,667, producing an increase in partnership minimum gain of $6,667 and an increase in partner nonrecourse debt minimum gain of $3,333. The nonrecourse deductions of $6,667 are allocated 10% to A and 90% to B under the partnership agreement. The partner nonrecourse deductions of $3,333 must be allocated entirely to A.

Exculpatory liabilities

The flip side, so to speak, of partner nonrecourse debt is debt that is recourse to the partnership but for which no partner bears economic risk of loss. The most common example (and it is very common) is the recourse debt of a limited liability company. A less common example, but which gives this kind of liabilities their name, is a recourse debt of a general or limited partnership, with respect to which the lender has entered into a separate agreement exculpating (releasing) the partners from personal responsibility on the debt, even though it would otherwise have existed under state law. It would seem that the tax treatment of such loans would be well settled, but in truth it is not. They are certainly nonrecourse debt for purposes of the allocation rules of Treas. Reg. § 1.704–2. But because they are not secured by any specific property, the calculation of partnership minimum gain, and thus of nonrecourse deductions, is challenging and uncertain. The IRS is well aware of this problem and for decades has allowed LLCs and other affected partnerships to treat allocations attributable to these liabilities in any manner that reasonably reflects the principles of section 704(b). Commonly, exculpatory liabilities are treated as secured by a "floating lien" on all of the assets of the LLC or other partnership. An exculpatory liability is illustrated in Question 4.4.6.

4.4.1   Eggsellent Poultry LP has two partners. Aidy, the general partner, makes an initial capital contribution of $10,000 and Bo, the limited partner, makes an initial contribution of $40,000. Neither Aidy nor Bo has a deficit-restoration obligation except as imposed by state law. The partnership is fortunate to borrow $200,000 on a nonrecourse basis, with which it purchases depreciable plant and equipment for $200,000. Repayment of the debt is secured by a lien on the plant and equipment. The allocation provisions in the partnership agreement satisfy the requirements of the alternate test for economic effect and include a minimum gain chargeback. Except to the extent otherwise provided by law, 20% of income, gains, losses and deductions are to be allocated to Aidy until such time as the aggregate amounts of income and gain so allocated equal the aggregate amounts of losses and deductions so allocated. Thereafter Aidy will be allocated 50% of all income, gains, losses and deductions. At the beginning 2017, after two years of operation during which it has made no distributions to partners, Eggsellent's balance sheet is as follows:

Assets			Liabilities		
	Tax	Book		Tax	Book
Cash	$ 4,000	$ 4,000	Bank Debt	$200,000	$200,000
Receivables	0	0			
Inventory	50,000	50,000	Capital		
Plant	88,000	88,000	Aidy	0	0
Equipment	58,000	58,000	Bo	0	0
Total Assets	$200,000	$200,000	Total Liabilities and Capital	$200,000	$200,000

What is the amount of nonrecourse deductions that have been allocated to Aidy and Bo during the first two years of operation?

a) Aidy, $0; Bo, $0

b) Aidy, $10,000; Bo, $40,000

c) Aidy, $10,800; Bo, $43,200

d) Aidy, $27,000; Bo, $27,000

4.4.2   Same facts as Question 4.4.1. Eggsellent incurs a tax loss of $36,000 for 2017, which includes depreciation on plant and equipment equal to $27,000. Pursuant to the partnership agreement, the partners seek to allocate $7,200 (20%) of this tax loss to Aidy and $28,800 (80%) to Bo. Can they?

a) No, Bo has no deficit-restoration obligation and already has a zero balance in his capital account. The entire $36,000 loss must be allocated to Aidy.

b) No, the allocation of nonrecourse deductions to Bo is acceptable, but the alternate test for economic effect does not allow any of the additional $9,000 in loss to be allocated to him.

c) No, the allocation of nonrecourse deductions does not meet the significant item consistency test.

d) Yes, the proposed allocation meets all applicable standards.

4.4.3   Same facts as Question 4.4.1, except that the Bank makes two $100,000 nonrecourse loans of equal priority. Eggsellent purchases $100,000 of equipment with the proceeds of one of these loans and purchases the plant for $100,000 with the other. Bo guarantees the repayment of the equipment loan. As in Question 4.4.1, the partnership claims depreciation of $42,000 on its equipment and $12,000 on its plant over the first two years of operation. What is the aggregate amount of nonrecourse deductions (including partner nonrecourse deductions) properly allocated to Aidy and Bo for these two years?

a)   Aidy, $0; Bo, $0

b)   Aidy, $2,400; Bo, $51,600

c)   Aidy, $10,800; Bo, $43,200

d)   Aidy, $14,000; Bo, $40,000

4.4.4   Same facts as Question 4.4.1. Eggsellent has an excellent year in 2017, with income of $80,000. It celebrates by paying down its nonrecourse debt by $80,000. What is the proper amount of income allocated to Aidy and Bo for 2017?

a)   Aidy, $16,000; Bo, $64,000

b)   Aidy, $23,800; Bo, $56,200

c)   Aidy, $25,000; Bo, $55,000

d)   Aidy, $35,800; Bo, $98,200

4.4.5   Axel and Bebe contribute $10,000 each to Computek LLC, a limited liability company taxed as a partnership, which borrows $80,000 on a nonrecourse basis, secured by a lien on all of its assets. In the ensuing years, Computek incurs an aggregate of $60,000 of losses (including depreciation), which it allocates equally to Axel and Bebe. Despite these tax losses, the value of Computek's assets has actually been increasing, and the net value of the assets is now $40,000. Axel and Bebe agree to revalue the assets of Computek and admit Conrad as a one-third member in exchange for a capital contribution of $20,000, which is used to pay down Computek's nonrecourse debt by $20,000. Computek's operating agreement contains a minimum gain chargeback. Pursuant thereto, how much income or gain must be allocated to each of Axel and Bebe with respect to the decrease in minimum gain created by these transactions?

a) $0

b) $10,000

c) $20,000

d) $30,000

4.4.6   Ajax, Bria and Charlene contribute $450,000, $450,000 and $100,000, respectively, to the capital of Eagle Ridge LLC, a Delaware limited liability company treated as a partnership for tax purposes. Eagle Ridge borrows $20 million on a recourse basis and purchases an office building for $21 million. Under the operating agreement, all income and loss of Eagle Ridge, other than nonrecourse deductions, are allocated among the members in proportion to their invested capital. No member has a deficit-restoration obligation. Based solely on these facts, what is the **maximum** amount of nonrecourse deductions that Eagle Ridge can realize and the **maximum** amount of such deductions that it can allocate to Charlene? If you believe that current law is not entirely clear, please give the best answer under current law.

a) Maximum nonrecourse deductions are $0, of which a maximum amount of $0 can be allocated to Charlene.

b) Maximum nonrecourse deductions are $20 million, of which a maximum amount of $100,000 can be allocated to Charlene.

c) Maximum nonrecourse deductions are $20 million, of which a maximum amount of $2 million can be allocated to Charlene.

d) Maximum nonrecourse deductions are $20 million, of which a maximum amount of $20 million can be allocated to Charlene.

CHAPTER 5
INSIDE AND OUTSIDE
BASIS REVISITED

5.1   THE IMPORTANCE OF INSIDE-OUTSIDE BASIS EQUALITY

When we reviewed contributions of property in Topic 2.2, the first provision we studied was section 723, which gives the partnership a basis in contributed, appreciated property equal to the contributor's basis. (A more complex rule applies where the property is depreciated, but that's for later.) This rule makes intuitive sense, because neither the partner nor the partnership recognizes gain on the contribution, so maintaining the basis of the contributed property preserves this gain for later taxation. Then came section 722, which gives the contributing partner a basis in her interest in the partnership equal to her prior basis in the contributed property. This is also an intuitive result. A higher (or lower) outside basis would cause her to realize less (or more) gain on a subsequent sale of her interest, although she recognized no gain on the contribution itself.

A third equality, which may have escaped your attention, is that inside and outside basis, because they are both equal to the basis of the contributed property, are also equal to each other. This is not an accident. In fact, the partnership tax law goes through a lot of trouble to ensure that this is always true (or can be, for a partnership that so elects). The list of Internal Revenue Code sections is formidable. In addition to sections 722 and 723, there is section 705, discussed in Topic 5.2, which adjusts outside basis upon the occurrence of events that change inside basis. Section 752, discussed in Topics 5.3, 5.4 and 5.5, includes a partnership's liabilities in the outside bases of the partners, because such liabilities are also included in the inside bases of the partnership's assets. Sections 732 and 733, which are bookends to sections 722 and 723, generally preserve the inside basis of property distributed to a partner and adjust the distributee's outside basis by reference to the inside basis of the distributed property. They are discussed in Topic 9.1. In cases where this does not happen, these provisions get help from section 734(b), a largely elective provision discussed in Topic 9.2. Rounding out the roster is section 743(b), discussed in Topic 6.5, another largely elective provision which re-establishes equality of aggregate inside basis and aggregate outside basis following the transfer of a partnership interest.

Professor Andrews encourages us to see the forest past this multitude of trees:

> Indeed the matter should be put even more strongly: Inside and outside basis should be the same because they are essentially the same thing, just divided up or allocated differently. Total inside or outside basis represents total tax-paid (and debt-financed) investment of the partners in a partnership enterprise. Inside basis represents that total allocated among partnership assets, while outside basis represents the same total allocated among the partners—like rows and columns in a rectangular array. Since there is only one level of tax imposed on partnership income, there is no need or room for more than one measure of total basis, although it is necessary to be able to arrive at that total differently for the purposes of taxing partner and partnership level transactions.

Andrews, *Inside Basis Adjustments and Hot Asset Exchanges in Partnership Distributions*, 47 TAX LAW REV. 3, 10 (1991). Pause for a moment on Professor Andrew's observation that there is "no need or room" for more than one measure of basis in partnership taxation. If Stella contributes to a partnership an investment asset with a value of $1,000 and an adjusted basis in her hands of $400 and the partnership sells that asset for $1,000, who realizes how much gain? Applying some provisions that we have already reviewed and some yet to come, the answer is that the partnership realizes $600 of gain, all of which it allocates to Stella—exactly the result had she sold the asset herself. Moreover, if the partnership then liquidates Stella's interest by distributing the $1,000 to her in cash, she realizes no further gain or loss. This is the goal of the partnership tax system—to tax all partnership income once and only once, as though the partners owned directly the partnership's assets and realized directly the income and loss from those assets.

Now consider two hypothetical variations in this example. In the first, the partnership takes a basis in the contributed asset equal to its fair market value, $1,000. When it sells this asset, the partnership realizes no gain. When it distributes the cash proceeds of sale to Stella, she realizes $600 of gain, assuming that she took a $400 basis in her partnership interest. Compared to direct ownership (or to current law), Stella ultimately realizes the correct amount of gain ($600), but only on the liquidation of her interest, an event that Stella would like to postpone for as long as possible. Alternatively, a different timing problem would occur if the partnership took a basis less than Stella's $400 basis in the asset. In that case, it would realize more than $600 of gain on sale of the asset. This overstated gain would be passed through to Stella currently and would be offset by a commensurately overstated loss that she would realize on liquidation, an event that Stella probably would not like to postpone at all.

These hypotheticals could be multiplied to cover many other situations where aggregate inside basis does not equal aggregate outside basis. In each situation, the inequality leads to under-taxation or over-taxation of partnership income, relative to the norm of direct ownership. There is "no need or room" for this result in a properly functioning partnership tax system.

5.2 OUTSIDE BASIS: SECTION 705

The outside-basis adjustments of section 705 can be entirely explained by the need for equality between inside basis and outside basis. Return for a moment to the case of Stella, whom we met in Topic 5.1. When her partnership sells for $1,000 the asset she contributed with an adjusted basis of $400, the partnership realizes a $600 gain, which it passes through to her. When the partnership distributes the $1,000 cash proceeds of sale to Stella, she is threatened with a second $600 gain, because the cash distribution exceeds her initial outside basis by that amount. *See* section 731(a)(1), discussed in Topic 9.1. The adjustment provided by section 705(a)(1)(A) forestalls this double taxation by increasing her outside basis from $400 to $1,000 as a result of the allocation to her of the $600 gain on sale by the partnership. It avoids double taxation, in other words, by equalizing inside and outside basis.

At first, it may seem that only *taxable* income, gains and losses realized by the partnership should produce adjustments to outside basis. This would still leave room, however, for double or no taxation, as illustrated by the following Questions.

5.2.1 Raj is a 5% partner in the All Weather Fund LP. In 2017, the Fund realizes $10,000 of tax-exempt interest on municipal bonds and $20,000 of fully taxable interest on US Treasuries. What is the total adjustment to Raj's outside basis from these two items?

a) $0

b) $500

c) $1,000

d) $1,500

5.2.2 One of the holdings of the All Weather Fund is a telecommunications company that is taken over in 2017. The Fund owns 10,000 shares with an adjusted basis of $2 million. In the merger, the Fund receives shares of the acquiring company valued at $3.5 million and recognizes no gain or loss. What is the adjustment to Raj's outside basis arising from this merger exchange?

a) $0

b) $75,000

c) $100,000

d) $175,000

5.2.3   In 2017, the All Weather Fund makes two charitable contributions, one consisting of $30,000 in cash and the other, 200 shares of stock, valued at $70,000 with an adjusted basis of $40,000. What is the total adjustment to Raj's outside basis from these two contributions?

a) $0

b)   ($2,000)

c)   ($3,500)

d)   ($5,000)

5.3   OUTSIDE BASIS: ALLOCATING RECOURSE DEBT UNDER SECTION 752

Please re-read the essay that begins Topic 2.4.

Thank you. Welcome back. As you now recall, section 752(a) includes a partner's share of partnership liabilities in the partner's outside basis, using the mechanism of a deemed contribution of cash to accomplish that purpose. Section 752(b) uses the mechanism of a deemed distribution of cash to decrease a partner's outside basis whenever her share of partnership liabilities decreases. Our main task in this Topic and the following two is to review the Treasury regulations that spell out how to determine a partner's share of partnership liabilities—an issue that is not addressed in the statute. But first, let's consider a prior question: just what is a "liability" for these purposes? Answering this question will help to illuminate the role that section 752 plays in Subchapter K.

Defining liabilities

Not every obligation of or undertaking by a partnership is a liability for purposes of section 752. Instead, that status is reserved for three particular types of obligations: those that (1) create or increase the basis of any partnership asset (including cash), (2) give rise to an immediate deduction, or (3) give rise to a nondeductible, noncapitalizable expense. Treas. Reg. § 1.752–1(a)(4). The rationale for this specification follows directly from the goal of section 752 to promote parity between aggregate inside basis and aggregate outside basis.

Say, for example, that a partnership borrows $1,000 from a bank, the transaction considered in Topic 2.4. This is a category (1) liability. The partnership's assets and liabilities are both increased by $1,000, satisfying the accounting identity. Section 752(a) sees to it that the partners' aggregate outside basis also increases by $1,000, thus ensuring that aggregate outside basis continues to equal aggregate inside basis.

Now consider an accrual-method partnership that incurs a $1,000 obligation to pay for services performed by an outside consultant. Assuming that this cost is properly accrued (and economic performance has occurred), and that it is not required to be capitalized, it does not create an asset on the partnership's balance sheet, but it does give rise to an immediate deduction.

The flow-through of this deduction to the partners decreases their outside bases. This obligation is a category (2) liability. Treating it as a liability of the partnership increases the aggregate outside basis of the partners under section 752(a), offsetting the decrease to aggregate outside basis caused by the flow-through of the deduction. Aggregate outside basis is therefore unchanged, as is aggregate inside basis.

Finally, imagine that a partnership using an accrual method agrees to donate $1,000 to a local charity. This is a category (3) liability. Under section 703(a)(2)(C), the partnership is not entitled to deduct this charitable contribution, but instead passes it through to the partners, who can deduct it on their own tax returns when and to the extent allowable. The flow-through of this item reduces the partners' aggregate outside basis by $1,000 under section 705(a)(2)(B). Treating the obligation as a liability creates an offsetting increase in aggregate outside basis under 752(a), leaving it unchanged. There is, meanwhile, no change in the partnership's assets, so inside-outside basis parity is maintained. When the partnership actually pays the promised amount, its assets (cash) and liabilities will each decline by $1,000. Aggregate inside basis will decline by $1,000 by virtue of the cash expenditure. Aggregate outside basis will also, under section 752(b).

Allocating recourse liabilities

Treas. Reg. § 1.752–2 governs allocation of the "recourse" debt of a partnership among its partners. It was promulgated in response to a 1984 Congressional directive that partnership debt be allocated in accordance with the "economic risk of loss" borne by each of the partners. For purposes of section 752, debt is "recourse" to the extent that any partner or related party bears the economic risk of loss.

In order to determine whether and to what extent a partner bears the economic risk of loss for a partnership liability, the Treasury regulations ask us to engage in a thought experiment, dubbed the "constructive liquidation." In a constructive liquidation, all of a partnership's liabilities become due in full, and the partnership sells all of its assets, allocates all items of income, gain, loss and deduction among its partners in accordance with the partnership agreement and applicable law, and thereafter liquidates. There is one catch: the partnership's assets (even cash) are assumed to be worthless and the partnership receives no consideration in the sale of its assets, other than relief from nonrecourse liabilities (but not recourse liabilities, which remain due and payable in full). Tax profs describe this scenario using colorful phrases that involve nuclear bombs, doomsday, Armageddon and the like. The point is that the constructive liquidation is not intended to reflect accurately the actual value of the partnership's assets. Instead, it is intended to ascertain where the buck would stop if the partnership suddenly had no assets at all—that is, which of the partners would bear the economic risk of loss for the partnership's debt if the partnership could not help defray it in any way.

In many cases, it is not hard to determine which partner or partners bear the economic risk of loss for a partnership debt. You will not always need to employ the constructive liquidation to make this determination. If, for instance, a limited partnership with one general partner incurs a recourse debt, you should not need a constructive liquidation to tell you that all of that debt should be allocated to the general partner. Like your mom, however, the constructive liquidation will always be there for you if you need it—and sometimes you *will* need it, as the following Questions demonstrate. All involve partnerships where the entire economic arrangement is set forth in the partnership agreement and the loan documentation. More complex cases involving guarantees and indemnifications are covered in Topic 5.5.

5.3.1   The Hyponix Company, a limited liability company taxed as a partnership, has a calendar taxable year and uses the cash method of tax accounting. The company has a loan on which interest is payable each year on January 31, April 30, July 31 and October 31. As of December 31, 2016, interest in the amount of $2,400 has accrued on this loan. During December 2016, the company acquires office supplies for $750, payment for which is due on standard terms in January 2017. Considering solely these two items, what is the amount of the company's liabilities for purposes of section 752?

a) $0

b) $750

c) $2,400

d) $3,150

5.3.2   Klix, a general partnership, has two partners, Xander and Zoe, each of whom makes an initial capital contribution of $100,000 in cash. The partnership agreement provides that all income, gains, losses and deductions will be allocated 75% to Xander until the total amount of income and gains allocated in such proportion equals the amount of losses and deductions so allocated, and then all further partnership items will be allocated 45% to Xander and 55% to Zoe. The partnership agreement requires the maintenance of proper capital accounts, which will govern liquidating distributions, and both partners have full, unconditional deficit-restoration obligations. The partnership borrows $700,000 on a recourse basis and uses the proceeds of this loan to acquire its plant and equipment. For section 752 purposes, how is this liability allocated between Xander and Zoe?

a)   Xander, $315,000; Zoe, $385,000

b)   Xander, $350,000; Zoe, $350,000

c)   Xander, $525,000; Zoe, $175,000

d)   Xander, $575,000; Zoe, $125,000

5.3.3   Same facts as Question 5.3.2, except that the partners are obligated to restore capital-account deficits only to the extent necessary to pay creditors, but not to pay the amount of the positive balance, if any, in the capital account of the other partner. The partnership agreement contains a qualified income offset. For section 752 purposes, how is the $700,000 recourse liability allocated between Xander and Zoe?

a)   Xander, $315,000; Zoe, $385,000

b)   Xander, $350,000; Zoe, $350,000

c)   Xander, $525,000; Zoe, $175,000

d)   Xander, $575,000; Zoe, $125,000

5.4 OUTSIDE BASIS: ALLOCATING NONRECOURSE DEBT UNDER SECTION 752

Recourse debt follows the loss allocations among partners, while nonrecourse debt follows profits. Although this statement is not exactly wrong, it leaves out all the most interesting parts of the allocation of nonrecourse debt. As you know, the nonrecourse debt of a partnership is allocated among the partners in three tiers: first, by shares of minimum gain; second, by shares of what is often called section 704(c) minimum gain; and, finally, under a multitude of rules for "excess nonrecourse liabilities," the most basic of which is allocation according to the partners' shares of partnership profit. It is this final rule that gives the allocation of nonrecourse debt its reputation. Let's spend some time investigating the other rules.

The first tier

If you have read Topic 4.4, you already know all you need to know about the first tier of nonrecourse debt allocation. Once a partner is determined to have a share of partnership minimum gain, she has the same share (by dollar amount) of the nonrecourse debt that funds it. Treas. Reg. § 1.752–3(a)(1). (If a partner has a share of partner nonrecourse debt minimum gain, she is allocated 100% of that partner nonrecourse debt, because it is considered to be a recourse debt, under rules that we reviewed in Topic 5.3.)

This is a rule with a purpose that may not be immediately obvious. You will recall from Topic 4.4 that a partner's share of the partnership's minimum gain is increased dollar-for-dollar by an allocation of a nonrecourse deduction or a distribution financed by nonrecourse borrowing. Allocating that partner a commensurate share of the partnership's nonrecourse debt affects the tax treatment of both transactions. In the case of an allocation of nonrecourse deductions, the allocation of nonrecourse debt *guarantees* that the partner will have outside basis sufficient to utilize the allocated deduction, even if the partner has no capital investment remaining in the partnership and no share of any other partnership debt. Similarly, in the case of a debt-financed distribution, the nonrecourse debt allocation provides the distributee-partner with basis to "cover" the distribution, so that it is not currently taxable even if it is made in cash. Of course, the partner will eventually have to pay the piper, when the partner's share of partnership minimum gain decreases and the minimum gain chargeback takes hold. This can occur, for example, when the property securing the nonrecourse debt is sold or when the debt itself is paid down in whole or in part.

When a partnership holds property with a book value that differs from its adjusted basis, the determination of minimum gain is made by reference to book value. *See* Topic 4.4. This affects the computation, and even the existence, of first-tier allocations of nonrecourse debt in such situations.

The second tier

The second tier in the allocation scheme for nonrecourse debt is as purposive as the first. Under Treas. Reg. § 1.752–3(a)(2), a partner is allocated a share of nonrecourse debt equal to the amount of taxable gain that would be allocated to the partner under section 704(c) if the partnership transferred the property subject to (*i.e.*, securing) the nonrecourse debt in a taxable transaction in full satisfaction of the debt and for no other consideration. This amount is not necessarily the partner's full responsibility for gain under section 704(c). Suppose, for example, that Sid contributes property to Luckman LLC, a limited liability company taxed as a partnership, which has a value of $1,000, an adjusted basis of $400 and is subject to nonrecourse debt of $700. If the company were to sell the property for $1,000 the next day, section 704(c) would require the $600 gain to be allocated to Sid. In the second-tier allocation, Sid is allocated not $600 of the nonrecourse debt, but only $300, which is the amount of gain the partnership would realize (and allocate to Sid) if it sold the property for $700, the amount of the debt. This is why this allocation is often referred to as the section 704(c) minimum gain, rather than simply the section 704(c) gain.

So what's the point? Imagine that Sid were allocated none of the nonrecourse debt. When he contributed the property to Luckman LLC, he would have a deemed cash distribution of $700, the amount of the debt, under section 752(b). He would have no deemed cash contribution under section 752(a), because we are assuming he would be allocated none of the debt once it has been assumed by the company. Accordingly, Sid would recognize a gain of $300 on this contribution, being the excess of the debt relief (deemed cash distribution under section 752(b)) of $700 over his basis in the contributed property (outside basis in the partnership under section 722) of $400. This is the problem (tax disaster, I remember calling it) that was the focus of discussion in Topic 2.5.

The second-tier allocation of nonrecourse debt allocates to Sid an amount of debt precisely equal to the amount of gain ($300) that he would recognize in this situation. This is not necessarily all that Sid will be allocated—he may receive a further allocation of the nonrecourse debt in the third tier, or even in the second tier if the partnership has adopted the remedial method. *See* Rev. Rul. 95–41, 1995–1 C.B. 132. But this minimum allocation assures Sid that he will not recognize gain on the contribution to a partnership of property encumbered by nonrecourse debt, no matter how large the debt or how small his adjusted basis in the property.

The third tier

The third tier offers a number of possibilities for allocating excess nonrecourse debt (*i.e.*, nonrecourse debt remaining to be allocated after application of the rules in the first two tiers). Excess nonrecourse debt is not required to be allocated under the same method every year. Treas. Reg. § 1.752–3(a)(3).

- ✓ *General profit share* (first two sentences). This is the default rule, but not terribly useful because of the difficulty in determining what is a partner's general profit share in all but the simplest cases. That said, the simplest cases often show up on partnership tax exams, so come prepared to apply this one.

- ✓ *Profit share specified in the partnership agreement* (third sentence). Many partnership agreements use this alternative. It is limited by the same "significant item consistency" test that applies in the allocation of nonrecourse deductions. *See* Topic 4.4. The specified profit shares must be "reasonably consistent with allocations (that have substantial economic effect under the section 704(b) regulations) of some other significant item of partnership income or gain."

- ✓ *Nonrecourse deductions* (fourth sentence). A very useful standard, this one allows nonrecourse debt to be allocated in the manner that the deductions funded by the nonrecourse debt are reasonably expected to be allocated. The chosen allocation is not reasonable if it does not pass the tests for the allocation of nonrecourse deductions under Treas. Reg. § 1.704–2. This choice allocates nonrecourse debt to the partners in advance of the allocations of nonrecourse deductions, avoiding the need to re-allocate nonrecourse debt under the first tier when the allocations of nonrecourse deductions actually occur.

- ✓ *Remaining section 704(c) gain* (fifth, sixth and seventh sentences). Unlike the preceding methods, this one can apply in addition to another method. It allows a contributing partner to be allocated not only the section 704(c) minimum gain, but the entire section 704(c) gain, on the contributed property. This method would allocate to Sid not only the $300 minimum, but the remaining $300 of his total section 704(c) gain of $600 (which is the excess of the $1,000 value of the property on contribution over its $400 adjusted basis). Thus, $600 of the nonrecourse debt would be allocated to Sid, with the remaining $100 to be allocated under another of the permissible methods.

5.4.1   Rancor Records LLC is a "partnership by shares" that was recently formed with cash contributions. The operating agreement, which meets the requirements of the alternate test for economic effect, provides that all items of partnership income, gain, loss and deduction will be allocated according to relative capital accounts. Rancor borrows $1 million on a recourse basis (meaning that the lender is not limited to pledged assets to collect its debt and can reach all of the partnership's assets in an insolvency or bankruptcy proceeding). Rancor has never revalued its assets. How is the $1 million liability shared among the partners and why?

a) According to relative capital accounts, because this is how economic risk of loss is shared

b) According to the sharing of economic risk of loss, which must be determined by applying the constructive liquidation test

c) According to relative capital accounts, because this measures the partners' interests in the partnership

d) According to relative capital accounts, because this measures the partners' shares of partnership profits

5.4.2 Naomi, Natalie and Natasha form the 3N Company LP, a limited partnership, to design and market office sundries. Naomi is the general partner and Natalie and Natasha are limited partners. Each partner makes a cash contribution of $100,000 and the partnership borrows $500,000 on a nonrecourse basis, secured by a pledge of all of its assets. Over the first three years of operation, the partnership incurs losses aggregating $500,000, including nonrecourse deductions of $200,000. Assume that all nonrecourse deductions have been and will be properly allocated to Naomi. Assume further that the partnership agreement provides that the partners' shares of partnership profits are equal for purposes of allocating excess nonrecourse liabilities, and that this specification is valid. At the end of the third year, what are the partners' shares of the $500,000 nonrecourse debt?

a) Naomi, $0; Natalie, $250,000; Natasha, $250,000

b) Naomi, $166,667; Natalie, $166,667; Natasha, $166,667

c) Naomi, $300,000; Natalie, $100,000; Natasha, $100,000

d) Naomi, $500,000; Natalie, $0; Natasha, $0

5.4.3 Same facts as Question 5.4.2. It is now the end of year five, and 3N has allocated an additional $100,000 of nonrecourse deductions to Naomi. What are the partners' shares of the $500,000 nonrecourse debt at the end of the fifth year?

a) Naomi, $0; Natalie, $250,000; Natasha, $250,000

b) Naomi, $166,667; Natalie, $166,667; Natasha, $166,667

c) Naomi, $300,000; Natalie, $100,000; Natasha, $100,000

d) Naomi, $366,667; Natalie, $66,667; Natasha, $66,667

5.4.4 Same facts as Question 5.4.2, except that, rather than providing partners' shares of partnership profits for purposes of allocating excess nonrecourse liabilities, the 3N partnership agreement provides that excess nonrecourse liabilities are allocated as nonrecourse deductions are expected to be allocated. At the end of the third year, what are the partners' shares of the $500,000 nonrecourse debt?

a) Naomi, $0; Natalie, $250,000; Natasha, $250,000

b)   Naomi, $166,667; Natalie, $166,667; Natasha, $166,667

c)   Naomi, $300,000; Natalie, $100,000; Natasha, $100,000

d)   Naomi, $500,000; Natalie, $0; Natasha, $0

5.4.5   Let's return to Sid, who contributes to Luckman LLC depreciable property worth $1,000, with an adjusted basis in Sid's hands of $400 and subject to nonrecourse debt of $700, in exchange for a 50% interest in Luckman. Estelle contributes $300 in cash for the other 50% interest. The operating agreement provides that all partnership items are to be shared equally between Sid and Estelle. The partnership uses the traditional method for purposes of section 704(c). On formation, what are the partners' respective shares of the nonrecourse debt?

a)   Sid, $300; Estelle, $400

b)   Sid, $400; Estelle, $300

c)   Sid, $500; Estelle, $200

d)   Sid, $700; Estelle, $0

5.4.6   Over the next several years, Luckman LLC operates at breakeven, except for depreciation, which reduces the book value of the depreciable property to $600 and its adjusted tax basis to $240. The principal balance of the nonrecourse debt remains $700. How is it allocated now?

a)   Sid, $500; Estelle, $200

b)   Sid, $530; Estelle, $170

c)   Sid, $580; Estelle, $120

d)   Sid, $700; Estelle, $0

5.4.7   *The earlier Questions asked you to assume that the allocations provided in the partnership agreement are respected for tax purposes. This and the following Questions require you to decide for yourself whether the allocations provided in the partnership agreement are acceptable and to use that conclusion in determining the allocation of the nonrecourse debt. Assume that a partnership exists in all Questions, even when one partner is allocated 100% of all tax items.* Addison, Bailey and Camellia form the Brighten Bleach Company, a general partnership that will make teeth-whitening products. They contribute $200,000 each to finance inventory and working capital. The partnership obtains a $400,000 nonrecourse loan to acquire a small manufacturing facility, which is mortgaged to secure repayment of the loan. The purchase price of this facility is $400,000, so it is 100% financed. The partnership agreement, which satisfies all three requirements of the safe harbor for establishing economic effect for its allocations and contains a minimum gain chargeback, provides that all items of partnership income, gain, loss and deduction (including depreciation) will be allocated to Addison until she has been allocated aggregate income and gain equal to aggregate losses and deductions (other than nonrecourse deductions), from which point all allocations (including depreciation) will be shared equally among the partners. The partners expect to expend most of their capital during the first two years of operation, then to turn profitable and to reach the crossover point for allocations by the end of four years. The partnership agreement provides that Addison's share of partnership profits is 100% for purposes of allocating excess nonrecourse liabilities. What is Addison's initial share of the $400,000 nonrecourse loan?

a) $400,000, pursuant to the specification of profit shares in the partnership agreement

b) $400,000, because this is how the partnership reasonably expects nonrecourse deductions will be allocated

c) $133,333, because this is Addison's share of partnership profits

d) More than $133,333 but less than $400,000, depending on one's view of Addison's general profit share

5.4.8 Same facts as Question 5.4.7, except the partnership agreement provides that all items of income, gain, loss, deduction and credit will be allocated equally among the three partners, except for depreciation on the manufacturing facility, which will be allocated entirely to Addison. The partnership agreement continues to provide that Addison's share of partnership profits is 100% for purposes of allocating excess nonrecourse liabilities. What is Addison's initial share of the $400,000 nonrecourse loan?

a) $400,000, pursuant to the specification of profit shares in the partnership agreement

b) $400,000, because this is how the partnership reasonably expects nonrecourse deductions will be allocated

c) $133,333, because this is Addison's share of partnership profits

d) More than $133,333 but less than $400,000, depending on one's view of Addison's general profit share

5.4.9 Brighten Bleach is capitalized differently this time. Addison contributes the manufacturing facility (value, $600,000; adjusted basis, $100,000; subject to a $400,000 nonrecourse loan) and Bailey and Camellia contribute $200,000 each in cash. The partnership agreement, which satisfies all three requirements of the safe harbor for establishing economic effect for its allocations and contains a minimum gain chargeback, provides that all items of income, gain, loss, deduction and credit will be allocated equally among the three partners, except for depreciation on the manufacturing facility, which will be allocated entirely to Addison. The partnership agreement continues to provide that Addison's share of partnership profits is 100% for purposes of allocating excess nonrecourse liabilities. The partnership uses the traditional method for purposes of section 704(c). What is Addison's initial share of the $400,000 nonrecourse loan?

a) $400,000

b) $333,333

c) $300,000

d) More than $300,000 but less than $400,000, depending on one's view of Addison's general profit share

5.4.10 Same facts as in Question 5.4.9. It is now five years later and Brighten Bleach's manufacturing facility has increased in value to $900,000. Depreciation has reduced its book value to $475,000 and its adjusted tax basis to $75,000. The partnership borrows $225,000 with a second mortgage on the facility and distributes the money to the partners, $75,000 each. The principal amount of the original debt remains at $400,000. What is each partner's share of the $625,000 nonrecourse debt of this partnership?

a) Addison, $625,000; Bailey, $0; Camellia, $0

b) Addison, $575,000; Bailey, $25,000; Camellia, $25,000

c) Addison, $525,000; Bailey, $50,000; Camellia, $50,000

d) Addison, $475,000; Bailey, $75,000; Camellia, $75,000

5.5   OUTSIDE BASIS: DEBT-SHIFTING ARRANGEMENTS

Why would a partner want a higher share of partnership debt? To have a higher outside basis, of course. What is outside basis good for? At least three things. A higher outside basis can reduce a partner's gain on a sale of her partnership interest. However, as we will discuss further in Chapter 6, increasing debt share to increase outside basis for this purpose is futile, because the increased debt share will also increase the partner's amount realized on the sale, leaving the gain unchanged.

The two remaining uses for outside basis are more interesting. The first is to enhance a partner's ability to take allocations of losses and deductions from the partnership without bumping into the limitation of section 704(d), discussed in Topic 5.6. Outside basis arising from partnership debt allows a partner to take aggregate loss deductions that exceed her investment in the partnership by two, three or more times. These losses can provide tax savings that reduce the after-tax cost of her investment and increase her after-tax return.

Nonrecourse debt is ideal for this purpose, because allocations of nonrecourse deductions—deductions funded by nonrecourse debt—provide their own basis through the first tier (minimum gain) allocations of nonrecourse debt under Treas. Reg. § 1.752–3(a)(1). *See* Topic 5.4. But not all debt can be nonrecourse, because the type and quality of the assets of the partnership may not justify lending with recourse only to those assets. If partnership debt is recourse, it must be allocated to the partner or partners who bear the economic risk of loss, bypassing limited partners who have no deficit-restoration obligation in favor of other partners who do, typically the general partner.

A final reason for a partner to want a greater share of the partnership's debt is to remove cash from the partnership without current tax cost. We will not review the tax treatment of partnership distributions in detail until Chapter 9. All you need to know for present purposes is that a partner can withdraw cash from a partnership up to the amount of her outside basis without paying tax. So, more debt equals more outside basis equals more tax-free cash. It is a compelling equation for many.

A recent variation on this theme has drawn significant attention in the tax community, not to mention scrutiny from the IRS and the Tax Court. Under the disguised-sale rules discussed in Topic 2.7, a partner can be treated as selling a portion of property which she contributes to a partnership subject to debt that she has incurred during the previous two years. Treas. Reg. § 1.707–5. The amount realized in the disguised sale is the excess of the amount of the liability over the portion that is allocated to the contributing partner under the rules of section 752. To take a simple example, suppose that Alice contributes property worth $1 million with an adjusted basis in her hands of $200,000, subject to debt of $600,000. Suppose further that her allocable share of the debt after it has been assumed by the partnership is $150,000. Thus, Alice's net debt relief is $450,000. Under Treas. Reg. § 1.707–5, Alice will be treated as selling 45% ($450,000/$1 million) of the property for $450,000. She will be entitled to recover 45% of her basis ($90,000) and will recognize gain of $360,000.

Obviously, if Alice can obtain a greater share of the debt after it has been assumed by the partnership, she can reduce the tax hit on this transaction. If, for example, her share of the debt is $400,000, she will be treated as selling only 20% of the property for $200,000. She will recover $30,000 of her basis and realize gain of $170,000, a reduction of $190,000. Treas. Reg. § 1.707–5(b) clarifies that the same analysis applies even if it is the partnership, rather than Alice, that borrows the money and distributes it to Alice shortly after her contribution of the property.

Techniques for shifting debt

Tax planners frequently face the task of moving debt from where it is to where they want it to be. There is no set pattern, and therefore no single plan or idea that works in all situations. The following are some common approaches.

- ✓ *Change the relationship with the lender.* Nonrecourse debt is allocated among the partners according to different rules than recourse debt. Changing from one type to the other, if the lender will allow it, may re-allocate debt shares in a useful way. Converting recourse debt to nonrecourse debt is particularly useful for getting basis to limited partners.

- ✓ *Change the borrowing entity.* Debt that is recourse to a limited liability company is allocated as nonrecourse debt under section 752. If converting the recourse debt of a limited partnership to nonrecourse is not possible, perhaps converting the limited partnership into a limited liability company is. This technique can be useful even if the lender requires some amount of credit support (*e.g.*, a guarantee) from one or more of the members.

✓ *Guarantee a nonrecourse debt.* In determining economic risk of loss, Treas. Reg. § 1.752–2(b) requires that you take into account not only the partnership agreement, but also all contractual arrangements outside the partnership agreement and all state-law obligations and reimbursement rights. This opens lots of possibilities. If a partner guarantees a nonrecourse debt, for instance, she assumes the economic risk of loss for the guaranteed portion. Under Treas. Reg. § 1.752–1(i), the debt is "bifurcated," meaning it is split between a recourse component, which is allocated entirely to the guarantor, and a nonrecourse component, which continues to be allocated under the three tiers of Treas. Reg. § 1.752–3(a).

✓ *Guarantee a recourse debt.* Careful! One of the rights you must consider is the right of subrogation, which gives a guarantor who has performed under the guarantee the right to proceed against the partnership to collect the guaranteed debt. If that debt is a recourse debt, there will be someone, probably the general partner, who will be responsible for paying the guarantor. This reimbursement right will frustrate your efforts to shift recourse debt with a guarantee. *See* Treas. Reg. § 1.752–2(f), example (4). The usual answer is for the guarantor to waive the right of subrogation, so that the buck stops with her.

✓ *Indemnify the partner who otherwise would bear the economic risk of loss.* A limited partner might, for example, indemnify the general partner for a portion of the general partner's obligation under state law to repay a recourse liability in the event of default. This will work, if the indemnitor has no right of reimbursement from anyone else.

✓ *Add a limited deficit-restoration obligation to the partnership agreement.* This is similar to an indemnification.

✓ *Shift nonrecourse debt by changing the specification of the partners' interests in partnership profits.* Under Treas. Reg. § 1.752–3(a)(3), excess nonrecourse liabilities are allocated as specified by the partnership agreement, so long as that specification meets the significant item consistency test. *See* "IRS response," below.

Evaluating techniques

Most of these techniques have both an economic effect and a tax effect. Any technique that shifts the economic risk of loss has the economic effect of imposing greater risk on the partner to whom it is shifted in the event of default. That is a negative, which must be weighed against the positive of the tax benefit of greater loss allocations or tax-free cash distributions. The winning strategies (from the perspective of the "shiftee") are those with the smallest increase in economic risk per dollar of debt shifted. This depends on the situation, of course, but the constructive liquidation test for determining economic risk of loss makes the tax planner's job easier. You will recall that that test determines who is responsible for a partnership debt on the assumption that the partnership's assets are entirely worthless. In reality, the assets of any given partnership may have substantial value, and a partner guaranteeing the partnership's debt may not judge that she is taking much of a risk.

The so-called "bottom dollar" guarantee is especially well designed for this purpose. Pursuant to such a guarantee, the guarantor agrees to pay the lender the guaranteed amount only to the extent that the lender does not receive at least that amount from the partnership. If, for example, the partnership's debt is $800,000 and the guarantee is $100,000, the liability of the guarantor ceases when the partnership pays the first $100,000 on the debt if the guarantee is bottom-dollar, whereas it does not cease until the partnership has paid the debt in full if it is a traditional, "top-dollar" guarantee. The difference in additional protection that these two guarantees offer to the lender is obvious. So too is the difference in risk that they entail for the guarantor. But for purposes of the constructive liquidation test, these two guarantees are exactly the same, as indeed they would be if the partnership had absolutely no assets.

IRS response

Although the tax rules under which debt shifting occurs are of the government's own making, the IRS currently seems to regard them with something between ambivalence and outright hostility. IRS concern has focused in particular on so-called "leveraged partnership" transactions under Treas. Reg. § 1.707–5(b), described above, in which a taxpayer's contribution of highly appreciated property to a newly formed partnership is followed in quick succession by (1) the partnership's borrowing of an amount nearly equal to the value of the contributed property, with debt-shifting mechanisms in place to the extent necessary to ensure that most of the borrowing is allocated to the contributor, and (2) distribution of most of the proceeds of the borrowing to the contributor. Despite the similarity of this transaction to a sale of the contributed property for cash, it is outside of the reach of the disguised-sale rules if the debt shifters work and the transaction otherwise complies with Treas. Reg. § 1.707–5(b).

In roughly chronological order, here is the IRS response:

✓ *Technical Advice Memorandum 2004–36–011 (Apr. 30, 2004).* In this and other administrative determinations that cannot be cited or used as precedent, the IRS has sought to redefine the significant item consistency test, so as to limit the flexibility of partnerships to specify profit shares, and therefore the allocation of excess nonrecourse liabilities, under Treas. Reg. § 1.752–3(a)(3). In these determinations, the IRS takes the position that a "significant item" of income should really mean a "significant class" of income, such as gain from the sale of property or tax-exempt income. A special allocation of only a portion of such a class of income should not, the

IRS reasons, justify allocating the partnership's excess nonrecourse debt the same way, even if the amount of income specially allocated is clearly large enough to be significant. This somewhat results-oriented redefinition of terms was intended to shut down the practice of using a preferred return to allocate all of a partnership's excess nonrecourse debt to the partner receiving the preferred return, a common tactic in "leveraged partnership" transactions. It is inconsistent with the interpretation of the same language in Treas. Reg. § 1.704–2(e)(2) by Treas. Reg. § 1.704–2(m), example (1).

✓ *Effect of a disregarded entity (Treas. Reg. § 1.752–2(k)).* One neat way for a partner to create the appearance of an economic risk of loss for partnership debt is to interpose a limited liability company between herself and the partnership and then to cause that LLC to guarantee or otherwise assume responsibility for the debt. So long as the existence of the LLC is recognized under state law, it affords the protection of limited liability to the partner. On the other hand, if the LLC is a disregarded entity for tax purposes, it appears that the partner herself should be treated as bearing the economic risk of loss. This regulation, finalized in 2006, provides that the LLC's obligation is taken into account only to the extent that it has net worth beyond its interest in the partnership. This is often called the "net value test."

✓ *Anti-abuse rule (Treas. Reg. § 1.752–2(j)).* This regulation provides that a partner's obligation to make a payment may be disregarded if it is part of an arrangement a principal purpose of which is to eliminate the partner's economic risk of loss with respect to that obligation or to create the appearance of an economic risk of loss when the substance of the arrangement is otherwise. In *Canal Corp. v. Commissioner,* 135 T.C. 199 (2010), which involved a "leveraged partnership" transaction, the IRS successfully urged the Tax Court to apply this regulation to disregard the taxpayer's indemnity agreement and thus to treat a $755 million distribution to the taxpayer as the proceeds of a disguised sale.

✓ *Proposed section 752 regulations.* In 2014, the IRS proposed its most forceful response to date: amendments to the regulations for allocating both recourse and nonrecourse debt. On the recourse side, the proposed regulations seek to distinguish "bona fide, commercial" obligations from those that are tax-driven. To do this, they would establish certain commercial indicia that an obligation must meet to be recognized for tax purposes, such as that the obligor must be paid an arm's-length price for assuming the obligation. They would disregard all forms of bottom-dollar guarantees. The proposed regulations would also extend the net-value test to all obligors other than individuals and decedent's estates. On the nonrecourse side, the proposed regulations would repeal the allocation of excess nonrecourse liabilities by profit shares specified in the partnership agreement, as well as allocation in accordance with the manner that nonrecourse deductions are reasonably expected to be allocated. In their place, the proposed regulations would substitute allocation in accordance with liquidation-value percentages—essentially, capital accounts adjusted to take into account a hypothetical sale of the partnership's assets at fair market value.

It would be an understatement to say that the proposed regulations are controversial, and at this writing there is no way to know what will become of them. At the very least, it seems clear that the IRS is not happy with the *status quo*, particularly with respect to "leveraged partnership" transactions. Revisions to the current rules for allocating debt in disguised sales seem likely. Whether the IRS ultimately chooses to modify the debt-allocation rules more broadly remains to be seen.

5.5.1   Homer's Ice Cream LP has one small shop with a loyal following. Homer, the general partner, has a 50% interest and Luke and Noah, the limited partners, have interests of 25% each. Their respective capital accounts stand in the same proportions. Homer's has borrowed $500,000 on a full recourse basis from the local bank to finance an aggressive expansion. The anticipated losses will exhaust all of the partners' capital accounts, and neither of the limited partners have a deficit-restoration obligation. Wishing to share some of the debt-financed losses, Luke agrees to a deficit-restoration obligation limited to $50,000. Assuming that the partnership generates losses of $300,000 beyond the partners' capital, what share of the partnership's debt and what share of the debt-financed losses properly will be allocated to Luke?

a) $0 of debt; $0 in debt-financed losses

b) $50,000 of debt; $50,000 in debt-financed losses

c) $75,000 of debt; $75,000 in debt-financed losses

d) $162,500 of debt; $97,500 in debt-financed losses

5.5.2   Same as Question 5.5.1, except that Luke executes a $50,000 guarantee in favor of the bank, without waiving rights of subrogation. What is Luke's share?

a) $0 of debt; $0 in debt-financed losses

b) $50,000 of debt; $50,000 in debt-financed losses

c) $75,000 of debt; $75,000 in debt-financed losses

d) $162,500 of debt; $97,500 debt-financed in losses

5.5.3   Same as Question 5.5.2, except that Homer's Ice Cream is a limited liability company treated as a partnership for tax purposes. What is Luke's share? Assume that Luke guarantees the repayment of 10 cents of every dollar of the bank loan (a so-called "vertical slice" guarantee).

a) $0 of debt; $0 in losses

b) $50,000 of debt; $50,000 in debt-financed losses

c) $75,000 of debt; $75,000 in debt-financed losses

d) $162,500 of debt; $97,500 in debt-financed losses

5.5.4   Calumet Manufacturing Company, Inc. is a leading producer of after-market auto parts. Willamette Fabrication, Inc. is the parent company of a consolidated group of corporations. Wilco, Inc., one of Willamette's subsidiaries, has a successful, though smaller, parts manufacturing business, which Calumet wishes to acquire. After discussing this transaction with their tax advisors, Calumet and Wilco decide to form Newco LLC, a limited liability company taxed as a partnership, to which Calumet will contribute its $190 million business and Wilco will contribute its $50 million business. Neither business has liabilities other than ordinary trade payables. Immediately after these contributions, Newco will borrow $40 million on a recourse basis and distribute this amount to Wilco. The lender demands that Calumet guarantee the payment of the entire $40 million principal amount of the debt. On the advice of tax counsel, Wilco indemnifies Calumet for any principal payments that Calumet might have to make under its guarantee. Neither the lender nor Calumet demands this indemnity, but the parties are willing to accommodate Wilco's request to offer it. The indemnity agreement requires Wilco to maintain a net worth, exclusive of its interest in Newco, of at least $40 million. At closing, the lender wires the $40 million directly to Willamette, but documents are put in place evidencing that Newco distributed the funds to Wilco, which loaned the funds to its parent, Willamette, on a ten-year note at 8% interest. Going forward, Calumet and Willamette hold interests in Newco of 95% and 5%, respectively. Newco continues to operate the auto parts manufacturing business. Assuming that Wilco had an adjusted tax basis of zero in its auto parts business, how much gain, if any, does it recognize in this transaction?

a)   None, because Wilco's allocable share of Newco's liability is $40 million under Treas. Reg. § 1.707–5(b).

b) $40 million, because Wilco's allocable share of Newco's liability is $0. Wilco's indemnity must be disregarded under the anti-abuse rule of Treas. Reg. § 1.752–2(j).

c) $40 million, because Wilco's allocable share of Newco's liability is $0. Wilco's indemnity is not a payment obligation under Treas. Reg. § 1.752–2(b).

d) $40 million, because Newco is a sham which cannot be treated as a partnership for tax purposes.

5.5.5   Same as Question 5.5.4, except that Wilco has no obligation to maintain any net worth; it can distribute all or any portion of Willamette's note at any time. How much gain, if any, does Wilco recognize in this transaction?

a)   None, because Wilco's allocable share of Newco's liability is $40 million under Treas. Reg. § 1.707–5(b).

b) $40 million, because Wilco's allocable share of Newco's liability is $0. Wilco's indemnity must be disregarded under the anti-abuse rule of Treas. Reg. § 1.752–2(j).

c) $40 million, because Wilco's allocable share of Newco's liability is $0. Wilco's indemnity is not a payment obligation under Treas. Reg. § 1.752–2(b).

d) $40 million, because Newco is a sham which cannot be treated as a partnership for tax purposes.

5.5.6 Same as Question 5.5.5, except that the regulations proposed under section 752 apply to this transaction as proposed. How much gain, if any, does Wilco recognize?

a) None, because Wilco's allocable share of Newco's liability is $40 million under Treas. Reg. § 1.707–5(b).

b) $40 million, because Wilco's allocable share of Newco's liability is $0. Wilco's indemnity must be disregarded under the anti-abuse rule of Treas. Reg. § 1.752–2(j).

c) $40 million, because Wilco's allocable share of Newco's liability is $0. Wilco's indemnity is not a payment obligation under Treas. Reg. § 1.752–2(b).

d) $40 million, because Newco is a sham which cannot be treated as a partnership for tax purposes.

5.5.7 Johnston & Johnston ("J&J"), a manufacturer of home health-care products, is the 50% general partner of a limited partnership which is about to introduce a new incontinence product called the iPeed. The 50% limited partner is Steve Hamilton, a venture-capital investor, who has no obligation to make additional contributions to the partnership under any circumstances. The partnership has a $5 million bank loan which is not a nonrecourse loan under section 1001—that is, the bank's rights of collection are not limited to any specific partnership assets and the bank is able to pursue the general partner to collect amounts unpaid by the partnership. Due to its concerns regarding exposure to certain commercial defamation claims, J&J transfers its partnership interest to a wholly owned limited liability company, Shellco LLC, along with $400,000 in cash to cover anticipated expenses and as a liability reserve. Shellco does not elect to be treated as a corporation for tax purposes. Following this action, how much of the $5 million bank loan is allocable to J&J under section 752?

a) $400,000

b) $2,700,000

c) $4,600,000

d) $5,000,000

5.5.8 The facts are the same as Question 5.5.7, except that J&J owns 92% of Shellco LLC, and a wholly owned subsidiary of J&J owns the other 8%. Under current law (*i.e.*, not taking into account the proposed regulations), how much of the $5 million bank loan is allocable to J&J under section 752?

  a) $400,000

  b) $2,700,000

  c) $4,600,000

  d) $5,000,000

5.5.9   The facts are the same as Question 5.5.8, except that J&J owns the limited partner interest in the iPeed partnership directly and owns the general partner interest indirectly through wholly owned Shellco LLC. Steve Hamilton is out of the picture in this variant of the facts. How much of the $5 million bank loan is allocable to J&J under section 752?

  a) $2,700,000

  b) $4,600,000

  c) $5,000,000

  d)   None of the above

5.6   OUTSIDE BASIS: SECTION 704(d)

This Chapter began with the observation that the equality of inside and outside basis is a fundamental principle of the partnership tax system. When inside and outside basis are unequal, partnership income will be overtaxed or undertaxed, at least temporarily, relative to the taxation of the same income earned directly by the partners without an intervening entity.

Because partnership debt is undeniably included in inside basis, it must be included in outside basis, so as not to frustrate the goal of basis equality. Granting that, partnership debt must be allocated among the partners. This issue has consumed us through Topics 5.3, 5.4 and 5.5. Over the course of this study, we have witnessed—although perhaps not noticed—a consistent organizing principle: debt allocations follow the allocations of debt-financed losses. In other words, if a partner properly is allocated losses or deductions that are financed by partnership debt, she can be sure that she will be allocated at least an equal share of the debt.

We saw this principle at work in the application of the constructive liquidation test for allocating recourse debt. The losses realized by the partnership in the constructive liquidation are allocated among the partners to determine who bears the economic risk of loss. These loss allocations must pass muster under section 704(b). If they do, they become the basis upon which the recourse debt is allocated.

What about nonrecourse debt, which, as everybody knows, is allocated in accordance with partnership profits, not losses? Actually, this generalization obscures the real picture. The first tier for allocation of nonrecourse debt is in accordance with the partners' shares of minimum gain, which include their shares of nonrecourse deductions, those deductions that are attributable to nonrecourse debt. Such allocations must pass muster under section 704(b). If they do, they become the basis upon which the nonrecourse debt is allocated.

This debt-allocation scheme follows from the general principle of inside-outside basis equality. For any tax year in which a partnership makes no distributions, its losses equal the reduction in the inside basis in its assets for the year. These items flow through to the partners and, under section 705(a)(2), they reduce each partner's outside basis. But not below zero. Accordingly, if a partner is allocated, say, a $10,000 share of the reduction in inside basis for the year, but has only $8,000 of outside basis, the zero-basis limitation will result in a $2,000 disparity between inside and outside basis. Although this is only one partner, allocations to the other partners cannot make up for this disparity. Under section 704(d), the $2,000 amount is not re-allocated to other partners who have positive outside basis. Instead, it is "suspended," to be available to the partner to whom it was originally allocated at such time as she acquires additional outside basis.

Thus, an allocation of losses in excess of outside basis to even a single partner creates a disparity between inside and outside basis for the partnership and the partners as a whole. If debt and the losses it finances were allocated among the partners according to two different systems, some partners would have more outside basis and fewer loss allocations, while others would have the opposite. Inside-outside basis disparities would not be the exception; they would be the general rule. By allocating debt in accordance with the losses it finances, the Treasury regulations seek to minimize this problem. In so doing, they seek to replicate the results of direct ownership, where all debt-financed losses must be taken into account annually by the owners.

So is that it for section 704(d)? Is there nothing left for it to do? No, section 704(d) still comes to work every morning. It applies, for example, when one partner is allocated losses financed by the capital provided by another partner. It can also apply whenever inside basis exceeds outside basis. Distributions can cause such disparities, as discussed in Topic 9.2. Transfers of partnership interests can do the same, as you will see in Topic 6.5.

5.6.1   Kylie is the general partner of RRK LP, a calendar-year limited partnership. Its balance sheet at year-end 2016 looks like this:

Assets			Liabilities		
	Tax	**Book**		**Tax**	**Book**
Cash	$ 25,000	$ 25,000	Recourse	$200,000	$200,000
Investments	125,000	125,000			
			Capital		
			Randy	100,000	100,000
			Rayliegh	100,000	100,000
			Kylie	(250,000)	(250,000)
Total Assets	$150,000	$150,000	**Total Liabilities and Capital**	$150,000	$150,000

The partnership maintains proper capital accounts, which govern liquidating distributions. Kylie has an unconditional deficit-restoration obligation, although Randy and Rayleigh, as limited partners, do not. The partners contributed $100,000 each to this investment partnership, which Kylie manages. In order to persuade Randy and Rayleigh to invest with her, Kylie agreed to be responsible for all investment losses incurred by the partnership, subject to a chargeback of an equal amount of gains. The partners are to share any further gains equally. Things have not gone well so far: the partnership has lost $350,000. What is Kylie's suspended loss?

a) $0

b) $50,000

c) $250,000

d) $350,000

5.6.2   In 2017, the bank threatens to call its loan and requires Kylie to contribute $25,000 to prevent that. During the year, the partnership recognizes $90,000 of investment gains. What amount of gain does Kylie take into account for 2017?

a) $0

b) $5,000

c) $40,000

d) $65,000

5.6.3   Instead, Kylie sells her interest in the partnership in early 2017 for $10,000 cash to an obviously over-eager young man who wants to get into the money-management business. The partnership's investment gain for the portion of the year preceding Kylie's sale is $20,000. What is Kylie's gain on this sale?

a) $10,000

    b) $160,000

    c) $180,000

    d) $210,000

CHAPTER 6
TRANSFERS OF PARTNERSHIP INTERESTS

6.1 THE VARYING INTERESTS RULE

A partnership in financial distress, reeling from losses and the demands of creditors, gets a life-line in the form of a substantial equity contribution from a new investor group specializing in distressed investments. The partnership has a calendar tax year, and the new investment is made on December 31. Most of the new equity goes to pay down the existing debt. The new investment sharply reduces the percentage ownership interests of the original partners and, as a special incentive for the new investors, the partnership agreement is amended to allocate to them 99% of the loss of the partnership for the year of their investment. The partnership duly reports losses to the new investor group for that year exceeding by about 40% the entire amount of their investment.

What's wrong with this picture? The IRS, the Tax Court and the Fifth Circuit Court of Appeals all thought that the 99% loss allocation to the new investors violated the "varying interests" rule. *Richardson v. Commissioner*, 76 T.C. 512 (1981), *aff'd*, 693 F.2d 1189 (5th Cir. 1982). This rule, now found in section 706(d), provides that the distributive shares of the partners for any tax year in which there is a change in any partner's interest in the partnership must be determined by the use of a method that takes into account the varying interests of the partners during such year. At its simplest, the purpose of the rule is to prohibit a partner from being allocated any share of the partnership's income or loss generated when she is not a partner. In the case of an existing partner whose interest increases, or decreases without being entirely eliminated, the rule is intended to ensure that the partner is allocated an appropriate share of the partnership's income or loss from each time period. The new investors in *Richardson* had no interest in the partnership prior to the last day of the year. The IRS argued, and the courts agreed, that their distributive share of the partnership's loss for the year should therefore be limited to 99% of 1/365 of the partnership's total loss.

The varying interests rule applies to almost any change in any partner's interest in the partnership, whether it occurs through sale or gift of an interest, by reason of the death of a partner, or on account of a contribution by or distribution to a partner. The rule applies whether the partner's interest is increased, decreased or eliminated entirely. It does not apply, however, to changes in partners' interests that occur on account of amendments to the partnership agreement or changes in interests that are provided for in the agreement, if unaccompanied by a contribution or distribution. This so-called "contemporaneous partner exception" was voiced in *Lipke v. Commissioner*, 81 T.C. 689 (1983), and is now reflected in Treas. Reg. § 1.706–4(b)(1).

The Treasury regulations permit partnerships to use either the "interim closing method" or the "proration method" to apply to varying interests rule. The former requires a partnership to close its books upon a variation in the partners' interests and is the default method, absent an agreement of the partners to use the proration method. Treas. Reg. § 1.706–4(a)(3)(iii). Such an agreement can be memorialized in the partnership agreement. It can, however, also be evidenced by a dated, written statement by an authorized person (such as the general partner) maintained with the partnership's books and records. Treas. Reg. § 1.706–4(f).

A partnership may choose between the two methods for each variation, subject to restrictions on this freedom that the IRS may impose by future revenue rulings. To keep the discussion manageable, let's assume that the partnership chooses either one method or the other. (If your tax prof wants more than this, she's being unreasonable, IMHO.)

If the chosen method is the interim closing method, each variation occurring in a taxable year divides the year into "segments." Thus, the taxable year of a partnership having two variations in the year is broken into three segments. The dates dividing these segments are not necessarily the dates on which the variations occur. Recognizing that closing the books may be costly and time-consuming, the regulations allow partnerships to adopt, by agreement of the partners, various conventions to determine when each variation is deemed to occur. For example, a partnership may adopt the monthly convention, pursuant to which all variations occurring on the 1st through the 15th of any month are deemed to take place on the last day of the preceding month (the first day of the current month in the case of a variation occurring in January), and all variations occurring on the 16th through the last day of any month are deemed to take place on such last day. The partnership must use the same convention for all variations for which it uses the interim closing method. The default convention is the calendar-day convention, which treats variations as occurring on the date they actually occur. Treas. Reg. § 1.706–4(c).

A partnership electing to use the proration method has only one segment, which includes its entire taxable year, but it may have multiple "proration periods." If, for example, the partnership experiences two variations in a single taxable year, it has three proration periods. The only allowable convention is the calendar-day convention. The partnership's income or loss for the year is allocated ratably to each day in the year and to each proration period based upon its length in days.

The interim closing method can badly misallocate certain items of a partnership that uses the cash method. These are items that accrue ratably but are paid from time to time, like interest and taxes. Section 706(d)(2) requires that such "allocable cash basis items" be prorated on a daily basis.

An important exception to the use of either the interim closing method or the proration method is the treatment of "extraordinary items." Regardless which method or convention the partnership may have chosen, it must allocate extraordinary items among the partners in proportion to their interests in the partnership *at the time of day* on which the extraordinary item occurred. Treas. Reg. § 1.706–4(e). This is a "safety net" for the IRS, which ensures that gains and losses from, for example, dispositions of assets outside of the ordinary course of business are not misallocated through the use of a less-precise method or convention.

Service partnerships are permitted to use any reasonable method to comply with the varying interests rule, reflecting the more relaxed attitude of the IRS regarding misallocations by partnerships for which capital is not a material income-producing factor. Treas. Reg. § 1.706–4(b)(2).

It is natural to think about the varying interests rule in the context of partnerships by shares—those whose partners are allocated all items of income, gain, loss and deduction in proportion to their capital accounts. But it also applies to partnerships with more complex allocations. These more complex settings present difficulties in applying the varying interests rule. How, for example, should a partnership allocate its depreciation for the year to a partner who is entitled to a special allocation of depreciation that is capped at a fixed dollar amount that was reached during the year but not during the period that she was a partner?

Furthermore, special allocations can at least partially un-do the results reached by the varying interests rule. Assume that Abner, Bette and Clarence own equal shares in Partnership ABC, which earns about the same amount of income every month. Mid-way through the year, Abner sells his interest to Dottie. A straightforward application of the proration method results in Abner and Dottie each being allocated one-sixth of the partnership's income for the year. What would be the result if the partnership agreement were amended to allocate no income to the Abner interest for the first half of the year and two-thirds of the partnership's income for the second half of the year to the Dotti interest? If respected, these special allocations would cause no income to be allocated to Abner and one-third of the partnership's income for the year to the allocated to Dottie. Bette and Clarence shouldn't care, because each gets one-third of the partnership's income for the year either way.

Even if it has substantial economic effect, this scheme of special allocations is a fairly transparent attempt to circumvent the varying interests rule and should not stand up to scrutiny. *See* Treas. Reg. § 1.704–1(b)(1)(ii) (allocations that are respected under section 704(b) may nevertheless be re-allocated under other operative provisions such as section 706(d)). Other, less egregious efforts will work. For example, either of the special allocations described above, standing alone, should be respected.

6.1.1   Abner, Bette and Clarence are equal partners in Partnership ABC, a general partnership in the business of manufacturing. The tax year of the partnership and all of its partners is the calendar year. For 2016 (which has 366 days), the partnership's operating income is $366,000. At 9:00 AM on February 29, Bette sells one-half of her interest to Clarence and at 2:00 PM on July 28, the partnership liquidates Clarence's entire interest for cash. By agreement of the partners, the partnership elects to use the proration method under section 706(d). How much of the partnership's income for 2016 is allocated to each of the partners?

a)   Abner, $147,500; Bette, $122,000; Clarence, $96,500

b)   Abner, $148,000; Bette, $122,833; Clarence, $95,167

c)   Abner, $148,000; Bette, $123,000; Clarence, $95,000

d)   Abner, $148,000; Bette, $148,000; Clarence, $70,000

6.1.2   Same facts as Question 6.1.1, except that the partnership closes the sale of a manufacturing plant at 4:00 PM on July 28, recognizing a gain of $900,000. How much of the partnership's income and gain for 2016 is allocated to each of the partners?

a)   Abner, $447,500; Bette, $272,000; Clarence, $546,500

b)   Abner, $448,000; Bette, $273,000; Clarence, $545,000

c)   Abner, $597,500; Bette, $572,000; Clarence, $96,500

d)   Abner, $598,000; Bette, $573,000; Clarence, $95,000

6.1.3   Abbey, Belinda and Cluny are equal partners in Partnership ABC, a general partnership in the business of acquiring and holding gas leases. The tax year of the partnership and all of its partners is the calendar year and all use the cash method of tax accounting. For 2016, the partnership's income is $366,000, broken down monthly as follows:

Month	Income	Month	Income
Jan	$25,000	Jul	$42,000
Feb	29,000	Aug	39,000
Mar	32,000	Sept	26,000
Apr	19,000	Oct	31,000
May	38,000	Nov	21,000
June	31,000	Dec	33,000

At 9:00 AM on February 29, Belinda sells one-half of her interest to Cluny and at 9:00 AM on July 10, the partnership liquidates Cluny's entire interest for cash. The partnership agreement contains no election regarding the partnership's section 706(d) method. In connection with her work on the partnership's tax return for 2016, Abbey puts a note in the partnership's tax file that it is using the monthly convention and dates it April 15, 2017. How

much of the partnership's income for 2016 is allocated to each of the partners?

a) Abbey, $151,000; Belinda, $129,000; Cluny, $86,000

b) Abbey, $154,000; Belinda, $134,000; Cluny, $78,000

c) Abbey, $154,000; Belinda, $154,000; Cluny, $58,000

d) Need more information; monthly convention is inapplicable

6.1.4 Same facts as Question 6.1.3, except that Partnership ABC has annual interest expense of $36,600, paid by the partnership in two semi-annual payments of $18,300 on January 5 and July 5. For simplicity, assume that this interest accrues ratably, $100 each day. How is this interest expense allocated to each of the partners?

a) Abbey, $12,200; Belinda, $9,150; Cluny, $15,250

b) Abbey, $15,100; Belinda, $12,900; Cluny, $8,600

c) Abbey, $15,116.67; Belinda, $12,916.67; Cluny, $8,566.67

d) Abbey, $15,250; Belinda, $15,250; Cluny, $6,100

6.2   TRANSFEROR: CALCULATING GAIN OR LOSS ON THE SALE OF A PARTNERSHIP INTEREST

A taxable disposition of a partnership interest produces gain or loss measured by the difference between the amount realized on the disposition and the partner's adjusted basis in her partnership interest. As to the character of this gain or loss, see Topic 6.3. As to whether a taxable disposition has occurred, see Topic 6.7.

A partner has a single, unitary basis in her interest in a partnership, even if she is both a general partner and a limited partner of the same partnership. Rev. Rul. 84–52, 1984–1 C.B. 157. If she sells her entire interest in a single transaction, the tax consequences are straightforward. Her amount realized includes the amount of money and the fair market value of any property she receives. Under section 752(d), it also includes her share of the liabilities of the partnership. Her adjusted basis includes exactly the same share of the partnership's liabilities, making this portion of the computation a wash (provided you remember to include it twice). Her basis is adjusted for all contributions and distributions she has made to or received from the partnership prior to the time of the disposition. It is also adjusted under section 705 for her share of partnership income, gains, losses and deductions for the period up to and including the date of the disposition.

The latter adjustment is accomplished through an ungainly mechanism found in section 706(c)(2)(A). The general rule of section 706(c)(1) is that a transfer of a partnership interest does not close the partnership's tax year unless it creates a partnership termination. *See* Topic 10.1. Absent termination, the partnership's income, gains, losses and deductions for the entire partnership tax year flow through to the partners who are partners at the end of the partnership's tax year, under the rules that we reviewed in Topic 4.2. This is obviously not the right answer for the partner who has sold her entire partnership interest mid-year, because she is not a partner at the end of the partnership's tax year. Section 706(c)(2)(A) modifies the general rule for this partner, providing that the partnership's tax year ends *as to her but only as to her* on the date of her sale. This causes her share of the partnership's tax items, determined in accordance with the varying interests rule, to flow through to her on the date of the sale. This flow-through, in turn, creates a section 705 adjustment to her outside basis as of that date, which she takes into account in computing her gain or loss on the sale.

The story is different, and more complicated, if the partner sells only a portion of her interest in the partnership. Watch out for two things in particular. First, the adjustment mechanism of section 706(c)(2)(A) does not apply on a disposition of less than a partner's entire interest. Section 706(c)(2)(B) says this explicitly. Therefore, the partner's outside basis is not adjusted to take into account any partnership tax items for the year of the sale. Whether this is a good thing or a bad thing depends on the situation. Generally, however, a partner selling an interest in a profitable partnership would prefer to have her share of the partnership's income for the pre-sale portion of the year included in outside basis, whereas a partner in a loss-generating partnership may have the opposite preference.

Assume, for example, that Shuyuan, a calendar-year partner in a calendar-year partnership, sells one-half of her partnership interest on June 30 for an amount realized (including liabilities) of $3,000. Her adjusted basis for this one-half interest, including liabilities but excluding any share of partnership income for the year of sale, is $1,000. Assume further that $500 of partnership income is properly allocable to the one-half interest that Shuyuan sells. Whether Shuyuan takes that share of income into account on June 30 or on December 31 will not change or accelerate her tax liability, because in either case she will include it in her taxable income for the same year. Taking it into account on June 30 will, however, reduce her gain on the sale by $500. How much this is worth to her depends on when she expects to sell the other half of her interest, because the $500 basis increase, if not available currently, will be available then. Regardless of the answer to that question, Shuyuan would likely prefer to have the basis adjustment now.

If, on the other hand, a $500 partnership loss is properly allocable to Shuyuan's one-half interest, taking it into account on June 30 will increase the amount of her gain on sale (or reduce the amount of her loss on sale). In this situation, Shuyuan is presumably happy not to have the basis adjustment at the time of her sale.

There are other variations to this fact pattern, of course, but these two are enough to demonstrate that the current rule of section 706(c)(2)(B) helps in some cases and hurts in others. This creates a strong incentive for taxpayers to argue (selectively) that the rule of section 706(c)(2)(A) applies, even to sales of partial interests. The sixth sentence of Treas. Reg. § 1.705–

1(a)(1) provides a basis for such an argument. It states that "where there has been a sale or exchange of *all or a part* of a partnership interest . . . the adjusted basis of the partner's interest should be determined as of the date of the sale or exchange" (emphasis added). This language plainly suggests that a partner's basis at the time of sale may be different than it was at the prior year-end, even in the case of a sale of a partial interest. This may support an inference that the selling partner's basis should be adjusted to take into account her pre-sale share of the partnership's income or loss, even when only a partial interest is sold.

This reading, however, conflicts with the structure of the statute—without a closing of the partnership's tax year as to the selling partner, there is no statutory mechanism for creating this basis adjustment. More likely, to the extent that this regulation is addressing sales of partial interests, it is intended to cover only contributions and distributions occurring before the sale—a reading of the regulation that has the great advantage of not making it inconsistent with the statute. A separate issue is whether the statute itself reaches appropriate conclusions. Questions 6.2.2 and 6.2.3 ask you to think about this issue.

The second complication for sales of partial interests is allocation of basis. Because a partnership interest has a single, unitary basis, the sale of only part of the interest requires that basis be apportioned equitably between the portion sold and the portion retained. Treas. Reg. § 1.61–6(a). Under Rev. Rul. 84–53, 1984–1 C.B. 159, this is achieved by allocating basis according to the relative fair market values of the portion of the interest sold and the portion retained. This is the same rule that would apply to the sale of a partial interest in land or other property.

So far, so good. Things get a little dicey when the selling partner has a share of partnership liabilities. Almost inevitably, this share will change when the partner sells a portion of her interest, sometimes declining in proportion to the interest sold and other times declining disproportionately, even to zero. The first step is to determine the selling partner's shares of partnership liabilities both before and after the sale. Any reduction in the liability share is included in amount realized. Under Rev. Rul. 84–53, it is also included in the adjusted basis of the portion of the interest sold. Thus, if you do the computations correctly, the same amount of liabilities appears in both amount realized and adjusted basis, so it is a wash—just as in the computation of gain or loss on the sale of an entire partnership interest. This is not quite the end of the story. If a partner's adjusted basis in her partnership interest is less than her share of partnership liabilities—that is, if she has negative tax capital—a portion of her negative tax capital is triggered on the sale of a partial interest, creating a larger gain or smaller loss. The portion triggered is proportional to the amount of the partnership liabilities discharged (*i.e.*, included in amount realized on the sale).

6.2.1   River Road Investors LP is a limited partnership that is a dealer in residential housing lots. Shuyuan is its general partner, holding a 50% interest, and Shelby and Shakira are limited partners, holding 25% interests each. The tax year of the partnership and all of its partners is the calendar year. As of December 31, 2015, the balance sheet of River Road is as follows:

Assets			Liabilities		
	Tax	Book		Tax	Book
Cash	$100,000	$100,000	[None]	$ 0	$ 0
Housing Lots	700,000	700,000			
			Capital		
			Shuyuan	400,000	400,000
			Shelby	200,000	200,000
			Shakira	200,000	200,000
Total Assets	**$800,000**	**$800,000**	**Total Liabilities and Capital**	**$800,000**	**$800,000**

On July 1, 2016, Shuyuan sells her entire interest in the partnership to Sherman for a cash payment of $500,000. By agreement of the partners, River Road elects to use the proration method under section 706(d). For its tax year 2016, the partnership earns income of $160,000 and has no extraordinary transactions. What is Shuyuan's share of the partnership's income for 2016 and what is her gain on the sale of her partnership interest?

a)   Income, $0; Gain, $100,000

b)   Income, $40,000; Gain, $60,000

c)   Income, $40,000; Gain, $100,000

d)   Income, $80,000; Gain, $20,000

6.2.2   *Answer this Question and the next with your best interpretation of current law. Then try putting on your "policy hat." Are you happy with these answers?* Same as Question 6.2.1, except that Shuyuan sells only one-half of her interest to Sherman for $250,000. What is Shuyuan's share of the partnership's income for 2016 and what is her gain on the sale of her partnership interest?

a)   Income, $40,000; Gain, $50,000

b)   Income, $60,000; Gain ($10,000)

c)   Income, $60,000; Gain, $30,000

d)   Income, $60,000; Gain, $50,000

6.2.3   In this variation of Question 6.2.1, River Road's tax year ends January 31, 2017, during which it earns income of $160,000. Shuyuan sells one-half of her interest for $250,000 on August 1, 2016. What is the share of the partnership's income for its tax year ending January 31, 2017 that Shuyuan must take into account in her tax year ending December 31, 2016, and what is her gain on the sale of her partnership interest?

a) Income, $0; Gain, $50,000

b) Income, $20,000; Gain, $50,000

c) Income, $20,000; Gain $30,000

d) Income, $60,000; Gain, $30,000

6.2.4 *Read Rev. Rul. 84–53 before answering this Question.* In this variation of Question 6.2.1, River Road's balance sheet as of December 31, 2015 is as follows:

Assets			Liabilities		
	Tax	**Book**		**Tax**	**Book**
Cash	$ 100,000	$ 100,000	Recourse	$ 500,000	$ 500,000
Housing Lots	1,200,000	1,200,000			
			Capital		
			Shuyuan	400,000	400,000
			Shelby	200,000	200,000
			Shakira	200,000	200,000
Total Assets	$1,300,000	$1,300,000	**Total Liabilities and Capital**	$1,300,000	$1,300,000

Neither Shelby nor Shakira has guaranteed or provided any other form of credit support for the partnership's liability. On July 1, 2016, Shuyuan sells one-half of her partnership interest to Sherman for $250,000. What is Shuyuan's gain on this sale?

a) $30,000

b) $50,000

c) $300,000

d) $550,000

6.2.5   In this variation, River Road's balance sheet as of December 31, 2015 is as follows:

Assets			Liabilities		
	Tax	Book		Tax	Book
Cash	$100,000	$100,000	Recourse	$500,000	$500,000
Housing Lots	200,000	200,000			
			Capital		
			Shuyuan	(100,000)	(100,000)
			Shelby	(50,000)	(50,000)
			Shakira	(50,000)	(50,000)
Total Assets	$300,000	$300,000	**Total Liabilities and Capital**	$300,000	$300,000

Neither Shelby nor Shakira has guaranteed or provided any other form of credit support for the partnership's liability. On July 1, 2016, Shuyuan sells one-half of her partnership interest to Sherman for $50,000. What is Shuyuan's gain on this sale?

a) $50,000

b) $100,000

c) $150,000

d) $350,000

6.3   TRANSFEROR: CHARACTERIZING GAIN UNDER SECTIONS 741 AND 751(a)

By now, you have become so used to thinking about a partnership as an entity separate from its owners that it is easy to forget that there is an alternative approach. This Topic will jog your memory.

Treating a partnership as an entity necessitates rules to spell out the tax consequences arising from the sale or other disposition of an interest in the entity, including computation of the amount of gain or loss, reviewed in Topic 6.2, and determination of the character of such gain or loss, reviewed here. The general rule of section 741 is that a partner recognizes capital gain or loss on the sale or other taxable disposition of her partnership interest. It is a bit surprising that the drafters of this statute took such a definitive position, rather than saying, for example, that the character of the gain or loss is to be determined under section 1221 by treating the partnership interest as an asset separate from the assets of the partnership. One apparent result is that there is no such thing (in the world of section 741) as a dealer in partnership interests.

The drafters of section 741 had a different and much more important issue on their minds. Their "always capital" rule created a substantial disconnect between the taxation of partners and the taxation of other co-owners of property. Suppose that Marion and Lillian offer home-decorating services on a joint basis. Their small business, which they do not treat as a partnership for tax purposes, has a few assets, including accounts receivable for consulting services rendered in the past for which they have not yet been paid. If Marion wished to sell her interest in the business to Adrian, she would be treated for tax purposes as selling her interest in each of the assets of the business. *Williams v. McGowan*, 152 F.2d 570 (2d Cir. 1945). The sale of her share of the accounts receivable would produce ordinary income. If, on the other hand, the business were a partnership, the general rule of section 741 would allow Marion to recognize only capital gain on the sale.

To avoid this sort of discontinuity, the drafters of section 741 included an exception by cross-reference to section 751. The relevant subsection, section 751(a), provides that the consideration received by the transferor of a partnership interest is treated as an amount realized from the sale or exchange of property other than a capital asset, to the extent it is attributable to "inventory items" or "unrealized receivables." Under section 751(a), Marion would recognize ordinary income on the amount that Adrian paid for her share of the receivables of the home-decoration business. As someone said eloquently in the essay in Topic 4.1, this is an aggregate result in an entity world.

"Inventory items" and "unrealized receivables" are terms of art—there are lots of exam questions lurking in these definitions. Together, they are commonly referred to "section 751 assets," "tainted assets" or "hot assets."

Inventory items are defined in section 751(d). Under section 751(d)(1), the concept includes conventional inventory as described in section 1221(a)(1). Under section 751(d)(2), it also includes basically any other asset that would produce ordinary income if sold by the partnership. Ironically, this means that all unrealized receivables are also "inventory items," but this overlap in the definitions does not require them to be included more than once in the ordinary-income computation. Finally, under section 751(d)(3), "inventory items" include any items of partnership property that would be inventory or otherwise produce ordinary income if owned directly and sold by the partner. The apparent purpose of this provision is to prevent taxpayers who are dealers in property from avoiding ordinary income by transferring that property to partnerships and dealing in partnership interests at capital-gains tax rates. The "always capital" rule of section 741 may have made this definition more necessary than it would have been if dealers in partnership interests were taxed at ordinary-income rates.

As long as they meet any of the foregoing definitions, items of property are "inventory items" regardless of the relationship between their values and adjusted bases. Appreciation is not required—an item of property can be depreciated (in the sense that it is worth less than its adjusted basis) and still be an "inventory item." A different rule applies to the application of section 751(b), discussed in Topic 9.6.

Unrealized receivables, on the other hand, must be "unrealized," which means that at least some portion of the right to payment represented by the receivable must not have been previously includible in the partnership's income under its method of accounting. Because a partnership using the cash method does not include an item in income until payment is received, it will typically have unrealized receivables. In order to qualify as an unrealized receivable, the right to payment must be for services or for property that produces ordinary income (*e.g.,* inventory). Thus, the right to receive an installment payment on the sale of a capital asset is not an unrealized receivable.

The "flush language" of section 751(c) identifies several other types of unrealized receivables, the most important of which is recapture. Treas. Reg. §§ 1.751–1(c)(4), –1(c)(5) treat recapture as a separate unrealized receivable with a basis of zero. Although these rules cover recapture under both section 1245 and section 1250, it is important to note that section 1250 recapture is unusual today, because it applies only to real-estate depreciation taken faster than straight-line. *See* section 1250(b)(1). Since 1986, the Modified Accelerated Cost Recovery System (MACRS) has required that real estate be depreciated on a straight-line basis. *See* section 168(b)(3). Straight-line depreciation on real estate is not subject to recapture as ordinary income, but instead is taxed as "section 1250 capital gain" at a higher rate than most other capital gains. *See* section 1(h)(6). Section 1250 capital gain is not an unrealized receivable and is therefore not subject to section 751(a). A parallel system applies, set forth in Treas. Reg. § 1.1(h)–1(b)(3).

The hypothetical sale is the mechanism that section 751(a) uses to determine the amount of ordinary income or loss realized by a transferor of an interest in a partnership holding section 751 assets. The transferor realizes ordinary income or loss equal to that which the partnership would have allocated to her if it had sold all of its section 751 assets, together with all of its other assets, in a fully taxable transaction for fair market value immediately prior to the transfer. The remainder of the transferor's gain or loss is capital under section 741. Treas. Reg. § 1.751–1(a)(2). The important thing to remember is that this is an entirely unconstrained computation. In the hypothetical sale, the partnership may realize gain on some section 751 assets and loss on others, which are all netted together to reach the final ordinary income or loss determination. The transferor partner may be required to take ordinary loss into account in a sale on which she realizes overall gain, in which case the ordinary loss increases the amount of the capital gain, so that the two net to the appropriate overall amount. Alternatively, there may be ordinary income with an overall loss, so that the ordinary income increases the amount of the capital loss.

6.3.1   The assets of Runners World LLC, a limited liability company taxed as a partnership that uses an accrual method to compute taxable income, are as follows:

	Adjusted Basis	Accumulated Depreciation	Fair Market Value
Cash	$ 20,000		$ 20,000
Accounts receivable	65,000		65,000
Equipment inventory	95,000		80,000
Clothing inventory	115,000		150,000
Equipment for on-site gym	32,000	$28,000	40,000
Building and improvements	312,000	32,000	400,000
Common stock investment	48,000		59,000
Land	45,000		60,000

The partnership has depreciated its building and improvements on a straight-line basis, so no recapture under section 1250 would occur on their sale; gain equal to the depreciation taken would, however, be classified as "section capital 1250 gain." Abe Abner, a local art dealer, was an early investor in the partnership's business but has since soured on the concept. If Abe sells his partnership interest, what is the total fair market value of the partnership's "unrealized receivables" that must be taken into account in determining the character of his gain or loss?

a) $0

b) $8,000

c) $28,000

d) $40,000

6.3.2   The assets of Globe Runners LLC, a limited liability company taxed as a partnership, are as follows:

	Adjusted Basis	Accumulated Depreciation	Fair Market Value
Cash	$ 20,000		$ 20,000
Accounts receivable	0		65,000
Equipment inventory	95,000		80,000
Clothing inventory	115,000		150,000
Equipment for on-site gym	32,000	$28,000	40,000
Building and improvements	312,000	32,000	400,000
Common stock investment	48,000		59,000
Land	45,000		60,000

The partnership generally uses an accrual method, but accounts for its personal-training business on the cash method. It has employed straight-line depreciation of its building and improvements. Sally Stiles, a Wall Street dealer in stocks and bonds, is selling her membership interest in Globe Runners. What is the total fair market value of the partnership's "inventory items" that must be taken into account in determining the character of Sally's gain or loss on this sale?

a) $150,000

b) $230,000

c) $289,000

d) $362,000

6.3.3 *Read Treas. Reg. § 1.1(h)–1(b)(3) prior to answering this Question.* Same facts as Question 6.3.1. Abe sells his 20% interest for $160,000 cash plus assumption of his $40,000 share of the partnership's liabilities. The partnership closes its taxable year as to Abe under section 706(c)(2)(A) and passes through his share of the partnership's income for the year of sale, computed in accordance with the varying interests rule of section 706(d). Taking this income into account under section 705(a)(1)(A), Abe's adjusted basis in his partnership interest (including his share of partnership liabilities) is $146,400. How much capital gain or loss and how much ordinary income or loss does Abe realize on this sale?

a) Ordinary income, $5,600; section 1250 capital gain, $6,400; capital gain $16,400

b) Ordinary income, $4,000; section 1250 capital gain, $6,400; capital gain, $43,200

c) Ordinary income, $5,600; section 1250 capital gain, $6,400; capital gain, $41,600

d) Ordinary income, $12,000; section 1250 capital gain, $0; capital gain, $41,600

6.3.4 Same facts as Question 6.3.3, except that Abe is desperate to get out and winds up selling his 20% interest for only $100,000 cash plus assumption of his $40,000 share of the partnership's liabilities. How much capital gain or loss and how much ordinary income or loss does Abe realize on this sale?

a) Ordinary loss, $3,000; section 1250 capital gain, $6,400; capital loss $9,800

b) Ordinary income, $4,000; section 1250 capital gain, $6,400; capital loss, $16,800

c) Ordinary income, $5,600; section 1250 capital gain, $6,400; capital loss, $18,400

d) Ordinary income, $5,600; section 1250 capital gain, $6,400; capital loss, $5,600

6.4   TRANSFEREE: DETERMINING THE BASIS OF AN ACQUIRED INTEREST

If you blink, you'll miss this Topic. Though slim, it stands apart because it deals solely with the outside basis of the transferee of an interest in a partnership—which stands apart from either the basis of the transferor in the transferred interest or the basis of the partnership in its assets.

By now, you have become accustomed to the "inter-connectedness" of basis in the system of Subchapter K. Changes to the adjusted bases of a partnership's assets (for example, through the generation of income) are reflected in changes in the outside bases of the partners. A partner's adjusted basis in property she contributes to a partnership generally becomes the partnership's basis in such property. Later, in Chapter 9 you will see this same inter-connectedness in the basis rules pertaining to property distributions. These inter-connected adjustments are what keep inside and outside basis in sync and are necessary to achieving the goal of taxing partnership income once and only once.

But all that is out the window when Stella makes a cash purchase of Rick's interest in the RTS Partnership. Stella's basis in the acquired interest is determined under exactly the same rules that would apply to her acquisition of any other property. *See* section 742. Because no nonrecognition rule applies to this transaction, Stella takes a cost basis under section 1012(a). (The exception for Subchapter K written into section 1012(a) leaves room for contributions and distributions, but has no application here.) Her cost includes the partnership liabilities attributable to the acquired interest. *See* section 752(d). Except for extraordinary coincidence, Stella's basis will not equal Rick's basis for the very same interest, nor will it equal that interest's share of the partnership's inside basis. The meticulously constructed partnership basis system has just fallen apart in front of your eyes, defeated by the simplest transaction imaginable.

6.5   EFFECT OF THE TRANSFER OF A PARTNERSHIP INTEREST ON INSIDE BASIS: SECTION 743

The drafters of the 1954 Internal Revenue Code understood the problem that transfers of partnership interests presented for their basis system. The first step they took, however, made things worse. Section 743(a), as enacted in 1954, established a general rule that a partnership's adjusted basis in its assets is unchanged by a transfer of interests. In other words, if the effect of a transfer of an interest is to cause inside and outside basis to be unequal, they will stay that way.

The effect is easy to see through a simple example, Stella's purchase of Rick's interest in the RTS Partnership from Topic 6.4. If Stella purchases the interest at full fair market value, she will recognize no gain or loss if she sells it at the same price to someone else, because her purchase has given her a fair-market-value basis in the interest. Similarly, if the RTS Partnership were not treated as an entity, but simply as a collection of assets, Stella's purchase would be treated as a purchase of Rick's share of each of these assets. She would have a fair-market-value basis in each asset and would recognize no gain or loss if the RTS Partnership later sold any (or all) of the assets at the same value.

But the RTS Partnership is an entity. When Stella buys Rick's interest, she obtains a fair-market-value basis in the purchased interest, but not in her share of the partnership's assets. Accordingly, if the partnership then sells any of its assets, it will allocate gain or loss to Stella, without regard to the fact that she has a fair-market-value basis in her interest. In this way, the inequality of inside and outside basis will cause Stella to recognize gain or loss on asset sales which she would not recognize if she owned the assets directly.

To correct this problem, the 1954 drafters offered section 743(b), pursuant to which a partnership that makes an election under section 754 *must* adjust the basis of its assets to take into account the difference between a transferee partner's outside basis and that partner's share of the partnership's inside basis. This is not an adjustment to the common basis of the partnership's assets, but rather an adjustment that is personal to the transferee partner. For this reason, it is often referred to as a "special basis adjustment." Because it is personal to the transferee, the special basis adjustment does not travel with the partnership interest. If there is another transfer of the same interest, a new special basis adjustment must be determined for the new transferee.

Accordingly, if the RTS Partnership has made a section 754 election, it will compute a special basis adjustment for Stella and allocate it among all of the partnership's assets. For each partnership asset, the sum of Stella's share of the partnership's common basis plus her special basis adjustment will equal the portion of her outside basis allocable to that asset. For Stella, inside basis will once again equal outside basis. Problem solved.

If this works so well, why is it not the general rule of section 743? Why does it take an election to reach the "right" result (the one that avoids under- or over-taxation relative to direct ownership of assets)? In 1954, the drafters evidently thought that the computations required to ascertain special basis adjustments and to allocate them among the assets of the partnership were too burdensome to impose on all partnerships. Their solution was to let partnerships decide for themselves—recognizing that the default rule of section 743(a) sacrifices accuracy for simplicity in any case that an election is not made. The computational burden has diminished significantly in the intervening 60-some years. This, in turn, has led many policy thinkers to recommend amending section 743 to require special basis adjustments in every case.

There is another impulse for reform. Partnerships do approach the question of whether to make a section 754 election as an academic exercise. For them, the issue is whether making such an election will save enough tax dollars to make the computational hassle worthwhile. Assume, for instance, that the RTS Partnership has many assets with built-in gains and few with built-in losses. Stella will surely favor making a section 754 election, because her special basis adjustment under section 743(b) will be positive—it will reduce or eliminate the amount of gain that she will be allocated on subsequent asset dispositions. Stella will be motivated to persuade her partners to make the election and she may prevail, perhaps by offering to fund the computations. If, on the other hand, the RTS Partnership has many assets with built-in losses and few with built-in gains, Stella will have no such motivation. In that case, her special basis adjustment would be negative—it would reduce or eliminate the amount of loss that she would otherwise be allocated on subsequent asset dispositions. The RTS Partnership is unlikely to make a section 754 election under these circumstances.

This sort of heads-I-win-tails-you-lose behavior is curtailed by the requirement that a section 754 election, once made, cannot be revoked without IRS approval. Treas. Reg. § 1.754–1(c)(1) ("no application for revocation of an election shall be approved when the purpose of the revocation is primarily to avoid stepping down the basis of partnership assets upon a transfer"). Nevertheless, there are situations where the existence or nonexistence of a section 754 election can make all the difference. This is particularly so where a transaction is planned to take advantage of electivity. For example, in a partnership constructed with built-in loss assets, the ability of one partner to sell her interest without diminishing the partnership's built-in loss in its assets was the foundation for many tax shelters in the 1990s and early 2000s. Congress reacted to this technique in 2004 by amending section 743 to *require* special basis adjustments to be made in any case in which a partnership has a "substantial built-in loss" (more than $250,000) immediately after the transfer of an interest.

Taking this amendment into account, it is not inaccurate to say that the law today requires special basis adjustments, except in cases where they may be beneficial to taxpayers. This is not an illogical position—partnerships are still free to capture the tax benefit of special basis adjustments by making a section 754 election. And the $250,000 threshold for substantial built-in losses spares small partnerships. Nevertheless, the asymmetry of current law strengthens the calls for change. P. Postlewaite, *Optional Basis Adjustments under Subchapter K: Trap for the Unwary, Tax Planning Tool, or Both? Should They Be Mandatory?* FLORIDA TAX REV. 105 (2014).

Computing the special basis adjustment

So what exactly are these computations that are so off-putting? There are two steps, calculating the special basis adjustment and allocating it among the partnership's assets. Both start with a mechanism that we are becoming ever more familiar with, the hypothetical sale for fair market value of all of the partnership's assets in a fully taxable transaction. In this case, the hypothetical sale takes place immediately after the interest transfer has occurred.

Under the statute, the special basis adjustment is measured by the difference between the transferee's outside basis in her partnership interest (determined as discussed in Topic 6.4) and the transferee's share of the partnership's inside basis in its assets. The statute uses the term "proportionate share." *See* sections 743(b)(1), (b)(2). This term seems appropriate in cases where all partners have fixed percentage interests in everything—capital, profits, losses, liabilities and inside basis—the sort of partnership that we have earlier described as a partnership by shares or a partnership with "straight-up" allocations. In this happy situation, it is easy to determine the transferee's share of inside basis: simply multiply the partnership's inside basis by the partner's percentage interest in the partnership.

Alas, partnerships are often more complex than that, with contributed properties, special allocations, carried interests and the like, so that determining the transferee's share of inside basis requires a more nuanced approach. Here is where the hypothetical sale comes in. Treas. Reg. § 1.743–1(d)(1) defines a transferee's share of inside basis as the sum of (1) her share of the partnership's liabilities and (2) her share of the partnership's "previously taxed capital." This should make some intuitive sense to you, because all of a partnership's inside basis comes either from capital or from liabilities, so you just have to figure out the transferee's share of each. The former is easy—or at least it is no different than the determination you have already learned to make under section 752.

To determine the latter, Treas. Reg. § 1.743–1(d) starts with the liquidating distribution that the transferee would receive if the partnership sold all of its assets in the hypothetical sale, allocated the resulting gains and losses, paid off the creditors and distributed the balance to the partners in accordance with the partnership agreement. For a partnership that makes liquidating distributions in accordance with capital accounts, this liquidating distribution is the same amount as the transferee's book capital account following revaluation. It measures the transferee's capital interest in the partnership, but not her "previously taxed" capital. To derive the latter amount, the regulation subtracts from the transferee's revalued book capital account the gain, if any, that she would be allocated in the hypothetical sale and adds the loss, if any, that she would be allocated in the hypothetical sale. It subtracts the gain, because gain measures the excess of the transferee's share of the partnership's capital over the transferee's share of the partnership's inside basis. It adds the loss, because loss measures the excess of the transferee's share of the partnership's inside basis over her share of the partnership's capital.

Sound complicated? Here's another way to approach it. The Treasury regulations could have saved us all some aggravation by providing simply that a transferee's share of the partnership's inside basis is the sum of (1) her share of the partnership's liabilities plus (2) her tax capital. You can read a partner's tax capital off any properly maintained balance sheet. Why not take the easy way out?

There are at least two reasons. First, despite its ubiquity, "tax capital" is not a term that is defined in the Internal Revenue Code or regulations. So the IRS was stuck with the need to create a definition in any event. The definition it chose, however, is not exactly how one would define tax capital. Tax capital is a balance-sheet concept and it is therefore historical. There are situations, which we have yet to study, in which changes in the values of a partnership's assets can shift among the partners the responsibility for paying tax on the gains or losses realized by the partnership. This is best illustrated by an example. Say that Arthur, Bertrand and Chauncey form a partnership. Arthur contributes property worth $100 with an adjusted basis of $40. Bertrand and Chauncey contribute $100 in cash each. The partnership's simple balance sheet is as follows:

FIGURE 6.5

Assets			Liabilities		
	Tax	**Book**		**Tax**	**Book**
Cash	$200	$200	[None]	$ 0	$ 0
Property	40	100			
			Capital		
			Arthur	40	100
			Bertrand	100	100
			Chauncey	100	100
Total Assets	$240	$300	**Total Liabilities and Capital**	$240	$300

Arthur's tax capital is $40; the tax capital of the other two partners is $100.

A year or so later, after the value of the contributed property has fallen to $91, the partnership sells all of its assets and liquidates. The book loss of $9 is allocated equally among the partners, $3 each, reducing their book capital accounts to $97 each. Following the sale, the partnership has cash of $291, exactly the right amount to distribute to each partner the positive balance in his capital account. Under the "traditional method" of section 704(c), which we will review in Topic 8.2, Arthur is allocated all $51 of the gain realized by the partnership on the sale.

If, just before the sale, Arthur sold his interest in the partnership to Danforth for $97 and the partnership made a section 754 election, what should Danforth's special basis adjustment be? If we use Danforth's tax capital (which would be the same as Arthur's), the answer is Danforth's outside basis ($97) less his tax capital ($40) equals $57. Assume that this special basis adjustment is allocated entirely to the contributed property. When it is then sold by the partnership for its fair market value of $91, Danforth will recognize a loss of $6 ($91 proceeds less $40 common basis less

$57 special basis adjustment). We have over-shot: the special basis adjustment is too big, producing a loss for Danforth on the sale.

What if we use instead Danforth's previously taxed capital, as defined in the Treasury regulation? This can be determined as Danforth's revalued book capital account ($97) less the gain that would be allocated to him in the hypothetical sale ($51) equals $46. The special basis adjustment is then Danforth's outside basis ($97) less his previously taxed capital ($46) equals $51. If this special basis adjustment is allocated entirely to the contributed property and the property is then sold, Danforth will realize no gain or loss ($91 proceeds less $40 common basis less $51 special basis adjustment). Bingo.

Thus, while tax capital and previously taxed capital are close kin, they are not exactly the same thing. Regrettably, for those of us that like to keep things simple, previously taxed capital is the correct measure for determining special basis adjustments. At this point, if you are like me and everyone I have ever met, you want to know when you can cheat. Are there circumstances in which tax capital (which is easy to find) and previously taxed capital (which takes some work) are reliably the same?

Sure. In a partnership that liquidates in accordance with capital-account balances, the two will be the same if the so-called "ceiling rule" of section 704(c) does not apply. We will review this rule in Topic 8.2. For now, suffice it to say that this will be the case if (1) the partnership has no section 704(c) property, (2) the values of the partnership's section 704(c) property have not moved in such a way as to cause the ceiling rule to apply or (3) the partnership has elected the so-called "remedial method" under section 704(c).

Allocating the special basis adjustment

Once we have determined an accurate special basis adjustment, it must be allocated among the assets of the partnership. Why is that? If the transferee had acquired an undivided interest in each of the assets of the partnership, she would have a cost basis in each of those assets. The process of allocating the special basis adjustment is meant generally to replicate that result.

Treas. Reg. § 1.755–1(b) allocates the special basis adjustment among the partnership's assets by using exactly the same hypothetical sale that is used to determine the amount of the special basis adjustment. The amount of the special basis adjustment allocated to each asset is generally the amount of the gain or loss that would be allocated to the transferee in the hypothetical sale of that asset. A gain yields a positive special basis adjustment; a loss yields a negative special basis adjustment. With respect to each asset, the sum of the transferor's share of the partnership's common basis plus the special basis adjustment (which is a subtraction when the special basis adjustment is negative) equals the transferor's share of the fair market value of the asset. When the partnership sells any (or all) of its assets with no further change in value, the transferor will be allocated no gain or loss.

Okay, that is actually an oversimplification. The foregoing statement is true if the transferee acquires the partnership interest for a price equal to the sum of the fair market values of the assets (less liabilities) attributable to that interest—*e.g.*, an acquisition price of $250 for a 25% interest in a partnership with net assets valued at $1,000. In that case, the sum of the allocations of the special basis adjustment under Treas. Reg. § 1.755–1(b) will exactly equal the total special basis adjustment determined under Treas. Reg. § 1.743–1(d). While it is not implausible that the acquisition price of an interest will reflect only the value of the net assets on the partnership's books ($250), it is just as likely for the acquisition to take place at $200, reflecting a minority discount, or $300, reflecting the value of some asset that is not on the partnership's books, like goodwill other than purchased goodwill.

In the former case (minority discount), the special basis adjustment determined under Treas. Reg. § 1.743–1(d) is smaller than the sum of the allocations determined under Treas. Reg. § 1.755–1(b). Treas. Reg. § 1.755–1(b) scales back the allocations to match the amount of the special basis adjustment. It does not do so proportionately. Instead, allocations of the special basis adjustment go first to ordinary income property, defined in Treas. Reg. § 1.755–1(a)(1) to mean property other than capital assets and section 1231 assets. Whatever is left goes to capital gain property (defined to mean capital assets and section 1231 assets), in proportion to the fair market values of such assets. Treas. Reg. §§ 1.755–1(b)(2)(i), –1(b)(3)(ii).

Thus, in the case of a minority discount, the transferee may indeed recognize gain on the partnership's later sale of assets, even without an intervening increase in asset value. This is not inconsistent with the goal of section 743(b). Due to the discount, the transferee has paid less for her partnership interest than the sum of the net asset values attributable to the transferred interest. On subsequent asset dispositions by the partnership, it is not unfair for her to recognize the gain arising from this discount.

In the premium case, the special basis adjustment determined under Treas. Reg. § 1.743–1(d) is larger than the sum of the allocations determined under Treas. Reg. § 1.755–1(b). Treas. Reg. §§ 1.755–1(a)(4), –1(a)(5)(i) provide that the excess is "residual section 197 intangibles value" which is to be allocated to section 197 intangibles, often goodwill and going-concern value. The allocated amount may be amortized under section 197.

Like the computations under section 751(a) that we reviewed in Topic 6.3, allocations of special basis adjustments under section 755 are unconstrained. It is entirely possible, and indeed likely, that an overall positive special basis adjustment will beget both positive and negative adjustments for specific assets. The same can be said for an overall negative adjustment. Even where the overall special basis adjustment turns out to be zero, positive and negative adjustments (netting to zero) must be made with respect to specific assets. A positive special basis adjustment allocated to depreciable or amortizable property generally is depreciated or amortized as if it were newly acquired property. Treas. Reg. § 1.743–1(j)(4)(i). A negative special basis adjustment allocated to depreciable or amortizable property is recovered over the remaining useful life of the property. Treas. Reg. § 1.743–1(j)(4)(ii).

6.5.1   Regina Cleaners LP is a successful dry-cleaning business with several retail locations, all in rented space, and a plant, which it owns. Riley is the general partner with a 50% interest and Skyler and Taylor are limited partners, each with a 25% interest. The partnership was formed with cash contributions several years ago and currently has the following balance sheet:

Assets				Liabilities		
	Tax	**Book**	**FMV**		**Tax**	**Book**
Cash	$ 10,000	$ 10,000	$ 10,000	Recourse	$200,000	$200,000
Receivables	0	0	26,000			
Inventory	20,000	20,000	16,000			
Dry Cleaning Equipment (accumulated depreciation $17,000)	40,000	40,000	38,000			
Building (accumulated depreciation $33,000)	230,000	230,000	342,000			
				Capital		
				Riley	50,000	50,000
				Skyler	25,000	25,000
				Taylor	25,000	25,000
Total Assets	$300,000	$300,000	$432,000	**Total Liabilities and Capital**	$300,000	$300,000

A qualifying taxpayer with annual gross receipts less than $1 million, the partnership uses the cash method. It takes straight-line depreciation on its building, has no section 704(c) property and has made an election under section 754. Riley sells her entire general partnership interest to Winona for a single cash payment of $116,000. What is the amount of Winona's special basis adjustment under section 743(b)?

a) $266,000

b) $166,000

c) $116,000

d) $66,000

6.5.2 Same facts as Question 6.5.1. Allocate Winona's special basis adjustment among the assets of the partnership.

	(a)	(b)	(c)	(d)
Receivables	$13,000	$13,000	$26,000	$13,000
Inventory	(2,000)	0	(4,000)	(2,000)
§ 1245 recapture	0	0	17,000	0
Equipment	(1,000)	0	(2,000)	(1,000)
§ 1250 recapture	0	0	0	16,500
Building	56,000	56,000	112,000	39,500

6.5.3 Same facts as Question 6.5.1, except that Winona's cash payment is only $80,000. Determine Winona's special basis adjustment and allocate it among the assets of the partnership.

	(a)	(b)	(c)	(d)
Receivables	$ 5,910	$13,000	$13,000	$13,000
Inventory	(910)	(2,000)	(2,000)	(2,000)
§ 1245 recapture	0	0	0	0
Equipment	(450)	(4,600)	(350)	(1,000)
§ 1250 recapture	0	0	0	0
Building	25,450	23,600	19,350	20,000
Total Special Basis Adjustment	$30,000	$30,000	$30,000	$30,000

6.5.4   Same facts as Question 6.5.1, except that Riley does not sell any portion of her interest to Winona. Instead, Winona agrees with the partnership that she will provide management services and in exchange she receives a 20% capital interest as a limited partner in the partnership. Regina Cleaners revalues its book assets immediately before Winona is admitted as a new partner, resulting in the following balance sheet (expanded to show asset values):

Assets				Liabilities		
	Tax	**Book**	**FMV**		**Tax**	**Book**
Cash	$ 10,000	$ 10,000	$ 10,000	Recourse	$200,000	$200,000
Receivables	0	26,000	26,000			
Inventory	20,000	16,000	16,000			
Dry Cleaning Equipment (accumulated depreciation $17,000)	40,000	38,000	38,000			
Building (accumulated depreciation $33,000)	230,000	342,000	342,000			
				Capital		
				Riley	50,000	116,000
				Skyler	25,000	58,000
				Taylor	25,000	58,000
Total Assets	$300,000	$432,000	$432,000	**Total Liabilities and Capital**	$300,000	$432,000

Upon admittance as a partner, Winona recognizes ordinary compensation income of $46,400 (the agreed value of her 20% interest). Assuming that this compensation is fully deductible by the partnership, its balance sheet and asset values now look like this:

Assets				Liabilities		
	Tax	**Book**	**FMV**		**Tax**	**Book**
Cash	$ 10,000	$ 10,000	$ 10,000	Recourse	$200,000	$200,000
Receivables	0	26,000	26,000			
Inventory	20,000	16,000	16,000			
Dry Cleaning Equipment (accumulated depreciation $17,000)	40,000	38,000	38,000			
Building (accumulated depreciation $33,000)	230,000	342,000	342,000			
				Capital		
				Riley	26,800	92,800
				Skyler	13,400	46,400
				Taylor	13,400	46,400
				Winona	46,400	46,400
Total Assets	$300,000	$432,000	$432,000	**Total Liabilities and Capital**	$300,000	$432,000

The partnership makes an election under section 754. What is the amount of Winona's special basis adjustment?

a) $0

b) $26,400

c) $46,400

d) No special basis adjustment is available in this case.

6.6   INSIDE BASIS: SECTION 704(c)(1)(C)

You have already met section 704(c)(1)(C) in passing in Topics 2.2 and 2.3, where we considered briefly its effect on setting up the opening balance sheets for a partnership that receives a contribution of built-in loss property. Now it's time to get better acquainted.

True or false? Section 704(c)(1)(C) requires a partnership that receives a contribution of an asset with a built-in loss to take an inside basis equal to the fair market value of that asset. Thus, the rule that you learned on the second day of partnership tax class is wrong. The inside basis of every contributed asset is not its adjusted basis in the hands of the contributor, but instead the lower of such adjusted basis or fair market value.

True or false? Where it applies, section 704(c)(1)(C) breaks the rule that a partner's outside basis is equal to the sum of her tax capital and her share of the partnership's liabilities.

True or false? Where it applies, section 704(c)(1)(C) creates an inequality of inside and outside basis. It is thus inconsistent with the fundamental tenant of partnership taxation that inside and outside basis should always be equal.

Like most sensational statements, these are all untrue, but each contains a kernel of truth. They just misunderstand the truth on which they are based. As interpreted by Treasury regulations proposed in 2014, section 704(c)(1)(C)(ii) does indeed establish the fair market value of a contributed built-in loss asset as the partnership's initial common basis. But the excess of the contributing partner's basis over that amount is not lost, as the foregoing statements would have you believe. Instead, as required by section 704(c)(1)(C)(i), it is preserved for the sole and exclusive use of the contributing partner. The proposed regulations accomplish this through the "section 704(c)(1)(C) basis adjustment." Prop. Treas. Reg. § 1.704–3(f). (As you will see, it could just as easily be called the "section 704(c)(1)(C) special basis adjustment," but I will defer to the regulatory term here.)

The section 704(c)(1)(C) basis adjustment is functionally identical to the section 743(b) special basis adjustment that you studied in Topic 6.5. It is personal to the contributing partner and dies when she transfers her partnership interest. In the world of section 743(b), it would be referred to as a "positive" adjustment: it augments the basis of the contributed asset, but only for the benefit of the contributing partner. If the partnership sells the contributed asset, it computes its gain or loss by reference to its common basis in the asset. The contributing partner's share of that gain is then decreased, or loss is increased, by the amount of her section 704(c)(1)(C) basis adjustment. If the contributed asset is depreciable or amortizable, so is the section 704(c)(1)(C) basis adjustment, using the same method and life. Prop. Treas. Reg. § 1.704–3(f)(3)(ii)(D).

According to the legislative history of section 704(c)(1)(C), the Congress that enacted it was concerned with "tax-shelter transactions" that took advantage of then-existing rules to transfer losses among partners inappropriately. STAFF OF THE JOINT COMMITTEE ON TAXATION, 109TH CONG., 1ST SESS., GENERAL EXPLANATION OF TAX LEGISLATION ENACTED IN THE 108TH CONGRESS 386 (Comm. Print 2005). In a typical case, a built-in loss asset would be contributed to a partnership that did not make a section 754 election. The contributing partner could sell her partnership interest and recognize exactly the same loss she would have recognized on the sale of asset. The partnership would then own a built-in loss asset that it could sell. The resulting loss would be allocated to the purchaser of the partnership interest, generally an executive or investor who had realized a capital gain on another asset and was looking for capital losses to offset it. To preserve her tax position, she ordinarily did not liquidate her partnership interest.

Alternatively, the partnership could contribute the built-in loss asset to another partnership and then sell its interest in that new partnership. This would produce a tax loss for the selling partnership and also allow the transaction to be replicated by the new partnership. In that way, a single built-in loss asset could produce many times the amount of its loss in tax benefits. Often, these partnership interests were preferred interests, to insulate them from risk of economic loss, and were marketed with droll accuracy as "viral preferreds."

As you learned in Topic 1.1, the IRS could attack these schemes as not being partnerships at all, for failure to meet the *Culbertson* test. Or it could challenge the status of the tax-loss-seeking investor as a partner. But the success of such challenges is not assured and Congress decided also to change the underlying rules on which such tax shelters were based. Actually, Congress made two changes to the underlying rules, both in the American Jobs Creation Act of 2004. First, as discussed in Topic 6.5, it made section 743(b) special basis adjustments mandatory whenever a partnership's built-in loss exceeds $250,000. Second, it enacted section 704(c)(1)(C).

Did it have to do both? Consider Viral Partnership LP. It has only two assets, cash contributed by its 1% general and limited partners (A and B, respectively) and a built-in loss asset contributed by its special limited partner (C). Prior to the enactment of section 704(c)(1)(C), its balance sheet, with asset values added, would have been as follows:

FIGURE 6.6.1

Assets				Liabilities		
	Tax	**Book**	**FMV**		**Tax**	**Book**
Cash	$ 2,000	$ 2,000	$ 2,000	[None]	$ 0	$ 0
Loss Asset	498,000	98,000	98,000			
				Capital		
				A	1,000	1,000
				B	1,000	1,000
				C	498,000	98,000
Total Assets	$500,000	$100,000	$100,000	**Total Liabilities and Capital**	$500,000	$100,000

Pursuant to plan, C sells her partnership interest to D, an investor looking for tax losses. The sale price is $98,000. Assume that a special basis adjustment is mandatory under the 2004 amendment to section 743, but that section 704(c)(1)(C) has not been enacted. D has an outside basis of $98,000. Her share of inside basis (previously taxed capital) is $498,000, which is the amount that she would receive on liquidation at fair market value ($98,000) plus the loss that would be allocated to her under section 704(c) in the hypothetical sale ($400,000). D's special basis adjustment is therefore $98,000 less $498,000, or a negative $400,000. It is allocated entirely to the built-in loss asset.

When the partnership sells this asset, the "step in the shoes" rule of Treas. Reg. § 1.704–3(a)(7) requires that the built-in loss must be allocated to D as it would have been allocated to C. Assume the partnership sells this asset immediately for $98,000. It recognizes a loss of $400,000, all of which it allocates to D. D's special basis adjustment completely offsets this allocation. D's net loss allocation is zero.

Now let's run through the same scenario assuming that the amendment to section 743 was not enacted, but section 704(c)(1)(C) was. Viral's opening balance sheet and asset values would now be as follows:

FIGURE 6.6.2

Assets				Liabilities		
	Tax	**Book**	**FMV**		**Tax**	**Book**
Cash	$ 2,000	$ 2,000	$ 2,000	[None]	$ 0	$ 0
Loss Asset	98,000	98,000	98,000			
				Capital		
				A	1,000	1,000
				B	1,000	1,000
				C	98,000	98,000
Total Assets	$100,000	$100,000	$100,000	**Total Liabilities and Capital**	$100,000	$100,000

The only difference—but it's quite a difference—is that the partnership's tax basis for the loss asset is now its fair market value of $98,000. C's tax capital changes accordingly. (Off to the side, out of view, C has a section 704(c)(1)(C) basis adjustment of $400,000. If the partnership were to sell the loss asset, C would recognize a $400,000 loss, courtesy of this basis adjustment.) When C sells her partnership interest to D, C still recognizes a $400,000 loss—section 704(c)(1)(C) does not modify or affect C's outside basis in any way. D still acquires the partnership interest with an outside basis of $98,000. When, however, the partnership sells the loss asset, it recognizes no loss. D's net loss allocation is zero.

Thus in this case, the duplication of loss that troubled Congress can be eliminated by either section 704(c)(1)(C) or a mandatory special basis adjustment with respect to the built-in loss property under section 743(b). It does not take both.

If Viral Partnership were more complex, with more assets and more partners, the computations would of course be more complex as well, but this simple example is representative. It does not, however, take *de minimis* rules into account. Both section 743 and section 704(c)(1)(C) have them. The former's, as you know, is $250,000 of built-in loss in the partnership's assets in the aggregate. The latter's is provided by the "small disparities" rule of Treas. Reg. § 1.704–3(e)(1) and it is considerably smaller. Thus, section 704(c)(1)(C) applies to more and smaller transactions than does the mandatory basis adjustment rule of section 743. It is hard to believe that Congress enacted section 704(c)(1)(C) only to prevent loss duplication by partnerships without significant built-in losses, but that is what it accomplished.

6.6.1 Alessa, Briana and Clarissa form a natural-gas investment partnership. Alessa and Briana contribute landowners' interests in various gas leases and Clarissa contributes publicly traded stock that is intended to be sold to finance the acquisition of additional gas leases. Each of these contributions is valued at $300,000. Because they were acquired at different times in the past, the gas leases have widely varying tax bases. Alessa's leases have an aggregate basis of $180,000; Briana's, $420,000. Clarissa's tax basis in the contributed stock is $560,000. Complete the opening balance sheet for this partnership, applying the 2014 proposed regulations.

Assets			**Liabilities**		
	Tax	**Book**		**Tax**	**Book**
A's leases	$	$	[None]	$ 0	$ 0
B's leases					
C's stock			**Capital**		
			Alessa		
			Briana		
			Clarissa		
Total Assets	$	$	**Total Liabilities and Capital**	$	$

6.6.2 As planned, the partnership sells the stock that Clarissa contributed, using the $300,000 proceeds of sale to acquire new gas leases. What is the amount of loss that Clarissa recognizes on this sale?

    a) $0

    b) $86,667

    c) $260,000

    d) $300,000

6.6.3 As natural-gas prices rise over the next year, the value of each of the sets of leases, including the newly acquired leases, increases from $300,000 to $400,000. At that point, Alessa sells her interest in the partnership to Daniella for $400,000. The partnership makes an election under section 754 in connection with this sale. What amount of gain or loss does Alessa recognize on the sale and what is Daniella's special basis adjustment?

a) Alessa, $120,000 gain; Daniella, $120,000 special basis adjustment

b) Alessa, $120,000 gain; Daniella, $220,000 special basis adjustment

c) Alessa, $220,000 gain; Daniella, $120,000 special basis adjustment

d) Alessa, $220,000 gain; Daniella, $220,000 special basis adjustment

6.6.4 Same facts as Question 6.6.3, but it is Briana who sells her partnership interest to Daniella for $400,000. What amount of gain or loss does Briana recognize on the sale and what is Daniella's special basis adjustment?

a) Briana, $100,000 gain; Daniella, ($20,000) special basis adjustment

b) Briana, $100,000 gain; Daniella, $100,000 special basis adjustment

c) Briana, $20,000 loss; Daniella, ($20,000) special basis adjustment

d) Briana, $20,000 loss; Daniella, $100,000 special basis adjustment

6.6.5 Same facts as Question 6.6.3, but it is Clarissa who sells her partnership interest to Daniella for $400,000. What amount of gain or loss does Clarissa recognize on the sale and what is Daniella's special basis adjustment? (Recall that the partnership sold for $300,000 the stock that Clarissa contributed on formation.)

a) Clarissa, $100,000 gain; Daniella, $100,000 special basis adjustment

b) Clarissa, $100,000 gain; Daniella, ($160,000) special basis adjustment

c) Clarissa, $160,000 loss; Daniella, $100,000 special basis adjustment

d) Clarissa, $160,000 loss; Daniella, ($160,000) special basis adjustment

6.7 DISGUISED SALES OF PARTNERSHIP INTERESTS

You are unlikely to see a question on disguised sales of partnership interests on your partnership tax exam. (That sound was my students turning to the next Chapter.) The reason is not that such transactions are unimportant. It is that the rules for deciding whether one has occurred are not well articulated. This is in contrast to the rules for analyzing disguised sales of property to and by partnerships, which attract exam questions like flies. *See* Topic 2.7.

In a sale (or exchange) of a partnership interest, the transferor transfers the interest to the transferee, who transfers cash (or property) back to the transferor. In a disguised sale, these transfers happen, not directly between the transferor and transferee of the interest, but indirectly through the partnership. Say, for instance, that Aria wishes sell her partnership interest to Bartholome. During their negotiations, it emerges that Aria would be perfectly willing to take Bartholome's seaside villa as full payment. If they make this exchange, however, both will recognize gain. A partnership interest cannot be used in a like-kind exchange. Section 1031(a)(2)(D). After consulting a soothsayer of tax, they decide that Bartholome will transfer his villa to the partnership in exchange for an interest in the partnership (equivalent in every way to Aria's interest). The partnership will then transfer the villa to Aria in liquidation of her interest. As you will see in Chapter 9, Aria is not currently taxable on this liquidating distribution of property (the villa). If this works, the non-tax results are identical to the desired direct transfer and the tax results are way better. *See Crenshaw v. United States*, 450 F.2d 472 (5th Cir. 1971) (similar scheme unsuccessful).

The last clause of section 707(a)(2)(B) contemplates the possibility of "a transaction between 2 or more partners acting other than in their capacity as members of the partnership." This is the statutory basis upon which the IRS might attack the foregoing transaction. There are no Treasury regulations—controversial proposed regulations that generally would have applied the standards of Treas. Reg. § 1.707–3 were withdrawn in 2009. This leaves the characterization of these transactions to depend on general principles of tax law, including the step-transaction doctrine.

As you sort your way through the facts of a question that may involve a disguised sale of a partnership interest, keep the following in mind:

✓ The transaction must involve, at a minimum, a contribution to a partnership and a distribution by the same partnership to a different person. If you see only a contribution, or only a distribution, or a contribution and distribution involving the same person, you are not looking at a disguised sale of a partnership interest (although you may be looking at a disguised sale of property to or by the partnership).

✓ In a disguised sale of a partnership interest, the partnership is being used as a conduit for the passage of consideration from transferor to transferee. The less risk there is that the consideration will get "stuck" in the partnership, the more likely the transaction is a disguised sale. So look for facts that indicate that the subsequent transfer is not subject to the entrepreneurial risks of the partnership's operations—such as that the two transfers are close in time. The factors of Treas. Reg. § 1.707–3(b) are useful here.

✓ Even if the contribution portion and the distribution portion of the transaction cannot be conclusively linked to form a disguised sale of a partnership interest, either one may be a disguised sale of property subject to challenge under Treas. Reg. § 1.707–3.

✓   Depending on the size and complexity of a partnership, it is possible that a contribution and distribution may take place at about the same time, but under circumstances that indicate that the putative transferor and transferee have never met. In the absence of some direct negotiations between the two (whether personally or through agents), it is unlikely that a court would find that they engaged in a disguised sale.

6.7.1   After a tour of the place, Aria decides that she doesn't want Bartholome's villa after all, but she will take $850,000 in cash for her partnership interest. The soothsayer of tax is busy that afternoon, so Aria and Bartholome take their problem to Bob's Barbershop and Tax Advisory Services. Bob opines that sending the cash through the partnership will still produce the best tax answer. So Bartholome transfers $850,000 in cash to the partnership, which transfers it to Aria in liquidation of her partnership interest. Aria's outside basis is $450,000, not including her share of the partnership's liabilities. How much gain does she recognize on this transaction?

a) $0, because this is not a disguised sale of Aria's interest

b) $400,000, because this is not a disguised sale of Aria's interest

c) $400,000, because this is a disguised sale of Aria's interest

d) $850,000, whether or not this is a disguised sale

6.7.2   Same facts as Question 6.7.1, except that Aria will only sell one-half of her partnership interest. Bartholome accordingly transfers $425,000 cash to the partnership, which transfers it to Aria in redemption of one-half of her interest. How much gain does Aria recognize?

a) $0, because this is not a disguised sale of one-half of Aria's interest

b) $200,000, because this is not a disguised sale of one-half of Aria's interest

c) $200,000, because this is a disguised sale of one-half of Aria's interest

d) $425,000, whether or not this is a disguised sale

6.7.3   Same facts as Question 6.7.2, except that the soothsayer has returned, having spent the day at a conference on partnership taxation. She advises Aria and Bartholome that a change in their transaction is in order. Bartholome transfers his villa to the partnership, even though Aria will not take it. The partnership will keep the villa and transfer $425,000 of its existing funds to Aria in redemption of one-half of her interest. How much gain does Aria recognize on this transaction?

a) $0, because it is not a disguised sale of one-half of Aria's interest

b) $200,000, because it is not a disguised sale of one-half of Aria's interest

    c) $200,000, because it is a disguised sale of one-half of Aria's interest

    d) $425,000, whether or not this is a disguised sale

CHAPTER 7
SAFEGUARDS

7.1   SEEING THE FOREST FOR THE TREES

We have passed the midpoint of our trip together, so it may be a good time to stop and take stock of what we have seen and what is still ahead. Most, but not all, of what we have reviewed so far is the basic structure of partnership taxation—those provisions of law that are necessary to describe the tax consequences of carrying on business in partnership. One the road ahead, we'll see many provisions that are not integral to the basic system, but are instead safeguards that prevent the basic system from reaching tax results that Congress believes are inappropriate. Call these latter provisions anti-abuse rules if you like, but that seems an unfair characterization. The inappropriate results addressed by these safeguards often are not abusive, as that word is customarily used to describe people who apply tax provisions in unintended ways to reach unintended results. In some instances the basic system, applied exactly as intended, simply produces answers that are not consistent with current notions of good tax policy. In many of those cases, Congress has intervened.

An example may help. Prior to 1985, when a partnership sold an asset that had been contributed to the partnership with a built-in gain, the partnership was free to allocate the gain from the sale in any way it chose, subject to general requirements that applied to all allocations. This meant that partnerships could be used to shift built-in gains among the partners. It is beyond doubt that the drafters of the Internal Revenue Code in 1954 knew that and they thought it was okay. By 1984, however, the growing importance of low-taxed and tax-exempt partners led Congress to re-think this judgment. The result was the amendment of what is now section 704(c)(1)(A) by the Tax Reform Act of 1984, which made the anti-shifting apparatus of that section universally applicable.

Partnership taxation is based on an accounting system. This system tells us how to determine inside and outside basis, how to account for partnership liabilities, how to compute partnership income and loss and allocate it among the partners, how to adjust the accounts for partnership distributions, and so forth. This goes a long way toward explaining the modifications to the system that have been made over the years. A system of accounts is blind to the identity of its owners—everybody is treated alike. As it turns out, that has not always worked for partnership tax. Moreover, an accounting system tends to be driven by labels—a "contribution" has certain tax consequences, as does a "distribution." If they both happen at the same time, are they something fundamentally different—a disguised sale, perhaps? An accounting system is not designed to answer that question.

The evolution of the rules for allocating partnership income and loss to partners, which we reviewed in Topic 4.3, provides an excellent illustration. At the heart of the section 704(b) apparatus is the capital-accounting system, which the Treasury regulations use to determine whether an allocation has "economic effect." If all partners were in exactly the same tax position, this would be enough. But often they are not. In a case where one partner is in a high tax bracket while another is not, the attributes (I hesitate to call them "defects") of the accounting system give the IRS heartburn. Capital accounts do not bear interest. So an allocation of loss to a partner in a higher tax bracket can be offset with an allocation of income or gain ten years, twenty years, or longer in the future, permitting that partner to enjoy the compounding benefit of the tax savings in the meantime without diminishing her ownership stake in the partnership. Moreover, since capital accounts are maintained on a pre-tax basis, the offsetting allocation need not have the same character as the initial allocation. Thus, an allocation of ordinary loss may be offset (perhaps years later) by an allocation of capital gain, or even tax-exempt interest.

Of course, if the second partner were in the same tax position as the first, her cost from this allocation scheme would equal the first partner's benefit. If, however, the second partner is in a lower tax bracket than the first, the special allocations will produce aggregate tax savings that they can divvy up.

The drafters of the 1954 Internal Revenue Code were aware of this potential, but did not blame the accounting system. Instead, they bolted on a safeguard, providing in section 704(b) that an allocation in the partnership agreement would not be respected for tax purposes if "the principal purpose [of the allocation] . . . is the avoidance or evasion of any tax." In the Tax Reform Act of 1976, Congress replaced this safeguard with a newer version, substantial economic effect. In the post-1976 world, the substantiality test, although not part of the accounting system, adjusts its effects in egregious cases of tax avoidance.

As you flip through your dog-eared copy of the Internal Revenue Code (is there an electronic version of that?), it is not always easy to tell whether a given provision is part of the basic partnership tax system or a safeguard to that system. It is a meaningful exercise, however, because it forces you to think systematically about what you are learning. Here is one attempt at that classification:

A TAXONOMY OF SUBCHAPTER K

Systemic Provisions		Safeguards	
Code Section	**Date**	**Code Section**	**Date**
701	*1954*		
702	*1954*		
703	*1954*		
704(a)	*1954*	704(b)	*1976*

Systemic Provisions		Safeguards	
Code Section	Date	Code Section	Date
		704(c)(1)(A)	*1984*
		704(c)(1)(B)	*1989*
		704(c)(1)(C)	*2004*
704(d)	*1954*	704(e)	*1954*
705	*1954*		
706	*1954*		
707(a)(1)	*1954*	707(a)(2)	*1984*
		707(b)	*1954*
707(c)	*1954*		
708	*1954*		
		709	*1976*
721(a)	*1954*	721(b)	*1976*
		721(c)-(d)	*1997*
722	*1954*		
723	*1954*		
		724	*1984*
731(a)(1)	*1954*	731(a)(2)	*1954*
732(b)	*1954*	731(c)	*1994*
732(a)-(e)	*1954*	732(f)	*1999*
733	*1954*		
734	*1954*	734(a)	*2004*
735(b)	*1954*	735(a)	*1954*
736	*1954*		
		737	*1992*
741	*1954*		
742	*1954*		
743	*1954*	743(a)	*2004*
		751	*1954*
752	*1954*		
		753	*1954*
754	*1954*		
755(a)-(b)	*1954*	755(c)	*2004*
761	*1954*		

Don't mistake this simple chart for more than it is. By no means does it contain all of the changes to Subchapter K that have occurred since 1954. Instead, it tries to capture just the most important ones—in some cases, the modification of an existing provision and, in others, the enactment of an entirely new provision.

The most obvious observation is that in 1954 the drafters of the Internal Revenue Code built a complete and coherent system for partnership taxation. There is not, by my reckoning, a single modification or addition since 1954 that should be counted as a necessary part of the basic partnership tax system. On the other hand, there was little in the 1954 statute that went beyond the basic system, making the safeguards included at that time all the more noteworthy. There were six, for family partnerships (section 704(e)), transactions between related parties (section 707(b)) and transactions that could shift ordinary income (sections 731(a)(2), 735, 751 and 753).

It is a testament to the enduring quality of the work done in 1954 that the additions and amendments in the subsequent sixty-plus years have not been more numerous. Most of these changes came in three tax acts, in 1976, 1984 and 2004. The safeguards added earlier in this period tended to enunciate changes in general principles. Examples include the 1976 amendment to section 704(b), establishing substantial economic effect as the touchstone for partnership allocations, the 1984 exhortation to the IRS to promulgate rules taxing disguised sales of property and service contracts in accordance with their substance, and the aforesaid 1984 change to section 704(c). In contrast, later amendments have generally tended to focus on shutting down the latest marketed tax scheme, *e.g.*, the "anti-mixing-bowl" rules of section 704(c)(1)(B) and section 737, the change in treatment for distributions of marketable securities in section 731(c) and the anti-loss duplication rules of section 704(c)(1)(C), section 734(a) and section 743(a). Some later amendments have addressed ways that partnerships might be used to thwart the objectives of other portions of the United States tax law, *e.g.*, section 732(f) (*General Utilities* repeal) and section 721(d) (international transfer pricing).

In 1994, the IRS finalized Treas. Reg. § 1.701–2, the so-called "general anti-abuse regulation." In it, the IRS asserts its right to disregard the existence of a partnership or the status of one or more of its owners as partners, to re-allocate tax items, or otherwise to adjust the tax treatment claimed by the partnership or its partners if the partnership "is formed or availed of in connection with a transaction a principal purpose of which is to reduce substantially the present value of the partners' aggregate federal tax liability in a manner that is inconsistent with the intent of subchapter K." Treas. Reg. § 1.701–2(b). Separately, the IRS asserts its right to "treat a partnership as an aggregate of its partners in whole or in part as appropriate to carry out the purpose of any provision of the Internal Revenue Code or the regulations promulgated thereunder." Treas. Reg. § 1.701–2(e).

This development was different in kind from the statutory amendments discussed above. The regulation did not seek to modify any particular statutory provision—nor could it, as doing so would be beyond the authority of the IRS. Nevertheless, it asserted the right of the IRS to recharacterize partnerships and the transactions they undertake so as to cause any given statutory provision not to apply or to apply differently than contemplated by the taxpayer. Although this caused consternation among taxpayers and their representatives, the IRS defended it as an articulation of its traditional power to tax transactions in accordance with their economic reality, taking into account business purpose, substance over form, step transactions and other judicial doctrines. Over its first twenty years, the general anti-abuse regulation has been oft-cited by the IRS but seldom used by courts. It may have played a larger role, however, by encouraging judges to use the tools created by other judges to determine the proper treatment of particularly tax-motivated transactions.

The remainder of this Chapter discusses a few statutory safeguards that do not fit conveniently into discussions elsewhere in the Reading Period. Chapter 8 then takes on what has become over the past thirty years the 500-pound gorilla of Subchapter K safeguards, section 704(c).

7.2   PRESERVING CHARACTER: SECTIONS 724 AND 735(a)

Section 724 and section 735 are twins, although they were born 30 years apart. Section 724, enacted in 1984, seeks to prevent untoward changes in character when property is contributed to a partnership. Section 735, enacted in 1954, tries to prevent much the same thing when property is distributed from a partnership. To borrow the international-tax lingo, section 724 deals with the "inbound" transactions, while section 735 deals with the "outbound."

Actually, these sections should be considered fraternal twins, because they are not identical. Section 724(c), which preserves the character of capital losses in property contributed to a partnership, has no parallel in section 735. Section 735(b), which is not a safeguard provision at all, but a definition of the holding period of distributed property which is necessary to the basic system, has no analogue in section 724.

The approach of these sections to preserving the character of ordinary income is simple and rough-cut. Property characterized as "unrealized receivables" in the hands of the transferor (the partner, in the case of a contribution, or the partnership, in the case of a distribution) keeps that character in the hands of the transferee, so that any gain or loss on the subsequent disposition of the property by the transferee is ordinary. Period. The size of the subsequent gain or loss does not matter, nor does the delay before it is recognized. Section 724(a), section 735(a)(1). The rule for inventory items is slightly different, because in that case the ordinary-income taint is lost if the subsequent disposition occurs more than five years after the contribution or distribution. Section 724(b), section 735(a)(2). "Unrealized receivables" and "inventory items" have the broad meanings assigned to them by section 751(c) and section 751(d), respectively.

The foregoing provisions in sections 724 and 735 are not limited to the gain or loss existing at the time the property in question is transferred. This may (and probably should) strike you as odd. The purpose of these provisions is to prevent a transferor in whose hands property would produce ordinary income from reducing her or its tax liability by transferring the property to a related party for whom it would produce capital gain. But the operation of the provisions is not so limited. Thus, for example, if Carmen, who is a dealer in real estate, contributes land worth $100,000 with an adjusted basis of $75,000 to a partnership that sells it a year later for $160,000, the entire $85,000 tax gain, not just the $25,000 built-in gain at the time of the contribution, will be ordinary income to the partnership and all of its partners—including partners for whom the land would have been a capital asset if held directly.

Section 724(c) is different. It maintains the character of capital losses only to the extent of the capital loss existing at the time of the contribution. The intended effect of section 724(c) can be illustrated by assuming that Daniel, who holds land worth $100,000 as a capital asset with an adjusted basis of $160,000, contributes the land to a partnership which holds it for sale to customers in the ordinary course of its business. The partnership sells the land a year later for $75,000. Prior to the enactment of section 704(c)(1)(C), the partnership would recognize a tax loss of $85,000 on this sale. Of that loss, $60,000 would be capital under section 724(c) and would be allocated entirely to Daniel under section 704(c). The remaining loss of $25,000 would be ordinary and would be allocated among the partners according to the partnership agreement and applicable law.

This result should not be disturbed by the enactment of section 704(c)(1)(C). The proposed Treasury regulations under that section, discussed in Topic 6.6, may create unintended confusion, however, by excluding the built-in loss in a property from that property's basis in the hands of the partnership—in other words, by setting the partnership's common basis equal to the fair market value of property. Prop. Treas. Reg. § 1.704–3(f)(3)(ii). This is awkward for the analysis under section 724(c), which maintains the capital character of certain "loss recognized by the partnership." Let's assume once again that the partnership sells the land Daniel contributed for $75,000. If the partnership's common basis in the land is $100,000 under section 704(c)(1)(C), the $60,000 tax loss that section 724(c) characterizes as capital is not recognized by the partnership at all, but is rather reflected only in Daniel's section 704(c)(1)(C) basis adjustment. *Id.* Yet it should retain its character as capital loss—a result that may be clarified when the proposed regulations are finalized.

7.2.1 *If you have no prior exposure to section 704(c), you should read the essay introducing Topic 8.2 before answering this Question.* Abilene is an art dealer. She contributes a painting from her shop to an investment partnership in exchange for a 10% interest. The partnership holds the painting as a capital asset. Abilene's adjusted basis in the contributed painting is $45,000 and its agreed value at the time of contribution is $95,000. Four years later, the partnership receives an unsolicited offer to sell the painting for $90,000. If it accepts this offer, what are the tax consequences to Abilene and the other partners? The partnership applies section 704(c) using the traditional method.

a) Abilene has ordinary income of $45,000; the other partners have no income, gain or loss.

b) Abilene has capital gain of $45,000; the other partners have no income, gain or loss.

c) Abilene has ordinary income of $4,500; the other partners have $40,500 of ordinary income.

d) Abilene has capital gain of $4,500; the other partners have $40,500 of capital gain.

7.2.2   Does it make any difference in Question 7.2.1 how long Abilene has held the painting before she contributes it to the partnership?

a) Yes. The partnership's holding period for the painting includes the period that Abilene held it under section 1223(2). If the partnership's holding period for the painting exceeds five years at the time of sale, section 724(b) does not apply, and all of the partnership's recognized gain is capital gain.

b) No. The partnership's holding period for the painting does not include the period that Abilene held it, because she did not hold the painting as a capital asset or as section 1231 property.

c) No. Although the partnership's holding period for the painting includes the period that Abilene held it, this is irrelevant for purposes of applying section 724(b).

d) No. The fact that the partnership sold the painting for a book loss (*i.e.*, for a price lower than the value of the painting when Abilene contributed it) means that section 724(b) is inapplicable in this case.

7.2.3   How would your answer to Question 7.2.1 change if the partnership sold the painting for $145,000?

a) Abilene has ordinary income equal to the original built-in gain of $50,000. Abilene and the other partners share $50,000 of capital gain.

b) Abilene has ordinary income equal to the original built-in gain of $50,000. Abilene and the other partners share $50,000 of ordinary income.

c) Abilene has ordinary income equal to the original built-in gain ($50,000) plus 10% of the remaining $50,000 of gain ($5,000), for a total of $55,000 of ordinary income. The other partners share $45,000 of capital gain.

d)   Abilene has $55,000 of capital gain. The other partners share $45,000 of capital gain.

7.2.4   Cheyenne owns a parcel of land in a depressed part of town. She paid $80,000 for it a few years ago and it is now worth only $35,000. She contributes the land, which is a capital asset in her hands, in exchange for a 10% interest in a partnership that constructs a plant on the land for the production of auto parts. Four years later, the partnership sells the plant and land in order to move its production facility overseas. Of the sale price, $25,000 is allocable to the land. What are the tax consequences of the sale of the land to Cheyenne and the other partners?

a)   Cheyenne has a capital loss of $55,000; the other partners have no income, gain or loss.

b)   Cheyenne has a section 1231 loss of $55,000; the other partners have no income, gain or loss.

c)   Cheyenne has a capital loss of $45,000; Cheyenne and the other partners share a section 1231 loss of $10,000.

d)   Cheyenne has capital loss equal to the original built-in loss ($45,000) plus 10% of the remaining $10,000 of loss ($1,000), for a total of $46,000 of capital loss. The other partners share a section 1231 loss of $9,000.

7.3   TIMING OF LOSSES OR DEDUCTIONS ON TRANSACTIONS BETWEEN RELATED PARTIES: SECTIONS 267 AND 707(b)

The rules covered in this Topic extend well beyond partnerships, although we will review them only in that context. They come in two basic flavors. The first is the matching of deductions with income. If the payor of a deductible payment and the recipient of that payment use different accounting methods, their income and deduction may not be matched, meaning that the recipient may take the income into account at a different point in time (earlier or later) than the payor takes the deduction. When the payor and the recipient are related parties, this mismatch may prevent the clear reflection of the income of the related parties as a group. Section 267(a)(2) defers the allowance of deductions to promote matching in some, but not all, cases.

The second basic concern is the recognition of losses in sales between related parties. The reasons for such concern should be obvious: there is no (or less) adversity of interests to coax the price in such a sale toward fair market value, and the IRS cannot audit everything. The solution of section 267(a)(1), which does not apply to partnerships, and section 707(b)(1), which does, is to disallow such losses, subject to an idiosyncratic loss-revival rule that is far more complicated than it looks.

Section 267

At first reading, it does not appear that section 267 applies to partnerships or their partners at all. You can read and re-read section 267(b), which describes the relationships covered by this statute, without finding a single reference to the relationship of partner and partnership. If you read a bit further, however, you will see that section 267(e), which was added in 1984, extends the reach of section 267 to partners and partnerships, but in a peculiar way. First, it extends section 267(a)(2), governing matching of deductions to income, but not section 267(a)(1), governing losses in related-party sales. Congress no doubt felt that the latter subject was sufficiently well covered by section 707(b)(1). Second, section 267(e) has no ownership or control trigger: a partner owning a miniscule partnership interest is treated as a party related to the partnership.

Indirect and constructive ownership rules apply that are specific to partnerships in some cases, but that invoke the general rules of section 267 in others. Sections 707(e)(1)(C), (e)(1)(D), (e)(3). It is possible, but quite unfair, to construct an intricate and time-consuming exam question requiring the application of these rules. I hope your tax prof thinks there are better things to test on a partnership tax exam.

Have a close look at the language of section 267(a)(2) and you may find that it does less than you were expecting. It defers only deductions, not income, and it never accelerates either deductions or income. Accordingly, it does not achieve matching of deductions and income in all cases. In fact, it establishes a regime of heads I win, tails you lose, by deferring deductions to match income, where an earlier deduction would be allowed by the taxpayer's method of accounting, but gleefully allowing deductions to trail income, where that is the result of the taxpayer's method of accounting.

Most of the regulations under section 267 are out-of-date, some having been superseded by five tax acts amending section 267 itself. Take, for example, Treas. Reg. § 1.267(a)–1. On reading it, you will be chagrined to learn that it disallows deductions for certain items that are not paid within two and a half months following the close of the tax year. That has not been the law since 1984.

One regulation that bears special attention is Treas. Reg. § 1.267(b)–1(b), which deals with the application of section 267 to partnerships. This regulation was promulgated 26 years before the legislation that extended section 267 to partnerships in 1984. It explicitly characterizes a partnership as an aggregate (as opposed to an entity) for purposes of applying section 267 to transactions between a partnership and one who is not a partner. Although this regulation has been supplanted to some extent by subsequent legislation, it has some remaining vitality. The operation of this regulation is explored in Questions 7.3.5 and 7.3.6 below.

Section 707(b)(1)

The allowance of losses on sales of property between partnerships and their partners is governed not by section 267(a)(1), but by section 707(b)(1).

Since its amendment in 1986, this section disallows losses from sales or exchanges of property between a partnership and "a person" owning, directly or indirectly, more than 50% of the capital interest *or* the profits interest in the partnership, or between two commonly controlled partnerships. The significance of the quoted language is that it extends the reach of the statute to include sales (or purchases) by persons who are not partners, but who nevertheless are treated as owning an interest in the partnership under the constructive-ownership rules of section 267(c), made applicable by section 707(b)(3).

Section 707(b)(1) disallows only losses, not gains. Moreover, loss disallowance under section 707(b)(1) is not necessarily permanent. Under section 267(d), made applicable by the penultimate sentence of section 707(b)(1), the buyer of the property may use the disallowed loss to offset some or all of any gain it recognizes on any subsequent disposition of the property. There is no time limit. On the other hand, the disallowed loss is permanently extinguished to the extent it exceeds the amount of the gain recognized on the buyer's subsequent disposition. This is a weird rule. Ordinarily, when the tax law permits or requires nonrecognition treatment on the disposition of property, the transferor's adjusted basis carries over to the transferee, to preserve the unrecognized gain or loss for future taxation. Here, in contrast, the transferee (buyer) of loss property takes a cost basis in the acquired property, together with a special dispensation to reduce future gain by the amount of the basis step-down. Why not just carry over the seller's basis to the buyer?

To illustrate, assume that Carl, who owns 75% of the Carlsbad Partnership, sells property to the partnership for $300. Carl's adjusted basis in the property is $500. Under section 707(b)(1), Carl recognizes no loss on this sale. The partnership takes the property with a cost basis of $300. If it later sells the property for $600, it will recognize $100 of gain—the same outcome that would result if the partnership had taken Carl's $500 basis in the property. If, on the other hand, the partnership sells the property for $400, it will recognize no gain or loss, and $100 of Carl's initial basis will evaporate.

In the partnership context, the problem is actually worse. If Carl contributes the property to Carlsbad, section 704(c)(1)(C) would give the partnership a basis equal to fair market value, and the excess of Carl's adjusted basis in the contributed property over that amount would be a section 704(c)(1)(C) basis adjustment that is personal to Carl. When the partnership sold the property, Carl's gain would be reduced, or his loss increased, by the amount of this basis adjustment. The other partners would recognize gain or loss based on the change in value of the property during the period of the partnership's ownership. In contrast to this tidy result, section 707(b)(1) allows—nay, requires—that some of the benefit of Carl's loss be shifted to the other partners. This is contrary to the legislative purpose of section 704(c).

To illustrate, assume the same facts as above and add the heroic assumption that the fair market value of the property is actually $300 when Carl sells it to the partnership for $300. If this transaction were governed by section 704(c)(1)(C), the partnership would take a $300 basis in the property and would recognize a $300 gain when it later resold the property for $600. It would allocate this gain $225 (75%) to Carl and $75 (25%) to the other partner. Taking into account Carl's section 704(c)(1)(C) basis adjustment of $200, he would have a gain of $25 and the other partner would have a gain of $75. Under section 707(b)(1), in contrast, Carl has a gain of $75 and the other partner has a gain of $25.

Let's assume instead that the "real" fair market value of the property is $400. (Recall that the basic reason for the existence of section 707(b)(1) is the difficulty of knowing fair market value in a related-party transaction, and that the parties may be incentivized to understate it.) Applying section 704(c)(1)(C), the partnership takes a basis of $400 and recognizes a gain of $200 on its sale of the property for $600. Taking Carl's section 704(c)(1)(C) basis adjustment of $100 into account, he has a gain of $50 and the other partner has a gain of $50.

Finally, let's assume that the "real" fair market value of the property is $500—*i.e.*, that the property is not a loss property at all, but is worth as much a Carl paid for it. Applying section 704(c)(1)(C), the partnership takes a basis of $500 and recognizes a gain of $100 on its sale of the property for $600. Carl has no section 704(c)(1)(C) basis adjustment. He is allocated a gain of $75 on the sale and the other partner is allocated a gain of $25—the results reached by section 707(b)(1).

Thus, viewed through the prism of partnership tax, section 707(b)(1) reaches an inappropriate result in any case in which the disallowed loss is real. It only comes out okay where the disallowed loss is a figment of Carl's imagination (or a creation of his tax planner), so that there is really no built-in loss for him to retain.

Section 707(b)(2)

Section 707(b)(2) is worried about a different problem that may arise when property is transferred between a partnership and a controlling partner. Say that the Carlsbad Partnership is in the business of buying widgets at $2 apiece and reselling them for $3. Carl personally is not engaged in that business. So Carl buys some widgets for $2 and sells them to the partnership for $2.75, which resells them to customers for $3. This simple scheme, if effective, would turn 75% of the profit on widget resales into capital gain. (A disproportionate share of the partnership's resale profit would have to be allocated to the minority partners in order not to adversely affect them.) There are at least three avenues of attack. First, the IRS could assert that Carl himself is a dealer, which would result in Carl's profit on sales to the partnership being taxed as ordinary income. Second, the IRS could challenge the price at which Carl sells to the partnership—a transfer-pricing case. Lastly, section 707(b)(2) makes these fact-intensive challenges unnecessary by treating all of Carl's profits as ordinary income.

As in the case in section 267, the Treasury regulations under section 707(b) are out-of-date to the point of confusion, and it is best simply to ignore them.

7.3.1   Natalie is a tax accountant who owns a 10% interest in Rosencrans LLC, a manufacturer of custom gift boxes. Rosencrans is concerned about complying with state sales tax laws and hires Natalie to prepare a study summarizing the laws of the states where Rosencrans has customers and giving her compliance recommendations. Natalie delivers her report in December 2016 and sends the partnership an invoice for $25,000, which it pays in February 2017. Rosencrans and Natalie are both cash-method, calendar-year taxpayers. What is the result?

a) $25,000 income to Natalie in 2016 and an equal deduction to the partnership in 2016

b) $25,000 income to Natalie in 2016 and an equal deduction to the partnership in 2017

c) $25,000 income to Natalie in 2017 and an equal deduction to the partnership in 2016

d) $25,000 income to Natalie in 2017 and an equal deduction to the partnership in 2017

7.3.2   Same facts as in Question 7.3.1, except that Natalie is on the cash method, while the partnership uses an accrual method. What result?

a) $25,000 income to Natalie in 2016 and an equal deduction to the partnership in 2016

b) $25,000 income to Natalie in 2016 and an equal deduction to the partnership in 2017

c) $25,000 income to Natalie in 2017 and an equal deduction to the partnership in 2016

d) $25,000 income to Natalie in 2017 and an equal deduction to the partnership in 2017

7.3.3   Same facts as in Question 7.3.1, except that Rosencrans is on the cash method, while Natalie uses an accrual method. What result?

a) $25,000 income to Natalie in 2016 and an equal deduction to the partnership in 2016

b) $25,000 income to Natalie in 2016 and an equal deduction to the partnership in 2017

c) $25,000 income to Natalie in 2017 and an equal deduction to the partnership in 2016

c) $25,000 income to Natalie in 2017 and an equal deduction to the partnership in 2017

7.3.4 *You may want to look again at Topic 3.5 before answering this Question.* Now Natalie is a designer and graphic artist who works regularly in the partnership's business, not an independent tax accountant. She agrees to design a new suite of gift boxes for the partnership for a fixed payment of $25,000. She delivers the new designs to the partnership in December 2016 and the partnership pays her in February 2017. Rosencrans is on the cash method, Natalie uses an accrual method and both are calendar-year taxpayers. What result?

    a) $25,000 income to Natalie in 2016 and an equal deduction to the partnership in 2016

    b) $25,000 income to Natalie in 2016 and an equal deduction to the partnership in 2017

    c) $25,000 income to Natalie in 2017 and an equal deduction to the partnership in 2016

    d) $25,000 income to Natalie in 2017 and an equal deduction to the partnership in 2017

7.3.5 Natalie's father, Nate, owns lithography equipment that he has used for two years in his business as a sole proprietor but no longer needs. He sells this equipment to Rosencrans for $12,000. At the time of the sale, Nate's adjusted basis in the equipment is $15,000. What is the result to Nate?

    a) Capital loss of $3,000

    b) Ordinary loss of $3,000 under section 1231(a)(2)

    c) Ordinary loss of $2,700; $300 of Nate's loss is disallowed under Treas. Reg. § 1.267(b)–1(b)

    d) All of Nate's loss is disallowed under section 707(b)(1)

7.3.6 Rather than paying cash, Rosencrans gives Nate its promissory note for $12,000, payable over five years in equal semi-annual installments on August 1 and February 1, with interest at an annual rate of 8%. Nate is on the cash method, the partnership uses an accrual method and both use the calendar year. What can you say about the interest on this promissory note that accrues for the period August 1, 2016 through December 31, 2016, which the partnership pays on February 1, 2017?

    a) The partnership can deduct this interest in its 2016 tax return.

    b) The partnership cannot deduct this interest, because it is "self-charged interest" under the passive-activity rules of Treas. Reg. § 1.469–7.

    c) Section 267(a)(2) defers the partnership's deduction until 2017.

    d) Treas. Reg. § 1.267(b)–1(b) permanently disallows Natalie from taking her share of the partnership's interest deduction.

7.3.7 Carl, who owns 75% of the Carlsbad Partnership, sells land to the partnership for $240,000 cash. Carl held the land as a capital asset with a tax basis of $160,000 and the partnership likewise will hold it as a capital asset. If the actual fair market value of the land at the time of Carl's sale was $320,000, what is the result to Carl?

    a)   Carl's gain is disallowed under section 707(b)(1), regardless of the actual value of the land.

    b)   Section 267(a)(2) requires the partnership to recognize $80,000 of gain.

    c)   Carl recognizes $120,000 capital gain and the partnership recognizes neither gain nor loss.

    d)   Carl recognizes $80,000 capital gain and the partnership recognizes neither gain nor loss.

CHAPTER 8
SECTION 704(c)

8.1 ACCOUNTING FOR BOOK-TAX DIFFERENCES

Over the past 30 years, section 704(c) has been "the" hot topic in partnership tax. The decision to make it mandatory in 1984 and the ramifications of that decision—both for accountants and lawyers who must apply the statute on a daily basis and government officials who are responsible for determining its proper scope—have used up enough brain power to send a dozen missions to Mars.

As enacted in 1954, old section 704(c)(1) provided that gain or loss recognized by a partnership on the sale of a contributed asset (as well as depreciation and depletion on such an asset) were to be allocated among the partners just as if the partnership had acquired the asset by a cash purchase. There were no special rules. The drafters realized, of course, that a taxpayer holding an asset with, say, a built-in gain could contribute it to a partnership and, through the application of old section 704(c)(1), shift at least a portion of that gain to other partners when the partnership sold the asset. The drafters viewed this as a potential problem for the partners, who might disagree with such gain-shifting, and therefore added old section 704(c)(2), which gave the partners permission to agree to such other allocations as they might choose to "take account of the variation between the basis of the property to the partnership and its fair market value at the time of contribution." But the drafters did not require allocations of this nature, presumably on the easy assumption that tax on the gain would be paid by one partner or another, and the government was indifferent who wrote the check.

Partnerships thus became, with the government's blessing, superhighways for transporting gains and losses between taxpayers. In time, more and more of those taxpayers turned out to be non-taxpayers, and the government realized it had a serious problem on its hands. The growing number and importance of tax-indifferent parties—foreign individuals and entities, tax-exempt organizations, pension plans and tax-advantaged US corporations—gave tax planners limitless opportunities to eliminate the tax on existing gains simply by pairing a partner who pays tax with one who does not. The government's first response was to make the elective rule of old section 704(c)(2) into the mandatory rule that is now found in section 704(c)(1)(A). At the same time, the language of old section 704(c)(2) was broadened to include "income, gain, loss, and deduction."

Later legislative responses have included the enactment of the so-called "anti-mixing-bowl" rules of section 704(c)(1)(B) and section 737 (Topic 9.4) and the anti-loss-duplication rule of section 704(c)(1)(C) (Topics 6.6 and 8.4).

On the administrative front, the Treasury Department and the IRS undertook the task of filling in the operational rules needed to implement these legislative provisions. But tax administrators are not without their own expansionist tendencies. Their chief contribution is the invention of the so-called "reverse section 704(c) layer," a concept that expands the scope of section 704(c) enormously, from gains and losses existing at the time of contribution to those arising upon any (and all) future revaluations (Topic 8.5).

The section 704(c) landscape

Until 2004, section 704(c)(1)(A) had the formidable job of policing the shifting of gains and losses that are accrued prior to the contribution of property to a partnership, as well as the shifting of gains and losses arising from revaluations of property already owned by a partnership. The enactment of section 704(c)(1)(C) in that year took one task off its hands. Section 704(c)(1)(C) is charged with preventing losses accrued prior to the contribution of property to a partnership from benefiting any partner other than the contributor. Section 704(c)(1)(A) continues to be responsible for built-in gains (but not losses) on contribution and revaluation gains and losses. This division of responsibilities is discussed in more detail in Topic 8.5.

The Treasury regulations governing section 704(c) methods were written before 2004. They speak of built-in gains and losses as though they were governed by the same set of rules. Although this is no longer strictly true, the regulations remain critically important for understanding and interpreting section 704(c)(1)(A) wherever it applies.

Section 704(c)(1)(A) boot camp

In this Topic, we begin with the most basic questions: how does a partnership keep track of the variation between the basis of property to the partnership and its fair market value at the time of contribution, and what on earth is it supposed to do to "take account" of that variation in making allocations to partners?

Happily, you already know the answer to the first of these questions. Topic 2.3 reviewed the rules for constructing a partnership's balance sheet. One of the many tasks accomplished by the balance sheet is to reflect the variation between the basis of contributed property and its value at the time of contribution. Take, for example, the balance sheet in Question 2.3.2:

FIGURE 8.1.1

Assets				Liabilities	
	(1) Tax	**(2)** Book	**(3)** FMV		**(4)** Tax	**(5)** Book
Cash	$120,000	$120,000	$120,000	[None]	$ 0	$ 0
Equipment	60,000	60,000	60,000			
Plant	190,000	220,000	220,000	**Capital**		
Land	110,000	140,000	140,000	Aaliyah	300,000	360,000
				Blake	120,000	120,000
				Carbury	60,000	60,000
Total Assets	$480,000	$540,000	$540,000	**Total Liabilities and Capital**	$480,000	$540,000

In this Question, Aaliyah, Blake and Carbury formed a limited partnership by contributing various assets. Aaliyah, the general partner, contributed a small plant, worth $220,000 with a basis of $190,000, on land worth $140,000 with a basis of $110,000. Blake and Carbury, both limited partners, contributed, respectively, cash of $120,000 and newly purchased manufacturing equipment with a value and basis of $60,000.

The inside basis of each asset (which equals the basis of the asset in the hands of the contributor) is reflected in column (1). The fair market value of each of the contributed assets at the time of its contribution is its initial book value, which is reflected in column (2). Moreover, the aggregate of these variations shows up in the capital of each partner. Aaliyah contributed assets that had an aggregate variation between tax basis and value of $60,000, as demonstrated by the difference between her book capital account in column (5) and her tax capital in column (4). Neither of the other partners contributed assets with such variation, so their respective book capital accounts equal their tax capital.

How is the partnership supposed to "take account" of these variations in making its allocations? The Treasury regulations begin their quest for clarity on this question with a simple statement of the statutory purpose: "The purpose of section 704(c) is to prevent the shifting of tax consequences among partners with respect to precontribution gain or loss." Treas. Reg. § 1.704–3(a). Therefore, because the variation between the tax basis and the value of a contributed property measures its built-in gain or loss, allocations that take account of that variation must assure, to the extent possible, that the built-in gain or loss is recognized by the partner who contributed that property (the "contributing partner").

Okay, how does the partnership do that? Let's take several different examples and see if we can build them into a general rule. Say, for example, that the partnership sells the land Aaliyah contributed for $140,000, its value at the time of contribution. The partnership realizes a tax gain of $30,000, all of it attributable to the built-in gain in existence at the time of contribution. The partnership should therefore allocate all $30,000 of tax gain to Aaliyah and none to Blake or Carbury.

Consider the changes to the balance sheet resulting from this sale and gain allocation:

FIGURE 8.1.2

Assets			Liabilities		
	Tax	**Book**		**Tax**	**Book**
Cash	$120,000	$120,000	[None]	$ 0	$ 0
Equipment	60,000	60,000			
Plant	190,000	220,000	**Capital**		
Cash from sale	140,000	140,000	Aaliyah	330,000	360,000
			Blake	120,000	120,000
			Carbury	60,000	60,000
Total Assets	$510,000	$540,000	**Total Liabilities and Capital**	$510,000	$540,000

The sale increases the aggregate tax basis of the partnership's assets by $30,000 and does not change the aggregate book value (because the land was sold at book value). Said differently, the difference between the book value of the partnership's assets and their tax basis, initially $60,000, has been reduced by $30,000 to $30,000. The effect on the other side of the balance sheet is similar. The book-tax difference in Aaliyah's capital, initially $60,000, is now $30,000. This is significant, because Aaliyah's book-tax difference measures the aggregate built-in gain in the assets she contributed to the partnership. She has now recognized $30,000 of that built-in gain and has $30,000 remaining.

We can generalize an important insight from even this simple example. Section 704(c)(1)(A) is concerned with built-in gain. (It used to be concerned with built-in loss as well, but that job has been taken over by section 704(c)(1)(C).) Consequently, it is concerned with book-tax differences, because the book-tax difference in an asset or in a partner's capital measures the amount of the built-in gain attributable to that asset or to that partner. The goal of section 704(c)(1)(A) is to prevent the shifting of built-in gain from one partner to any other partner. Said another way, the goal of section 704(c)(1)(A) is to eliminate the book-tax difference in the contributing partner's capital. When the contributing partner's book-tax difference is eliminated, she has been allocated all of the built-in gain attributable to the assets she contributed to the partnership, and the goal of section 704(c)(1)(A) is met.

It is easier for accountants to understand section 704(c)(1)(A) than it is for lawyers. At root, it is about making one number (tax capital) equal to another number (book capital). All the rest is details.

Let's try another example. Say the partnership sells the land for $170,000, instead of $140,000. Its tax gain is $60,000, equal to the excess of the selling price over the partnership's tax basis in the land. How should it allocate this gain? Your first impulse may be that it should be allocated entirely to Aaliyah, because this allocation would completely eliminate her book-tax difference. Not a bad idea, but a little over-eager. Only $30,000 of the partnership's $60,000 tax gain is built-in gain. The remaining $30,000 of gain represents the increase in the value of the land while it has been owned by the partnership, and all of the partners should get a share of that. To determine how much, it is helpful to introduce a new term, "book gain." Book gain is the gain calculated by reference not to the tax basis of the land, but instead its book basis. The book gain on this sale is $30,000. It is allocated in whatever way the partnership agreement provides, as long as that allocation has substantial economic effect or is otherwise in accordance with the partners' interests in the partnership. It appears from the partner's respective book capital accounts that Aaliyah has two-thirds of the partnership's total capital, Blake has two-ninths and Carbury has one-ninth. Assuming that their respective interests in partnership profits and losses are in these proportions, Aaliyah is allocated $20,000 of the $30,000 book gain, Blake is allocated $6,667 and Carbury is allocated $3,333.

If each of the three partners is allocated tax gain equaling the amount of book gain allocated to that partner, there will be $30,000 of tax gain remaining to be allocated. This is exactly the built-in gain in the land, and it should all be allocated to Aaliyah. The resulting balance sheet is as follows:

FIGURE 8.1.3

Assets			Liabilities		
	Tax	Book		Tax	Book
Cash	$120,000	$120,000	[None]	$ 0	$ 0
Equipment	60,000	60,000			
Plant	190,000	220,000	Capital		
Cash from sale	170,000	170,000	Aaliyah	350,000	380,000
			Blake	126,667	126,667
			Carbury	63,333	63,333
Total Assets	$540,000	$570,000	Total Liabilities and Capital	$540,000	$570,000

Each of the partner's tax and book capital accounts have been increased by the amounts of tax gain and book gain, respectively, allocated to them. The bottom line is that the book-tax difference on both the left side and the right side of the balance sheet has been reduced by $30,000. On the right side of the balance sheet, the entire reduction is located in Aaliyah's accounts, where her book-tax difference has been reduced by the entire amount of the built-in gain on the land she contributed.

There is another important generalization that can be drawn from Figure 8.1.3. Have a look at Blake and Carbury's accounts. Both started with no book-tax difference, and neither has one now. This is the result of allocating to each of them an amount of tax gain that is equal to book gain. This has two salutary effects. First, it prevents the creation of an artificial book-tax difference when neither partner contributed assets with built-in gain. Second, it assures that Aaliyah is allocated all, but not more than all, of the built-in gain attributable to the land she contributed. The tax gain of $60,000 is composed of two parts, the book gain of $30,000 and the built-in gain of $30,000. By allocating tax gain equal to book gain to each of the partners, you are assured that Aaliyah, the contributing partner, will be allocated the entire built-in gain. In fact, you will have the same assurance if you simply allocate equal amounts of tax gain and book gain to each of Blake and Carbury, the noncontributing partners. And so arises the most famous maxim of section 704(c), one that you have doubtless heard from your tax prof: *"Tax follows book to the noncontributing partners."*

Now, a third variation. Let's say that the partnership agreement states that the first $30,000 of the partnership's gain on the sale of the land is to be allocated two-thirds to Blake and one-third to Carbury. Your first question should be, is that tax gain or book gain? If the partnership agreement is referring to tax gain, the allocation is contrary to section 704(c)(1)(A) and cannot stand. An allocation of book gain in this manner, on the other hand, is fine if it passes muster under section 704(b). The tests for substantial economic effect appear satisfied here, so when the partnership sells the land for $170,000, the resulting $30,000 of book gain will be allocated $20,000 to Blake and $10,000 to Carbury. The tax gain will follow this allocation of book gain, $20,000 to Blake and $10,000 to Carbury. The $30,000 remaining tax gain will be allocated to Aaliyah, satisfying section 704(c)(1)(A). The resulting balance sheet will look like this:

FIGURE 8.1.4

Assets			Liabilities		
	Tax	**Book**		**Tax**	**Book**
Cash	$120,000	$120,000	[None]	$ 0	$ 0
Equipment	60,000	60,000			
Plant	190,000	220,000	**Capital**		
Cash from sale	170,000	170,000	Aaliyah	330,000	360,000
			Blake	140,000	140,000
			Carbury	70,000	70,000
Total Assets	**$540,000**	**$570,000**	**Total Liabilities and Capital**	**$540,000**	**$570,000**

Once again, Aaliyah's book-tax difference has been reduced by $30,000, and no book-tax difference has emerged for either Blake or Carbury.

Sometimes, it is not possible to allocate to the noncontributing partners an amount of tax gain equal to book gain. Consider a partnership sale of the land for $131,000. This sale creates a tax gain of $21,000, but a book *loss* of $9,000. Let's say the partnership agreement provides for this book loss to be allocated two-thirds to Aaliyah ($6,000), two-ninths to Blake ($2,000) and one-ninth to Carbury ($1,000). When we attempt to allocate an amount of tax loss equal to the amount of book loss allocated to Blake and Carbury, we find that there is no tax loss, only tax gain. Traditionally, that has been the end of the story. A partnership cannot allocate what it does not have—a common-sense limitation known as the "ceiling rule."

(Your common sense may lead you to a different conclusion. You may see two components in the partnership's tax gain of $21,000: a tax loss equal to the book loss of $9,000 and a tax gain of $30,000, equal to Aaliyah's built-in gain in the land. Implicitly, the ceiling rule requires these two components to be netted together. The remedial method, discussed in Topic 8.2, separates them.)

Applying the ceiling rule, the partnership allocates no tax gain to either Blake or Carbury and all of the tax gain ($21,000) to Aaliyah. Its balance sheet then looks like this:

FIGURE 8.1.5

Assets			Liabilities		
	Tax	**Book**		**Tax**	**Book**
Cash	$120,000	$120,000	[None]	$ 0	$ 0
Equipment	60,000	60,000			
Plant	190,000	220,000	**Capital**		
Cash from sale	131,000	131,000	Aaliyah	321,000	354,000
			Blake	120,000	118,000
			Carbury	60,000	59,000
Total Assets	$501,000	$531,000	**Total Liabilities and Capital**	$501,000	$531,000

The book-tax difference in the partnership's assets in the aggregate has been reduced from $60,000 to $30,000, reflecting the elimination of the book-tax difference in the land through its sale. Because the balance sheet satisfies the accounting identity, the book-tax difference in the partner's capital in the aggregate has also been reduced by $30,000. But this reduction is not entirely attributable to Aaliyah, as it has been in every previous example. Instead, her book-tax difference in Figure 8.1.5 is $33,000 rather than $30,000 as in the previous examples. Blake and Carbury have book-tax differences aggregating a negative $3,000, reflecting the fact that they received no tax loss to match their aggregate book loss of $3,000.

Relative to the goal of section 704(c)(1)(A) to eliminate book-tax differences, $3,000 too little gain has been allocated to Aaliyah and $3,000 too much gain (or too little loss) has been allocated to Blake and Carbury. The ceiling rule thus frustrates the application of section 704(c)(1)(A), creating "distortions," to use the word chosen by the Treasury regulations. Such distortions can be reduced or eliminated by optional methods, if a partnership elects to use them. These methods are the subject of Topic 8.2.

Looking at the big picture, this is all a matter of timing. If the partnership were to sell all of its remaining assets at their book values and liquidate, Blake and Carbury would recognize tax losses on the liquidation of $2,000 and $1,000, respectively. These are exactly the tax losses denied to them by the ceiling rule. It is too cavalier, however, to conclude that Blake and Carbury have nothing to complain about, or that the goal of section 704(c) really has not been frustrated. Liquidation of the partnership may not be desirable for, or within the control of, these minority partners and it seems in all events a draconian solution to their problem. From Aaliyah's perspective, liquidation of the partnership would be her day of reckoning, because she would at that time recognize her entire remaining book-tax difference of $33,000, consisting of the remaining amount of her built-in gain on the land ($9,000), reduced by her share of the loss on the sale of the land ($6,000), plus her entire built-in gain on the plant ($30,000). She thus has an incentive to put off that day for as long as possible.

One final example illustrates a situation where it is not immediately clear what is required to take account of the variation between tax basis and fair market value on contribution. Assume that the partnership sells the land for $95,000, producing a book loss of $45,000 and a tax loss of $15,000. The book loss is allocated $30,000 to Aaliyah, $10,000 to Blake and $5,000 to Carbury. How should the tax loss be allocated? The presence of a book loss at least equal to the tax loss demonstrates that the tax loss arose during the period that the partnership owned the land. Thus, allocating this tax loss under section 704(c) might appear to violate the purpose of that provision, which is to avoid the shifting of *precontribution* tax gain or loss. Treas. Reg. § 1.704–3(a). In this way of thinking, section 704(c) should not be involved with the allocation of *post-contribution* tax gain or loss. The $15,000 of tax loss would therefore follow the allocation of a like amount of book loss, $10,000 to Aaliyah, $3,333 to Blake and $1,667 to Carbury. The balance sheet would then look like this:

FIGURE 8.1.6

Assets			Liabilities		
	Tax	**Book**		**Tax**	**Book**
Cash	$120,000	$120,000	[None]	$ 0	$ 0
Equipment	60,000	60,000			
Plant	190,000	220,000	**Capital**		
Cash from sale	95,000	95,000	Aaliyah	290,000	330,000
			Blake	116,667	110,000
			Carbury	58,333	55,000
Total Assets	$465,000	$495,000	**Total Liabilities and Capital**	$465,000	$495,000

This balance sheet shows that the foregoing analysis is wrong. Allocating in this manner leaves Aaliyah with a book-tax difference of $40,000 rather than $30,000 and it also produces book-tax differences for Blake and Carbury aggregating a negative $10,000. Thus, it results in the shifting of $10,000 of the $30,000 precontribution tax gain attributable to the land.

To avoid this result, the Treasury regulations require the partnership to allocate its tax loss to the noncontributing partners up to the amount of their book loss. Treas. Reg. § 1.704–3(d)(7), example (3)(i). *Tax follows book to the noncontributing partners.* Accordingly, the partnership allocates $10,000 of tax loss to Blake, $5,000 to Carbury and none to Aaliyah. The resulting balance sheet is:

FIGURE 8.1.7

Assets			Liabilities		
	Tax	**Book**		**Tax**	**Book**
Cash	$120,000	$120,000	[None]	$ 0	$ 0
Equipment	60,000	60,000			
Plant	190,000	220,000	**Capital**		
Cash from sale	95,000	95,000	Aaliyah	300,000	330,000
			Blake	110,000	110,000
			Carbury	55,000	55,000
Total Assets	$465,000	$495,000	**Total Liabilities and Capital**	$465,000	$495,000

Notice how this application of section 704(c)(1)(A) takes account of the built-in gain. It allocates the same amount of tax loss and book loss to each of the noncontributing partners. It allocates $30,000 of book loss to Aaliyah, but no tax loss. In effect, Aaliyah recognizes her full $30,000 of built-in gain on the land, because she is allocated $30,000 less tax loss than book loss.

With the foregoing examples in mind, we can identify the situations where the ceiling rule will apply to the sale of the partnership's land:

- ✓ Land sold for more than $140,000, its book value. There is book gain as well as tax gain. The ceiling rule does not apply.

- ✓ Land sold for less than $140,000 but more than $110,000, its adjusted tax basis. There is book loss and tax gain. The ceiling rule applies.

- ✓ Land sold for less than $110,000 but more than $95,000. There is both book loss and tax loss, but the tax loss is less than the amount of book loss that will be allocated to the noncontributing partners. The ceiling rule applies.

- ✓ Land sold for $95,000 or less. The total tax loss equals or exceeds the amount of book loss that will be allocated to the noncontributing partners. The ceiling rule does not apply.

The "cross-over point" (here, $95,000) where the ceiling rule ceases to apply can only be determined by reference to the terms of the partnership agreement. Here, the noncontributing partners are allocated one-third of book losses in the aggregate, so the cross-over point occurs where the total tax loss equals one-third of the total book loss. At a sale price of $95,000, the partnership will have a book loss of $45,000 and a tax loss of $15,000. The noncontributing partners will be allocated one-third, or $15,000, of the book loss and all $15,000 of the tax loss.

Depreciation

Tax profs sometimes teach the application of section 704(c)(1)(A) to depreciation as a whole new subject, separate and different from the application of that section to gain and loss on sale. It really is not. In fact, if you look at depreciation as a series of sales occurring every year throughout the depreciation period, it is exactly the same. The amount realized on each of these sales is zero. The book loss and the tax loss incurred on each sale are the amounts of the book depreciation and the tax depreciation. At the end of the depreciation period, the entire depreciable asset has been "sold" and its book value and adjusted tax basis are both zero.

Let's try an example to prove the point. In this instance, Aaliyah's partnership does not sell the land. Instead, in the first year of its existence, the partnership claims depreciation on its plant and its equipment and does nothing else. Assume that the equipment is depreciated on a straight-line basis over a five-year life, so that (ignoring depreciation conventions) the partnership claims $12,000 of book depreciation and $12,000 of tax depreciation on the equipment. Assume that the plant is depreciated on a straight-line basis over 10 years and (again ignoring conventions) the partnership claims $22,000 of book depreciation and $19,000 of tax depreciation on the plant.

Because there is no book-tax difference in the equipment, section 704(c) has no role in determining the allocation of the depreciation on the equipment. This is governed exclusively by section 704(b). Let's assume that the allocation is, as before, two-thirds ($8,000) to Aaliyah, two-ninths ($2,667) to Blake and one-ninth ($1,333) to Carbury.

The depreciation on the plant is a different matter. If we are to take account of the built-in gain with which Aaliyah contributed this property to the partnership, we must apply section 704(c)(1)(A) to this depreciation. The depreciation will slowly reduce both the book value and the tax basis of the plant to zero. At that point, the book-tax difference in the plant will be gone and, if we have not already applied section 704(c)(1)(A), it will be too late.

From this point, the process is familiar. Allocating depreciation is exactly like allocating loss from the sale of the property. There will always be both book loss (book depreciation) and tax loss (tax depreciation). In other words, if the depreciable property has built-in gain, you will always find yourself in the third or fourth bullet point from the list above, never in the first or second. Let's assume that the partnership allocates two-thirds of the book depreciation on the plant ($14,667) to Aaliyah, two-ninths ($4,889) to Blake and one-ninth ($2,444) to Carbury. How should it allocate the tax depreciation? *Tax follows book to the noncontributing partners.* The partnership allocates $4,889 of the tax depreciation to Blake and $2,444 to

Carbury. The remainder ($11,667) goes to Aaliyah. The resulting balance sheet after the first year of depreciation is:

FIGURE 8.1.8

Assets			Liabilities		
	Tax	**Book**		**Tax**	**Book**
Cash	$120,000	$120,000	[None]	$ 0	$ 0
Equipment	48,000	48,000			
Plant	171,000	198,000	**Capital**		
Land	110,000	140,000	Aaliyah	280,333	337,333
			Blake	112,444	112,444
			Carbury	56,223	56,223
Total Assets	$449,000	$506,000	**Total Liabilities and Capital**	$449,000	$506,000

At the outset, the book-tax difference in the partnership's depreciable property was $30,000, as shown in Figure 8.1.1. Now, as a result of depreciation alone, it is down to $27,000. One-tenth ($3,000) of the book-tax difference in the plant has disappeared, and the same thing will happen each year throughout the plant's 10-year depreciable life. The book-tax difference in the partners' capital has dropped by $3,000 as well, and all of this reduction can be traced to Aaliyah. She has been allocated $3,000 more book loss ($22,667) than tax loss ($19,667). Just as in the sale at a book and tax loss, Aaliyah has in effect borne $3,000 of her built-in gain on the plant by receiving an allocation of tax depreciation that is $3,000 less than her allocation of book depreciation.

———————

8.1.1   Clara, Dyson, Ellie and Frank organize Waves LLC, a limited liability company treated as a partnership for tax purposes, to continue and expand Clara's business of designing and manufacturing surfboards. Clara contributes her inventory and accounts receivable and the partnership assumes her $10,000 of accounts payable. Dyson contributes a small building near the beach where the partnership will install its workshop. Ellie contributes cash and Frank contributes appreciated stock that the partnership will use as an additional source of funds. Under the partnership agreement, each partner is allocated 25% of book income and loss. The adjusted bases and initial fair market values of the contributed assets are reflected on the partnership's opening balance sheet, which is as follows:

Assets			Liabilities		
	Tax	**Book**		**Tax**	**Book**
Cash	$ 80,000	$ 80,000	Payables	$ 0	$ 10,000
Receivables	0	30,000			
Inventory	60,000	60,000	**Capital**		
Building	40,000	80,000	Clara	60,000	80,000
Stock	50,000	80,000	Dyson	40,000	80,000
			Ellie	80,000	80,000
			Frank	50,000	80,000
Total Assets	$230,000	$330,000	**Total Liabilities and Capital**	$230,000	$330,000

(The somewhat odd treatment of the accounts payable as liabilities on the partnership's opening balance sheet is discussed in the Answer to Question 8.1.5.) The partnership and all the partners use the cash method and a calendar year. The partnership has not elected a section 704(c) method. Soon after the partnership's formation, it sells the stock, as planned, for a price that was not planned, $70,000. What book and tax amounts should the partnership allocate to Frank?

   a)   Book, ($2,500); Tax, (2,500)

   b)   Book, ($2,500); Tax, $20,000

   c)   Book, ($2,500); Tax, $30,000

   d)   Book, ($10,000); Tax, $20,000

8.1.2   At the formation of Waves LLC, Frank has a book-tax difference of $30,000. What is this difference immediately following the partnership's sale of stock for $70,000?

   a) $0

   b) $7,500

   c) $10,000

d) $30,000

8.1.3   What book and tax amounts should the partnership allocate to Dyson on the sale of the stock for $70,000?

a)   Book, ($2,500); Tax, $0

b)   Book, ($2,500); Tax, ($2,500)

c)   Book, ($2,500); Tax, $20,000

d)   Book, ($10,000); Tax, $20,000

8.1.4   At the formation of Waves LLC, Dyson has a book-tax difference of $40,000. What is this difference immediately following the partnership's sale of stock for $70,000?

a) $0

b) $37,500

c) $40,000

d) $42,500

8.1.5   *Read section 704(c)(3) before answering this Question.* In due course, the partnership collects all $30,000 of the accounts receivable contributed by Clara and pays off all $10,000 of the accounts payable it assumed from her. What is the amount of taxable income allocated to Clara from these collections and payments?

a)   ($2,500) ordinary loss

b) $5,000 ordinary income

c) $20,000 ordinary income

d) $27,500 ordinary income

8.1.6   How does Dyson's book-tax difference change as a result of the partnership's collection of the $30,000 accounts receivable and payment of the $10,000 accounts payable?

a)   Increases by $5,000

b)   No change

c)   Decreases by $5,000

d)   Decreases by $10,000

8.1.7   The partnership depreciates the building over a 20-year period and for the first four years claims aggregate book depreciation of $16,000 and aggregate tax depreciation of $8,000. What amounts of depreciation does the partnership allocate to Dyson for these four years?

a)   Book, $4,000; Tax, $0

b)   Book, $4,000; Tax, $2,000

c)   Book, $4,000; Tax, ($4,000) (*i.e.*, $4,000 taxable ordinary income)

d)   Book, $16,000; Tax, $8,000

8.1.8   How does Dyson's book-tax difference change as a result of this depreciation?

   a)   No change

   b)   Decreases by $2,000

   c)   Decreases by $4,000

   d)   Decreases by $8,000

8.1.9   At the beginning of year 5, Waves LLC sells its building to move to larger quarters. The sale price is $140,000. Immediately prior to the sale, the partnership's balance sheet looks like this, assuming unrealistically that the partnership has had no profit or loss from operations during this period:

Assets			Liabilities		
	Tax	**Book**		**Tax**	**Book**
Inventory	$ 60,000	$ 60,000	[None]	$ 0	$ 0
Building	32,000	64,000			
Assets acquired with initial cash and proceeds from other asset sales and net collections	170,000	170,000			
			Capital		
			Clara	77,334	73,500
			Dyson	40,000	73,500
			Ellie	77,333	73,500
			Frank	67,333	73,500
Total Assets	$262,000	$294,000	**Total Liabilities and Capital**	$262,000	$294,000

The partnership realizes a book gain of $76,000 and a tax gain of $108,000 on the sale of its building. What book and tax gains does it allocate to Dyson?

   a)   Book, $0; Tax, $32,000

   b)   Book, $0; Tax, $33,500

   c)   Book, $19,000; Tax, $51,000

   d)   Book, $19,000; Tax, $52,500

8.2   SECTION 704(c) METHODS

When you first hear it, the ceiling rule seems self-evident. How can a partnership allocate more income, gain, loss or deduction than it has? If Gabriella contributes property with $400 of built-in gain to a partnership, which the partnership later sells, recognizing a tax gain of $300, but a book loss of $100, due to a post-contribution decline in the value of the property, the partnership will of course allocate all $300 of tax gain to Gabriella. But the other $100 of built-in gain has disappeared through no fault of Gabriella's—and certainly not as the result of some nefarious tax plan to shift that gain to another partner. How can section 704(c)(1)(A) require the allocation to Gabriella of gain that is no longer there?

The answer is, it does not. Partnerships and partners generally are free to apply the ceiling rule, if they do so consistently. Not everyone is happy about that. Topping the list of unhappy people are Gabriella's partners. They have suffered a real loss on account of the decline in value of the asset that Gabriella contributed—on the partnership's balance sheet, the $100 book loss is allocated in part to each of them, as well as to Gabriella. Yet none of Gabriella's partners has received an allocation of tax loss to match their shares of this book loss. Instead, Gabriella has been allocated 100% of this tax loss, a benefit she has received in the form of a lesser allocation of gain, relative to the original built-in gain.

Many tax-policy thinkers are unhappy too. They argue that the contribution of appreciated property to a partnership is plainly a realization event for tax purposes, although the gain is not recognized currently under section 721(a). The ceiling rule expands the role (or effect) of section 721(a) beyond deferral of a fixed amount of gain to a complex tax-sharing arrangement. Assume, for example, that the partnership agreement allocates Gabriella 25% of book gain and loss. She has:

- ✓   A 25% interest in tax gain arising from appreciation in the value of her property after contribution. (There is no ceiling rule issue here, where there is both book gain and tax gain.)

- ✓   A 100% interest in tax loss (lesser tax gain, from her perspective) arising from any decline in the value of the property, up to $400, at which point the sale would produce no tax gain. (The ceiling rule applies in this region, where there is book loss and tax gain.)

- ✓   A 0% interest in tax loss arising from the next $1,200 decline in value, all of which is allocated to the noncontributing partners. (The ceiling rule continues to apply in this region, where the noncontributing partners are allocated all of the tax loss, but it is less than their 75% share of the book loss. Once the tax loss equals 75% of the book loss, the ceiling rule ceases to apply.)

- ✓   A 25% interest in all tax loss thereafter.

Gabriella's partners are in the mirror position. None of the tax allocations affect their capital accounts or the amounts that the partners will receive on liquidation of their partnership interests. None of the tax allocations, in other words, have substantial economic effect. But they certainly affect the partners' respective tax liabilities. So, the ceiling rule actually is a device to shift tax gains and losses—whether you think it is nefarious is up to you.

In 1993 and 1994, the IRS issued proposed and temporary regulations intended to give partnerships greater flexibility in making allocations under section 704(c). As finalized, these regulations describe three allocation methods, while noting that other methods may also be acceptable if they are reasonable and consistent with the purpose of section 704(c). The regulations dub the method reviewed in Topic 8.1—the only method that had been described in regulations up to that time—the "traditional" method. The two new methods are the "traditional method with curative allocations" and the "remedial method." These methods provide partnerships with the tools to minimize or avoid the effects of the ceiling rule, if they elect to use them. Partnerships are free to use whichever method they choose, subject to the general condition of reasonableness. *See* Topic 8.3. A partnership may use different methods with respect to different items of contributed property, although once the partnership chooses a method for an item of contributed property, the partnership and its partners must continue to apply that method consistently to that item. *See generally* Treas. Reg. § 1.704–3(a).

Remedial method

Of the two new methods, the remedial method is more straightforward, although it is also more revolutionary. It goes like this. First, apply the traditional method, just as we have learned it (with one exception relating to the computation of book depreciation, to which we will return shortly). Then, see if the ceiling rule applies—*i.e.*, whether there is enough tax gain or loss to be able to allocate an amount of tax gain or loss equal to the amount of book gain or loss allocated to each of the noncontributing partners. If the ceiling rule does not apply, there is no need for remedial allocations. If, however, there is insufficient tax gain or loss, remedial allocations bridge the gap. A partnership using the remedial method simply allocates tax (not book) gain or loss to the noncontributing partners as needed to make up the deficit and allocates the same aggregate tax amount (with the opposite sign) to the contributing partner. Done.

Assume Gabriella's partnership elects to apply the remedial method to its sale of the property she contributed. As before, the partnership realizes $100 of book loss on that sale. It allocates $25 of the book loss to Gabriella and $75 to the other partners and all $300 of tax gain to Gabriela, following the traditional method. It then makes a remedial allocation of $75 of tax loss to the other partners in the aggregate and $75 of tax gain to Gabriella. If the partnership's gain on the sale of Gabriella's property is capital gain, these remedial allocations are capital gain and loss.

Points to remember about remedial allocations:

✓ Remedial allocations do not depend on the partnership actually realizing the items subject to the allocation. Remedial items are "notional" tax items created solely for making remedial allocations. There are no corresponding book items. Remedial items do not affect the partners' book capital accounts.

✓ Remedial allocations to all partners must sum to zero (counting remedial losses and deductions as negative remedial income and gains).

✓ A remedial allocation must have the same tax attributes (character, source, etc.) as the item limited by the ceiling rule, the effect of which the remedial allocation corrects. If, for example, the ceiling rule limits an allocation of tax depreciation on the contributed property, the remedial allocations to the noncontributing partners must have the same tax attributes as depreciation on such property and the offsetting remedial allocation to the contributing partner must be of income of the type produced by such property.

✓ Remedial items are taken into account by the partners like actual tax items. They affect the partners' taxable income, tax capital accounts and outside bases.

✓ Remedial items do not affect the computation of the partnership's taxable income or the partnership's adjusted basis in any asset.

✓ Because the remedial method involves the creation of notional tax items, the IRS does not believe it has authority to force partnerships to use this method and it has undertaken not to do so, even if the partnership's chosen method is unreasonable.

See generally Treas. Reg. § 1.704–3(d).

The remedial method requires a special computation of book depreciation. Rather than the usual rule of Treas. Reg. § 1.704–1(b)(2)(iv)(g)(3), which determines book depreciation simply by applying the tax depreciation method and recovery period to the book value of an asset, the remedial method requires that the book value be divided into two pieces. The first, equal to the tax basis of the asset, is depreciated using the tax method and period. The second, equal to the excess, if any, of the book value of the asset over its tax basis, is depreciated like newly acquired property. Treas. Reg. § 1.704–3(d)(2). The total amount of book depreciation is unchanged by this computation, but its pattern over time is changed, relative to that which would be computed using the tax depreciation method and period. For properties whose book value exceeds their adjusted tax basis (*i.e.*, built-in gain properties), book depreciation under the remedial method is smaller in the early years and larger in the later years than that which would be computed using the tax depreciation method and period. For built-in gain properties, book depreciation under the remedial method continues for a longer period than tax depreciation. Questions 8.2.4 and 8.2.5 explore the application of this rule.

Traditional method with curative allocations

A curative allocation is an allocation of a tax item that differs from the allocation of the corresponding book item. *See generally* Treas. Reg. § 1.704–3(c). After applying the traditional method and finding that the ceiling rule applies to an allocation, a partnership that has elected to use the traditional method with curative allocations may allocate some other tax item or items differently than the corresponding book item or items in an effort to correct the distortion caused by the ceiling rule. Under Treas. Reg. § 1.704–3(c)(3)(iii)(A), an acceptable curative allocation must be expected to have substantially the same effect on each partner's tax liability as the item limited by the ceiling rule. An exception is gain on the sale of depreciable property, which may be allocated so as to correct the effect of a ceiling-rule limitation on the allocation of the depreciation on that property. Treas. Reg. § 1.704–3(c)(3)(iii)(B).

If Gabriella's partnership elects to apply the traditional method with curative allocations, the initial question is whether it has any other gains or losses for the year (which must be capital if that is the character of the partnership's gain on the sale of the property Gabriella contributed). Such gains or losses can arise from the disposition of either a contributed property or a property that is not a contributed property. The key is that any such gain or loss must have equal book and tax components that would otherwise be allocated under section 704(b).

If the partnership has such items, it must allocate the book gain or loss in accordance with the partnership agreement and section 704(b). It may allocate the corresponding tax gain or loss differently—this is the curative allocation. If the partnership has a capital loss, for example, it may allocate its tax loss so as to achieve an allocation of $100 more tax loss than book loss to the noncontributing partners as a group and $100 less tax loss than book loss to Gabriella. If the partnership has a capital gain instead, it may allocate its tax gain so as to achieve an allocation of $100 less tax gain than book gain to the noncontributing partners as a group and $100 more tax gain than book gain to Gabriella.

If the partnership has insufficient capital gain or loss to offset entirely the effect of the ceiling rule in the year of sale, it may still make curative allocations of whatever capital gain or loss it has. Curative allocations may be made in future years to "finish the job" if they are provided for in the partnership agreement in effect for the year of the contribution. Treas. Reg. § 1.704–3(c)(3)(ii). (A further requirement that the curative allocations must be made over a reasonable period of time is not relevant in the case of a ceiling-rule distortion that arises from the sale of contributed property. *See* Topic 8.3.)

It should be evident that the choice of section 704(c) method is a subject for negotiation among the partners. As the contributor of property with built-in gain, Gabriella can be expected to prefer the traditional method, because the ceiling rule in effect allocates to her all of the tax losses on the sale of the contributed property up to the amount of the built-in gain. The other partners can be expected to prefer anything but. The remedial method is likely to be their first choice, because it guarantees them their tax losses, should the value of Gabriella's property decline, regardless of the existence of any other partnership gain or loss. When the contributed property is depreciable, on the other hand, curative allocations are likely to be larger than remedial allocations in the early years, because the computation of book depreciation is not subject to the special rule applicable to the remedial method. Indeed, there are situations where curative allocations would be permitted, even though remedial allocations would not, as illustrated by Questions 8.2.5 and 8.2.6. Then again, curative allocations will be smaller than remedial allocations in later years. And curative allocations cannot be made at all, unless the partnership generates book and tax items of the required type to make them. You can see why the partners need to come to this negotiating session equipped with spreadsheets and a crystal ball.

8.2.1   Ava, Bella and Cora form a general partnership. The partnership agreement provides that each of these three individuals has an equal, one-third interest in profits and losses. Cora contributes land, Bella cash and Ava some used equipment. The partnership uses Bella's cash to purchase an investment asset. After this purchase, the partnership's balance sheet is as follows:

Assets			**Liabilities**		
	Tax	**Book**		**Tax**	**Book**
Equipment	$ 400,000	$ 750,000	[None]	$ 0	$ 0
Investment Asset	750,000	750,000			
Land	350,000	750,000	**Capital**		
			Ava	400,000	750,000
			Bella	750,000	750,000
			Cora	350,000	750,000
Total Assets	$1,500,000	$2,250,000	**Total Liabilities and Capital**	$1,500,000	$2,250,000

The partnership sells its land for $600,000. If it elects to apply the remedial method, what is the remedial allocation to Cora from this sale?

a) Taxable ordinary income, $100,000; Book income, $0

b) Tax gain, $100,000; Book gain, $0

c) Tax gain, $100,000; Book gain, $100,000

d) Tax gain, $350,000; Book loss $50,000

8.2.2   Now assume that the partnership has adopted the traditional method with curative allocations. In addition to selling its land for $600,000, it sells its investment asset for $900,000. If it chooses to use the latter sale to make curative allocations, what is the curative allocation of tax gain to Cora?

a) $0

b) $100,000

c) $150,000

d) $400,000

8.2.3 Same as Question 8.2.2, except that, in addition to selling its land for $600,000, the partnership sells the investment asset for $600,000. What is the curative allocation to Cora?

a) Tax loss, $0

b) Tax gain, $50,000

c) Book loss, $50,000

d) Cannot use this sale for curative allocations

8.2.4 *Read section 168(i)(7) before answering this Question.* The partnership in Question 8.2.1 sells no assets, but it does claim depreciation on its equipment and earns income from operation of the equipment. Assume for simplicity that the equipment is depreciable on a straight-line basis over 10 years with 5 years remaining at the time of Ava's contribution, that the property's remaining economic life is approximately five years, and that the partnership is entitled to a full year's depreciation in the year of contribution and each year thereafter. For purposes of the remedial method, what is the amount of the book depreciation for the first year?

a) $75,000

b) $80,000

c) $115,000

d) $150,000

8.2.5 If the partnership elects to apply the remedial method, what is the remedial allocation to Ava in the first year?

a) Taxable ordinary income, $0

b) Taxable ordinary loss, $3,333

c) Taxable ordinary income, $20,000

d) Taxable ordinary loss, $10,000

8.2.6 If the partnership instead elects to apply the traditional method with curative allocations and chooses to use $105,000 of operating income to correct distortions caused by the ceiling rule, what is the curative allocation of operating income to Ava in the first year?

a) Taxable income, $0

b) Taxable income, $25,000

c)   Taxable income, $35,000

d)   Taxable income, $55,000

8.3   UNREASONABLE SECTION 704(c) METHODS

The most basic rule regarding section 704(c) methods is that a partnership can employ any reasonable method that is consistent with the purpose of section 704(c). Treas. Reg. § 1.704–3(a)(1) (third sentence). The three methods that are described in the Treasury regulations are not always or necessarily reasonable and there are other methods (or variations or extensions) that may be reasonable under the circumstances. Because a partnership is generally free to use different methods for different items of contributed property, it is possible for the partnership's combination of methods to be unreasonable, even though each method, taken separately or applied consistently to all items of property, would be just fine.

"Any reasonable method that is consistent with the purpose of section 704(c)." This language seems to say that there is a class of reasonable methods, which can be determined by the application of some knowable standards, only some of which are consistent with the purpose of section 704(c) and therefore permissible. Read as a whole, however, Treas. Reg. § 1.704–3 suggests a different interpretation. The standard for determining whether a chosen method is reasonable appears to be whether it is consistent with the purpose of section 704(c). That purpose, as interpreted by the Treasury regulations, is to prevent the shifting of tax consequences among partners with respect to precontribution gain or loss. Treas. Reg. § 1.704–3(a)(1) (first sentence). This interpretation is confirmed by Treas. Reg. § 1.704–3(a)(10)(i):

> An allocation method (or combination of methods) is not reasonable if the contribution of property . . . and the corresponding allocation of tax items with respect to the property are made with a view to shifting the tax consequences of built-in gain or loss among the partners in a manner that substantially reduces the present value of the partners' aggregate tax liability.

A word of caution. These general principles may lead you to conclusions that are incorrect. For example, one operating rule that you could infer from the language quoted above is that any section 704(c) method that results in a lower aggregate tax liability than other available methods is *per se* unreasonable. That inference is explicitly rejected by the Treasury regulations. Treas. Reg. § 1.704–3(a)(1) (fifth sentence). An allocation method is not necessarily unreasonable merely because another method would result in a higher aggregate tax liability. A partnership's choice, for example, of the traditional method over the remedial method will have one tax effect on the contributing partner and an opposite tax effect on the noncontributing partners and, depending on their respective tax profiles and post-contribution developments, this choice may end up reducing the partners' aggregate tax liability. The IRS is not interested in second-guessing the partnership's choice of method solely on that basis. If, however, the facts suggest that the reduction in aggregate tax liability was a substantial, intended and predictable consequence of the choice of the traditional method, then reasonableness will be a concern.

Treas. Reg. § 1.704-3(a)(1) provides that the purpose of section 704(c) is to "prevent" the shifting of built-in gain or loss. You might infer from this statement that any section 704(c) method that is less successful than another available method in accomplishing that goal is *per se* unreasonable. This, too, is incorrect. As should be clear from the review of methods in Topic 8.2, the remedial method is the only method that "prevents" such shifting, so this interpretation would render unreasonable all other methods. This is plainly not the intent of the Treasury regulations, which describe the traditional method and the traditional method with curative allocations as "generally reasonable." Treas. Reg. § 1.704–3(a)(1) (sixth sentence). Thus the ceiling rule, for all its faults, is generally okay—but not when its application results in a substantial, intended and predictable shifting of built-in gain or loss.

It is not necessary for the IRS to prove that a partnership's allocation method has actually produced a reduction in aggregate tax liability in order to find that the method is unreasonable. Statements and examples in the Treasury regulations suggest that, in order to be reasonable, a section 704(c) method must produce allocations that are reasonable in amount, in "type," and in timing.

Reasonable in amount. Allocations of tax items under section 704(c) must not exceed those needed to prevent the shifting of built-in gain. Allocations of tax items to the noncontributing partners should not exceed their allocations of book items. Say, for example, that Owen and Terrill form the OT Partnership. Owen contributes nondepreciable property worth $1,000 with an adjusted basis of $300. Terrill contributes $1,000 cash. If the partnership later sells the property for $1,400, recognizing a book gain of $400, the partnership should not allocate Terrill more than $200 of tax gain, which equals Terrill's share of the book gain. Doing so would shift a portion of Owen's built-in gain to Terrill.

If, on the other hand, the OT Partnership sells the contributed property for $800, recognizing a book loss of $200, the ceiling rule compels it to allocate Terrill less tax loss ($0) than his share of the book loss ($100). At this point, Owen has recognized less than his original built-in gain of $700. If the partnership elects to make curative allocations from, say, a $400 book and tax loss recognized on the sale of another asset, its allocation of tax loss to Terrill should not exceed his allocation of book loss by more than $100. A larger allocation would be greater than that required to offset the effect of the ceiling rule and would cause Owen in effect to recognize more than the amount of his original built-in gain:

FIGURE 8.3.1

	Owen		Terrill	
	Tax	Book	Tax	Book
Initial	$ 300	$1,000	$1,000	$1,000
Property sale	500	(100)	0	(100)
Subtotal	800	900	1,000	900
Reasonable curative allocation	(100)	(200)	(300)	(200)
Ending	$ 700	$ 700	$ 700	$ 700

FIGURE 8.3.2

	Owen		Terrill	
	Tax	Book	Tax	Book
Initial	$ 300	$1,000	$1,000	$1,000
Property sale	500	(100)	0	(100)
Subtotal	800	900	1,000	900
Unreasonable curative allocation	(0)	(200)	(400)	(200)
Ending	$ 800	$ 700	$ 600	$ 700

Owen is allocated $500 of tax gain on the sale and receives no tax loss to match his $100 allocation of book loss, thereby effectively recognizing another $100 of the built-in gain, for a total of $600. The reasonable curative allocation in Figure 8.3.1 gives Owen $100 less tax loss than book loss, thereby causing him, in effect, to recognize the final $100 of his built-in gain. The unreasonable curative allocation in Figure 8.3.2 gives Owen $200 less tax loss than book loss, causing him to recognize, in effect, $200 of tax gain, overshooting his built-in gain by $100.

Do not miss the forest for the trees here. Before you starting reading this essay, you probably would have said that the unreasonable curative allocation in Figure 8.3.2 is "wrong." By that, you would have meant that the partnership has allocated too much tax loss to Terrill and too little to Owen.

The Treasury regulations would not disagree with you, but they would use a different word. Under the regulations, the allocation shown in Figure 8.3.2 not reasonable, because it is in the wrong amount to carry out the purpose of section 704(c).

Reasonable in "type." To be reasonable, a curative allocation must be expected to have substantially the same effect on each partner's tax liability as the tax item limited by the ceiling rule. Treas. Reg. § 1.704–3(c)(iii)(A). This is the basis for saying that, if the item limited by the ceiling rule is a capital gain for tax purposes, the curative allocation must also consist of capital gain (or loss). This requirement extends beyond character, narrowly construed, to encompass any characteristic or quality of a tax item that may be expected to affect a partner's tax liability. Treas. Reg. § 1.704–3(c)(iii)(A) contains further examples. This requirement applies to any section 704(c) method that involves the allocation of realized tax items to offset ceiling-rule limitations. Similarly, reasonable remedial allocations must have the same tax attributes as the tax items limited by the ceiling rule. Treas. Reg. § 1.704–3(d)(3).

Reasonable in timing. The timing concern involves contributed property that is depreciable for book purposes over a short recovery period—specifically, a recovery period significantly shorter than the economic life of the property remaining when the property is contributed to the partnership. In this case, the book depreciation on the contributed property overstates the actual decline in its value. This sets the stage for two different kinds of mischief.

First, let's assume that the property Owen contributes to the OT Partnership is depreciable over the five years following its contribution (for both book and tax purposes). If the partnership adopts the traditional method, its allocations of tax depreciation will be ceiling-limited. If the partnership sells the property at the beginning of year 6 for its book value of $0, Owen will succeed in shifting $200 of his original built-in gain to Terrill, courtesy of the ceiling rule:

FIGURE 8.3.3

	Owen		Terrill	
	Tax	Book	Tax	Book
Initial	$300	$1,000	$1,000	$1,000
Five years of depreciation	0	(500)	(300)	(500)
Subtotal	300	500	700	500
Sale of property	0	0	0	0
Ending	$300	$ 500	$ 700	$ 500

Owen will continue to enjoy this benefit until he liquidates his partnership interest.

But what if the book depreciation mis-measures the decline in value of this property? If the partnership sells the property in year 6 for its initial $1,000 value, its book and tax gain will be $1,000. There will be no section 704(c) allocation on this sale, because the property's book-tax difference will have been eliminated by the depreciation.

FIGURE 8.3.4

	Owen		Terrill	
	Tax	Book	Tax	Book
Initial	$300	$1,000	$1,000	$1,000
Five years of depreciation	0	(500)	(300)	(500)
Subtotal	300	500	700	500
Sale of property	500	500	500	500
Ending	$800	$1,000	$1,200	$1,000

In Figure 8.3.3, Owen's gain-shifting is merely that allowed by the ceiling rule—the result is no different than if the partnership had received nondepreciable property from Owen and sold it for $0. In Figure 8.3.4, however, the property actually did not decline in value at all. If the partnership had received nondepreciable property from Owen and sold it for $1,000, he would have been allocated the entire amount of his original built-in gain of $700. The application of the ceiling rule to the (economically) overstated depreciation created a gain-shifting opportunity out of thin air.

In such a case, the IRS is likely to assert that the use of the traditional method is unreasonable, particularly if it reduces the aggregate tax liability of the partners. An example suggests that the OT Partnership could use the traditional method if it supplemented it with a requirement that Owen be allocated tax gain from the sale of the property in sufficient amount (here, an additional $200) to offset the effect of the ceiling rule. Treas. Reg. § 1.704–3(b)(2), example (2).

We can use the same facts to illustrate a second "timing" issue. Assume that the OT Partnership elects to use the traditional method with curative allocations. For this purpose, the partnership allocates $400 of taxable operating income all to Owen, while splitting the corresponding book income equally between the two partners:

FIGURE 8.3.5

	Owen		Terrill	
	Tax	Book	Tax	Book
Initial	$300	$1,000	$1,000	$1,000
Five years of depreciation	0	(500)	(300)	(500)
Subtotal	300	500	700	500
Curative allocation of operating income	400	200	0	200
Ending	$700	$ 700	$ 700	$ 700

In this case, the partnership has allocated $400 of taxable operating income to Owen and none to Terrill, causing Owen effectively to recognize his entire original built-in gain of $700 (although not as capital gain), even though the partnership still owns the property that he contributed. This would be an unexceptional example of curative allocations, if the contributed property were actually worthless at the end of the depreciation period. If it is not, however, the curative allocations accelerate Owen's recognition of the built-in gain and create an opportunity to shift operating income from Terrill to Owen.

In such a case, the IRS is likely to assert that the use of the traditional method with curative allocations is unreasonable, particularly if it reduces the aggregate tax liability of the partners. An example in the Treasury regulations suggests that the OT Partnership could salvage its curative allocations by agreeing to spread them over the remaining economic life (rather than the depreciable life) of the contributed property. Treas. Reg. § 1.704–3(c)(4), example (3).

As these examples demonstrate, determining whether an allocation relating to the depreciation of contributed property is reasonable in timing requires you to take into account the remaining economic life of the property at the time of its contribution. The focus of this inquiry is on the expected decline in the actual value of the property. For this reason, the remaining economic life of the property is probably not its remaining recovery period under the MACRS depreciation system and may not be the MACRS recovery period for newly purchased property in the same class as the contributed property.

Conceptually, remedial allocations could be subject to the same "timing" challenge as traditional and curative allocations. The calculation of book depreciation under the remedial method corrects most of the problem, however, because the excess of the fair market value of contributed property over its adjusted tax basis (which is the portion of the book value that can create a ceiling rule limitation) is recovered over the MACRS recovery period applicable to newly purchased property. Treas. Reg. § 1.704–3(d)(2). This reduces the excess of book depreciation over tax depreciation in the early years, thereby decreasing the chance that remedial allocations will be necessary and reducing their size if they are. Probably for this reason, the Treasury regulations do not contain an example of the remedial method raising a "timing" problem.

8.3.1   Edison and Franklin form a partnership. Edison contributes depreciable property with a value of $9,000 and an adjusted basis in her hands of $6,000 in exchange for a two-thirds interest in the partnership. Franklin contributes cash of $4,500 for a one-third interest. Edison's equipment is depreciable on a straight-line basis over 10 years, with five years remaining at the time of her contribution. Assume, as always in these Questions, that the partnership takes a full year of book and tax depreciation on the equipment in its first year of ownership and in every year thereafter. The partnership elects to apply the traditional method and in the first year allocates $1,200 of book depreciation and $0 of tax depreciation to Edison. The partnership's allocation method is:

a)   Reasonable. It is the traditional method.

b)   Unreasonable. It ignores the application of the ceiling rule, which is part of the traditional method.

c)   Reasonable. Although the partnership's allocation method does not follow the traditional method, it eliminates Edison's book-tax difference as quickly as possible, and therefore is consistent with the purpose of section 704(c).

d)   Unreasonable. It creates a book-tax difference for Franklin, the noncontributing partner.

8.3.2   *Read Treas. Reg. § 1.704–3(d)(5) before answering this Question.* Same facts as Question 8.3.1, but the partnership instead allocates $1,000 of book depreciation and $700 of tax depreciation to Edison. It then allocates $700 notional ordinary income to Edison and $700 notional ordinary loss to Franklin. The partnership's allocation method is:

a)   Reasonable. It is the remedial method.

b)   Unreasonable. The allocation required to correct the distortion caused by the ceiling rule is only $600, so the partnership's $700 allocation is unreasonably large.

c)   Reasonable. Although the partnership's method does not follow the remedial method, it eliminates Edison's book-tax difference as quickly as possible, and therefore is consistent with the purpose of section 704(c).

d) Unreasonable. The creation of notional tax items is prohibited, except under the remedial method.

8.3.3 *Read Treas. Reg. § 1.704–3(c)(3)(ii) before answering this Question.* Same facts (other than partnership allocations) as Question 8.3.1, but Edison's adjusted basis in the equipment is $1,500. Assume that the remaining economic life of the equipment is approximately five years at the time of its contribution. In its first year of operations, the partnership's business generates $750 of book income, which is taxable as ordinary income. In its second year, it makes $1,050. Pursuant to the partnership agreement, the partnership makes curative allocations to Edison of all of its ordinary taxable income for both years. The partnership's allocation method is:

a) Reasonable. These are permissible curative allocations.

b) Unreasonable. These curative allocations are not made over a reasonable period of time.

c) Unreasonable. The curative allocation of taxable income in the second year is intended to correct the ceiling-rule distortion that arose in the first year. That is not permissible.

d) Reasonable. Although these allocations are not permitted under the traditional method with curative allocations, they fully correct the ceiling-rule distortions that arise in the first two years and therefore are consistent with the purpose of section 704(c).

8.3.4 Same facts as Question 8.3.3, except that the remaining economic life of the property is approximately 25 years at the time of its contribution. The partnership's allocation method is:

a) Reasonable. These are permissible curative allocations.

b) Unreasonable. These curative allocations are not made over a reasonable period of time.

c) Unreasonable. The allocation of taxable income in the second year is intended to correct the ceiling-rule distortion that arose in the first year. This is not permissible.

d) Reasonable. Although these allocations are not permitted under the traditional method with curative allocations, they fully correct the ceiling-rule distortions that arise in the first two years and therefore are consistent with the purpose of section 704(c).

8.3.5 Same facts as Question 8.3.1 (other than partnership allocations), but Edison's adjusted basis in the equipment is $1,500. Assume that the remaining economic life of the equipment is approximately five years at the time of its contribution. The partnership invests Franklin's cash contribution in a capital asset, which it sells during the first year for a book and tax gain of $900. Pursuant to its agreement, the partnership makes a curative allocation of all of the tax gain to Edison. The partnership's allocation method is:

a) Reasonable. This is the traditional method with curative allocations.

b) Unreasonable. Although the allocations are permissible in amount, they are of the wrong character.

c) Unreasonable. These curative allocations are not made over a reasonable period of time.

d) Reasonable. Although these allocations are not permitted under the traditional method with curative allocations, they are consistent with the purpose of section 704(c), because the partnership has no other available income or gain with which to correct the distortion caused by the ceiling rule.

8.3.6   *Read Treas. Reg. § 1.704–3(c)(3)(iii)(B) before answering this Question.* Same facts as Question 8.3.1, but Edison's adjusted basis in the equipment is $1,500. Assume that the remaining economic life of the equipment is approximately 25 years at the time of its contribution. On the first day of year 2, the partnership sells the equipment contributed by Edison, recognizing a book and tax gain of $900. Pursuant to its agreement, the partnership makes a curative allocation of all of the tax gain to Edison. The partnership's allocation method is:

a) Reasonable. This is the traditional method with curative allocations.

b) Unreasonable. Although the allocations are permissible in amount, they are of the wrong character.

c) Unreasonable. These curative allocations are not made over a reasonable period of time.

d) Reasonable. Although these allocations are not permitted under the traditional method with curative allocations, they are consistent with the purpose of section 704(c), because the partnership has no other available income or gain with which to correct the distortion caused by the ceiling rule.

8.4   BUILT-IN LOSS ASSETS: SECTION 704(c)(1)(C)

It seems like every time you and I are having a good talk about partnership tax, we turn around and there's section 704(c)(1)(C) trying to butt his way into our conversation. I remember when we were talking about how to determine a partnership's initial basis in a contributed asset—it was in Topic 2.2 and we were really just getting to know each other—and I said that the partnership's basis equals the contributor's basis, like it has since the beginning of time. Then section 704(c)(1)(C) piped up and said that, since he arrived in town, a partnership's initial basis in a contributed asset cannot be any higher than its fair market value on the date of contribution. In Topic 2.3, we had to listen to how section 704(c)(1)(C) affects something as basic as the determination of a partner's tax capital. In that discussion, I made the innocent observation that a contributing partner's tax capital is her share of the inside basis of the partnership's properties, if the partnership has no liabilities—and there was section 704(c)(1)(C) spouting off about how you really have to add the section 704(c)(1)(C) basis adjustment, if there is one, to make that statement true. In Topic 6.6 we gave section 704(c)(1)(C) the floor and learned about where he came from and why he had moved into town and, after all that, we still weren't sure what he's doing here.

Now that we're talking about section 704(c), it's only natural that section 704(c)(1)(C) would feel that he has to make another appearance. And sure enough, here he is. He heard us talking about section 704(c) allocation methods and came right over. In a nutshell, what he has to say is this: as interpreted by the Treasury regulations proposed in 2014, section 704(c)(1)(C) makes the remedial method mandatory for all assets contributed to a partnership with built-in loss.

It makes sense if you think about it. Take it in two steps. First, under section 704(c)(1)(C)(ii), the partnership's initial basis for a built-in loss asset is the asset's fair market value at the time of contribution. Prop. Treas. Reg. § 1.704–3(f)(3)(ii)(A). Thus, such an asset has no book-tax difference and no allocations are required or permitted under section 704(c)(1)(A). Although the built-in loss is entirely excluded from the operation of section 704(c)(1)(A), that is not the end of the story.

The second step in this analysis is to take into account the effect of the section 704(c)(1)(C) basis adjustment provided by Prop. Treas. Reg. § 1.704–3(f)(2)(iii). This basis adjustment is recognized by the contributing partner if and when the partnership sells the loss asset, thereby reducing her share of the gain or increasing her share of the loss recognized by the partnership by an amount equal to the entire amount of the initial built-in loss. Prop. Treas. Reg. § 1.704–3(f)(3)(ii)(C). If the contributed loss asset is depreciable, the basis adjustment is depreciable by the contributing partner under the depreciation method used by the partnership for the contributed asset, thus augmenting her share of the partnership's depreciation by an amount that, in total, equals the entire amount of the initial built-in loss. Prop. Treas. Reg. § 1.704–3(f)(3)(ii)(D).

At the end of the day, every noncontributing partner is allocated taxable income, gain, loss or deduction equal to the book amount allocated to that partner. This is true for the contributing partner as well, because, for the partnership as a whole, there is no difference between the book value and the adjusted tax basis of any contributed loss asset. In addition, the contributing partner recognizes tax loss or deduction equal to the entire excess of the adjusted basis of the contributed property over its fair market value at the time of contribution. These are exactly the same results as the remedial method.

You see why none of the examples in Chapter 8 have involved property contributed to a partnership with a built-in loss. In its heavy-handed way, section 704(c)(1)(C) (or the proposed regulations thereunder) have simply replaced the half of section 704(c)(1)(A) that used to apply to built-in losses with an entirely different approach. Whether this approach is better or worse is a worthy subject for debate, as a matter of both policy (Is it time to kill off the ceiling rule?) and administration (Are special basis adjustments easier to understand or track than book-tax differences? What about after a revaluation?). It seems undebatable, however, that Subchapter K does not need the added complexity of two different systems running in parallel.

It is hard to avoid the conclusion that Congressional rage at tax shelters overflowed in 2004. In enacting section 704(c)(1)(C), Congress accomplished almost nothing to curtail shelters that was not achieved by the amendments to sections 734 and 743 enacted at the same time. It did, however, make Subchapter K even more formidable.

8.5   REVERSE SECTION 704(c) ALLOCATIONS

You are familiar with revaluations from Topic 2.6. As you learned there, revaluations have a history and purpose that have nothing to do with section 704(c). When a partnership revalues all of its book assets, however, consequences under section 704(c) do ensue. This is because such a revaluation (called a "general revaluation" in Topic 2.6) creates or changes book-tax differences for all of the partnership's assets whose fair market value on the revaluation date is different than their book value on that date. The resulting book-tax differences are subject to section 704(c)(1)(A).

The purpose for applying section 704(c) to revaluation gains and losses is to cause the persons who were partners when a change in the value of partnership property occurred to bear the tax consequences of that change. This is similar to the original purpose of section 704(c), which is to cause a partner who contributes property to a partnership to bear the tax consequences of the change in the value of that property prior to the contribution. It is, however, an extension of the original purpose that is by no means dictated by the statute. The application of section 704(c) to revaluation gains and losses has been effectuated entirely by Treasury regulations, unbidden by either statutory change or legislative history.

The terminology in this area is a bit confusing. Logically, there is a need to distinguish a book-tax difference that exists when property is contributed to the partnership from a book-tax difference that arises when the book value of that property is changed by a revaluation. Conventionally, the former difference has been called a "forward section 704(c) layer" and allocations pertaining thereto are known as "forward section 704(c) allocations." A book-tax difference arising from a revaluation is known as a "reverse section 704(c) layer" and the corresponding allocations are "reverse section 704(c) allocations." These naming conventions have made their way into the Treasury regulations, so we are probably not getting rid of them any time soon. Prop. Treas. Reg. §§ 1.704–3(a)(3)(ii), –3(a)(6)(i). There is, however, nothing inverted in the way that reverse section 704(c) allocations operate. With one important exception, they are identical to forward section 704(c) allocations, but they target post-contribution, rather than precontribution, gain or loss.

And what is that exception? Naturally, it is section 704(c)(1)(C). Under the proposed Treasury regulations that would implement that section, it does not apply to revaluations. Thus, under the proposed regulations, a forward section 704(c) layer can only reflect built-in gain, not built-in loss, because the latter is governed by section 704(c)(1)(C), which eliminates the forward layer in the case of a loss asset by setting the partnership's tax basis in the contributed asset equal to its book value. In contrast, a reverse section 704(c) layer can reflect either a gain or a loss, because section 704(c)(1)(C) does not apply.

Taking a step back from all this detail, one thing should be clear. The extension of section 704(c) from forward layers to reverse layers expands the potential reach of the section enormously. An asset can be contributed to a partnership only once. But it can be revalued many times. Thus, while any given partnership asset can only have one forward layer, it can have many reverse layers, each created by a new revaluation. Revaluations are hardly once-in-a-lifetime events. Although they do not occur in connection with a mere transfer of an interest in a partnership, they do occur in connection with any contribution or distribution that changes the interest of any partner by more than a *de minimis* amount. Treas. Reg. §§ 1.704–1(b)(2)(iv)(*f*)(5)(*i*), (*ii*). For securities partnerships, revaluations occur quarterly under generally accepted industry accounting practices. Treas. Reg. § 1.704–1(b)(2)(iv)(*f*)(5)(*v*). Proposed Treasury regulations would allow revaluations to occur on partnership "recapitalizations"—any agreement to change (other than a *de minimis* change) the manner in which the partners share an item of partnership income, gain, loss, deduction or credit. Prop. Treas. Reg. § 1.704–1(b)(2)(iv)(*f*)(5)(*v*). That's a lot of potential revaluations.

This may paint a picture in your mind of section 704(c) slowly swallowing the world of partnership tax. While some embrace this development, others have pushed back in at least three ways. The first, one suspects, is noncompliance. The second, more respectable, effort is a successful lobbying push to allow securities partnerships, which revalue their assets regularly, to aggregate the resulting gains and losses for purposes making reverse section 704(c) allocations. Treas. Reg. § 1.704–3(e)(3). Though important to this industry, this is a specialized rule that we will not consider further.

That brings us to the question of maintaining the separate section 704(c) layers, the third pushback. Let's say that Cephus contributes to a partnership an asset that has an adjusted basis in his hands of $250 and a value of $750. This creates a forward section 704(c) gain layer of $500. Later, when a new partner joins the partnership, the book value of the asset is revalued to $1,000, creating a reverse section 704(c) gain layer of $250. Still later, another revaluation resets the book value of the asset to $700. How many layers are there now? One answer is three, a forward gain layer of $500, a reverse gain layer of $250 and a reverse loss layer of $300. But a traditionalist, steeped in the ceiling rule, might argue that there is only one, a forward gain layer of $450, representing the amount of gain that section 704(c) would require the partnership to allocate to Cephus if it sold the asset for its current $700 value.

Some commentators, concerned in part with the growing complexity of the section 704(c) requirements, have urged this latter interpretation on the IRS and Treasury Department. To date, they have not met with success. Proposed Treasury regulations require partnerships to track every section 704(c) layer, forward and reverse, separately from every other layer. These regulations specifically acknowledge that this rule may cause a single asset to have both gain and loss layers. Prop. Treas. Reg. § 1.704–3(a)(6)(i).

A partnership may use different section 704(c) methods for forward and reverse layers in the same asset—for example, using the traditional method for the forward layer in an asset, the traditional method with curative allocations for one reverse layer in that asset, and the remedial method for all other reverse layers. Likewise, a partnership is not required to use the same method for all property each time it undertakes a revaluation. This Mardi Gras of electivity is limited by the constraint that the overall combination of methods must be reasonable. Treas. Reg. § 1.704–3(a)(6).

Let's say that Cephus' partnership has elected to apply the traditional method to all of its section 704(c) layers and sells the asset he contributed for $800, which is $100 more than its value on the latest revaluation. The partnership recognizes a book gain of $100 and a tax gain of $550 on this sale. The partnership allocates its book gain among its current partners in accordance with the partnership agreement and section 704(b). It has a number of different possibilities for allocating its tax gain. (Because the partnership has adopted the traditional method, it will not allocate tax loss to any partner with respect to the reverse loss layer of $300, because it has no tax loss to allocate.) The $500 forward gain layer, the $250 reverse gain layer and the $100 book gain add up to $850—well more than the actual tax gain of $550.

Your first impulse might be to allocate to some or all of the partners an amount of tax gain equal to their share of the $100 book gain, because, as we all know, *tax follows book to the noncontributing partners*. While that maxim is not wrong in this context, it is not very helpful. One problem is figuring out who the noncontributing partners are. Every partner (except Cephus) is a noncontributing partner with respect to one or more of the section 704(c) layers in the asset that Cephus contributed to the partnership. A second problem is that the $100 book gain realized on the sale represents only the increase in the value of the asset since its last revaluation, not its change in value since contribution or any earlier revaluation. For these and other reasons, it is easier to keep track of the various forward and reverse layers directly and allocate them to the appropriate partners on sale.

But how? In the present case, there is $550 tax gain to be allocated to section 704(c) gain layers totaling $750 plus a book gain of $100 (which should be considered another gain layer for purposes of allocating the tax gain). The partnership must find some way to allocate the tax gain among these layers. The proposed regulations say simply that the partnership may use any reasonable method. Prop. Treas. Reg. § 1.704–3(a)(6)(ii). The preamble to the proposed regulations repeats three suggestions made by commenters: (1) allocate tax items to the oldest layer first, (2) allocate tax items to the newest layer first, or (3) allocate tax items among all the layers pro-rata according to the amount in each layer. The Questions explore the application of these different approaches.

8.5.1   Cephus and Dan form the Target Partnership for making speculative investments in land. Cephus contributes land ("Parcel C") worth $750,000 with an adjusted basis of $250,000. Dan contributes $750,000 in cash. Target purchases additional land with the cash that Dan contributed, which does not change in value during the time period considered in these Questions. Parcel C, however, increases in value to $1,000,000, at which point Target receives an offer from Errol to make a cash contribution of $875,000 for a one-third interest. Target revalues its book assets and capital accounts and accepts Errol's contribution, which it continues to hold in cash during the time period considered in these Questions. Shortly thereafter, the partnership receives an offer to sell Parcel C for $1,150,000, which it accepts. Target uses the traditional method for section 704(c) allocations and chooses to allocate tax items to the oldest layer first. What is the tax gain allocated to Cephus on this sale?

     a) $50,000

     b) $125,000

     c) $500,000

     d) $675,000

8.5.2   Same as Question 8.5.1, except that Target sells Parcel C for $850,000. What is the tax gain allocated to Cephus?

     a) $50,000

     b) $500,000

     c) $550,000

     d) $675,000

8.5.3   Same as Question 8.5.2, except that the partnership chooses to allocate tax items to the newest layer first. What is the tax gain allocated to Cephus on the sale of Parcel C?

     a) $50,000

     b) $125,000

    c) $475,000

    d) $550,000

8.5.4   Same as Question 8.5.3, except that the partnership uses the remedial method for section 704(c) allocations. As in Question 8.5.3, the partnership uses a newest-first approach in allocating tax items to section 704(c) layers. What is the remedial allocation to Cephus on the sale of Parcel C?

    a) $0

    b) $100,000

    c) $475,000

    d) $575,000

8.5.5   A proposed development project for Parcel C collapses and its value falls to $700,000. Target receives an offer from Frank to acquire a 25% partnership interest for a cash investment of $775,000. The partnership revalues and takes Frank's cash. Assume for simplicity that the value of all of the partnership's other assets remains unchanged at $1,625,000 (*i.e.*, they have neither appreciated nor depreciated during the period of time the partnership has owned them). Further assume that the partnership uses the traditional method under section 704(c) and chooses to allocate tax items to the oldest layer first. What is the tax gain allocated to Cephus on the sale of Parcel C for $800,000?

    a) $25,000

    b) $325,000

    c) $475,000

    d) $525,000

8.5.6.   Same as Question 8.5.5, except that the partnership uses the remedial method. As in Question 8.5.5, the partnership uses an oldest-first approach in allocating tax items to section 704(c) layers. What is the correct remedial allocation of tax gain to Cephus on the sale of Parcel C?

    a) $0

    b) $25,000

    c) $75,000

    d) $100,000

8.6   NONCOMPENSATORY OPTIONS REVISITED

A "noncompensatory option" is an option issued by a partnership, other than one issued in connection with the performance of services. Treas. Reg. § 1.721–2(f). The most common noncompensatory option is the conversion feature of convertible debt (*i.e.*, debt that may be surrendered to the issuer at the option of the holder in exchange for an equity interest). Convertible debt is often issued by partnerships that cannot afford to pay a high current interest rate on their debt. The addition of a conversion feature reduces the interest rate demanded by the lender, often substantially. The partnership can thereby raise funds at a lower current cash cost, albeit by giving up equity that may turn out in the long run to be far more valuable than the cash interest saved.

In 2013, the Treasury Department issued final regulations on the tax treatment of noncompensatory options. In Topic 2.8, we reviewed some aspects of these regulations, but left for later their significant contribution to section 704(c) policy development. We return to that topic now.

Revaluations

The approach to revaluations taken by the noncompensatory-option regulations is unprecedented—which is not to say that it will not be repeated. It seems to reflect growing confidence on the part of the IRS and the Treasury Department that revaluations are not only appropriate, but necessary, to the maintenance of proper capital accounts.

First, the business background. When we first studied revaluations in Topic 2.6, you were introduced to Puff Unlimited, a partnership in which Peter, Paul and Mary each had equal interests. After prospering for some years, the partnership was approached by Jackie Paper, who offered to contribute money to the partnership in exchange for a 25% interest. Because of the increase in the value of the partnership, Jackie was willing to contribute more (a lot more) than the others had contributed at the beginning, although all were to be equal partners going forward. Jackie's capital account would be relatively too big without a revaluation, and the original partners could be expected to make a revaluation as part of the deal.

Now let's change the story. Instead of making a capital contribution, suppose that Jackie loans money to the partnership at the outset. Jackie obtains a convertible debt instrument, which entitles him to convert his loan into an equity interest in the partnership if he wants, although he can also choose not to convert and receive interest and principal on the loan until it is repaid in full. What are the terms on which Jackie's loan can be converted? Well, that's for Jackie to negotiate with the partnership, but commonly a convertible debt instrument entitles the holder to an equity interest that is somewhat less valuable than the amount of the loan at the outset. (This difference is called a "conversion premium.") The investor (Jackie, in this case) hopes that the equity interest will become more valuable over time, at some point exceeding (perhaps by a lot) the amount of the loan. At that point, or later, the investor will convert. If the hoped-for appreciation in the equity value does not occur, the investor will simply hold the loan to maturity.

In this case, Puff Unlimited does well, and as Jackie's loan approaches maturity he decides to convert. In the conversion he receives, let's assume, a 25% interest that is worth twice the amount of his loan. Absent a revaluation, Jackie's capital account will equal the principal amount of his loan. It is hard to draw a generalized conclusion about the relative size of this capital account. If the partnership has made no revaluations while Jackie's loan was outstanding, Jackie's capital account will be slightly larger than the other partners', reflecting his conversion premium. If there have been intervening revaluations, however, it will be smaller, because prior increases in the value of the partnership's assets will have been captured in the capital accounts of the other partners. Although it is hard to know in advance who will negotiate for a revaluation, it is likely that at least one party will favor making one.

The noncompensatory-option regulations establish two rules for revaluations in this situation. First, the partnership *must* revalue its assets upon the exercise of a noncompensatory option. Second, this revaluation must take place *immediately after* the exercise. Treas. Reg. § 1.704–1(b)(2)(iv)(s). Both of these rules are contrary to those that usually apply to revaluations. And both are in service to the government's ultimate goal, which is that the exercising option holder's capital account reflects her right to share in partnership capital under the partnership agreement as of the exercise (conversion) date. To this end, if the required revaluation is not enough to reach the desired goal, the other partners must shift their book capital to the option holder and the partnership must make something called "corrective allocations" to attend to the book-tax differences that arise from that capital shift. Let's take a look at each of these innovations in turn.

  ✓ *Mandatory revaluation.* As the simple case of Puff Unlimited illustrates, there are economic incentives for partnerships to make revaluations in almost every case that a new partner is admitted to the partnership. Prior to the noncompensatory-option regulations, the IRS and Treasury Department were content to allow these incentives to govern the maintenance of partnership capital accounts—albeit with a strong warning that failures to revalue would be scrutinized. The noncompensatory-option regulations seem to reflect a growing commitment that revaluations are necessary for proper capital-account maintenance and a waning concern for the record-keeping costs of revaluations. Underlying all this is section 704(c). Every revaluation brings with it a new reverse section 704(c) layer. As the government becomes more confident in its apparatus for allocating and taxing such layers, it is natural for it to want to create more of them.

  ✓ *Revaluation immediately after.* If Puff Unlimited revalued in the usual way—that is, immediately before Jackie converts—all of the increase in the value of the partnership's assets would be captured in the capital accounts of the existing partners, Peter, Paul and Mary. Then, when Jackie converts and becomes a partner, the only way for his capital account to reflect his full, 25% interest in the partnership's capital would be to shift capital from the other three partners to him. If, on the other hand, the partnership waits to revalue until after Jackie is in, it is far more likely that there will be sufficient book gain available to set Jackie's opening capital account at the correct amount. Accordingly, one way to understand the requirement to revalue immediately after the exercise, rather than immediately before, is that this approach minimizes the need for capital shifts.

Why would the government want to do that? A practical answer is that, if the revaluation occurred immediately before the conversion, some or all of the book gain allocated to Peter, Paul and Mary would then have to be re-allocated to Jackie. Revaluing immediately after the conversion minimizes the need for this do-over. More fundamentally, Jackie owns a share of this gain through his option contract. Although he is not a partner prior to the conversion, the terms of his convertible debt (in particular, his right to acquire a fixed share of the partnership's equity for a fixed price) give him a right to a share in the appreciation of the partnership's assets just as surely as if he were a partner holding that interest. By revaluing immediately after the conversion, the partnership can allocate to him book gain in the amount necessary to raise his capital account from the amount of his investment (here, the amount of Jackie's loan) to his bargained-for share of the partnership's equity value (here, 25%).

In order to achieve that goal, the partnership allocates the book gain arising from the revaluation first to Jackie in an amount necessary to set his capital account at the appropriate level. It allocates the remaining book gain to the other partners according to their shares under the partnership agreement. Treas. Reg. § 1.704–1(b)(2)(iv)(s)(*2*).

Capital shifts

If revaluing immediately after the exercise of a noncompensatory option does not do the trick, the partnership must shift book (not tax) capital among the partners until the exercising option holder's capital account reflects her right to share in partnership capital under the partnership agreement. Treas. Reg. § 1.704–1(b)(2)(iv)(s)(*3*). Generally this will involve an allocation of book capital from the existing partners to the exercising option holder. This capital shift is not currently taxable or deductible to or by any partner, being a shift of book capital only. It does, however, create a book-tax disparity for all partners. If Peter, Paul and Mary must shift book capital to Jackie, each of them suffers a reduction in book capital relative to tax capital, while Jackie enjoys an increase in book capital relative to tax capital.

One could imagine a variety of ways these new book-tax differences might be handled. They might, for example, be treated as a new reverse section 704(c) layer, to be taken into account under the rules applicable to such layers if and when the partnership sells or depreciates its assets. If so treated, this layer would be akin to the reverse layer created in the revaluation itself. The Treasury regulations do not adopt this approach, choosing instead a more draconian alternative, known as corrective allocations.

Corrective allocations

A corrective allocation is an allocation of tax items that differs from the allocation of the corresponding book items that is made to reverse the book-tax differences arising from the re-allocation of book capital described above. A partnership that has made a re-allocation of book capital must make corrective allocations in the taxable year of the option exercise and in all succeeding years until the required allocations have all been made. Treas. Reg. § 1.704–1(b)(4)(x). If the capital account re-allocation is from the historic partners to the exercising option holder, the corrective allocations must first be made with gross income and gain. If that is not enough, corrective allocations of gross loss and deduction are required. Treas. Reg. § 1.704–1(b)(4)(x)(*c*).

This is not good news for Jackie. The book capital shifted to him brings with it an immediate tax bill, in the form of an allocation of "gross income and gain" equal to the amount of the capital shift. Any partnership that is still breathing has gross income, so it will be difficult for Jackie to avoid this tax burden. The regulations are silent as to the split of the corrective allocation between ordinary income and gain, so there may be some room for Jackie to negotiate with his partners on that issue. There is no question, however, that this treatment is more onerous than Jackie would receive if the capital shift were treated as a reverse section 704(c) layer—or the treatment that he does receive on the reverse layer created in the revaluation itself.

What is bad for Jackie is good for Peter, Paul and Mary, who receive a lesser allocation of taxable income and gain, equal to the book capital that they have shifted to Jackie. This sets up a conflict between the two sides that capable tax counsel will anticipate even as they negotiate the terms of Jackie's convertible debt. The historic partners will favor, for example, revaluations while Jackie's convertible debt instrument remains outstanding. These revaluations will soak up book gain, leaving less for Jackie if and when he converts, therefore maximizing the possibility of corrective allocations. Anticipating this, the regulations mandate an artificial valuation technique that is meant to reserve book gain ("headroom" as it has come to be called) on Jackie's behalf. Treas. Reg. § 1.704–1(b)(2)(iv)(*h*)(*2*). At the same time, however, the regulations open up a significant opportunity for competitive gamesmanship by allowing the partnership to revalue immediately before issuing the convertible debt instrument. Treas. Reg. § 1.704–1(b)(2)(iv)(*f*)(*5*)(*iv*). The headroom regulation does not apply to this revaluation, because the convertible debt is not yet outstanding, so it is the last clear chance for the historic partners to suck the existing book gain out of the partnership and, potentially, enjoy the benefit of corrective allocations somewhere down the road.

8.6.1 The balance sheet of Puff Unlimited and the fair market value of its assets are as follows:

Assets				Liabilities		
	Tax	**Book**	**FMV**		**Tax**	**Book**
Cash	$ 2,000	$ 2,000	$ 2,000	Convertible Debt	$12,000	$12,000
Equipment	10,000	10,000	30,000			
Plant	18,000	18,000	48,000	**Capital**		
Land	12,000	12,000	16,000	Peter	10,000	10,000
				Paul	10,000	10,000
				Mary	10,000	10,000
Total Assets	$42,000	$42,000	$96,000	**Total Liabilities and Capital**	$42,000	$42,000

At formation, Peter, Paul and Mary each contributed $10,000 in cash to the partnership in exchange for equal, one-third interests. Jackie made a loan in the amount of $12,000 that is convertible into a 25% interest in the partnership. How will the balance sheet appear immediately after Jackie converts, taking into account the revaluation required by Treas. Reg. § 1.704–1(b)(2)(iv)(*s*)?

Assets				Liabilities		
	Tax	**Book**	**FMV**		**Tax**	**Book**
Cash	$	$	$ 2,000	Convertible Debt	$	$
Equipment			30,000			
Plant			48,000	**Capital**		
Land			16,000	Peter		
				Paul		
				Mary		
				Jackie		
Total Assets	$	$	$96,000	**Total Liabilities and Capital**	$	$

8.6.2   Same as Question 8.6.1, but Jackie's initial loan amount was only $8,000. Nevertheless, he has the right to a 25% partnership interest on conversion. The balance sheet immediately before Jackie converts is as follows:

Assets				Liabilities		
	Tax	**Book**	**FMV**		**Tax**	**Book**
Cash	$ 1,000	$ 1,000	$ 1,000	Convertible Debt	$ 8,000	$ 8,000
Equipment	9,000	9,000	31,000			
Plant	17,000	17,000	48,000	**Capital**		
Land	11,000	11,000	16,000	Peter	10,000	10,000
				Paul	10,000	10,000
				Mary	10,000	10,000
Total Assets	$38,000	$38,000	$96,000	**Total Liabilities and Capital**	$38,000	$38,000

How will the balance sheet appear immediately after Jackie converts, taking into account the required revaluation?

Assets				Liabilities		
	Tax	**Book**	**FMV**		**Tax**	**Book**
Cash	$	$	$ 1,000	Convertible Debt	$	$
Equipment			31,000			
Plant			48,000	**Capital**		
Land			16,000	Peter		
				Paul		
				Mary		
				Jackie ·		
Total Assets	$	$	$96,000	**Total Liabilities and Capital**	$	$

8.6.3   In Question 8.6.1, Jackie's debt had a conversion premium at issuance, because the equity interest he was entitled to receive on conversion had at that time a lower value ($10,500 on a book basis) than the amount of the debt he would have to surrender to obtain it ($12,000). In Question 8.6.2, Jackie's debt had a conversion discount at issuance, because the equity interest he would obtain on conversion would be worth more ($9,500 on a book basis) than the amount of the loan ($8,000). What difference does this make to the tax positions of the parties?

a)   It makes no difference.

b) Following conversion, Jackie's book capital is $4,000 lower in the discount case.

c) In the discount case, Jackie will receive corrective allocations of $4,000 of partnership gross income or gain.

d) In the discount case, Jackie must take an additional $4,000 book-tax difference into account under the principles of section 704(c).

8.6.4 Same facts as Question 8.6.3 regarding the formation of Puff Unlimited. The partnership's business does not prosper, however, and there is no change in the value of its assets. The balance sheet immediately before Jackie converts is as follows:

Assets				Liabilities		
	Tax	**Book**	**FMV**		**Tax**	**Book**
Cash	$ 1,000	$ 1,000	$ 1,000	Convertible Debt	$ 8,000	$ 8,000
Equipment	9,000	9,000	9,000			
Plant	17,000	17,000	17,000	**Capital**		
Land	11,000	11,000	11,000	Peter	10,000	10,000
				Paul	10,000	10,000
				Mary	10,000	10,000
Total Assets	$38,000	$38,000	$38,000	**Total Liabilities and Capital**	$38,000	$38,000

How will the balance sheet appear immediately after Jackie converts, taking into account the required revaluation?

Assets				Liabilities		
	Tax	**Book**	**FMV**		**Tax**	**Book**
Cash	$	$	$ 1,000	Convertible Debt	$	$
Equipment			9,000			
Plant			17,000	**Capital**		
Land			11,000	Peter		
				Paul		
				Mary		
				Jackie		
Total Assets	$	$	$38,000	**Total Liabilities and Capital**	$	$

8.6.5 What can you say about Jackie's tax position in Question 8.6.4?

a) He will receive corrective allocations of $1,500 of partnership gross income or gain.

b) He must take a $1,500 book-tax difference into account under the principles of section 704(c).

c) His book capital account will be $1,500 less than 25% of the partnership's total book capital, but it will be increased to the appropriate level as corrective allocations are made to him.

d) The "headroom" regulation will require the partnership to allocate to him a book gain of $1,500, even though there is zero overall book gain realized in this revaluation. The other partners will be allocated an offsetting $1,500 book loss.

CHAPTER 9
PARTNERSHIP DISTRIBUTIONS

9.1   SECTIONS 731, 732 AND 733: THE OTHER HALF OF THE BASIS STORY

Whenever you confront a partnership distribution, ask yourself three questions. What is the distributee-partner's outside basis immediately before the distribution? Is the distribution currently taxable? And, what is the basis of the distributed property and of the distributee's remaining partnership interest following the distribution? The question of tax basis, always a critical inquiry in partnership taxation, is particularly important here.

On their face, the rules for partnership distributions are not very hard, especially when compared to the elaborate taxonomy that applies to corporate distributions. You do not have to worry about whether the partnership has current or accumulated earnings and profits; whether the distribution is a redemption or essentially equivalent to a dividend; whether the distribution is substantially disproportionate or in partial liquidation; or whether the distribution is pursuant to a plan of complete liquidation. With exceptions that are themselves intended to protect the corporate tax base, you need not be concerned about the identity of the distributee or how much of the partnership the distributee holds. In the world of partnership tax, there are only two kinds of distributions: liquidating and current. A liquidating distribution terminates the interest of the distributee in the partnership, whether or not as part of a larger transaction that liquidates the entire partnership. A current distribution is any distribution that is not a liquidating distribution. The tax treatment of these two types of distributions is very similar, although not identical.

Question 1: What is the distributee-partner's outside basis?

Ordinarily, a partner's outside basis is determined at the close of the partnership's tax year. Treas. Reg. § 1.705–1(a). A partner receiving a distribution of cash or property must, however, determine her outside basis immediately before the distribution, in order to know whether and to what extent the distribution is taxable and also to determine the tax basis of distributed property.

If the partner's interest is liquidated by the distribution, her share of the partnership's income or loss for the year flows through to her and she takes the corresponding adjustments to outside basis into account prior to determining the tax effects of the distribution. The applicable rule in this case is section 706(c)(2)(A), the same rule that applies to a partner's sale of her entire interest in the partnership, which we reviewed in Topic 6.2.

A current distribution, on the other hand, does not cause partnership income or loss to flow through to the distributee-partner. The applicable rule here is section 706(c)(2)(B), which also applies to sales of less than a partner's entire interest. As a result, the tax effects of the distribution are determined without any adjustment of outside basis for the distributee's share of predistribution income or loss. This rule is mitigated in the case of "advances" or "draws" against the partner's anticipated share of partnership income, as discussed under the following heading.

Question 2: Is the distribution currently taxable?

Under section 731(b), a partnership never recognizes gain or loss on a distribution of money or property. This is, of course, not the rule for corporations—indeed, even S corporations, which are in some ways similar to partnerships, recognize gain on the distribution of appreciated property. *See* section 311(b). The ability of a partnership not only to take property from its partners on a tax-free basis, but to give it back to them as well, is certainly one of the primary reasons for a tax advisor to recommend the use of a partnership or limited liability company in preference to an S corporation.

A distributee-partner can recognize gain in either a current distribution or a liquidating distribution, but only if the amount of cash distributed (including cash deemed distributed under section 752(b)) exceeds the distributee's tax basis in her partnership interest immediately before the distribution. Section 731(a)(1). Cash distributions not in excess of outside basis do not produce taxable gain. Neither do property distributions, even if the value (or the tax basis) of the distributed property exceeds the distributee's outside basis. (We are talking here about the basic rules for partnership distributions. There are exceptions to these rules, including one we have already reviewed (recall the discussion of disguised sales in Topic 2.7) and several that we will review later in this Chapter.)

A distributee-partner can recognize loss only in a liquidating distribution, not in a current distribution. Under section 731(a)(2), a liquidating distribution of cash in an amount that is less than the distributee's outside basis produces a recognized loss to the distributee. So does a distribution of section 751 assets (unrealized receivables and/or inventory items) having a basis in the hands of the partnership that is less than the distributee's outside basis. (This is not exactly what the statutory language says, but it is what it means. *See* Treas. Reg. § 1.732–1(c)(3).) Not surprisingly, a liquidating distribution consisting of both money and section 751 assets also produces recognized loss, if the sum of the cash and the basis of the distributed property is less than the distributee's outside basis.

The gain or loss recognized by the distributee-partner under section 731(a) is capital gain or loss. Section 731(a)(2) (last sentence). If, however, the distributee-partner does not receive her share of certain section 751 assets, she may be required to recognize ordinary income or loss under the complex rules of section 751(b), discussed in Topic 9.6.

In an effort to ease the taxation of current distributions, the IRS permits "advances" or "draws" against a partner's anticipated share of the partnership's income for the year to be treated as current distributions made on the last day of the partnership's tax year. Treas. Reg. § 1.731–1(a)(1)(ii). Universally known as the "drawings rule," this regulation is particularly useful for partners of service partnerships who receive monthly cash payments against the current year's earnings. The rule allows them to increase outside basis by their share of the partnership's income for the entire year before determining the tax treatment of the cash distributed to them during the year. In Rev. Rul. 94–4, 1994–1 C.B. 195, the IRS extended this treatment to deemed cash distributions under section 752(b).

Question 3: What about basis?

Under ordinary tax principles, if the gain or loss realized on an exchange of properties is not recognized, basis is not adjusted, thereby preserving the unrecognized gain or loss for future recognition. We saw this principle at work in the contribution of property to a partnership in Topic 2.2. A partnership takes the contributing partner's basis in appreciated property, so that the gain unrecognized on the contribution can be recognized by the partnership (and allocated to the contributor under section 704(c)) on any subsequent sale or other taxable disposition of the property.

And so it is with property distributions by a partnership. Just like contributions, partnership distributions occur for tax purposes "at basis"— *i.e.*, the amount of a distribution is the tax basis of the property distributed. I do not know why, but this important fact—foundational, really—is hard for students to keep in mind. Maybe it is because corporate distributions, because they are taxed, occur "at fair market value." *See* section 301(b)(1). Or maybe it is that the book treatment of a partnership property distribution requires that it be taken into account at fair market value, as discussed below. Regardless, for purposes of determining the tax consequences to the distributee, the amount of a partnership's distribution is the sum of the amount of money and the adjusted basis to the partnership of any property distributed. Let's see how this works in current and liquidating distributions.

Current distributions. Under section 732(a)(1), a partner receiving a current distribution takes a basis in the distributed property equal to the partnership's prior basis in that property. In the parlance of section 7701(a)(43), such property is "transferred basis property." If the distributee-partner later sells the distributed property, she will recognize exactly the same gain or loss that the partnership would have recognized had it sold the property for the same price. In such a distribution, the basis system has preserved the exact amount of the partnership's gain or loss for future recognition. The distribution has, however, changed the party who recognizes it. There is no analogue to section 704(c) at work here: the distribution shifts to the distributee gain or loss that would have been shared by the partners in accordance with the partnership agreement and applicable law (including section 704(c)).

Under section 732(a)(2), if the partnership's aggregate adjusted basis in the property distributed in a current distribution exceeds the distributee-partner's outside basis, which is first reduced by the cash distributed in the same distribution, the distributee's basis in the distributed property is not equal to the partnership's prior basis. Instead, it equals the distributee's outside basis as so reduced. This provision of the statute acts as a "cap" on the aggregate basis of the distributed property. In the parlance of section 7701(a)(44), the distributed property in this case is "exchanged basis property." Section 732(a)(2) is true to the basic concept of a tax-free exchange: because the distributee-partner recognizes no gain, she cannot take a tax basis in the property received (the distributed property) that is bigger than her basis in the property exchanged (her partnership interest). In this case, the basis system does not preserve the partnership's gain or loss for future recognition, but instead causes it to change by an amount equal to the excess of the partnership's basis in the distributed property over the distributee's outside basis (after a reduction for cash distributed). Thus, the distribution in this case changes both the amount of the gain or loss and the identity of the party who will recognize it.

Because a partnership is an entity for tax purposes, we must also be concerned about effects of a distribution on the partner's basis in her partnership interest. In a current distribution, the outside basis of the distributee is reduced, first, by the amount of cash distributed and then by the adjusted basis to the distributee (not the fair market value) of distributed property. Generally, this means that outside basis is reduced by the partnership's prior basis in the distributed property. But in any case that the distributee's basis in distributed property is limited by section 732(a)(2), the reduction in the distributee's outside basis is also limited. This prevents the distributee's outside basis from becoming negative.

To illustrate, assume that Gaylord is a partner in the RRD Partnership. His adjusted basis in his partnership interest is $100,000. The partnership distributes to Gaylord $20,000 cash and an item of property with a value of $70,000 and an adjusted basis of $25,000 in the partnership's hands. As long as this distribution does not liquidate Gaylord's interest, it is a current distribution, regardless whether his percentage interest in the partnership is reduced by reason of the distribution. Neither Gaylord nor RRD recognizes any gain or loss on this distribution. The cash distribution reduces Gaylord's outside basis to $80,000 under section 733(1). He takes the distributed property with a basis of $25,000 under section 732(a)(1). If Gaylord later sells the distributed property for $70,000, he will recognize a gain of $45,000, in which the other partners will not share.

If, contrary to this analysis, Gaylord's basis in the distributed property were not its $25,000 basis to the partnership but instead its value of $70,000, Gaylord would enjoy a basis step-up of $45,000 in that property, despite the fact that neither he nor the partnership recognized any gain on the distribution. That would clearly be the wrong answer.

On receipt of the distributed property, Gaylord's outside basis is reduced by a further $25,000 under section 733(2), to $55,000. Thus, his original outside basis of $100,000 has been fragmented into three pieces: (1) $20,000 of cash, (2) $25,000 basis in the distributed property and (3) $55,000 remaining basis in his interest in the RRD Partnership. If his outside basis were reduced by the $70,000 value of the distributed property instead, Gaylord would be left with only $10,000 basis remaining in his partnership interest ($100,000 less $20,000 for the cash and $70,000 for the property), and he would have $55,000 basis in total ($20,000 in the cash, $25,000 in the property and $10,000 in his partnership interest). In that case, $45,000 of Gaylord's outside basis would disappear in a transaction in which he recognizes no loss for tax purposes—again, clearly the wrong answer.

Now assume that the value and basis of the property distributed to Gaylord is $100,000. As before, the cash distribution reduces his outside basis by $20,000 to $80,000. But now he cannot take the partnership's full $100,000 basis in the distributed property, because of the limitation of section 731(a)(2). (If he did so, he would have $20,000 more basis in cash and property after the transaction than he had before it, without recognizing any gain.) Applying that limitation, Gaylord takes the property with a basis of $80,000, and reduces his outside basis to zero. If Gaylord sells the property thereafter for $100,000, he will recognize $20,000 gain, whereas the partnership would have recognized no gain on its sale of the property for the same price.

Liquidating distributions. Turning now to a liquidating distribution, the rules are happily much the same. In fact, there are only two differences. First, a distributee-partner can recognize capital loss on a liquidating distribution, but not on a current distribution, as discussed above. Second, the property received in a liquidating distribution is always "exchanged basis property." Under section 732(b), the recipient of a liquidating distribution takes an aggregate basis in the distributed property equal to her outside basis, as reduced by any cash distributed. A moment's thought will confirm that this is a slightly different rule than the one that applies to current distributions under section 732(a)(2). The latter rule is a cap, which applies only if the distributee's outside basis (reduced by distributed cash) is smaller than the aggregate basis of the distributed properties. Section 732(b), by contrast, can either increase or decrease the basis of the distributed properties.

Allocating tax basis among the distributed properties. In current distributions governed by section 732(a)(2), and in all liquidating distributions, a protocol is required for spreading the distributee-partner's outside basis among the distributed properties. Section 732(c) supplies it. It assigns each distributed property a tentative tax basis equal to the partnership's former basis. Decreases, which can be mandated by either section 731(a)(2) or section 732(b), are allocated, first, in proportion to the depreciation in the value, if any, of the distributed assets and then in proportion to their respective adjusted bases. Increases, which can only be mandated by section 732(b), are allocated, first, in proportion to the appreciation in the value, if any, of the distributed assets and then in proportion to their respective fair market values.

Two special rules apply to section 751 assets. Under section 732(c)(1)(A), outside basis is assigned first to section 751 assets and increases are never assigned to section 751 assets. The purpose of these two rules is to assure to the greatest possible extent that the basis of each section 751 asset in the hands of the distributee will be the same as it was in the hands of the partnership and, therefore, the distribution will neither create nor destroy unrealized ordinary income or loss. Loss recognition under section 731(a)(2) is a corollary to the rule that increases cannot be allocated to section 751 assets. The issue arises in a liquidating distribution in which the distributee's outside basis exceeds the partnership's aggregate basis in the distributed assets, so that increases are required, but the only properties distributed are section 751 assets, which cannot accept increases. The solution of section 731(a)(2) is to allow the distributee-partner to recognize a loss equal to the amount that would otherwise be allocated as increases to the basis of section 751 assets. Because this loss is a capital loss, the net amount of ordinary income or loss is unaffected.

To illustrate, suppose that the asset distributed to Gaylord is inventory with a value and tax basis to the partnership of $100,000. It is the partnership's only section 751 asset and Gaylord is receiving exactly his share of it. That asset and $100,000 in cash liquidate Gaylord's partnership interest, in which he has a basis of $250,000. After reducing Gaylord's outside basis by the amount of the cash, he still has $150,000 left. If he took the distributed inventory with a basis of $150,000, however, he would have a $50,000 built-in ordinary loss, which would exceed (by $50,000) the amount of the ordinary loss inherent in the inventory when the partnership owned it. In this case, section 732(c)(1)(A) prohibits the allocation of the $50,000 increase to the inventory, and section 731(a)(2) allows Gaylord to claim a $50,000 capital loss on the liquidation. If, on the other hand, the asset distributed to Gaylord were a capital asset, the $50,000 increase would be permitted (and required) by section 732(c)(1)(B). He would take the capital asset with a tax basis of $150,000 (*i.e.*, a built-in loss of $50,000) and would claim no loss on the liquidation.

The book effect of a distribution

Every transaction between a partnership and one of its partners has both a tax effect (often, an adjustment to tax basis; less frequently, gain or loss recognition) and a book effect. In the case of a contribution, the partner's book capital account increases by the amount of money and the fair market value of the property contributed, and the partnership takes a book value in the contributed property equal to fair market value. *See* Topic 2.3. The book effects of a distribution are parallel to those of a contribution. The distributee-partner's book capital account is reduced by the amount of money and the fair market value of property distributed to her. Treas. Reg. § 1.704–1(b)(2)(iv)(*b*). For this purpose, every distributed property is revalued immediately before it is distributed, and the book gain or loss arising from the revaluation is allocated among all of the partners according to the partnership agreement and applicable law. We reviewed this "distributed-property revaluation" in Topic 2.6.

_____

The first few Questions are based on the following fact pattern:

Load 'n Lock LLC ("LnL") operates a chain of self-service laundromats. Taxed as a partnership, LnL has a simple business model. It rents commercial washers and dryers in bulk from an equipment supplier and locates them in rented storefronts, mainly in strip malls. Most of its income is in quarters that patrons pay to operate the machines; a smaller amount comes from commercial cleaning contracts, which LnL accounts for using an accrual method. The business has struggled lately and several partners are looking to reduce or liquidate their interests. LnL has no liabilities and no unrealized receivables or inventory items within the meaning of sections 751(c) and (d).

_____

9.1.1 LnL distributes $15,000 cash and an account receivable (value $5,000, inside basis $5,000) in liquidation of the partnership interest of Partner S, whose outside basis is $10,000. What are the tax consequences to Partner S and the partnership?

a) S, no gain or loss; LnL, no gain or loss

b) S, $5,000 ordinary income; LnL, $5,000 ordinary loss

c) S, $5,000 capital gain; LnL, no gain or loss

d) S, $10,000 capital gain; LnL, no gain or loss

9.1.2 In Question 9.1.1, what is Partner S's tax basis in the distributed receivable?

a) $10,000

b) $5,000

c) $0

d) ($5,000)

9.1.3 Partner M, who has an outside basis of $40,000, receives $20,000 cash in liquidation of her interest. What are the tax consequences to her and the partnership?

a) M, no gain or loss; LnL, no gain or loss

b) M, $20,000 ordinary loss; LnL, $20,000 ordinary income

c) M, $20,000 capital loss; LnL, no gain or loss

d) M, $20,000 capital loss; LnL, $20,000 capital gain

9.1.4 Partner P, who has an outside basis of $30,000, receives $10,000 cash and an account receivable on a cleaning contract in liquidation of her interest. The tax basis of the receivable in the partnership's hands is $5,000 and its value is also $5,000. What are the tax consequences to Partner P and the partnership?

a) P, no gain or loss; LnL, no gain or loss

b) P, $15,000 ordinary loss; LnL, $15,000 ordinary income

c) P, $15,000 capital loss; LnL, no gain or loss

d) P, $15,000 capital loss; LnL, $15,000 capital gain

9.1.5 In Question 9.1.4, what is Partner P's tax basis in the distributed receivable?

a) $30,000

b) $20,000

c) $5,000

d) $0

9.1.6 Assume in Question 9.1.4 that the partnership uses the cash method to account for the commercial contracts. Its tax basis for the receivable distributed to Partner P is $0, although the amount of the receivable is still $5,000. Assume that the receivable distributed to Partner P represents her share of the partnership's receivables. What are the tax consequences to Partner P and the partnership?

a) P, no gain or loss; LnL, no gain or loss

b) P, $15,000 ordinary loss; LnL, $15,000 ordinary income

c) P, $15,000 capital loss; LnL, no gain or loss

d) P, $20,000 capital loss; LnL, no gain or loss

9.1.7 LnL is back on the accrual method. Partner T, who has an outside basis of $40,000, receives a distribution of $10,000 cash and an account receivable (value $5,000, inside basis $5,000). As a result of this distribution, Partner T's partnership interest is reduced from 10% to 2%. What is Partner T's tax basis in the distributed receivable?

a) $40,000

b) $30,000

c) $5,000

d) $0

The next two Questions are based on the following modifications to the fact pattern:

Load 'n Lock's business model is now a bit more complex. It owns most of its locations and all of its own equipment. It uses the cash method, so it has two types of unrealized receivables: accounts receivable whose value exceeds their tax basis and recapture on the washers and dryers. Its business is no better than before, and more partners want out.

9.1.8   In liquidation of her partnership interest, Partner Q has agreed to take ownership of three buildings owned by LnL where it has discontinued operations, as follows:

Location	Inside Basis	Fair Market Value
Third St.	$ 90,000	$60,000
Fifth St.	60,000	80,000
Ninth Ave.	100,000	60,000

Partner Q will also receive accounts receivable (value $30,000, inside basis $0), which is exactly her share of the partnership's total unrealized receivables. Partner Q's outside basis prior to this distribution is $120,000. Following the distribution, what is the tax basis of these three properties?

a)   Third St., $30,000; Fifth St., $30,000; Ninth Ave., $30,000

b)   Third St., $40,000; Fifth St., $40,000; Ninth Ave., $40,000

c)   Third St., $43,200; Fifth St., $28,800; Ninth Ave., $48,000

d)   Third St., $51,000; Fifth St., $8,000; Ninth Ave., $61,000

9.1.9   Partner W wants to start her own laundry business with some of LnL's old washing machines. In liquidation of her interest, she takes ownership of 100 used machines, having an aggregate adjusted basis to the partnership of $2,000 and a value of $10,000. If the partnership were to sell these machines for $10,000, it would have $8,000 of recapture under section 1245. This amount of recapture, which is an unrealized receivable under section 751(c), exactly equals Partner W's share of the partnership's total unrealized receivables. Partner W's outside basis is $20,000. What are the tax consequences to her of this distribution?

a)   No gain or loss; $20,000 tax basis in the washing machines; no responsibility for $8,000 recapture

b)   Same as **(a)**, except that Partner W must take up to $8,000 recapture into account on any future sale of the washing machines

c)   No gain or loss; $2,000 tax basis in the washing machines; Partner W may add $18,000 to the tax basis of a nondepreciable capital asset of her choice

d) $18,000 capital loss; $2,000 tax basis in the washing machines

9.2   INSIDE BASIS ADJUSTMENTS UNDER SECTION 734(b)

Section 734(b) applies to liquidating distributions and, less commonly, to current distributions. It only applies to a partnership that has made an election under section 754 or that has a "substantial basis reduction" with respect to the distribution. If applicable, section 734(b) can lead to either an increase or a decrease in the partnership's tax basis in the properties remaining after the distribution.

If you want to appreciate (or even understand) section 734(b), you have to look past its flaws. The ink was not yet dry on the Internal Revenue Code in 1954 when the principal drafters of Subchapter K disavowed the formula in section 734(b). *See* Jackson, Johnson, Surrey, Tenen & Warren, *The Internal Revenue Code of 1954: Partnerships*, 54 COLUM. L. REV. 1183, 1230 n. 90 (1954). Averring that the statutory formula for inside basis adjustment only works correctly in cases where the distributee's outside basis equals her pro-rata share of the partnership's aggregate inside basis, the authors suggested that, in the case of a liquidating distribution:

> Perhaps a better formula would be to increase or decrease the remaining partnership assets [basis] by the difference between (1) any money received by the distributee plus the partnership basis for any distributed property and (2) the distributee's pro rata share of the aggregate partnership basis for its assets.

So let's start there. Item (1) in the formula is straightforward. Item (2) is the sum of the distributee-partner's tax capital and her share of the partnership's liabilities. In simplest terms, the formula says that when a partnership distributes, in liquidation of a partner's interest, money and asset basis that exceed in the aggregate the partner's tax capital and debt share, the partnership increases the basis of its remaining assets by the excess. If, on the other hand, the money and asset basis distributed are less than the partner's tax capital and debt share, the partnership decreases the basis of its remaining assets by the amount of the deficit. Thus, in the case of a liquidating distribution, the section 734(b) adjustment to be made by the partnership can be either positive or negative.

Sound mysterious? It's really just another application of the general rules that govern tax-free exchanges. You will recall from Topic 9.1 that a partner receiving a liquidating distribution treats the property received as "exchanged basis property," in which she takes a basis equal to her prior basis in her partnership interest. Any other result would be inappropriate. To the extent that she does not recognize gain or loss on the exchange, the tax basis in the property she receives should not be different than the tax basis in the partnership interest she surrenders in the exchange.

A liquidating distribution is an exchange from the perspective of the partnership as well. In that exchange, the partnership relinquishes whatever money and property it distributes to the partner. It gets back her interest in the partnership. The partnership recognizes no gain or loss on this exchange. Applying to the partnership the same rule that we applied to the distributee-partner, the partnership should take a basis in the property received in this exchange equal to the basis of the property it relinquishes. But what is the property the partnership receives?

An aggregate approach, in which every partner is treated as owning a pro-rata "interest" in each of the partnership's assets, could be used to answer this question. But that would be complex at best and, in any event, the "interest" of a partner in any particular partnership asset might be difficult or impossible to identify. A simpler approach, consistent with the treatment of the partnership as an entity, is to determine the adjustment by reference to the total amounts. Overall, the partnership surrenders to the distributee property with tax basis equal to the amount identified in item (1) in the formula. And overall, it receives back from the distributee-partner her claim on property with a tax basis equal to the amount identified in item (2) of the formula. Therefore, the partnership should adjust the basis of its remaining properties by the difference between these two. This ensures that the partnership's tax basis in the properties it is deemed to receive in the exchange is neither greater nor less than its tax basis in the properties it is deemed to surrender.

(If you are unpersuaded, try the following thought experiment. In the liquidating distribution the partnership transfers to the partner (i) her "interest" in those partnership properties actually distributed to her and (ii) the "interest" of the other partners in the properties actually distributed to her. It receives in exchange (iii) her "interest" in those partnership properties not actually distributed to her. There is no transfer of the fourth property element, which is (iv) the "interest" of the other partners in the properties not actually distributed. Item (1) in the formula includes items (i) and (ii) above. Item (2) in the formula includes items (i) and (iii) above. Item (i) is common to both and is eliminated in the subtraction. Without need to determine any partner's "interest" in any partnership asset, the formula isolates the partnership's exchange of item (ii) for item (iii) and, through the basis adjustment, causes them to be equal.)

Section 734(b) can also apply to a current distribution. Although Mr. Jackson *et al.* did not offer a formula to apply to that case, a relatively small adjustment does the trick:

> [I]ncrease or decrease the remaining partnership assets [basis] by the difference between (1) any money received by the distributee plus the partnership basis for any distributed property and (2) the amount by which the distributee's pro rata share of the aggregate partnership basis for its assets is reduced by the distribution.

This formulation would apply to liquidating distributions in exactly the same manner as the earlier one. In current distributions, it would limit the availability of a section 734(b) basis adjustment to cases in which the amount of money and distributed basis exceed the distributee-partner's tax capital and debt share. This can occur when the amount of money distributed exceeds the outside basis of the distributee, who recognizes gain under section 731(a)(1). It can also occur in the situation described in section 732(a)(2), where the distributee's basis in the distributed property is limited by her outside basis. In both situations, the partnership's section 734(b) adjustment is always positive, because item (1) in the formula (basis surrendered by the partnership) is always larger than item (2) in the formula (basis acquired). In the great majority of current distributions, the distributee-partner simply takes the partnership's prior tax basis in the distributed property and reduces her tax capital by a like amount. No section 734(b) adjustment is available.

So that's the theory. What about the actual statute? Here's the good part: the statute works exactly like the theory in every case that the distributee-partner's outside basis equals her share of the partnership's inside basis. That's a lot of cases—and likely includes anything you will see on an exam. Let's look at the kind of example you are likely to confront. (In this and following examples, there are no differences between tax and book amounts, so to save space they are shown together in a single column.)

FIGURE 9.2.1

Assets			Liabilities		
	Tax/Book	**FMV**		**Tax/Book**	
Property Q1	$ 700	$ 700	Recourse	$ 900	
Property Q2	300	300			
Property R	700	1,000	**Capital**		**Outside Basis**
Property S	100	1,000	Albert	300	$ 600
			Brooks	300	600
			Celine	300	600
Total Assets	$1,800	$3,000	**Total Liabilities and Capital**	$1,800	$1,800

Albert, Brooks and Celine formed this equal general partnership with contributions of $300 cash each. It is an investment partnership and all of its properties are capital assets in its hands. Assuming that the partnership has made a section 754 election, what is the adjustment under section 734(b) if the partnership distributes Property Q1 to Celine in liquidation of her interest in the partnership?

In this distribution, Celine is deemed to receive $300 in cash under section 752(b), which reduces her outside basis to $300. Under section 732(b), this becomes her basis in Property Q1. Under section 734(b)(1)(B), the partnership has a positive adjustment of $400. This comports perfectly with the theory. Prior to the distribution, Celine had a $600 share of the partnership's asset basis, equal to the sum of her tax capital ($300) and her share of the debt (also $300). In the distribution, she received money and property that together had a $1,000 tax basis to the partnership. Thus, she took $400 more than her share of the partnership's inside basis, so the partnership should have a positive adjustment of $400 to the basis of its remaining assets.

Prior to the distribution, each of the three partners had a $400 share of the partnership's gain in its assets (one-third of $1,200). The distribution of Property Q1 to Celine increases those shares to $600 for each of Albert and Brooks (one-half of $2,300 value less $1,100 inside basis). The $400 section 734(b) adjustment returns those shares to $400 (one-half of $2,300 value less $1,500 inside basis).

The section 734(b) adjustment would be the same, under both the statute and the theory, if Property Q1 happened to be cash. In that case, Celine would receive actual and deemed cash distributions totaling $1,000 and would recognize $400 of gain under section 731(a)(1). Under section 734(b)(1)(A), that would be the amount of the partnership's positive basis adjustment.

If Celine instead received a current distribution of Property Q2, reducing her percentage interest in the partnership from one-third to 22.2%, she would have a deemed distribution of $100 cash under section 752(b) which, together with the distribution of Property Q2, would reduce her outside basis to $200. Celine would recognize no gain or loss on the distribution and her tax basis in the distributed Property Q2 would be the same as that of the partnership. No section 734(b) adjustment would be forthcoming under either the statute or the theory.

To see a case where the statute and the theory diverge, consider the following:

FIGURE 9.2.2

Assets			Liabilities		
	Tax/Book	**FMV**		**Tax/Book**	
Property Q1	$ 700	$ 700	Recourse	$ 900	
Property Q2	300	300			
Property R	700	1,000	**Capital**		**Outside Basis**
Property S	100	1,000	Albert	300	$ 600
			Brooks	300	600
			Dion	300	1,000
Total Assets	$1,800	$3,000	**Total Liabilities and Capital**	$1,800	$2,200

Before we arrived, Celine sold her partnership interest to Dion for its fair market value of $700. Dion thus has an outside basis (including debt share) of $1,000. The partnership has no section 754 election, so Dion has no special basis adjustment. If the partnership now distributes Property Q1 to Dion in liquidation of the purchased interest and makes a section 754 election in connection with the distribution, what is the section 734(b) adjustment? The theory says it is $400, as before, because the partnership has distributed to Dion property with a tax basis that exceeds Dion's share of inside basis by $400.

Under the statute, however, there is no section 734(b) adjustment. The section 752(b) cash distribution ($300) plus the basis of the property ($700) distributed to Dion equal her outside basis, so that neither section 734(b)(1)(A) nor section 734(b)(1)(B) applies. This is not good news for Albert and Brooks, who, as before, see their shares of the partnership's remaining gain rise to $600 each, but now without relief from section 734(b).

Unlike special basis adjustments under section 743(b), adjustments under section 734(b) are not personal to any particular partner, but instead affect the partnership's common basis for its properties. They are allocated among the partnership's assets under the rules of Treas. Reg. § 1.755–1(c). For this purpose, the partnership's property is divided into two classes, capital assets and section 1231 property ("capital gain property") and all other property ("ordinary income property"). Treas. Reg. § 1.755–1(a)(1). Allocations arising from the distributee's recognized gain or loss are allocated solely to the partnership's capital gain property. Treas. Reg. § 1.755– 1(c)(1)(ii). Allocations arising from the distributee taking property with a basis that is higher or lower than the partnership's basis in such property are allocated solely to partnership property having the same character as such property. Treas. Reg. § 1.755–1(c)(1)(i).

Within each class of property (capital gain property or ordinary income property), allocations of the section 734(b) adjustment follow the same approach as section 732(c). Positive adjustments are allocated, first, in proportion to the appreciation in the value, if any, of the partnership's properties in the appropriate class and, then, in proportion to their respective fair market values. Negative adjustments are allocated, first, in proportion to the depreciation in value, if any, of the partnership's properties in the appropriate class and, then, in proportion to their respective adjusted bases. The tax basis of a property, as adjusted, cannot be less than zero. If a partnership does not have any property of the appropriate class, or if the basis of property in the appropriate class has been reduced to zero, further adjustments are held in abeyance until the partnership acquires additional property in that class. Treas. Reg. § 1.751–1(c)(4).

If a distribution would produce a negative adjustment under section 734(b) exceeding $250,000 (termed a "substantial basis reduction" by an amendment to section 734(a) enacted in 2004), the partnership must make such adjustment, whether or not it has made an election under section 754. In all other cases, the application of section 734(b) depends on the presence of a section 754 election. In the past, this has opened the door to some significant tax avoidance, as discussed in the next Topic.

———————

9.2.1   Austin, Benjamin, Cooper and Devon are equal partners in East Side Investments LLC, a limited liability company taxed as a partnership that makes real estate investments in prominent residential neighborhoods. The balance sheet of the partnership (expanded to show property values and outside bases) looks like this:

Assets			Liabilities		
	Tax/Book	FMV		Tax/Book	
Cash	$ 1,000,000	$ 1,000,000	Bank Debt	$ 2,000,000	
Property 1	1,300,000	500,000			
Property 2	600,000	2,000,000	Capital		Outside Basis
Property 3	600,000	1,600,000	Austin	400,000	$ 900,000
Property 4	100,000	900,000	Benjamin	400,000	900,000
			Cooper	400,000	900,000
			Devon	400,000	900,000
Total Assets	$ 3,600,000	$ 6,000,000	Total Liabilities and Capital	$ 3,600,000	$ 3,600,000

The partnership distributes its cash to Austin in liquidation of her interest. If the partnership has made an election under section 754, what is the amount of the adjustment under section 734(b)?

a) ($100,000)

b) $100,000

c) ($600,000)

d) $600,000

9.2.2 In Question 9.2.1, what is the amount of the adjustment allocated to Property 3?

a) $0

b) $187,500

c) $192,000

d) $213,333

9.2.3 In Question 9.2.1, assume alternatively that the partnership distributes Property 4 and cash of $100,000 to Austin in liquidation of her interest. If the partnership has made an election under section 754, what is the amount of the adjustment under section 734(b)?

a) ($200,000)

b) $200,000

c) ($700,000)

d) $700,000

9.2.4   In Question 9.2.3, what is the amount of the adjustment allocated to Property 3?

a) $0

b)   ($48,000)

c) $83,333

d) $88,888

9.2.5   How does your answer to Question 9.2.3 change if the partnership has not made a section 754 election?

a)   My answer does not change.

b)   There is no section 734(b) adjustment in this case. No adjustment can occur absent a section 754 election.

c)   There is no section 734(b) adjustment in this case. An adjustment, if made, would not produce a substantial basis reduction.

d)   There is no section 734(b) adjustment in this case. Absent a section 754 election, Austin would take Property 4 with the partnership's inside basis.

9.2.6   In Question 9.2.1, assume alternatively that the partnership distributes Property 1 to Austin. This distribution reduces, but does not liquidate, her interest in the partnership. In connection with the distribution, Austin executes a guarantee, such that her share of the bank debt remains at $500,000. If the partnership has made an election under section 754, what is the amount of the adjustment under section 734(b)?

a) $0

b) $400,000

c) $900,000

d) $1,300,000

9.2.7 McKayla, McKyra and McKenna own and operate a children's amusement park through their partnership, Sunny Daze LLC. Things have not been going well, and McKyra wants out. The partnership's sorry balance sheet (with added asset values and outside bases) looks like this:

Assets			Liabilities		
	Tax/Book	FMV		Tax/Book	
Cash	$ 15,000	$ 15,000	Bank Debt	$ 150,000	
Receivables	0	90,000			
Equipment	185,000	65,000	**Capital**		**Outside Basis**
Land	250,000	115,000	Albert	100,000	$ 150,000
			Brooks	100,000	150,000
			Celine	100,000	150,000
Total Assets	**$450,000**	**$285,000**	**Total Liabilities and Capital**	**$ 450,000**	**$ 450,000**

It is not clear that the receivables—mostly for pre-sales of "Hot Summer Daze" ticket packages—are collectible given the condition of the park, but McKyra is willing to take them. If the partnership distributes $30,000 of these receivables and $15,000 in cash to liquidate McKyra's interest and makes a section 754 election, what is the amount of its section 734(b) adjustment?

a) $0

b) $85,000

c) ($85,000)

d) ($135,000)

9.3 THE TRICKS OF THE TRADE: GAIN, LOSS AND BASIS SHIFTING

Well, that's it. You have learned all there is to know about the partnership tax-basis system. You are probably thinking how perfect and inevitable it is, and how you are a better person for having mastered it. Or something like that. But before we declare victory and move on, I encourage you to consider that the basis rules governing partnership distributions serve the general nonrecognition rule of section 731. That rule causes most property distributions to be treated as tax-deferred exchanges. The consequences for tax basis follow directly from that characterization. Initially concentrated in the partnership interest, outside basis is spread among the distributed properties and the remaining partnership interest, if any, with the goal that the distributee-partner's ultimate gain or loss will be determined by the difference between the value of her investment (whether it is held in one or several different properties) and the cost to her of that investment.

In other words, the basis system for partnership distributions preserves the amount of gain or loss at the level of the individual partners ("partner gain or loss"). It can do no more, because the nonrecognition rule allows partners to "swap" their partnership interests (or portions thereof) for partnership properties without recognizing gain or loss. Therefore, the gain or loss that exists in a partnership property ("partnership gain or loss") can be transferred among partners or even eliminated through a distribution. While the tax-basis system can and does preserve partner gain or loss on a partner-by-partner basis, it is powerless to preserve partnership gain or loss on an asset-by-asset basis.

Professor Andrews has called section 731 "a nonrecognition rule of stunning scope and flexibility." Andrews, *Inside Basis Adjustments and Hot Asset Exchanges in Partnership Distributions*, 47 TAX L. REV. 3, 3 (1991). It is not a fair appraisal of this rule to say that it merely bestows tax-free treatment on distributions that would happen in any event. Instead, like any nonrecognition provision, it encourages the subject transaction (here, property distributions by partnerships) to occur in a manner and with a frequency that would not be observed in its absence. In the hands of a skilled tax advisor, the results are eye-popping. Here are a few examples.

ELIMINATING PARTNERSHIP GAIN OR LOSS

Amelia, Brody and Corbett are equal partners in the ABC Partnership, a general partnership formed with cash contributions to buy and sell investments. The balance sheet (expanded to show the fair market values of assets) is as follows:

FIGURE 9.3.1

Assets				Liabilities		
	Tax	Book	FMV		Tax	Book
Cash	$ 3,000	$ 3,000	$ 3,000	[None]	$ 0	$ 0
Property X	1,000	1,000	7,000			
Property Y	6,000	6,000	7,000	**Capital**		
Property Z	8,000	8,000	7,000	Amelia	6,000	6,000
				Brody	6,000	6,000
				Corbett	6,000	6,000
Total Assets	$18,000	$18,000	$24,000	**Total Liabilities and Capital**	$18,000	$18,000

Amelia wants to exit the partnership for a cash distribution of $8,000. Because the partnership does not have that much cash, the partners consider which asset to sell to raise the required $5,000. The partners believe that

Property X, which has done very well, has little potential for further appreciation and it should be sold, but they would prefer not to recognize the gain.

What if the partnership distributes Property X and $1,000 in cash to Amelia in liquidation of her partnership interest? The total value of this distribution, $8,000, is what she wants. After reducing Amelia's outside basis by $1,000 for the cash, she takes a tax basis in Property X of $5,000. If she then sells that property, she recognizes no more gain than she would have recognized on the cash distribution she asked for. If the partnership has not made an election under section 754, however, its gain in Property X simply disappears, and with it the tax that Brody and Corbett would have paid when the partnership sold it. This is easy to see from the balance sheet of the partnership following the distribution:

FIGURE 9.3.2

Assets				Liabilities		
	Tax	**Book**	**FMV**		**Tax**	**Book**
Cash	$ 2,000	$ 2,000	$ 2,000	[None]	$ 0	$ 0
Property X	0	0	0			
Property Y	6,000	7,000	7,000	**Capital**		
Property Z	8,000	7,000	7,000	Amelia	0	0
				Brody	6,000	8,000
				Corbett	6,000	8,000
Total Assets	$16,000	$16,000	$16,000	**Total Liabilities and Capital**	$12,000	$16,000

The general revaluation of all of the partnership's assets immediately before the distribution resets to fair market value the book values of all of the partnership's assets and increases the book capital accounts of all three partners to $8,000. Amelia's book capital account is then reduced to zero by the distribution of cash and property having a total book value of $8,000. Following the distribution, the aggregate book value of the assets equals the aggregate book capital accounts of Brody and Corbett, due to the deemed book sale of all the partnership's assets. Inside book basis equals outside book basis.

Not so for tax basis. There has been, of course, no deemed sale of any of the partnership's assets and no adjustment of either inside basis or tax capital. In the distribution, Amelia takes cash and partnership property with an aggregate tax basis that is $4,000 less than her tax capital. In other words, she takes $4,000 less than her share of the inside basis. For this reason, the inside basis of the partnership's assets exceeds the partners' aggregate tax capital (and outside basis) by $4,000 following the distribution. Inside tax basis does not equal outside tax basis. When this happens, trouble follows, as you learned in Topic 5.1. Through the simple expedient of keeping the partnership alive, Brody and Corbett can defer recognition of $4,000 of gain for as long as they like. In this instance, the partnership tax system has failed to live up to its goal, which is to tax each of the partners as though they owned the partnership's property directly.

There also has been no adjustment to Brody's or Corbett's outside basis. If and when their partnership interests are liquidated by cash distributions (assuming that comes before the basis step-up at death afforded by section 1014), they will each recognize their shares of the $4,000 deferred gain. If their partnership interests are liquidated with property distributions instead, the distributed property will take a substituted basis in their hands, preserving the deferred gain for taxation if and when they sell the distributed property (again, assuming no section 1014 step-up). As you can see, death can play a big role in partnership tax planning, because of the relative ease of deferring partner gain until that unfortunate event erases the deferred gain for good.

The viability of this technique for eliminating partnership gain was limited by the 2004 amendment of section 734, to require adjustments under section 734(b) whenever there is a "substantial basis reduction." *See* Topic 9.2. Proposals have been made to require section 734(b) adjustments in all cases. Even if this occurred, however, it would not eliminate all (or even most) of the opportunities for adult recreation.

SHIFTING PARTNERSHIP GAIN OR LOSS AMONG PARTNERS

Distributions that change the basis of the distributed property: Exploiting defects in section 734(b)

Shifting can take several forms, as you will see in the coming examples. Here, we are concerned with the use of a distribution to change the total amount of partnership gain or loss for which a particular partner is responsible, even in cases where a section 734(b) adjustment is required to be made. The examples in this category rely on defects in the adjustment mechanism.

Let's begin with the ABC Partnership from the prior example (Figure 9.3.1) and give it $3,000 more cash:

FIGURE 9.3.3

Assets				Liabilities		
	Tax	**Book**	**FMV**		**Tax**	**Book**
Cash	$ 6,000	$ 6,000	$ 6,000	[None]	$ 0	$ 0
Property X	1,000	1,000	7,000			
Property Y	6,000	6,000	7,000	**Capital**		
Property Z	8,000	8,000	7,000	Amelia	7,000	7,000
				Brody	7,000	7,000
				Corbett	7,000	7,000
Total Assets	$21,000	$21,000	$27,000	**Total Liabilities and Capital**	$21,000	$21,000

Instead of liquidating Amelia's interest, the partnership makes a current distribution to her of $5,000 of cash and one-half of Property Y (value $3,500, basis $3,000). This significant distribution will change Amelia's percentage interest, so the partnership makes a general revaluation of all of its assets immediately before the distribution. Taking this revaluation and the distribution into account, the balance sheet looks like this:

FIGURE 9.3.4

Assets				Liabilities		
	Tax	**Book**	**FMV**		**Tax**	**Book**
Cash	$ 1,000	$ 1,000	$ 1,000	[None]	$ 0	$ 0
Property X	1,000	7,000	7,000			
Property Y	3,000	3,500	3,500	**Capital**		
Property Z	8,000	7,000	7,000	Amelia	0	500
				Brody	7,000	9,000
				Corbett	7,000	9,000
Total Assets	$13,000	$18,500	$18,500	**Total Liabilities and Capital**	$14,000	$18,500

Amelia takes her one-half of Property Y with a tax basis of $2,000, which is her original outside basis of $7,000 reduced by the $5,000 cash distribution. Because this is $1,000 less than the partnership's inside basis for one-half of Property Y, there is a positive adjustment of $1,000 under section 734(b)(1)(B). This positive adjustment is allocated between Property X and the remaining portion of Property Y under the rules of Treas. Reg. § 1.755–1(c). Following this adjustment, the aggregate basis of all of the partnership's properties is $14,000. Aggregate inside basis is equalized with aggregate outside basis, and you might think that all is right with the world.

Not quite. The general revaluation created a reverse section 704(c) layer in all of the partnership's assets, for which each of the three partners is equally responsible. Following the distributions and the section 734(b) adjustment, the partnership has aggregate gain in its properties of $4,500. Each of the partners is responsible for $1,500. Overall, the section 734(b) adjustment has ensured that the total amount ($6,000) of partnership gain has been preserved, as shown in Figure 9.3.5. This is an improvement over the earlier example. On the other hand, the gain has been shifted among the partners, as follows:

FIGURE 9.3.5

	Gain Before Distribution			Gain After Distribution		
	Distributed Property	Retained Property	Total	Distributed Property	Retained Property	Total
Amelia	$0	$2,000	$2,000	$1,500	$1,500	$3,000
Brody	0	2,000	2,000	0	1,500	1,500
Corbett	0	2,000	2,000	0	1,500	1,500
TOTAL	$0	$6,000	$6,000	$1,500	$4,500	$6,000

Amelia's share of the total gain has increased by $1,000, while those of Brody and Corbett have decreased by $500 each. The fly in the ointment here is the allocation of the section 734(b) adjustment to the common basis of the partnership's remaining properties. If it were personal to Amelia, like the section 743(b) special basis adjustment, her responsibility for the gain in the remaining partnership properties would drop to $500 and the responsibility of Brody and Corbett would increase to $2,000 each, thus preserving the *status quo ante.* This defect in the application of section 734(b) to current distributions is widely known and may be fixed by a future legislative change.

Another defect in section 734(b) affects its application to distributions where the outside basis of the distributee-partner is not equal to her share of the partnership's basis in its assets. This defect was illustrated in the partnership among Albert, Brooks and Dion discussed in Topic 9.2. It, too, can lead to shifts in aggregate partnership gain or loss among the partners, as it did in that example. And it, too, may be the subject of future legislative attention.

Distributions that change the basis of the distributed property: Shifting partnership gain or loss among assets (aka basis shifting)

A liquidating distribution can shift tax basis to a partnership property that is about to be sold, thereby reducing the current tax cost of the sale. Even if the section 734(b) adjustment mechanism functions perfectly, it can only ensure that the amount of basis added to the sale property is subtracted from the bases of the partnership's other properties. This is hardly onerous. It is akin to allowing an investor in, say, common stock to add basis to those shares that she is planning to sell—on the condition that she must subtract the same amount from the basis of those shares she plans to keep. There is nobody who would not take that deal.

This particular trick was on display in the first example in this Topic (Figure 9.3.1 and Figure 9.3.2). There, Amelia took a liquidating distribution that included Property X, an asset for sale that had a tax basis in the partnership's hands of $1,000. In the liquidating distribution, its tax basis increased to $5,000, so that Amelia recognized only $2,000 gain on its sale, $4,000 less than the partnership's gain would have been. If the partnership in that example had made a section 754 election, it would have been required to reduce the bases of its remaining properties, Property Y and Property Z, by the same $4,000, thus keeping total partnership gain constant at $6,000 ($4,000 remaining in the partnership and $2,000 realized by Amelia on the sale of Property X). The partnership tax-basis system would have done its job in this case, preserving both the aggregate amount of partnership gain ($6,000) and each partner's share of it ($2,000). The basis system is powerless, however, to stop the deferral of gain that is permitted by the nonrecognition rule. Therefore, rather than recognizing the full $6,000 of partnership gain on the sale of Property X, the partners recognize only $2,000 of it now, deferring the remaining $4,000 into the indefinite future.

Distributions that do not change the basis of the distributed property: Specially allocating partnership gain or loss (without substantial economic effect)

Suppose that the partnership does not liquidate Amelia's partnership interest, but instead distributes Property X to her in a current distribution. Because she takes the partnership's basis in Property X under section 732(a)(1), there is no section 734(b) adjustment, even if the partnership has made a section 754 election. This distribution does not change the tax basis of any partnership property. It does not change the total amount of partnership gain, which remains $6,000. It does, however, shift all of this gain to Amelia. Why would she agree to such a thing? If Amelia is a foreign individual not subject to US tax, she may not care. (In a different case, a partnership holding an asset with a built-in loss could distribute it to a partner, who by selling it would avail herself of the entire loss. In that case, the other partners would have to agree to this loss-shifting, which might occur because the distributee is in a higher tax bracket than they.)

Following the general revaluation of the partnership's assets, the balance sheet looks like this:

FIGURE 9.3.6

Assets			Liabilities		
	Tax	Book	FMV		Tax	Book
Cash	$ 3,000	$ 3,000	$ 3,000	[None]	$ 0	$ 0
Property X	1,000	7,000	7,000			
Property Y	6,000	7,000	7,000	**Capital**		
Property Z	8,000	7,000	7,000	Amelia	6,000	8,000
				Brody	6,000	8,000
				Corbett	6,000	8,000
Total Assets	$18,000	$24,000	$24,000	**Total Liabilities and Capital**	$18,000	$24,000

The distribution of Property X affects only Amelia's capital accounts:

FIGURE 9.3.7

Assets			Liabilities		
	Tax	Book	FMV		Tax	Book
Cash	$ 3,000	$ 3,000	$ 3,000	[None]	$ 0	$ 0
Property X	0	0	0			
Property Y	6,000	7,000	7,000	**Capital**		
Property Z	8,000	7,000	7,000	Amelia	5,000	1,000
				Brody	6,000	8,000
				Corbett	6,000	8,000
Total Assets	$17,000	$17,000	$17,000	**Total Liabilities and Capital**	$17,000	$17,000

When Amelia sells Property X (value $7,000, basis $1,000), she will recognize gain of $6,000. Meanwhile, the net gain remaining in the partnership is reduced to zero. As before, the basis system is doing what it can. There has been no change in the outside basis of either Brody or Corbett, so if and when their partnership interests are liquidated for $8,000 in cash (the current amount of their book capital accounts), they will each recognize $2,000 of gain, assuming they have not died in the meantime. Amelia will harvest a corresponding $4,000 loss on the taxable liquidation of her partnership interest.

It is illuminating to consider the other way the partnership could have shifted to Amelia the gain in Property X. A special allocation of that gain would be permissible under section 704(b), assuming that it met the standards for substantial economic effect. (Prior to the distribution, Property X does not have a book-tax difference, so section 704(c) would not interfere with this special allocation of gain.) As we reviewed in Topic 4.3, this would require that the allocation of gain be reflected in Amelia's capital account. Following the sale of Property X for cash and the special allocation of the gain, the partnership's balance sheet would look like this:

FIGURE 9.3.8

Assets				Liabilities		
	Tax	**Book**	**FMV**		**Tax**	**Book**
Cash	$10,000	$10,000	$10,000	[None]	$ 0	$ 0
Property X	0	0	0			
Property Y	6,000	6,000	7,000	**Capital**		
Property Z	8,000	8,000	7,000	Amelia	12,000	12,000
				Brody	6,000	6,000
				Corbett	6,000	6,000
Total Assets	$24,000	$24,000	$24,000	**Total Liabilities and Capital**	$24,000	$24,000

The distribution of the $7,000 proceeds from the sale of Property X would reduce Amelia's tax and book capital to $5,000. Her tax capital would be the same as in the property distribution, but her book capital would be $4,000 higher. Why? In order to have economic effect under Treas. Reg. § 1.704–1(b)(2)(ii), the special allocation of the $6,000 gain must be reflected in Amelia's book capital account. In the distribution scenario, by contrast, only Amelia's $2,000 share of the revaluation gain on Property X is so reflected. The $4,000 difference is the other partners' share of the $6,000 gain. The economic-effect regulations require this $4,000 difference to be included in Amelia's book capital account. Upon liquidation of the partnership if not sooner, she must be paid this amount. This is an expensive proposition for Brody and Corbett, and it is unlikely they would be willing to pay Amelia $4,000, even on a deferred basis, for deflecting $4,000 of gain. No matter—by simply distributing the built-in gain asset to Amelia, they can accomplish the same effect and pay Amelia only such compensation, if any, as she actually demands.

Distributions that do not change the basis of the distributed property: Erasing reverse section 704(c) layers

All the examples to this point—those that featured a change in the tax basis of the distributed property as well as those that did not—have involved the distribution of property with a reverse section 704(c) layer arising from the revaluation occasioned by the distribution itself. Consider, for example, Figure 9.3.6. The general revaluation of the partnership's assets creates book-tax differences for all of the partnership's properties except its cash. Under Treas. Reg. § 1.704–3(a)(6), the partnership must make reverse section 704(c) allocations to its partners so as to take into account these differences. That means, for example, that the partnership must allocate equally among its partners the first $6,000 of tax gain arising on its sale of Property X.

This obligation ceases when the partnership distributes Property X— section 704(c) does not "follow" the property out of the partnership. Further, the nonrecognition rule ensures that neither the partnership nor its partners recognize any of this gain on the distribution itself. This frustrates the policy of section 704(c) as it is expressed in the Treasury regulations. The exact effect can be seen by looking again at Figure 9.3.7. Following the distribution of Property X to Amelia, there are book-tax differences throughout the capital accounts. Amelia's tax capital is $4,000 greater than her book capital. The tax capital of the other two partners is, in the aggregate, $4,000 less than their aggregate book capital. On the assets side of the balance sheet, however, there is no aggregate book-tax difference. In Topic 8.2, you saw how the ceiling rule creates exactly this situation—book-tax differences in the partners' capital with no remaining book-tax difference in the contributed asset—and you learned how remedial or curative allocations can be used to address it. No remedial or curative allocations would be allowed here.

A property distribution can just as easily erase one or many reverse section 704(c) layers that have existed since long before the distribution. Imagine, for example, that Partnership ABC had revalued its assets at some time in the past, immediately before it admitted, say, Daniel as a new partner. The purpose and effect of the reverse section 704(c) layer created by this revaluation is to ensure that the original partners are allocated all of the gain or loss existing in the partnership's assets at the time that Daniel joined the partnership and that Daniel is allocated none of such gain or loss. Now suppose that the partnership distributes to Daniel some of that property. He immediately inherits all of the pre-existing gain or loss in the distributed property and the original partners are responsible for none of it.

This prompts two observations. First, section 704(c) is one of the most complex provisions in Subchapter K, made more so by the elaborations in Treasury regulations issued over the past 30 years or so. A good deal of that complexity comes from the presence of ever-multiplying reverse section 704(c) layers. Given that reverse layers can be readily eliminated by property distributions, it appears that the Treasury Department and IRS have been building their edifice on some pretty soft ground.

Second, one wonders how Congress feels about this. The ready availability of property distributions as a "back door" to escape from reverse section 704(c) layers may suggest that Congress either has never heard of reverse section 704(c) layers or does not much care. The former seems unlikely. As to the latter, it is perhaps telling that Congress has enacted not one, but two statutes to prevent property distributions from eliminating *forward* section 704(c) layers. These are section 704(c)(1)(B) and section 737, which we will review next, in Topic 9.4. As we will see there, Congress clearly understands how partnership distributions might be used to defer the recognition of precontribution gains and wants to prevent it. The level of Congressional commitment to, or even interest in, preventing partnership distributions from doing the same thing to gains that arise post-contribution is far less clear.

9.4 SECTIONS 704(c)(1)(B) AND 737: THE "ANTI-MIXING-BOWL" STATUTES

Section 704(c)(1)(B) was enacted in 1989 and section 737 followed close behind in 1992. They are joined together in the minds of tax lawyers as the "anti-mixing-bowl" rules, sometimes shortened to the "amb(e)rs." I prefer to think of them as "the joint strike force to protect forward section 704(c) layers," but please do not repeat that to anyone. To understand these labels, you need some history.

Two events in the mid-1980s conspired to create section 704(c)(1)(B). You already know the first one, which was the 1984 amendment of section 704(c) to make it mandatory. As we reviewed in Topic 8.1, Congress had been quite happy during the three decades prior to that date to let taxpayers use partnerships to shift gains and losses among themselves. By 1984, the growing numbers of tax-indifferent partners caused Congress to re-think that decision. For the first time, Congress got serious about tracking "the variation between the basis of property to the partnership and its fair market value at the time of contribution" and making sure that the contributing partner could not shift to other partners the gain or loss represented by that variation.

This shift in Congressional perspective might have been enough by itself to beget section 704(c)(1)(B). As it turned out, however, the pace of legislative change got a boost from a likely suspect, the investment bankers. They were marketing a technique to accomplish a tax-free exchange of business assets through the use of a partnership. They called it a "mixing-bowl" transaction. In oversimplified terms, Corporation A and Corporation B would contribute appreciated Business A and appreciated Business B, respectively, to a partnership. After a decent interval, the partnership would liquidate, distributing Business A to Corporation B and Business B to Corporation A. Under the usual nonrecognition and basis rules, neither corporation would recognize gain or loss and each would take the assets of the distributed business with an aggregate tax basis equal to its outside basis in the partnership (which itself equaled, or closely approximated, its prior tax basis in the contributed business). This duplicated the results of a like-kind exchange of the assets of the businesses—without the need for those assets to be like-kind.

In truth, this transaction was more often discussed than executed and suffered from numerous tax and non-tax complexities. Nevertheless, it was just the sort of threat that could rouse Congress to action and it did. Section 704(c)(1)(B) requires a contributing partner to recognize gain or loss on the partnership's distribution to another partner of the contributed property, just as if the partnership had sold that property in a fully taxable transaction for fair market value. The required basis adjustments mimic those that would occur on such a sale. Because all of this happens "as if" the partnership had engaged in a taxable sale, section 731(b) remains intact, and the partnership itself recognizes nothing.

There are three very important limitations on this gain or loss recognition. The first limitation is temporal. Section 704(c)(1)(B) applies only if the distribution of the contributed property occurs within seven years after the contribution. This is a rough-hewn (and fairly aggressive) way to measure whether the contribution and distribution are likely to have been part of a single plan and reflects the origin of the statute as an anti-abuse rule targeted at a particular transaction.

Second, the amount of gain the contributor recognizes is limited to the gain she would have been allocated on a taxable sale by reason of the "variation" described in section 704(c)(1)(A)—which in this context is interpreted to mean her forward section 704(c) layer, the precontribution gain. The partnership uses its chosen section 704(c) method in making this allocation. *See* Treas. Reg. § 1.704–4(a)(5), example (3) (illustrating use of the remedial method in this context). Gain is neither recognized nor allocated with respect to any post-contribution appreciation in the value of the contributed property, whether or not encapsulated in a reverse section 704(c) layer. This significant limitation on the scope of section 704(c)(1)(B) reflects the nature of Congressional concern, which was to prevent the shifting of precontribution gain or loss, consistent with the 1984 amendment. *See* Prop. Treas. Reg. §§ 1.704–4(c)(7), 1.737–2(f) (statutes do not apply to reverse section 704(c) gain).

The third limitation on the scope of section 704(c)(1)(B) is our old friend section 704(c)(1)(C). As we reviewed in Topic 8.4, that section, as interpreted by proposed regulations, has eliminated book-tax differences for all assets contributed to a partnership with a built-in loss. Thus, no allocations are required or permitted under section 704(c)(1)(A) with respect to such an asset. Because section 704(c)(1)(B) triggers recognition of the section 704(c)(1)(A) amount upon a distribution of the contributed property, there is nothing to trigger in the case of a built-in loss asset. Accordingly, although the statutory language of section 704(c)(1)(B) continues to read "gain or loss," it actually only applies to built-in gains. For clarity, I will refer to it that way going forward.

Applying section 704(c)(1)(B) to the above example, both Corporation A and Corporation B would recognize the full amount of the gain inherent in their respective businesses. They could, of course, remain partners for more than 7 years in order to escape gain recognition. Yet this presents several obstacles, including allocating profits, losses, management responsibilities and changes in the relative values of Business A and Business B while they remain in partnership. Ultimately, most parties find that this particular tax-savings game is not worth the candle.

There are, however, other games and other candles. Assume, for example, that Corporation A forms a partnership with its subsidiary,

Corporation A1, to which it contributes cash equal to the amount it is willing to pay for Business B. The partnership purchases an asset, Asset A (which, until 1994, could have been marketable securities), as directed by Corporation B. Corporation B contributes its business to the partnership and, after a decent interval, takes Asset A as a liquidating distribution. If this transaction is successful, Corporation B recognizes no gain or loss and gets Asset A with a tax basis approximately equal to its former tax basis in Business B. Corporation A acquires Business B, which it continues to hold in partnership with its subsidiary.

There are reasons to think that this transaction would not be successful. The business purpose of the partnership and the role of Corporation B as a partner might be challenged under traditional tax principles. Beginning in 1994, the general anti-abuse regulation might buttress this argument. *See* Treas. Reg. § 1.701–2(d), example (7). As you saw in Topic 2.7, this transaction could be challenged as a disguised sale of Business B by Corporation B to the partnership and of Asset A by the partnership to Corporation B. Indeed, beginning with the publication of final regulations under section 707(a)(2)(B) in 1992, this transaction would be *presumed* to be a disguised sale if the contribution and distribution occurred within two years. Treas. Reg. § 1.707–3(c).

Nevertheless, Congress continued to be concerned with distributions through which a contributing partner could exit the partnership prior to the partnership's sale or distribution of the contributed property and thus could avoid recognizing the precontribution gain in that property. Section 737 was its response to that concern.

Under section 737(a), a partner who receives a distribution of property within seven years following a property contribution must recognize gain (even as enacted, this statute did not cover built-in losses) equal to the lesser of (1) her "excess distribution" and (2) her "net precontribution gain." The first implication—so obvious that it can be missed—is that section 737 does not apply to a distribution to a partner who has *not* contributed property in the past seven years, either because she has never contributed property or because her last contribution was more than seven years ago. The amount of gain recognized under section 737 cannot exceed the distributee-partner's excess distribution. This is the amount of gain the distributee-partner would recognize if the property distribution were instead cash equal to the fair market value of the distributed property. Treas. Reg. § 1.737–1(b). Finally, the amount of gain recognized cannot exceed the distributee-partner's net precontribution gain. This is the amount of gain that the distributee-partner would have to recognize under section 704(c)(1)(B) if the partnership distributed to another partner (or sold) all of the property it now owns which the distributee-partner contributed to the partnership over the past seven years. Treas. Reg. § 1.737–1(c). As with section 704(c)(1)(B), correlative basis adjustments are required under section 737(c). Section 737(d)(1) provides an exception for distributions of previously contributed property.

It is a bit surprising that section 737 applies to current distributions, because a current distribution does not break the distributee-partner's link with the partnership and she remains responsible for her forward section 704(c) layer (as well as for any reverse layers for which she has responsibility). Both the language of the statute and its legislative history leave no doubt, however, that current distributions are covered. Perhaps Congress was wary of the application of the statute turning on the retention of a small partnership interest, the value of which might be less than the tax liability under section 704(c) that came with it.

Section 704(c)(1)(B) and section 737 can both apply in a single distribution, and sometimes to the same partner. Imagine, for example, that Corporation A and Corporation B contribute Business A and Business B, respectively, to a partnership. Other, perhaps related, parties also own small partnership interests. Within seven years, the partnership distributes Business A to Corporation B in liquidation of its interest. Business B says put in the partnership. In this distribution, section 704(c)(1)(B) applies to Corporation A and section 737 applies to Corporation B. Now imagine the full Monty, with the partnership also distributing Business B to Corporation A. In this, the classic mixing-bowl transaction, both section 704(c)(1)(B) and section 737 apply to each partner. In such case, section 704(c)(1)(B) applies first. Treas. Reg. § 1.737–1(c)(2)(iv).

The anti-mixing-bowl statutes reflect a developing vision regarding the proper tax treatment of precontribution gain and loss. In 1984, by making section 704(c) mandatory, Congress decided that a contributing partner must be responsible for recognizing any precontribution gain or loss in the contributed property. In 1989, by enacting section 704(c)(1)(B), it decided that the contributing partner could not avoid this responsibility by causing the partnership to dispose of the contributed property in an otherwise tax-free distribution. With the enactment of section 737 in 1992, Congress decided that a contributing partner could not avoid this responsibility by leaving the partnership.

Taken together, the anti-mixing-bowl statutes evidence a willingness on the part of Congress to police not only the allocation of precontribution gain and loss, but also the timing of its recognition by the contributing partner. As we saw in our study of the tax basis system earlier in this Chapter, the contributing partner could not really shake her precontribution gain or loss, even prior to the enactment of the anti-mixing-bowl statutes. In the case of a distribution now governed by section 704(c)(1)(B), the contributing partner's precontribution gain or loss remained embedded in her partnership interest following the distribution, to be recognized when she sold her partnership interest or the partnership liquidated it for cash. Similarly, in the case of a distribution now governed by section 737, the distributee-partner took a tax basis in the distributed property that approximated her basis in the contributed property, so that her precontribution gain or loss was preserved in the distributed property. Congress seems to have recognized both of these as transactions that shifted the contributing partner's forward layer from the contributed property to some other property, which might well be retained long after the contributed property was gone. This struck Congress as fundamentally inconsistent with its decision in 1984 to hold contributing partners responsible for the precontribution gain or loss in the contributed property. As we saw in Topic 9.3, gain- and loss-shifting are alive and well for reverse section 704(c) layers. Since 1992, the same cannot be said for forward layers.

9.4.1 Theo's Supermarket and Osgood's Automall are on opposite ends of the fast-growing town of Drinkwater. By a quirk of fate, Osgood used to own a large parcel of land next to Theo and Theo owned a similar parcel next to Osgood. Both were suitable for development, either by the business next door or by one of the many new businesses that were springing up in town. Three years ago, Theo and Osgood formed a real estate development partnership with Raeburn, to which Theo and Osgood contributed their parcels, Land T and Land O, respectively, and Raeburn contributed cash to purchase new properties. It was an equal, general partnership, whose balance sheet (expanded to show asset values) looks like this today:

Assets				Liabilities		
	Tax	**Book**	**FMV**		**Tax**	**Book**
Parcel O	$ 20,000	$ 80,000	$120,000	[None]	$ 0	$ 0
Parcel T	30,000	80,000	120,000			
New Property A	50,000	50,000	80,000	**Capital**		
New Property B	30,000	30,000	40,000	Osgood	20,000	80,000
				Theo	30,000	80,000
				Raeburn	80,000	80,000
Total Assets	$130,000	$240,000	$360,000	**Total Liabilities and Capital**	$130,000	$240,000

After three years of looking, the partnership has not found a buyer for any of its properties. Discouraged, Theo approaches the other partners with a request to withdraw from the partnership, taking New Properties A and B as a liquidating distribution. If he does that, what are the tax consequences?

a) Theo, $50,000 gain; Raeburn, $0 gain

b) Theo, $50,000 gain; Raeburn, $40,000 gain

c) Theo, $90,000 gain; Raeburn, $0 gain

d) Theo, $90,000 gain; Raeburn, $40,000 gain

9.4.2   In Question 9.4.1, what is Theo's aggregate basis in New Properties A and B and what is the partnership's inside basis in Parcel T immediately following the distribution?

a)   Theo's basis, $30,000; partnership's basis, $30,000

b)   Theo's basis, $80,000; partnership's basis, $80,000

c)   Theo's basis, $80,000; partnership's basis, $120,000

d)   Theo's basis, $120,000; partnership's basis, $120,000

9.4.3   How does your answer to Question 9.4.1 change if Theo takes Parcel O as a liquidating distribution instead?

a)   Theo, $50,000 gain; Osgood, $0 gain

b)   Theo, $50,000 gain; Osgood, $60,000 gain

c)   Theo, $50,000 gain; Osgood, $100,000 gain

d)   Theo, $90,000 gain; Osgood, $100,000 gain

9.4.4   How does your answer to Question 9.4.1 change if the partnership liquidates Raeburn's interest by distributing Parcel T?

a)   Theo, $0 gain; Raeburn, $0 gain

b)   Theo, $50,000 gain; Raeburn, $0 gain

c)   Theo, $50,000 gain; Raeburn, $40,000 gain

d)   Theo, $90,000 gain; Raeburn, $40,000 gain

9.4.5   In Question 9.4.4, what is Theo's outside basis and what is Raeburn's tax basis in Parcel T immediately following the distribution?

a)   Theo's basis, $30,000; Raeburn's basis, $30,000

b)   Theo's basis, $30,000; Raeburn's basis, $80,000

c)   Theo's basis, $80,000; Raeburn's basis, $30,000

d)   Theo's basis, $80,000; Raeburn's basis, $80,000

9.4.6   In Question 9.4.1, what are the tax consequences to all three partners if the partnership liquidates, distributing Parcel T to Raeburn, Parcel O to Theo, and New Properties A and B to Osgood?

a)   Raeburn, $0 gain; Theo, $50,000 gain; Osgood, $60,000 gain

b)   Raeburn, $0 gain; Theo, $100,000 gain; Osgood, $120,000 gain

c)   Raeburn, $40,000 gain; Theo, $50,000 gain; Osgood, $60,000 gain

d)   Raeburn, $50,000 gain; Theo, $0 gain; Osgood, $60,000 gain

9.4.7   In Question 9.4.1, what are the tax consequences to Theo and Osgood if the partnership makes a current distribution to each partner, consisting of a one-third interest in Parcel O?

a)   Theo, $10,000 gain; Osgood, $40,000 gain

b)   Theo, $33,333 gain; Osgood, $40,000 gain

    c)   Theo, $33,333 gain; Osgood, $60,000 gain

    d)   Theo, $50,000 gain; Osgood, $60,000 gain

9.4.8   In this variation, Parcel O has enjoyed appreciation that outstrips that of the other properties, and the partnership has not yet deployed $30,000 of Raeburn's cash contribution. The partnership's balance sheet (with asset values) looks like this:

Assets				Liabilities		
	Tax	**Book**	**FMV**		**Tax**	**Book**
Cash	$ 30,000	$ 30,000	$ 30,000	[None]	$ 0	$ 0
Parcel O	20,000	80,000	210,000			
Parcel T	30,000	80,000	120,000	**Capital**		
New Property A	50,000	50,000	90,000	Osgood	20,000	80,000
				Theo	30,000	80,000
				Raeburn	80,000	80,000
Total Assets	$130,000	$240,000	$450,000	**Total Liabilities and Capital**	$130,000	$240,000

Osgood withdraws from the partnership, taking a liquidating distribution of Parcel T and $30,000 in cash. What are the tax consequences to Osgood and Theo?

    a)   Theo, $0 gain; Osgood, $50,000 gain

    b)   Theo, $40,000 gain; Osgood, $60,000 gain

    c)   Theo, $50,000 gain; Osgood, $60,000 gain

    d)   Theo, $50,000 gain; Osgood, $70,000 gain

9.5 DISTRIBUTIONS OF MARKETABLE SECURITIES: SECTION 731(c)

The main limit on the use of tax planning like that described in Topic 9.3 is not the flexibility of the tax law or the imagination of tax advisors, but instead the availability of partnership assets that partners would actually want to own themselves. Indeed, the most routine example of the deferral offered by section 731(a)(1)—the distribution of property in liquidation of the interest of a partner who would recognize gain if she took cash instead—is entirely hypothetical if that partner will only take cash.

Shrewd tax planners in the 1980s publicized a way around this problem. United States Treasury bonds, investment-grade corporate bonds and even stock in blue-chip companies are very much like cash, being easily valued and highly liquid, but are assuredly "property" for purposes of the partnership distribution rules. Even the most cash-insistent partner is likely to be happy with a distribution of assets like these. No matter if the partnership did not own such assets—it could use the cash it was planning to distribute to buy them or, if it did not have cash, it could borrow.

It is easy to over-sell the advantages of a distribution of this sort. Although the nonrecognition rule would apply to the distribution of marketable securities, so too would the basis rules. In a liquidating distribution, the distributee-partner would take the distributed securities with a tax basis equal to her outside basis in the partnership under section 732(b). If she immediately sold them, the very gain that the transaction was meant to defer would be triggered. Securities of this nature have, however, another significant advantage—they make very good collateral for a loan. A patient partner could receive such assets, borrow against them for living necessities and the occasional Porsche, and wait to die.

In the halls of government, this was an unwelcome development. The Joint Committee on Taxation, the Treasury Department Office of Tax Policy and the IRS are, of course, aware of the tax advantages of partnership property distributions. But the availability of these advantages has always been limited by the idiosyncrasies of partnerships and their partners. Simply put, cash distributions are more common than property distributions. As long as it stays that way, the damage, from the government's perspective, is contained. The marketable securities gambit posed a threat to this fragile truce, because it made property distributions "scalable."

Congress responded in 1994 with the enactment of new section 731(c). It treats marketable securities like money for purposes of applying section 731(a)(1) (and not applying section 737). This is a surgical strike. If you remember nothing else about section 731(c), remember this: it does not treat marketable securities like money for all purposes, but only for the limited purpose of computing the amount of gain, if any, under section 731(a)(1). For all other purposes, marketable securities are still property. To see why this matters, consider the follow examples.

Jack Fracker is a partner in a partnership that owns gas leases, which it hopes to sell at a profit to gas companies wishing to drill. The leases are capital assets in the partnership's hands. The price of gas soars, making both the partnership's leases and Jack's interest in the partnership more valuable. Jack approaches the partnership with a request to liquidate his interest for a cash payment of $1 million. Jack's outside basis is $300,000. After consulting with tax counsel, the partnership offers Jack $900,000 in 30-year Treasury bonds. Jack takes the deal.

Prior to 1994, Jack would have recognized no gain on the liquidation and taken the Treasuries with a tax basis of $300,000. Assuming that he did not make an election under section 1278(b) to include market discount ratably in income, his $600,000 gain would be deferred until the maturity of the bonds in 30 years. If he died in the meantime, so much the better.

Under new section 731(c), Jack treats the Treasuries as cash for purposes of computing his gain on the distribution. The $600,000 gain is taxed to him as capital gain in the year of the distribution. To determine his tax basis in the Treasuries, he begins with the basis determined under section 732(b), which is $300,000, and adds the recognized gain, which is $600,000, resulting in a tax basis of $900,000. *See* section 731(c)(4). Although Jack's tax basis in the Treasuries is in this case equal to their fair market value, that is not how it is determined. As we will see, there are lots of cases in which the distributee-partner's tax basis in distributed marketable securities is different than fair market value.

Now assume the price of gas goes down, not up. The partnership distributes Treasury bonds with a value of $250,000 in liquidation of Jack's interest. Jack recognizes no loss on this distribution under section 731(a)(2), because the Treasuries are not considered to be money for purposes of applying that section. Instead, Jack takes a $300,000 tax basis in the distributed securities under section 732(b) and holds them with a $50,000 built-in loss.

Finally, assume that Jack's partnership interest is worth $900,000, but he wants to keep half of it. The partnership distributes to him $450,000 in Treasury bonds and reduces his percentage interest in the partnership to 20%. Under section 731(a)(1), as modified by section 731(c), Jack recognizes, at most, $150,000 of capital gain, which is the excess of the value of the Treasuries ($450,000) over Jack's outside basis ($300,000). The amount of Jack's gain, and his tax basis in the Treasuries, will depend on the partnership's inside basis in the Treasuries. Let's examine two alternatives.

In the likely case that the partnership bought the Treasury bonds in order to distribute them to Jack, their basis to the partnership will be $450,000. In this case, Jack's gain will be $150,000. His basis in the Treasuries will be $450,000, but not because this is the value, or even the inside basis, of the Treasuries. Rather, under section 731(c)(4), Jack will take a basis in the Treasuries of $300,000 under section 732(a)(2) and then increase it by his $150,000 recognized gain to $450,000. In other words, Jack determines his tax basis in the Treasuries by applying the usual rules and then adding the gain he recognizes under section 731(c).

If the inside basis of the Treasuries is, say, $200,000, Jack's basis in them will depend on the amount of gain he recognizes, which in turn depends on the application of section 731(c)(3)(B). We will get to that in a minute. In any event, it will be far less than their value—Jack will hold the Treasuries with a built-in gain. By the same token, Jack's remaining basis in his partnership interest will be $100,000, which is his initial outside basis of $300,000, reduced under section 733 by the $200,000 inside basis of the Treasury securities distributed to him. In other words, Jack determines his remaining outside basis under the usual rules, ignoring section 731(c) altogether. *See* section 731(c)(5). This has the very desirable effect of adjusting Jack's outside basis by no more than the inside basis of the property distributed to him. Thus, if his outside basis equaled his share of the inside basis prior to the distribution, it will continue to do so after the distribution. Section 731(c) does not disturb an existing equality of inside and outside basis.

The definition of what is a "marketable security" is expansive and seems written by hounds who, having cornered the fox, were loath to let him get away. Expanding beyond the particular transactions that apparently moved Congress to action, the definition is entirely agnostic regarding whether the security in question is long-held or newly acquired, or whether it is appreciated, depreciated or neither. This definition is explored in the Questions below. Section 731(c) has, however, several exceptions for partnerships or transactions that are not meant to be the quarry of the hunt. Subject to some qualifications and an anti-stuffing rule, section 731(c) does not apply to a distribution of securities contributed to the partnership by the distributee-partner, securities acquired by the partnership in exchange for business assets in a nonrecognition exchange, or property that was not a marketable security when it was acquired by the partnership. Sections 731(c)(3)(A)(i) and (ii); Treas. Reg. § 1.731–2(d).

Section 731(c)(3)(A)(iii) provides an important exception for investment partnerships. You might wonder why this exception exists at all. A distribution of a marketable security by an investment partnership provides the same deferral benefit as such a distribution by any other partnership, and investment partnerships are most likely to have marketable securities close at hand for distribution. The answer can only be that this advantage was historically available to such partnerships, rather than newly created by the tax alchemists of the 1980s, and Congress did not think it necessary to curtail this longstanding privilege.

The most pervasive exception is section 731(c)(3)(B). Under the statute, the amount of marketable securities treated as cash is reduced by the excess of (1) the distributee's share of the partnership's gain in its marketable securities immediately before the distribution over (2) the same share immediately after the distribution. (Although the statutory formulation leaves room for applying this rule by issuer and class of security, the Treasury regulations lump all marketable securities together for this purpose. Treas. Reg. § 1.731–2(b)(1).) Therefore, the distributee's recognized gain on the distribution is reduced dollar-for-dollar by the reduction in her share of the partnership's built-in gain in its marketable securities on account of the distribution.

This exception is different in kind than those identified earlier. It is not limited to special situations. It changes the computation of the amount of gain recognized in most, although not all, distributions of marketable securities. Sorry, but you can't skip it. There is also virtually no chance that you will understand the next few paragraphs on first reading. Skim them and focus on the Jack Fracker example that follows. Then come back and read these paragraphs again, when, I hope, they will make more sense.

It is important to know what the section 731(c)(3)(B) exception is not. It is not a gross-value test—*i.e.*, it is not focused on whether the distributee receives more or less than her share of the value of the marketable securities held by the partnership. It measures changes in the distributee's share of the gain, not the value, of marketable securities. The less appreciation in the marketable securities, relative to the other assets of the partnership, the less helpful this exception will be. If the marketable securities are not appreciated at all, the exception is useless, because the distributee's share of gain both before and after the distribution is zero.

On the other hand, the section 731(c)(3)(B) exception can be very helpful for a partnership (for example, a venture-capital fund that does not qualify as an investment partnership because of its other activities) that owns a marketable security with substantial appreciation and distributes it pro-rata to all of its partners. In this case, the exception reduces the amount of the distribution treated as cash from the value of the distributed securities down to their inside basis. If each of the partners has an outside basis at least equal to their share of this amount, no partner recognizes gain on the distribution. The partners take the distributed securities with the partnership's basis and reduce their outside bases by a like amount—the same results they would achieve had section 731(c) never been enacted.

The section 731(c)(3)(B) exception does not take into account the distributee's share of gain in directly held marketable securities immediately following the distribution. Instead, it looks only to her share of the gain in the marketable securities that remain in the partnership. Thus, this test is not attempting to measure the distributee's total exposure to gain in marketable securities before and after the distribution, although it might appear logical to do so. Its purpose is best understood by reading the legislative history, which justifies this exception as follows:

> It is not intended that a partner be taxed under the provision [section 731(c)] on the partnership's gain attributable to his share of the marketable securities distributed to him, because he has not exchanged his share of any other partnership asset for an increased share of the partnership's marketable securities.

H.R. REP. NO. 103–826, 103d Cong., 2d Sess., Part 1, at 188 (1994). Taking an aggregate approach, this legislative history views a partnership's distribution of marketable securities, to the extent that it exceeds the distributee's share of the partnership's marketable securities, as an exchange of the distributee's share of other partnership assets for an additional share of marketable securities. It measures such shares by gain, not by gross value. The statute does not treat a distributee's exchange of some or all of her share of the gain in other partnership assets for more gain in the distributed marketable securities as a fair trade. It refuses to give the distributee "credit" for assuming gain in distributed marketable securities. This may be because of the perceived ease in borrowing against such securities and deferring, perhaps for a long time, the gain built into them. Whatever the reason, the result is that a partner receiving a distribution of marketable securities that causes her share of the partnership's gain in its assets as a whole to increase can still pay current tax under section 731(c).

   This is particularly so in a current distribution. Take Jack Fracker's partnership. After the value of its leases has increased sufficiently to give Jack's interest a $900,000 value, the partnership's balance sheet (expanded to show asset values) might look like this:

FIGURE 9.5.1

Assets				Liabilities		
	Tax	**Book**	**FMV**		**Tax**	**Book**
Cash	$100,000	$100,000	$ 100,000	[None]	$ 0	$ 0
Treasuries	200,000	200,000	450,000			
Leases	600,000	600,000	2,150,000	**Capital**		
				Earle	300,000	300,000
				Bobby Ray	300,000	300,000
				Jack	300,000	300,000
Total Assets	$900,000	$900,000	$2,700,000	**Total Liabilities and Capital**	$900,000	$900,000

   Prior to distributing its Treasury securities to Jack in redemption of one-half of his interest, the partnership revalues:

FIGURE 9.5.2

Assets				Liabilities		
	Tax	**Book**	**FMV**		**Tax**	**Book**
Cash	$100,000	$ 100,000	$ 100,000	[None]	$ 0	$ 0
Treasuries	200,000	450,000	450,000			
Leases	600,000	2,150,000	2,150,000	**Capital**		
				Earle	300,000	900,000
				Bobby Ray	300,000	900,000
				Jack	300,000	900,000
Total Assets	$900,000	$2,700,000	$2,700,000	**Total Liabilities and Capital**	$900,000	$2,700,000

It then makes the distribution to Jack:

FIGURE 9.5.3

Assets				Liabilities		
	Tax	Book	FMV		Tax	Book
Cash	$100,000	$ 100,000	$ 100,000	[None]	$ 0	$ 0
Leases	600,000	2,150,000	2,150,000			
				Capital		
				Earle	300,000	900,000
				Bobby Ray	300,000	900,000
				Jack	100,000	450,000
Total Assets				**Total Liabilities and Capital**		
	$700,000	$2,250,000	$2,250,000		$700,000	$2,250,000

Applying the exception of section 731(c)(3)(B), Jack's share of the gain in the partnership's Treasury securities immediately before the distribution was $83,333 (one-third of $250,000). His share of the gain in the Treasury securities held by the partnership immediately after is $0. The amount of the distribution that is treated as cash therefore is reduced by $83,333, from $450,000 to $366,667, and Jack's recognized gain is the difference between that and his outside basis of $300,000, or $66,667. Jack takes the distributed Treasury securities with a tax basis of $266,667 ($200,000 inside basis plus $66,667 gain recognized), and a built-in gain of $183,333 ($450,000 value less $266,667 tax basis). His remaining outside basis is $100,000.

Take a step back and consider the tax effect of this distribution on Jack. Before the distribution, his share of the partnership's gain in its assets was $600,000, which is one-third of the excess of the value of the partnership's assets over their inside bases. After the distribution, he is responsible for gain in two different "pockets." First, he has $183,333 built-in gain in the Treasury securities that he now owns directly. Second, he is still a partner in the partnership and, as such, is responsible for one-third of the reverse section 704(c) layer created by the revaluation. This layer is $1,550,000 (entirely attributable to the partnership's leases) and Jack's share of that is $516,667. Even if the partnership has made a section 754 election, there is no adjustment of the basis of the leases under section 734(b), because gain recognized under section 731(c) is ignored for purposes of section 734(b). *See* section 731(c)(5).

Adding these two amounts together, Jack's share of the gain in the partnership's assets is now $700,000—$100,000 more than his share before the transaction. Jack's reward for taking a bigger share of the partnership's gain is a current tax bill. He recognizes gain of $66,667 under section 731(c).

Jack can trace his tax trouble to the reverse layer created by the revaluation. Without responsibility for that layer, his total share of the partnership's gain would not be increased by the distribution. But why does section 731(c) not take that into account? For a statute enacted in 1994, it seems curiously blind to section 704(c) principles. The formula in section 731(c)(3)(B) is built on the assumptions that total partnership gain is always constant and that such gain is always proportionately allocated among partners, so that a distributee who takes more than her share of the gain in marketable securities must perforce have less than her share of the gain in other partnership properties. Both assumptions are wrong, or at least not necessarily right. As you saw in Topic 9.2, total partnership gain increases in any case that a partner takes an asset with a stepped-down basis and the partnership does not make a section 734(b) adjustment. And as Jack has learned, distributions have a way of changing partners' shares of partnership gain.

So why isn't section 731(c)(3)(B) more precise? The simple answer is that section 731(c) is an anti-abuse rule, meant to discourage a particular transaction, the distribution of marketable securities, that Congress doubts has a strong commercial purpose, or much of any purpose other than tax avoidance. For all its faults, Jack is still way better off with section 731(c)(3)(B) than without it. (Do the math and see for yourself.) And in the end it is hard to feel too sorry for Jack, other than maybe for his last name, because self-help is available. First, he may not actually recognize the built-in gain in the Treasury bonds he now owns, for the reasons explained earlier. Even if he does, if he liquidates his remaining partnership interest for cash, he will recognize only $350,000 of additional gain, bringing his total to $600,000—exactly the right amount. If the partnership recognizes all of the gain in its assets prior to that time, Jack will recognize an offsetting loss on the liquidation, which will again bring his total gain to $600,000.

9.5.1   Which of the following is a *not* a marketable security within the meaning of section 731(c)(2)? (Mark all that apply.)

   a)   Stock traded on the London Stock Exchange

   b)   Membership interest in a closely held LLC that has elected to be taxed as a corporation

   c)   Gold

   d)   Derivative, not actively traded, that is based on the S&P 500

9.5.2   Which of the following is *not to any extent* a marketable security within the meaning of section 731(c)(2)? (Mark all that apply.)

   a)   Stock in a corporation, 95% of whose assets by value consist of marketable securities

   b)   Stock in a corporation, 35% of whose assets by value consist of marketable securities

   c)   Long-term debt that is part of an issue not exceeding $25 million

   d)   Swiss Franc

9.5.3 Megaron LLC, a limited liability company taxed as a partnership, sells its successful LCD glassmaking business for $300 million and invests the proceeds in a diversified portfolio of publicly traded stocks and bonds. Five years and a day later, it distributes its demand note for $50 million to its founder, who many years ago had contributed a similarly diversified portfolio to provide Megaron with funds to get started. This distribution:

a) Is covered by section 731(c)

b) Is not covered by section 731(c), because at the time of the distribution Megaron is an investment partnership

c) Is not covered by section 731(c), because the demand note is not a marketable security

d) Is not covered by section 731(c), because the distribution is made to a partner who contributed marketable securities to Megaron

9.5.4 Instead of selling its glassmaking business, Megaron contributes it to a newly formed corporation in a transaction governed by section 351. As part of the same transaction, the new corporation, Megaron Inc., issues shares to the public in an IPO. Shortly thereafter, Megaron LLC distributes all of its shares to its members. This distribution:

a) Is covered by section 731(c)

b) Is not covered by section 731(c), because at the time of the distribution Megaron is an investment partnership

c) Is not covered by section 731(c), because the shares of Megaron Inc. that are owned by Megaron LLC are not publicly traded and therefore are not marketable securities

d) Is not covered by section 731(c), because the shares of Megaron Inc. that are owned by Megaron LLC were acquired in a nonrecognition transaction

9.5.5   Alinea, Beatrix and Coco are equal partners in Near North Eateries LLC, a limited liability company taxed as a partnership that owns and operates an upscale restaurant. The balance sheet of the partnership (expanded to show the fair market values of its assets) is as follows:

Assets				Liabilities		
	Tax	**Book**	**FMV**		**Tax**	**Book**
Cash	$ 20,000	$ 20,000	$ 20,000	[None]	$ 0	$ 0
Treasuries	30,000	30,000	30,000			
Equipment	130,000	130,000	120,000	**Capital**		
Premises	180,000	180,000	640,000	Alinea	120,000	120,000
				Beatrix	120,000	120,000
				Coco	120,000	120,000
Total Assets	$360,000	$360,000	$810,000	**Total Liabilities and Capital**	$360,000	$360,000

Beatrix wants to leave the partnership, but recognizes that she will have a taxable gain if her interest is redeemed for cash. What are the tax consequences to Beatrix if the partnership borrows $270,000 to purchase shares of an equity mutual fund and distributes those shares to Beatrix in liquidation of her interest?

a)   Beatrix recognizes no gain and takes the shares with a tax basis of $120,000.

b)   Beatrix recognizes $150,000 gain and takes the shares with a tax basis of $120,000.

c)   Beatrix recognizes $60,000 gain and takes the shares with a tax basis of $270,000.

d)   Beatrix recognizes $150,000 gain and takes the shares with a tax basis of $270,000.

9.5.6   Assume alternatively that the balance sheet of Near North Eateries (expanded to show the values of its assets) is as follows:

Assets				Liabilities		
	Tax	**Book**	**FMV**		**Tax**	**Book**
Cash	$ 20,000	$ 20,000	$ 20,000	[None]	$ 0	$ 0
Treasuries	30,000	30,000	30,000			
Equipment	90,000	90,000	80,000	**Capital**		
Premises	110,000	110,000	410,000	Alinea	150,000	150,000
Mutual Fund	200,000	200,000	390,000	Beatrix	150,000	150,000
				Coco	150,000	150,000
Total Assets	$450,000	$450,000	$930,000	**Total Liabilities and Capital**	$450,000	$450,000

Business has been good and the partnership has retained earnings, which it has invested in a mutual fund. This investment has also done well. The partnership distributes one-half of its mutual fund shares ($195,000 value, $100,000 tax basis) to Beatrix. This current distribution reduces, but does not liquidate, Beatrix' interest in the partnership. Near North Eateries revalues its book assets and capital accounts in connection with this distribution. What is Beatrix' tax basis in the distributed shares? What is the tax basis of her remaining partnership interest?

a)   Distributed shares, $113,333; Outside basis, $50,000

b)   Distributed shares, $145,000; Outside basis, $0

c)   Distributed shares, $145,000; Outside basis, $50,000

d)   Distributed shares, $145,000; Outside basis, $95,000

9.5.7   If Near North Eateries has made a section 754 election in Question 9.5.6, what is its basis in the premises after making this distribution?

a) $110,000

b) $120,126

c) $123,333

d) $155,000

9.6   PREVENTING THE SHIFTING OF ORDINARY INCOME: SECTION 751(b)

Chances are, your tax prof skipped section 751(b). Or went through it at lightning speed and took no questions. Everything about section 751(b) is hard—it is hard to teach, hard to learn and hard to apply in practice. For that reason, it is the most overlooked provision in Subchapter K. This, despite the fact that section 751(b) is supposed to apply to a great many commonplace transactions, including distributions that liquidate a partnership, distributions that liquidate a partner's interest in a partnership, and current distributions that involve a change in the distributee's interest in the partnership.

I come not to bury section 751(b), but to praise it. It is significant in an historical context, because it stands as the sole exception to the nonrecognition treatment prescribed by the Internal Revenue Code in 1954 for distributions of capital assets. As discussed in Topic 9.1 and Topic 9.2, the system for partnership distributions worked out in 1954 was a perfect model of nonrecognition, going well beyond that which is permitted in other areas of the tax law, including in particular the treatment of property distributions from C corporations and even S corporations. But the drafters drew the line at distributions that could shift the partners' respective interests in property producing ordinary income. In an era when the statutory maximum tax rate on ordinary income exceeded 90%, they must have felt they had no choice.

The existence of section 751(b) refutes, in my judgment, the argument that there is something unique and immutable about the generous tax treatment given to partnership property distributions. This argument is raised against every proposal to change the status quo. In truth, nonrecognition treatment is simply a legislative choice. Even in 1954, it gave way to a policy that Congress believed was more important, which was to prevent the use of distributions to shift rights to ordinary income. In subsequent years, the favorable treatment has eroded further, as we have seen in Topic 9.4 and Topic 9.5.

Its historical importance aside, there is reason to believe that section 751(b) may be less widely ignored in the future. A decade of study by the Treasury Department and the IRS culminated in the issuance of proposed Treasury regulations in 2014. These regulations address many of the problems with the existing regulations and promise, if not a kinder and gentler section 751(b), at least a more workable one.

The statute

The target of section 751(b) is the shifting of rights to ordinary income and its remedy is harsh. If a distribution results in the distributee-partner's escaping from her share of the partnership's unrealized, ordinary income, the goal of section 751(b) is to tax her on that amount of ordinary income immediately. If the distribution results in the distributee-partner taking more than her share of such income with her, the goal of section 751(b) is to tax the partnership (and therefore the remaining partners) on the avoided amount of ordinary income immediately. The intent of the partners is irrelevant. So also is whether the distributee-partner has received (or the partnership has retained) enough cash to pay the tax due.

Somewhat surprisingly, section 751(b) does not apply to a partnership that has only ordinary losses. It focuses on unrealized receivables and inventory items which have appreciated substantially in value (hereafter, "section 751(b) assets"), both of which produce only ordinary income, not loss. For this purpose, inventory items have appreciated substantially if they are worth more than 120% of their adjusted basis. The existence of substantial appreciation is determined on an aggregate basis, not item-by-item. Under current Treasury regulations all receivables, whether realized or unrealized, are included in this calculation. Treas. Reg. §§ 1.751–1(d)(2)(ii), –1(g), example (2)(b). This can produce unexpected results. Say, for example, that a partnership using the cash method holds conventional inventory with a value and adjusted basis of $100 and an uncollected account receivable of $25. On its own, the partnership's inventory is not substantially appreciated. Taken together with the unrealized receivable, however, it is.

A proposed Treasury regulation is apparently intended to change this rule, by excluding unrealized receivables from the definition of "inventory items which have substantially appreciated in value." Prop. Treas. Reg. § 1.751–1(d). This intention is less than clear, however, because the proposed regulation would continue to include unrealized receivables in the determination of whether inventory items are considered to have appreciated substantially in value. Treas. Reg. § 1.751–1(d)(1) (first sentence, unchanged by the proposed regulation). Worse than the unclear language is the unclear rationale for the proposed regulation. Its apparent purpose is to limit the application of section 751(b). However, while the proposed regulation would doubtless allow the appreciation in conventional inventory to escape the grasp of section 751(b) in some cases, it would not prevent the application of section 751(b) in a single one of those cases, due to the presence of unrealized receivables, to which no *de minimis* rule applies. Putting that problem aside, it is ironic that the Treasury Department and the IRS would think that the issuance of proposed regulations that promise to make section 751(b) workable presents the right opportunity to limit the statute's scope.

Just as including unrealized receivables in the computation of substantial appreciation broadens the scope of section 751(b) under current law, including realized receivables narrows it. Consider a partnership using an accrual method that holds conventional inventory (value $100, basis $80) and an account receivable for $25, which the partnership has already included in income following its method of accounting. This is not an unrealized receivable and therefore is not described in section 751(c). It is, however, an inventory item described in section 751(d)(2) and must be taken into account in determining whether, on an aggregate basis, the partnership's inventory items are substantially appreciated. On its own, the partnership's inventory is substantially appreciated. Taken together with the realized receivables, however, it is not. The proposed regulations would not change this rule.

Topic 2.1 explored the difference between the aggregate view of a partnership, which treats the partners as owning undivided interests in each of the partnership's assets, and the entity view, which treats the partnership as the owner of all of its assets and each of the partners as the owner of an interest in the entity. In its effort to prevent the shifting of rights to ordinary income, section 751(b) takes an explicitly aggregate approach. The statutory language requires a determination of the distributee-partner's "interest" in the properties owned by the partnership. If a distribution causes the distributee to receive less than her "interest" in the section 751(b) assets and more than her "interest" in other partnership property, she is deemed to have exchanged with the partnership the section 751(b) assets that she did not receive for the excess of other property that she did receive. If, on the other hand, the distributee-partner receives more than her "interest" in section 751(b) assets and less than her "interest" in other partnership property, she is deemed to have exchanged with the partnership the other property that she did not receive for the excess of section 751(b) assets that she did receive. These exchanges are fully taxable transactions for both the distributee-partner and the partnership.

To take a simple example, suppose Albert, Bethany and Charlize are equal partners in Partnership ABC. The partnership holds $3,000 of section 751(b) assets and $15,000 of other property. It has no liabilities. Albert receives a distribution of $6,000 of other property in liquidation of his interest. Taking an aggregate view, Albert owned $1,000 of section 751(b) assets and $5,000 of other property prior to the distribution. So the $6,000 of other property distributed to him really represented two things: (1) $5,000 was simply a return to him of property that he had owned all along and (2) the other $1,000 was paid to him in exchange for his prior interest in section 751(b) assets. Following this approach, section 751(b) treats Albert and the partnership as engaging in an exchange, in which Albert gives up his prior $1,000 interest in section 751(b) assets and receives $1,000 of other property, while the partnership gives up $1,000 of other property in exchange for $1,000 of section 751(b) assets. This exchange is fully taxable to Albert and the partnership.

The 1956 regulations

That doesn't sound so bad, right? The trouble is, however, that Albert doesn't actually own any of the partnership's property. So how is Albert supposed to sell something he doesn't own? The problem is to implement the aggregate approach of the statute in a world that otherwise treats partnerships as entities. The drafters directed the Treasury Department to figure this out in regulations. Section 751(b)(1) (flush language).

Those regulations, issued in 1956, solve this problem by deeming the partnership to make a distribution to Albert of the property that, under the statute, he is deemed to sell to the partnership. In the present case, the regulations would treat Albert as receiving a distribution of his "interest" in the section 751(b) assets. This deemed distribution is a current distribution and is governed by the rules that govern current distributions generally, including the basis rules of section 732(a). Treas. Reg. §§ 1.751–1(b)(3)(iii), –1(g), example (2)(d). Following this deemed distribution, Albert owns directly his "interest" in the partnership's section 751(b) assets. His tax basis in these assets is likely to be the partnership's former basis under section 732(a)(1), although it might be limited to his outside basis by section 732(a)(2). This sets the stage for the taxable exchange called for by the statute.

In that exchange, Albert gives up the $1,000 of section 751(b) assets deemed distributed to him in exchange for $1,000 of other partnership property. It's easy to think that Albert recognizes no gain on this exchange, because he is exchanging assets of like value. Crucially, however, Albert's tax basis in the section 751(b) assets he gives up in the exchange is not their fair market value. It is the basis he took in the current distribution from the partnership, which is no greater, and may be less, than the partnership's former basis in these assets. Thus, in the deemed exchange, Albert realizes at least as much gain as the partnership would have realized if it had sold the assets itself. Albert's gain in the deemed exchange is ordinary under Treas. Reg. § 1.751–1(b)(3)(iii). Thus, Albert recognizes ordinary income with respect to his "interest" in the partnership's section 751(b) assets. This is the goal of the statute—to tax Albert currently to the extent that the distribution separates him from his share of the partnership's ordinary income.

The partnership also takes part in this exchange. It gives up $1,000 of other property in exchange for $1,000 of section 751(b) assets received from Albert. This exchange is fully taxable to the partnership as well. Its amount realized is $1,000, the value of the section 751(b) assets received. Its tax basis in the other property surrendered is its adjusted basis in those assets. Depending on the relationship between those two numbers, the partnership could recognize either gain or loss on the exchange. Its character is determined by the character of the property treated as sold under Treas. Reg. § 1.751–1(b)(3)(ii), and thus is mostly likely capital gain or loss or section 1231 gain or loss. Later, we will return to this example to consider whether this recognition of such gain or loss is required by the statute.

The remainder of the partnership's actual distribution of property to Albert in liquidation of his interest—that portion of the distribution which has not been accounted for by the deemed current distribution and exchange—is governed by the usual rules for partnership distributions. Treas. Reg. § 1.751–1(b)(1)(iii). In this case, the remainder of the distribution is $5,000 of other property. Albert receives this property without paying tax under section 731(a). He takes a tax basis in this property equal to his remaining outside basis under section 732(b), *after* his initial outside basis has been reduced under section 733 to take into account the current distribution of section 751(b) assets that he is deemed to have received.

In a different case, the distributee-partner might receive only section 751(b) assets in the actual liquidating distribution. In that case, the statute would treat the distributee-partner as selling her "interest" in other partnership property in exchange for section 751(b) assets in excess of her "interest" therein. To implement this exchange, the regulations would deem the partnership to make a current distribution of the distributee's "interest" in other property. Treas. Reg. § 1.751–1(b)(2)(iii). The distributee would then exchange the other property deemed distributed for the amount of section 751(b) assets in excess of her "interest" in such assets. The distributee would most likely recognize capital or section 1231 gain or loss on this exchange. For its part, the partnership would recognize ordinary income on its deemed exchange of section 751(b) assets for other property. The partnership's recognition of ordinary income carries out the purpose of the statute, because this distribution leaves the partners remaining in the partnership with less than their "interest" in the section 751(b) assets. Whether the distributee's recognition of gain or loss is intended by the statute remains to be discussed.

The foregoing are simple examples, in which the distributee-partner receives only section 751(b) assets or only other partnership property. In many cases, the distributee will receive some of each, but not exactly her "interest" in every item or type of partnership property. Even in simple cases, you must be able to answer a number of questions in order to apply the statutory/regulatory scheme:

✓ *What is a partner's "interest" in partnership property?* This is not a question that normally needs to be answered, because the partnership as an entity is considered to own all of the partnership's property. A partner's book capital account measures her interest in the aggregate book value of the partnership's assets, less liabilities, and her tax capital measures her interest in the partnership's aggregate tax basis in its assets, other than that attributable to debt. There is no ready measure of a partner's "interest" in any particular asset or group of assets. The examples in the Treasury regulations illustrate the operation of section 751(b) with relatively simple partnerships by shares, in which all partners hold equal percentage interests in everything. In such a setting, it is not difficult to conclude that a partner with a 25% interest in partnership capital, income, gains, losses and deductions has an "interest" of 25% in the partnership's section 751(b) assets. Guidance is lacking in more complex cases. For example, if a partner is entitled to an allocation of all of the income (or depreciation) generated by a partnership asset, does she have a 100% "interest" in that asset?

✓ *Is a partner's "interest" in partnership property measured by its value or its appreciation?* It is measured by its gross value. Treas. Reg. §§ 1.751–1(b)(1)(ii), –1(g), example (2)(c).

✓ *Is it important whether the distributee-partner receives her share of the value of each of the partnership's section 751(b) assets?* No. The distributee-partner's "interest" in section 751(b) assets is measured in the aggregate. Partnership ABC, discussed above, has $3,000 of section 751(b) assets and Albert's "interest" therein is $1,000. Let's say that the partnership's section 751(b) assets consist of $1,500 of conventional inventory with a tax basis of $1,500 and $1,500 of unrealized receivables with a zero tax basis. If Albert receives $1,000 worth of inventory, section 751(b) is satisfied. If Albert receives $1,000 worth of receivables, section 751(b) is satisfied. Indeed, section 751(b) is satisfied if Albert receives any combination of inventory and receivables totaling $1,000 in value.

✓ *If section 751(b) applies to a distribution, what partnership assets are deemed to be distributed in the current distribution and then sold back to the partnership?* If a distributee-partner receives excess section 751(b) assets, the current distribution consists of other partnership property. What other property? The default answer under the Treasury regulations is that this distribution consists of a proportional amount of the value of every item of partnership property (other than section 751(b) assets) in which the distributee-partner has relinquished an interest. Treas. Reg. §§ 1.751–1(g), examples (4)(c), (5)(c). Recognizing that that could be a lot of properties, and could potentially cause the distributee-partner to recognize a considerable capital gain, the regulations permit the partners to reach an agreement which identifies the specific other property or properties that the partnership will be deemed to have transferred in the current distribution and that the distributee-partner will be deemed to have sold back to the partnership. Treas. Reg. § 1.751–1(g), example (3)(c).

If a distributee-partner receives excess other property, the current distribution consists of section 751(b) assets. The default rule is the same: the current distribution consists of a proportional amount of the value of each section 751(b) asset. Treas. Reg. § 1.751–1(g), example (2)(c). The Treasury regulations do not specifically permit the identification of the distributed section 751(b) assets by agreement of the partners, and there seems to be good reason for this omission. Consider, for example, Partnership ABC, which has $1,500 of full-basis inventory and $1,500 of zero-basis receivables. The partnership makes a liquidating distribution to Albert, which consists entirely of other property. Albert has exchanged a $1,000 "interest" in section 751(b) assets for $1,000 of other property. If Albert could agree with the other partners that the section 751(b) assets deemed distributed to him consist entirely of inventory, he would recognize no ordinary income on his deemed exchange of the distributed inventory for an additional interest in other partnership property. Thus, he could shift the partnership's ordinary income entirely to the other partners. This seems inconsistent with the purpose of section 751(b) and would in fact render its application elective by agreement of the partners.

✓ *If section 751(b) applies to a distribution, what partnership assets are deemed to be distributed (other than in the current distribution) and what partnership assets are deemed to be acquired by the distributee in the deemed exchange?* If a distributee-partner receives excess section 751(b) assets, she will be deemed to have acquired the excess in the deemed exchange. Although the Treasury regulations do not address this issue, it stands to reason that the distributee should be treated as acquiring in this manner a proportional amount of the value of each section 751(b) asset she actually receives. This approach has the effect of spreading the step-up in basis obtained in the deemed exchange proportionally among all of the section 751(b) assets. It also means that the partnership is deemed to have sold a proportionate value of each of its section 751(b) assets in the deemed exchange, thereby recognizing an appropriate amount of ordinary income.

If a distributee-partner receives excess other property, she too will be deemed to have acquired the excess in the deemed exchange. While the default rule should be that the distributee is deemed to have acquired a proportional amount of the value of each item of other property that she actually receives, there should be room for side agreements in this case. An agreement among the partners that the partnership has sold, and the distributee-partner has acquired, a single, high-basis capital asset in the deemed exchange would both simplify the accounting for the transaction and minimize the recognition of capital gain by the partnership. These are laudable goals in themselves and not inconsistent with the purpose of section 751(b).

To summarize, applying section 751(b) is a two-step process. First, you must decide whether the statute applies to the distribution at hand. If that distribution is a liquidating distribution, like the one to Albert, section 751(b) applies only if the distributee-partner takes more or less than her "interest" in the value of the partnership's section 751(b) assets in the aggregate in exchange for less or more than her "interest" in the value of the partnership's other property in the aggregate. Thus, if a distributee-partner has an "interest" in the section 751(b) assets that is valued in the aggregate at $12,000 prior to the distribution, section 751(b) will not apply if the partnership distributes to her exactly $12,000 worth of section 751(b) assets (regardless which ones it distributes). If the partnership distributes $11,999.99 (or less) or $12,000.01 (or more) of such assets, however, section 751(b) will apply. (This assumes that the entire distribution is made for the distributee's interest in the partnership, rather than, for example, as compensation for services or as a retirement payment under section 736(a).)

The analysis of a current distribution is different. A current distribution does not entail an exchange of section 751(b) assets in the aggregate for other property in the aggregate if every partner receives property with a value that is proportional to that partner's predistribution "interest" in such property, whether the distributed property consists entirely of section 751(b) property, of other partnership property, or of a combination of both. In other words, section 751(b) does not apply to pro-rata current distributions. As with liquidating distributions, section 751(b) also does not apply to a current distribution to a single partner, if that partner receives both section 751(b) assets and other property, in each case of a value that is proportional to her predistribution "interest" in that type of property.

Once you have decided that section 751(b) applies to a distribution, you must apply it. This, in turn, takes three steps:

1.   *The deemed current distribution.* You have already concluded that the distributee-partner has received more (or less) than her "interest" in the value of the partnership's section 751(b) assets in the aggregate. The deemed current distribution is an aggregate value of partnership property that equals the excess (or deficit) in the aggregate value of the section 751(b) assets actually distributed compared to the distributee's "interest" in such assets. If the distributee actually receives more than her "interest" in the partnership's section 751(b) assets, the current distribution consists of other partnership property; if the distributee actually receives less than her "interest" in the partnership's section 751(b) assets, the current distribution consists of section 751(b) assets. The important point is that the deemed current distribution is just this excess or deficit value—it is not the distributee's entire "interest" in all of the partnership's assets, or the entire amount of the actual distribution. Remember that the purpose of the deemed current distribution is to transfer ownership to the distributee of that property—and only that property—which the distributee is deemed to sell in the deemed exchange.

2.   *The deemed exchange.* In this step, the distributee engages in a fully taxable exchange with the partnership. The distributee sells the property deemed received in the current distribution back to the partnership in exchange for an equal value of the property actually distributed. Both the distributee and the partnership may recognize income, gain or loss, which, to the extent recognized by the partnership, is allocated among the partners in accordance with their interests after the distribution.

3.   *The remaining distribution.* To the extent not accounted for in the deemed current distribution and the exchange, the distribution is governed by the usual rules for distributions. Generally, the distributee's outside basis will have been reduced by the current distribution, and this reduction must be taken into account in determining the gain, if any, recognized by the distributee and her basis in the properties distributed in this step. The distributee's tax basis in one or more properties will be composed partly of the cost basis obtained in the deemed exchange and partly of the transferred or substituted basis prescribed by section 732 for distributed property. Capital assets may have a split holding period. The partnership may have a stepped-up basis for some of its properties, which also may have a split holding period.

In the Questions that follow, you will have an opportunity to try your hand at analyzing a section 751(b) distribution.

Weaknesses of the 1956 regulations

It has been more than half a century since the 1956 regulations were promulgated and they are showing their age. In 2006, the IRS took the somewhat unusual step of issuing a public call for assistance in addressing their numerous deficiencies. Notice 2006–14, 2006–1 C.B. 498. Among the problems that have been identified are the following:

✓ *Fearsome complexity.* The 1956 regulations are hard to understand conceptually. They are even harder to apply in practice, particularly if a distributing partnership has more than just a few assets. The 1956 regulations attempt to limit this complexity with simplifying assumptions, such as measuring the distributee-partner's "interest" in section 751(b) assets by reference to the gross value of all of those assets in the aggregate, but this has introduced its own problems.

✓ *Under-inclusiveness.* The purpose of section 751(b) is to prevent the shifting of ordinary income. By focusing on the gross value of section 751(b) assets, however, the regulations sometimes permit what the statute is intended to prevent. A distribution of high-basis inventory and a distribution of zero-basis receivables are treated in the same way by the 1956 regulations, despite the fact that the former distribution transfers less ordinary income to the distributee than the latter.

✓ *Over-inclusiveness.* The 1956 regulations cause section 751(b) to apply to current distributions of cash (or other non-section 751(b) property) in which no ordinary income is being shifted. The reason is that the 1956 regulations do not take section 704(c) into account. While this is understandable, given that the 1956 regulations were issued 28 years before Congress made section 704(c) mandatory, it is out of step with the current tax reality. Prior to making a current distribution that changes the partners' respective interests in the partnership, partnerships quite routinely revalue their assets, which has the effect of embedding in the book capital accounts of all of the partners, including those of the distributee(s), all of the existing appreciation in the partnership's assets, including its section 751(b) assets. When the partnership recognizes this income or gain for tax purposes, it must allocate the taxable income and gain to follow the previously allocated book gain. Treas. Reg. § 1.704–1(b)(4)(i). Accordingly, the distributee-partner(s) cannot actually avoid paying tax on the income from the partnership's section 751(b) assets, if such partner(s) remain partners in the partnership and the partnership continues to hold its section 751(b) assets. Current taxation of the distribution is unnecessary to carry out the purpose of section 751(b) in these circumstances.

✓ *Needless recognition of capital gain or loss.* The remedy of section 751(b) to the shifting of ordinary income is to cause the partner or partners who would otherwise avoid ordinary income to pay tax on it immediately. No statutory purpose is served by requiring the other partners to recognize capital gain or loss. Nevertheless, this happens routinely under the 1956 regulations. It is "collateral damage" from the explicitly aggregate approach of the statute, which requires an exchange of properties that has tax consequences for both of the exchanging parties.

✓ *Reliance on the aggregate approach.* More generally, the aggregate approach of the statute, carried over into the 1956 regulations, has at its root a question with no readily apparent answer: what is the "interest" of the distributee-partner in any given item of partnership property? Worse, this does not seem to be a question that needs to be answered. The statutory concern is whether the distributee-partner, or the remaining partners, are avoiding paying tax on their respective shares of the ordinary income of the partnership. Focusing on the distributee's "interest" in partnership property (a question with no clear answer) rather than her share of the partnership's unrealized ordinary income (a question to which there is a clear answer) not only complicates the analysis and makes it uncertain, but can in some cases cause the statute to fail to achieve its essential purpose.

The proposed regulations

So section 751(b), as interpreted by the 1956 regulations, is basically a train wreck. Its goal, however, is the same as that of section 751(a), and the fact that this goal is harder to meet in the context of a distribution does not make it less worthwhile. The IRS and the Treasury Department have worked for years to come up with a better approach. The issuance of proposed regulations in 2014 signals their confidence in a radical new alternative, which utilizes a high-tech arsenal of modern partnership tax administration, including revaluations, hypothetical sales, allocations of notional tax items, elective recognition of capital gain and, of course, an anti-abuse rule.

Under the proposed regulations, applying section 751(b) is still a two-step process, first determining whether section 751(b) applies to a distribution and then applying it. The proposed regulations are not yet law—they are proposed to be effective on finalization. It is reasonable to expect modifications, perhaps significant, between now and then. That said, taxpayers can elect to apply from November 3, 2014 that portion of the proposed regulations which identifies the distributions to which section 751(b) applies. Prop. Treas. Reg. § 1.751–1(f). It seems unlikely that your tax prof will expect you to have detailed knowledge of the proposed regulations prior to their finalization, so the following is a brief summary with emphasis on the efforts made to correct the deficiencies of the 1956 regulations.

In order to determine whether section 751(b) applies to a distribution, the proposed regulations borrow a technique from the Treasury regulations under section 751(a)—specifically, the hypothetical sale of Treas. Reg. § 1.751–1(a)(2), which we reviewed in Topic 6.3. The idea is refreshingly straightforward: if the purpose of section 751(b) is to tax currently a shift of rights to ordinary income, then determine whether it applies by seeing whether the distribution has shifted such rights. The proposed regulations do this by comparing the amount of ordinary income from the sale of section 751(b) assets that each partner would be allocated on the partnership's sale of all of its assets for fair market value immediately before the distribution in question with the amount of ordinary income that each partner would be allocated or would recognize directly on the sale of the same assets by the partnership and the distributee-partner(s) immediately after the distribution. Any partner for whom the distribution reduces ordinary income (or increases ordinary loss) so determined is said to have a "section 751(b) amount." Prop. Treas. Reg. § 1.751–1(b)(2); *see* Prop. Treas. Reg. § 1.751–1(g), example (3)(iv).

Once it is determined that section 751(b) applies to a distribution, the partnership must use "a reasonable approach that is consistent with the purpose of section 751(b) under which each partner with a section 751(b) amount recognizes ordinary income . . . equal to that section 751(b) amount immediately prior to the section 751(b) distribution." Prop. Treas. Reg. § 1.751–1(b)(3)(i). This is disappointing to folks yearning for a single and definitive answer, though it is reminiscent of the approach taken to section 704(c) methods, reviewed in Topic 8.3, and to section 704(c) layers, reviewed in Topic 8.5. The preamble to the proposed regulations expresses a slight preference for what it calls the "deemed gain" approach, under which each partner with a section 751(b) amount recognizes (out of thin air) an amount of ordinary income equal to that partner's section 751(b) amount. The partnership makes appropriate adjustments to the tax basis of its assets to reflect this ordinary income recognition. The outside basis of the partner is similarly adjusted. *See* Prop. Treas. Reg. § 1.751–1(g), example (3)(v). Although such an approach might have been abhorrent in 1956 (or at least unimaginable), it has more recent antecedents in the Treasury regulations under the "anti-mixing-bowl" rule of section 704(c)(1)(B), which we reviewed in Topic 9.5, and in the remedial method under section 704(c)(1)(A), which we reviewed in Topic 8.2.

The new generation of tax technology is on full display in the proposed regulations. One example is their requirement that any partnership that maintains capital accounts and will hold any section 751(b) assets after the distribution must revalue its assets immediately prior to the distribution, if the distribution is consideration for an interest in the partnership. Prop. Treas. Reg. § 1.751–1(b)(2)(iv). Another is an anti-abuse rule that applies if a partner avoids the application of section 751(b) by holding through the operation of section 704(c) a relatively large interest in unrealized partnership ordinary income through a relatively small economic interest in the partnership. Prop. Treas. Reg. § 1.751–1(b)(4). The proposed regulations require the distributee to recognize capital gain in carefully defined circumstances, and permit her to do so in others. Prop. Treas. Reg. § 1.751–1(b)(3)(ii).

The proposed regulations address the weaknesses of the 1956 regulations:

✓ *Complexity.* While this topic will never be easy, the boldly straightforward approach of the proposed regulations avoids many of the complications and uncertainties presented by the deemed exchange utilized in the 1956 regulations. Further simplification would be achieved by specification of a single method for applying section 751(b), although it is understandable that the IRS and the Treasury Department may be hesitant to mandate the use of a method that involves the creation of notional ordinary income.

✓ *Under-inclusiveness.* The replacement of the gross-value approach of the 1956 regulations with the hypothetical-sale approach is a major improvement and seems to solve the problem of income-shifting transactions escaping the grasp of section 751(b).

✓ *Over-inclusiveness.* Mandatory revaluations create reverse section 704(c) layers that are attributable to the existing partners, including the distributee-partner(s) in current distributions, and thus limit the scope of section 751(b). Interestingly, the proposed regulations call for revaluations even in the case of liquidating distributions, although the distributee-partner(s) in such circumstances will have no interest in the reverse layer created by the revaluation. This may simply reflect the growing confidence of the IRS and the Treasury Department in the revaluation technique and their desire to see it more widely used.

✓ *Recognition of capital gains and losses.* The partnership never recognizes capital gains or losses under the proposed regulations. The distributee-partner recognizes capital gain in only a small class of cases that the proposed regulations define with precision.

✓ *Use of aggregate approach.* Overall, the proposed regulations move the implementation of section 751(b) away from a concept that is not well developed in the tax law—a partner's "interest" in partnership property—back to a concept that is exquisitely well developed—a partner's distributive share of partnership income. For this reason alone, the proposed regulations are a vast improvement over the regulations that they will someday supersede.

———————

9.6.1   The balance sheet of Partnership ABC, a general partnership which uses an accrual method and has not made an election under section 754, is as follows:

Assets	Tax	Book	FMV	Liabilities	Tax	Book
Cash	$ 75,000	$ 75,000	$ 75,000	Debt	$ 72,000	$ 72,000
Receivables	27,000	27,000	27,000			
Inventory	21,000	21,000	33,000	**Capital**		
Equipment	45,000	45,000	42,000	Albert	62,000	62,000
Plant	90,000	90,000	120,000	Bethany	62,000	62,000
				Charlize	62,000	62,000
Total Assets	$258,000	$258,000	$297,000	**Total Liabilities and Capital**	$258,000	$258,000

The partnership's plant is real property which it has depreciated on a straight-line basis; such depreciation is not subject to recapture under section 1250. Identify the partnership's section 751(b) assets under the 1956 regulations.

a)   Inventory

b)   Inventory and receivables

c)   Inventory and recapture

d)   Inventory, receivables and recapture

9.6.2   The partnership distributes cash of $75,000 to Bethany in liquidation of her partnership interest. Under the 1956 regulations, what properties is Bethany deemed to have exchanged?

a) $20,000 of section 751(b) assets for other property

b) $16,000 of section 751(b) assets for other property

c) $4,000 of section 751(b) assets for other property

d) $9,000 of receivables, $11,000 of inventory, $14,000 of equipment and $40,000 of plant for like amounts of cash

9.6.3   Assuming the partners make no agreement regarding the properties deemed distributed to Bethany and exchanged by her with the partnership, how much taxable ordinary income and capital gain or loss do Bethany and the partnership recognize on the deemed exchange under the 1956 regulations?

a)   Bethany, $0 income; ABC, $0 income

b)   Bethany, $4,000 income; ABC, $0 gain

c)   Bethany, $4,000 income; ABC, $4,000 income

d)   Bethany, $4,000 income; ABC, $4,000 gain

9.6.4   Assuming the partners make no agreement regarding the properties deemed distributed to Bethany and exchanged by her with the partnership, how much taxable ordinary income and capital gain or loss do Bethany and the partnership recognize on this entire distribution under the 1956 regulations?

a)   Bethany, $0 income, $13,000 gain; ABC, $4,000 income

b)   Bethany, $4,000 income, $7,000 loss; ABC, $0 income

c)   Bethany, $4,000 income, $0 gain; ABC, $8,000 income

d)   Bethany, $4,000 income, $9,000 gain; ABC, $0 income

9.6.5   Assume that the partners reach an agreement that the sole section 751(b) asset deemed distributed to Bethany and exchanged by her with the partnership is accounts receivable. How much ordinary income and capital gain do Bethany and the partnership recognize on this distribution under the 1956 regulations?

a)   Bethany, $0 income, $13,000 gain; ABC, $0 income

b)   Bethany, $0 income, $13,000 gain; ABC, $4,000 income

c)   Bethany, $0 income, $9,000 gain; ABC, $0 income

d)   Bethany, $4,000 income, $9,000 gain; ABC, $0 income

9.6.6   How much ordinary income and capital gain or loss would Bethany and the partnership recognize on the distribution in Question 9.6.2 under the proposed regulations?

a)   Bethany, $0 income, $13,000 gain; ABC, $4,000 income

b)   Bethany, $4,000 income, $7,000 loss; ABC, $0 income

c)   Bethany, $4,000 income, $0 gain; ABC, $8,000 income

d)   Bethany, $4,000 income, $9,000 gain; ABC, $0 income

9.6.7   Assume that Partnership ABC distributes to Bethany $55,000 in cash and receivables valued at $20,000 in liquidation of her partnership interest. How much ordinary income and capital gain or loss do Bethany and the partnership recognize on this distribution under the 1956 regulations?

a)   Bethany, $0 income, $13,000 gain; ABC, $0 income

b)   Bethany, $0 income, $0 gain; ABC, $0 income

c)   Bethany, $0 income, $0 gain; ABC, $4,000 income

d)   Bethany, $4,000 income, $9,000 gain; ABC, $0 income

9.6.8   Assume now that Partnership ABC distributes to Bethany all of its receivables and inventory, plus $15,000 in cash, in liquidation of her interest in the partnership. Under the 1956 regulations, what properties is Bethany deemed to have exchanged?

a) $40,000 of section 751(b) assets for other property

b) $60,000 of other property for section 751(b) assets

c) $8,000 of other property for section 751(b) assets

d) $40,000 of other property for section 751 assets

9.6.9   Assuming the partners make no agreement regarding the properties deemed distributed to Bethany and exchanged by her with the partnership, how much ordinary income and capital gain do Bethany and the partnership recognize under the 1956 regulations on the distribution described in Question 9.6.8?

a)   Bethany, $0 income, $5,000 capital gain; ABC, $0 income

b)   Bethany, $0 income, $6,667 net section 1231 gain, $1,667 capital loss; ABC, $8,000 income

c)   Bethany, $0 income, $6,667 net section 1231 gain; ABC, $0 income

d)   Bethany, $0 income, $0 gain; ABC, $8,000 income

9.6.10   Assume that the partners reach an agreement that the sole asset deemed distributed to Bethany and exchanged by her with the partnership is $40,000 in cash. How much ordinary income and capital gain do Bethany and the partnership recognize under the 1956 regulations on the distribution described in Question 9.6.8?

a)   Bethany, $0 income, $5,000 gain; ABC, $0 income

b)   Bethany, $0 income, $6,667 net section 1231 gain, $1,667 capital loss; ABC, $8,000 income

c)   Bethany, $0 income, $6,667 net section 1231 gain; ABC, $0 income

d)   Bethany, $0 income, $0 gain; ABC, $8,000 income

9.6.11   How much ordinary income and capital gain would Bethany and the partnership be required to recognize under the proposed regulations on the distribution described in Question 9.6.8?

a)   Bethany, $0 income, $5,000 gain; ABC, $0 income

b)   Bethany, $0 income, $6,667 net section 1231 gain, $1,667 capital loss; ABC, $8,000 income

c)   Bethany, $0 income, $6,667 net section 1231 gain; ABC, $0 income

d)   Bethany, $0 income, $0 gain; ABC, $8,000 income

9.7   DISGUISED SALES:
SECTION 707(a)(2)(B) REDUX

This Topic is a cross-reference with a warning. As we saw in Topic 2.7, a disguised sale takes place when a contribution is coupled with a related distribution. At that time, our focus was on contributions to a partnership, and disguised sales stood as examples of contributions that are not taxed like contributions. Now our focus is on distributions, but the message is the same. If a distribution is found to be part of a disguised sale, it will not be taxed under the rules reviewed in this Chapter 9, but instead under the rules applicable to disguised sales.

Labeling a distribution as part of a disguised sale fundamentally changes the nature of the transaction for tax purposes. If a cash transfer to a partner (or liability assumption from a partner) is treated as a distribution, the partner can recover her outside basis in full before recognizing gain. Any excess distribution is treated as gain from the sale of her partnership interest, and taxed as capital gain under section 741. Section 751(b) may apply to require recognition of ordinary income. If, on the other hand, the transfer of cash (or assumption) is treated as the consideration for a disguised sale, the asset sold is not a partnership interest, but instead the contributed property. Under the rules applicable to disguised sales, only a portion of the transferor's tax basis in the property can be recovered. The character of any gain recognized is not determined under section 741 and section 751(b), but depends instead on the property sold. This gain can be capital gain, if the transferor held the property as a capital asset prior to transferring it to the partnership. But it might instead be gain from the disposition of section 1231 property (to which recapture may apply) or even ordinary income from the disposition of inventory or other non-capital asset.

So, whenever you confront a question involving what seems to be a simple partnership distribution, always check to see whether any partner has contributed property to the partnership in the past seven years. If so, you may be dealing with more than a simple distribution. It may be a distribution to which the anti-mixing-bowl statues apply. Or it may only partly a distribution, the remainder being the proceeds of a disguised sale of property to the partnership.

9.8   RETIREMENT DISTRIBUTIONS UNDER SECTION 736

Despite the fact that section 736 contains more words than ever, it is a shadow of its former self. In olden times, section 736 gave all partnerships the opportunity to deduct the portion, if any, of a liquidating distribution that was attributable to the distributee-partner's interest in the partnership's goodwill. This result was all the more startling in a world in which goodwill was not amortizable for tax purposes, let alone deductible. That all changed in 1993, with the enactment of section 736(b)(3), which eliminated this opportunity for almost all partnerships that were likely to take advantage of it. Ironically, section 197, which for the first time permitted the amortization of goodwill, was enacted the same year.

The statutory pattern

Section 736 became part of the Internal Revenue Code in 1954. Its original purpose was to answer a single, vexing question that had arisen repeatedly in litigation prior to that date: if a retiring partner (or her estate) receives a liquidating payment that exceeds her share of the value of the partnership's tangible assets, how should the excess amount be taxed?

Section 736 applies only to liquidating distributions, not current distributions. But you must consider it, perhaps only briefly, every time a partnership—any partnership—makes a liquidating distribution.

The title of section 736, "Payments to a Retiring Partner . . ." suggests that the section applies only to some special kind of transaction, a "retirement"—whatever that is. Do not be fooled. There are only two kinds of distributions, current and liquidating. Section 736 applies to the latter. Its novel nomenclature reflects the fact that partnerships, then and now, often refer to liquidating distributions that exceed a partner's interest in the partnership's assets as retirement payments.

The first step is to segregate the liquidating distribution into two parts. The first (the "section 736(b) amount") is the amount paid to the distributee with respect to her interest in the partnership's assets. The IRS will generally go along with the agreement of the parties as to what that amount is. Treas. Reg. § 1.736–1(b)(1). You already know all you need to know about how the section 736(b) amount is taxed, because its tax treatment follows the ordinary rules for liquidating distributions that we have reviewed in this Chapter. Section 736(b)(1), Treas. Reg. § 1.736–1(b)(1). In all the prior examples of liquidating distributions, the distributee is paid only for her interest in the partnership's assets—*i.e.*, the entire liquidating distribution is a section 736(b) amount. Although section 736 technically applied to all these distributions, you did not need to worry about it.

The second part of the liquidating distribution (the "section 736(a) amount") is the excess, if any, of the entire liquidating distribution over the section 736(b) amount. Establishing clear rules for taxing this excess was the original purpose of the statute. Consistent with that purpose, the rules are simple. If the excess payment is determined with regard to the income of the partnership, section 736(a)(1) treats it as a distributive share of partnership income. If not, section 736(a)(2) treats it as a guaranteed payment under section 707(c). These payments are generally ordinary income to the recipient. Treas. Reg. § 1.736–1(a)(4).

Section 736(b)(2) smashes into this simple structure like a wrecking ball. Although motivated by understandable concerns, this subsection is the source of most of the complexity—and the gamesmanship—that has given section 736 its reputation as a tricky statute. Under section 736(b)(2)(A), the section 736(b) amount never includes any payment for the distributee's interest in the unrealized receivables of the partnership. Under section 736(b)(2)(B), it also does not include any payment for the distributee's interest in the partnership's goodwill, unless the partnership agreement explicitly provides for a payment for goodwill. Let's try to understand each of these provisions in turn.

Section 736(b)(2)(A). This provision is factually incorrect—withdrawing partners do not simply walk away from their interest in unrealized receivables without being paid. Of course, it is not the purpose of this provision to claim that they do. Instead, it seeks to ensure that any payment the withdrawing partner receives for unrealized receivables is treated, not as a section 736(b) amount, but as a section 736(a) amount. Consequently, the withdrawing partner includes this payment as income (either as a distributive share or as a guaranteed payment) and the partnership has either a deduction (if the payment is treated as a guaranteed payment) or the equivalent thereof (if the payment is treated as a distributive share of partnership income, thereby reducing the distributive shares of the remaining partners).

The intriguing question is why the drafters felt the need to include this provision in section 736 at all. If the partnership's payment for unrealized receivables were treated as a section 736(b) amount, it would be subject to section 751(b), which would also create ordinary income for the recipient. That is, in fact, the approach that applies to payments for the withdrawing partner's share of the partnership's substantially appreciated inventory items, which is not excluded from the section 736(b) amount and is subject to section 751(b). Treas. Reg. § 1.736–1(b)(4).

The answer to this question may lie on the partnership's side of the transaction. If section 751(b) applies, the partnership takes a stepped-up basis in the portion of its receivables that it is deemed to have purchased from the withdrawing partner. The partnership's recovery of this additional basis will depend on the speed at which the receivables are collected by the partnership and will require the partnership to keep track of the step-up in the meantime. The drafters had seen the effect of this treatment in *Wilkes v. Commissioner*, 7 T.C. 519 (1946), *aff'd*, 161 F.2d 830 (1st Cir. 1947), a case decided under the 1939 Internal Revenue Code, which held that the estate of a deceased law partner receiving a payment intended to approximate his interest in the firm's uncollected receivables should be treated as having sold such receivables to the partnership. In reaching this holding, the Tax Court expressed its regret over the "detailed and possibly intricate accounting process [that] will be required on the part of the firm." 7 T.C. at 524. It is entirely possible that the drafters excluded payments for unrealized receivables from the section 736(b) amount in order to avail the partnership of the far simpler deduction mechanism available under section 736(a). All section 736(a) amounts are excluded from treatment under section 751(b) by section 751(b)(2)(B). The drafters may not have had the same concern regarding the application of section 751(b) to substantially appreciated inventory, because a partnership that has adopted a method of accounting for inventory has shown that it can put up with a little complexity.

Section 736(b)(2)(B). This provision may or may not be factually incorrect. Strange as it may seem, it is not uncommon for the partners in service partnerships—think law firms and accounting firms—to walk away from their shares of the partnership's goodwill without getting paid for it. Their justification is that the generation of partners that came before them did the same thing, so, having not paid for goodwill on the way in, they have little claim to be paid for it on the way out. Section 736(b)(2)(B) is agnostic on this issue, not caring whether or not partnerships pay withdrawing partners for their shares of goodwill. It does, however, require partnerships to declare what they are doing, and it determines the tax treatment of both the partnership and the withdrawing partner based on that declaration.

The purpose of this provision is to eliminate the potential for whipsawing the government that was apparent in the years before 1954. No clear rules applied to payments to a withdrawing partner in excess of her share of the value of the partnership's tangible assets. When excess payments were made, the withdrawing partner could cogently argue that they were in exchange for her interest in the goodwill of the partnership—and therefore capital gain—while the partnership would maintain that they were merely a distributive share of partnership income—and therefore effectively deductible. *See* Jackson, Johnson, Surrey, Tenen & Warren, *The Internal Revenue Code of 1954: Partnerships*, 54 COLUM. L. REV. 1183, 1225–26 (1954). Section 736(b)(2)(B) establishes a default rule that payments in excess of the value of the withdrawing partner's share of the partnership's identifiable tangible and intangible assets are section 736(a) amounts, creating a consistent rule for the treatment of both the partnership and the withdrawing partner. If a partnership so chooses, however, it may provide for payments for goodwill in its partnership agreement. Under Treas. Reg. § 1.736–1(b)(3), such payments must be reasonable and goodwill can generally be valued as agreed by the parties. In this event, the stated amount paid for the withdrawing partner's share of goodwill is treated as a section 736(b) amount by both the partnership and the withdrawing partner.

1993 amendment

Although section 736(b)(2)(B) achieved its original purpose of curtailing the opportunities for withdrawing partners and remaining partners to take inconsistent positions regarding the tax treatment of payments for partnership goodwill, it created opportunities for tax arbitrage in the planning of liquidating distributions. This is simplest to see where the withdrawing partner pays tax at a significantly higher or lower rate than the remaining partners. If, for example, the withdrawing partner is in a lower tax bracket, treating a payment for goodwill as a section 736(a) amount may save taxes in the aggregate, because of the greater value of the deduction to the other partners.

Even where all partners pay tax at the same rate, however, good planning can produce overall tax savings. Say, for example, that Alvin receives a liquidating distribution which includes $200,000 with respect to his interest in the partnership's goodwill, all of which exceeds his outside basis. Alvin and all other partners pay tax at 40% on ordinary income and at 20% on capital gains. For Alvin, treating the goodwill payment as a section 736(b) amount saves $40,000 in tax as compared to treating it as a section 736(a) amount, due to the difference between the applicable tax rates on capital gains and ordinary income. For the other partners, however, section 736(b) treatment of the goodwill payment costs $80,000, relative to section 736(a) treatment—twice as much as the benefit to Alvin. This is because the partnership cannot deduct any of the $200,000 payment if it is described in section 736(b), and therefore loses a deduction equal to 40% of $200,000, or

$80,000. (This example assumes the partnership has not made a section 754 election or, if it has, that the entire basis adjustment is allocable to nondepreciable, nonamortizable assets.) In fact, in exchange for his agreement to treat the goodwill payment as a section 736(a) amount, the other partners could afford to pay Alvin $266,667, which would net him the same amount after tax ($160,000) as a $200,000 payment taxed as capital gain. This payment, however, would cost the other partners only $160,000 on an after-tax basis ($266,667 less the value of a 40% deduction, $106,667), thus saving them $40,000. This $40,000 saving is the direct result of the "tax-deductible goodwill" created by section 736(a). Depending on his savvy and negotiating strength, Alvin could share part of the tax savings, in the form of a still-higher payment for goodwill—bounded only by the general restriction that the amount of the payment be reasonable.

This bothered Congress, which in 1993 moved to eliminate electivity in the treatment of payments for goodwill. In theory, Congress could have gone either way—mandating either section 736(a) treatment or section 736(b) treatment for payments of goodwill—and still preserved the anti-whipsaw effect achieved in 1954. Congress opted to mandate section 736(b) treatment for most partnerships, thus eliminating "tax-deductible goodwill" in this context. It did this by adding section 736(b)(3), which jettisons section 736(b)(2), except in the case of liquidating distributions to general partners in service partnerships.

Curiously, perhaps, the same 1993 tax act that added section 736(b)(3) also included section 197, which provides for the amortization of purchased goodwill. This new amortization substantially changes the tax-arbitrage calculus. Assume, for example, that Alvin's partnership includes $200,000 in his liquidating distribution with respect to goodwill and the payment is treated in its entirety as a section 736(b) amount. Assume further that the partnership makes a section 754 election and that the entire $200,000 basis adjustment arising from this payment under section 734(b)(1)(A) is allocated to the partnership's goodwill. As before, section 736(b) treatment saves Alvin $40,000 in tax. Due to the 15-year amortization of the basis adjustment to goodwill, however, the cost to the partnership is substantially less than before. In fact, the present value of the amortization deductions is about $65,000 (using a 5% after-tax discount rate), so that the additional cost to the partnership of section 736(b) treatment is only about $15,000. Comparing this to Alvin's savings of $40,000, this means that section 736(b) treatment is actually favorable for this partnership, and if you gave it a free choice, it would choose this treatment over the "tax-deductible goodwill" offered by section 736(a).

Why did Congress keep the old rules in effect for service partnerships? In small part, perhaps, Congress wanted to keep simple rules for payments related to unrealized receivables. These are common in service partnerships. More important is the statement in the legislative history that "service partnerships do not ordinarily value goodwill in liquidating partners." H.R. REP. NO. 103–111, 103d Cong., 1st Sess. 782 (1993). Stated in words that sound less like they came from Tony Soprano, the legislative history is saying that service partnerships typically do not include any payment for the partnership's goodwill in the liquidating distributions they make to their general partners. For such partnerships, the excess of any liquidating distribution over the value of the partner's interest in the firm's identifiable assets should not be treated as a section 736(b) amount, because such excess is not paid for the withdrawing partner's interest in any partnership asset. If the legislative history is correct about this habit of service partnerships (and there is every indication that it is), Congress left electivity in place for the class of partnerships that is the least likely to use it.

Service partnerships

9.8.1 The balance sheet (enhanced to show asset values) of ABC LLP, a calendar-year limited liability partnership offering legal services, is as follows:

Assets	Tax	Book	FMV	Liabilities	Tax	Book
Cash	$ 27,000	$ 27,000	$ 27,000	[None]	$ 0	$ 0
Receivables	0	0	96,000			
Equipment	147,000	147,000	120,000	**Capital**		
[Goodwill]	0	0	300,000	Audrey	58,000	58,000
				Brody	58,000	58,000
				Cooper	58,000	58,000
Total Assets	$174,000	$174,000	$543,000	**Total Liabilities and Capital**	$174,000	$174,000

The partnership does not revalue its assets in connection with partner retirements and the only mention of goodwill in the partnership agreement is a prohibition against a retired partner holding herself out as affiliated with the partnership. The partnership distributes $181,000 in liquidation of Brody's interest, an amount which equals the value of her interest in the partnership's assets, including goodwill. How much of this distribution is treated as a guaranteed payment under section 736(a)(2)?

a)   None. The partnership uses equipment of significant value in its business. Therefore, capital is a material income-producing factor, within the meaning of section 736(b)(3)(A). Section 736(b)(2) does not apply to this distribution, which is treated in its entirety as a section 736(b) amount.

b)   None. Because the partnership is an LLP, Brody is not a "general partner" within the meaning of section 736(b)(3)(B). Therefore, section 736(b)(2) does not apply to this distribution and all of it is treated as a section 736(b) amount.

   c) $32,000, Brody's interest in the partnership's unrealized receivables.

   d) $132,000, the excess of the $181,000 cash distribution over Brody's $49,000 interest in the partnership's cash and equipment.

   9.8.2   The partnership is the same as in Question 9.8.1, except that it has not gotten around to settling some payables for office supplies and the like. The cash to do so is on its balance sheet, which now looks like this:

Assets				Liabilities		
	Tax	**Book**	**FMV**		**Tax**	**Book**
Cash	$ 66,000	$ 66,000	$ 66,000	Payables	$ 39,000	$ 39,000
Receivables	0	0	96,000			
Equipment	147,000	147,000	120,000	**Capital**		
[Goodwill]	0	0	300,000	Audrey	58,000	58,000
				Brody	58,000	58,000
				Cooper	58,000	58,000
Total Assets	$213,000	$213,000	$582,000	**Total Liabilities and Capital**	$213,000	$213,000

   The partnership makes the same $181,000 cash distribution to Brody in liquidation of her interest. What are the tax consequences to her of this distribution?

   a) Ordinary income, $132,000; capital loss, $9,000

   b) Ordinary income, $132,000; capital loss, $22,000

   c) Ordinary income, $123,000; capital gain, $0

   d) Ordinary income, $119,000; capital gain, $4,000

   9.8.3   How does your answer to Question 9.8.2 change if ABC LLP has no goodwill on its balance sheet, but the partners amend their agreement to provide that $50,000 of the $181,000 distribution to Brody is attributable to partnership goodwill? Assume that this is a reasonable valuation for the goodwill.

   a) No change

   b) Ordinary income, $82,000; capital gain, $41,000

   c) Ordinary income, $69,000; capital gain, $54,000

   d) Ordinary income, $32,000; capital gain, $91,000

9.8.4 What are the tax consequences to the partnership of the distribution described in Question 9.8.1? Assume that the partnership has not made a section 754 election.

	Deduction	Basis Adjustment		
		Receivables	Equipment	Goodwill
a)	$132,000	$ 0	$ 0	$ 0
b)	132,000	0	(9,000)	0
c)	100,000	32,000	(9,000)	0
d)	0	32,000	0	91,000

9.8.5 What are the tax consequences to the partnership of the distribution described in Question 9.8.1 if the partnership has made a section 754 election?

	Deduction	Basis Adjustment		
		Receivables	Equipment	Goodwill
a)	$132,000	$ 0	$ 0	$ 0
b)	132,000	0	(9,000)	0
c)	100,000	32,000	(9,000)	0
d)	0	32,000	0	91,000

9.8.6 *Before answering this Question, please read Treas. Reg. § 1.736–1(b)(5).* The facts are the same as in Question 9.8.1, except that the partnership does not make the $181,000 distribution in a lump sum. Instead, on June 30, 2016, the partnership pays Brody $40,000 and agrees to pay her five percent of its net profits for the second half of 2016 and for each of the following two years. On the same date, Brody resigns from the firm and withdraws from the partnership. The profit-sharing payments turn out to be $25,000 (which the partnership pays to Brody on December 31, 2016), $45,000 (paid in 2017) and $60,000 (paid in 2018). What are the tax consequences of this arrangement to Brody for her 2016 tax year? The partners have no agreement regarding the allocation of annual payments between section 736(a) and section 736(b).

a) Ordinary income, $25,000; capital gain, $0

b) Ordinary income, $25,000; capital loss, $18,000

c) Ordinary income, $22,000; capital gain, $0

d) Ordinary income, $16,000; capital loss, $9,000

Capital-intensive partnerships

9.8.7 The facts are the same as Question 9.8.1, except that the nature of the partnership's activities compels a conclusion that capital is a material income-producing factor. The partnership makes its $181,000 liquidating distribution to Brody. What are the tax consequences of this distribution to her?

a) Ordinary income, $132,000; capital loss, $9,000

b) Ordinary income, $123,000; capital gain, $0

c) Ordinary income, $32,000; capital gain, $91,000

d) Ordinary income, $0; capital gain, $123,000

9.8.8 What are the tax consequences to the partnership of the liquidating distribution described in Question 9.8.7? Assume the partnership has made a section 754 election.

	Deduction	Basis Adjustment		
		Receivables	Equipment	Goodwill
a)	$132,000	$ 0	$ 0	$ 0
b)	132,000	0	(9,000)	0
c)	100,000	32,000	(9,000)	0
d)	0	32,000	0	91,000

9.8.9 The facts are the same as in Question 9.8.7, except that the partnership distributes $200,000 to Brody in liquidation of her interest. Assume that the values of all of the partnership's assets, including goodwill, are exactly as shown on the expanded balance sheet. What are the tax consequences of this distribution to Brody?

a) Ordinary income, $151,000; capital loss, $9,000

b) Ordinary income, $51,000; capital gain, $91,000

c) Ordinary income, $32,000; capital gain, $110,000

d) Ordinary income, $0; capital gain, $142,000

CHAPTER 10
PARTNERSHIP TERMINATIONS, MERGERS AND DIVISIONS

10.1 TERMINATIONS

You may be curious about the title of section 708, "Continuation of Partnership." It derives from the fact that partnerships historically were frail creatures, which "dissolved" upon the occurrence of many commonplace events, including the withdrawal, death, bankruptcy or legal incompetence of any partner. Following dissolution, a partnership wound up its business and liquidated, absent an agreement among the remaining partners to continue. Although the Revised Uniform Partnership Act of 1997 significantly modified this historical pattern, it was what the drafters of subchapter K confronted in 1954. They believed, sensibly enough, that this was no way to run a tax system. They expressed that belief in section 708(a), which provides that for tax purposes a partnership continues unless and until it is "terminated"—a word intentionally chosen to be different than the state-law concept of "dissolution."

Having so provided in section 708(a), the drafters faced the task of defining—exhaustively, with no help from state law—what constitutes a termination for tax purposes. In section 708(b), they settled on only two events, the cessation of business activity in a partnership and the sale or exchange of 50% or more of the partnership interests within a 12-month period. A partnership ceases to exist for tax purposes on the date of its termination, whether or not that date happens to coincide with the last day of the partnership's regular tax year. On the date of termination, the partnership passes through to its partners all of its income, gains, losses, deductions and credits for the period ending with the termination. If the remaining partners chose to continue business in a partnership after this date, that partnership will be considered a new partnership for tax purposes.

Termination through cessation

This is the obvious one. A partnership terminates for tax purposes as of the date on which the winding up of the affairs of the partnership is completed. This can be later—much later—than the date that the partners resolve to wind up the business and liquidate. Moreover, a partnership terminates only when "no part of any business, financial operation, or venture" continues to be carried on, not merely when it ceases to conduct its historic business. Section 708(b)(1)(A). Thus, a partnership can sell its historic business and reinvest the proceeds in a new business, or become an investment partnership—all without terminating for tax purposes.

The fate of a two-person partnership, which terminates on account of the liquidation of the interest of one partner or the purchase of one partner's interest by the other, has garnered inordinate attention over the years. The rules that have emerged put off the terminating event until the partner or her successors are no longer sharing in the fruits of the partnership's business. *See* Treas. Reg. § 1.708–1(b)(1). This is a useful rule when retirement payments are spread over more than one year, or when the settlement of a partner-decedent's estate is delayed. In contrast to these sensible results, the analysis of the sale of one partner's interest to another is one of the most bizarre in all of federal tax law. It was hatched by the Tax Court in *McCauslen v. Commissioner*, 45 T.C. 588 (1966), and regrettably perpetuated by the IRS in Rev. Rul. 99–6, 1999–1 C.B. 432. The seller treats this transaction as a mere sale of her partnership interest. For the buyer, however, it is not a purchase of a partnership interest. Instead, for the purpose of determining the buyer's tax treatment, the entire transaction is treated as a liquidation. In this liquidation, the partnership distributes all of its assets to the buyer and the seller in accordance with their interests. The buyer then purchases the seller's share of the distributed assets from the seller. You will have a chance to apply this analysis in Question 10.1.6. The partnership terminates under section 708(b)(1)(A), not section 708(b)(1)(B), because no part of the partnership's business, financial operation or venture is thereafter carried on "in a partnership"—a partnership must have at least two partners, which this one no longer does. If the buyer carries on the partnership's activities, it will be as a sole proprietor.

Technical termination

The termination described in section 708(b)(1)(B) does not involve the cessation of business activities in a partnership, but instead the transfer of partnership interests. It is often referred to as a "technical termination" or, worse, a "tech term." The statute defines this type of termination to involve a transfer of 50% or more of the total interest in partnership capital and profits within a 12-month period; the relevant period is any period of 12 consecutive calendar months, whether or not coinciding with the calendar year or the partnership's tax year, if different. This is an entirely mechanical test. A technical termination does not occur if, for example, 100% of the profits interests but only 49% of the capital interests change hands within any 12-month period. This is true, even if the partnership or its partners fully intend to transfer the remaining 51% of the capital interests during the following 12-month period, and indeed even if they are legally obligated to do so.

The origin of the technical termination is obscure. It was added (actually, an election to avoid it was removed) by the Conference Committee in 1954, without published explanation. It is widely agreed that it was intended to prevent trafficking (it's always spelled that way) in partnership taxable years. The idea is that a partnership with a really juicy tax year, like January 31, could be sold to a bunch of calendar-year partners, who would forever after enjoy the 11 months of deferral which such a partnership tax year would provide. As discussed in Topic 4.2, however, current law generally would require such a partnership to change its tax year to the calendar year, beginning with the tax year immediately following the year of the sale. Moreover, as discussed in Topic 6.1, the varying interests rule would require the selling partners to pay tax on their shares of the partnership's income for the period prior to the sale. The advantage of trafficking in tax years is thus greatly limited by current law, and it is hard to justify the continuing existence of section 708(b)(1)(B) on this basis alone. Partnerships might still be used to traffick in depreciable lives, however, without a contrary rule in section 168, discussed below, which makes use of the notion of a technical termination.

The IRS and the Treasury Department have been doing what they can to limit the damage caused by a technical termination. It all has to do with the transactions that are deemed to occur when a technical termination takes place. Under Treasury regulations promulgated in 1997, the terminating partnership is deemed to contribute its assets subject to its liabilities to a new partnership in exchange for all of the interests in the new partnership, which the terminating partnership then distributes to the continuing partners in liquidation of their respective interests in the terminating partnership. Treas. Reg. § 1.708–1(b)(4). We will see in Topic 10.2 that this form of deemed transaction is commonly called "assets over."

Under this characterization, the new partnership takes the old partnership's tax bases and holding periods in partnership assets, and the continuing partners recognize no gain or loss and take outside bases in their interests in the new partnership equal to their respective outside bases in the old partnership. The entire transaction is ignored for purposes of capital-account maintenance. Treas. Reg. §§ 1.704–1(b)(2)(iv)(*l*) and –1(b)(5), example (13). Further, no new section 704(c) layer is created by the deemed contribution of property by the old partnership to the new partnership. Treas. Reg. § 1.704–3(a)(3)(i); *see generally* Treas. Reg. § 1.708–1(b)(4), example; *see also* Treas. Reg. §§ 1.704–4(c)(3) (section 704(c)(1)(B) gain, if any, not triggered by deemed distribution); 1.737–2(a) (ditto for section 737 gain); 1.704–4(a)(4)(ii) (no new seven-year periods created by deemed contribution); Prop. Treas. Reg. § 1.737–1(c)(3)(ii) (ditto).

These regulations do not, however, eliminate all of the tax effects of a technical termination. Of note are the following:

✓ *Bunching of income.* The old partnership's tax year (indeed, its very existence for tax purposes) ends on the date of the termination, which is the date of the sale or exchange that created the technical termination. Treas. Reg. § 1.708–1(b)(3)(ii). On that date, all of the income or loss of the old partnership is passed through to the partners. This creates a "bunching" of income or loss for any partner whose tax year is not the same as the partnership's tax year, so called because such a partner must report, in a single return, income or loss from more than one partnership tax year. Say, for example, that Leon, a calendar-year taxpayer, is a partner in Worldbook LLC, a partnership with a September 30 tax year. If Worldbook suffers a technical termination on December 31, 2016,

Leon will be forced to pick up 15 months of partnership income in his 2016 return—12 months from the partnership tax year ended September 30, 2016, and another three months from the short tax period ended December 31, 2016.

✓ *Re-starting of depreciation.* Normally, when depreciable property is contributed to a partnership, the partnership "steps into the shoes" of the contributor, meaning that the partnership can continue to depreciate the property using the same method of depreciation over the remaining depreciable life. By statute, this rule does not apply in the case of a technical termination. Section 168(i)(7)(B) (flush language). The important practical consequence is that the new partnership must re-start the depreciable lives of all its properties, which can have the effect of reducing significantly the amount of depreciation that may be claimed in the first years following the technical termination. Think of this as a sort of "anti-churning rule" through which Congress prevents purchasers of depreciable property owned through partnerships from avoiding the need to re-start the depreciation on such properties by buying partnership interests rather than interests in the properties themselves. The presence of this rule probably explains why the notion of a technical termination hangs on in the Internal Revenue Code.

✓ *Elimination of elections.* When a partnership terminates, all of its tax elections terminate with it. Of course, depending on the elections that the partnership has made in the past, this can be a good thing or a bad thing. For example, a technical termination can free a partnership from a prior section 754 election that could otherwise be revoked only with IRS permission.

✓ *Tax consequences of sale.* All partners (not just those involved in the sale) may have tax consequences arising from the sale of the partnership interest which caused the technical termination. For example, the re-arranging of partnership liabilities may cause basis adjustments to all partners under sections 752(a) and (b), and may even require one or more partners to recognize gain. This is not strictly a result of the termination itself, but you should not forget about it.

This is all good to know, but it may or may not appear on your partnership tax exam. You are at least as likely to be tested on whether a technical termination has taken place and, more specifically, whether a given event or transaction is a sale or exchange of a partnership interest that must be taken into account in deciding if the 50% threshold has been breached. The following Questions test your understanding of these issues. Before answering them, please re-read Treas. Reg. §§ 1.708–1(b)(1) through –1(b)(3).

10.1.1   Which of the following transactions or events count as a sale or exchange of a partnership interest for purposes of section 708(b)(1)(B)? Mark all that apply.

a)   A partner's gift of a capital interest to a family member

b)   A partnership's issuance of a capital interest in exchange for a contribution of property

c)   A corporate partner's distribution of a capital interest to its parent corporation in a liquidation that is tax-free pursuant to section 332

d)   A partner's pledge of a capital interest to a bank as security for a nonrecourse loan

10.1.2   Alvin, Boris, Michael and Marvin are equal partners in Partnership ABMM, a general partnership. Prior to February 1, 2016, there have been no transfers of any interest in Partnership ABMM. On that date, Alvin sells his interest in the partnership to Michael for cash, raising Michael's interest to 50%. On June 26, Michael sells the interest he acquired from Alvin to Bill, who previously has not been a partner. On August 1, Marvin withdraws from the partnership, taking a cash liquidating distribution and thereby increasing the partnership interests of Michael, Boris and Bill to 33.3% each. On September 8, Boris dies and his interest passes under his will to his son, who is not admitted to the partnership as a partner, but continues to share in its profits. Finally, on January 27, 2017, Michael assigns his interest in the partnership to his bank, in partial satisfaction of a personal loan. When does Partnership ABMM terminate under section 708(b)(1)(B)?

a)   June 26

b)   August 1

c)   September 8

d)   January 27

10.1.3   Aaron and Ben are partners in Partnership AB, with interests in capital and profits of 75% and 25%, respectively. Cam and Dworkin are partners in Partnership CD, with interests in capital and profits of 62.5% and 37.5%, respectively. Cam contributes his interest in Partnership CD to the Partnership AB (now renamed Partnership ABC) in exchange for a 20% interest therein. This reduces the interests of Aaron and Ben to 60% and 20%, respectively. For purposes of applying section 708(b)(1)(B), which interests have been sold or exchanged?

a)   Cam's new interest in Partnership AB

b)   Cam's old interest in Partnership CD

c)   Both of these interests

d)   Neither of these interests

10.1.4   Later, Aaron sells his interest in Partnership ABC to Eugenie for cash and it is renamed Partnership BCE. Which partnership(s) terminate under section 708(b)(1)(B)?

a)   Partnership ABC

b)   Partnership CD

c)   Both

d)   Neither

10.1.5   Later still, Partnership BCE liquidates Ben's interest by distributing to him its entire interest in Partnership CD. For purposes of applying section 708(b)(1)(B), which interests have been sold or exchanged?

a)   Ben's interest in Partnership BCE

b)   Partnership BCE's interest in Partnership CD

c)   Both of these interests

d)   Neither of these interests

10.1.6   Duo-Tone LLC operates a large photo-processing business. Its assets comprise cash, receivables, plant and equipment and a sizeable investment portfolio. Duo-Tone has and will continue to have its default classification for federal income tax purposes. A and B are its only members, each holding a 50% interest in capital and profits. If A sells all of her interest in Duo-Tone to B for cash, who owns the assets for tax purposes and what are their holding periods?

a)   Duo-Tone owns the assets, and their holding periods are unaffected by the transaction.

b)   Duo-Tone owns the assets, and its holding periods for all of the assets begin the day after the transaction.

c)   B owns the assets, and B's holding periods for all of the assets include Duo-Tone's holding periods for such assets.

d)   B owns the assets; B's holding periods for one-half of the assets begin the day after the transaction; B's holding periods for the remaining one-half of the assets include Duo-Tone's holding periods for such assets.

10.2   MERGERS: IDENTIFYING THE CONTINUING AND TERMINATED PARTNERSHIPS AND CONSTRUCTING THE TRANSACTION

What is deemed to happen for federal income tax purposes when two or more partnerships merge or consolidate? What are the federal income tax consequences of the transaction? The two questions are obviously related. We will consider the first in this Topic and the second in Topic 10.3.

What is a "merger or consolidation"?

This term, which appears in section 708(b)(2)(A), is not defined further by statute or regulation. In this respect, partnership tax law differs greatly from corporate tax law. This reflects the profound differences between the two tax regimes. Without a statutory nonrecognition rule, a corporate merger would be a taxable transaction. The transactions that benefit from nonrecognition therefore must be defined with care, which begets section 368, regulations, court decisions and published and private rulings by the thousands. There is no analogue to section 368 in Subchapter K. The generally benign rules of partnership tax allow for the combination of the assets of two or more partnerships to proceed as a lightly taxed or entirely non-taxed transaction, without the need for any special nonrecognition rule for mergers.

Nonetheless, the rules discussed in this Topic regarding the characterization of mergers and consolidations apply only to those transactions, so it is useful to have some idea of what they are. As a working definition, think of a merger or consolidation (hereafter referred to simply as a merger) as a transaction in which substantially all of the assets of two or more partnerships are combined in a single, multi-step transaction into a single entity. The most straightforward example is a statutory merger, which is provided by the laws of many states. Partnership tax lawyers often refer to a statutory merger as "formless," because state merger statutes do not describe or characterize the transfers that are deemed to have taken place in order to put the partnerships together. A merger can also be accomplished through actual transfers of partnership interests and assets.

Identifying the continuing and terminated partnerships

No matter how many partnerships participate in a merger, only one is left standing at the end, which section 708(b)(2)(A) refers to as the "resulting partnership." Looking at the language of section 708(b)(2)(A), it appears that the resulting partnership may be treated for tax purposes as a continuation of any number of the merging partnerships, from none of them to all of them. A quick peek at the Treasury regulations will disabuse you of that idea. Under Treas. Reg. § 1.708–1(c)(1), one (at most) of the merging partnerships survives the merger and the other merging partnerships are treated as terminated for tax purposes. It is possible that none survive. In that event, the resulting partnership is treated as an entirely new partnership for tax purposes.

What difference does it make whether any merging partnership survives the merger, or which one it is? If the resulting partnership is treated as the continuation of a merging partnership, the existence and elections of that merging partnership continue for tax purposes and its tax year ends on its normal date, unaffected by the merger. Treas. Reg. § 1.708–1(c)(2). In contrast, the fate of merging partnerships that are terminated is that of all terminated partnerships: their tax years, their tax elections and their very existence for tax purposes come to an end on the date of the merger. On that date, they pass through to their partners their income, gains, losses, deductions and credits for the short taxable period then ending, and their partners may suffer bunching of income as a result.

In one significant respect, however, termination by merger is less painful than termination resulting from the sale or exchange of partnership interests. In Topic 10.1, you met the final sentence of section 168(i)(7)(B), which requires a partnership subject to technical termination to restart depreciation on all of its properties. That rule applies only to technical terminations under section 708(b)(1)(B), not to terminations pursuant to mergers (or divisions) under section 708(b)(2).

Identifying the continuing partnership, if any, and the terminated partnership or partnerships is the first step in determining what is deemed to have taken place for tax purposes in the merger transaction. Here are the alternatives that you may face on an exam:

- ✓ *Two merging partnerships with no overlapping ownership.* The resulting partnership is treated as the continuation of any merging partnership whose partners own more than 50% of the capital and profits of the resulting partnership. If no partner has an interest in more than one of the merging partnerships (that is what is meant by no overlapping ownership), one partnership will usually survive. In the unusual case that the ownership of the resulting partnership is split equally between the two partner groups, both merging partnerships will terminate and a new partnership will result.

- ✓ *More than two merging partnerships with no overlapping ownership.* The more merging partnerships there are, the less likely it is that any partner group will own more than 50% of the capital and profits of the resulting partnership. If none does, all of the merging partnerships will terminate and a new partnership will result.

- ✓ *Two merging partnerships with overlapping ownership.* Under the statute, both merging partnerships may survive. In this case, Treas. Reg. § 1.708–1(c)(1) provides that the surviving partnership will be the one with the higher net asset value. In the unlikely situation that both merging partnerships have exactly the same net asset values, both will terminate, unless the IRS determines otherwise (by, for example, a private letter ruling). *See* Treas. Reg. § 1.708–1(c)(1) (second sentence) (net asset values control "unless the Commissioner permits otherwise").

- ✓ *More than two merging partnerships with overlapping ownership.* Overlapping ownership increases the chances that the partners of one (or more) of the merging partnerships will cross the 50% threshold, because in counting the ownership interest in the resulting partnership obtained by the partners of any merging partnership, the interests in the resulting partnership received by the overlap partner(s) on account of their interests in the other merging partnership(s) are included in the count. If more than one

of the merging partnerships survives under the statute, apply the
regulatory tiebreaker, so that the merging partnership with the
higher (highest) net asset value continues.

You can try your hand at analyzing some of these alternatives in the
Questions below.

Constructing the transaction

There are four ways to accomplish a merger. First, a merging
partnership can transfer its assets to the resulting partnership in exchange
for interests in the resulting partnership, which it distributes to its partners
in liquidation ("assets over"). Second, a merging partnership can distribute
its assets to its partners in liquidation, and they can contribute those assets
to the resulting partnership ("assets up"). Third, the partners of a merging
partnership can transfer their partnership interests to the resulting
partnership in exchange for interests in the resulting partnership ("interests
over"). The transferred partnership, now owned solely by the resulting
partnership, terminates. Fourth, the partnerships can engage in a formless
merger under a state merger statute.

The Treasury regulations could have taxed the first three of these in
accordance with their form, leaving only the job of deciding what is deemed to
have happened in the formless merger. Instead, the regulations register a
strong preference for the assets-over characterization. Under Treas. Reg.
§ 1.708–1(c)(3), unless the parties follow a specified version of the assets-up
approach, discussed below, the following steps are deemed to occur in the
merger of two (or more) partnerships:

1. Each terminated partnership contributes all of its assets to the
    resulting partnership in exchange for interests in the resulting
    partnership, and

2. Each terminated partnership distributes the interests in the
    resulting partnership obtained in step 1. to its partners in
    liquidation of their interests in the terminated partnership.

Notice how this default characterization depends on the identification of
the terminated partnership(s) in the merger. Each terminated partnership is
a transferor of assets, either to the continuing partnership, if there is one, or
to a new partnership resulting from the merger. These transfers are deemed
to take place for tax purposes, whether or not they actually occur under
governing state law. Say, for example, that two partnerships, Saltco and
Pepperco, merge by means of a transfer of all of Saltco's assets to Pepperco. If
Saltco is the continuing partnership under the rules we reviewed earlier, the
merger must be analyzed for tax purposes as though Pepperco transferred its
assets to Saltco, even though that is not what actually happened. Further, if
neither Saltco nor Pepperco is a continuing partnership, both are considered
to have transferred their assets to a new partnership for tax purposes.

The default characterization does not apply, and the transaction will be
taxed in accordance with its form, if a terminated partnership distributes all
of its assets to its partners in liquidation and they immediately contribute all

of the distributed assets to the resulting partnership. "Direct deeding" (a transfer of title directly from the terminated partnership to the resulting partnership directed by the partners) will not work: the transfer to the partners must cause them, however briefly, to be treated as the owners of the assets under state law. They need not, however, assume the terminated partnership's liabilities (except to the extent such liability arises from their momentary ownership of the partnership's assets). Treas. Reg. §§ 1.708–1(c)(3)(ii), –1(c)(5), example (3).

10.2.1   AB LP is a limited partnership, the partners of which are A, the general partner, and B, the limited partner. AB operates an active business which has generated substantial profits over the years. AB has retained most of these profits as investment assets. CD LLC is a limited liability company treated as a partnership for tax purposes, the members of which are C and D. Pursuant to an agreement, AB transfers all of its business assets to CD in exchange for CD interests which it distributes to its partners. AB retains its investment assets, because CD does not want to pay for them and they can be managed more effectively by the partnership than by A and B individually. For tax purposes, this transaction is:

a)   Not a merger, because two legal entities survive the transaction

b)   Not a merger, because it was not undertaken in the proper assets-up form

c)   A merger in which AB is treated as distributing all of its assets to A and B, who then contribute them to CD

d)   A merger in which AB is treated as transferring all of its assets to CD and terminating

10.2.2   AB LLC is a limited liability company treated as a partnership for tax purposes. Its members are A and B. CD LP is a limited partnership, the partners of which are C, the general partner, and D, the limited partner. A and B transfer their interests in AB to CD in exchange for limited partnership interests amounting to 35% of the total interests in capital and profits of CD after the transaction. CD owns all of the interests in AB, which it does not liquidate but instead operates as a wholly owned subsidiary. AB does not make a "check the box" election to be treated as a corporation. For tax purposes, this transaction is:

a)   Not a merger, because two legal entities survive the transaction

b)   Not a merger, because a merger cannot be accomplished in interests-over form

c)   A merger in which CD is treated as the continuation of AB

d)   A merger in which AB terminates

10.2.3   Three partnerships combine under the governing state merger statute. They are Partnership AB, Partnership CD and Partnership EFG. A and B each own 25% of the capital and profits interests in the resulting partnership, and C, D, E, F and G each own 10%. For tax purposes, the resulting partnership is treated as a continuation of:

a)   Partnership AB

b)   Partnership CD

c)   Partnership EFG

d)   None of the above

10.2.4   What is deemed to have happened for tax purposes in the transaction described in Question 10.2.3?

a)   Partnership CD and Partnership EFG transfer all of their assets to Partnership AB in exchange for interests therein, which they distribute to their respective partners in liquidation.

b)   Same as **Answer (a)**, but Partnership AB thereafter transfers all of its assets to a new partnership.

c)   Partnership CD and Partnership EFG distribute all of their assets to their respective partners in liquidation, and the partners immediately transfer the distributed assets to Partnership AB in exchange for interests therein.

d)   Partnership AB, Partnership CD and Partnership EFG transfer all of their assets to a new partnership in exchange for interests therein, which they distribute to their respective partners in liquidation.

10.2.5   Partnership AB has a net asset value of $300,000 and is owned 60% by A and 40% by B. Partnership BCD has a net asset value of $200,000 and is owned 40% by B and 30% by each of C and D. Partnership AB transfers all of its assets to Partnership BCD in exchange for interests therein, which it distributes in liquidation to its partners. The ownership of capital and profits interests in the resulting partnership is A, 36%; B, 40%; C, 12% and D, 12%. For tax purposes, the partnership resulting from this transaction is treated as a continuation of:

a)   Partnership AB

b)   Partnership CD

c)   Both

d)   Neither

10.2.6   What is deemed to have happened for tax purposes in the merger described in Question 10.2.5?

a)   The merger is taxed in accordance with its form, an asset transfer by Partnership AB to Partnership CD.

b)   The merger is recharacterized as asset transfers by both Partnership AB and Partnership CD to a new partnership.

c)   The merger is recharacterized as an asset transfer by Partnership CD to Partnership AB.

d)   The merger is recharacterized as a distribution of the assets of Partnership CD to its partners, followed by their contribution of the assets to Partnership AB.

10.2.7   Partnerships AB, BCD and EF combine. Partnership BCD transfers all of its assets to Partnership AB in exchange for interests therein, which it distributes to its partners in liquidation. Partnership EF makes liquidating distributions of all of its assets to its partners, who immediately contribute all of the distributed assets to partnership AB in exchange for interests therein. The ownership of capital and profits interests in the resulting partnership is A, 25%; B, 40%; C, 5%; D, 5%; E, 5% and F, 20%. What is deemed to have happened for tax purposes in these transactions?

a)   The transactions are taxed in accordance with their form, as an asset transfer by Partnership BCD and a distribution (and recontribution) by Partnership EF (and its partners)+.

b)   The transactions are recharacterized, because the assets-up form was not followed uniformly. Partnership BCD and Partnership EF are both treated as transferring assets to Partnership AB in assets-over transfers.

c)   The transactions are recharacterized, because assets were not transferred to the continuing partnership. Partnership AB and Partnership EF are both treated as transferring assets to Partnership BCD in assets-over transfers.

d)   The transactions are recharacterized, because assets were not transferred to the continuing partnership. Partnership AB is treated as transferring assets to Partnership BCD in an assets-over transfer. Partnership EF is treated as making liquidating distributions of all of its assets to its partners, who recontribute the assets to Partnership BCD in an assets-up transfer.

10.3   MERGERS: TAX TREATMENT

Chances are, you are not reading this. It is sitting back here toward the end of the Reading Period, untouched by (many) human eyes. But don't feel sorry for this lonely little essay—save that for the one on divisions in Topic 10.5.

The likely reason for this neglect is that you did not cover either mergers or divisions in your partnership tax class. Most do not, and those that do may focus only on Treas. Reg. §§ 1.708–1(c) and –1(d), which we covered in Topic 10.2 and will cover in Topic 10.4. This Topic provides a short primer on what can seem to be a very complex subject, the tax treatment of partnership mergers.

Assets-over

If you remember nothing else, remember this: there are almost no special rules for the taxation of partnership mergers. Instead, you apply the ordinary rules of partnership taxation to the transactions that are deemed to have occurred under Treas. Reg. § 1.708–1(c), just as though they actually happened. For example, in the default assets-over form for the merger of two partnerships, the terminated partnership ("T") transfers all of its assets and liabilities to the continuing partnership ("C") in exchange for interests in C, which T distributes to its partners in liquidation of their T interests. The deemed asset transfer from T to C is a contribution, generally tax-free under section 721. (Watch out, however, if T has a lot of debt relative to tax basis. (The tip-off will be that the T partners have negative tax capital.) Whenever T has liabilities that are assumed by C, there will be deemed contributions and distributions under sections 751(a) and (b), respectively. *See* Topic 2.5. It is possible that T, and therefore its partners, may recognize gain as a result of the shifting of liability shares to the historic partners of C.)

Under the ordinary rules applicable to contributions of property, C takes a tax basis in the contributed assets equal to T's prior tax basis. T takes a tax basis in the C interests it receives equal to the amount of money and the aggregate basis of the property contributed. T's outside basis in C is more elusive than the Higgs boson, however, because it flashes out of existence instantly when T distributes the C interests to its partners. T recognizes no tax gain or loss on this distribution, nor do T's partners. (Those 14 words capture the essential difference between partnership tax and corporate tax, and explain why they need mountains of rules on tax-free reorganizations and we do not.) Under section 732(b), T's basis in the C interests disappears and T's partners take the C interests with bases equal to their prior bases in the T interests.

The ordinary rules for book accounting also apply to mergers. From C's perspective, the merger is the receipt of a property contribution. As with any property contribution, C will likely revalue its book assets and the book capital accounts of its partners immediately prior to the merger. *See* Topic 2.6. Accordingly, C's partners may realize book gain or loss, although it is not recognized for tax purposes. Whether or not a revaluation takes place, the assets contributed by T will be reflected on C's books at fair market value as of the date of the merger.

Section 704(c) layers, both forward and reverse, can arise in a merger. When C revalues its book assets immediately before the merger, it creates a reverse section 704(c) layer, which reflects the changes in values of its assets since the time of their contribution or last revaluation. When the partnership sells these assets, this reverse layer of gain or loss will be allocable under the principles of section 704(c) only to the partners of C prior to the merger, not to the partners who join as a result of the merger. This is, of course, exactly the effect of a revaluation before any other sort of contribution. *See* Topic 8.5.

T's deemed contribution of its properties to C can create a forward section 704(c) layer, just like any contribution of property to a partnership.

As we have seen in past discussions, this forward layer will only exist for assets with built-in gain; built-in loss assets are separately tended by section 704(c)(1)(C). *See* Topic 8.4. It seems obvious that the former partners of T should be responsible for that layer, but it takes a close reading of the Treasury regulations to see how that happens. Treas. Reg. § 1.704–3(a)(7) provides that, if a contributing partner transfers her interest in the partnership to which the contribution was made, the transferee of the interest inherits her section 704(c) responsibility. Accordingly, when T (the contributing partnership) distributes (transfers) the C interests to T's partners (the transferees), they are responsible for this forward section 704(c) layer in proportion to their former interests in T.

Assets-up

If accomplished in just the right way, it is possible for a merger to be an assets-up transaction. *See* Topic 10.2. The ordinary partnership tax rules apply here as well, but to a transaction composed of different steps. T's distribution of its assets and liabilities to its partners in liquidation of their interests does not normally produce a tax liability. In unusual cases, however, the amount of cash distributed to a given partner might exceed her basis, resulting in recognized gain under section 731(a)(1). A deemed cash distribution under section 752(b) could produce the same result, if not matched by the amount of partnership liabilities the distributee-partner assumes. Note also the discussion of the "anti-mixing-bowl" statutes, below.

Setting aside for a moment the effects of taxing this distribution, each of T's partners takes an aggregate basis in the distributed assets which under section 732(b) equals her outside basis in T, reduced by any cash actually distributed and reduced or increased by the net section 752 amount. This adjusted outside basis is allocated among the distributed assets in accordance with the rules of section 732(c). An inside-outside basis differential, if present, will create a step-up (or step-down) in the tax basis of T's assets in the aggregate. Whether or not there is such a disparity, basis will be "rearranged" among T's assets by the section 732(c) allocation mechanism. This restated (possibly), rearranged (probably) tax basis is inherited by C when T's partners contribute the assets to C.

This might appear to be a significant difference from the tax treatment of an assets-over merger, and a significant advantage if the aggregate outside basis of T's partners is greater than T's inside basis in its assets. And so it may be. If, on the other hand, C has in place or is willing to make an election under section 754, a similar step-up in asset basis can be achieved in an assets-over merger. This is because the deemed distribution by T of the C interests in an assets-over merger is a sale or exchange for purposes of section 743(b), creating special basis adjustments for each of T's partners. *See* section 761(e)(2). In the aggregate, these special basis adjustments equal the excess of the T partners' aggregate outside basis over their aggregate share of C's inside basis. *See* Topic 6.5. This should equal, or closely approximate, T's inside-outside basis differential. The special basis adjustments will, however, be allocated among all of C's assets under section 755, rather than being concentrated in only T's historic assets, as is the step-up in the assets-up merger. Depending on the composition of those assets, this may be either an advantage or a disadvantage.

The book treatment of an assets-up merger is straightforward. T's partners contribute T's assets to C, receiving book capital accounts equal to the fair market value of the contributed assets. C may, and normally does, revalue immediately prior to this contribution. The new section 704(c) layers are easy to see. A new forward layer arises from the asset contribution by T's partners and is traceable only to them. A new reverse layer arises from C's revaluation and is traceable only to C's partners before the merger.

The "anti-mixing-bowl" rules

Application of the anti-mixing-bowl rules of sections 704(c)(1)(B) and 737 to partnership mergers is a complex and in some ways controversial subject. We touch on it here, with the goal of answering just one of many possible questions: Does a merger in either assets-over form or assets-up form trigger gain under either section 704(c)(1)(B) or section 737? You may find it helpful to look again at Topic 9.4 before continuing here.

Assets-over merger. Let's begin with the case where A, a partner of T, contributed Asset X to T with built-in gain. That contribution was less than seven years ago, so the section 704(c)(1)(B) "clock" is still running. It is not self-evident why A should worry about an assets-over merger triggering this built-in gain. You will recall that section 704(c)(1)(B) applies when a built-in gain asset is distributed to a partner other than the contributing partner within seven years of its contribution. There is no distribution of any T asset in an assets-over merger, so what is the problem? When T transfers Asset X along with all of its other assets to C, it receives C interests in exchange. Treas. Reg. §§ 1.704–3(a)(8) and –4(d)(1) provide in this instance that the C interests are treated as section 704(c) property with the same amount of built-in gain as Asset X. Under this general rule, it appears that A, the contributing partner, would recognize gain under section 704(c)(1)(B) to the extent that any other T partner receives C interests when they are distributed by T. The regulations provide no clear way to "trace" the built-in gain in Asset X solely to the C interests that A receives. If A is a 10% partner of T, 90% of the C interests will be distributed to the other T partners. It appears that A would recognize 90% of the built-in gain on Asset X under this analysis.

This is, of course, the wrong result. Neither A nor Asset X has gone anywhere—the former is a partner, and the latter is an asset, of C following the merger and that partnership will be able to allocate to A the appropriate amount of gain if it sells or distributes Asset X prior the end of the seven-year period. Happily, Treas. Reg. § 1.704–4(c)(4)(i) moots the foregoing analysis and provides simply that section 704(c)(1)(B) does not apply to an assets-over merger.

The pattern is generally the same under section 737. You will recall that section 737 causes the contributor of a built-in gain asset to recognize the lesser of the net precontribution gain or the excess distribution when she receives a distribution within seven years following the contribution. A distribution of the contributed property is exempted. A, the contributing partner of Asset X, plainly receives a distribution in an assets-over merger, but it is a distribution of an interest in C, not Asset X. Under Treas. Reg. § 1.737–2(d)(3)(i), the C interests A receives from T will be treated as Asset X, but A will not receive all of them. Nevertheless, Treas. Reg. § 1.737–2(b)(1) provides that section 737 does not apply to an assets-over merger—not a surprising result, given the IRS' decision not to apply section 704(c)(1)(B).

What if A had instead been a partner of C and had contributed Asset X to that partnership? In that case, no issue would arise under either section 704(c)(1)(B) or section 737, because C is not treated as distributing any assets or partnership interests in the merger.

Assets-up merger. The analysis is shorter here, but not ultimately as sweet. In an assets-up merger, T's assets are actually distributed to the partners of T. If A is a partner in T, she will recognize gain on this distribution under section 704(c)(1)(B) or section 737 unless her entire distribution consists of the contributed property, Asset X. If A's interest in T is worth less than Asset X, the distribution should be a fractional interest in Asset X. If A's interest in T is more valuable than Asset X alone, the distribution can presumably consist of other assets in addition to Asset X. If this is not commercially feasible or if it is overlooked, A will recognize gain on the merger. Unlike in the case of assets-over mergers, there is no regulatory rule that reverses this result—even though the net result of both forms of merger is the same (one partnership with all of the assets and all of the partners).

The answer is different, however, if A is a partner in C. As the continuing partnership, C makes no distributions of assets and thus does not trigger gain for its partners under either section 704(c)(1)(B) or section 737.

10.3.1   On January 5, 2011, Ainslie contributed Land 1 (value $100,000, basis $40,000) and Briana contributed $100,000 in cash to form AB LLC, in which each has a 50% interest in capital and profits. Shortly thereafter, AB LLC purchased Land 2 for $400,000, $300,000 borrowed from a local bank. Its balance sheet as of April 29, 2016 (expanded to show asset values) is as follows.

Assets				Liabilities		
	Tax	**Book**	**FMV**		**Tax**	**Book**
Land 1	$ 40,000	$100,000	$240,000	Bank Debt	$300,000	$300,000
Land 2	400,000	400,000	460,000			
				Capital		
				Ainslie	40,000	100,000
				Briana	100,000	100,000
Total Assets	$440,000	$500,000	$700,000	**Total Liabilities and Capital**	$440,000	$500,000

On July 29, 2010, Colin contributed Land 3 (value $200,000, basis $60,000) and Dylan contributed $200,000 in cash to form CD LLC, in which each has a 50% interest in capital and profits. Like AB LLC, CD LLC used its cash to acquire additional land, although it did not borrow. Its balance sheet as of April 29, 2016 (expanded to show asset values) is as follows.

Assets				Liabilities		
	Tax	**Book**	**FMV**		**Tax**	**Book**
Land 3	$ 60,000	$200,000	$250,000	Bank Debt	$ 0	$ 0
Land 4	200,000	200,000	350,000			
				Capital		
				Colin	60,000	200,000
				Dylan	200,000	200,000
Total Assets	$260,000	$400,000	$600,000	**Total Liabilities and Capital**	$260,000	$400,000

Both of these companies are treated as partnerships for tax purposes and they hold all parcels of land for investment. On April 29, 2016, the companies merge pursuant to the merger provision of governing state law, forming ABCD LLC. Ownership interests in the new entity are proportional to the net asset values contributed. Which is the continuing partnership in this merger?

a)   AB LLC

b)   CD LLC

c)   Both

d)   Neither

10.3.2   For tax purposes, what is deemed to happen in this merger?

a)   AB LLC contributes all of its assets to CD LLC in exchange for interests therein, which AB LLC distributes to its members in liquidation.

b)   CD LLC contributes all of its assets to AB LLC in exchange for interests therein, which CD LLC distributes to its members in liquidation.

c)   AB LLC distributes its assets to its members in liquidation, and they immediately contribute all of the distributed assets to CD LLC in exchange for interests therein.

d)   CD LLC distributes its assets to its members in liquidation, and they immediately contribute all of the distributed assets to AB LLC in exchange for interests therein.

10.3.3   How much book gain does Ainslie realize in this merger, and how much is recognized for tax purposes?

a) $100,000 book gain; $0 tax gain

b) $100,000 book gain; $60,000 tax gain

c) $140,000 book gain; $0 tax gain

d) $140,000 book gain; $200,000 tax gain

10.3.4   What is Ainslie's outside basis in ABCD LLC?

a) $40,000

b) $90,000

c) $100,000

d) $190,000

10.3.5   Assuming that CD revalues its book assets in connection with this merger, how much book gain does Colin realize, and how much is recognized for tax purposes?

a) $0 book gain; $0 tax gain

b) $50,000 book gain; $140,000 tax gain

c) $100,000 book gain; $140,000 tax gain

d) $100,000 book gain; $0 tax gain

10.3.6   What is Colin's outside basis in ABCD LLC?

a) $60,000

b) $135,000

c) $150,000

d) $160,000

10.4 DIVISIONS: IDENTIFYING THE CONTINUING, TERMINATED, NEW AND DIVIDED PARTNERSHIPS AND CONSTRUCTING THE TRANSACTION

Let's discuss divisions as we did mergers. This Topic covers the tax characterization of a division. Topic 10.5 considers the tax consequences that follow from that characterization.

What is a "division"?

Just as with mergers, there is no statutory or regulatory definition of a partnership "division." But just as with mergers, it is useful to have a working definition of the type of transaction to which the rules discussed in this Topic apply. So think of a division this way: it is a single, multi-step transaction in which the assets of one partnership (in the terminology of section 708(b)(2)(B), the "prior partnership") are divided between two or more partnerships, each of which has at least two partners who were partners of the prior partnership. In the simplest form of division, a partnership transfers a portion (less than all) of its assets to a partnership in formation, all of the interests in which are issued pro-rata to the partners of the prior partnership. This corresponds roughly to what is called a "spin-off" in the corporate world, but without all of the bells and whistles needed to satisfy the requirements for nonrecognition under section 355 and section 368(a)(1)(D). Alternatively, the prior partnership could do a "split-off" by causing interests in the new partnership to be issued to two or more of its partners in liquidation of their interests in the prior partnership. Another possibility is a "split-up," in which the prior partnership transfers all of its assets to two or more new partnerships and causes interests in these new partnerships to be issued in some combination to all of its partners, in exchange for all of their interests in the prior partnership. There are, of course, other variants that would also be considered divisions.

Identifying the continuing, terminated and new partnerships

Unlike in the case of mergers, more than one of the partnerships resulting from a division can be a continuation of the prior partnership. This result is established in section 708(b)(2)(B) and is not disturbed by the Treasury regulations. Any partnership resulting from a division whose partners owned more than 50% of the interests in the capital and profits of the prior partnership is a continuation of the prior partnership. Thus, for example, both partnerships resulting from the spin-off described above are continuations of the prior partnership, because the same partners own 100% of each partnership.

This is not so in the split-off, however, because that type of division splits the partners of the prior partnership into two groups, who cannot both have owned more than 50% of the interests in the prior partnership. Accordingly, only one (at most) of the two resulting partnerships in a split-off is considered to be a continuation of the prior partnership. The other resulting partnership is treated as a new partnership for tax purposes. If the liquidated interests account for exactly 50% of the total interests in the prior partnership, it terminates for tax purposes and two new partnerships result from the division. This triggers the usual consequences of tax termination, ending the prior partnership's tax year and elections and creating possible bunching of income for all its partners. As with mergers, the restarting of depreciation periods is not required.

To take a third example, consider the split-up transaction described above. There, the prior partnership disappears for purposes of state law, but it lives on for tax purposes in any of the two or more resulting partnerships that is considered to be a continuation of the prior partnership. If, on the other hand, none of these partnerships is a continuation, the prior partnership terminates for tax purposes and each of the resulting partnerships is treated as a new partnership.

Identifying the divided partnership

As we saw in Topic 10.2, a merger creates, at most, only one continuing partnership. All of the terminated partnerships are deemed to transfer their assets to the continuing partnership (or to a new partnership, if there is no continuing partnership). Thus, in a merger, once you have identified the terminated partnerships, you have identified the transferors of assets and you can describe the transaction for tax purposes. Divisions are similar, but different. They are similar in that identifying the continuing, terminated and new partnerships is the first step in characterizing the transaction for tax purposes. Divisions are different than mergers in two important ways. First, as a broad generalization, it is the continuing partnership, rather than the terminated partnership, that is treated as the transferor of assets in a division. Second, because there can be more than one continuing partnership—or none—in a division, you need a way to sort among them to identify the transferor uniquely.

The Treasury regulations do this with the concept of the "divided partnership." Treas. Reg. § 1.708–1(d)(4)(i). With one exception, the divided partnership is the transferor of assets in a division. Here is how to identify the divided partnership:

✓   If only one of the resulting partnerships is a continuation of the prior partnership, the divided partnership is that one. This rule applies, for example, to the split-off described above.

✓   If more than one of the resulting partnerships is a continuation of the prior partnership, and one of these continuing partnerships actually made the asset transfer, the divided partnership is that one. This rule applies, for example, to the spin-off described above.

✓   If more than one of the resulting partnerships is a continuation of the prior partnership, but the partnership that actually made the asset transfer is not a continuing partnership, the divided partnership is whichever of the continuing partnerships has the greatest net asset value.

✓ If more than one of the resulting partnerships is a continuation of
the prior partnership, and the division was "formless" pursuant to
governing state law, the divided partnership is whichever of the
continuing partnerships has the greatest net asset value.

✓ If none of the resulting partnerships is a continuation of the prior
partnership, there is no divided partnership, and a different
approach (described under the next heading) is needed to determine
the deemed transferor of assets. This rule might apply, for example,
to the split-up described above.

The Questions below will give you an opportunity to test your
understanding of these rules, which are actually a lot more intuitive than
they may appear at first.

Constructing the transaction

As in the case of mergers, assets-over is the default characterization of
divisions in the Treasury regulations. Under Treas. Reg. § 1.708–1(d)(3),
unless the parties follow a specified version of the assets-up approach,
discussed below, the following steps are deemed to occur in every division in
which there is a divided partnership:

1. The divided partnership contributes certain assets to one (or more)
recipient partnerships in exchange for interests in such
partnership(s), and

2. The divided partnership distributes the interests in the recipient
partnership(s) received in step 1. to some or all of its partners, as
current or liquidating distributions.

In some divisions, there will be no divided partnership, because no
resulting partnership is a continuation of the prior partnership. In this case,
the prior partnership is treated as transferring all of its assets to two (or
more) resulting partnerships, all of which are new partnerships for tax
purposes, and then distributing the interests in all of the resulting
partnerships to its partners in complete liquidation of all of their interests.
Treas. Reg. § 1.708–1(d)(3)(i)(B).

Just as with mergers, the default characterization applies, whether or
not it reflects what was actually done. Say, for example, that Pepperco LLC
transfers 60% of its assets to a new entity, Saltco LLC, in exchange for all of
the interests in Saltco, which Pepperco then distributes to partners holding
60% of the total interests in capital and profits of Pepperco in liquidation of
those interests. Despite the manner in which this transaction is executed,
Treas. Reg. § 1.708–1(d)(3) treats it as a transfer by Saltco to Pepperco of the
40% of the assets that were not actually transferred, because Saltco is the
divided partnership in this transaction and thus must be treated as the asset
transferor. Saltco is then deemed to distribute Pepperco interests, not to the
distributees in the actual transaction (who actually received Saltco interests),
but instead to the other partners, who will ultimately own Pepperco.

Treas. Reg. § 1.708–1(d)(3)(ii) provides an exception to the default characterization for certain assets-up division transactions. This exception mirrors that available for assets-up mergers. *See* Treas. Reg. § 1.708–1(c)(3)(ii). This exception applies only if the divided partnership (or, if there is none, the prior partnership) distributes assets to its partners, who immediately contribute all they get to a recipient partnership. As with mergers, direct deeding will not do. If it is consummated so as to fit this exception, the form of the assets-up division will be respected for federal income tax purposes.

10.4.1   Marcellus Drilling LP, a limited partnership, transfers gas leases on 10,000 acres of Ohio farmland to Utica Shale LLC, a limited liability company taxed as a partnership, in exchange for membership interests in Utica Shale LLC amounting to 10% of its total interests in capital and profits. Marcellus Drilling LP distributes these interests to Jack Fracker in liquidation of his limited partnership interest in Marcellus Drilling LP. No other partners of Marcellus Drilling LP have an interest in Utica Shale LLC, either before or after this transaction. For tax purposes, this transaction is:

a)   A division in which Marcellus Drilling LP is treating as the divided partnership

b)   A division, pursuant to which Marcellus Drilling LP is treated as distributing the leases to Jack in liquidation of his interest as a limited partner

c)   Not a division, because it was not accomplished in required assets-up form

d)   Not a division, because Utica Shale LLC does not have at least two partners in common with Marcellus Drilling LP and is therefore not a resulting partnership.

10.4.2   Following its transaction with Jack, Marcellus Drilling LP has 100,000 acres under lease remaining, 75,000 in Pennsylvania and 25,000 in Ohio, and no other assets. Assume for purposes of this and the following Questions that all acres are of equal value, regardless where they are located. In order to reorganize its operations on a regional basis, Marcellus Drilling LP transfers all of its properties in Pennsylvania to a new limited liability company, Marcellus (PA) Drilling LLC, the interests in which it distributes to all of its partners in proportion to their interests in Marcellus Drilling LP. It retains all of its properties in Ohio and is renamed Marcellus (Ohio) Drilling LP. For tax purposes, which, if any, partnership is treated as a continuation of Marcellus Drilling LP?

a)   Marcellus (Ohio) Drilling LP

b)   Marcellus (PA) Drilling LLC

c)   Both

d) Neither

10.4.3 What is deemed to have happened for tax purposes in the transaction described in Question 10.4.2?

a) Marcellus Drilling LP distributed its Pennsylvania acreage pro-rata to its partners, who contributed the acreage to a recipient partnership that is a new partnership.

b) Marcellus Drilling LP distributed its Pennsylvania acreage pro-rata to its partners, who contributed the acreage to a recipient partnership that is a continuation of Marcellus Drilling LP.

c) Marcellus Drilling LP transferred its Pennsylvania acreage to a recipient partnership that is a new partnership, in exchange for interests in which it distributed pro-rata to its partners.

d) Marcellus Drilling LP transferred its Pennsylvania acreage to a recipient partnership that is a continuation of Marcellus Drilling LP, in exchange for interests in which it distributed pro-rata to its partners.

10.4.4 Same facts as Question 10.4.2, but Marcellus Drilling LP accomplishes its regional reorganization in a different fashion. It distributes the Pennsylvania acreage to partners (the "Pennsylvania partners") owning limited partnership interests equal, in the aggregate, to 75% of the interests in capital and profits of Marcellus Drilling LP. This distribution liquidates the interests of the Pennsylvania partners. Immediately thereafter, they contribute all of the distributed assets to Marcellus (PA) Drilling LLC, a limited liability company treated as a partnership for tax purposes, in exchange for all of the membership interests therein. As before, Marcellus Drilling LP changes its name to Marcellus (Ohio) Drilling LP and it is owned by its remaining partners (the "Ohio partners"). For tax purposes, which, if any, partnership is treated as a continuation of Marcellus Drilling LP?

a) Marcellus (Ohio) Drilling LP

b) Marcellus (PA) Drilling LLC

c) Both

d) Neither

10.4.5 What is deemed to have happened for tax purposes in the transaction described in Question 10.4.4?

a) Marcellus Drilling LP distributed its Pennsylvania acreage to the Pennsylvania partners, who contributed the acreage to a recipient partnership that is a new partnership.

b) Marcellus Drilling LP distributed its Ohio acreage to the Ohio partners, who contributed the acreage to a recipient partnership that is a new partnership.

c) Marcellus Drilling LP transferred its Pennsylvania acreage to a recipient partnership that is a new partnership in exchange for interests therein, which it distributed to its Pennsylvania partners in liquidation of their interests in Marcellus Drilling LP.

d) Marcellus Drilling LP transferred its Ohio acreage to a recipient partnership that is a new partnership in exchange for interests therein, which it distributed to its Ohio partners in liquidation of their interests in Marcellus Drilling LP.

10.4.6 This time, Marcellus Drilling LP accomplishes its regional reorganization by distributing its Ohio acreage to the Ohio partners in liquidation of their interests; they promptly contribute it to a new partnership, Marcellus (Ohio) Drilling LP. Marcellus Drilling LP also wishes to separate its properties in Northeastern Pennsylvania from those in Southwestern Pennsylvania. To do so, it transfers 40,000 acres in Northeastern Pennsylvania to a new entity, Marcellus (NE PA) Drilling LLC and distributes interests in that entity in liquidation of interests of equal value owned by its own partners. Marcellus Drilling LP then changes its name to Marcellus (SW PA) Drilling LP. What is deemed to have happened for tax purposes in these transactions?

a) Marcellus Drilling LP transferred Pennsylvania and Ohio acreage to two recipient partnerships, each of which is a new partnership.

b) Marcellus Drilling LP transferred Pennsylvania and Ohio acreage to three recipient partnerships, each of which is a new partnership.

c) Marcellus Drilling LP transferred Pennsylvania acreage to one recipient partnership, which is a new partnership, and distributed Ohio acreage to the Ohio partners.

d) Marcellus Drilling LP transferred Pennsylvania acreage to two recipient partnerships and distributed the Ohio acreage to the Ohio partners.

10.5 DIVISIONS: TAX TREATMENT

If you have read the essay at the beginning of Topic 10.3, you already know much of what is covered here—and you will find the remainder easier to understand. Divisions, like mergers, are governed by the tax provisions that ordinarily apply to the actual transactions that are deemed to occur in a division. So, as with mergers, the steps in the analysis are, first, to determine the transactions that are deemed to take place and, second, to apply the tax rules you already know to these transactions. We covered the first of these steps in Topic 10.4. Now we turn to a short primer on the second.

Assets-over

In an assets-over division, the transferor partnership, which is usually but not always the divided partnership (D), transfers a portion of its assets to one or more recipient partnerships (R) in exchange for R interests, which D distributes to some or all of its partners as current or liquidating distributions. For concreteness, let's consider a division that is a split-off, in which D transfers 40% of its assets and liabilities to a single R. D receives R interests in exchange for its contribution, which it distributes in liquidation of the interests of 40% of D's partners (the retiring partners).

R recognizes no gain on the contribution. D doesn't either, even if the liabilities transferred to R exceed the aggregate basis of the transferred assets, because at this point all of the liabilities of R still are allocated to D, its sole partner. R takes a tax basis in the contributed assets equal to D's prior tax basis, except to the extent that section 704(c)(1)(C) requires otherwise. D takes a tax basis in the R interests equal to the amount of money and the aggregate tax basis of the properties contributed. As in the case of the assets-over merger, D's tax basis in R interests has only a momentary existence, because under section 732(b), the retiring partners will replace D's basis with their own outside basis in D when the R interests are distributed to them.

D's distribution of the R interests to its retiring partners can create a variety of tax problems. If D transfers a disproportionately large amount of liabilities to R, there will be deemed distributions to the non-retiring partners of D under section 752(b), perhaps sufficient to cause them to recognize gain. Conversely, a disproportionate retention of liabilities by D can create the same issue for the retiring partners. Section 751(b) is an issue, as are the anti-mixing-bowl rules. Each of these is discussed separately below.

For book purposes, R receives all of the contributed assets with a book value equal to fair market value. The book value of the R interests on D's books is also fair market value. The contribution is not an occasion for D to revalue all of its book assets (termed a "general revaluation" in Topic 2.6), but the distribution, being non-pro-rata in this case, is such an occasion under Treas. Reg. § 1.704–1(b)(2)(iv)(*f*)(*5*)(*ii*). D can be expected to take advantage of this opportunity, so the book capital accounts of the retiring partners equal the book value of the liquidating distributions made to them.

The contribution of assets to R creates a forward section 704(c) layer in R, for assets with built-in gain, or a section 704(c)(1)(C) basis adjustment, for assets with built-in loss. *See* Topics 8.4 and 8.5. D's revaluation creates a reverse section 704(c) layer, whether gain or loss. Momentarily, R's forward layer of gain, if any, is allocable to D and, through D, to all of D's partners, retiring and non-retiring, under Treas. Reg. § 1.704–3(a)(9). After the distribution, it is allocable only to R's partners. Likewise, following the distribution, D's reverse layer of gain or loss is allocable only to D's non-retiring partners, because the retiring partners lose their section 704(c) responsibilities for D's assets when they leave the partnership.

Assets-up

A division can also be structured as an assets-up transaction. *See* Topic 10.4. It is entirely possible that the distribution of D's assets to the retiring partners will be taxed to some extent. There may be actual cash distributions, or deemed distributions under section 752(b), that exceed outside basis. Section 751(b) and the anti-mixing-bowl rules are also a concern, as discussed below.

The distribution otherwise follows the usual model for a property distribution. Under section 732(b), each of the retiring partners takes an aggregate basis in the distributed assets equal to her outside basis in D, reduced by any cash actually distributed and increased or reduced by the net contribution or distribution under sections 752(a) and (b). The adjusted outside basis is allocated among the distributed assets in accordance with the rules of section 732(c). If the retiring partners' aggregate outside basis in D is greater than the inside basis of the assets distributed to them, the distribution will create a basis step-up. This step-up will follow the assets into R when the retiring partners contribute them. If the aggregate outside basis of the retiring partners is less than the inside basis of the assets that D distributes to them, a basis step-down will result.

Just as with mergers, it is possible to use a section 754 election to replicate the effect of a basis step-up (or step-down, but who wants to replicate that?) in an assets-over division. Here, R makes the election. D's distribution of the R interests is a sale of exchange under section 761(e)(2), justifying a special basis adjustment for each retiring partner under section 743(b). Indeed, a section 754 election works even better here than in the merger context. The special basis adjustments will be allocated under section 755 only among R's assets—the same assets for which the retiring partners would receive a step-up (or step-down) in an assets-up division.

For book purposes, D may undertake a general revaluation immediately prior to the distribution of assets to the retiring partners. Only the non-retiring partners of D will be responsible for the reverse section 704(c) layer thus created in the undistributed assets. The retiring partners contribute the distributed assets to R, which accepts them with book values equaling fair market value. The forward section 704(c) layer thus created is the sole responsibility of the retiring partners, who are now the only partners of R.

Section 751(b)

In a merger, all of the assets of all combining partnerships wind up in the resulting partnership, and all of the partners of all of the combining partnerships are partners of the resulting partnership. There is thus no principled reason for section 751(b) to apply, whether the merger is consummated in assets-over or assets-up form. The same cannot necessarily be said for divisions. The proper question is not whether the division is assets-over or assets-up, but instead whether it reduces the exposure to ordinary income of any partner. The split-off division we have been considering may do exactly that. If, for example, D retains after the division more than 60% of its total unrealized ordinary income prior to the division, then the division has shifted unrealized ordinary income from the retiring partners to the non-retiring partners. The retiring partners should recognize ordinary income under section 751(b) on the division. If, on the other hand, D transfers to R more than 40% of its total unrealized ordinary income prior the division, then the division has had the opposite effect, and it is the non-retiring partners who should recognize ordinary income.

The "anti-mixing-bowl" rules

In our review of mergers in Topic 10.3, we found that assets-up mergers have some potential exposure under the anti-mixing-bowl statutes, which can be avoided by using assets-over mergers under a regulatory safe harbor. In contrast, assets-over divisions create exposure to current taxation under section 704(c)(1)(B) and section 737. This exposure may be reduced by using the assets-up form. Before diving too far into the details, it may be useful to consider why the IRS has been unwilling to draft a safe harbor for divisions comparable to that for mergers. The distributions that take place as part of a division permanently separate assets from the dividing partnership, just like the property distributions that are the focus of section 704(c)(1)(B) and section 737. The distributions that occur in the course of a merger do not do this—they are merely a step in a larger transaction that brings all of the assets into a single resulting partnership.

Assets-over division. A is a partner of D. Less than seven year ago, A contributed Asset X to D with built-in gain. In an assets-over division, D contributes assets other than Asset X to R in exchange for R interests, which D distributes to A and the other retiring partners in liquidation of their interests in D. Section 737 applies to this division, because the property that A receives in liquidation of her interest in D—whether that property is viewed as a partnership interest in R or as an undivided interest in each of R's assets—is not Asset X, for the simple reason that R does not own Asset X. A recognizes gain equal to the lesser of her net precontribution gain or the excess distribution.

Now assume that D contributes Asset X and other assets to R and distributes the R interests to A and other retiring partners. Does the analysis change? Maybe. The "substitute property" rule of Treas. Reg. §§ 1.704–3(a)(8), –4(d)(1) and 1.737–2(d)(3)(i) provides that the R interests are treated as section 704(c) property with the same amount of built-in gain as Asset X. Asset X is not the only property R owns, however, and A does not own all of R following the distribution. It is unclear to what extent the R interest should be treated as substitute property for Asset X in these circumstances, and therefore how much, if any, gain A should be forced to recognize under section 704(c)(1)(B) and section 737. Question 10.5.5 examines this issue in more detail.

As a final variation, assume that A is a non-retiring partner of D who does not receive any distribution. If D contributes Asset X to R, A clearly will be subject to tax under section 704(c)(1)(B). If D does not contribute Asset X to R, it seems equally clear that A has no current liability under either of the anti-mixing-bowl statutes.

Assets-up division. From A's perspective, a division in assets-up form holds promise for eliminating the tax risk that may be present in assets-over divisions. Imagine that D distributes to A only Asset X (or only a fractional interest in Asset X, if Asset X is worth more than A's partnership interest, or Asset X plus other assets, if A's partnership interest is worth more than Asset X). It may be possible for A to satisfy the previously contributed property exception in section 737(d)(1), thus escaping taxation under section 737, and at the same time avoid having any portion of Asset X distributed to another partner, thus escaping section 704(c)(1)(B). Ordinarily, one would worry whether this distribution technique would be subject to challenge as a step transaction, given that Asset X will find its way into R in short order, so the distribution of Asset X to A is not in substance different from the distribution of an interest in R. The final section 708 regulations seem to foreclose this argument, however, as Treas. Reg. § 1.708–1(d)(3)(ii) provides that the assets-up form of a division will be respected, "despite the partners' transitory ownership of some of the prior partnership's assets."

10.5.1   Duquesne Power Blinds LLC manufactures and sells window blinds for commercial and residential applications. Its Duquesne Ducora® brand is famous throughout western Pennsylvania, if not beyond. Bryce Shirzer and Dumol Godard started the company 15 years ago with contributions of cash. The company prospered, providing regular cash distributions to its founders with enough left over for the company to buy a dilapidated shopping center nearby. It demolished the old buildings and now holds the empty parcel for investment (Land D). As years went by, the company's neighborhood "gentrified," which increased the value of Land D substantially and gave Bryce and Dumol the idea to expand the company's business to include investing in, and possibly developing, local real estate.

The two approached Albany and Chubb, who owned development lots, Land A and Land C, respectively, across the highway from Land D. They reached an agreement to admit Albany and Chubb as 20% members of the company in exchange for contributing those two parcels. The company revalued its book assets immediately before admitting Albany and Chubb, creating book-tax differences in its equipment, plant and Land D totaling $1,050,000. Albany and Chubb became members five years ago.

The company's blinds business has continued strong, generating $2 million in undistributed profits in the years since Albany and Chubb joined. The property investments have done even better—and that has created discord among the owners. Albany and Bryce are anxious to move forward with some development ideas; Chubb and Dumol are content to run the blinds business and watch the value of the undeveloped lots continue to rise.

Here is the company's current balance sheet, enhanced to show asset values:

Assets (000s)				Liabilities (000s)		
	Tax	Book	FMV		Tax	Book
Cash	$ 30	$ 30	$ 30	Bank Debt	$3,000	$ 3,000
Rec'bles	370	370	370			
Inventory	850	850	1,300			
Equipment	3,800	4,000	3,400	Capital (000s)		
Plant	1,400	2,000	4,100	Albany (20%)	1,000	1,400
Land A	600	1,000	2,800	Bryce (20%)	1,050	1,400
Land C	600	1,000	2,800	Chubb (20%)	1,000	1,400
Land D	500	750	2,200	Dumol (40%)	2,100	2,800
Total Assets	$8,150	$10,000	$17,000	Total Liabilities and Capital	$8,150	$10,000

The members have agreed to form a new limited liability company, Westside Properties LLC, to which Duquesne will transfer ownership of Land A and Land C, free and clear of debt. Duquesne will then distribute all of the Westside interests equally to Albany and Bryce in liquidation of their entire interests in Duquesne. Assume that both of these limited liability companies are treated as partnerships for tax purposes and neither makes a section 754 election. Which is the divided partnership in this division?

a) Duquesne Power Blinds LLC

b) Westside Properties LLC

c) Both

d) Neither

10.5.2 For tax purposes, what is deemed to take place in this division?

a) The transaction is taxed in accordance with its form: the divided partnership transfers properties to a new partnership in exchange for interests therein, which it then distributes to Albany and Bryce in liquidation of their interests in the divided partnership.

b) The transaction is recharacterized: the divided partnership transfers properties to a new partnership in exchange for interests therein, which it then distributes to Chubb and Dumol in liquidation of their interests in the divided partnership.

c) The transaction is recharacterized: the prior partnership transfers properties to two new partnerships in exchange for interests therein, which it distributes to all of its partners in complete liquidation.

d) The transaction is recharacterized: the divided partnership distributes properties to Albany and Bryce in liquidation of their interests; Albany and Bryce thereupon contribute all of the distributed properties to a new partnership.

10.5.3 Does any partner have exposure to section 751(b) in this division? Who has what exposure? The Answers below apply the 1956 regulations under section 751(b), not the proposed regulations issued in 2014.

a) No exposure

b) Albany and Bryce have $90,000 ordinary income each.

c) Albany and Bryce have $90,000 ordinary income each; Albany and Chubb have about $262,430 capital gain each.

d) Albany and Bryce have $90,000 ordinary income each; Chubb and Dumol have about $175,000 and $350,000, respectively, of capital gain.

10.5.4 How much book gain does Dumol likely realize in this division?

a) $0

b) $1,400,000

c) $1,450,000

d) $2,800,000

10.5.5 How much tax gain, if any, does Albany recognize in this division under the anti-mixing-bowl statutes?

a) $0

b) $200,000

c) $400,000

d) $1,000,000

10.5.6 What is Bryce's outside basis in her interest in Westside Properties LLC immediately following the division?

a) $1,050,000

b) $1,140,000

c) $1,384,000

d) $1,740,000

10.5.7 How much tax gain, if any, does Chubb recognize in this division under the anti-mixing-bowl statutes?

a) $0

b) $400,000

c) $1,800,000

d) $2,200,000

10.5.8   How much tax gain would Albany and Chubb recognize under the anti-mixing-bowl statutes if this division were accomplished in the most tax-efficient, assets-up form?

   a)   Albany, $0; Chubb, $0

   b)   Albany, $0; Chubb, $400,000

   c)   Albany, $200,000; Chubb, $0

   d)   Albany, $200,000; Chubb, $400,000

ANSWERS TO STUDY QUESTIONS

QWIKCHECK

CHAPTER 1	
Question	Answer
1.1.1	C
1.1.2	A
1.1.3	C
1.1.4	D
1.2.1	B,C,D
1.2.2	C
1.2.3	C
1.2.4	A,B,C
1.2.5	B
1.3.1	A
1.3.2	B
1.3.3	C
1.3.4	A
1.3.5	D
1.4.1	D
1.4.2	B
1.4.3	C

CHAPTER 2	
Question	Answer
2.1.1	C
2.1.2	A
2.1.3	D
2.2.1	A
2.2.2	D
2.3.1	B/S
2.3.2	B/S
2.3.3	B/S
2.4.1	B/S
2.4.2	B/S
2.4.3	B/S
2.4.4	B/S
2.5.1	B/S
2.5.2	B/S
2.5.3	B/S
2.5.4	B/S
2.6.1	B/S
2.7.1	C
2.7.2	C
2.7.3	D
2.7.4	B
2.7.5	A
2.7.6	A
2.7.7	B
2.8.1	A
2.8.2	B
2.8.3	C
2.8.4	C

CHAPTER 3	
Question	Answer
3.1.1	D
3.1.2	A
3.1.3	A
3.1.4	C
3.1.5	D
3.2.1	B/S
3.2.2	B/S
3.2.3	B/S
3.2.4	B/S
3.2.5	B/S
3.3.1	B
3.3.2	C
3.3.3	C
3.3.4	B
3.4.1	D
3.4.2	B
3.4.3	D
3.4.4	A
3.4.5	C
3.4.6	A
3.4.7	A
3.4.8	A,B,D
3.5.1	B
3.5.2	C
3.5.3	A
3.5.4	D

CHAPTER 4	
Question	Answer
4.1.1	B
4.1.2	D
4.1.3	D
4.2.1	A
4.2.2	B
4.2.3	C
4.2.4	C
4.3.1	A
4.3.2	B
4.3.3	D
4.3.4	D
4.3.5	A
4.3.6	A
4.3.7	D
4.3.8	D
4.3.9	D
4.3.10	B
4.3.11	B
4.4.1	C
4.4.2	D
4.4.3	B
4.4.4	B
4.4.5	B
4.4.6	C

CHAPTER 5	
Question	Answer
5.2.1	D
5.2.2	A
5.2.3	C
5.3.1	B
5.3.2	D
5.3.3	C
5.4.1	D
5.4.2	C
5.4.3	D
5.4.4	D
5.4.5	C
5.4.6	B
5.4.7	A
5.4.8	C
5.4.9	A
5.4.10	C
5.5.1	B
5.5.2	A
5.5.3	D
5.5.4	A
5.5.5	B
5.5.6	C
5.5.7	B
5.5.8	C
5.5.9	D
5.6.1	B
5.6.2	C
5.6.3	D

CHAPTER 6	
Question	Answer
6.1.1	C
6.1.2	D
6.1.3	B
6.1.4	C
6.2.1	B
6.2.2	D
6.2.3	A
6.2.4	B
6.2.5	B
6.3.1	B
6.3.2	D
6.3.3	C
6.3.4	C
6.5.1	D
6.5.2	A
6.5.3	B
6.5.4	D
6.6.1	B/S
6.6.2	C
6.6.3	D
6.6.4	D
6.6.5	A
6.7.1	C
6.7.2	C
6.7.3	A

CHAPTER 7		CHAPTER 8		CHAPTER 9	
Question	Answer	Question	Answer	Question	Answer
7.2.1	A	8.1.1	B	9.1.1	C
7.2.2	C	8.1.2	B	9.1.2	A
7.2.3	B	8.1.3	A	9.1.3	B
7.2.4	C	8.1.4	B	9.1.4	D
7.3.1	D	8.1.5	C	9.1.5	C
7.3.2	D	8.1.6	B	9.1.6	C
7.3.3	B	8.1.7	A	9.1.7	C
7.3.4	D	8.1.8	C	9.1.8	B
7.3.5	C	8.1.9	C	9.1.9	B
7.3.6	C	8.2.1	B	9.2.1	D
7.3.7	C	8.2.2	C	9.2.2	B
		8.2.3	A	9.2.3	A
		8.2.4	C	9.2.4	A
		8.2.5	A	9.2.5	C
		8.2.6	D	9.2.6	B
		8.2.7	D	9.2.7	C
		8.3.1	D	9.4.1	A
		8.3.2	D	9.4.2	B
		8.3.3	A	9.4.3	B
		8.3.4	B	9.4.4	B
		8.3.5	B	9.4.5	D
		8.3.6	A	9.4.6	A
		8.5.1	D	9.4.7	A
		8.5.2	C	9.4.8	D
		8.5.3	C	9.5.1	B
		8.5.4	B	9.5.2	C
		8.5.5	D	9.5.3	A
		8.5.6	B	9.5.4	D
		8.6.1	B/S	9.5.5	D
		8.6.2	B/S	9.5.6	A
		8.6.3	D	9.5.7	A
		8.6.4	B/S		
		8.6.5	A		

CHAPTER 9			CHAPTER 10	
Question	Answer		Question	Answer
9.6.1	B		10.1.1	C
9.6.2	A		10.1.2	D
9.6.3	B		10.1.3	B
9.6.4	D		10.1.4	C
9.6.5	D		10.1.5	B
9.6.6	D		10.1.6	D
9.6.7	B		10.2.1	A
9.6.8	D		10.2.2	D
9.6.9	B		10.2.3	D
9.6.10	B		10.2.4	D
9.6.11	D		10.2.5	A
9.8.1	D		10.2.6	C
9.8.2	A		10.2.7	A
9.8.3	B		10.3.1	B
9.8.4	A		10.3.2	A
9.8.5	B		10.3.3	A
9.8.6	D		10.3.4	C
9.8.7	C		10.3.5	D
9.8.8	D		10.3.6	C
9.8.9	B		10.4.1	D
			10.4.2	C
			10.4.3	D
			10.4.4	B
			10.4.5	D
			10.4.6	B
			10.5.1	A
			10.5.2	A
			10.5.3	D
			10.5.4	D
			10.5.5	A
			10.5.6	B
			10.5.7	B
			10.5.8	B

Note: In this context, B/S does not have its usual meaning. It indicates that the Answer to this Question is not a letter, but a completed balance sheet, which can be found in the Complete Explanations.

COMPLETE EXPLANATIONS OF ANSWERS TO STUDY QUESTIONS

1.1.1 **The correct Answer is (c).** Let's proceed by process of elimination. **Answer (a)** is incorrect, because a partnership agreement need not be written. If it is not, of course, the partners may have a difficult time proving its existence and terms. In this case, the very simplicity of the undertaking is helpful to resist the IRS's contention. **Answer (b)** is incorrect. Treas. Reg. § 301.7701–1(a)(2) provides in part that a "joint venture or other contractual arrangement may create a separate entity for federal tax purposes if the participants carry on a trade, business, financial operation, or venture and divide the profits therefrom." The family in this Question is carrying on a simple venture ("investing" in lottery tickets) and in their informal discussions the family members have contemplated a division of the profits. You can love your partners and still be in a partnership with them—it might even help. **Answer (d)** is close, but incorrect. State law may provide that, in the absence of a contrary agreement, equal sharing among partners is presumed. The family members here do not appear to have reached any definitive agreement on this point before visiting their lawyer. Section 761(c) provides, however, that a partnership agreement includes all modifications agreed upon prior to the date for filing of the partnership return. Since the clarification or modification was agreed upon by all partners prior to such date, it is effective in determining the family members' shares of the partnership's income for that year. The inspiration for this Question is *Estate of Winkler v. Commissioner*, T.C. Memo 1997–4.

1.1.2 **The correct Answer is (a).** There is no doubt that this is a bona fide, commercial enterprise. But is it an entity? The parties have the good idea of compensating Lyle with a share of the profits on the development—an idea that could be the basis of a partnership if they took the trouble to create one. But it takes more than an agreement to create a partnership. In this case, the parties seem to have taken no actions consistent with the treatment of Lyle as a partner. Although the enterprise has plenty of contact with the public, it does not hold itself out as a partnership. It is not fatal that ACRE holds title to the property in its own name—there are lots of examples where partnerships use a partner or affiliated entity as a titleholder—but ACRE's failure to transfer title creates substantial doubt whether it considers this arrangement to be a partnership at all. *See Mayhew v. Commissioner*, T.C. Memo 1992–68.

Answers (b) and (d) are incorrect, because the arrangement is not an entity for federal income tax purposes. **Answer (b)** is, however, the result you would be shooting for if you were representing Lyle, and it is perfectly attainable with good planning. *See* Topic 3.1. **Answer (c)** is incorrect, because the same factors apply in determining if this arrangement is an entity for federal income tax purposes, regardless whether the parties call it a "partnership" or a "joint venture."

1.1.3 **The correct Answer is (c).** This is a great answer for Debra, who can report her share of the profits received over the next five years as proceeds of sale, taxed as capital gain (save for a little imputed interest), rather than as ordinary business income, as would be the case if she were a partner in the event-planning business. It is less beneficial for AM, which will pay tax on all of the business profits and capitalize the amounts it pays to Debra when the payments are made (again, save for a little imputed interest, which it can deduct).

How do we get to this answer? By considering all the facts and circumstances. There is no exhaustive list of what to look for, but the classic statement of factors evidencing the existence of an entity was made by the Tax Court in *Luna v. Commissioner*, 42 T.C. 1067, 1077–78 (1964):

> The agreement of the parties and their conduct in executing its terms; the contributions, if any, which each party has made to the venture; the parties' control over income and capital and the right of each to make withdrawals; whether each party was a principal and coproprietor, sharing a mutual proprietary interest in the net profits and having an obligation to share losses, or whether one party was the agent or employee of the other, receiving for his services contingent compensation in the form of a percentage of income; whether business was conducted in the joint names of the parties; whether the parties filed Federal partnership returns or otherwise represented to respondent [the IRS] or to persons with whom they dealt that they were joint venturers; whether separate books of account were maintained for the venture; and whether the parties exercised mutual control over and assumed mutual responsibilities for the enterprise.

We don't know all the facts, of course, and those that we do know are not entirely consistent with any single answer. The strongest factors favoring entity characterization are Debra's sharing in the net income of the business and her role in its management. The fact that Debra shares in the net, rather than the gross, income of the business gives her at least some exposure to expenses (to the point that they equal the gross income), which is significant. On the other hand, she has no responsibility for losses and has made no capital contribution—if the business were to shut down the next day, Debra would not be entitled to any return of capital (although she might sue for the value of her lost profit share). Debra's management rights are less than they might appear. On analysis, they seem to be the sorts of rights that a creditor might wish to retain to protect the value of the collateral. As in Question 1.1.2, the parties have not held this arrangement out to customers or others as a partnership.

The conclusion that this is not an entity is facilitated by the fact that there is an easy alternative characterization of these facts. Debra's arrangement with AM is a common commercial arrangement called an "earn-out." Earn-outs are typically used when, as here, the parties to a purchase and sale are unable to agree on a price. The higher the profits of the business, the larger the earn-out payments.

Answer (a) is incorrect, because this is not an entity for federal income tax purposes. **Answer (d)** is incorrect, because the attributes of tax ownership pass to AM at the closing. **Answer (b)** is interesting but wrong. It does not seem plausible that the kind of services that Debra is supplying (which mainly protect her earn-out payments) are worth a 20% share of net income.

1.1.4 	 **The correct Answer is (d).** On the face of it, the parties seem to have done all that was necessary to constitute the Rupert Rudier Venture as a partnership for tax purposes. They have executed a written agreement and acted with due regard for the existence of the venture as a separate entity, including holding themselves out to the public as partners. Although there is not a great deal of business activity, the partnership undertakes in its own name such activity as is appropriate for its investment purpose. There is no doubt that an investment partnership can qualify as a partnership for tax purposes. *See* Treas. Reg. § 1.701–2(a) ("Subchapter K is intended to permit taxpayers to conduct joint business (including investment) activities through a flexible economic arrangement without incurring entity-level tax.").

This analysis, however, seems superficial. The facts suggest that Guy planned to use the joint venture as a mechanism to convert the ordinary income that he otherwise would have realized on the resale of the Rodin as an art dealer into an allocation of capital gain from a partnership holding the sculpture as a capital asset. And, indeed, that is exactly how it worked out. In a case like this, the *Culbertson* test requires a weighing of the tax motivations of the parties against whatever else they may have been doing. It is hard to see what Guy received from the joint venture other than tax savings. Rupert was not a significant source of capital, art expertise or even, it appears, legal services. In essence, Guy gave up 1% of the potential profits on the Rodin in exchange for cutting his tax rate in half. It is therefore difficult to conclude that Guy acted with the business purpose needed to pass the *Culbertson* test. For an example of a court decision that disregarded a purported partnership arrangement whose sole function was the avoidance of taxes, see *ASA Investerings Partnership v. Commissioner,* 201 F.3d 505 (D.C. Cir.), *cert. denied,* 531 U.S. 871 (2000).

Answer (a) is incorrect, because it misapplies, or fails to apply at all, the *Culbertson* analysis. **Answer (b)** is based on a false premise—that the Rupert Rudier Venture is properly treated as a partnership for tax purposes—and even on its own terms seems incorrect. The venture does not appear to have held the sculpture primarily for sale to customers, given its utter lack of marketing efforts and the fact that it did not place the sculpture with Guy's other artwork for sale. **Answer (c)** is surely wrong—it is quite difficult to conclude that an entity is a sham for tax purposes. The worst fact here is that Rupert's interest in the venture is only 1%, but that ought to be enough for him to be recognized as a real partner. *See* Treas. Reg. § 1.701–2(d), example (1) (99/1 ownership of limited partnership formed to conduct bona fide business; partnership treatment upheld, despite fact that 99% partner retained, indirectly, substantially all benefits and burdens of ownership of contributed money or property).

1.2.1 **The correct Answers are (b), (c) and (d).** Under Treas. Reg. § 301.7701–2(a), a business entity is an entity that is not a trust or otherwise subject to special treatment under the Internal Revenue Code. Whether or not organized as a trust, the real estate investment trust in **Answer (a)** is not a business entity, because of its special tax treatment under sections 856–59. Not all of the remaining entities identified in **Answers (b), (c) and (d)** are eligible entities. But they do pass the relatively simple test for being business entities.

1.2.2 **The correct Answer is (c).** Under Treas. Reg. § 301.7701–3(a), an eligible entity must be a business entity. It also must not be classified as a corporation under Treas. Reg. § 301.7701–2(b); entities so classified are often referred to as "*per se* corporations." The domestic limited liability company in **Answer (c)** is a prime example of an eligible entity. Indeed, the rising popularity of limited liability companies in the United States throughout the 1990s was the main impetus for the promulgation of the check-the-box regulations. **Answer (a)** is incorrect, because REITs are subject to special treatment under sections 856–59. Thus, they are not business entities and so cannot possibly be eligible entities. **Answer (b)** is also incorrect. Although a corporation formed under state law is a business entity, it is not an eligible entity, because it is a *per se* corporation under Treas. Reg. § 301.7701–2(b)(1). Finally, **Answer (d)** is incorrect. A publicly traded partnership is a business entity. Under section 7704, however, it is treated as a corporation for federal income tax purposes. It is therefore a *per se* corporation under Treas. Reg. § 301.7701–2(b)(7).

1.2.3 **The correct Answer is (c).** As before, the limited liability company is the poster child of eligible entities. In this particular case, the limited liability company is owned by a single member. This will prevent it from ever being a partnership for tax purposes, as you will see in Topic 1.3, but it is still an eligible entity. **Answer (a)** is incorrect. The French Societe Anonyme is identified as a *per se* corporation in Treas. Reg. § 301.7701–2(b)(8). The only sure way to know whether a non-US entity is a *per se* corporation is to check the list in that regulation and run a quick search for clarifying revenue rulings. *See, e.g.,* Rev. Rul. 2006–3, 2006–1 C.B. 276 (classification of Japanese TYK). **Answer (b)** is incorrect. As provided in section 851(a), a regulated investment company must be a domestic corporation. This knocks it out of contention for eligible- entity status under Treas. Reg. § 301.7701–2(b)(7). Finally, **Answer (d)** is incorrect, because insurance companies are *per se* corporations under Treas. Reg. § 301.7701–2(b)(4).

1.2.4 **The correct Answers are (a), (b) and (c).** The Nova Scotia Unlimited Liability Company in **Answer (a)** is a business entity, so the only question is whether it is a *per se* corporation. As it turns out, these entities are specifically included in the category of eligible entities by Treas. Reg. § 301.7701–2(b)(8)(ii)(A)(1). How would you know that? Look it up. Although the Delaware business trust in **Answer (b)** sounds like it would be a trust and therefore not a business entity, such is not the case. *See* Treas. Reg. § 301.7701–4(b) ("These trusts, which are often known as business or commercial trusts, generally are created by the beneficiaries simply as a device to carry on a profit-making business which normally would have been carried on through business organizations that are classified as corporations or partnerships under the Internal Revenue Code."). The Austrian GmbH in **Answer (c)** is a business entity that is not classified as a *per se* corporation under Treas. Reg. § 301.7701–2(b)(8). **Answer (d)** is incorrect. You might think that a federally chartered bank is not a *per se* corporation, because Treas. Reg. § 301.7701–2(b)(5) refers only to state-chartered banks. Not so fast. The national banking statute, pursuant to which federally chartered banks are formed, describes such an entity as a "body corporate" and treats it in all relevant respects as a corporation. 12 U.S.C. § 21. A national bank is thus a *per se* corporation under Treas. Reg. § 301.7701–2(b)(1).

1.2.5   **The correct Answer is (b).** A New York limited liability partnership is a business entity that is not classified as a *per se* corporation under Treas. Reg. § 301.7701–2(b). **Answer (a)** is incorrect. An "investment" trust is classified as a trust if the trustee has no power to vary its investment. Treas. Reg. § 301.7701–4(c). Accordingly, it is not a business entity and cannot be an eligible entity. **Answer (c)** is incorrect, because the Korean Chusik Hoesa is classified as a *per se* corporation under Treas. Reg. § 301.7701–2(b)(8). **Answer (d)** is also incorrect. An Illinois land trust is essentially a title-holding vehicle, which is not even classified as an entity for federal income tax purposes. Rev. Rul. 92–105, 1992–2 C.B. 204.

1.3.1   **The correct Answer is (a).** Because all of the shareholders of Opco BV have limited liability under Dutch law, it is classified as a corporation under the default rule of Treas. Reg. § 301.7701–3(b)(2)(i)(B). This is true, regardless whether Opco BV has one or many owners. **Answer (b)** is incorrect, because all of the Opco shareholders have limited liability. (How are you supposed to know this? One of three ways. First, if your instructor is fair-minded and thinks of it, he or she will tell you as part of the exam question. Second, you can confirm it with a quick internet search, if your exam rules allow. Third, it is reasonable to assume that foreign corporate laws provide limited liability to all, just as corporate laws do in the United States. If possible, state that you have made this assumption in your exam answer.) **Answers (c) and (d)** are incorrect, because the default classification of Opco as a corporation precludes classifying it as a disregarded entity.

1.3.2   **The correct Answer is (b).** This change in the facts changes the default rule for Opco. Because Opco does not provide limited liability to all of its owners, its default classification is either disregarded entity (if it has one owner) or partnership (if it has more than one). Treas. Reg. §§ 301.7701–3(b)(2)(i)(A), (C). Topco is classified as a corporation under Treas. Reg. § 301.7701–2(b)(1). Under the default rule of Treas. Reg. § 301.7701–3(b)(2)(i)(B), Subco is classified as a corporation because all of its members have limited liability. Therefore, for federal income tax purposes, Opco has two owners, Topco and Subco, and is classified as a partnership. **Answer (a)** is incorrect, because of the aforementioned change in the default classification rule for Opco. **Answers (c) and (d)** are incorrect, because Opco has more than one owner and therefore cannot be a disregarded entity.

1.3.3   The correct Answer is (c). Topco is classified as a corporation under Treas. Reg. § 301.7701–2(b)(1). Under the default rule of Treas. Reg. § 301.7701–3(b)(1)(ii), Subco is classified as a disregarded entity. Therefore, for federal income tax purposes, Opco has but a single owner, Topco. Absent a contrary election, an eligible entity with one owner is treated as a disregarded entity. Where the single owner is a corporation, the disregarded entity is treated in the same manner as a branch of that corporation. **Answer (a)** is incorrect, because the default rule for domestic entities does not treat them as corporations, even if they provide limited liability to all owners. **Answer (b)** is incorrect, because Opco does not have more than one owner for tax purposes. **Answer (d)** is incorrect, because Subco itself is a disregarded entity in this case.

1.3.4   The correct Answer is (a). A disregarded entity is not disregarded for all purposes. It is still liable for employment taxes, for withholding from wages and associated penalties and for most excise taxes. Treas. Reg. §§ 301.7701–2(c)(iv), (v). Additionally, a disregarded entity remains liable for any federal taxes (including income taxes) for which it was liable with respect to a period when it was not disregarded and for any taxes of other entities for which it is liable (for example, under joint and several liability). **Answers (b), (c) and (d)** are incorrect, because they are inconsistent with these regulations.

1.3.5   The correct Answer is (d). This Question raises two issues. The first is that eligible entities generally can elect to change their classification only once every five years—more precisely, every 60 months. Treas. Reg. § 301.7701–3(c)(1)(iv). But a newly formed entity's initial election, if effective on the date of formation, does not count for this purpose. Thus, in the present case, LLC may change its election even though only four years have passed since it initially checked the box. (Note that the application of a default classification upon formation would not count, either.) The second issue is identifying the transaction that is deemed to happen upon the change in classification. Once this identification is made, all parties will be taxed as if that transaction had actually happened. Here, LLC changes its classification from corporation to disregarded entity. Unsurprisingly, this is treated as a corporate liquidation. Treas. Reg. § 301.7701–3(g)(1)(iii). Because the sole owner of LLC is an individual, both A and LLC recognize gain or loss. **Answer (a)** is incorrect, because LLC is an eligible entity. **Answer (b)** is incorrect, because of the special exception to the 60-month rule described above. **Answer (c)** is incorrect, because the deemed liquidation of LLC is taxed as though it had actually happened. If LLC were the wholly owned subsidiary of a corporation, gain and loss recognition would be avoided by application of section 332.

1.4.1   The correct Answer is (d). Section 761(a)(1) allows an election by an entity availed of for investment purposes only and not for the active conduct of a business. The Treasury regulations refer to such an organization as an "investing partnership," and this is the category of electing organization that is closest to Bryce Hardware Company. Alas, it is not very close. The flush language at the end of section 761(a) further limits the election to situations where the income of the members of the organization may be adequately determined without the computation of partnership taxable income. Treas. Reg. § 1.761–2(a)(2) adds the further requirements that the members own the property as co-owners and reserve the right separately to take or dispose of their shares of the property. Bryce Hardware fails each of these requirements, except for the requirement that the members own the property as co-owners. (It is worth noting, however, that the IRS takes the position that limited partners are not co-owners of the property held by a limited partnership, so that it is impossible for a limited partnership to be an "investing partnership.") **Answers (a), (b) and (c)** are correct but incomplete.

1.4.2   The best Answer is (b). This Question illustrates the irony that just about the only organizations that qualify to elect out of Subchapter K as "investing partnerships" are those that don't need to. The investing activity of the Goethe Street Club is so sporadic and informal that there is a good argument that no entity exists for federal income tax purposes. The principal purpose of an election out in a case like this is to give the members comfort that they are not required to file a partnership tax return. Of course, the election out would also be available to an investing partnership that is considerably more active. If trading decisions are centralized, however, the ability to elect out may be jeopardized. *See* Treas. Reg. § 1.761–2(a)(2)(iii) (any such delegations of authority cannot exceed one year's duration). **Answer (a)** is also an acceptable answer. It is uncertainty on this very point that might lead the club members to make the election out. **Answer (c)** is incorrect, because through its careful records the club is able to determine each member's income or loss without resort to the aggregate income or loss of the club. **Answer (d)** is also incorrect, but emphasizes an important point. In order to be a partnership, an organization must engage in a business. In order to elect out as an "investing partnership," it must not engage in an active business. This distinction may seem paper-thin to you. You are not alone. It seems a fair surmise, however, that simply doing more of the same activity (investing) should not be disqualifying. Branching out—for example, selling subscriptions to the club's newsletter ("Hot Stocks for the Well-Heeled")—would spell trouble.

1.4.3   Answer (c) is correct and that's a shame. The K Street Investment Club seems to be just what Congress had in mind as the type of organization that should be able to elect out. But electing out is a disaster for K Street. The problem, of course, is that K Street has chosen to live without any of Subchapter K, which includes section 721. So when Ron joins the club by contributing appreciated securities, the tax treatment of the transaction must be determined by reference to the change in the economic position of each of the parties. Ron is exchanging 90% of his securities for a 10% interest in all of the securities previously held by the club (an aggregate analysis). The other members of the club are exchanging 10% of their previously held securities for 90% of Ron's securities. All parties recognize gain. **Answer (a)** is incorrect, because section 721 does not apply. **Answer (b)** is incorrect: the rules of section 706(b) relating to required tax years do not apply to an organization that has elected out of Subchapter K. **Answer (d)** is also incorrect. Once made, an election out is irrevocable, except with the consent of the IRS. Treas. Reg. § 1.761–2(b)(3).

2.1.1   The correct Answer is (c). This transaction is governed by section 721(b), which together with its corporate cousin section 351(e)(1) was enacted to check the rise of so-called "swap funds"—investment partnerships (or corporations) that provide tax-free diversification for holdings in appreciated financial instruments. The trickiest part of this analysis is knowing where to look for guidance. There are no regulations under section 721(b), but there are regulations under section 351(e)(1), last amended in 1996. Treas. Reg. § 1.351–1(c). These regulations have been superseded in important part by legislative changes to section 351(e)(1) in 1997. Putting this all together, we see that a transfer to an investment partnership is one that (1) provides diversification to the transferor (certainly the case here) if (2) the transferee is a partnership more than 80% of the value of whose assets consists of certain listed (bad) assets. Confusingly, the list of assets is found not in the regulation, but in the superseding statute. For purposes of answering this Question, the important statutory change is the elimination of the requirement (found in the 1996 regulations) that the transferred stock must be "readily marketable" in order to count as a listed asset. Thus, while this partnership would not have been a section 721(b) investment partnership in 1996, it is today. **Answer (a)** is incorrect, because it applies the general rule of nonrecognition of section 721(a), which is inapplicable here. **Answer (b)** seems like it should be the right answer, but it is not. A close look at section 721(b) will show you that this provision does not call off nonrecognition entirely. It requires the recognition of gains, but does not allow the recognition of losses. **Answer (d)** is unnecessary.

2.1.2   The correct Answer is (a). The 1997 statutory change widened the class of listed assets to include virtually every imaginable sort of financial instrument (and some that you may feel are unimaginable). It did not call off the protection of section 721(a) where the transferee partnership holds a significant amount (20% or more by value) of other assets. Business assets such as inventory, plant and equipment are on the good side of this line, because they are not "held for investment." *See* Treas. Reg. § 1.351–1(c)(1)(ii). So is land—even land held for investment. This answer cannot be intuited; the only way to know for sure is to read carefully the list of assets in section 351(e)(1)(B). **Answer (b)** is incorrect, because it reflects full recognition of both gain and loss. **Answer (c)** is incorrect, because it reflects the results of applying section 721(b). **Answer (d)** is still unnecessary.

2.1.3   The correct Answer is (d). The list of assets in section 351(e)(1)(B) includes (and even begins with) money. But that is not the end of the story. The legislative history of the 1997 expansion of listed assets indicates that it was intended only to expand the types of assets considered in the definition of an investment company and not to override the regulations in other respects. Thus, Treas. Reg. § 1.351–1(c)(2) remains relevant to the analysis. It provides that the determination of the status as an investment company normally is made immediately after all transfers have been made. "However," it continues, "where circumstances change thereafter pursuant to a plan in existence at the time of the transfer, this determination shall be made by reference to the later circumstances." Accordingly, if the partnership has a plan to invest the contributed cash in an asset or assets that are not listed, this planned investment would be enough to save the partnership from investment company status. **Answer (a)** is incorrect, because it applies section 721(a), which may or may not apply, depending on the partnership's plans for the cash and its ability to prove them. **Answer (b)** is incorrect, because it reflects full recognition of gain and loss, which is certainly wrong. **Answer (c)** is incorrect, because it applies section 721(b), which may be right, but may not be.

2.2.1 **The correct Answer is (a).** A partner has a single basis in her partnership interest, even if such partner is both a general partner and a limited partner of the same partnership. Rev. Rul. 84–53, 1984–1 C.B. 159. This is very different from the rule in corporate taxation, which allows the basis of individual shares, or lots, of stock to be separately maintained. When a partner sells less than all of her partnership interest, she is entitled to recover a fraction of her unitary basis that is equal to the fraction of the fair market value of her entire interest that she has sold, adjusted for liabilities. *Id.* The partnership interest is bifurcated, however, for the purpose of determining holding periods. This bifurcation is based on relative fair market values. Treas. Reg. § 1.1223–3(b)(1). Thus, if a partner contributes property with a long-term holding period in exchange for one-half of her partnership interest by value, she takes a long-term holding period in one-half of her partnership interest. Here, Aubrey exchanged land that she held as a capital asset with a long-term holding period for $100,000/$150,000, or 2/3, of the value of her partnership interest immediately following the exchange. She therefore takes a long-term holding period in two-thirds of her interest and a short-term holding period in the remaining one-third. **Answers (b) and (d)** are incorrect, because they conclude that Aubrey has two partnership interests. **Answer (c)** is incorrect, because it allocates the holding period according to the relative bases of the properties contributed, rather than according to the relative values of the partnership interests received in exchange therefor.

2.2.2 **The correct Answer is (d).** Section 1223(1) provides that the contributing partner receives a tacked holding period only if she held the contributed property as a capital asset or as section 1231 property. Looking at the list of properties that Grayson contributed, the only one that fits this description is his studio, which appears to be real property used in his trade or business and held for more than one year. *See* section 1231(b)(1). (Extra credit for noticing that this property is not subject to depreciation recapture, which, if present, would complicate this analysis.) The other items are not section 1231 property and are disqualified as capital assets by paragraphs (1), (3), (4) or (8) of section 1221(a). Accordingly, bifurcation of the holding period of Grayson's partnership interest is necessary. His shop constitutes $45,000/$125,000 or 36% of the value of his contributed property and presumably 36% of the value of the partnership interest he receives in exchange. Therefore, 36% of his partnership interest has a long-term holding period and the remaining 64% has a short-term holding period. **Answer (a)** is plainly incorrect, since it attempts no bifurcation at all. While **Answer (b)** does bifurcate based on fair market values, it does so by counting all assets that Grayson acquired more than one year before the contribution as long-term, without regard to whether they are capital assets or section 1231 property. **Answer (c)** takes into account the proper assets, but bifurcates according to bases rather than fair market values.

2.3.1   The completed balance sheet is as follows:

Assets				Liabilities		
	(1) **Tax**	**(2)** **Book**	**(3)** **FMV**		**(4)** **Tax**	**(5)** **Book**
Cash	$50,000	$50,000	$50,000	[None]	$ 0	$ 0
Land	25,000	25,000	25,000			
				Capital		
				Addison	50,000	50,000
				Benchley	25,000	25,000
Total Assets	$75,000	$75,000	$75,000	**Total Liabilities and Capital**	$75,000	$75,000

Let's start with the book accounts. Treas. Reg. § 1.704–1(b)(2)(iv)(*b*) tells us that the capital accounts of the partners must reflect the amount of money and the fair market value of the property that they contribute. These amounts are reflected in column (5) of the balance sheet. The initial book values of the partnership's assets must be their respective fair market values, because then and only then do Assets = Liabilities + Capital. These values are shown in column (2) of the balance sheet, and the book accounts of the partnership (column (2) and column (5)) satisfy the accounting identity.

The tax accounts of the partnership are shown in column (1) and column (4). (It would of course be possible to keep the book and tax accounts on entirely separate balance sheets. Combining them into one balance sheet not only saved paper (in the old days), but facilitates the application of section 704(c), which we will study in Chapter 8.) Column (1) shows the partnership's initial basis in its assets (inside basis). The amounts are determined by applying the "transferred basis" rule of section 723. The numbers in column (4) are the tax capital accounts for Addison and Benchley. They reflect the contribution that each of the partners has made to the basis of the partnership's assets: Addison contributed $50,000 of basis in the form of cash and Benchley contributed $25,000 of basis in the form of land. As you can see, the tax accounts also independently satisfy the accounting identity that Assets = Liabilities + Capital.

Where on this balance sheet are the partners' outside bases? They are not directly shown anywhere. In this simple partnership, which has no liabilities, the outside basis of each partner equals his or her tax capital. If a partnership has liabilities, the outside basis of any partner includes her share of the partnership's liabilities. In the following Topic 2.4, where liabilities are present, we will modify the presentation of the balance sheet to be able to display outside basis directly.

2.3.2 The completed balance sheet is as follows:

	Assets			Liabilities		
	(1) **Tax**	**(2)** **Book**	**(3)** **FMV**		**(4)** **Tax**	**(5)** **Book**
Cash	$120,000	$120,000	$120,000	[None]	$ 0	$ 0
Equipment	60,000	60,000	60,000			
Plant	190,000	220,000	220,000	**Capital**		
Land	110,000	140,000	140,000	Aaliyah	300,000	360,000
				Blake	120,000	120,000
				Carbury	60,000	60,000
Total Assets	$480,000	$540,000	$540,000	**Total Liabilities and Capital**	$480,000	$540,000

The book accounts are completed as before, with the amount of money and the fair market values of the contributed assets reflected in columns (2) and (5). Although she contributed two separate assets, Aaliyah has a single capital account. The tax accounts in columns (1) and (4) reflect, as before, the amount of money and the adjusted basis of the contributed properties. The only real difference between this balance sheet and the one in Question 2.3.1 is that the tax amounts do not in all cases match the book amounts. The values of the manufacturing plant and the land that Aaliyah contributed have each appreciated by $30,000 over her purchase price. This appreciation is "captured" on the asset side of the balance sheet in the $30,000 difference between the book value and the tax basis of each of these two assets. On the liabilities side of the balance sheet, this pre-contribution appreciation is reflected in the $60,000 difference between Aaliyah's book capital account and her tax capital. These so-called "book-tax differences" play the starring role in the analysis under section 704(c) discussed in Chapter 8.

Assuming that the partners negotiate no special allocations, what do you think Aaliyah's percentage interest should be in this partnership's income and loss? One possibility is 62.5%, which is the fraction of the tax basis that she brings to the partnership ($300,000/$480,000). But this would not give Aaliyah any credit for the $60,000 of value in addition to basis that she has contributed. So what about 66.7% ($360,000/$540,000)? The trouble with this answer is that Aaliyah seems to have brought to the partnership $60,000 of built-in gain, which the partnership (and therefore its partners) will have to recognize when the partnership disposes of these assets. You would think the partners would have to take this built-in tax liability into account in determining Aaliyah's share, which would then wind up someplace between 62.5% and 66.7%. In fact, section 704(c) solves this problem by requiring Aaliyah to be responsible for the entire built-in gain. The partnership would therefore be expected to award her a full 66.7% interest.

2.3.3   The completed balance sheet is as follows:

Assets				Liabilities		
	(1) **Tax**	**(2)** **Book**	**(3)** **FMV**		**(4)** **Tax**	**(5)** **Book**
Cash	$200,000	$200,000	$200,000	[None]	$ 0	$ 0
Land	150,000	200,000	200,000			
Stock	200,000	200,000	200,000	**Capital**		
				Aiden	200,000	200,000
				Brooklyn	150,000	200,000
				Caleb	200,000	200,000
Total Assets	$550,000	$600,000	$600,000	**Total Liabilities and Capital**	$550,000	$600,000

The book accounts in this balance sheet are as we would expect them, but the tax accounts are not. Caleb is the problem. His tax capital in column (4) is only $200,000, not the $250,000 that we would expect from the fact that he contributes to the partnership stock with a basis in his hands of $250,000. In column (1), the partnership's basis in this stock is $200,000, not $250,000, which also seems to be wrong.

This balance sheet reflects the application of Treasury regulations proposed in 2014 to implement section 704(c)(1)(C). Prop. Treas. Reg. § 1.704–3(f). These proposed regulations are discussed in Topic 6.6. For present purposes, it is sufficient to note that they limit the partnership's "common basis" for any property contributed with a built-in loss to the fair market value of such property. Presumably, the contributing partner's tax capital is subject to similar limitation (to maintain the accounting identity in the tax books). In that case, Caleb's tax capital ($200,000) does not match his outside basis ($250,000 under section 722). The proposed regulations create a "section 704(c)(1)(C) basis adjustment" equal to this difference, which is taken into account in determining Caleb's (and only Caleb's) share of partnership income, gain, loss and deduction. In this somewhat technical sense, the inside basis of the stock is "really" $250,000, which matches Caleb's outside basis in his partnership interest.

2.4.1   The revised balance sheet looks like this:

Assets			
	Tax	Book	FMV
Cash	$ 20,000	$ 20,000	$ 20,000
Receivables	0	0	30,000
Plant & Equipment	490,000	490,000	490,000
Total Assets	**$510,000**	**$510,000**	**$510,000**
Liabilities			
[None]	$150,000	$150,000	$150,000

Capital			Outside Basis
Aaron	120,000	120,000	$170,000
Butch	120,000	120,000	170,000
Cassidy	120,000	120,000	170,000
Total Liabilities and Capital	**$510,000**	**$510,000**	**$510,000**

The effect of the transactions is to add $150,000 to book and tax assets (under Plant & Equipment) and $150,000 to liabilities. There is no change in any of the partners' book or tax capital. The company's basis in its assets increases by $150,000 on account of the truck purchase. Under section 752(a), the partners' aggregate outside basis matches this increase, as they are considered to have contributed an aggregate of $150,000 in cash to the company by reason of the increase in their shares of the company's liabilities. The aggregate $150,000 increase must be allocated among the partners under rules that we will study in Chapter 5. For now, it is a reasonable assumption that the partners share this increase equally, $50,000 each.

2.4.2   The revised balance sheet looks like this:

Assets			
	Tax	**Book**	**FMV**
Cash	$ 6,000	$ 6,000	$ 6,000
Receivables	150,000	150,000	150,000
Inventory	870,000	870,000	870,000
Showroom	290,000	290,000	290,000
Investment Land	0	0	0
Total Assets	$1,316,000	$1,316,000	$1,316,000

Liabilities			
Bank Debt	$ 580,000	$ 580,000	$ 580,000

Capital				**Outside Basis**
Alison	184,000	184,000		$ 329,000
Bailey	184,000	184,000		329,000
Wally	368,000	368,000		658,000
Total Liabilities and Capital	$1,316,000	$1,316,000		$1,316,000

The sale of the land and repayment of $360,000 of the debt reduces the company's book and tax assets and its liabilities by the same amount, $360,000. Accordingly, there is no adjustment in the partners' book or tax capital. The transactions reduce the inside basis of the company's assets by $360,000. Section 752(b) reduces the partners' aggregate outside basis by the same amount, because they are considered to have received an aggregate distribution of $360,000 by reason of their reduced shares of partnership liabilities. In the initial balance sheet, 25% of total liabilities were allocated to each of Alison and Bailey and 50% went to Wally. The reduction is allocated in the same proportions.

2.4.3 Revised to reflect this alternative transaction, the balance sheet is as follows:

Assets			
	Tax	**Book**	**FMV**
Cash	$ 6,000	$ 6,000	$ 6,000
Receivables	150,000	150,000	150,000
Inventory	870,000	870,000	870,000
Showroom	290,000	290,000	290,000
Investment Land	360,000	360,000	360,000
Total Assets	$1,676,000	$1,676,000	$1,676,000

Liabilities			
Bank Debt	$ 580,000	$ 580,000	$ 580,000

Capital			**Outside Basis**
Alison	184,000	184,000	$ 329,000
Bailey	184,000	184,000	329,000
Wally	728,000	728,000	1,018,000
Total Liabilities and Capital	$1,676,000	$1,676,000	$1,676,000

This workout illustrates an increase in a partner's individual liabilities by reason of the assumption of a partnership liability. Unlike in Question 2.4.2, the workout causes no reduction in the company's assets. It does result, however, in exactly the same reduction in the company's liabilities ($360,000). This means, of course, that the partners' capital must increase by $360,000. The requisite increase in capital is provided in Treas. Reg. § 1.704–1(b)(2)(iv)(c). The increase affects solely Wally's capital, because only he assumed partnership debt. Alison and Bailey's capital accounts are unaffected by Wally's assumption.

Wally's outside basis increases by $360,000, on account of the increase in his tax capital, and decreases by $180,000, on account of the reduction in his share of the partnership's liabilities (50% of $360,000, or $180,000). The net increase in Wally's outside basis is $180,000, from $838,000 to $1,018,000. Alison and Bailey's outside bases are reduced by their respective shares of the amount assumed (25% of $360,000, or $90,000), from $419,000 to $329,000. There is no change in aggregate outside basis.

2.4.4 Although this assumption agreement may help Wally's partners relax, it has absolutely no effect on the company's balance sheet or on anyone's outside basis. The reason is that it is not really an assumption of the company's bank debt. Treas. Reg. § 1.704–1(b)(2)(iv)(c) establishes several sensible requirements for an agreement regarding a partnership's debt to be regarded as an assumption. Among these are that the bank must know about it and be able directly to enforce the assuming party's obligation. Neither is true here. If, on the other hand, Wally had entered into an agreement like this with the bank, it would qualify as a guarantee that would affect the partners' outside bases, although not their capital accounts. Guarantees of that sort are discussed in Topic 5.5.

2.5.1   The opening balance sheet for this partnership is as follows:

Assets			
	Tax	**Book**	**FMV**
Cash	$400,000	$ 400,000	$ 400,000
Building	500,000	800,000	800,000
Total Assets	$900,000	$1,200,000	$1,200,000
Liabilities			
Mortgage Debt	$400,000	$ 400,000	$ 400,000

Capital			**Outside Basis**
Alan	100,000	400,000	$300,000
Bethany	400,000	400,000	600,000
Total Liabilities and Capital	$900,000	$1,200,000	$900,000

Under these facts, the amount of Alan's liabilities assumed by the partnership does not exceed his basis in the property contributed. Said differently, Alan has positive, not negative, tax capital. There is no possibility of gain recognition.

2.5.2   With the increase in the amount of the debt to $700,000, the opening balance sheet is as follows:

Assets			
	Tax	**Book**	**FMV**
Cash	$400,000	$ 400,000	$ 400,000
Building	500,000	800,000	800,000
Total Assets	$900,000	$1,200,000	$1,200,000

Liabilities			
Mortgage Debt	$700,000	$700,000	$700,000

Capital			**Outside Basis**
Alan	(200,000)	100,000	$ 0
Bethany	400,000	400,000	960,000
Total Liabilities and Capital	$900,000	$1,200,000	$ 960,000

In this case, Alan's tax capital is negative, so trouble lurks. Based on the value of his net capital contribution, he is a 20% partner in this partnership, so he is allocated 20% of the $700,000 liability that the partnership has assumed. This reduces the net liability assumed to $560,000 ($700,000—$140,000), which exceeds Alan's basis in the property contributed by $60,000. He recognizes gain in this amount, which restores his outside basis to zero. *See* Treas. Reg. § 1.722–1, example (2). An alternative way to reach this result is to add Alan's share of the partnership's liability ($140,000) to his tax capital (negative $200,000), resulting in a "negative outside basis" of $60,000, which measures Alan's gain recognition.

Notice that the aggregate outside basis of the partners now exceeds the aggregate inside basis of the partnership's assets by the amount of gain Alan has recognized. Later in the Reading Period, you will see in Topic 9.2 that section 734(b)(1)(A) would provide an upward adjustment to the inside basis of an electing partnership that would eliminate this differential.

2.5.3   Adding the debt owed to the brokerage firm and the borrowed cash, the opening balance sheet looks like this:

Assets			
	Tax	**Book**	**FMV**
Cash	$ 700,000	$ 700,000	$ 700,000
Building	500,000	800,000	800,000
Total Assets	$1,200,000	$1,500,000	$1,500,000
Liabilities			
Mortgage Debt	$ 700,000	$ 700,000	$ 700,000
Brokerage Debt	300,000	300,000	300,000

Capital			**Outside Basis**
Alan	(200,000)	100,000	$ 0
Bethany	400,000	400,000	1,200,000
Total Liabilities and Capital	$1,200,000	$1,500,000	$1,200,000

Alan's problem need not be solved by a greater allocation of the same mortgage debt that encumbers the property he contributed. Salvation can and often does come in the form of a share of an entirely unrelated partnership debt. Here, Alan receives an allocation of 20% of the $300,000 of brokerage debt. This additional $60,000 of outside basis is exactly the right amount to eliminate his gain recognition. Inside and outside basis are equal.

2.5.4 The debt needed to cover Alan's negative tax capital need not come from new partnership borrowing, as it did in Question 2.5.3; it can come instead from the debt encumbering another partner's contribution. The facts of this Question illustrate a successful application of this technique. The opening balance sheet looks like this:

Assets	Tax	Book	FMV	
Land	$ 500,000	$ 800,000	$ 800,000	
Building	500,000	800,000	800,000	
Total Assets	$1,000,000	$1,600,000	$1,600,000	
Liabilities				
Mortgage Debt	$ 700,000	$ 700,000	$ 700,000	
Mortgage Debt	700,000	700,000	700,000	
Capital				**Outside Basis**
Alan	(200,000)	100,000		$ 500,000
Bethany	(200,000)	100,000		500,000
Total Liabilities and Capital	$1,000,000	$1,600,000		$1,000,000

At first, this may strike you as an impossible result. Bethany is just like Alan: both partners have liabilities assumed by the partnership that exceed their basis in the contributed property by $200,000. How can they *both* avoid gain recognition? Do not make the mistake of thinking that a partner's share of partnership liabilities under section 752(a) must be greater than the amount of liabilities the partnership assumes from her in order to avoid gain recognition. The partner's share of liabilities must only be greater than the excess of the liabilities assumed over her basis. For each of Alan and Bethany, this is only $200,000 (their negative tax capital), and the partnership has $1.4 million of liabilities to allocate between them. In this equal partnership, each of the partners is allocated an amount of partnership liabilities that equals the liabilities assumed, leaving each partner with the same basis in the partnership interest that he or she had in the contributed property—a perfect aggregate result.

2.6.1   The revaluation takes place immediately before Dualla's entry into the partnership. Following the revaluation, the partnership's balance sheet appears as follows:

	Assets			Liabilities		
	Tax	**Book**	**FMV**		**Tax**	**Book**
Cash	$ 40,000	$ 40,000	$ 40,000	Bank Debt	$200,000	$200,000
Equipment	160,000	130,000	130,000			
Plant	340,000	400,000	400,000	**Capital**		
Land	120,000	420,000	420,000	Adama	180,000	395,000
				Baltar	140,000	197,500
				Cally	140,000	197,500
Total Assets	$660,000	$990,000	$990,000	**Total Liabilities and Capital**	$660,000	$990,000

Net book gain is $230,000, which is allocated under the partnership agreement and applicable law 50% to Adama ($115,000) and 25% to each of Baltar and Cally ($57,500 each). Following the revaluation, the book value of each partnership asset equals its fair market value, and the book capital accounts of the partners include the net revaluation gain. Prior to the revaluation, there was a book-tax disparity in only one partnership asset, the land. Now there is such a disparity in every asset except cash. (Notice that the equipment has been revalued downward, reflecting the decline in its fair market value.) Similarly, prior to the revaluation, only Adama had a book-tax disparity in his capital accounts. (Although the facts do not explicitly state, it appears from the balance sheet that Adama contributed the appreciated land to the company.) Following the revaluation, every partner has a book-tax disparity, reflecting the addition of the net revaluation gain to the book, but not the tax, capital accounts.

Immediately after Dualla's cash contribution, the balance sheet is as follows:

	Assets			Liabilities		
	Tax	**Book**	**FMV**		**Tax**	**Book**
Cash	$ 435,000	$ 435,000	$ 435,000	Bank Debt	$ 200,000	$ 200,000
Equipment	160,000	130,000	130,000			
Plant	340,000	400,000	400,000	**Capital**		
Land	120,000	420,000	420,000	Adama	180,000	395,000
				Baltar	140,000	197,500
				Cally	140,000	197,500
				Dualla	395,000	395,000
Total Assets	$1,055,000	$1,385,000	$1,385,000	**Total Liabilities and Capital**	$1,055,000	$1,385,000

On the assets side, the only change is the addition of Dualla's cash. The liabilities side reflects Dualla's admission to the partnership. Dualla has no book-tax disparity, because her contribution consists solely of cash.

2.7.1   The correct Answer is (c). Here, there appear to be simultaneous transfers of the land (one way) and the cash (the other). Even if the transfers are not simultaneous, they are agreed from the outset, so this is plainly a disguised sale. Of what? To determine the portion of the land that Jacob has sold, compare the cash payment of $500,000 to the value of the land, $2,000,000. Jacob has sold 25% of his land and can recover 25% of his basis, or $50,000. Jacob's gain is $500,000 less $50,000, or $450,000. **Answer (a)** is incorrect, because it ignores the cash distribution and thus the possibility that there is a disguised sale. **Answer (b)** is incorrect, because it uses Jacob's entire basis in the contributed property to determine the amount of his gain in the disguised sale. **Answer (d)** is incorrect, because it uses none of Jacob's basis in computing his gain.

2.7.2   The correct Answer is (c). Sunbelt's basis in the transferred land is composed of two parts, its basis for the land deemed purchased and its basis for the land contributed. The former is $500,000. The latter is Jacob's remaining basis after subtracting the portion used in determining his gain on the sale. This is $200,000 less $50,000, or $150,000. Thus, Sunbelt's aggregate basis in the land is $500,000 plus $150,000, or $650,000. **Answer (a)** is incorrect, because $200,000 is the transferred basis that would apply if Jacob recognized no gain on the contribution. **Answer (b)** is the correct answer to the wrong question (the amount of Jacob's gain). **Answer (d)** is incorrect, because it gives Sunbelt credit for the $500,000 purchased basis plus Jacob's entire basis, unreduced by the portion of Jacob's basis used up in the disguised sale.

2.7.3   The correct Answer is (d). There are no facts to indicate that the $60,000 nonrecourse liability is a "qualified liability" within the meaning of Treas. Reg. § 1.707–5(a)(6). So this is a disguised sale. Under Treas. Reg. § 1.707–5(a)(1), the consideration in this sale is the excess of the amount of the nonqualified liability ($60,000) over Stevie's share of that liability after the contribution ($15,000), or $45,000. This represents half of the value of the contributed equipment, so Stevie can use half of her basis in calculating her gain on sale, which is $45,000 less $12,000, or $33,000. Note that section 1245 applies to this sale in determining the character of Stevie's gain. **Answer (a)** is incorrect, because it does not take into account the disguised sale. **Answer (b)** and **Answer (c)** are incorrect, because they allow Stevie to use 100% and 75%, respectively, of her basis to compute the gain on sale.

2.7.4   The correct Answer is (b). You may think that the source of the partnership's cash distribution should have no bearing on the amount of gain that Jacob recognizes in this transaction. But imagine if Jacob had borrowed $500,000 against his land before contributing it to the partnership and that his share of the debt after the contribution were $125,000. Applying the rules of Treas. Reg. § 1.707–5(a) exactly as we did in answering Question 2.7.3, we would conclude that the consideration in this disguised sale is $375,000, not $500,000. Treas. Reg. § 1.707–5(b) reaches the same answer here. It provides that the cash distributed to Jacob is not disguised-sale proceeds to the extent it can be traced to his share of the indebtedness incurred to fund the distribution. Jacob has thus sold $375,000/$2,000,000, or 18.75%, of his land to the partnership and contributed the remainder. Against the $375,000 amount realized, he can apply 18.75%, or $37,500, of his basis, resulting in a recognized gain of $337,500. **Answer (a)** is incorrect, because it allows Jacob to use his entire outside basis in computing the gain on this disguised sale. **Answer (c)** is incorrect, because it does not take into account any portion of Jacob's basis in computing his gain. **Answer (d)** is incorrect, because it does not take into account the fact that this distribution is debt-financed.

2.7.5   The correct Answer is (a). The issue in this Question is whether Cody has engaged in a disguised sale of a portion of the arena. This issue is raised by the fact that Cody incurred the debt during the same calendar year that he contributed the arena to Frontier Days—plainly within the two-year presumption that this debt is not a qualified liability. Treas. Reg. § 1.707–5(a)(7). Here, however, the entire amount borrowed was invested in capital improvements to the arena, so the debt is, in fact, a qualified liability under Treas. Reg. § 1.707–5(a)(6)(i)(C). The transaction in this Question is thus an innocent capital contribution governed by section 721(a). **Answer (b)** would be correct if this liability were not a qualified liability. The consideration in the disguised sale would be the excess of the amount of the liability ($300,000) over Cody's share of the liability after the contribution ($60,000), or $240,000. The value of the refurbished arena is $1 million. Thus, this would be a disguised sale of 24% of the arena and Cody would be entitled to recover 24% of his adjusted basis, or $132,000. His gain would be $240,000 less $132,000, or $108,000. **Answers (c) and (d)** both apply the disguised sale approach, but reflect errors in the computations. **Answer (c)** treats the consideration in the disguised sale as $300,000. **Answer (d)** treats Cody's adjusted basis in the refurbished arena as $250,000.

2.7.6 **The correct Answer is (a).** Eli has not parted with ownership of his toolshop and the payments to him that are characterized as partnership distributions are properly viewed as rent paid by the partnership for its use of Eli's toolshop for ten years. Section 707(a)(1) requires that the payments be treated as rent, paid to Eli other than in his capacity as a partner. One clue to the correct analysis is the specification of the amount of the cash payment as 5% of the partnership's gross income. This is far different than 5% of the partnership's net income, because it does not cause Eli to bear any portion of the expenses of the partnership. Specifying at least a portion of rent in this manner is, in fact, common in commercial leases. Even more important is the fact that Eli has not contributed any capital to the partnership in this transaction. Far from having ownership of the toolshop, the partnership simply has the right to use it for ten years and to buy it at fair market value at the end of the lease term. **Answers (b) and (d)** require the partnership to acquire a present ownership interest in the toolshop. Since it does not, these answers are incorrect. **Answer (c)** is also incorrect, because Eli, though a partner, is not acting in his capacity as a partner in this transaction.

2.7.7 **The correct Answer is (b).** If the IRS succeeds in characterizing this as a disguised sale, it is an installment sale of the lot that Isaac contributed. This may have one small effect on the character of Isaac's gain and one big one. The former is that interest must be imputed under section 483 or section 1274 if Isaac has engaged in an installment sale, but not if the cash payment to Isaac is treated as a partnership distribution. More importantly, all of Isaac's gain on the disguised sale is ordinary income, because the lot appears to have been section 1221(a)(1) property in his hands. If treated as a distribution, however, the cash payment produces capital gain, except to the extent required by section 751(b), discussed in Topic 9.6. **Answer (a)** is incorrect, because both the distribution and the installment sale cause Isaac to recognize income or gain in the year he receives the payment. **Answer (c)** is incorrect, because Isaac has no basis in the contributed property, and therefore no basis in his partnership interest. Whether the cash transfer by the partnership is treated as a distribution or as sales proceeds, all of it will be income or gain to Isaac. This is a corollary to the point that the disguised-sale rules are essentially rules regarding basis recovery. **Answer (d)** is incorrect, because **Answer (b)** is correct.

2.8.1 **The correct Answer is (a).** The option issued by Speedee Messenger Services is a noncompensatory option, because it is issued for cash, not services provided or to be provided by Lillian. The issuance of a noncompensatory option does not result in recognized gain to either the partnership or the option holder. Rev. Rul. 58–234, 1958–1 C.B. 279 (option issuance is part of an open transaction; taxation held in abeyance until the transaction closes through the lapse or exercise of the option). Moreover, section 721(a) generally applies to the exercise of a noncompensatory option by the delivery of cash or property to the partnership. Treas. Reg. § 1.721–2(a)(1). **Answers (b), (c) and (d)** are incorrect, because all reflect recognition of gain by Lillian, Speedee or both.

2.8.2   **The correct Answer is (b).** Section 721(a) does not generally apply to the transfer of property to a partnership in exchange for (*i.e.*, to acquire) a noncompensatory option. Treas. Reg. § 1.721–2(b)(1). Lillian recognizes the $8,000 gain inherent in her Apple stock when she acquires the option in 2017, and Speedee takes the Apple stock with a basis equal to its fair market value, $10,000. Notice the discontinuity between this result and that in Question 2.8.1. In both cases, the partnership ends up with Apple stock and cash and Lillian gets an interest in the partnership. If, consistent with Rev. Rul. 58–234, one were to view Lillian's acquisition and exercise of the noncompensatory option as two steps in a single, open transaction, one might expect that the answers to the two Questions would be the same. But they are not. In this case, but not in Question 2.8.1, Lillian recognizes gain and the partnership takes a stepped-up basis in the Apple stock. **Answer (a)** applies this open-transaction approach to Lillian's acquisition of the option, which is inconsistent with the cited Treasury regulation. **Answer (c)** is incorrect, because it treats Speedee, rather than Lillian, as the seller in 2017. **Answer (d)** is incorrect for this reason and also because it fails to give Speedee the benefit of section 721(a) in 2019.

2.8.3   **The correct Answer is (c).** It should be clear that Lillian loses from the lapse of her option, because her $10,000 investment has vanished. It should also be clear that Speedee gains something, because it can keep Lillian's $10,000 with no further obligation to her. But how are this loss and this gain taxed? There are no unique rules for the taxing the lapse of a noncompensatory option issued by a partnership. Answering this Question therefore requires a basic knowledge of the operation of section 1234, which sets forth the general rules for the taxation of options. Under section 1234(a)(1), Lillian recognizes capital loss on the lapse of her option, which is long-term capital loss under section 1234(a)(2). Under section 1234(b)(1), Speedee's gain is short-term capital gain, even though it results from a transaction that spread over three years. **Answer (a)** is incorrect, because it is inconsistent not only with section 1234 but with the fundamental economics of the transaction. **Answers (b) and (d)** are appealing, because they reach consistent results for both Lillian and Speedee, but these are not the results produced by section 1234.

2.8.4   **The correct Answer is (c).** Treas. Reg. § 1.721–2(e) provides that section 721 does not apply to the transfer of a partnership interest to a noncompensatory option holder upon conversion of convertible debt to the extent that the transfer is in satisfaction of the partnership's indebtedness for accrued but unpaid interest. Thus, Devon must recognize the $4,000 of interest income paid by delivery of an interest in the partnership and the partnership can deduct it. **Answers (a) and (b)** are inconsistent with this analysis and are therefore incorrect statements of the law. So is **Answer (d)**, although many have argued that it is the correct answer in a case like this, reasoning that the partnership should, in effect, be deemed to have transferred an undivided $4,000 interest in all of its assets to Devon, who should in turn be deemed to have transferred such assets back to the partnership in exchange for an additional partnership interest. This characterization would result in the partnership recognizing gain or loss on the deemed disposition of its assets. It was not adopted by the Treasury regulations. Treas. Reg. § 1.721–2(e) ("The debtor partnership will not, however, recognize gain or loss upon such conversion.").

3.1.1   The correct Answer is (d). Beatrice's cash compensation appears to be paid to her as a guaranteed payment for services under section 707(c), includible in Beatrice's income and deductible by the company as a business expense. This type of payment is discussed in more detail in Topic 3.5. There is no indication in the facts that the partnership interest transferred to Beatrice is anything other than a capital interest. This conclusion is supported by the fact that she views it as a "signing bonus"— something of clear, current value in the nature of cash, rather than a more speculative interest in future company profits. Beatrice's income thus includes her cash compensation ($350,000) and the value of the partnership interest ($600,000). The situation for Box is a bit more complicated. The cash compensation is deductible. Capitalization of the $600,000 value of the partnership interest is required only if and to the extent that the partnership has acquired a benefit that extends beyond 12 months. Treas. Reg. §§ 1.263(a)–4(d)(6), –4(f). Beatrice can terminate her services at will, so capitalization should not generally be required. Her agreement not to compete does, however, provide a multi-year benefit to the partnership, which it values at $175,000 (half of her annual salary). This portion of the $600,000 is therefore not deductible. It is also not currently amortizable, because of its indefinite duration. Treas. Reg. § 1.167(a) –3(a). The partnership's current deduction is thus $350,000 plus $600,000 less $175,000, or $775,000. **Answer (a)** is incorrect, because it includes only the cash compensation in the partnership's deduction. **Answer (b)** is incorrect, because it allows the partnership to deduct the entire amount it paid for Beatrice's agreement not to compete, and mistakenly adds, rather than subtracts, the value of Beatrice's covenant not to compete. **Answer (c)** is also incorrect, because it erroneously reduces Beatrice's compensation income by the amount paid for her noncompete.

3.1.2   The correct Answer is (a). The partnership interest issued to James in this case appears to be a capital interest, so he will recognize compensation income. The question is: how much? Reasonable estimates of the value of the interest at the time it is granted to James could range from $100,000 (his 10% share of the partnership's $1 million in capital) to $1,500,000 (the high end of ultimate value). The parties would probably adopt the liquidation-value approach here. This choice helps James, who is receiving no cash to pay his current tax liability, and hurts the partnership less, because it must capitalize into the basis of the building whatever amount is chosen. **Answers (b) and (c)** are incorrect, because they overlook the requirement for the partnership to capitalize the compensation of its construction manager. **Answer (d)** is plausible, but even if the parties do not use the liquidation-value approach, they are unlikely to choose the highest estimate of ultimate value for the interest granted to James, without discounting it for either time or risk.

3.1.3   The correct Answer is (a). The interest that James receives here is a profits interest and, assuming the parties use the liquidation-value approach, he does not include any amount in his income for the year of the grant. Notice the symmetry in the analysis of the last two Questions. In Question 3.1.2, James receives a current interest in the partnership's capital and he pays tax on that. In both Question 3.1.2 and Question 3.1.3, James receives a 10% interest in the future profits of the partnership and in neither case does he pay tax on that. **Answers (b), (c) and (d)** all reflect valuations of James' profits interest that are more or less plausible, but unlikely to be adopted by the parties. For further discussion of this point, see Questions 3.2.3 and 3.2.4 and the Answers thereto.

3.1.4   The correct Answer is (c). Relative to either of the prior approaches, this one is a pretty bad idea for James. Under Treas. Reg. § 1.83–7, James is not subject to tax on the receipt of the option. This might seem like a good thing, comparable to the treatment of a profits interest. Unfortunately, that is where the good news ends. The effect of the option is to hold taxation in abeyance until the option is exercised. Thus, when James exercises, he is subject to tax on the receipt of a capital interest for services, but based on the valuation at the time of exercise, not at the time of grant. Accordingly, James recognizes ordinary, compensation income equal to the excess of the value of the interest received ($1,250,000) over what he pays for it ($100,000).

Answer (a) is the result of receiving a profits interest, not an option. **Answer (b)** is the result of receiving a capital interest rather than an option. **Answer (d)** addresses the correct transaction, but does not give James credit for paying the $100,000 exercise price of the option.

What if the partnership issued a profits interest to James and thereafter sold its building at a price that resulted in an allocation of $1,150,000 of gain to James? As you will see in Topic 4.1, the character of James' gain would be determined at the partnership level under section 702(b) and would likely be capital gain. This is the second big advantage of profits interests for service providers (the first being that they are not taxed on receipt).

The option granted to James in this Question would, in the corporate context, be called a "nonqualified stock option." Cash aside, such options are the most common form of executive compensation in U.S. public companies. Like partnership profits interests, they are not taxable on receipt. They are uncommon in the partnership context, however, because they produce ordinary income on exercise, as we witnessed in this Question. This can be avoided through the use of profits interests in partnerships which generate capital gains—a method of compensation that is not available to corporations.

3.1.5   If Sam asked me, I'd say Answer (d). When Sam transfers a 25% interest in his limited liability company to Myra, he is converting a disregarded entity into a partnership. Rev. Rul. 99–5, 1999–1 C.B. 434. In so doing, he raises "the *McDougal* problem." In that case, the owner of a racehorse granted his trainer a one-half interest in the horse for services provided to the owner up to that time. The Tax Court characterized the transaction as a transfer of an appreciated asset (the one-half interest in the horse) from the owner to the trainer, followed by contributions by each of them of one-half interests in the horse to a new partnership. On the deemed transfer to the trainer, the owner recognized gain measured by the excess of the value of the one-half interest transferred over the owner's adjusted basis therein. The owner could claim a compensation deduction equal to the value of the one-half interest he transferred and the trainer, although he was not a party to the lawsuit, presumably had corresponding compensation income. *McDougal v. Commissioner*, 62 T.C. 720 (1974). The IRS agrees with the result of this case. Although the 2005 proposed regulations would shield a partnership holding appreciated assets from recognizing gain when it grants a capital interest to a provider of services *to the partnership*, such protection would not extend to a partner granting a capital interest in a new or existing partnership to a provider of services *to the partner*. Unfortunately, that is what Sam is proposing to do.

It is not entirely clear that Sam can avoid recognizing gain on 25% of the assets in his accounting business. There is no problem, of course, if he simply pays Myra in cash. The issue arises when she invests the cash in the business (now a partnership) for a 25% interest. If the cash that Sam pays to Myra comes from the business, the IRS may seek to disregard the "circle of cash" and treat Sam as though he had simply transferred a 25% partnership interest (and thus, under the *McDougal* analysis, 25% of the business assets) to Myra. Sam's position will be enhanced if he uses cash from outside the business to pay Myra and does not withdraw it after she contributes the cash to the partnership. **Answer (a)** may make Sam like you until he (or Myra) learns that it is wrong. Myra has the same amount of compensation income whether she is paid in cash or property. **Answer (b)** is wrong, because Sam has the same deduction whether Myra is paid in cash or property. **Answer (c)** is correct as far as it goes, but misses the *McDougal* problem.

3.2.1   After accounting for compensation income and deduction, the opening balance sheet is as follows:

Assets				Liabilities		
	Tax	**Book**	**FMV**		**Tax**	**Book**
Cash	$180,000	$180,000	$180,000	[None]	$ 0	$ 0
Property	120,000	180,000	180,000			
				Capital		
				Adair	60,000	120,000
				Blair	120,000	120,000
				Claire	120,000	120,000
Total Assets	$300,000	$360,000	$360,000	**Total Liabilities and Capital**	$300,000	$360,000

The partnership's initial basis in the property is $120,000, which was Adair's adjusted basis in the property when she contributed it. Adair's initial tax capital is also $120,000. Blair, who contributed only cash, has an initial tax capital of $180,000. The initial book capital accounts of Adair and Blair are both $180,000, reflecting the value of their contributions.

Claire recognizes compensation income of $120,000, the value of the one-third interest she receives for her promise to perform services for the partnership. This is the amount of her opening tax capital and book capital account. If you have trouble seeing this, imagine that the partnership paid $120,000 to Claire for her promise to perform services and then she contributed that amount to the partnership for her capital interest.

The final piece in the puzzle is the adjustment in the accounts of Adair and Blair. As a result of issuing the capital interest to Claire, the partnership has a deduction of $120,000, which it allocates equally to Adair and Blair. This reduces both the tax capital and the book capital of each partner by $60,000.

Stepping back, we can see that there has been a "capital shift" of $120,000 to Claire, $60,000 from each of Adair and Blair. This shift of capital reflects compensation for Clair's services and is taxable to her and deductible by the other partners.

3.2.2 As discussed in Topic 3.1, the amount paid to Claire for her covenant not to compete cannot be deducted, but must be added to the adjusted basis of that asset. The resulting balance sheet is as follows:

Assets				Liabilities		
	Tax	Book	FMV		Tax	Book
Cash	$180,000	$180,000	$180,000	[None]	$ 0	$ 0
Property	120,000	180,000	180,000			
Covenant	60,000	60,000	60,000	Capital		
				Adair	90,000	150,000
				Blair	150,000	150,000
				Claire	120,000	120,000
Total Assets	$360,000	$420,000	$420,000	Total Liabilities and Capital	$360,000	$420,000

The difference between this balance sheet and the one in the prior Question is not attributable to Claire—she recognizes compensation income, whether the amount paid to her is in respect to her agreement to render services to the partnership or her agreement not to compete with it. Claire has exactly the same tax and book capital as before. The difference is rather that Adair's and Blair's tax capital and book capital are each $30,000 higher, reflecting the reduction in the current deduction from $120,000 to $60,000. This gives them the capacity to take a special allocation of the amortization of the partnership's investment in Claire's covenant not to compete, when available, under the rules reviewed in Topic 4.3.

3.2.3 If Claire instead received a profits interest that is valued at zero using the liquidation-value approach, she would recognize no compensation income and the partnership would have no amount to deduct or capitalize. The opening balance sheet would be as follows:

Assets				Liabilities		
	Tax	Book	FMV		Tax	Book
Cash	$180,000	$180,000	$180,000	[None]	$ 0	$ 0
Property	120,000	180,000	180,000			
				Capital		
				Adair	120,000	180,000
				Blair	180,000	180,000
				Claire	0	0
Total Assets	$300,000	$360,000	$360,000	Total Liabilities and Capital	$300,000	$360,000

If the partnership were to sell its property at fair market value and liquidate, there would be no book gain or loss, so the partners' book capital accounts would remain unchanged. If the partnership thereupon liquidated, distributing to the partners the values in their respective capital accounts, Adair and Blair would each get $180,000 and Claire would get nothing. This is consistent with the parties' agreement that Claire is entitled to an equal share of future profits, but none of the partnership's current capital. The partnership would recognize $60,000 of tax gain on such a sale, the allocation of which is the subject of Chapter 8.

3.2.4 There is no law that the value of Claire's profits interest must be determined by the liquidation-value approach. There is, in fact, common-sense appeal to using a number higher than zero for the value of her interest. It represents, after all, the right to one-third of the partnership's future profits—surely that is worth something. So, taking this "option value" into account, the parties value Claire's profits interest at $40,000. She recognizes this much compensation income and the partnership has a corresponding deduction. The balance sheet looks like this:

	Assets			Liabilities		
	Tax	**Book**	**FMV**		**Tax**	**Book**
Cash	$180,000	$180,000	$180,000	[None]	$ 0	$ 0
Property	120,000	180,000	180,000			
				Capital		
				Adair	100,000	160,000
				Blair	160,000	160,000
				Claire	40,000	40,000
Total Assets	$300,000	$360,000	$360,000	**Total Liabilities and Capital**	$300,000	$360,000

This new valuation has changed the economic position of the parties. If the partnership were to sell its property at fair market value and liquidate, Claire would get $40,000, rather than nothing, and each of the other partners would get $20,000 less. This is exactly the same "capital shift" we witnessed in Question 3.2.1, and it calls into question whether the interest Claire has received should even be called a profits interest. Because the value placed by the parties on Claire's interest ($40,000) becomes her opening book capital account ($40,000), it gives her a claim on the partnership's assets on liquidation in the same amount ($40,000). In other words, by placing a value on Claire's profits interest that is greater than zero, the partners have, in effect, converted it into a capital interest. This is a good deal for Claire, who now has a right to $40,000 of the partnership's assets simply because she has paid tax on that amount. It is not such a good deal for the other partners, who have surrendered $40,000 of partnership assets and received only a deduction—a bad trade at any tax rate less than 100%.

3.2.5   The grant of an interest in a partnership as consideration for the provision of services to or for the benefit of the partnership is a revaluation event. Treas. Reg. § 1.704–1(b)(2)(iv)(*f*)(*5*)(*iii*). This is true whether the interest is a capital interest or a profits interest. Failure to revalue in either case can result in the service partner having a capital account that is out of proportion with her percentage interest in the partnership, or an interest in unrealized appreciation that is unintended. This is exactly the same problem that was discussed in Topic 2.6 in connection with subsequent contributions of money or property.

Just as in Topic 2.6, the revaluation should occur *immediately before* the service provider joins the partnership. After such revaluation, and before the issuance of Dr. Bork's interest, the balance sheet of Suncoast appears as follows:

Assets (000s)				Liabilities (000s)		
	Tax	Book	FMV		Tax	Book
Cash	$ 500	$ 500	$ 500	Bank Debt	$ 60,000	$ 60,000
Plant & Equipment	114,500	117,000	117,000			
Land	5,000	12,500	12,500	Capital (000s)		
				CEG, Inc.	30,000	35,000
				Datalon, Inc.	30,000	35,000
Total Assets	$120,000	$130,000	$130,000	Total Liabilities and Capital	$120,000	$130,000

With the admittance of Dr. Bork, the balance sheet becomes:

Assets (000s)				Liabilities (000s)		
	Tax	Book	FMV		Tax	Book
Cash	$ 500	$ 500	$ 500	Bank Debt	$ 60,000	$ 60,000
Plant & Equipment	114,500	117,000	117,000			
Land	5,000	12,500	12,500	Capital (000s)		
				CEG, Inc.	30,000	35,000
				Datalon, Inc.	30,000	35,000
				Bork	0	0
Total Assets	$120,000	$130,000	$130,000	Total Liabilities and Capital	$120,000	$130,000

Absent a revaluation, Suncoast would have $10 million of unrealized book gain, in which Dr. Bork would have a 5% share when realized. Using the liquidation-value approach, his interest would be worth $500,000 when issued. He would recognize compensation income in this amount and the other partners would have a corresponding deduction. Hence, the revaluation is necessary to establish that Dr. Bork's interest is, in fact, a profits interest.

3.3.1   The correct Answer is (b). If this worked, nobody would ever recognize ordinary income on the provision of services to a partnership. If section 721(a) applied, Ann would take a basis of zero in her partnership interest and would generally recognize capital gain when the partnership distributed the $45,000 that it owes her. It can't be that easy. But why not? There are two possible reasons that section 721(a) does not apply here. First, it is possible that the receivable from the partnership is not property in Ann's hands, but this approach would run afoul of the fact that accounts receivable are routinely considered to be property in other contexts. *See, e.g.,* section 1221(a)(4). More likely, the exchange would be disqualified from section 721(a) treatment, perhaps on the grounds that the $45,000 capital interest that Ann receives is a "substitute for ordinary income." *Hort v. Commissioner,* 313 U.S. 28 (1941) (payment by tenant to terminate lease favorable to landlord was ordinary income to landlord); *see also* Treas. Reg. § 1.721–1(d)(2) (section 721(a) does not apply to partnership interests issued in exchange for the partnership's indebtedness for unpaid rent, royalties or interest). Disqualified from section 721(a) treatment, Ann's contribution of the receivable is treated in exactly the same manner as her contribution of the services themselves. Because she acquires a capital interest in the partnership, she recognizes compensation income and the partnership has a corresponding deduction. **Answer (a)** is incorrect, because section 721(a) does not apply, for the reasons suggested above. **Answers (c) and (d)** are both incorrect for two reasons. First, section 721(a) does not apply to Ann's contribution. Second, the partnership does not have cancellation of debt income, because it pays in full the amount that it owes to Ann, with a capital interest worth $45,000, valued using the liquidation-value approach. Treas. Reg. § 1.108–8(b)(2) (use of liquidation-value approach is generally permitted in this context).

3.3.2   The correct Answer is (c). Conceivably, Ann has made an assignment of income to Winken in the amount of $45,000. *Lucas v. Earl,* 281 U.S. 111 (1930). More recent authority suggests, however, that assignments of receivables to corporations and partnerships will be given nonrecognition treatment if accomplished for a valid business purpose and not for a tax-avoidance motive. Rev. Rul. 80–198, 1980–2 C.B. 113; *see also Schneer v. Commissioner,* 97 T.C. 643 (1991) (declining to apply assignment-of-income principles in a case somewhat similar to this one). The addition of section 704(c)(3) in 1984 has, however, diminished the significance of *Lucas v. Earl* in cases like this. Even if Ann is considered to have contributed property (the receivable) to Winken, she, and she alone, will be taxed on the $45,000 income when it is realized by the partnership. **Answer (a)** is incorrect, because the attribution of the $45,000 of income to Ann (whether by application of the assignment-of-income doctrine or by allocation under section 704(c)) does not create a deduction for Winken. The effect, however, is similar to a deduction, because none of the other Winken partners will be responsible for paying tax on any part of the $45,000. **Answer (b)** is incorrect, because section 704(c)(3) requires the allocation of the $45,000 only to Ann. **Answer (d)** is incorrect, because Ann cannot write off any portion of her capital account (or, better said, her outside basis) until she liquidates or sells her partnership interest.

It may be helpful at this point to review Ann's capital accounting. Upon contribution of the receivable, Ann has book capital of $45,000 and tax capital of $0. When the partnership is paid $45,000 by Taxes, it recognizes no book income and $45,000 of taxable income, which it allocates to Ann pursuant to section 704(c)(3), equalizing her book and tax capital at $45,000. Presumably, the partnership will distribute this amount in cash to Ann at some point, although the facts do not indicate that it is obligated to do so. If and when it does, Ann's book capital and tax capital will each decline by $45,000, to zero if she is allocated no further income or loss (or if future allocations of income are matched by cash distributions). No loss would be allowable if she left the partnership in these circumstances.

3.3.3 **The correct Answer is (c).** Dickie receives his partnership interest partly for services and partly for property. He recognizes compensation income only with respect to the former. We cannot measure this amount directly, but instead must "back out" the interest he receives for property. The tricky part is identifying the property that Dickie contributes. Surely, he will argue (or perhaps have the horse argue for him) that his property contribution is the exclusivity contracts that he negotiated, worth $200,000. The problem with this argument is that Dickie negotiated the contracts, not for himself, but for the partnership. Acting as an agent of the partnership, he captured the value of those contracts for the partnership directly, so he cannot be viewed as contributing that value in exchange for a partnership interest. Dickie's only contribution of property is the $70,000 of cash that came from his own pocket. His compensation income is thus $450,000 less $70,000, or $380,000. This is an issue that arises frequently in real cases and was in fact present in the *Stafford* case itself. The problem is that promoters, anticipating the formation of a partnership as a financing vehicle down the road, are wont to negotiate agreements for the entity "in formation." If the trier of fact concludes that this course of action makes the promoter an agent, his ability to claim a substantial contribution of property evaporates. **Answer (a)** is incorrect, because it treats Dickie's entire transaction as a property contribution. **Answer (b)** is incorrect, because it improperly identifies the property Dickie contributes as the contracts rather than the cash. **Answer (d)** is incorrect, because it ignores Dickie's cash contribution.

3.3.4 **The correct Answer is (b).** There's a lot going on here, because Hunter, like most real estate developers, is a busy person. The total value of the property she contributes is $300,000, consisting of her lot ($180,000), the hotel contract ($40,000) and the financing commitments ($80,000). Unlike Dickie in Question 3.3.3, Hunter negotiated all contracts on her own behalf, so there is no issue of her acting as agent of the partnership. Hunter has not contributed the organizational expenses she fronted for the partnership ($60,000), which all parties have treated as, in effect, a loan. She does not appear to have incurred any cost in negotiating the other contracts.

Hunter receives an initial book capital account of $500,000. Applying the liquidation-value approach, this is also the value of her partnership interest. She recognizes compensation income of $500,000 less $300,000, or $200,000. Because Hunter has contributed appreciated property (her lot) to the partnership, we would ordinarily be worried about the presence of a disguised sale when the partnership makes a distribution of cash to her within two years. Treas. Reg. § 1.707–3(c) (two-year presumption). In this case, however, a special exception applies. Under Treas. Reg. § 1.707–4(d), a partnership can reimburse a partner for organizational or syndication costs that the partner has incurred within the two-year period preceding the partner's contribution of property to the partnership without triggering a disguised sale. **Answer (a)** is incorrect, because in ascertaining the amount of Hunter's compensation income, it gives her credit for a contribution of $60,000 of organizational expenses, which appears inconsistent with the agreement of the parties. **Answer (d)** is incorrect, because it treats the $60,000 expense reimbursement as part of a disguised sale. **Answer (c)** is incorrect for both of these reasons.

3.4.1   The correct Answer is (d). The existence of a substantial risk of forfeiture holds taxation in abeyance until the risk is eliminated. Here, that occurs at the end of two years. At that time, James recognizes ordinary compensation income equal to the value of his interest at that time ($1,250,000) less the amount he paid for it ($0). The result is similar to the result in Question 3.1.4, where the partnership gave James an option to acquire a capital interest. In both cases, taxation is deferred until a later event (here, vesting; there, option exercise), at which time James recognizes ordinary income based on the current value of his interest. The numbers are not exactly the same in the two Questions, because James is required in Question 3.1.4 to pay $100,000 to exercise the option, whereas the partnership requires no monetary contribution from James here. **Answer (a)** is incorrect, because James will be taxed at vesting, absent an election under section 83(b). **Answer (b)** is incorrect, because James is not taxed at the time of the grant, due to the existence of a substantial risk of forfeiture. **Answer (c)** is incorrect for that same reason, and it also mis-measures the amount of James' income at vesting.

3.4.2   The correct Answer is (b). As the recipient of a capital interest for services, James cannot entirely avoid recognizing compensation income. He can, however, substantially improve his position by making a section 83(b) election. The election makes vesting a non-event, which eliminates the large inclusion of ordinary income that vexes him in Questions 3.1.4 and 3.4.1. **Answer (a)** reflects the results obtained through use of a profits interest, unattainable here. **Answers (c) and (d)** both show income inclusions at the time of vesting, which is exactly what the section 83(b) election avoids.

3.4.3   **The correct Answer is (d).** As we saw in Question 3.1.2, the partnership would have to capitalize the value of the interest granted to James because of the nature of the services he is providing. Setting that requirement aside, the timing of James' compensation income and the partnership's compensation deduction would be matched. Exactly how they would be matched is a detail that is in flux. Historically, James' income has been considered a guaranteed payment, which passes through to him, as the partnership's deduction passes through to the other partners, at the end of the partnership's tax year. *See* section 706(a); Treas. Reg. § 1.721–1(b)(2). The 2005 proposed regulations would alter the traditional treatment by giving primacy to the approach of section 83, under which James includes income according to his method of accounting and the partnership takes its deduction for its year in which or with which ends James' tax year of inclusion. Treas. Reg. § 1.83–6(a)(1). The subtle difference between these two approaches can be illustrated by assuming that the tax years of all the partners, including James, end December 31 and the partnership's tax year ends June 30. (Topic 4.2 discusses how such a mismatched partnership tax year could come to pass.) All are cash method. James receives his partnership interest on October 1, 2016 and makes a section 83(b) election. Under the traditional approach, James has income, and the other partners have deductions, for their tax years ending December 31, 2017. Under the section 83 approach, James has income for his tax year ending December 31, 2016. The partnership deducts that amount and passes it through to the other partners for its year ending June 30, 2017, which gives the other partners the benefit of the deduction for their tax years ending December 31, 2017. **Answer (a)** is incorrect. As you have seen throughout this Chapter, partnerships deduct (or capitalize) the value of compensation paid to partners acting in their capacity as partners. As you will see in Topic 3.5, partnerships also deduct (or capitalize) the value of compensation paid to partners not acting in their capacity as partners. The two are not mutually exclusive. **Answers (b) and (c)** are incorrect statements of the law.

3.4.4   **The correct Answer is (a).** This is one downside of the section 83(b) election. The only loss that James could claim would be for the amount of money and the adjusted basis of any property that he transferred to the partnership in exchange for his interest—none in this case. No current or proposed rule would allow James to claim a loss with respect to the $100,000 he included as compensation income by reason of making the election. The 2005 proposed regulations, even if currently effective, would not help James. In fact, they would hurt. Because James has been allocated losses during his brief tenure as a partner, the required "forfeiture allocation" would actually be an allocation of income to him. *See* Prop. Treas. Reg. § 1.704–1(b)(4)(xii)(*c*). **Answer (b)** reflects the forfeiture allocation of income that would be made under the proposed regulations. **Answer (c)** reflects the forfeiture allocation of loss would be made under the proposed regulations if James had been allocated $32,000 of partnership income. **Answer (d)** incorrectly gives James a loss for the $100,000 of income that he included on making the section 83(b) election.

3.4.5   The correct Answer is (c). Here's how to goof up a good thing. Using the liquidation-value approach for valuing a profits interest, it is worthless (by definition) at issuance. Unfortunately, the presence of a substantial risk of forfeiture at that time pushes the date for determining James' taxation to the date of vesting. The liquidation value of James' interest is unlikely to be zero on that date, because the valuation must take into account the intervening change in the value of the partnership's property. Here, we are told that the value of James' interest at vesting is $1,150,000, so that is the amount that he must report as compensation income. **Answer (a)** would be correct if James' interest were not subject to forfeiture. **Answers (b) and (d)** use incorrect valuations for James' interest on the vesting date.

3.4.6   The correct Answer is (a). The risk of forfeiture creates the tax problem and the section 83(b) election solves it. By moving the date for valuation to the issuance date for the interest, the election restores a zero valuation, eliminating compensation income both at issuance and at vesting. This solution is so good, it would be nuts (or malpractice) not to consider it. Indeed, Rev. Proc. 2001–43, 2001–2 C.B. 191, which, in effect, treats the section 83(b) election as having been made if the partnership treats the service provider as a partner for tax purposes during the vesting period, seems based on the notion that the election should be the default rule in this case. **Answer (b)** is the best that can be achieved with a capital interest in this case. **Answer (c)** reflects over-taxation, even for a capital interest. **Answer (d)** is the result if there is no election.

3.4.7   The correct Answer is (a). Never pass up a networking opportunity. **Answer (d) is also pretty good.** Caroline's question is whether there is any downside at all in making a section 83(b) election for a nonvested profits interest. The upsides are pretty obvious. Using the liquidation-value approach for valuing her profits interest, Caroline will have no compensation income on issuance, **Answer (b)** notwithstanding. As a result of the election, she will be treated as a partner and therefore can enjoy the benefit of substantial capital-gain allocations. What can go wrong? **Answer (c)** says nothing can go wrong. **Answer (d)** anticipates the likely course of negotiations between Caroline and Mid-American. If Caroline makes the election and thus receives allocations of the partnership's income and gains, she will, of course, have to pay tax on those allocations. If she later forfeits her interest (as unthinkable as that may seem in the rosy present), she can claim no loss with respect to that tax liability, at least until forfeiture allocations become law. In other words, she will be worse off in the event of forfeiture than if she had made no election. To protect herself, she should negotiate for distributions during her vesting period that (1) are large enough to cover her tax liability on the allocated income and gains and (2) are not required to be returned to the partnership in the event of forfeiture. The partnership should be willing to go along with this request, because the income and gains that are allocated to Caroline are not allocated to the other partners. By electing, she is, in effect, agreeing to pay the other partners' tax liability on such income and gain, whether she ultimately gets to keep it or not.

3.4.8 **The correct Answers are (a), (b) and (d).** By now, you may have the idea that making a section 83(b) election is always a good idea. The STD Partnership may present a case where it is not. A section 83(b) election often requires the service provider to report compensation income before it would otherwise be due. Strike one. Moreover, if forfeiture occurs, no tax loss is allowed with respect to the amount so reported. Strike two. What can offset these potentially serious disadvantages? In the prior Questions, the partnerships held capital assets that were expected to appreciate and the service provider expected these gains to be realized for tax purposes during his or her period of ownership. By making a section 83(b) election, the service provider could enjoy capital-gains treatment with respect to gains accrued during the vesting period, which would be taxed as compensation income in the absence of an election. This tipped the balance in favor of an election in James' case, because 406 West Madison LP promised a substantial capital gain from the sale of its building. The decision was even easier for Caroline. Her private-equity partnership generated lots of capital gains. Further, she did not need to report any compensation income on making a section 83(b) election because she owned a profits interest. Roy, on the other hand, is receiving a capital interest in a partnership that is likely to produce solely ordinary income for him. Unless its business assets (including goodwill) are expected to appreciate significantly in value over Roy's three-year vesting period (and he expects the partnership to sell such assets while he is an owner), a section 83(b) election may not be worthwhile in his case.

Answers (a) and (b) identify detriments of making a section 83(b) election and **Answer (d)** identifies a possible benefit. **Answer (c)** misses the mark—a section 83(b) election cannot convert ordinary income earned by a partnership into capital gains for one of its partners.

3.5.1 **The correct Answer is (b).** The starting point is to determine whether Samantha is a partner of RB&N for tax purposes. The designation of her base pay as "salary" may suggest that she is not, but this fact is overwhelmed by her substantial participation in the profits of the partnership. Samantha is a partner, and her $300,000 profit allocation is her distributive share of partnership income. The next step is to decide whether her salary is best characterized as a section 707(a) payment or as a guaranteed payment under section 707(c). Because Samantha's work as a tax lawyer is part of the business of RB&N, the latter characterization is correct. **Answer (a)** is incorrect, because it treats Samantha's "salary" as wages. This presents two problems. First, the IRS maintains a decades-old position that a partner cannot also be an employee of the partnership. Rev. Rul. 69–184, 1969–1 C.B. 256. Second, even if this position could be overcome, a necessary first step would be to demonstrate that Samantha's salary is properly considered a section 707(a) payment. Because her services are rendered in the scope of the partnership's own business, this characterization is unlikely. **Answer (c)** is incorrect for the same reasons. **Answer (d)** is incorrect, because it reflects the wrong timing for inclusion of Samantha's distributive share under section 706(a).

3.5.2   The correct Answer is (c). In Question 3.5.1, we established that Samantha is a partner. Can she also be an "employee" for purposes of section 106, which would allow her to exclude from her income the $19,000 premium that RB&N pays for her health coverage? The IRS thinks not, and there is no authority to the contrary. Rev. Rul. 91–26, 1991–1 C.B. 184. Don't feel sorry for Samantha—section 162(*l*) will likely allow her to take the $19,000 premium as a "self-employed health insurance deduction." **Answers (a) and (b)** are incorrect, because they treat Samantha as an employee of the partnership. **Answer (d)** is incorrect, because it, in effect, allows Samantha to claim the section 106 exclusion with respect to the $19,000 premium.

3.5.3   The correct Answer is (a). We must return to the question of whether Samantha is a partner. Here, there are indications that she is: (1) she signed the partnership agreement and she may be viewed as a partner under state law; (2) she attends partner meetings; and (3) her compensation is ambiguously referred to as a "draw," a term usually reserved for a partner's compensation. One suspects, however, that these trappings were designed by human resources to make Samantha feel important. The facts remain that she does not share in partnership profits and has no role in the management of the partnership's business. Under these circumstances, Samantha is best classified as an employee of the partnership, and thus entitled to the section 106 exclusion for health coverage. **Answer (b)** correctly classifies Samantha, but fails to give her the benefit of section 106. **Answers (c) and (d)** incorrectly classify Samantha as a partner.

3.5.4   The correct Answer is (d). The issue in this Question is whether an allocation of partnership gross income can be used to circumvent section 709, which prohibits the deduction of so-called "syndication fees"—expenses to promote the sale of partnership interests. Addressing this issue (in this and other contexts) was the principal concern of Congress in enacting section 707(a)(2)(A) in 1984. It appears from the facts that Pratt Marketing is taking little entrepreneurial risk in this transaction, because (1) the contracts that will generate partnership income are already in place; (2) Pratt will be allocated gross, not net, income and will therefore not be exposed to fluctuations in partnership expenses; and (3) the three-year time period of the pay-out is relatively short, leaving less room for estimation error. Thus, under section 707(a)(2)(A), Pratt Marketing should be considered to receive a "related allocation and distribution" which, taken together, should be treated as a transaction between MAP and a service provider acting other than in its capacity as a partner. Under section 709, the partnership is not entitled to deduct its payments to Pratt Marketing. **Answer (a)** is the result avoided by the application of section 707(a)(2)(A). **Answer (b)** is incorrect, because it ignores the application of section 709. Even if the payments to Pratt Marketing were guaranteed payments, they would not automatically be deductible by the partnership. They must independently satisfy the requirements for deduction under section 162(a), which a syndication fee cannot. **Answer (c)** is not bad. In substance, it is the same as **Answer (d)**. **Answer (c)** is not quite correct, however, because Pratt Marketing is acting as an independent contractor, performing services that it renders to others, rather than as an integral part of MAP's business.

4.1.1 **The correct Answer is (b).** The guiding principle is that Sunflour must report separately to all of its partners every item that might be subject to special treatment in any partner's tax return. That can be a lot of work and, regrettably, requires an encyclopedic knowledge of the tax law. In practice, many partnerships opt for more separate reporting rather than less, so Schedules K-1 can swell from the single page suggested by the IRS form to small books with attached statements, schedules and instructions. In this relatively simple case, separate reporting is required for the section 179 expense, because the limitations on the amount that can be expensed apply at the partner level as well as the partnership level. Separate reporting is also required for the section 1231 loss, because each partner must combine it with any other section 1231 gains or losses which that partner may have incurred for the year in determining whether the partner has net section 1231 gain (taxed as capital gain) or net section 1231 loss (allowed as ordinary loss). All remaining items are lumped together under section 702(a)(8) into what is often called "bottom-line" income or loss (which, ironically, is reported on top line of Schedule K-1). **Answer (a)** is incorrect, because the deductibility of mortgage interest on business property (as opposed to personal residences) is not subject to any special limitation. **Answers (c) and (d)** are incorrect because they fail to state separately all required items.

4.1.2 **The correct Answer is (d).** Under section 702(b), we look to the partnership to determine not only the character, but the holding period, of the stock positions that Scythe sold on December 15. From the partnership's perspective these were capital assets with a long-term holding period, so that is what they are to Jack as well. It is immaterial that his holding period for his partnership interest is not yet long-term. Rev. Rul. 68–79, 1968–1 C.B. 310. Note that this is not the "aggregate answer" that would be obtained by treating Jack as the direct owner of an undivided interest in the partnership's assets. **Answers (a) and (c)** are incorrect, because they reduce Jack's gain share to one-fourth of $37,000, which is contrary to the statement in the facts that $37,000 represents Jack's share of the gain under the partnership agreement and applicable law. **Answer (b)** is incorrect, because it uses Jack's holding period, rather than the partnership's, to determine whether the partnership's gain is long-term or short-term.

4.1.3 **The correct Answer, regrettably, seems to be (d).** This Question is patterned after the facts in *Podell v. Commissioner*, 55 T.C. 429 (1970). It raises at least three issues. First, did Abe and Mort form a partnership? Although there is no written partnership agreement, it appears that they did. There are (1) co-owners, (2) engaged in a business, (3) for profit. It might be argued that the whole enterprise is eleemosynary, but that is belied by the fact that a profit was in fact made and Mort and Abe could do with it what they wanted. Second, what was the character of the gains generated by this partnership? Here, the Tax Court in *Podell* was perhaps a bit uncharitable itself. It found that the partnership was formed "for the purpose of purchasing, renovating, and selling certain residential real estate in the ordinary course of trade or business." This finding meant that the townhouses were not capital assets under section 1221(a)(1) and the gains from selling them were taxable as ordinary income. Under section 702(b), this characterization carried over to Abe and Mort. This may come as a particular surprise to Abe, who did not do anything but give his friend money. Yet it is the partnership's activities, not Abe's, that determine the character of the gains in Abe's hands. Perhaps the Tax Court would have decided the case differently if the partnership had been a bit less successful and renovated only one or two properties as capital assets. Finally, what was the nature of Mort's partnership interest—was it a capital interest or a profits interest? If the former, Mort would have $100,000 of compensation income (and a $100,000 capital account) on formation and the partnership would be entitled to capitalize a like amount into the basis of the renovated townhouses. This would reduce its $90,000 gain on the sale of the townhouses to a $10,000 loss. It seems relatively clear, however, that Mort's interest was simply in the profits, if any, earned by this well-meaning venture. **Answer (a)** is incorrect, because this partnership generates income that is not tax-exempt. **Answer (b)** reflects two errors. First, it treats Mort's interest as a capital interest. Second, it treats the townhouses as capital assets in the hands of the partnership. **Answer (c)** is incorrect, because it too treats the townhouses as capital assets.

4.2.1   The correct Answer is (a). From afar, it appears that roughly 20% of InSight's members have taxable years ending in each of March, September, October, November and December. If minimizing aggregate deferral were the single-minded goal of section 706(b), it might not matter much which of these months were chosen as the required taxable year-end and, indeed, it might be fine to allow any of them. In order to be confident of this conclusion, however, one would need to collect information regarding the interest and taxable year of every InSight member. In its effort to achieve a degree of simplicity, the "waterfall" of section 706(b)(1)(B) takes a more mechanical approach. It asks first if there is a "majority interest taxable year." Here, there is not. In the absence of a single taxable year representing more than 50% of partnership capital and profits, it asks next whether all of the principal partners have the same taxable year. Here there is only one partner holding an interest of at least five percent, and its taxable year ends March 31. At that point, we stop. The partnership's required taxable year is March 31. **Answers (b)**, **(c)** or **(d)** might result from a careful application of the "least aggregate deferral" test, but because InSight satisfies a test higher up the waterfall, the least-aggregate-deferral test is inapplicable.

4.2.2   The correct Answer is (b). The facts in this case do not satisfy either the majority-interest rule or the all-principal-partners rule. (There are two principal partners, and they do not have the same taxable year.) The least-aggregate-deferral test thus applies, but its application is unusually simple here. If the partnership choses as its taxable year the taxable year of Corp X, Corp X will have no deferral and Corp Y will have seven months of deferral (April through October). If the partnership choses as its taxable year the taxable year of Corp Y, Corp Y will have no deferral and Corp X will have five months of deferral (November through March). Because Corp X and Corp Y have equal interests, the least aggregate deferral will be achieved if the partnership adopts the taxable year of Corp Y, ending in October. **Answer (a)** is incorrect, because it is the taxable year of Corp X, which would result in slightly greater aggregate deferral. **Answer (c)** is incorrect, because under the least-aggregate-deferral test the required taxable year of the partnership must be the taxable year of at least one of the partners. Treas. Reg. § 1.706–1(b)(3)(i). **Answer (d)** is incorrect, because an October year-end results in slightly less aggregate deferral than a March year-end.

4.2.3 **The correct Answer is (c).** As in the preceding Question, there is no majority interest taxable year or taxable year shared by all of the principal partners. Thus, the least-aggregate-deferral test applies, and you must run the numbers. They follow:

Partner	% Interest	Taxable Year	Months of Deferral if Partnership Taxable Year Is:			% Interest × Months if Partnership Taxable Year Is:		
			Oct.	June	Dec.	Oct.	June	Dec.
Corp Q	0.42	Oct.	0	4	10	0	1.68	4.20
Corp R	0.42	June	8	0	6	3.36	0	2.52
Corp S	0.16	Dec.	2	6	0	0.32	0.96	0
Aggregate Deferral						3.68	2.64	6.72

The computation is straightforward, but it may be worth pausing on the determination of the months of deferral. When the partnership's taxable year and the partner's taxable year coincide, there is zero deferral. In every other case, the months of deferral equal the number of months between the beginning of the partnership's taxable year (or, more accurately, the end of the partnership's preceding year), when income is first earned that will be deferred into the following year, and the end of the partner's taxable year, when the deferral stops. Always count "forward" from the partnership's year-end to the partner's year-end. Treas. Reg. § 1.706–1(b)(3)(i) (last sentence). If you get confused, you can always draw a picture like the one in the essay that begins this Topic. **Answers (a), (b) and (d)** are incorrect, because they are inconsistent with the foregoing calculation.

4.2.4 **The correct Answer is (c).** The required taxable year ends in December, because that is the majority interest taxable year. There are two possible ways that the Cheese Factory could have a different taxable year. First, it might elect a year other than the required taxable year under section 444 and make the necessary payments under section 7519. Under section 444(b)(2), however, a partnership that has already established a taxable year cannot elect a taxable year that would produce greater deferral than the existing year. Because every other year would entail greater deferral than a year ending in December, the Cheese Factory cannot avail itself of the section 444 election. Second, the Cheese Factory could attempt to establish a business purpose for a new taxable year under section 706(b)(1)(C). This, too, is unlikely to succeed. As explained in Situation 2 of Rev. Rul. 87–57, saving accounting fees is not a business purpose, but merely a "convenience" to the taxpayer. (Said differently, if that worked, everybody would do it, and the concept of a required taxable year would simply disappear.) More promising is the possibility that the Cheese Factory has a natural business cycle that ends sometime other than December 31. This is illustrated in Situation 7 of Rev. Rul. 87–57 and the "natural business year" concept is found in revenue procedures granting permission for automatic changes to that year. *See, e.g.,* Rev. Proc. 2006–46, 2006–2 C.B. 859, § 5.07. Unfortunately, the Cheese Factory's natural business cycle seems to end on December 31, when annual sales have concluded and the company shuts down for a mid-winter snooze. **Answer (a)** is incorrect. It reflects the result that would be available under section 444(b)(1) if the company had not yet established its taxable year. **Answer (b)** is incorrect, because February is the end of the period of dormancy for the company, which is not the end of its natural business year. **Answer (d)** is incorrect, because it includes all of these incorrect answers.

4.3.1   The correct Answer is (a). The first step in answering this Question is to decide which allocations must be tested. It's tempting to think that the annual allocations of operating loss are immune from challenge under section 704(b)(2), because they are proportional to the partners' capital contributions and therefore are in accord with the partners' interests in the partnership. But it's not that easy—or maybe it's easier. Once the first allocation of depreciation is made (100% to Caden), the capital accounts are no longer proportional to the initial capital contributions, and neither are the partners' economic interests in the partnership. Accordingly, all of this partnership's allocations must be tested for substantial economic effect. In this case, all three of the elements of the safe harbor for economic effect are present and there is nothing to indicate that substantiality is an issue. The allocations provided in the partnership agreement are respected for tax purposes.

The opening balance sheet of the partnership looks like this:

Assets			Liabilities		
	Tax	Book		Tax	Book
Cash	$100,000	$100,000	Bank Debt	$500,000	$500,000
Building	500,000	500,000			
			Capital		
			Aiden	25,000	25,000
			Brayden	25,000	25,000
			Caden	50,000	50,000
Total Assets	$600,000	$600,000	**Total Liabilities and Capital**	$600,000	$600,000

Each year, the operating loss of the partnership reduces its cash holding by $20,000 and depreciation reduces the tax basis and the book value of the building by $20,000. The amount of the bank debt does not change, so, in order to preserve the accounting identity that Assets = Liabilities + Capital, the capital accounts of the partners are reduced by an aggregate of $40,000, allocated as provided in the partnership agreement. At the end of three years, the balance sheet looks like this:

Assets			Liabilities		
	Tax	Book		Tax	Book
Cash	$ 40,000	$ 40,000	Bank Debt	$500,000	$500,000
Building	440,000	440,000			
			Capital		
			Aiden	10,000	10,000
			Brayden	10,000	10,000
			Caden	(40,000)	(40,000)
Total Assets	$480,000	$480,000	**Total Liabilities and Capital**	$480,000	$480,000

The year-by-year capital-account adjustments are as follows:

		Aiden	Brayden	Caden
Initial Capital Acc't		$25,000	$25,000	$50,000
Year 1	Operating Loss	(5,000)	(5,000)	(10,000)
	Depreciation	(0)	(0)	(20,000)
End of Year 1		20,000	20,000	20,000
Year 2	Operating Loss	(5,000)	(5,000)	(10,000)
	Depreciation	(0)	(0)	(20,000)
End of Year 2		15,000	15,000	(10,000)
Year 3	Operating Loss	(5,000)	(5,000)	(10,000)
	Depreciation	(0)	(0)	(20,000)
End of Year 3		10,000	10,000	(40,000)
Total Allocated		($15,000)	($15,000)	($90,000)

If the partnership liquidates at the end of its third year, Caden will owe $40,000 pursuant to his deficit-restoration obligation. That amount, added to the $480,000 book value of the partnership's assets, will give it $520,000. From the latter amount, the partnership will pay $500,000 to the bank to retire the debt and $10,000 to each of Aiden and Brayden to return to them the positive balances in their capital accounts.

Over the three-year life of the partnership, Caden will be allocated $90,000 of loss and deduction, while Aiden and Caden together will be allocated $30,000 of loss. Caden's special allocation of $60,000 depreciation will cost him $60,000 in cash—$40,000 in the form of a deficit-restoration payment and $20,000 in forgone liquidating distributions. In this manner, Caden bears the economic burden corresponding to the special allocation of depreciation.

4.3.2   The correct Answer is (b). In this Question, the partners have modified their economic deal slightly. No partner has an obligation to restore a deficit balance in his capital account, to the extent that it would be used to pay another partner. Let's use what we know about partnership accounting to understand the nature of this agreement. Assets = Liabilities + Capital. Therefore, if a partnership in liquidation has satisfied all of its liabilities and in so doing has exhausted all of its assets (including perhaps amounts contributed by the partners to cover payments to creditors), then its aggregate capital must be zero. 0 = 0 + 0. This does not mean, however, that each partner's capital account must be zero—they must simply sum to zero. It may be that one partner has a positive capital account and another has a negative capital account of the same amount. In Question 4.3.1, the partners' unlimited deficit-restoration obligation would require the partner with the negative capital account to contribute that amount to the partnership so that it could be distributed to the partner with the positive capital account. In this Question 4.3.2, that is not the deal. Each partner has agreed to take the risk that he will receive nothing if the partnership has no assets remaining after paying its creditors, even if he has a positive balance in his capital account.

It is significant that state law permits the partners to limit their obligations in this manner. If it did not, the greater obligation under state law would be controlling, not only for purposes of determining the partners' real economic exposure to the partnership, but also for the analysis of the economic effect of its tax allocations. Under Treas. Reg. § 1.704–1(b)(2)(ii)(*h*) (fourth sentence), the "partnership agreement" includes all provisions of federal, state or local law that govern the affairs of the partnership.

What difference does this new economic deal make in the allocation of the partnership's losses and deductions? In the absence of an unconditional obligation to restore deficits, this partnership is out of the general safe harbor and must rely on the alternate test for economic effect. For further discussion, see Rev. Rul. 97–38, 1997–2 C.B. 69.

Caden can take allocations of losses until his capital account reaches zero, which occurs in year 2, when an allocation of only half of the annual depreciation exhausts his capital account:

		Aiden	Brayden	Caden
Initial Capital Acc't		$25,000	$25,000	$50,000
Year 1	Operating Loss	(5,000)	(5,000)	(10,000)
	Depreciation	(0)	(0)	(20,000)
End of Year 1		20,000	20,000	20,000
Year 2	Operating Loss	(5,000)	(5,000)	(10,000)
	½ Depreciation	(0)	(0)	(10,000)
	½ Depreciation	?	?	?

The remaining $10,000 of depreciation for year 2 must be allocated in accordance with the partners' interests in the partnership. Here, you may be tempted to conclude that 25% should be allocated to each of Aiden and Brayden and 50% to Caden. That is not right. To see why, try applying the comparative-liquidation test. At the end of year 1, the partnership's balance sheet looks like this:

Assets			Liabilities		
	Tax	**Book**		**Tax**	**Book**
Cash	$ 80,000	$ 80,000	Bank Debt	$500,000	$500,000
Building	480,000	480,000			
			Capital		
			Aiden	20,000	20,000
			Brayden	20,000	20,000
			Caden	20,000	20,000
Total Assets	$560,000	$560,000	**Total Liabilities and Capital**	$560,000	$560,000

If depreciation is allocated as suggested above, the partnership's balance sheet will look like this at the end of year 2:

Assets			Liabilities		
	Tax	**Book**		**Tax**	**Book**
Cash	$ 60,000	$ 60,000	Bank Debt	$500,000	$500,000
Building	460,000	460,000			
			Capital		
			Aiden	12,500	12,500
			Brayden	12,500	12,500
			Caden	(5,000)	(5,000)
Total Assets	$520,000	$520,000	**Total Liabilities and Capital**	$520,000	$520,000

If the partnership sells its assets for book value and liquidates at the end of year 2, it will have enough cash to repay the bank with $20,000 left over. Presumably, it will distribute this equally to Aiden and Brayden, leaving them each with a $2,500 positive capital-account balance. And that's where it ends, if Caden has no obligation to restore his deficit balance. Caden has not borne the economic burden of the last $5,000 of depreciation that the partnership allocated to him. It has been borne by Aiden and Brayden, who will never receive the last $5,000 ($2,500 each) in their capital accounts. To avoid this result, the Treasury regulations require the partnership to allocate the final $10,000 of depreciation in year 2 entirely to Aiden and Brayden, because they together have 100% of the economic interest in that deduction.

Indeed, the partnership must continue to allocate 100% of its losses and deductions to Aiden and Brayden until their capital accounts are exhausted. At that point, the capital accounts of all of the partners equal zero, and something magical happens. A deficit-restoration obligation springs to life for Caden as well as each of the other partners. The next dollar of loss or deduction will be attributable to the partnership's debt, and all three partners are obligated to restore deficit balances in their capital accounts in order to pay off that debt. Supported by that obligation, Caden can once again take the depreciation deductions called for by the partnership agreement:

		Aiden	Brayden	Caden
Initial Capital Acc't		$25,000	$25,000	$50,000
Year 1	Operating Loss	(5,000)	(5,000)	(10,000)
	Depreciation	(0)	(0)	(20,000)
End of Year 1		20,000	20,000	20,000
Year 2	Operating Loss	(5,000)	(5,000)	(10,000)
	Depreciation	(5,000)	(5,000)	(10,000)
End of Year 2		10,000	10,000	0
Year 3	Operating Loss	(10,000)	(10,000)	(0)
	Depreciation	(0)	(0)	(20,000)
End of Year 3		0	0	(20,000)
Total Allocated		($25,000)	($25,000)	($70,000)

At the end of year 3, the partnership's balance sheet looks like this:

Assets			**Liabilities**		
	Tax	Book		Tax	Book
Cash	$ 40,000	$ 40,000	Bank Debt	$500,000	$500,000
Building	440,000	440,000			
			Capital		
			Aiden	0	0
			Brayden	0	0
			Caden	(20,000)	(20,000)
Total Assets	$480,000	$480,000	**Total Liabilities and Capital**	$480,000	$480,000

If the partnership liquidates at this point, Caden will owe the partnership $20,000. That amount, added to the $480,000 book value of the partnership's assets, will be just enough to repay the bank debt. Aiden and Brayden are owed nothing.

4.3.3   The correct Answer is (d). Here, Cayden has no deficit-restoration obligation imposed either by state law or under the partnership agreement. As a result, the total allocation of losses and deductions to him cannot exceed his positive capital account under the alternate test. The year-by-year allocations are as follows:

		Aiden	Brayden	Caden
Initial Capital Acc't		$25,000	$25,000	$50,000
Year 1	Operating Loss	(5,000)	(5,000)	(10,000)
	Depreciation	(0)	(0)	(20,000)
End of Year 1		20,000	20,000	20,000
Year 2	Operating Loss	(5,000)	(5,000)	(10,000)
	Depreciation	(5,000)	(5,000)	(10,000)
End of Year 2		10,000	10,000	0
Year 3	Operating Loss	(10,000)	(10,000)	(0)
	Depreciation	(10,000)	(10,000)	(0)
End of Year 3		(10,000)	(10,000)	0
Total Allocated		($35,000)	($35,000)	($50,000)

4.3.4   The correct Answer is (d). It seems a shame that a foot-fault in the drafting of the partnership agreement could prevent Caden from receiving special allocations of losses or deductions that are fully supported by amounts in his capital account. Much to the relief of the drafter, that is not the result here. Using the comparative-liquidation test of Treas. Reg. § 1.704–1(b)(3)(iii), you can see that Caden will bear the economic burden of losses and deductions allocated to him while his capital account is still positive. Such allocations are therefore in accord with Caden's interest in the partnership and should be respected. This ceases when Caden's capital account reaches zero, resulting in the same allowable pattern of deductions as the alternate test in this case.

4.3.5   The correct Answer is (a). This is a classic partnership by shares—a partnership that allocates profit and loss in the same proportions as capital. Under section 704, the allocations provided in the partnership agreement will be respected unless they do not have substantial economic effect. Plainly, this partnership fails to satisfy the safe harbor for economic effect. What then? There are two ways to analyze this situation, both leading to the same conclusion.

First, imagine that this partnership met the safe harbor, in that it maintained capital accounts that governed liquidations and contained an unconditional deficit-restoration obligation for all partners. How would the allocations in such a partnership be different than the ones provided for here? A few moments thought should persuade you that they would not be different at all. With losses allocated proportionally to the capital contributions, the partners' capital accounts all reach zero at the same time, at which point the joint and several liability of state law provides a deficit-restoration obligation to support the remaining allocations. Under the economic-effect equivalence test of Treas. Reg. § 1.704–1(b)(2)(ii)(*i*), sometimes called the "dumb but lucky" test, the proportional allocations provided by this partnership agreement should therefore be deemed to have economic effect.

Alternatively, and more simply, assume that the allocations provided in this partnership agreement do not have economic effect. In such case, section 704(b)(2) requires allocations in accordance with the partners' interests in the partnership. What are those? With capital, profits and losses all in lock-step proportions, there can be no doubt that these proportions measure the interests of the three partners.

Can anything go wrong? If future capital contributions or distributions change the proportions of the capital accounts and the partnership does not make a corresponding change to the profit and loss shares, then the preceding analysis will no longer apply. For this reason, it might be prudent for the partnership agreement explicitly to link profit and loss shares to capital shares or, if that is not the economic deal that the partners have made, to spend more time with the tax provisions in the partnership agreement.

4.3.6   The correct Answer is (a). Under the shifting test, the economic effect of special allocations is not substantial if there is a strong likelihood that (1) the allocations will not substantially affect the net changes in the capital-account balances of the affected partners for the year at issue, and (2) the aggregate tax liability of those partners will be reduced. The allocations of a disproportionate amount of tax-exempt interest to Gabriel and a disproportionate amount of taxable interest to Peter will be reflected in their respective capital accounts. The trouble is, the effect on their capital accounts would be exactly the same if they had each received their proportionate shares of both types of income. In addition, the special allocations will reduce the aggregate tax liability of Gabriel and Peter, because Gabriel, who receives a disproportionate amount of tax-exempt interest, is in a higher tax bracket than Peter. The special allocations thus fail the shifting test and do not have substantial economic effect. **Answer (b)** is incorrect, because the overall-tax-effect test requires that the special allocations make no partner worse off on an after-tax basis. Plainly, Peter is worse off because of these special allocations. **Answer (c)** is incorrect, because the transitory test applies only to multi-year special allocations, not to those that occur in a single year. **Answer (d)** is incorrect, because the shifting test is not satisfied.

4.3.7   I think the correct Answer is (d). Although these special allocations do not affect the net changes in Gabriel's and Peter's capital accounts, they also do not reduce their tax liability in the aggregate, because Gabriel and Peter are now in the same tax bracket. Accordingly, the shifting test is not violated, and **Answer (a)** is incorrect. **Answer (b)** is incorrect, because Peter is worse off. The pre-tax-effect test referenced in **Answer (c)**

presents the only viable challenge to these special allocations. Under the pre-tax-effect test, in order for the economic effect of an allocation to be substantial, there must be a reasonable possibility that the allocation will affect substantially the dollar amounts to be received by the partners, tax consequences aside. Arcadia's special allocations will not have this effect, because they will not cause adjustments to the partners' capital accounts that are any different than those that would have been made anyway. Thus, if the pre-tax-effect test is an independent test of substantiality, the special allocations do not have substantial economic effect and **Answer (c)** is correct. If, on the other hand, the pre-tax-effect test is not an independent test, **Answer (c)** is incorrect. What do you think?

4.3.8   The correct Answer is (d). The biggest mistake that students make with the substantiality tests is to apply them more broadly than they should. The facts of this Question suggest a subtle, tax-driven plan to allocate early taxable income to the low-bracket partner and later taxable income to the high-bracket partner. In this way, it is reminiscent of the Goldome scheme (so named for one of the participants in an early series of these transactions) described in Treas. Reg. § 1.704–1(b)(5), example (9). The critical difference here, however, is that Arcadia and its partners have no assurance regarding the amounts of taxable interest income to be received in any of the next six years. Given that lack of knowledge, the special allocations represent a risky business deal in which the high-bracket partner is forgoing her share of taxable interest income for the first three years in hopes of receiving at least an equal and hopefully greater amount during the next three. **Answer (a)** is incorrect, because the shifting test does not apply to multi-year special allocations. **Answer (b)** is incorrect, because there is not a "strong likelihood" that neither partner will be worse off on a present-value, after-tax basis as a result of the special allocations. **Answer (c)** is incorrect, because there is not a "strong likelihood" that the special allocations will not have a meaningful effect on the capital accounts of the affected partners.

4.3.9   The correct Answer is (d) in my opinion. With the changed facts, we now know that Arcadia's stream of taxable interest income is constant on an annual basis. Thus, the excess amount that each of the two affected partners will receive for three years will be exactly offset by the deficit amount for the other three years. This seems the ideal case to apply the transitory test. **Answer (a)** is incorrect, however, for the simple reason that the transitory test does not have a present-value component. Ignoring time value, front-loading taxable income to the low-bracket taxpayer does not create a tax advantage. This is a silly conclusion, of course, but it appears to be the answer under the transitory test as written. **Answer (b)** is incorrect, because it does not appear from the facts of this Question that the low-bracket partner is compensated in any manner for agreeing to take an early allocation of taxable income. Thus, she is worse off on an after-tax, present-value basis if her tax rate is higher than zero, and this fails to satisfy the requirement of the overall-tax-effect test that no partner be worse off. Contrast Treas. Reg. § 1.708–1(b)(5), example (9), where the low-bracket partner is compensated through the crediting of interest on its capital account, and the overall-tax-effect test is found to apply. **Answer (c)** invokes the pre-tax-effect test, which once again is the last and only hope. There does not seem to be a reasonable possibility that Arcadia's special allocations will affect substantially the dollar amounts to be received by the affected partners, independent of tax consequences. So, **Answer (c)** is correct if the pre-tax-effect test is an independent test, and incorrect if it is not.

4.3.10   **The correct Answer is (b).** The facts of this Question state that the chargeback of depreciation specially allocated to Bianca in years 1 through 5 will occur ratably from income in years 6 through 15. In other words, the special allocation of each year's depreciation in the earlier period will be offset by a special allocation of income from two years in the later period. For purposes of applying the five-year presumption, we are to assume that this offset takes place on a first-in, first-out basis. Therefore, the specially allocated depreciation from year 1 is deemed to be offset by the specially allocated income from year 6 and year 7, and so forth as follows:

Depreciation	Income
Year 1	Year 6
	Year 7
Year 2	Year 8
	Year 9
Year 3	Year 10
	Year 11
Year 4	Year 12
	Year 13
Year 5	Year 14
	Year 15

There are two interpretative questions. First, the five-year presumption requires there be a strong likelihood that the income allocations will not "in large part" be made within five years of the depreciation allocations. Half of the depreciation for year 1 will be offset in year 6 (within five years) and half in year 7 (beyond five years). Does 50% constitute a "large part" for this purpose? The Treasury regulation provides no answer. The second interpretative question is whether the special allocations stand or fall as a whole, rather than year-by-year. In this case, an affirmative answer to the second question produces an easy answer to the first. Viewed as a whole, only 10% of the special allocations of depreciation will be offset within five years and 90%—clearly a "large part"—will not be. An example in the regulation suggests (but does not clearly state) that this is the appropriate analysis. Treas. Reg. § 1.704–1(b)(5), example (2).

Answer (a) is incorrect, and it is important to understand why. You might think that the value-equals-basis presumption protects all special allocations of depreciation from a substantiality challenge. It does not. It only protects depreciation which is to be offset by a chargeback of gain from the sale of the depreciated property. Here, the chargeback of income is from the partnership's lease of the depreciated property—there is no suggestion in the facts that Cloudeez intends to dispose of the network servers or that it could expect to realize a gain if it did so. **Answer (c)** is incorrect for two reasons. First, the five-year presumption does apply. Second, even if it did not, the transitory test would not present a problem here, due to its failure to incorporate time value into its analysis of aggregate tax savings. **Answer (d)** is incorrect, but interesting. It is entirely possible that the five-year presumption does not cover the overall-tax-effect test. The language of the presumption states that it applies to the transitory test and the pre-tax-effect test and is silent regarding the overall-tax-effect test. Even so, there are no facts in this Question to show that the overall-tax-effect test is not satisfied. In particular, there is no mention of compensation to any of the other partners for the special allocation of a tax benefit to Bianca. Without more, this suggests that they are worse off on an after-tax, present-value basis, causing the overall-tax-effect test to be satisfied.

4.3.11 **The correct Answer is (b).** An allocation of the character of gain (*e.g.*, capital gain vs. recapture income) cannot have economic effect, because, like all character allocations, it does not affect the capital-account balances. The regulations under section 1245 avoid a potentially difficult substantiality analysis by providing a rule in this case. Under Treas. Reg. § 1.1245–1(e)(2)(i), the partnership must allocate recapture income to Mikayla equal to the lesser of (1) the amount of depreciation previously allocated to her or (2) her share of the gain on sale of the asset. If the partnership agreement provides otherwise, its allocation must be corrected. Here, the partnership agreement provides an allocation of gain, but not of character. Total recapture income is $26,000, which equals the prior depreciation, and the total gain on sale is $38,000. Mikayla has been allocated $26,000 of depreciation and her share of the gain on sale is $19,000. Applying Treas. Reg. § 1.1245–1(e)(2)(i), she must be allocated $19,000 of the $26,000 of recapture income and the remaining $7,000 goes to Miles. **Answer (a)** is incorrect, because it allocates more recapture income to Makayla than she has gain. **Answer (c)** is incorrect, because it represents the allocation of the partnership's entire gain, not its recapture income. **Answer (d)** is incorrect, because it splits the recapture income equally between Mikayla and Miles, violating Treas. Reg. § 1.1245–1(e)(2)(i).

4.4.1 **The correct Answer is (c).** Because this partnership has made no distributions, the aggregate amount of its nonrecourse deductions is simply the overall increase in the amount of the minimum gain. Minimum gain was zero at the outset ($200,000 debt less $200,000 adjusted basis of plant and equipment) and it is $54,000 at the beginning of 2017 ($200,000 debt less $146,000 adjusted basis). The partnership agreement calls for the $54,000 of nonrecourse deductions to be allocated 20% (or $10,800) to Aidy and 80% (or $43,200) to Bo. This allocation should be respected under the safe harbor of Treas. Reg. § 1.704–2(e). The various provisions required to be included in the partnership agreement are all there, and the significant item consistency test does not seem to be a problem, because all losses and deductions will be allocated in the same proportions, regardless of whether they are funded by nonrecourse debt or by the partner's capital. **Answer (a)** is incorrect. It confuses equity in the partnership with equity in the encumbered property. Here, the plant and equipment are entirely debt-financed—they have zero equity at the outset. The partnership, by contrast, has $50,000 of equity. The first dollar of depreciation on the plant and equipment creates a dollar of minimum gain and therefore of nonrecourse deduction, despite the fact that the partnership still has plenty of capital. **Answer (b)** caps the amount of deductions available to Aidy and Bo at the amount of their initial capital contributions. This would be a relevant limitation, at least for Bo, if nonrecourse deductions were required to have substantial economic effect, but they are not. **Answer (d)** reflects an incorrect reading of the partnership agreement.

As you can see from the balance sheet, as of the end of 2016, the partnership has incurred a net loss of $50,000—coincidently, exactly the amount of its original equity. Of that amount, $54,000 was nonrecourse deductions. This must mean that the partnership had net income, excluding nonrecourse deductions, of $4,000.

4.4.2   The correct Answer is (d). The remaining Answers list the counter-arguments. **Answer (a)** suggests that the allocations of both nonrecourse deductions and other losses are limited by the alternate test and that both fail this test. The first proposition is wrong: nonrecourse deductions do not have economic effect and cannot be limited by tests of substantial economic effect. The allocation of the other losses ($9,000) is subject to the alternate test but, in fact, it passes that test. This may seem peculiar, given that Bo has no deficit-restoration obligation and his capital account balance is zero. Denying him these losses would be harsh, however, given that he contributed $40,000 of capital to the partnership and the only reason that his capital account is zero is that he has been allocated $43,200 of nonrecourse deductions (along with $3,200 of income). Treas. Reg. § 1.704–2(g)(1) addresses this situation, by allowing Bo to treat his share of partnership minimum gain as a deficit-restoration obligation. Therefore, under the alternate test, Bo can be allocated up to $43,200 of losses with economic effect in 2017. In addition to being Bo's share of partnership minimum gain, this figure equals the sum of his initial capital contribution ($40,000) plus his share of pre-2017 partnership income ($3,200). **Answer (b)** is subsumed by **Answer (a)** and is incorrect.

Answer (c) raises the significant item consistency test—that is, whether the 20:80 allocation of nonrecourse deductions between Aidy and Bo is "reasonably consistent with allocations that have substantial economic effect of some other significant partnership item attributable to the property securing the nonrecourse liabilities." It is always a little hard to tell when that test has been satisfied—interpretative problems abound. One glib answer is that *all* items of the partnership's income, gain, loss and deduction will be allocated in the same 20:80 proportions until overall breakeven is achieved, so that the requirement of a significant allocation in those proportions is by definition satisfied. More cautiously, one might ask whether the 20:80 allocations that have substantial economic effect are expected to be significant in magnitude. Here, it seems enough that Aidy and Bo have exposed $50,000 of capital (one-fifth of the partnership's total funding) to 20:80 allocations. If their capital contributions were much smaller (that is, if the ratio of the partnership's contributed capital to its nonrecourse debt were much smaller), there would be room for concern. *See* Treas. Reg. § 1.704–2(m), example (1) (20% equity okay).

4.4.3   The correct Answer is (b). The equipment loan is nonrecourse from the perspective of the partnership, but Bo bears the risk of loss as guarantor. Thus it is a partner nonrecourse debt. As in the prior Questions, there is no equity in the plant or in the equipment, so minimum gain and thus nonrecourse deductions are present from the first dollar of depreciation. Here, however, the depreciation on the equipment is a partner nonrecourse deduction, allocable entirely to Bo. The depreciation on the plant is a partnership nonrecourse deduction, allocable under the partnership agreement 20% to Aidy and 80% to Bo. Accordingly, Bo's allocation of nonrecourse deductions is $42,000 (equipment) plus $9,600 (plant) or $51,600. Aidy's allocation is $0 (equipment) plus $2,400 (plant) or $2,400. **Answer (a)** is incorrect, because nonrecourse deductions exist, even though Aidy and Bo each have positive capital. **Answer (c)** in incorrect, as it reflects the allocation of nonrecourse deductions that would exist in the absence of Bo's guarantee. **Answer (d)** is incorrect, because the allocation of nonrecourse deductions, even partner nonrecourse deductions, is not limited by the alternate test.

4.4.4   The correct Answer is (b). The debt repayment decreases amount of the nonrecourse debt to $120,000, which is less than the $146,000 adjusted basis of the plant and equipment. The partnership minimum gain thus decreases from $54,000 to zero, which results in a minimum-gain chargeback of $54,000. This chargeback is made in accordance with the partners' respective shares of partnership minimum gain, which are $10,800 for Aidy (20%) and $43,200 for Bo (80%). The remainder of the partnership's income for 2017 ($80,000 less $54,000, or $26,000) is allocated in accordance with the partnership agreement, which provides for an equal split after overall breakeven. That has now occurred, as the total income allocated in the 20:80 proportion ($54,000) now exceeds the total losses ($50,000) allocated in that proportion. Therefore, the remaining income is allocated $13,000 each to Aidy and Bo. Their total income allocations for 2017 are $23,800 ($10,800 plus $13,000) for Aidy and $56,200 ($43,200 plus $13,000) for Bo. **Answer (a)** is incorrect, because it fails to follow the partnership agreement and allocates the entire 2017 income in the 20:80 proportion. **Answer (c)** is incorrect, because it neglects the minimum gain chargeback, applying the partnership agreement alone to allocate the first $50,000 of income (equal to prior net losses) in the 20:80 ratio and the remainder equally. **Answer (d)** is incorrect and it is important to understand why. **Answer (d)** treats total 2017 income as being $54,000 (minimum gain chargeback) plus $80,000 (partnership income) or $134,000. The minimum gain chargeback is not an independent source of income. Instead, like any chargeback, it is merely a requirement that income or gain, when realized, must be allocated to the partners in a particular manner.

4.4.5   The correct Answer is (b). The $80,000 loan in this case is nonrecourse to Computek. It is secured not by any single asset, but by a lien on all of the assets. The adjusted basis of those assets is now $40,000 which, compared to the $80,000 principal amount of the debt, yields minimum gain of $40,000. Just before Conrad arrives on the scene, Computek's balance sheet (expanded to show the fair market value of the assets) looks like this:

Assets				Liabilities		
	Tax	Book	FMV		Tax	Book
Assets	$40,000	$40,000	$120,000	Bank Debt	$ 80,000	$ 80,000
				Capital		
				Axel	(20,000)	(20,000)
				Bebe	(20,000)	(20,000)
Total Assets	$40,000	$40,000	$120,000	Total Liabilities and Capital	$ 40,000	$ 40,000

The revaluation changes the book value of the assets and the partners' book capital accounts, as follows:

Assets				Liabilities		
	Tax	Book	FMV		Tax	Book
Assets	$40,000	$120,000	$120,000	Bank Debt	$ 80,000	$ 80,000
				Capital		
				Axel	(20,000)	20,000
				Bebe	(20,000)	20,000
Total Assets	$40,000	$120,000	$120,000	Total Liabilities and Capital	$ 40,000	$120,000

There is now a disparity between the adjusted tax basis and the book values of Computek's assets. In these circumstances, Treas. Reg. § 1.704–2(d)(3) directs us to use the book values to determine, among other things, partnership minimum gain. It appears that, by reason of the revaluation alone, partnership minimum gain has decreased to zero, because the book value of the assets ($120,000) exceeds the amount of the nonrecourse debt ($80,000). Ordinarily, this would require a minimum gain chargeback of $40,000. Treas. Reg. § 1.704–2(d)(4) calls off this chargeback, by eliminating the decrease in partnership minimum gain arising from the revaluation. This is not as crazy as it may sound. The $40,000 tax gain is still there, as you can see by comparing the adjusted tax basis of the assets ($40,000) with the nonrecourse debt ($80,000). As you will see in Topic 8.5, which discusses the application of section 704(c) to so-called "reverse layers" created by a revaluation, Axel and Bebe, and not Conrad, will be responsible for this tax gain when the partnership realizes it.

Now Conrad joins Computek and his capital contribution of $20,000 is used to pay down a like amount of the debt. The balance sheet is now:

Assets				Liabilities		
	Tax	**Book**	**FMV**		**Tax**	**Book**
Assets	$40,000	$120,000	$120,000	Bank Debt	$ 60,000	$ 60,000
				Capital		
				Axel	(20,000)	20,000
				Bebe	(20,000)	20,000
				Conrad	20,000	20,000
Total Assets	$40,000	$120,000	$120,000	**Total Liabilities and Capital**	$ 40,000	$120,000

Again, partnership minimum gain has decreased, this time by $20,000 due to the loan repayment. And this time, a minimum gain chargeback is required, allocated $10,000 to Axel and $10,000 to Bebe in accordance with their shares of the minimum gain. The exception for capital contributions provided by Treas. Reg. § 1.704–2(f)(3) is no help, because the capital contribution is made by Conrad, a partner who has no share of partnership minimum gain.

Answer (a) is incorrect, although it would be right if the exception for capital contributions applied in this case. **Answer (c)** is incorrect, because it treats the revaluation as giving rise to a $40,000 decrease in partnership minimum gain. **Answer (d)** is incorrect. It recaptures all $60,000 of prior losses and deductions allocated to Axel and Bebe, a result that is not required by any construction of the minimum gain chargeback.

4.4.6   The correct Answer is (c). The $20 million loan is described in the facts as "recourse" to Eagle Ridge, meaning that the lender's rights are not limited to any particular asset of Eagle Ridge, but instead extend to all of its assets which may be reached in an insolvency or bankruptcy proceeding. Nevertheless, the members themselves have no personal responsibility for this debt. It is thus a so-called "exculpatory liability." The treatment of these loans is not entirely clear under current law. They are clearly treated as nonrecourse loans under section 704(b) and for that purpose are probably best thought of as being secured by all of Eagle Ridge's assets, including the office building and any other asset it may own. Depreciation of the office building, as well as other losses, will create nonrecourse deductions as the aggregate adjusted basis of Eagle Ridge's assets falls below the principal amount of the debt. The maximum amount of nonrecourse deductions that Eagle Ridge can generate is capped by the amount of its debt, here $20 million. The maximum amount that Eagle Ridge can allocate to Charlene is limited by the significant item consistency test. In this case, Charlene receives 10% of all allocations of partnership items having substantial economic effect. Thus her share of nonrecourse deductions should be similarly limited to 10%, or $2 million. **Answer (a)** is incorrect, because it does not treat the $20 million loan as a nonrecourse loan for purposes of section 704(b). **Answer (b)** is incorrect, because it limits Charlene's allocation of nonrecourse deductions to the amount of her capital, in effect applying the alternate test. Allocations of nonrecourse deductions, however, do not have economic effect and are not subject to the limitations applicable to deductions that do have economic effect. **Answer (d)** is incorrect, because it fails to take account of the significant item consistency test.

    5.2.1   **The correct Answer is (d).** Raj's $1,000 share of the taxable interest increases his outside basis under section 705(a)(1)(A). So does his share of the interest on the municipal bonds. There are three ways to justify this latter answer. First, and simplest, is that section 705(a)(1)(B) says so. But why does it say that? Imagine that Raj sells his interest after the partnership's receipt of the municipal interest. One would expect that the price he receives will be increased by approximately $500, his share of that interest. If he is not granted a $500 increase in outside basis, Raj will, in effect, pay tax on his share of the municipal interest, depriving it of the tax exemption that Congress approved in enacting section 103. This suggests the third, and most satisfying, way to justify or explain this answer. Section 705(a)(1)(B) re-establishes equality of inside and outside basis. Receipt of the municipal interest increases the partnership's basis in its assets by $10,000, so an aggregate increase of $10,000 in outside basis is required to prevent double taxation. **Answer (a)** misses the boat completely. **Answer (b)**, which increases Raj's outside basis only for the municipal interest, and **Answer (c)**, which increases it only for the taxable interest, are both incorrect.

    5.2.2   **The correct Answer is (a).** In the merger, the Fund takes shares of the acquiring company with an aggregate basis equal to that of the shares of the telecommunications company it surrendered. Section 358(a)(1). There is no change in the inside basis of the Fund's assets, so there should be no change in outside basis, either. **Answer (b)** would allow Raj to step up his outside basis to the fair market value of his share of the acquiror's stock. This would, in effect, create for him a tax exemption on the merger gain, rather than just a deferral. **Answers (c) and (d)** would go even further, giving Raj a built-in loss with respect to his share of the acquiror's stock. Both are incorrect.

    5.2.3   **The correct Answer is (c).** It is the sum of Raj's share of the cash contribution ($1,500) plus Raj's share of the adjusted basis of the contributed stock ($2,000). The former component is straightforward; the latter was sufficiently uncertain that the IRS published a Revenue Ruling to clarify it. Rev. Rul. 96–11, 1996–1 C.B. 140. The pattern should be clear by now: the charitable contribution of the shares of stock reduces the partnership's inside basis in its assets by $40,000, so outside basis should be reduced by a like amount. **Answer (a)** is a throwaway. **Answer (b)** neglects the cash contribution. **Answer (d)** includes the cash contribution, but adds to it the value, rather than the adjusted basis, of the contributed property.

5.3.1   The correct Answer is (b). The accrual of interest does not create or enhance any asset of a cash-method partnership, nor is it deductible prior to payment. Therefore, the accrual of interest expense does not create a liability for purposes of section 752. *See* Rev. Rul. 88–77, 1988–2 C.B. 128 (predating the promulgation of Treas. Reg. § 1.752–1(a)(4), but reaching the same conclusion on these facts). The office supplies, on the other hand, are assets of the partnership that are properly reflected on the balance sheet with an adjusted basis equal to their cost, even if payment is not due until the following year. Treas. Reg. § 1.1012–1(g)(1). Thus, the partnership's obligation to make this payment is a liability for purposes of section 752.

Answer (a) is incorrect, because the obligation to pay for the office supplies is treated as a liability. **Answers (c) and (d)** are incorrect, because the accrued interest is not so treated.

5.3.2   The correct Answer is (d). Upon formation, the balance sheet of Klix looks like this:

Assets			Liabilities		
	Tax	**Book**		**Tax**	**Book**
Cash	$200,000	$200,000	Recourse Debt	$700,000	$700,000
Plant & Equipment	700,000	700,000			
			Capital		
			Xander	100,000	100,000
			Zoe	100,000	100,000
Total Assets	$900,000	$900,000	**Total Liabilities and Capital**	$900,000	$900,000

Upon constructive liquidation, the partnership sells its assets for $0 and recognizes a loss of $900,000, which it must allocate to the partners. The partnership agreement meets all of the requirements for the safe harbor for economic effect and there are no facts to suggest that substantiality is an issue. Therefore, the $900,000 loss is allocated $675,000 (75%) to Xander and $225,000 (25%) to Zoe. After this allocation, the balance sheet appears as follows:

Assets			Liabilities		
	Tax	Book		Tax	Book
Cash	$0	$0	Recourse Debt	$ 700,000	$ 700,000
Plant & Equipment	0	0			
			Capital		
			Xander	(575,000)	(575,000)
			Zoe	(125,000)	(125,000)
Total Assets	$0	$0	**Total Liabilities and Capital**	$ 0	$ 0

Pursuant to their deficit-restoration obligations, Xander contributes $575,000 and Zoe contributes $125,000 to the partnership, which uses these contributions to pay off its $700,000 debt. The economic risk of loss for this recourse liability is shared in these proportions. **Answer (a)** incorrectly applies the partnership agreement, because it uses the final ratio in which the partners share profits and losses (45:55) to determine economic risk of loss. This ratio is inapplicable here, because the partnership has not generated any profits, let alone profits that equal or exceed its loss on the constructive liquidation. **Answer (b)** is incorrect, because it uses the ratio of the partners' capital contributions (50:50) for this purpose. **Answer (c)** is the siren song that will send you crashing upon the rocks (or at least to an incorrect exam answer). It results from applying the current loss-sharing ratio (75:25) directly to the amount of the recourse liability, rather than working through the constructive liquidation. This Question illustrates a common situation where that shortcut will not work, because the ratio of capital contributions is different than the ratio in which the partners share losses.

5.3.3 The correct Answer is (c). This Question demonstrates the close connection between the allocation of losses and the allocation of recourse debt. The issue is the same as in Question 5.3.2—how do you allocate the $900,000 loss recognized by the partnership on the constructive liquidation? Here, however, the absence of a full deficit-restoration obligation changes the answer. Allocation of the first $133,333 of the loss will reduce Xander's capital account to zero. Absent an obligation to restore a deficit capital account for the benefit of another partner, the next $66,667 of the loss must be allocated to Zoe, reducing her capital account to zero. Remaining losses may be allocated 75% to Xander. See Topic 4.3 and, in particular, Question 4.3.2. The resulting partnership balance sheet is as follows:

Assets			Liabilities		
	Tax	Book		Tax	Book
Cash	$0	$0	Recourse Debt	$ 700,000	$ 700,000
Plant & Equipment	0	0			
			Capital		
			Xander	(525,000)	(525,000)
			Zoe	(175,000)	(175,000)
Total Assets	$0	$0	**Total Liabilities and Capital**	$ 0	$ 0

Ironically, the correct answer to this Question is the siren song from the last Question. What happened? The allocation of the first $200,000 of loss equally to the two partners offsets their capital contributions. The remaining $700,000 of loss is properly allocated 75% to Xander and 25% to Zoe.

Answer (a) is incorrect, because it uses the final ratio in which the partners share profits and losses to determine economic risk of loss. **Answer (b)** is incorrect, because it uses the ratio of the partners' capital contributions for this purpose. **Answer (d)** is incorrect, because it improperly allows loss from the constructive liquidation to be allocated to Xander after his capital is exhausted but Zoe's is not.

5.4.1   The correct Answer is (d). The initial question: Is the $1 million liability recourse or nonrecourse for purposes of section 752? Despite the fact that it is "recourse" to the partnership and its assets, this liability is nonrecourse for section 752 purposes, because no partner of Rancor has any personal responsibility for this partnership debt due to the limited liability provided by state law. This sort of liability is often called an "exculpatory liability," a category of liabilities discussed briefly in Topic 4.4 and illustrated in Question 4.4.6. The analysis would change, of course, if the partners surrendered their liability protection by taking on obligations to restore deficits in their capital accounts, but there is no indication that they have done this.

As a nonrecourse liability, the $1 million liability is shared among the partners under the three-tier protocol of Treas. Reg. § 1.752–3. There are no allocations in the first two tiers. The partnership agreement contains no special provisions for the allocation of excess nonrecourse liabilities in the third tier, so the partners' general profit shares control. **Answers (a) and (b)** are incorrect, because this liability is not a recourse liability for purposes of section 752. **Answer (c)** is incorrect, because the partnership agreement provides for allocations of profits that are given effect under section 704(a).

5.4.2   The correct Answer is (c). Naomi's share of 3N's minimum gain is $200,000, because she has been allocated nonrecourse deductions in this amount. She is therefore allocated $200,000 of the nonrecourse debt in the first tier. There is no second-tier allocation. The remaining $300,000 of the nonrecourse debt is allocated equally among the partners pursuant to the specification in the partnership agreement. **Answer (a)** allocates all of the nonrecourse debt to the limited partners. This is incorrect—there is no reason that a general partner cannot be allocated a share (or all) of the partnership's nonrecourse debt. **Answer (b)** is incorrect, because it overlooks the allocation of debt to Naomi in the first tier. **Answer (d)** is incorrect, because it neglects the allocation of debt to Natalie and Natasha in the third tier.

5.4.3   The correct Answer is (d). This Question illustrates the "leakage" of nonrecourse debt share (and outside basis) away from partners who are not allocated nonrecourse deductions toward those who are. In this case, an additional $100,000 of nonrecourse deductions to Naomi brings her another $100,000 of debt share in the first tier (now totaling $300,000). Of course, this reduces the amount of debt left to be allocated in the third tier from $300,000 to $200,000, which is split equally among the three partners ($66,667 to each partner). **Answers (a) and (b)** are still wrong, for the same reasons they were wrong before. **Answer (c)** is incorrect, because it does not take into account the "leakage." Notice how Naomi benefits from the allocation scheme for nonrecourse debt. She takes debt share and outside basis away from the other partners in an amount that is just sufficient to allow her to utilize her allocation of nonrecourse deductions, even if she has no other source for outside basis.

5.4.4   The correct Answer is (d). One feature of the "leakage" described in the previous Question is that the nonrecourse debt shares of the partners are continuously changing—an administrative headache if nothing else. A partnership may avoid this by allocating excess nonrecourse liabilities in the manner that nonrecourse deductions are expected to be allocated. This is allowed by Treas. Reg. § 1.752–3(a)(3) if the partnership's expectation is reasonable. Here, we and the partnership know that 100% of the nonrecourse deductions attributable to this $500,000 nonrecourse debt will be allocated to Naomi, so it is permissible to allocate to her 100% of the excess of this debt over the amount allocated in the first tier. Accordingly, Naomi gets all of the debt, $200,000 in the first tier and $300,000 in the third. Obviously, as debt "leaks" from the third tier to the first tier over time, there will be no change in the overall allocation to Naomi, which will remain at 100% throughout. **Answers (a) and (b)** remain incorrect. **Answer (c)** is incorrect, because it does not take into account the partnership's new specification for allocating excess nonrecourse liabilities.

5.4.5   The correct Answer is (c). In the first tier, the partners are allocated their respective shares of the partnership's minimum gain. This concept is defined in Treas. Reg. § 1.704–2(d) as the gain that Luckman LLC would realize if it sold the property securing its $700 nonrecourse debt for the amount of the debt and no other consideration. This may suggest that the amount of the partnership's minimum gain is $300, the excess of the amount of the debt ($700) over the partnership's adjusted basis in the property ($400). Nope. The partnership holds this property with a disparity between book value ($1,000, its fair market value on contribution) and adjusted basis ($400). In this situation, Treas. Reg. § 1.704–2(d)(3) requires that minimum gain be determined by reference to the property's book value. So measured, there is no partnership minimum gain here, because the book value of the property ($1,000) actually exceeds the amount of the debt ($700), so on a sale for the amount of the debt, the partnership would realize a $300 book loss. Thus, there is no first-tier allocation of the nonrecourse debt.

In the second tier, Sid is allocated the amount of gain that he would be allocated under section 704(c) if the partnership sold the contributed property for the amount of the debt and no other consideration. This calculation does use the adjusted tax basis of the property, and produces a $300 allocation of nonrecourse debt to Sid.

The remaining $400 of the nonrecourse debt should be allocated equally, $200 to Sid and $200 to Estelle, according to their general shares of partnership profits. **Answer (a)** is incorrect, because it allocates nothing to Sid in the third tier. **Answers (b) and (d)** also make incorrect allocations of the $400 excess nonrecourse liability.

5.4.6   The correct Answer is (b). The partnership's minimum gain has increased to $100, which is the excess of the principal amount of the debt ($700) over the book value of the property after depreciation ($600). Under the partnership agreement, this minimum gain is shared equally, $50 each, by Sid and Estelle. Thus, each is allocated this amount of the debt in the first tier. Depreciation has also changed the allocation to Sid in the second tier, which now appears to be the excess of the amount of the debt ($700) over the tax basis of the property, adjusted by the depreciation ($240), or $460. This is not quite right, however. Of that $460, $100 has already been allocated in the first tier, so only $360 remains to be allocated in the second tier. This amount is allocated entirely to Sid. The remaining amount of the debt, $240, is allocated equally between Sid and Estelle, $120 each. **Answer (a)** is incorrect, because it takes none of these adjustments into account. **Answer (c)** is incorrect, because it allocates $460, rather than $360, to Sid in the second tier. **Answer (d)** is incorrect, because it allocates the entire nonrecourse liability to Sid.

A visualization of these nonrecourse debt tiers may be helpful. Picture a flagpole. The top of the pole is $700, the total amount of the nonrecourse debt. Moving toward the ground, there is a line on the pole, marked "book value $600." The portion of the pole above that line is the first tier. Moving further down the pole, the next line is marked, "adjusted tax basis $240." The portion of the pole between that line and the line above it is the second tier. The portion of the pole below the second line all the way down to the ground is the third tier. As time goes on, depreciation will cause both lines to move toward the ground (*i.e.*, the book value and the tax basis of the property will decrease by the amounts of book and tax depreciation). As they do, the first tier will grow at the expense of the second. The second tier will not shrink commensurately, however, because it will take over some of the pole that used to belong to the third tier. The final year's depreciation will eliminate both the second tier and the third tier, so that all that will be left is the first tier.

5.4.7   **The correct Answer is (a).** The opening balance sheet of Brighten Bleach looks like this:

Assets			Liabilities		
	Tax	**Book**		**Tax**	**Book**
Cash	$ 600,000	$ 600,000	Mortgage Debt	$ 400,000	$ 400,000
Manu. Facility	400,000	400,000			
			Capital		
			Addison	200,000	200,000
			Bailey	200,000	200,000
			Camellia	200,000	200,000
Total Assets	$1,000,000	$1,000,000	**Total Liabilities and Capital**	$1,000,000	$1,000,000

At the outset, there are no allocations of the nonrecourse debt in either of the first or second tiers. So, this Question comes down to the partnership's attempt to specify that 100% of excess nonrecourse liabilities—which in this case is the entire $400,000 nonrecourse debt—will be allocated to Addison. Under Treas. Reg. § 1.752–3(a)(3) (third sentence), the partnership's specification will be given effect if it is "reasonably consistent with allocations (that have substantial economic effect under the section 704(b) regulations) of some other significant item of partnership income or gain."

The partnership's allocation of depreciation (100% to Addison) will not satisfy this test. Because there is no equity in the partnership's manufacturing facility, depreciation from the first dollar will be a nonrecourse deduction, allocations of which do not have economic effect. The same goes for allocations of income and gains under the minimum gain chargeback, because they simply reverse allocations of nonrecourse deductions that themselves do not have economic effect. Treas. Reg. § 1.704–2(b)(2) (fourth sentence).

All is not lost. According to its business plan, the partnership anticipates that it will incur start-up losses approaching $600,000, all of which will be funded by partners' capital and all of which will be allocated to Addison. These allocations will have economic effect, and this effect should be substantial. The chargeback of income and gains to Addison may give you pause. The partnership expects that this chargeback will be complete within four years, so it falls outside of the five-year presumption of Treas. Reg. § 1.704–1(b)(2)(ii)(*c*). Nevertheless, the business of Brighten Bleach seems sufficiently risky (and badly named) that substantiality should not be a concern. *See* Topic 4.3.

Finally, is the anticipated allocation of start-up losses big enough to be a "significant item"? Absolutely. The anticipated amount will approach the partnership's entire initial capital—you can't get much more "significant" than that. Hence, the partnership's specification granting Addison a 100% share of the $400,000 nonrecourse debt should work. **Answer (b)** is incorrect, because it does not appear from the facts that the partnership expects to allocate all of its nonrecourse deductions to Addison. To be sure, it will allocate them entirely to her until breakeven, but thereafter she is entitled only to the same one-third share as the other two partners. **Answer (c)** is incorrect, because the partnership's specification of 100% should be respected for tax purposes. **Answer (d)** is incorrect for the same reason, but it is probably better than **Answer (c)**. In the event that the partnership's specification failed the significant item consistency test, the partnership would have to determine Addison's share of the nonrecourse debt by reference to her general profit share. One-third seems to be the lowest share that would fit this description and it could be higher, given her 100% share of the start-up losses. It is precisely to avoid imponderables like this that partnerships routinely specify each partner's profit share under Treas. Reg. § 1.752–3(a)(3).

5.4.8   The correct Answer is (c). In this case, the partnership's allocation of depreciation will not fly. Recall that any proposed allocation of nonrecourse deductions must meet the significant item consistency test under Treas. Reg. § 1.704–2(e)(2). *See* Topic 4.4. Trouble is, the partnership here proposes to make all allocations that have economic effect equally among the three partners and to allocate nonrecourse deductions only to Addison. It is to be expected, then, that depreciation will have to be re-allocated in accordance with the partners' respective interests in the partnership—presumably, equally. With all items of partnership income, gain, loss, deduction and credit allocated in equal thirds, the partnership's nonrecourse debt must be allocated the same way. **Answer (a)** is incorrect, because the partnership's specification of profit shares fails to meet the significant item consistency test. **Answer (b)** is incorrect, because the partnership's proposed allocation of nonrecourse deductions fails the same test. **Answer (d)** is incorrect, because there seems little doubt that the partners' general profit shares are one-third each.

5.4.9 **The correct Answer is (a).** Now, the opening balance sheet of Brighten Bleach is as follows:

Assets	Tax	Book	Liabilities	Tax	Book
Cash	$400,000	$ 400,000	Mortgage Debt	$ 400,000	$ 400,000
Manu. Facility	100,000	600,000			
			Capital		
			Addison	(300,000)	200,000
			Bailey	200,000	200,000
			Camellia	200,000	200,000
Total Assets	$500,000	$1,000,000	**Total Liabilities and Capital**	$ 500,000	$1,000,000

Notice that the partnership still has $600,000 of book capital, but it is deployed differently. Rather than having $600,000 in cash and no equity in the manufacturing facility, the partnership now has only $400,000 in cash, and $200,000 of equity in its facility. This seemingly small difference will make a big difference in the tax outcome.

Following the same analysis as in Question 5.4.5, there is no first-tier allocation of the nonrecourse debt. The second-tier allocation is $300,000, being the excess of the amount of the debt ($400,000) over the adjusted tax basis of the manufacturing facility ($100,000). This amount is allocated entirely to Addison.

As before, the partnership wants to allocate the entire third tier to Addison. In Question 5.4.8, this was impossible under the significant item consistency test. How about now? The first $200,000 of depreciation will not consist of nonrecourse deductions, because it will be funded by the partnership's equity in the facility. These deductions will, in fact, have economic effect and they will be allocated entirely to Addison. These allocations, equal in aggregate to Addison's initial book capital, seem clearly large enough to be a "significant item" for purposes of passing the significant item consistency test.

Accordingly, Addison should be allocated the remaining $100,000 of the nonrecourse debt in the third tier, which, together with her $300,000 share in the second tier, gives her a $400,000 (100%) share of the debt in total. **Answer (b)** is incorrect, because Addison is entitled to more than one-third of the third tier allocation. **Answer (c)** is incorrect, because it gives Addison no share in the third tier. **Answer (d)** is incorrect, because under the foregoing analysis, Addison is entitled to 100% of the third-tier allocation, not some lesser share of it.

5.4.10 **The correct Answer is (c).** Prior to the new borrowing, the partnership has no minimum gain, because the book value of the manufacturing facility ($475,000) is more than the nonrecourse debt it secures ($400,000). Thus, the partnership has not yet incurred any nonrecourse deductions. Partnership minimum gain appears with the new borrowing, in the amount of $150,000, the excess of the partnership's nonrecourse debt ($625,000) over the book value of the property securing the debt ($475,000). This increase in minimum gain is shared among the partners in the proportions that they receive distributions funded by that loan. Treas. Reg. § 1.704–2(g)(1)(i). Because the partners take equal distributions, they share the $150,000 increase in minimum gain equally, $50,000 each. (Notice that this is smaller than the amount of their distributions, due to the presence of some equity in the property at the time the loan is incurred.)

Accordingly, each of the partners has an allocation of $50,000 of nonrecourse debt in the first tier, because each has a $50,000 share of partnership minimum gain. The amount allocated to Addison in the second tier is, as an initial matter, the excess of the principal amounts of the two loans ($625,000) over the adjusted tax basis of the manufacturing facility ($75,000), or $550,000. But $150,000 of this amount has already been allocated in the first tier, so the amount allocated in the second tier cannot exceed $400,000. This amount goes entirely to Addison.

There is $75,000 left to be allocated in the third tier. The partnership agreement continues to provide, as it did in Question 5.4.9, that this amount is allocated to Addison and, for the reasons discussed there, this allocation should be respected. Altogether, Addison gets $50,000 in the first tier, $400,000 in the second and $75,000 in the third, for a total of $525,000. Bailey and Camellia each get $50,000 in the first tier. **Answer (a)** is incorrect, because it fails to allocate the first tier equally, in accordance with distributions, instead allocating it entirely to Addison. **Answer (b)** also makes this error and then compounds it by allocating the third tier equally to each of the three partners. **Answer (d)** is also incorrect. It allocates the first tier equally, which is correct, but allocates the third tier the same way, which is incorrect.

5.5.1   The correct Answer is (b). Under the economic risk of loss standard of Treas. Reg. § 1.752–2, Luke's share of the bank loan depends upon the amount of the losses that he would be allocated in a constructive liquidation. So you should start there. Upon a constructive liquidation, Homer's would suffer a loss that exceeded the partner's aggregate capital by $500,000, the amount of the bank loan. Under the alternative test for economic effect, Luke could be allocated his share (25%) of this loss until his capital account reached a $50,000 deficit, the limit of his restoration obligation. Remaining losses would have to be allocated elsewhere. Thus, the maximum amount of losses in excess of capital that can be allocated to Luke is $50,000. He will reach this limit when Homer's losses in excess of capital reach $200,000. Luke's share of the bank loan is also $50,000, because that is his economic risk of loss on the loan. **Answer (a)** is incorrect, because it would allocate no losses to Luke, despite his deficit-restoration obligation. **Answer (c)** is incorrect, because it would allocate losses to Luke exceeding his deficit-restoration obligation. **Answer (d)** is incorrect for the same reason.

 5.5.2 **The correct Answer is (a).** Again, start with the loss allocation. Is Luke's guarantee a deficit-restoration obligation that would justify the allocation to him of loss exceeding the positive balance in his capital account? It is not. Consider the alternatives. If the partnership's assets were worthless, the bank might proceed against Homer, the general partner, for the full amount of the loan or against Luke, the guarantor, for $50,000, the amount of the guarantee. In the former case, Homer would have no right of reimbursement from Luke. In the latter case, Luke would have a right of reimbursement (subrogation) against the partnership and, therefore, against Homer. In both cases, Luke keeps his $50,000. Therefore, under the alternate test no losses may be allocated to Luke in excess of his capital account and, under the constructive liquidation test, his share of the bank loan is zero. **Answer (b)** would be the correct answer if Luke had waived rights of subrogation. In that case, Luke would have no right to receive reimbursement from the partnership or Homer in the event that Luke were called upon to pay on his guarantee, and the partnership or Homer would have a right of reimbursement from Luke in the event that either paid the bank debt in full (and the conditions for Luke's obligations under the guarantee were otherwise satisfied). In either event, Luke would be out $50,000. He would be allocated losses and debt in this amount under the analysis described in the Answer to Question 5.5.1. **Answers (c) and (d)** are incorrect, because both allocate losses to Luke exceeding his deficit-restoration obligation.

 5.5.3 **The correct Answer is (d).** The rebirth of Homer's Ice Cream as a limited liability company changes a lot of this analysis. The debt of a limited liability company taxed as a partnership is nonrecourse for purposes of the debt-allocation rules of section 752. Luke's guarantee of $50,000 of the debt causes the debt to be "bifurcated" under Treas. Reg. § 1.752–1(i) into a $50,000 recourse debt and a $450,000 nonrecourse debt. This is because Luke bears the economic risk of loss for the guaranteed portion of the bank loan, whether or not he waives subrogation. Subrogation cannot give Luke greater rights than the lender's rights. On constructive liquidation, Luke would be called upon to honor his guarantee and, even with a right of subrogation, he could not reach any assets outside of the partnership.

 Because he bears the economic risk of loss, Luke's share of the $50,000 recourse debt is 100%. He should also be allocated 25% ($112,500) of the nonrecourse debt, because that is his interest in partnership profits. Luke's total share of the partnership's debt is $162,500.

 What about Luke's share of the first $300,000 of losses financed by the nonrecourse debt? All of these losses are nonrecourse deductions. Because of the guarantee, some are partner nonrecourse deductions, which must be allocated entirely to Luke under Treas. Reg. § 1.704–2(i), and the rest belong to the partnership, to be allocated among the partners with Luke's share being 25%. On the assumption that Luke has given a "vertical slice" guarantee, the partner nonrecourse deductions are 10% ($50,000/$500,000) of total nonrecourse deductions. Therefore, Luke's allocation of the first $300,000 of debt-financed losses is $30,000 plus $67,500 (25% of $270,000) or $97,500.

If that seems difficult—and it should—rest assured that it's often harder. You might well think that the percentage of total nonrecourse deductions that are partner nonrecourse deductions will always be the same as the percentage of the nonrecourse debt that is guaranteed. Not necessarily. Subsequent to Luke's guarantee, there are deemed to be two loans, one of $50,000 and one of $450,000. These two loans have equal priority, because Luke guarantees a "vertical slice" of the partnership's debt. If Luke had given either a traditional, "top dollar" guarantee or a "bottom dollar" guarantee, the results would have been different. *See* Treas. Reg. §§ 1.704–2(d)(2)(ii), –2(m), example (1)(vii).

Answer (a) is incorrect, because Luke is entitled to substantial nonrecourse deductions. Indeed, Luke would be entitled to $75,000 of debt-financed losses (25% of $300,000) even without a guarantee—proving the point that much can be accomplished by simply changing the entity from a limited partnership to an LLC. **Answer (b)** is incorrect, because it does not take into account this change in entity. **Answer (c)** reflects the losses that would be allocated to Luke with no guarantee, although his share of the debt in that case would be $125,000 (25% of $500,000).

5.5.4 **The correct Answer is (a).** Obviously, this is a highly structured transaction in which tax considerations play an important role. It is fair to assume that the structure of the transaction would have been quite different had the tax advisors not been involved. Ignoring Wilco's share of Newco's $40 million debt, this is a disguised sale, in which Wilco transfers its manufacturing business to Newco in exchange for $40 million in cash and a 5% interest in Newco. Wilco's adjusted basis in the contributed assets is zero, so it is unnecessary to allocate basis between the assets deemed contributed and the assets deemed sold to the partnership for cash. Wilco recognizes $40 million in gain and has an outside basis of zero in its Newco interest.

But Wilco's share of Newco's $40 million debt cannot be ignored. Under Treas. Reg. § 1.707–5(b), Wilco is entitled to take a cash distribution up to the amount of its debt share without recognizing gain. (Alternatively, Wilco could borrow $40 million first, keep the cash and contribute its assets to Newco subject to the debt. Under Treas. Reg. § 1.707–5(a), Wilco would realize proceeds of a disguised sale only to the extent that its share of Newco's debt is less than $40 million.)

The tax planners intended that Wilco's share of Newco's debt be $40 million, and it appears that they have succeeded. The other possible answers to this Question raise counter-arguments. **Answer (b)** concludes that this arrangement creates the appearance that Wilco bears a $40 million risk of loss when the reality is otherwise. While this argument was a winner for the government in *Canal Corp. v. Commissioner*, 135 T.C. 199 (2010), there seems to be no basis for it here. Because the borrowing entity is a limited liability company, neither Calumet nor Wilco had any risk of loss initially. That changed when Calumet guaranteed the entire debt and changed again when Wilco indemnified Calumet for its entire liability under the guarantee. There is no suggestion that these are not valid and binding agreements. Wilco took the further step of agreeing to maintain net worth sufficient to enable it to pay the full amount of the indemnity if called on. This will not require anything extraordinary of Wilco—it can do this by simply holding onto the Willamette note. There is no indication that Willamette is not creditworthy or that Wilco has any other liabilities that might diminish its assets.

Answer (c) presents the counter-argument that Wilco's indemnity is not the sort of obligation that should be taken into account in the constructive sale analysis. Treas. Reg. § 1.752–2(b)(3) requires taking into account "all statutory and contractual obligations" in this analysis, and specifically mentions guarantees and indemnifications. Obligations that are "stacked" in a manner that moves the economic risk of loss on a liability from one person to another and then to another—like the guarantee and the indemnification here—must all be considered. The fact that neither the lender nor Calumet demanded Wilco's indemnity does not cause it to be treated as other than an obligation if it is a valid and binding agreement. Treas. Reg. § 1.752–2(b)(4) disregards obligations subject to contingencies that make it unlikely they will ever be discharged. The financial health of the partnership (and thus the likelihood that it will default so that guarantees and indemnifications will be called on) is not such a contingency—the constructive liquidation test demands that we consider this possibility. Nor is the speculation that Calumet, having not asked for Wilco's indemnification, will not enforce it. Sure it will, happily, if Calumet is required to make good on its guarantee.

Answer (d) suggests that this partnership is a sham. While this argument might be strong in some other cases, it is not here. The partnership will hold $240 million in assets and operate a substantial business. Both its partners will hold meaningful stakes in the partnership by reason of substantial equity contributions. There is no indication in the facts that either is planning a quick exit—indeed, the deferral of Wilco's tax gain requires that it remains in the partnership with an undiminished debt share. Students and, unfortunately, IRS agents are often too quick to declare a highly structured transaction is a "sham" when what they really mean is they don't like that the taxpayer got away with it.

5.5.5 **The correct Answer is (b).** One little change and it all falls apart. This variation in the facts presents a classic confrontation between two principles in the economic risk of loss analysis. The first is the "deemed satisfaction" rule of Treas. Reg. § 1.752–2(b)(6), whereby it is assumed that persons obligated to make payments will actually make them, "irrespective of their actual net worth." The second is the anti-abuse rule of Treas. Reg. § 1.752–2(j), discussed above, which is explicitly identified as an exception to the deemed satisfaction rule. So how big a hole does the anti-abuse rule leave in the deemed satisfaction rule? Put another way, when can you rely on the deemed satisfaction rule and when can't you? This is a question without a clear answer and the IRS doesn't want to provide one. At its core, however, the deemed satisfaction rule is intended to forestall endless arguments between taxpayers and the IRS regarding whether an obligor's net worth is just bigger or just less than a particular payment obligation. It does not seem intended to validate allocations of partnership debt to an obligor that, when called upon to honor the payment obligation, turns out to be just an empty bag.

5.5.6 **The correct Answer is (c).** While the proposed regulations, if finalized in their current form, would not repeal the anti-abuse rule of Treas. Reg. § 1.752–2(j) or otherwise cause it to be inapplicable, they would render its application unnecessary in this case. That is because Wilco's indemnification would fail several of the tests in the proposed regulation for a "bona fide, commercial" obligation and would therefore not be recognized in applying the constructive liquidation test. Prop. Treas. Reg. § 1.752–2(b)(3)(ii). In addition, Wilco would likely fail the "net value" test of the proposed regulations, if and when it canceled any significant part of Willamette's note, causing Wilco to lose its prior debt share and recognize the gain deferred in the original transaction under section 752(b). Prop. Treas. Reg. § 1.752–2(b)(3)(iii)(B), Treas. Reg. § 1.752–2(k)(2)(iii)(B). As of this writing, there is no way of knowing whether, when or with what changes these proposed regulations will be finalized.

5.5.7 **The correct Answer is (b).** Since it has not elected to the contrary, Shellco is a disregarded entity for tax purposes. It is a "liability blocker," inserted into the structure between J&J and the general partnership in order to limit J&J's responsibility for partnership liabilities. Although J&J's professed concern is with contingent liabilities, the blocker will work equally well for known liabilities such as the $5 million bank loan. The allocation of that loan is governed by Treas. Reg. § 1.752–2(k), which provides that Shellco's economic risk of loss (and therefore that of J&J, since Shellco is a disregarded entity) cannot exceed Shellco's "net value," which in this case is $400,000, ignoring as required by this regulation the value of Shellco's interest in the partnership. As a limited partner, Mr. Hamilton does not have economic risk of loss for any portion of the partnership's liabilities. Accordingly, the remaining $4,600,000 of the bank loan is allocated between the partners as though it were nonrecourse, 50% to each. J&J's aggregate share is $400,000 plus $2,300,000, or $2,700,000. **Answer (a)** reflects a misreading of Treas. Reg. § 1.752–2(k). This regulation does not say that Shellco's share of the partnership's liabilities cannot exceed $400,000, but rather that its payment obligation (and therefore its economic risk of loss) cannot exceed $400,000. This leaves $4,600,000 to be allocated as nonrecourse debt. **Answer (c)** reflects a more substantial misunderstanding of this regulation. **Answer (d)** would be correct if J&J had not introduced Shellco into the ownership chain.

5.5.8 **The correct Answer is (c).** Shellco is now not a disregarded entity, but a partnership for tax purposes. The net-value rule that is applicable to disregarded entities does not apply to partnerships under current law. Accordingly, the $5 million liability of the iPeed partnership is allocated entirely to Shellco, because it is the sole general partner of the partnership. From there, it is allocated between the members of Shellco as a nonrecourse liability—92% ($4,600,000) to J&J and 8% ($400,000) to the J&J subsidiary. **Answer (a)** is incorrect, because current law considers the entire $5 million liability to be a recourse liability, regardless of the net value of Shellco. **Answer (b)** is incorrect under current law, although it would be the correct answer under the proposed section 752 regulations, which would apply the net-value test in this case. Prop. Treas. Reg. § 1.752–2(b)(3)(iii)(B). **Answer (d)** is incorrect, because Shellco is required to allocate a portion of the $5 million liability to J&J's wholly owned subsidiary.

    5.5.9   **The correct Answer is (d).** In this instance, J&J owns all of the iPeed partnership, directly and indirectly through Shellco. Shellco, however, is a disregarded entity. Thus, for tax purposes, J&J is considered to own, directly, all of the partnership interests. Whatever its characterization under local law, the iPeed partnership is not a partnership for tax purposes, but instead a branch of J&J. *See* Topic 1.3. Accordingly, J&J is considered to have incurred the $5 million liability itself. **Answers (a) and (b)** are incorrect, because they are inconsistent with this analysis. **Answer (c)** has the correct dollar figure, but it is inaccurate to say that this amount is allocated to J&J under section 752. Because J&J is treated for tax purposes as incurring this liability directly for its own account, section 752 is inapplicable in this case.

    5.6.1   **The correct Answer is (b).** In order to answer this Question, you must extrapolate Kylie's outside basis from the information provided on the partnership's balance sheet. Kylie's tax capital is a negative $250,000. As the only general partner, her share of the partnership's recourse debt is $200,000. The sum of these two would ordinarily give you Kylie's outside basis. Here, however, that sum is a negative $50,000, which section 705(a)(2) does not allow. Kylie's outside basis is zero, and her "suspended loss" under section 704(d) is $50,000. **Answer (a)** is incorrect, because it would cause Kylie to have a negative outside basis. **Answer (c)** is incorrect, because it gives Kylie no basis credit for her share of the partnership's debt. **Answer (d)** compounds this error by giving her no credit for her own capital contribution.

    5.6.2   **The correct Answer is (c).** Section 704(d) states that Kylie is allowed to use her suspended loss when that amount is "repaid" to the partnership. This suggests that Kylie must make a capital contribution. While that surely is one way a suspended loss can become available, it is not the only way. An allocation of partnership income or gain works as well. Here, all $50,000 of Kylie's suspended loss is freed, $25,000 by capital contribution and $25,000 by gain allocation. The partnership allocates her all $90,000 of its 2017 gain pursuant to the gain chargeback. Kylie offsets $50,000 of this gain with her now "unsuspended" loss, and takes into account a net $40,000 of gain. **Answers (a) and (b)** seem based on an incorrect allocation to Kylie of only $30,000 of the partnership's gain (one-third of $90,000). **Answer (b)** compounds this error by allowing Kylie to use only

$25,000 of her suspended loss. **Answer (d)** makes the same mistake, after properly allocating the partnership's gain.

5.6.3   The correct Answer is (d). Kylie's suspended loss of $50,000 is reduced to $30,000 by her 100% share of the partnership's $20,000 investment gain for the pre-sale period. But no matter—she cannot use any of this loss to offset her gain on sale. To see this, imagine that there were no zero-basis limitation and no concept of suspended loss. In that case, Kylie would have been able to use an additional $30,000 in partnership losses (those suspended under existing law) and her outside basis at the time of sale would be a negative $30,000. This would increase the amount of gain she would realize on the sale by an equal amount. Under existing law, she is unable to use the $30,000 in partnership losses, either when allocated to her or at the time of sale, but her gain on sale is $30,000 less. Put another way, if Kylie wanted to use her suspended loss to reduce her gain on sale, she would first have to increase such gain by an amount equal to the suspended loss—a wash.

Because Kylie has a suspended loss, the adjusted basis in her partnership interest is, by definition, zero. The amount she realizes on the sale is $210,000, the sum of the $10,000 cash consideration and her $200,000 share of the partnership's recourse debt. *See* section 752(d). Her gain is therefore $210,000. **Answer (a)** neglects to include Kylie's share of the partnership's debt in amount realized. **Answers (b) and (c)** each incorrectly use an amount of suspended loss to reduce Kylie's gain on sale.

6.1.1   The correct Answer is (c). Partnership ABC has chosen to use the proration method for all of its variations, so there's not much that can go wrong here if you know how to count the days. The Treasury regulations treat a partner who disposes of a partnership interest as owning it through the end of the date of the disposition. Treas. Reg. § 1.706–4(a)(4), example (ix). Therefore, Partnership ABC has three proration periods in 2016, one beginning on January 1, one beginning on March 1 and one beginning on July 29. The proration is as follows:

			Allocation Among Partners		
Period	Days	Prorated Income	Abner	Bette	Clarence
1	60	$ 60,000	$ 20,000	$ 20,000	$20,000
2	150	150,000	50,000	25,000	75,000
3	156	156,000	78,000	78,000	0
		$366,000	$148,000	$123,000	$95,000

The other answers explore some of the missteps you may have made in applying the proration method. **Answer (a)** is incorrect, because it applies the monthly convention, treating the liquidation of Clarence's interest as occurring on July 31 rather than July 28. No conventions are allowed with the proration method—only the actual dates of variations can be used. **Answer (b)** is the most beguiling of the incorrect answers. It counts days based on the time of the disposition, treating the transferor as the owner of an interest for the entire day only if the disposition takes place after noon. This is a perfectly logical approach, but it is not the one adopted by the varying-interests regulation. **Answer (d)** is the result you get if you mistakenly believe that the varying interests rule only applies to dispositions of all of a partner's interest, and therefore does not apply to Bette's sale of one-half of her interest on July 28.

6.1.2   The correct Answer is (d). Unlike the proration of operating income, the allocation of extraordinary items, such as Partnership ABC's gain on the sale of its manufacturing plant, depends very much on the time of day of the variation. Here, the partnership liquidated Clarence's interest at 2:00 PM and sold its plant at 4:00 PM on the same day. Under the proration rule, Clarence would be treated as the owner of his interest until the close of the day and would accordingly be allocated his share of the extraordinary gain. But under the time-of-day rule of Treas. Reg. § 1.706–4(e), Clarence is allocated none of this extraordinary gain, which instead goes half to Abner and half to Bette. The allocation of 2016 operating income is unchanged from Question 6.1.1. **Answer (a)** is incorrect for two reasons. First, it allocates operating income using the monthly convention, like incorrect **Answer (a)** in Question 6.1.1. It also allocates a share of the extraordinary gain to Clarence. **Answer (b)** makes only the second of these two errors. **Answer (c)** gets the allocation of the extraordinary gain right, but uses the monthly convention for the proration of 2016 operating income.

6.1.3   The correct Answer is (b). A partnership that does not elect to apply the proration method must apply the interim closing method. Partnership ABC's 2016 tax year has three segments. Under the monthly convention (more on that later), Partnership ABC treats the variation which occurs on February 29 as occurring on that date, which happens to be the last day of the calendar month, and treats the variation occurring on July 10 as occurring on June 30, the last day of the preceding calendar month. Thus, the first segment of Partnership ABC's tax year includes the months of January and February, the second includes the months from March through June and the third includes the months from July through December. The apportionment of the partnership's income to these segments and the allocation of that income to each of the partners is as follows:

| Segment | Months | Apportioned Income | Allocation Among Partners | | |
			Abbey	Belinda	Cluny
1	Jan-Feb	$ 54,000	$ 18,000	$ 18,000	$18,000
2	Mar-June	120,000	40,000	20,000	60,000
3	Jul-Dec	192,000	96,000	96,000	0
		$366,000	$154,000	$134,000	$78,000

Answer (a) is incorrect. It properly applies the proration method, but that method is not applicable here because Partnership ABC has not elected to apply it. **Answer (c)** is incorrect, because it fails to treat Belinda's sale of one-half of her interest to Cluny as a variation. **Answer (d)** explores what is required to have "agreement of the partners." Such an agreement is necessary for a partnership to adopt, among other things, the monthly convention. Although the action of Partnership ABC is certainly informal, it appears to be sufficient. Abbey is a general partner who has authority to bind the partnership, and there is no indication in the facts that her authority is limited by the partnership agreement or otherwise. Her election is written, dated, kept with the records of the partnership and made on or before the due date of the partnership's tax return (including extensions). It therefore meets the minimalist requirements of Treas. Reg. § 1.706–4(f).

6.1.4   The correct Answer is (c), regrettably. Interest is an "allocable cash basis item" which must be prorated under section 706(d)(2). Unlike the Treasury regulations, however, this statute counts days by seeing who holds a transferred partnership interest at the end of the day of transfer—meaning that the transferee, not the transferor, is treated as owning the interest on that day. Thus, the proration is just the tiniest bit different. The first proration period has 59 days rather than 60 and the last has 175 rather than 174. The proration of the interest expense is as follows:

Period	Days	Prorated Expense	Allocation Among Partners		
			Abbey	Belinda	Cluny
1	59	$ 5,900	$ 1,966.67	$ 1,966.67	$1,966.67
2	132	13,200	4,400.00	2,200.00	6,600.00
3	175	17,500	8,750.00	8,750.00	0
		$36,600	$15,166.67	$12,916.67	$8,566.67

Answers (a) and (d) are incorrect, because they use the interim closing method. **Answer (a)** employs the calendar-day convention and **Answer (d)** the monthly convention. The divergence between these answers and **Answer (c)** shows the distortion that occurs when the interim closing method takes account of the entire amount of an interest payment on the date it happens to be paid. This distortion is the reason that section 706(d)(2) was enacted. **Answer (b)** is incorrect, because it uses the approach of the Treasury regulations in counting days, thus finding 60 days in the first proration period and 174 in the last. The divergence between this and **Answer (c)** is virtually meaningless.

6.2.1   The correct Answer is (b). When Shuyuan sells her entire interest, the partnership's tax year closes with respect to her under section 706(c)(2)(A). Conveniently, she has chosen to sell at exactly the mid-point of the year 2016 (day 183 of 366), so the proration method chosen by the partnership assigns one-half of the year's income—$80,000 of $160,000—to the pre-sale period. As a 50% partner, Shuyuan is allocated $40,000 of this amount. Under section 705(a)(1)(A), her outside basis is adjusted by this amount, from $400,000 to $440,000, producing gain of $60,000 on the sale of her interest. **Answer (a)** is incorrect, because it fails to apply the rule of section 706(c)(2)(A). This results in Shuyuan being taxed on none of the partnership's income for 2016, because she is no longer a partner at year-end, when the flow-through ordinarily takes place. **Answer (c)** is incorrect, because it fails to apply the rule of section 705(a)(1)(A). This results in over-taxation in the amount of $40,000. This is yet another example of the distortions that appear when inside basis does not equal outside basis (here, because of a failure to adjust outside basis to take into account an increase in inside basis). **Answer (d)** is incorrect in a different way. It properly applies section 706(c)(2)(A) and section 705(a)(1)(A), but to the wrong amount of income.

6.2.2 **The correct Answer is (d).** When Shuyuan sells only a portion of her interest, rather than all of it, there is no closing of the partnership's tax year. Therefore, Shuyuan's share of the partnership's income for the year will flow through to her only at the end of the year (December 31). The partnership must allocate its income for the year so as to take into account Shuyuan's varying interests throughout the year. Shuyuan should get 50% of the $80,000 partnership income for the pre-sale period ($40,000) and 25% of the $80,000 partnership income for the post-sale period ($20,000), a total of $60,000.

Calculating Shuyuan's gain on sale simply requires allocating her outside basis between the interest sold (one-half) and the interest retained (one-half). Hence, she can apply $200,000 of her $400,000 basis against the cash amount realized of $250,000, yielding a gain of $50,000.

Considering both the income allocated to Shuyuan ($60,000) and the gain she realizes on the sale ($50,000), Shuyuan actually realizes more total income and gain here than in Question 6.2.1, although here she has sold only one-half rather than all of her interest. This is the inevitable result of denying her an outside basis increase for the income earned on the portion of the partnership interest that she has sold. It will all work out in the end. Her basis in her remaining partnership interest will increase by the amount of the partnership income flowed through to her at year-end (December 31), giving her an outside basis of $260,000. This is $10,000 more than the current value of her remaining interest—a built-in loss that, if realized, would reduce her total gain back to $100,000. In the meantime, however, Shuyuan is over-taxed.

Answer (a) mis-measures Shuyuan's share of the partnership's income for 2016, apparently losing track of the $20,000 share derived from the partnership interest she sold. **Answer (b)** allows Shuyuan to increase her outside basis for the interest sold, not only by the amount of the partnership's income attributable to that interest, but also by the income attributable to her remaining interest. As discussed further in the analysis of Question 6.2.3 below, **Answer (c)** measures Shuyuan's income for 2016 more accurately than any of the alternatives, including **Answer (d)**. It allows her to increase her outside basis for the interest sold by only the amount of the partnership's income attributable to that interest before it was sold. The fact that **Answer (c)** is seemingly the right answer does not, however, make it the law.

6.2.3   The correct Answer is (a). Determining the correct answer under current law is not too hard here. There is no closing of the partnership's tax year, so Shuyuan's share of the partnership's income is passed through to her at the partnership's year-end (January 31, 2017). This is after the end of Shuyuan's 2016 tax year (December 31, 2016), so she takes nothing into account for that year. (Presumably, she includes in her 2016 personal tax return her share of the partnership's income for its year ended January 31, 2016, but this is outside the scope of the facts we are given.) Shuyuan has no adjustment to outside basis, so her gain is $50,000.

Determining the right answer is harder. For its tax year ending January 31, 2017, the partnership will allocate $60,000 to Shuyuan, which is the sum of her 50% share of the $80,000 partnership income for the pre-sale period ($40,000) and her 25% share of the $80,000 partnership income for the post-sale period ($20,000). Shuyuan still winds up realizing total income and gain of $110,000, as in Question 6.2.2. The timing is different, however, as the $60,000 inclusion is deferred by one year. Does this justify not increasing her basis in the interest sold by the income attributable to that interest before it was sold? Perhaps. It can be argued that such an increase would be premature, because it would be allowed in the year prior to the year that Shuyuan must include that income in her personal return. On the other hand, it is unlikely that the benefit of deferring this income for one year equals the detriment of increasing currently realized gain by an equal amount.

The right answer seems to be to close the partnership's tax year with respect to only the interest that Shuyuan has sold. This would require her to include $20,000 of the partnership's income in her personal return for 2016, which is a 25% share of the $80,000 partnership income for the pre-sale period. That income inclusion would give her a corresponding $20,000 basis increase, reducing her realized 2016 gain to $30,000. The income attributable to her remaining interest ($40,000) would flow through to her on January 31, 2017, increasing her outside basis to $240,000 and leaving $10,000 of built-in gain. Following this approach, each half of Shuyuan's interest would account for exactly $50,000 of income or gain (built-in gain, in the case of Shuyuan's retained interest). The total of $100,000 would match the result under current law for a sale of Shuyuan's entire interest and would entail no double taxation.

In the end, two wrongs (deferral and mis-measurement) do not make a right, but they do accurately describe the current state of the law. **Answer (c)** takes the approach just suggested, but it is not the law. **Answer (b)** assumes that the income from the interest sold flows through to Shuyuan but does not increase her outside basis. This is neither the law nor the right answer. **Answer (d)** includes Shuyuan's entire share of the partnership's income—that attributable to the interest retained as well as that attributable to the interest sold—in her 2016 income and reduces her gain by $20,000, the portion of the income attributable to the interest sold. This accelerates income to a greater extent than necessary to fix the problem.

6.2.4   The correct Answer is (b). Under current law, Shuyuan's sale of a partial interest produces no adjustment to her outside basis that can be taken into account in calculating her gain. Ignoring liabilities, her amount realized is $250,000 and her apportioned basis in the interest sold is $200,000, resulting in gain of $50,000. Under the sensible approach of Rev. Rul. 84–53, that's all there is to it. Under this ruling, the portion of Shuyuan's liability share that is included in the basis of the interest sold equals the portion of Shuyuan's liability share that is included in the amount realized on the sale. In other words, a wash.

To spell it out, Shuyuan is the only general partner of River Road, so her initial share of the partnership's recourse liabilities is 100%, or $500,000. On the sale of a one-half interest, her amount realized equals one-half of this liability share ($250,000) plus the cash sale price ($250,000), or $500,000. Her basis equals the same liability share ($250,000) plus her apportioned basis ($200,000), or $450,000. Her gain on the sale is $50,000.

Think of the mess if Rev. Rul. 84–53 had not taken this approach. Let's say, for example, that Shuyuan were permitted to include only $200,000 of the partnership's liability in her basis for purposes of computing her gain. She would recognize an additional $50,000 of gain on the sale, but that would not be the worst of it. Her basis for her remaining interest would presumably include $300,000 of the partnership's liability—$50,000 more than her share of that liability following the sale. If her liability share were capped at $250,000 following the sale, she would be deprived of $50,000 of basis with no tax benefit.

Answer (a) is incorrect, because it apparently allows a section 705 adjustment in computing Shuyuan's outside basis. **Answer (c)** is incorrect, because it does not allow Shuyuan to include in her basis any portion of her liability share that is attributable to the interest sold. **Answer (d)** compounds this error by also including in Shuyuan's amount realized the full amount of her liability share, rather than just the portion of her liability share attributable to the interest sold.

6.2.5   The correct Answer is (b). Here again, current law allows no adjustment to Shuyuan's outside basis that can be taken into account in computing her gain. The difference here is that, ignoring liabilities, Shuyuan's basis in her partnership interest is negative—as evidenced by her negative tax capital. In this situation, Rev. Rul. 84–53 provides that the adjusted basis of the transferred portion of Shuyuan's partnership interest ($x) equals an amount that bears the same relationship to her basis in her entire interest ($400,000) as the share of liabilities attributable to the interest transferred ($250,000) bears to her entire share of liabilities ($500,000). Solving for $x, Shuyuan can take $200,000 of her outside basis into account, against an amount realized equal to the sum of the cash consideration ($50,000) and the liability share attributable to the interest sold ($250,000) or $300,000. Her gain is thus $100,000.

This approach, which only applies where the transferor has negative tax capital, has the effect of triggering gain equal to the sum of (1) the cash consideration and (2) a portion of the transferor's negative tax capital equal to the portion of the liabilities discharged (*i.e.*, included in the amount realized). By selling half of her partnership interest, Shuyuan is ridding herself of half of her negative tax capital—half of her negative basis, if you will. It is entirely appropriate that she include this as amount realized and gain on this transaction, plus the value of any other consideration she may receive.

Answer (a) is incorrect, because its gain calculation includes only the cash consideration. **Answer (c)** is incorrect because it triggers Shuyuan's entire negative tax capital into gain (in addition to the cash), thus over-taxing her on the transaction. **Answer (d)** is worse, allowing Shuyuan to use none of her $400,000 basis to offset any of the amount realized on the sale.

6.3.1   The correct Answer is (b). The only unrealized receivable of this partnership is the section 1245 recapture on its depreciable equipment. The amount of this recapture is the lower of the accumulated depreciation ($28,000) or the gain realized on the hypothetical sale at fair market value of this equipment ($8,000). *See* section 1245(a)(1). Under Treas. Reg. §§ 1.751–1(c)(4), –1(c)(5), the amount of this unrealized receivable is $8,000 and its adjusted basis is zero. The accounts receivable of $65,000 are not unrealized—their entire value has already been taken into income by this accrual-method partnership. The $32,000 of section 1250 capital gain is not an unrealized receivable. **Answer (a)** is incorrect, because it focuses only on the accounts receivable and misses the recapture. **Answer (c)** is almost right. It correctly identifies the section 1245 recapture as the sole unrealized receivable, but then miscalculates the amount of the recapture. **Answer (d)** is incorrect, because it includes in unrealized receivables the section 1250 capital gain as well as the section 1245 recapture.

6.3.2   The correct Answer is (d). "Inventory items" include all items described in sections 751(d)(1), (2) and (3). Section 751(d)(1) covers the equipment inventory and the clothing inventory—it is irrelevant that one is appreciated and the other is depreciated. Section 751(d)(2) covers all other ordinary-income items, which include the accounts receivable (which have zero basis and $65,000 of inherent ordinary income for this cash-method partnership) and the section 1245 recapture on the equipment. Section 751(d)(3) covers the common stock investment—it would be inventory in Sally's hands, because she is a dealer in stock. "Inventory items" do not include the partnership's section 1250 capital gain. **Answer (a)** is incorrect, because it includes only the appreciated inventory. **Answer (b)** includes also the depreciated inventory, but that is still not enough. **Answer (c)** adds the common stock investment, but fails to include either the accounts receivable or the section 1245 recapture.

6.3.3   The correct Answer is (c). In the hypothetical sale, Runners World would recognize $0 on the sale of its accounts receivable, $20,000 of the sale of its inventory (Abe's share is $4,000), $8,000 of gain on the sale of its depreciable gym equipment, all of it recapture (Abe's share is $1,600), $32,000 of section 1250 capital gain on the sale of its building and improvements (Abe's share is $6,400) and capital gain on the sale of other assets in the aggregate amount of $82,000 (Abe's share is $16,400). Thus, Abe's ordinary income is $5,600 ($4,000 plus $1,600), his section 1250 capital gain is $6,400 and his capital gain is the remainder of his gain.

You may be tempted (I certainly was) to jump to the conclusion that Abe's capital gain must be $16,400, which is his share of the partnership's capital gain on the hypothetical sale. This seems to make sense, because the purpose of section 751(a) is to mimic the results that would be obtained in co-ownership. This hasty conclusion overlooks the fact that Abe sold his partnership interest for $200,000, which is more—$25,200 more, to be precise—than his share of the value of the partnership's stated assets. This premium may reflect assets that are not found on the partnership's balance sheet (like goodwill) or it may be derived from some special characteristic of Abe's partnership interest (voting or managerial rights, for example) that make it more valuable. In any event, Abe's total gain on the transaction is $200,000 amount realized less $146,400 adjusted basis, or $53,600. Subtracting the components of ordinary income and section 1250 capital gain leaves capital gain of $41,600.

Answer (a) makes the mistake discussed in the preceding paragraph. **Answer (b)** correctly computes Abe's overall gain, but neglects to include Abe's share of the section 1245 recapture in ordinary income. **Answer (d)** correctly computes Abe's overall gain and includes all of the correct components in ordinary income, but erroneously adds Abe's share of the section 1250 capital gain.

6.3.4 **The correct Answer is (c).** The amounts of ordinary income and section 1250 capital gain are identical to those in Question 6.3.3. The only issue is computing Abe's residual capital gain or loss. Overall, he has a loss on the transaction equal to the excess of his adjusted basis ($146,400) over his amount realized ($140,000), or $6,400. His capital loss is the dollar amount which, when added to Abe's share of ordinary income ($5,600) and section 1250 capital gain ($6,400), yields Abe's overall loss of $6,400. That amount is a capital loss of $18,400. Check: $5,600 + $6,400 + ($18,400) = ($6,400). **Answer (a)** includes only Abe's share of the loss on the depreciated inventory. Though strangely compelling in a transaction which yields an overall loss, this is incorrect. **Answer (b)** includes also Abe's share of the gain on the appreciated inventory, but neglects his share of the section 1245 recapture. **Answer (d)** evidences the sort of brain cramp that can happen all too easily in an exam. After correctly identifying all components of ordinary income and section 1250 capital gain, it evidently changes the sign of the $6,400 overall loss to a $6,400 overall gain, resulting in a capital loss of only $5,600, rather than $18,400. All that good work wasted.

6.5.1 **The correct Answer is (d).** Winona's special basis adjustment is the excess of her outside basis over her share of the partnership's inside basis. Winona's outside basis is $316,000, the sum of her cash purchase price ($116,000) plus her share as the sole general partner of the partnership's recourse debt ($200,000). Under Treas. Reg. § 1.743–1(d), Winona's share of inside basis is her share of the partnership's debt plus her share of the partnership's previously taxed capital. The latter amount equals the distribution Winona would receive following the hypothetical sale, plus the losses and minus the gains that would be allocated to her in the hypothetical sale. If the partnership sold all of its assets at fair market value ($432,000) and paid off its $200,000 debt, it would have $232,000 to distribute to the partners, of which Winona would get 50%, or $116,000. In the hypothetical sale, she would be allocated losses of $2,000 and $1,000 with respect to the inventory and the dry-cleaning equipment, respectively, and gains of $13,000 and $56,000 with respect to the receivables and the building, respectively. Winona's previously taxed capital is thus $116,000 + $2,000 + $1,000 − $13,000 − $56,000 = $50,000. Her special basis adjustment is:

Outside basis			$316,000
less share of inside basis			
Share of previously taxed capital			
Cash on hypo. sale	$ 116,000		
plus losses	3,000		
minus gains	(69,000)		
		$ 50,000	
plus share of liabilities		200,000	
			(250,000)
Special basis adjustment			$ 66,000

Or you can cheat. Regency Cleaners has no section 704(c) property. In this case, Winona's special basis adjustment can be determined by subtracting the tax capital account she inherits from Riley ($50,000) from her cash purchase price ($116,000). Notice that this simplified computation ignores Winona's liability share entirely. Including it would add $200,000 to each number in the subtraction, but would not change the result.

Answer (a) makes the dreaded mistake of including Winona's liability share only once, in this case in her outside basis but not in her share of inside basis. **Answer (b)** subtracts Winona's tax capital not from her outside basis, but from her share of the value of the assets of the partnership. **Answer (c)** is also incorrect, because it would give Winona a special basis adjustment equal to the distribution she would receive following the hypothetical sale.

6.5.2   The correct Answer is (a). Under Treas. Reg. § 1.755–1(b), the allocation of the special basis adjustment to each asset begins with the amount of gain or loss that would be allocated to the transferee in the hypothetical sale of that asset. These allocations will sum to the actual special basis adjustment calculated under Treas. Reg. § 1.743–1(d) in only one case: where the purchase price for the transferred interest equals the

5

interest's share of the fair market value of the partnership's assets, less liabilities, without discount or premium. This is that case. Winona pays $116,000 for Riley's interest, which is exactly the amount that she would receive in a liquidation following the hypothetical sale of all of the partnership's assets for their respective fair market values. Accordingly, the full amount of the hypothetical gain or loss can be allocated to every partnership asset. Note that the special basis adjustment is positive for assets with gain and negative for assets with loss. In each case, the special basis adjustment, when added to Winona's share of the partnership's common basis for an asset (which is a subtraction for a negative special basis adjustment), equals Winona's share of the fair market value of the asset.

Answer (b) is incorrect, because it allocates special basis adjustment only to partnership assets with inherent gain. This may once have been the correct answer, but that was changed by Treasury regulations issued in 1999. **Answer (c)** is incorrect for two reasons. First, its allocations reflect the full amount of the partnership's gain or loss on its assets, not just Winona's share. Second, it makes an allocation to section 1245 recapture. This is not incorrect in concept. The regulations provide that recapture is treated for allocation purposes as a separate asset. Treas. Reg. § 1.755–1(a) (sixth sentence). The trouble is that there is no recapture present in this case, because the value of the dry-cleaning equipment is less than its adjusted basis. **Answer (d)** is incorrect for a similar reason. It makes an allocation to section 1250 recapture, but there is no such recapture in this case, because the partnership has depreciated its building on a straight-line basis.

> **6.5.3**   **Answer (b) is correct; Answers (c) and (d) are better.** Using the simplified method, the special basis adjustment is the excess of Winona's outside basis excluding liabilities ($80,000) over the tax capital attributable to the transferred interest ($50,000), or $30,000. The problem is to allocate it. The sum of the allocations initially determined under Treas. Reg. § 1.755–1(b) is $66,000, just as in Question 6.5.2, but there is only $30,000 of special basis adjustment—not enough to go around. The allocations must be trimmed down, which is the job of Treas. Reg. §§ 1.755–1(b)(2) and (3). These provisions are not models of clarity. Moreover, in the present case they seem to get the answer wrong.

We can dismiss **Answer (a)** out of hand, because it does not follow the mandate of Treas. Reg. § 1.755–1(b)(2) to allocate the special basis adjustment first to ordinary income property, but instead scales back the allocations to ordinary income property and capital gain property alike. **Answer (b) is a correct answer under current law**. It is the result of applying Treas. Reg. § 1.755–1(b)(3) according to its terms. Full allocations of $13,000 and ($2,000) are first made to the receivables and inventory, respectively. This uses up $11,000 of the special basis adjustment, leaving $19,000 to be allocated to the capital gain property—here, the equipment and the building. Unconstrained, the allocations to these two assets would be ($1,000) and $56,000, respectively. The trick is to scale them back so they total not $55,000, but only $19,000.

Treas. Reg. § 1.755–1(b)(3)(ii) takes a three-step approach. First, determine the full allocation to each capital gain asset. Second, determine the "scale back"—the amount by which the sum of the full allocations to all capital gain assets exceeds the actual special allocation available for capital gain assets. Third, allocate this "scale back" proportionately among the capital gain assets according to their fair market values.

That sounds sensible, but the manner in which the regulation sets out this approach only works if all of the capital gain assets are actually gain assets—*i.e.*, none of them have a built-in loss. Unfortunately, in the present case, the equipment is a loss asset. The result of applying the Treasury regulation is not pretty. Contrary to logic, the allocation to the equipment balloons to a negative $4,600, which not only eliminates Winona's built-in loss in that asset, but produces a built-in gain of $3,600. The allocation to the building is correspondingly larger, although happily not large enough to turn it into a built-in loss asset.

Answer (c) sets out an alternative approach, which reaches a better result from a policy perspective. Under the facts of this case, the actual special basis adjustment available for capital gain assets is $19,000 and the sum of the full allocations to capital gain assets is $55,000. **Answer (c)** simply multiplies each of the full allocations by 19/55.

Answer (d) seems to carry out best the policy of section 755. There is no reason to constrain the allocation of special basis adjustment to the equipment, because it is a negative adjustment. Indeed, the more that is allocated to the equipment, the more is available to allocate to the building. **Answer (d)** therefore makes the full allocation of negative $1,000 to the equipment and then allocates the remaining special basis adjustment (as augmented by the negative allocation to the equipment) to the building. This approach has the effect of diminishing to the greatest possible extent the difference between the fair market value and the adjusted basis of each of the partnership's properties. Section 755(a)(1) establishes this as the goal of the allocation process. **Answers (c) and (d) both implement this goal in a manner that appears superior to the approach of the Treasury regulation and both should be acceptable under the authority granted by section 755(a)(1).**

6.5.4   The correct Answer is (d). A special basis adjustment becomes available by reason of a sale or exchange of an interest in an electing partnership. The issuance of a partnership interest is not a sale or exchange for this purpose. Treas. Reg. § 1.743–1(a). Before you start feeling sorry for Winona, look again at the partnership's balance sheet. Inside and outside basis are equal. The issuance of a 20% partnership interest to Winona has shifted capital within the partnership's accounts (increasing Winona's capital and decreasing that of the other partners), but it has created no imbalance between inside and outside basis. Granting Winona a special basis adjustment greater than zero would, in effect, increase inside basis and thus introduce an imbalance that is not there now. This is inconsistent with the underlying policy of the partnership tax system.

Let's go a step further and investigate what would be the amount of Winona's special basis adjustment if one were allowed. This involves some section 704(c) thinking that will be clearer to you after you have reviewed Chapter 8. The revaluation of the partnership's book assets immediately before Winona joins the partnership creates a layer of gain and loss, represented by the difference between the book values of the assets and the partnership's adjusted basis therein. Under section 704(c), the existing partners (Riley, Skyler and Taylor), *but not Winona*, are responsible for this gain and loss. Accordingly, if the partnership engaged in a hypothetical sale of its assets immediately after Winona joined, Winona would be allocated no gain or loss. Her special basis adjustment is:

Outside basis		$46,400
less share of inside basis		
Share of previously taxed capital		
Cash on hypo. sale	$46,400	
plus losses	0	
minus gains	(0)	
	$46,400	
plus share of liabilities	0	
		(46,400)
Special basis adjustment		$ 0

As you learned in Topic 2.6, the partnership is not required to revalue. If it didn't, Winona would presumably be responsible for 20% of the gains and losses inherent in the partnership's assets—in the aggregate, a gain of $26,400. In this event, the amount of the special basis adjustment, were one allowed, would be $26,400 and it would protect Winona from the subsequent gain. Although she might find that useful, the tax law is having none of it. The gain from which Winona seeks protection is actually gain that is shifted from the other partners. If they can shift this gain to Winona and she can shelter it with a special basis adjustment, the gain is eliminated from the tax system, at least until partnership interests are liquidated.

Answer (a) would be correct if a special basis adjustment were permitted in this case. **Answer (b)** would be correct if a special basis adjustment were permitted and no revaluation had been made. **Answer (c)**, reflecting the amount of Winona's compensation income, would not be a correct measure of her special basis adjustment, even if one were allowed.

6.6.1   The opening balance sheet is as follows:

Assets			Liabilities		
	Tax	Book		Tax	Book
A's leases	$180,000	$300,000	[None]	$ 0	$ 0
B's leases	300,000	300,000			
C's stock	300,000	300,000	**Capital**		
			Alessa	180,000	300,000
			Briana	300,000	300,000
			Clarissa	300,000	300,000
Total Assets	$780,000	$900,000	**Total Liabilities and Capital**	$780,000	$900,000

The partnership's basis for Briana's leases and for Clarissa's stock is limited to fair market value under section 704(c)(1)(C). Briana has a section 704(c)(1)(C) basis adjustment of $120,000. Clarissa has a section 704(c)(1)(C) basis adjustment of $260,000.

6.6.2   **The correct Answer is (c).** Clarissa's loss is the sum of her allocable share of the partnership's loss on the sale of the stock and her section 704(c)(1)(C) basis adjustment. The former amount is zero, because the partnership recognizes no book or tax gain or loss on its stock sale. The latter amount is $260,000, which represents the excess of the adjusted basis of the stock in Clarissa's hands at the time she contributed it ($560,000) over the inside basis allowed by section 704(c)(1)(C) ($300,000). **Answer (a)** is incorrect, because it neglects Clarissa's section 704(c)(1)(C) basis adjustment. **Answer (b)** appears to make two errors. It gives the partnership a full carryover basis of $560,000 for the stock, which is contrary to section 704(c)(1)(C). It then splits the resulting partnership loss of $260,000 equally among the three partners, which is contrary to section 704(c)(1)(A). *See* Chapter 8. **Answer (d)** is just plain wrong. Sorry.

6.6.3   **The correct Answer is (d).** Alessa's gain is the excess of the cash purchase price ($400,000) over her outside basis ($180,000), or $220,000. Let's try determining Daniella's special basis adjustment two ways. First, employing the approach of Treas. Reg. § 1.743–1(d), we need to compute the amount of the tax gain Daniella would recognize on the hypothetical sale of all of the partnership's assets at fair market value. This requires some knowledge of section 704(c)(1)(A). As Alessa's transferee, Daniella assumes her section 704(c) responsibility under Treas. Reg. § 1.704–3(a)(7). If the partnership sold the leases Alessa contributed for their fair market value of $400,000, it would realize a book gain of $100,000 and a tax gain of $220,000. The excess of the tax gain over the book gain ($120,000) would be allocated to Daniella, as it would have been to Alessa. It represents the amount of built-in gain in the leases at the time Alessa contributed them. The remaining tax gain ($100,000), together with the tax gain on the sales of all the other leases ($200,000), would be allocated equally to the three partners, $100,000 each.

Thus, Daniella would be allocated a total gain of $220,000 on the hypothetical sale.

We can now finish the computation of Daniella's special basis adjustment. It is the excess of her outside basis ($400,000) over her previously taxed capital, which itself is her book capital account restated to fair market value ($400,000), reduced by the gain she would recognize on the hypothetical sale ($220,000), or $180,000. Her special basis adjustment is therefore $220,000.

The second approach to determining Daniella's special basis adjustment is to cheat. Although this partnership does hold section 704(c) property, the ceiling rule does not apply. (You can trust me on this, or go read Chapter 8 now.) Therefore, we can determine Daniella's special basis adjustment by simply comparing her outside basis ($400,000) with her (formerly Alessa's) tax capital ($180,000). It comes out to $220,000 either way, but this way you have time for a second cup of coffee.

Answers (a) and (b) miscalculate Alessa's gain and can be dismissed out of hand. **Answer (c)** gets Alessa's gain right, but misses with its calculation of Daniella's special basis adjustment, apparently by failing to take into account the $100,000 portion of the tax gain on the hypothetical sale of Alessa's leases that is *not* subject to section 704(c).

Is it a coincidence that **Answer (d)**, the correct answer, reports equal gain and special basis adjustment? Not at all. Inside and outside basis are equal. Alessa's outside basis equals her share of the inside basis. In computing both the gain and the special basis adjustment, we are subtracting the same basis number ($180,000) from the same value number ($400,000).

6.6.4   **The correct Answer is (d).** Briana realizes $400,000 on the sale and has an outside basis of $420,000, so her loss is $20,000. (The difference between her outside basis and her tax capital is made up by her section 704(c)(1)(C) basis adjustment of $120,000.) As the transferee of Briana's partnership interest, Daniella has no section 704(c) responsibility. This may seem strange, because Briana's gas leases were built-in loss assets when contributed to the partnership. But the effect of section 704(c)(1)(C) is to equalize inside basis with fair market value on contribution, thus removing the section 704(c) taint from the contributed property. Daniella's gain on the hypothetical sale would be only $100,000, which is the amount of her special basis adjustment. Here again, you can determine Daniella's special basis adjustment by comparing her outside basis ($400,000) with her tax capital ($300,000).

Answers (a) and (b) miscalculate Briana's gain. That's an easy mistake to make, because you are used to tax capital (here, $300,000) equaling outside basis in a partnership without liabilities. But when section 704(c)(1)(C) scales back inside basis, it does the same to tax capital.

Answer (c) is also incorrect. In this Question, unlike in Question 6.6.3, the correct answer does not entail equal amounts of gain and special basis adjustment. Why not? Inside and outside basis are still equal on formation, but a portion of the inside basis in this Question takes the form of Briana's $120,000 section 704(c)(1)(C) basis adjustment. Daniella does not succeed to that basis adjustment. Thus, there is a $120,000 shortfall in inside basis that must be made up by Daniella's special basis adjustment. That accounts for the $120,000 difference between Briana's $20,000 loss and Daniella's $100,000 special basis adjustment. If that deficiency in inside basis were not present (in other words, if section 704(c)(1)(C) did not apply), Daniella's special basis adjustment would indeed be ($20,000).

6.6.5 **The correct Answer is (a).** Clarissa realized $400,000 on the sale. Her initial outside basis was $560,000, but it was reduced to $300,000 by the loss allocated to her from the partnership's sale of the stock she contributed. Her gain is therefore $100,000. Daniella would be allocated $100,000 of gain on the hypothetical sale, which is the amount of her special basis adjustment. Alternatively, you can determine Daniella's special basis adjustment by comparing her outside basis ($400,000) with her tax capital ($300,000). The gain realized once again matches the special basis adjustment, for the simple reason that Clarissa no longer has a section 704(c)(1)(C) basis adjustment, having used it up on the sale of the contributed stock.

Answer (b) miscalculates Daniella's special basis adjustment. **Answers (c) and (d)** miscalculate Clarissa's gain.

6.7.1 **The correct Answer is (c).** There is nothing in the facts to challenge the contention that this is a disguised sale of Aria's entire partnership interest. Her amount realized on this disguised sale is $850,000 (plus her share of partnership liabilities, if any), her basis is $450,000 (plus such share, if any), and her recognized gain is $400,000. But really, so what? If this transaction were not characterized as a disguised sale, Aria would have recognized exactly the same amount of gain on the partnership's cash distribution in liquidation of her entire interest in the partnership. *See* section 731(a)(1), discussed in Topic 9.1. There is no point in arguing about characterization in this case, because Aria's (and Bartholome's) tax consequences are the same either way. This refreshes a point made in Topic 2.7: disguised sales are all about limiting basis recovery. Here, Aria will recover her entire basis either way. **Answer (a)** is incorrect, both because this is a disguised sale and because, even if it were not, Aria would recognize $400,000 of gain. **Answer (b)** is incorrect, because this is a disguised sale. **Answer (d)** is incorrect, because it allows no basis recovery at all (other than for one-half of Aria's share of partnership liabilities).

6.7.2 **The correct Answer is (c).** This is a case where characterization matters. If the transaction is taxed in accordance with its form as a distribution, Aria can apply her entire outside basis against the distribution, recognizing no gain under section 731(a)(1). If, on the other hand, it is a disguised sale of one-half of her partnership interest, she can use only one-half of her outside basis ($225,000, plus one-half of her share of partnership liabilities) in computing her gain, and she will recognize $200,000 of gain. There are no facts that would allow Aria seriously to challenge the existence of a disguised sale here. **Answer (a)** is incorrect, because this is a disguised sale. If it were not, however, Aria's gain would be $0. **Answer (b)** is incorrect, both because this is a disguised sale and because, if it were not, Aria's gain would be $0, not $200,000, because of the allowable basis recovery under section 731(a)(1). **Answer (d)** is incorrect, because it allows no basis recovery at all (other than for one-half of Aria's share of partnership liabilities).

6.7.3 **The correct Answer (a).** Since the withdrawal of the proposed Treasury regulations on disguised sales of partnership interests, the analysis of these transactions is fundamentally an application of the step-transaction doctrine. And when the asset that Bartholome transfers to the partnership is not the same asset that the partnership transfers to Aria, the step-transaction doctrine is hard to apply. The proposed regulations would have characterized this transaction as a disguised sale by imputing additional transactions. Without the assistance of those regulations, it is doubtful that a court would reach the same conclusion. **Answer (b)** is incorrect, because it mis-measures Aria's gain. **Answer (c)** is incorrect, because this transaction should not be treated as a disguised sale. **Answer (d)** is incorrect, because it allows no basis recovery at all (other than for one-half of Aria's share of partnership liabilities).

7.2.1 **The correct Answer is (a).** Under the traditional method, the partnership must allocate its first tax gain on the sale of the painting to Abilene, up to $50,000, which is the excess of the painting's fair market value over its adjusted basis (the "built-in gain") at the time of contribution. Here, the partnership recognizes only $45,000 of gain, all of which goes to Abilene. Under section 724(b), this gain is treated as ordinary income, because (1) the painting was inventory in Abilene's hands and (2) the partnership sold it within five years following the contribution. **Answer (b)** is incorrect, because it fails to apply section 724(b). **Answer (c)** is incorrect, because it fails to apply section 704(c). **Answer (d)** is incorrect, because it applies neither statute.

7.2.2 **The correct Answer is (c).** The partnership holds the painting as a capital asset. Under section 1223(2), the partnership's holding period includes the period that Abilene held the painting, whether or not she held it as a capital asset. This is all irrelevant, however, for purposes of applying section 724(b), which looks solely to the amount of time between the date of the painting's contribution and the date of its sale. **Answer (a)** is incorrect, because it misinterprets section 724(b) to apply by reference to the partnership's holding period for the painting. **Answer (b)** is incorrect for the same reason. It also miscalculates the partnership's holding period for the painting. Whether Abilene held the painting as a capital asset or as section 1231 property would be relevant in determining her holding period for her interest in the partnership under section 1223(1), but it is irrelevant in determining the partnership's holding period for the painting under section 1223(2). **Answer (d)** has no basis in the language of section 724(b).

7.2.3   The correct Answer is (b). As in Question 7.2.1, you must first apply section 704(c) to determine the amount of gain allocated to Abilene and the other partners and then apply section 724(b) to determine its character. Under the traditional method, $50,000 of tax gain is allocated to Abilene. The remainder of the gain (also $50,000) is allocated among all of the partners, including Abilene. Under section 724(b), all of the gain, whether allocated to Abilene or the others, is treated as ordinary income. **Answer (a)** is incorrect, because it limits the ordinary characterization to the original built-in gain. While this is a very sensible approach, it is not the law. **Answer (c)** embodies another interesting, though wrong, approach. It allocates the correct amount of gain to Abilene and treats it all as ordinary income. So far, so good. It then treats the remaining gain allocated to the other partners as capital gain. This is contrary to the simple, rough approach of section 724(b). **Answer (d)** fails to apply section 724(b) at all.

7.2.4   The correct Answer is (c). Under section 704(c)(1)(C) as interpreted by the proposed Treasury regulations, the partnership takes Cheyenne's land with a tax basis equal to the land's fair market value at contribution, $35,000. The partnership thus has no book-tax difference in the contributed land and therefore no further obligation under section 704(c). When the partnership sells the land, it recognizes a tax loss and a book loss equal to $10,000, which is allocated among all of the partners, including Cheyenne, in accordance with their distributive shares. Cheyenne herself recognizes an additional loss of $45,000, which is the amount of the built-in loss on contribution, through the elimination of her section 704(c)(1)(C) basis adjustment. Prop. Treas. Reg. § 1.704–3(f)(3)(ii)(C). *See* Topic 6.6.

Assuming that the enactment of section 704(c)(1)(C) did not disturb the functioning of section 724(c) in this context, Cheyenne's $45,000 loss is capital loss under section 724(c). In stark contrast to the results in Question 7.2.3, the remaining $10,000 of the partnership's loss retains its character as determined under section 702(b)—here, as loss on the sale of section 1231 property (land used in a trade or business and held for more than one year).

Answer (a) is incorrect. It misapplies section 704(c) by allocating all of the recognized loss, not just the built-in loss, only to Cheyenne. It also misapplies section 724(c) in characterizing all of the recognized loss, not just the built-in loss, as capital loss. **Answer (b)** misapplies section 704(c) and does not apply section 724(c) at all. **Answer (d)** applies section 704(c) correctly. It applies section 724(c) so as to preserve the character taint for all gain allocated to Cheyenne, not just for the built-in gain. This is close, but incorrect.

7.3.1   The correct Answer is (d). Natalie is acting as an independent contractor. Under section 707(a)(1), the partnership's payment to her is treated as made to a person who is acting other than in her role as a partner. The partnership deducts the payment and Natalie takes it into income according to their respective methods of tax accounting. Because both use the cash method, the correct date for both is the date of the payment in February 2017. Because both use the same accounting method, there is no mismatching of income and deduction, and section 267(a)(2) plays no role. **Answer (a)** would be correct if both Natalie and the partnership used an accrual method and section 267(a)(2) would not apply in that case either. **Answers (b) and (c)** misapply the cash method.

7.3.2 **The correct Answer is (d).** Under their respective accounting methods, the partnership would accrue the deduction in 2016 but Natalie would not take the income into account until 2017. This is the mismatch that section 267(a)(2) was built to correct. It defers the partnership's deduction until 2017 to match Natalie's income pickup. Note that section 267(a)(2) applies, even though Natalie owns far less than 50% of Rosencrans. **Answer (a)** is incorrect, because it accelerates Natalie's income rather than deferring the partnership's deduction. **Answer (b)** treats Natalie as an accrual taxpayer and the partnership as a cash taxpayer, contrary to the facts. **Answer (c)** fails to apply section 267(a)(2).

7.3.3 **The correct Answer is (b).** Section 267(a)(2) does not provide matching in all cases. Here, the income precedes the deduction by a year under the parties' methods of tax accounting. The statute is just fine with that—it does not accelerate the deduction to match the income, as in **Answer (a)**, or defer the income to match the deduction, as in **Answer (d)**. **Answer (c)** is also incorrect, because, *inter alia*, it treats Natalie as a cash-method taxpayer.

7.3.4 **The correct Answer is (d).** The matching of income and deduction in this case is not accomplished by consistent methods of tax accounting or by the application of section 267(a)(2). Instead, it arises from the nature of the payment that the partnership is making to Natalie. Natalie is working in the business of the partnership, rather than working in an independent business that provides services to the partnership, like a tax accountant. Thus, the $25,000 payment to her should probably be classified as a guaranteed payment under section 707(c). As discussed in Topic 3.5, a service provider includes a section 707(c) guaranteed payment in income in the taxable year within or with which ends the taxable year of the partnership in which the partnership deducts or capitalizes the payment. Treas. Reg. § 1.707–1(c). In the present case, Rosencrans, which uses the cash method, will deduct the payment in 2017. It will report the guaranteed payment to Natalie on the Schedule K-1 it distributes to her at year-end 2017 and she will include it in income for that year. **Answer (a)** is incorrect, because it accelerates the partnership's deduction, which is not the approach of either section 267(a)(2) or Treas. Reg. § 1.707–1(c). **Answer (b)** is incorrect, because it treats the $25,000 as a payment governed by section 707(a)(1), rather than by section 707(c). The resulting mismatch is the same one we saw in the correct Answer to Question 7.3.3. **Answer (c)** is incorrect because, *inter alia*, it treats Natalie as a cash-method taxpayer.

7.3.5 **The correct Answer is (c).** The first step in answering this Question is to recognize that section 707(b)(1) does not apply. Although Natalie's ownership interest in the partnership is attributed to her father, that interest is only 10%—well short of the 50%+ interest required for section

707(b)(1) to apply. Nate is not out of the woods. Although section 267(a)(1) does not apply to disallow losses in sales between partners and partnerships, Treas. Reg. § 1.267(b)–1(b) applies section 267(a)(1), surprisingly, to disallow losses in transactions between partnerships and persons related to partners. It explains its explicitly aggregate approach in the following language: "Any transaction described in section 267(a) between a partnership and a person other than a partner shall be considered as occurring between the other person and the members of the partnership separately." Accordingly, Nate's loss in this transaction is disallowed to the extent of Natalie's 10% interest in the partnership. Nate's allowed loss is ordinary in character under section 1231(a)(2).

Answer (a) is incorrect because it treats the lithography equipment as a capital asset in Nate's hands. **Answer (b)** is incorrect, because it fails to apply Treas. Reg. § 1.267(b)–1(b). **Answer (d)** is incorrect, because section 707(b)(1) does not apply in this case, as explained above.

7.3.6   The best Answer is (c). Treas. Reg. § 1.267(b)–1(b) was promulgated in 1958, many years before the reach of section 267(a)(2) was extended to partnerships by the addition of section 267(e). It has not been amended since 1984 to take that development into account.

In the present case, section 267(a)(2) would defer the partnership's entire interest deduction until 2017, to match the date of Nate's inclusion of the interest income. As Natalie's father, Nate is on the list of persons related to the partnership for this purpose. *See* section 267(e)(1)(D). Treas. Reg. § 1.267(b)–1(b)(1)(i), on the other hand, would permanently disallow Natalie's 10% share of the interest deduction, but would not affect the remainder of the partnership's deduction at all. The worst of all worlds would be to apply the statute to defer 90% of the partnership's interest deduction and the regulation to disallow permanently the remaining 10%.

While that is a possibility, a better reading of history is that the regulation has been superseded by the legislation in any case covered by section 267(e), because the statute has adopted an explicitly entity approach to this issue which is contrary to the aggregate approach reflected in the regulation. Perhaps the IRS will confirm this conclusion if these regulations are ever again amended.

Answer (a) is incorrect, because it fails to apply section 267(a)(2) at all. **Answer (b)** is incorrect, because the self-charged interest rules do not affect the deductibility of interest expense, but rather its treatment under the passive-activity rules. **Answer (d)** is probably incorrect, because Treas. Reg. § 1.267(b)–1(b)(1)(i) should not apply in a case where section 267(a)(2) applies according to its terms.

7.3.7   The correct Answer is (c). Section 707(b)(1) does not change the tax treatment of realized gains. This may seem odd, because an understated gain in a related-party transaction seems to raise the same concern as an overstated loss. In the gain scenario, however, an IRS agent must make the case for underpricing and follow where it leads. In the present case, that path should reach the conclusions that (1) Carl sold land worth $240,000 to the partnership for cash and contributed land worth $80,000; (2) Carl was entitled to recover $240,000/$320,000, or 75%, of his tax basis on the sale of the land and therefore recognized gain equal to $240,000 less $120,000 (.75 x $160,000), or $120,000; (3) under section 721(a), neither Carl nor the partnership recognized gain or loss on the contribution; and (4) Carl's outside basis in the partnership increased by $40,000 as a result of the contribution. Note the similarity of this analysis to that of disguised sales in Topic 2.7. In this transaction, however, the sale is out in the open—it is the contribution that the parties have attempted to disguise.

Notice that this reconstruction of the transaction causes Carl to recognize $120,000 rather than $80,000 of gain on the sale and to have an additional $40,000 of gain built into his partnership interest, thereby correcting the gain understatement of $80,000 in the original transaction. In a different case, the same reconstruction could correct an overstated loss, but it is unnecessary (and not permitted?) because of the existence of section 707(b)(1).

Answer (a) is incorrect, because section 707(b)(1) does not disturb gain transactions. **Answer (b)** is incorrect, because section 267(b)(2) deals with payments of deductible amounts, not realized losses, which are the province of section 267(a)(1). **Answer (d)** is the result if the transaction is not recharacterized in the manner suggested above.

    8.1.1   **The correct Answer is (b).** On this sale, the partnership recognizes a book loss of $10,000 and a tax gain of $20,000. It allocates the book loss equally, $2,500 to each partner. The goal of section 704(c)(1)(A) is to allocate the entire built-in tax gain of $30,000 to Frank, the contributing partner of the stock. Because the partnership has not elected an optional section 704(c) method, it must apply the so-called "traditional" method, which includes the ceiling rule. The ceiling rule prevents the allocation of tax gain to Frank in excess of that which the partnership actually recognizes, $20,000. At the same time, the ceiling rule prevents the allocation of tax losses to match the book losses allocated to the noncontributing partners, because the partnership has recognized no tax loss. **Answer (a)** reflects the allocations that the partnership would like to make to each of the noncontributing partners, were it not foreclosed by the ceiling rule. **Answer (c)** reflects an allocation of tax gain equal to the entire built-in gain with which Frank contributed the stock. There are two problems with this allocation. First, the partnership, limited by the ceiling rule, does not have that much tax gain to allocate. Second, this is in any event an excessive allocation of tax gain to Frank, because he, like all the other partners, has recognized a book loss of $2,500 on the sale. Therefore, even if the ceiling rule did not constrain tax allocations in any way, it would be wrong for the partnership to allocate more than $27,500 of tax gain to Frank, which is the sum of his $30,000 built-in gain and his $2,500 share of the partnership's book loss. **Answer (d)** shows the total book and tax amounts that the partnership has to allocate, rather than the correct allocation to Frank.

8.1.2 **The correct Answer is (b).** Ordinarily, the allocation required by section 704(c)(1)(A) on the sale of a contributed asset eliminates the book-tax difference in the capital account of the contributing partner, to the extent that it is attributable to that asset. This is not the case, however, whenever the ceiling rule applies. Immediately following the partnership's sale of the stock, its balance sheet is as follows:

Assets			**Liabilities**		
	Tax	**Book**		**Tax**	**Book**
Cash	$ 80,000	$ 80,000	Payables	$ 0	$ 0
Receivables	0	30,000			
Inventory	60,000	60,000			
Building	40,000	80,000			
Cash from sale of stock	70,000	70,000			
			Capital		
			Clara	60,000	87,500
			Dyson	40,000	77,500
			Ellie	80,000	77,500
			Frank	70,000	77,500
Total Assets	**$250,000**	**$320,000**	**Total Liabilities and Capital**	**$250,000**	**$320,000**

You would expect the application of section 704(c)(1)(A) to eliminate Frank's book-tax difference entirely. Instead, it is $7,500, which reflects two factors: (1) Frank has not recognized $10,000 of the initial built-in gain on the stock, and (2) Frank, like all of the partners, has not recognized a tax loss equal to his $2,500 share of the book loss suffered by the partnership on the stock sale. **Answer (a)** would be correct if the ceiling rule did not apply. **Answer (c)** reflects only the first of the two factors mentioned above. Frank's remaining book-tax difference is not $10,000, even though he has not recognized $10,000 of the initial built-in gain on the stock, because he has suffered a $2,500 book loss without a corresponding tax loss. This latter factor reduces his remaining book-tax difference from $10,000 to $7,500. **Answer (d)** is Frank's initial book-tax difference, not that remaining after the foregoing adjustments.

8.1.3 **The correct Answer is (a).** The goal of section 704(c)(1)(A), which is to allocate the entire $30,000 of built-in gain on the stock to Frank, can be accomplished by allocating tax loss equal to the book loss allocated to each of the noncontributing partners, Clara, Dyson and Ellie. Here, however, the ceiling rule prevents the allocation of tax loss to Dyson and the other noncontributing partners, because the partnership has not recognized any tax loss. Therefore, Dyson (like the other noncontributing partners) is allocated a book loss of $2,500 and no tax gain or loss. **Answer (b)** reflects the application of an optional section 704(c) method, the "remedial" method, which we will review in Topic 8.2. **Answer (c)** reflects the allocations that the partnership will make to Frank, the contributing partner, not to Dyson. **Answer (d)** shows the total book and tax amounts that the partnership has to allocate, rather than the correct allocation to Dyson.

8.1.4 **The correct Answer is (b).** Ordinarily, the allocation of equal book and tax amounts to the noncontributing partners results in no change to the book-tax difference, if any, in each of their capital accounts. This is not the case, however, whenever the ceiling rule applies. The partnership's allocation of $2,500 of book loss, but no tax loss, to each of the noncontributing partners reduces by $2,500 the book-tax difference in Clara's and Dyson's capital accounts and creates a book-tax difference in Ellie's capital account where none was present before. **Answer (a)** reflects the elimination of the book-tax difference in Dyson's capital. That would be the goal of section 704(c)(1)(A) if the partnership had sold the building that Dyson contributed. Upon the sale of the land, however, section 704(c)(1)(A) does not seek to change Dyson's book-tax difference at all. Any increase or decrease in Dyson's book-tax difference arising from the partnership's allocations of book and tax items from the sale of the land is a "distortion" caused by the application of the ceiling rule. **Answer (c)** reflects the goal of section 704(c)(1)(A), which cannot be achieved in this case. **Answer (d)** reverses tax and book amounts, allocating to Dyson a tax loss of $2,500 and no book loss.

8.1.5 **The correct Answer is (c).** Because it uses the cash method, the partnership is not entitled to a deduction with respect to the assumed accounts payable until it pays them. This obligation to pay is thus not a "liability" within the meaning of Treas. Reg. § 1.752-1(a)(4). *See* Topic 5.3. Although the payables do not appear on the balance sheet as liabilities for tax purposes, they should be reflected as liabilities for book purposes. Their book value is the amount of cash that a willing assignor would pay to a willing assignee to assume them—here, $10,000. As a result of this "dual" treatment of the cash-method payables, Clara's initial book capital is reduced by the amount of the payables, from $90,000 to $80,000, while her tax capital is undiminished. *See* Treas. Reg. § 1.752-7(c).

This treatment, in turn, creates a book-tax difference for Clara that is attributable solely to the payables. This difference is a negative $10,000 (*i.e.*, Clara's tax capital is higher than her book capital by $10,000) and is akin to a built-in loss. Clara also has a book-tax difference that is attributable to the contributed accounts receivable. This difference is a positive $30,000 (*i.e.*, Clara's book capital is higher than her tax capital by $30,000). The two book-tax differences net to $20,000, and both are addressed by section 704(c).

The partnership recognizes $30,000 of ordinary income on the collection of the accounts receivable and $10,000 of ordinary deduction on the satisfaction of the accounts payable. Section 704(c)(1)(A) applies to the former and section 704(c)(3) to the latter. The partnership must allocate all of this income and deduction to Clara, the "contributing" partner for this property. (It may seem odd to refer to the partnership's assumption of Clara's accounts payable as her "contribution" of such accounts, but this is the language used by both section 704(c)(3) and Treas. Reg. § 1.704–3(a)(4), presumably to emphasize the similarity between this and other applications of section 704(c).) **Answer (a)** is incorrect, because it does not apply section 704(c)(1)(A) to the $30,000 ordinary income, allocating only 25% of it to Clara. **Answer (b)** is incorrect, because it does not apply either section 704(c)(1)(A) to the $30,000 ordinary income or section 704(c)(3) to the $10,000 ordinary deduction, allocating Clara 25% of the net income. **Answer (d)** is incorrect, because it does not apply section 704(c)(3) to the $10,000 ordinary deduction, allocating only 25% of it to Clara.

8.1.6   The correct Answer is (b). On the collection of the accounts receivable, the partnership has no book income and $30,000 of taxable income. Clara is allocated all of the taxable income. On the payment of the accounts payable, the partnership has no book deduction and a tax deduction of $10,000. Clara is allocated all of the tax deduction. Treas. Reg. § 1.752-7(c). The ceiling rule does not apply, so that no other partner's book or tax capital is affected. Here is the partnership's balance sheet immediately after the allocation of these items. It reflects the sale of the stock that Frank contributed, but disregards book and tax depreciation on the building, which are taken up in the following Questions:

Assets			Liabilities		
	Tax	**Book**		**Tax**	**Book**
Initial cash plus stock sale proceeds	$150,000	$150,000	[None]	$ 0	$ 0
Net cash from receivables and payables	20,000	20,000			
Inventory	60,000	60,000	**Capital**		
Building	40,000	80,000	Clara	80,000	77,500
			Dyson	40,000	77,500
			Ellie	80,000	77,500
			Frank	70,000	77,500
Total Assets	$270,000	$310,000	**Total Liabilities and Capital**	$270,000	$310,000

8.1.7   The correct Answer is (a). The partnership allocates its book depreciation equally among the partners, $4,000 to each. It endeavors to allocate an equal amount of tax depreciation to each of Clara, Ellie and Frank, the noncontributing partners with respect to the building, but it cannot. Because of the ceiling rule, it is limited to allocating only $2,667 (which is one-third of $8,000) of tax depreciation to each of these partners.

There is no tax depreciation left to allocate to Dyson. **Answer (b)** reflects an equal 25% sharing of both book and tax depreciation to each of the partners, which is contrary to section 704(c)(1)(A). **Answer (c)** is the result of applying the remedial method. **Answer (d)** is the unallocated, total amount of book and tax depreciation claimed by the partnership over this period.

    8.1.8   **The correct Answer is (c).** Because Dyson is allocated $4,000 of book depreciation and no tax depreciation, his book-tax difference decreases by $4,000 during this period. **Answer (a)** seems to neglect to allocate book depreciation to Dyson. **Answer (b)** allocates him too little and **Answer (d)** allocates him too much.

    8.1.9   **The correct Answer is (c).** The partnership's book gain of $76,000 is split equally among the partners, $19,000 each. That is the easy part. It is more challenging to determine the amount of tax gain that should be allocated to Dyson as the contributing partner of the building that the partnership has just sold. The main problem is the intuition that this is the partnership's "last clear chance" to eliminate Dyson's book-tax difference, which arose in the first place from his contribution of the building. The amount of tax gain needed to do this is $19,000 (to match the allocation of book gain from the sale) plus $33,500 (Dyson's existing book-tax difference) equals $52,500. Resist this impulse! You cannot cure all of the world's problems and neither can section 704(c). The current value of Dyson's book-tax difference is attributable a number of factors: his contribution of the building, the effect of the ceiling rule on the allocations from the stock sale (which increased the book-tax difference), and the depreciation of the building (which decreased it).

    There are two ways to determine the correct allocation of tax gain to Dyson. The first stems from the observation that section 704(c)(1)(A) applies on a property-by-property basis, not on a partner-by-partner basis. On the sale of the building, the amount of tax gain that is subject to allocation under section 704(c)(1)(A) is only the remaining built-in gain in the building. Treas. Reg. § 1.704–3(a)(3)(ii). This is the initial built-in gain ($40,000) reduced by the excess of book depreciation claimed ($16,000) over tax depreciation claimed ($8,000). The remaining built-in gain in the building can be determined easily by noting the difference between its book value and its adjusted tax basis on the balance sheet. It is $32,000. Allocating this amount to Dyson in addition to the $19,000 required to match his allocation of book gain yields $51,000 tax gain.

    I bet you can guess the second way to determine the correct allocation of tax gain to Dyson. *Tax follows book to the noncontributing partners.* So allocate tax gain to the partners other than Dyson equal to their allocations of book gain. This is a total allocation of $57,000 tax gain to the other partners. The remaining tax gain, $51,000, goes to Dyson.

    Answers (a) and (b) are incorrect, because they allocate no book gain to Dyson. **Answer (d)** is incorrect, because it bases its allocation of tax gain on Dyson's remaining book-tax difference, rather than the remaining book-tax difference in the building.

8.2.1   **The correct Answer is (b).** On the sale of its land for $600,000, the partnership recognizes a book loss of $150,000, which it allocates equally among the partners pursuant to the partnership agreement. It recognizes a tax gain of $250,000, all of which it allocates to Cora, the contributing partner. This allocation, however, does not eliminate Cora's book-tax difference—a "distortion" caused by the ceiling rule that remedial allocations can fix. An allocation of a notional tax gain of $100,000 to Cora, with offsetting allocations of notional tax loss of $50,000 to each of Ava and Bella, does the trick. Notice that these remedial allocations eliminate the book-tax differences in both Bella's and Cora's capital accounts, while restoring Ava's book-tax difference to $350,000. This is the correct result under section 704(c). Because the property that Ava contributed has been neither sold nor depreciated, its initial book-tax difference of $350,000 should be undiminished.

	Ava		Bella		Cora	
	Tax	**Book**	**Tax**	**Book**	**Tax**	**Book**
Initial	$400,000	$750,000	$750,000	$750,000	$350,000	$750,000
Land sale	0	(50,000)	0	(50,000)	250,000	(50,000)
Subtotal	400,000	700,000	750,000	700,000	600,000	700,000
Remedial	(50,000)	0	(50,000)	0	100,000	0
Ending	$350,000	$700,000	$700,000	$700,000	$700,000	$700,000

Answer (a) is correct in magnitude, but its character is wrong. A reasonable remedial allocation has the same character as the item limited by the ceiling rule—here, capital gain on the sale of the land. **Answer (c)** is incorrect, because it contains a book allocation. Remedial allocations always consist of tax items only. **Answer (d)** represents the total allocation of book and tax gain to Cora, not the remedial allocation.

8.2.2   **The correct Answer is (c).** The partnership recognizes a book gain of $150,000 on the sale of its investment asset, which it allocates $50,000 to each partner under the partnership agreement. The tax gain recognized by the partnership on this sale is also $150,000. The goal of the partnership in making curative allocations of this tax gain is to eliminate, if possible, the book-tax difference remaining in Cora's capital following the sale of the land. It can do this by allocating Cora all of the tax gain:

	Ava		Bella		Cora	
	Tax	**Book**	**Tax**	**Book**	**Tax**	**Book**
Initial	$400,000	$750,000	$750,000	$750,000	$350,000	$750,000
Land sale	0	(50,000)	0	(50,000)	250,000	(50,000)
Subtotal	400,000	700,000	750,000	700,000	600,000	700,000
Inv. asset sale	0	50,000	0	50,000	150,000	50,000
Ending	$400,000	$750,000	$750,000	$750,000	$750,000	$750,000

These curative allocations result in no tax gain being allocated to Bella, which has the effect of eliminating her book-tax difference, or to Ava, which restores her book-tax difference to $350,000. **Answer (a)** is the correct answer for Ava and Bella, but not for Cora. **Answer (b)** is the correct remedial allocation to Cora, not the correct curative allocation. **Answer (d)** is the correct total allocation of tax gain to Cora from the sale of both the land and the investment asset.

8.2.3   **The correct Answer is (a).** On the sale of the investment asset for $600,000, the partnership recognizes book and tax loss of $150,000. It may seem that losses would be no good for curative allocations in this case, because the ceiling rule has caused Cora to be allocated insufficient gain, not insufficient loss. By allocating none of its tax loss to Cora, however, the partnership can at least move things along:

	Ava		Bella		Cora	
	Tax	Book	Tax	Book	Tax	Book
Initial	$400,000	$750,000	$750,000	$750,000	$350,000	$750,000
Land sale	0	(50,000)	0	(50,000)	250,000	(50,000)
Subtotal	400,000	700,000	750,000	700,000	600,000	700,000
Inv. asset sale	(75,000)	(50,000)	(75,000)	(50,000)	0	(50,000)
Ending	$325,000	$650,000	$675,000	$650,000	$600,000	$650,000

These curative allocations reduce Cora's book-tax difference from $100,000 to $50,000, reduce Bella's book-tax difference from $50,000 to $25,000 and cause Ava's book-tax difference to increase from $300,000 to $325,000—all steps in the right direction, although not big enough to cure entirely the effects of the ceiling rule on the sale of the land. The partnership may be able to do more later. Assume that the partnership recognizes another $150,000 of book and tax loss from the disposition of an investment asset in a subsequent year. An allocation to Cora of her share of the book loss ($50,000) and none of the tax loss would eliminate her remaining book-tax difference and should be a reasonable curative allocation. *See* Treas. Reg. § 1.704–3(c)(3)(ii).

In making the curative allocation for the year of the sale, you may be tempted to allocate $100,000 of tax loss, rather than $75,000, to either Ava or Bella, and $50,000 of tax loss, rather than $75,000, to the other of these two partners. Your rationale would be to "fix" the ceiling-rule distortion for the chosen partner, while admittedly exacerbating the problem for the other. Don't play favorites. It is likely that this would be viewed as an unreasonable section 704(c) method—all the more likely if your choice just happened to allocate more tax loss to the partner in a higher tax bracket. *See* Topic 8.3.

Answer (b) reflects a possible allocation that would eliminate Cora's book-tax difference. But it allocates to Cora something that the partnership does not have: tax gain from the sale of its investment asset. The traditional method with curative allocations does not allow this. In common with the traditional method itself, it allows the partnership to allocate to its partners only tax gain or tax loss that the partnership actually recognizes. **Answer (c)** is also incorrect. It is the book loss that that partnership allocates to each of its partners on the sale of the investment asset. You might have interpreted **Answer (c)** to mean that the partnership should allocate an additional $50,000 of book loss to Cora. From a numerical standpoint, this would eliminate Cora's book-tax difference. There are two problems with this interpretation. The first is that curative allocations are always tax items, not book items. The second problem is more fundamental. The partnership's election to use the traditional method with curative allocations for purposes of section 704(c) does not allow it to tamper with the allocations of book gain or loss. The partnership recognizes only $150,000 of book loss on the sale of its investment asset, which must be allocated equally among the partners under the partnership agreement. Of course, the partners could independently agree to allocate to Cora the first $100,000 of book loss on the sale of the investment asset. There is nothing in the facts, however, to suggest that they have reached such an agreement. **Answer (d)** is also incorrect. Curative allocations are permitted, even if they are insufficient to eliminate the disparities created by the ceiling rule.

8.2.4   The correct Answer is (c). Tax depreciation is computed in the same manner under all three of the section 704(c) methods specified in the Treasury regulations. Under the traditional method, with or without curative allocations, book depreciation is computed simply by applying the tax depreciation method and recovery period to the property's book value. Treas. Reg. § 1.704–1(b)(2)(iv)(*g*)(*3*). Under the remedial method, however, book depreciation is determined by, first, splitting the book value into two components, one equal to the property's adjusted tax basis and the other equal to the excess, if any, of the book value over the adjusted tax basis. Book depreciation on the first of these components is determined by applying the tax depreciation method and period. Book depreciation on the second is determined as though it were newly acquired property. Book depreciation on the property as a whole is the sum of these two. Treas. Reg. § 1.704–3(d)(2).

In the present case, the adjusted basis of the equipment upon contribution is $400,000, which, under the "step in the shoes" rule of section 168(i)(7), the partnership will continue to depreciate for tax purposes on a straight-line basis over the remaining 5 years of the recovery period. The amount of tax depreciation in the first year is $80,000. Book depreciation equals the sum of this amount plus depreciation computed on the excess of the book value of the equipment over its tax basis, which is $350,000, as if the equipment were newly purchased. According to the statement of facts in this Question, newly acquired property of this type would be depreciable on a straight-line basis over 10 years, yielding $35,000 of depreciation in the first year. For purposes of applying the remedial method, the partnership's total book deprecation on the equipment for the first year is the sum of these two amounts, $115,000.

Answer (a) is incorrect. It is one year's depreciation on the book value of the equipment, if it is depreciated on a straight-line basis over 10 years. **Answer (b)** is also incorrect. It is one year's depreciation on the adjusted tax basis of the equipment, if it is depreciated on a straight-line basis over 10 years. **Answer (d)** is the most beguiling of the incorrect answers, because it would be the correct amount of book depreciation under the traditional method or the traditional method with curative allocations. It equals one year's depreciation on the book value of the equipment, depreciated on a straight-line basis over 5 years.

8.2.5 **The correct Answer is (a).** Because this partnership has elected to use the remedial method, it uses that method, rather than the traditional method, to determine its book depreciation. As computed in the preceding Question, that amount is $115,000 for the first year. Tax depreciation is $80,000. The partnership allocates its book depreciation equally among the partners under the partnership agreement and section 704(b). The partnership attempts to allocate tax depreciation to the noncontributing partners, Bella and Cora, equal to their shares of the book depreciation:

	Ava		Bella		Cora	
	Tax	**Book**	**Tax**	**Book**	**Tax**	**Book**
Initial	$400,000	$750,000	$750,000	$750,000	$350,000	$750,000
Depreciation	(3,333)	(38,333)	(38,333)	(38,333)	(38,333)	(38,333)
Subtotal	396,667	711,667	711,667	711,667	311,667	711,667
Remedial	0	0	0	0	0	0
Ending	$396,667	$711,667	$711,667	$711,667	$311,667	$711,667

Taking into account the remedial method's reduced book depreciation, there is enough tax depreciation to allocate tax depreciation equal to book depreciation to the noncontributing partners. No remedial allocations are required or permitted. The partnership must adopt the book computations under the remedial method, however, so that the book value of the equipment at the end of the first year is $635,000, not $600,000 as it would be under the traditional method, and the book capital account of each of the three partners is $711,667, not $700,000 as it would be under the traditional method. Treas. Reg. § 1.704–3(d)(7), example (1).

Answer (b) is incorrect. It reflects the actual allocation of tax depreciation to Ava, not the remedial allocation. **Answer (c)** is incorrect is a complex way. It is the answer you would get if you forgot to use the special computation of book depreciation required under the remedial method, but then applied remedial allocations anyway. *See* Question 8.2.6 below. This is not a reasonable remedial allocation to Ava. Likewise, **Answer (d)** would be the remedial allocation to each of Bella and Cora if you forgot to compute book depreciation under the special rule for the remedial method.

8.2.6   The correct Answer is (d). The starting point for this partnership is to compute depreciation under the traditional method. Book depreciation under that method is $150,000 for the first year and tax depreciation is $80,000. The ceiling rule applies:

	Ava		Bella		Cora	
	Tax	**Book**	**Tax**	**Book**	**Tax**	**Book**
Initial	$400,000	$750,000	$750,000	$750,000	$350,000	$750,000
Depreciation	0	(50,000)	(40,000)	(50,000)	(40,000)	(50,000)
Subtotal	400,000	700,000	710,000	700,000	310,000	700,000
Operating income	55,000	35,000	25,000	35,000	25,000	35,000
Ending	$455,000	$735,000	$735,000	$735,000	$335,000	$735,000

In making curative allocations of operating income, the partnership's aim is to allocate total tax items (including tax depreciation and operating income) to the noncontributing partners equal to the total book items (including book depreciation and operating income) allocated to them. It can accomplish this by allocating $25,000 of taxable operating income to each of Bella and Cora and the remaining $55,000 of taxable operating income to Ava. Bella's book-tax difference disappears and Cora's is restored to $400,000. The most interesting change is in Ava's book-tax difference, which originally was $350,000 and has now been reduced to $280,000, a reduction of $70,000, or one-fifth of the original amount. In this first year, Ava receives allocations of book loss and taxable income of $15,000 and $55,000, respectively. Thus, her taxable income exceeds her book income by $70,000 and Ava has, in effect, recognized one-fifth of the equipment's original $350,000 built-in gain. Each year during the equipment's five-year recovery period, Ava will recognize another one-fifth ($70,000) of the original built-in gain, so that, when the equipment is fully depreciated, she will have recognized all of its built-in gain. At the end of the equipment's recovery period, its book value and tax basis will both be reduced to zero. At exactly the same time, Ava's book-tax difference will be eliminated.

Answer (a) would be the correct remedial allocation, if this partnership had elected the remedial method. It is the correct answer for Bella or Cora, but not for Ava. **Answer (b)** is the correct curative allocation of operating income to Bella or Cora, but not to Ava. **Answer (c)** is the correct allocation of book operating income to each of the three partners, but does not represent the curative allocation of taxable operating income.

8.3.1   The correct Answer is (d). The partnership's book depreciation in the first year is $1,800, which it allocates $1,200 to Edison and $600 to Franklin. Its tax depreciation is $1,200. An allocation of $600 of tax depreciation to Franklin will equal his book depreciation and thus is the correct amount. Any larger allocation of tax depreciation to Franklin (such as the partnership's $1,200 allocation) is unreasonable in amount. **Answer (a)** is incorrect, because the partnership's allocation of tax depreciation is not that which is called for by the traditional method. Under the traditional method, Franklin would be allocated $600 of tax depreciation, which would equal his book depreciation, and Edison would be allocated the remaining $600. **Answer (b)** is incorrect—there is no ceiling-rule issue in this example. **Answer (c)** is beguiling and wrong. Do not be impatient in applying section 704(c) to depreciation. The goal is not to eliminate Edison's book-tax difference as quickly as possible, but rather to eliminate it ratably over the remaining book life of the contributed equipment (assuming that this is not significantly shorter than its remaining economic life).

    8.3.2   **The correct Answer is (d).** There is no ceiling-rule limitation on the facts of this example, regardless whether book depreciation on the contributed property is determined under the traditional method or under the slower approach mandated by the remedial method, because the partnership has plenty of tax depreciation to go around. Remedial allocations are only permitted to the extent necessary to offset distortions caused by the ceiling rule. Thus, the partnership's method is something other than the remedial method. Trouble is, the Treasury regulations prohibit the creation of notional tax items except pursuant to the remedial method. Treas. Reg. § 1.704–3(d)(5)(i). **Answer (a)** is incorrect, because the partnership is not using the remedial method. **Answer (b)** is incorrect, because the ceiling rule does not apply on these facts. **Answer (c)** is wrong for the same reason that the same answer was wrong in Question 8.3.1. Fundamentally, the allocations employed by the partnership in this case do not advance the policy of section 704(c), because they cause Edison to recognize her built-in gain over a period that is shorter than the life of the contributed equipment. See the answer to Question 8.3.4 for more discussion of this issue.

    8.3.3   **The correct Answer is (a).** Now, finally, there is a ceiling-rule limitation and curative allocations are permissible. But at what rate?

	Edison		Franklin	
	Tax	Book	Tax	Book
Initial	$ 1,500	$ 9,000	$ 4,500	$ 4,500
First year's depreciation	0	(1,200)	(300)	(600)
Subtotal	1,500	7,800	4,200	3,900
Curative allocation of $750 operating income	750	500	0	250
End of first year	2,250	8,300	4,200	4,150
Second year's depreciation	0	(1,200)	(300)	(600)
Subtotal	2,250	7,100	3,900	3,550
Curative allocation of $1,050 operating income	1,050	700	0	350
End of second year	$ 3,300	$ 7,800	$ 3,900	$ 3,900

The curative allocations in the first year are not quite large enough to offset the ceiling rule's effect. (Notice the $50 book-tax difference that has appeared in Franklin's capital.) In the second year, the curative allocations are large enough to offset not only the effect of the ceiling rule in that year, but the remaining effect from the first year as well. Ordinarily, curative allocations in subsequent years cannot offset ceiling-rule effects left over from earlier years. Treas. Reg. § 1.704–3(c)(i). Notwithstanding this general rule, a partnership may make such allocations if they are made over a reasonable period of time, such as over the property's economic life, and are provided for in the partnership agreement. Treas. Reg. § 1.704–3(c)(ii). This special rule applies here. The economic life of the contributed equipment approximates its depreciable life. The curative allocations in the second year merely "catch up" to the equipment's depreciation. Larger curative allocations would be unreasonable, because they would be more than necessary to undo the effect of the ceiling rule.

Taking into account the curative allocations, by the end of the second year Edison has picked up $3,000 of her original built-in gain, as evidenced by the reduction in her book-tax difference from $7,500 to $4,500. At this rate, she will pick up the remaining $4,500 of built-in gain over the remaining three years of the economic life of the equipment. She is right on schedule.

Answer (b) is incorrect, for the reason explained above. **Answer (c)** properly states the general rule for curative allocations, but neglects the exception that controls this case. **Answer (d)** is technically incorrect, because these allocations actually are permissible curative allocations. However, **Answer (d)** correctly explains the reason why they are permissible.

8.3.4   The correct Answer is probably (b). The preceding Questions have illustrated the principle that the purpose of section 704(c) is to capture the built-in gain in contributed property over the life of the property. But there are at least three different lives to choose from: the cost recovery period for tax depreciation, the book life (which is the same as the tax life under the traditional method, but longer under the remedial method) and the economic life. Allocating tax depreciation equal to book depreciation to the noncontributing partners causes the contributing partner to recognize the built-in gain over the book life of the contributed property. While this is generally fine, if the book life is significantly shorter than the economic life, that allocation method may be unreasonable. Treas. Reg. § 1.704–3(c)(3)(ii). Such is probably the case here, where the remaining economic life of the contributed equipment is five times longer than its book life (25 years versus five years). On the other hand, two factors weigh against this conclusion. First, the only example in the Treasury regulations that illustrates this issue features a one-year book life and a 10-year economic life—a 10:1 ratio compared to the 5:1 ratio here. Treas. Reg. § 1.704–3(c)(4), example (3). Second, the facts give no information regarding the relative tax positions of Edison and Franklin, so it is not possible to determine whether the curative allocations here reduce, or increase, their aggregate tax liability. Such reduction is present in the regulatory example and is necessary in order to apply the anti-abuse rule of Treas. Reg. § 1.704–3(a)(10), although not the basic rule of Treas. Reg. § 1.704–3(c)(3)(ii).

If these factors are controlling, then **Answer (a)** is correct. **Answer (c)** is incorrect in any event, because, as we saw in Question 8.3.3, curative allocations can sometimes be made to offset earlier ceiling-rule distortions. Whether **Answer (d)** is right or wrong depends on whether causing Edison to pick up her entire built-in gain over five years is reasonable in this case.

8.3.5   **The correct Answer is (b).** The $900 curative allocation is the correct amount:

	Edison		Franklin	
	Tax	**Book**	**Tax**	**Book**
Initial	$ 1,500	$ 9,000	$ 4,500	$ 4,500
First year's depreciation	0	(1,200)	(300)	(600)
Subtotal	1,500	7,800	4,200	3,900
Curative allocation of $900 capital gain	900	600	0	300
End of first year	$ 3,400	$ 8,400	$ 4,200	$ 4,200

Because it is capital gain, however, the curative allocation does not satisfy the character-matching requirement of Treas. Reg. § 1.704–3(c)(3)(iii). The partnership's allocation method is therefore unreasonable. **Answer (a)** is incorrect. **Answer (c)** is incorrect, because these curative allocations exactly offset the ceiling rule limitation in the same year, which means that Edison is recognizing her built-in gain ratably over the book life of the contributed property, which approximates the economic life of that property. **Answer (d)** is incorrect. Every partnership choosing to make use of curative allocations runs the risk that there may be insufficient income of the proper "type." This method does not allow for making up a deficit with allocations of income of the improper type.

8.3.6   **The correct Answer is (a).** At first blush, this appears to be the same question as Question 8.3.5. The Treasury regulations, however, contain an exception that allows a partnership to use curative allocations of gain from the disposition of a property to offset the effect of the ceiling rule on the allocation of depreciation from that same property. Treas. Reg. § 1.704–3(c)(3)(iii)(B). In the present case, it appears that the partnership's gain on the sale of the equipment will be characterized as ordinary income under the section 1245 recapture rules, thereby creating a character match with the depreciation, but this is not necessary in order for the special exception to apply. If, for example, the contributed property were real estate subject to straight-line depreciation, there would be no section 1250 recapture, but the partnership would still be free to make curative allocations of the gain from its sale. **Answer (b)** is incorrect, because it does not take this special exception into account. **Answer (c)** is incorrect, even though the book depreciation period for the equipment (five years) significantly understates its estimated economic life (25 years). This is because the sale of the property provides the last opportunity to take into account Edison's built-in gain. **Answer (d)** is incorrect, because curative allocations of gain on the sale of the equipment are permitted.

    8.5.1   **The correct Answer is (d).** In the revaluation, the $250,000 book gain is allocated equally between Cephus and Dan, increasing Cephus' book-tax difference and creating one for Dan. When the partnership sells Parcel C, it realizes $150,000 of book gain, which is the excess of the sale price ($1,150,000) over the book value established in the revaluation ($1,000,000). It allocates this book gain equally among the three partners. Its tax gain is $900,000, which is the excess of the sale price ($1,150,000) over the adjusted basis of Parcel C ($250,000). Under the partnership's oldest-first approach, the first tax gain goes to Cephus in an amount equal to his forward gain layer ($500,000). The next $250,000 of gain is split equally between Cephus and Dan to equal their shares of the reverse gain layer created in the revaluation. Finally, the partnership allocates its last $150,000 of tax gain equally to the partners, as they share a like amount of book gain under the partnership agreement. The total tax gain allocated to Cephus is the sum of these three allocations to him, which is $675,000. There is sufficient tax gain generated by this sale to eliminate the book-tax differences for all partners:

(in 000s)	Cephus		Dan		Errol	
	Tax	**Book**	**Tax**	**Book**	**Tax**	**Book**
Initial	$250	$750	$750	$750		
Revaluation	0	125	0	125		
Subtotal	250	875	750	875	$875	$875
Sell Parcel C		50		50		50
Forward gain layer	500		0		0	
Reverse gain layer	125		125		0	
"Book layer"	50		50		50	
Ending	$925	$925	$925	$925	$925	$925

    8.5.2   **The correct Answer is (c).** The partnership's sale of Parcel C for $850,000 produces a book loss of $150,000 and a tax gain of $600,000. The book loss is allocated $50,000 to each partner. Because this partnership uses the traditional method, it cannot allocate tax loss to any of the partners, because it has recognized no tax loss. The partnership will therefore make no tax allocation to Errol. It allocates $500,000 of tax gain to Cephus with respect to his forward gain layer. It splits the remaining $100,000 of tax gain between Cephus and Dan with respect to their reverse gain layer, but this allocation falls short (by $150,000) of eliminating the book-tax difference in that layer. The total allocation of tax gain to Cephus is $550,000. Due to the application of the ceiling rule, all three partners have book-tax differences:

(in 000s)	Cephus		Dan		Errol	
	Tax	Book	Tax	Book	Tax	Book
Initial	$250	$750	$750	$750		
Revaluation	0	125	0	125		
Subtotal	250	875	750	875	$875	$875
Sell Parcel C		(50)		(50)		(50)
Forward gain layer	500		0		0	
Reverse gain layer	50		50		0	
"Book layer"	0		0		0	
Ending	$800	$825	$800	$825	$875	$825

8.5.3   **The correct Answer is (c).** The partnership's decision to allocate tax items to the newest layer first does not cure the book-tax difference for any partner, but it does shuffle the allocation of tax gain among them. In particular, Dan is allocated more tax gain and Cephus is allocated less, compared to the oldest-first allocation:

(in 000s)	Cephus		Dan		Errol	
	Tax	Book	Tax	Book	Tax	Book
Initial	$250	$750	$750	$750		
Revaluation	0	125	0	125		
Subtotal	250	875	750	875	$875	$875
Sell Parcel C		(50)		(50)		(50)
"Book layer"	0		0		0	
Reverse gain layer	125		125		0	
Forward gain layer	350		0		0	
Ending	$725	$825	$875	$825	$875	$825

Without knowing more, it appears that either of the allocation methods employed in Question 8.5.2 and Question 8.5.3 is reasonable in this case. Conceivably, the IRS could conclude that the oldest-first method (which allocates more gain to Cephus) is unreasonable if Dan is in the higher tax bracket and the newest-first allocation (which allocates more gain to Dan) is unreasonable if Cephus is in the higher tax bracket. Treas. Reg. § 1.704–3(a)(10). The IRS and the Treasury Department have not yet indicated their views on this issue in regulation, ruling or otherwise. A concerned partnership might opt for the pro-rata method, which in this case would spread the $600,000 tax gain between Cephus and Dan in the ratio of $625,000:$125,000, or 5:1.

   8.5.4   The correct Answer is (b). Another way for Target to avoid any concern about unreasonableness is to choose to make remedial allocations. After completing allocations under the traditional method, including its newest-first choice as to the stacking of layers, the partnership finds that each partner has a book-tax difference. These can be eliminated by a remedial allocation of $100,000 tax gain to Cephus and $50,000 tax loss to each of Dan and Errol:

(in 000s)	Cephus		Dan		Errol	
	Tax	Book	Tax	Book	Tax	Book
Initial	$250	$750	$750	$750		
Revaluation	0	125	0	125		
Subtotal	250	875	750	875	$875	$875
Sell Parcel C		(50)		(50)		(50)
"Book layer"	0		0		0	
Reverse gain layer	125		125		0	
Forward gain layer	350		0		0	
Subtotal	725	825	875	825	875	825
Remedial	100	0	(50)	0	(50)	0
Ending	$825	$825	$825	$825	$825	$825

   8.5.5   The correct Answer is (d). On its revaluation prior to Frank's entry, the partnership realizes a book loss of $300,000, which it allocates equally to Cephus, Dan and Errol. Because the partnership has chosen the traditional method, it will allocate no tax loss to any of these partners, because it has recognized only tax gain. The sale of Parcel C results in a book gain of $100,000 and a tax gain of $550,000. As the partnership considers how to allocate its tax gain, it must consider a question that has not come up before, because it has not mattered. Is the entire $550,000 tax gain allocated under section 704(c)? Or is $100,000 of tax gain allocated under section 704(b), leaving only $450,000 to be allocated under section 704(c)? The fact that the partnership recognizes $100,000 of book gain on the sale of Parcel C may suggest that an equal amount of tax gain must be allocated among the partners under section 704(b). That is not correct. The $100,000 of book gain simply reflects the appreciation in the value of Parcel C since its last revaluation. Previously, the partnership has realized other amounts of book gain and loss, which have become reverse section 704(c) gain and loss layers. The $100,000 book gain on the sale is really no different, although it cannot technically be called either a forward layer or a reverse layer, because it arises from a sale, not a contribution or revaluation. Prop. Treas. Reg. § 1.704–3(a)(6)(i) (forward layers arise from contributions; reverse layers arise from any other revaluation). Allocating $100,000 of tax gain to this layer of book gain would mean allocating less to earlier layers. This may be a reasonable choice, but it is not the only choice available to the partnership.

Using an oldest-first approach, the partnership allocates $500,000 of tax gain to Cephus. It splits the remaining $50,000 of tax gain equally between Cephus and Dan with respect to the next-oldest layer:

(in 000s)	Cephus		Dan		Errol		Frank	
	Tax	Book	Tax	Book	Tax	Book	Tax	Book
Initial	$250	$750	$750	$750				
Revaluation	0	125	0	125				
Subtotal	250	875	750	875	$875	$875		
Revaluation	0	(100)	0	(100)	0	(100)		
Subtotal	250	775	750	775	875	775	$775	$775
Sell Parcel C		25		25		25		25
Forward gain layer	500		0		0		0	
Reverse gain layer	25		25		0		0	
Reverse loss layer	0		0		0		0	
"Book layer"	0		0		0		0	
Ending	$775	$800	$775	$800	$875	$800	$775	$800

8.5.6   **The correct Answer is (b).** As you can see from the last line of the table immediately above, remedial allocations of $25,000 of tax gain to Cephus, Dan and Frank and $75,000 of tax loss to Errol will eliminate the book-tax differences for all partners.

8.6.1   Immediately after Jackie converts, the partnership's balance sheet, expanded to show asset values, appears as follows:

Assets				Liabilities		
	Tax	Book	FMV		Tax	Book
Cash	$ 2,000	$ 2,000	$ 2,000	Convertible Debt	$ 0	$ 0
Equipment	10,000	30,000	30,000			
Plant	18,000	48,000	48,000	**Capital**		
Land	12,000	16,000	16,000	Peter	10,000	24,000
				Paul	10,000	24,000
				Mary	10,000	24,000
				Jackie	12,000	24,000
Total Assets	$42,000	$96,000	$96,000	**Total Liabilities and Capital**	$42,000	$96,000

Jackie's tax capital and initial book capital both equal the adjusted issue price of the convertible debt instrument, $12,000. Treas. Reg. §§ 1.721–2(g)(5), 1.1273–2(j). Following the procedure of Treas. Reg. § 1.704–1(b)(2)(iv)(s), the partnership revalues all of its book assets immediately after Jackie converts his debt. It allocates the resulting book gain, $54,000, first to Jackie in the amount needed to increase his book capital to 25% of the partnership's aggregate revalued book capital. This allocation is $12,000 of book gain, increasing Jackie's book capital to $24,000 and leaving $42,000 of book gain to be allocated equally among the other three partners. On these facts, there is no need for book capital shifts or corrective allocations, because there is plenty of book gain to establish Jackie's book capital account at the correct level.

8.6.2   Immediately after Jackie converts, the partnership's balance sheet, expanded to show asset values, appears as follows:

Assets				Liabilities		
	Tax	Book	FMV		Tax	Book
Cash	$ 1,000	$ 1,000	$ 1,000	Convertible Debt	$ 0	$ 0
Equipment	9,000	31,000	31,000			
Plant	17,000	48,000	48,000	**Capital**		
Land	11,000	16,000	16,000	Peter	24,000	24,000
				Paul	24,000	24,000
				Mary	24,000	24,000
				Jackie	24,000	24,000
Total Assets	$38,000	$96,000	$96,000	**Total Liabilities and Capital**	$96,000	$96,000

Jackie's tax capital and initial book capital both equal the adjusted issue price of the convertible debt instrument, $8,000. The partnership revalues all of its book assets immediately after Jackie converts his debt. It allocates the resulting book gain, $58,000, first to Jackie in the amount needed to increase his book capital to 25% of the partnership's aggregate revalued book capital. This allocation is $16,000 of book gain, increasing Jackie's book capital to $24,000 and leaving $42,000 of book gain to be allocated equally among the other three partners. On these facts, there is again no need for book capital shifts or corrective allocations.

8.6.3   **The correct Answer is (d).** As can be seen by comparing the balance sheets of the partnership immediately after the conversions in Question 8.6.1 and Question 8.6.2, as the issue price of Jackie's convertible debt decreases, Jackie's tax capital in the partnership following conversion decreases as well. This creates a commensurately higher book-tax difference for Jackie that he must take into account as a reverse section 704(c) layer. This is not the obviously correct tax treatment for this situation. By issuing to Jackie a debt instrument with a conversion discount, the partnership and therefore the other partners are essentially transferring to him some of their existing book capital. You can see this by noting what would happen if Jackie converted immediately upon receiving his convertible debt: he would own 25% of the partnership (value $9,500) for an investment of $8,000, whereas each of the other partners would own the same $9,500 share for an investment of $10,000. Nevertheless, under the approach taken by the regulations, Jackie is permitted to avoid any immediate tax consequence from this capital shift, either upon the issuance of the convertible debt instrument or upon its exercise, so long as the partnership generates sufficient book gain during the period that Jackie holds the convertible debt to "fill up" his book capital account to the required level upon exercise. **Answer (b)** is incorrect, because Jackie's book capital account is exactly the same following the conversions in Question 8.6.1 and Question 8.6.2. **Answer (c)** is incorrect, because there is no capital shift and thus no corrective allocations in Question 8.6.2.

The existence of the conversion discount creates a possibility—a slim one, based on the facts provided—that Jackie should be treated as a partner of Puff Unlimited from the outset. *See* Topic 2.8.

8.6.4   Immediately after the conversion, the partnership's balance sheet looks like this:

	Assets			Liabilities		
	Tax	**Book**	**FMV**		**Tax**	**Book**
Cash	$ 1,000	$ 1,000	$ 1,000	Convertible Debt	$ 0	$ 0
Equipment	9,000	9,000	9,000			
Plant	17,000	17,000	17,000	**Capital**		
Land	11,000	11,000	11,000	Peter	10,000	9,500
				Paul	10,000	9,500
				Mary	10,000	9,500
				Jackie	8,000	9,500
Total Assets	$38,000	$38,000	$38,000	**Total Liabilities and Capital**	$38,000	$38,000

In this case, there is no book gain from the revaluation to allocate to Jackie's capital account. Beginning at $8,000, it must be increased to $9,500, which is 25% of the partnership's aggregate book capital immediately following the revaluation. This can only be accomplished by shifting $500 of book capital from each of the other three partners to Jackie.

8.6.5   **The correct Answer is (a).** The shift of book capital to Jackie begets corrective allocations to Jackie under Treas. Reg. 1.704–1(b)(4)(x). This is less favorable treatment for Jackie than the reverse section 704(c) layer he obtained in Question 8.6.3, for two reasons. First, corrective allocations must begin immediately, in the taxable year of the conversion, rather than awaiting the partnership's sale or depreciation of the assets on hand on the date of the revaluation. Second, corrective allocations are made from "gross income and gain"—meaning that at least some are likely to be ordinary in character. **Answer (b)** is incorrect, although Jackie cannot be happy about that. **Answer (c)** is incorrect, because in this case, as in all those before it, the regulations see to it that Jackie has an opening book capital account that equals his share of the partnership's total. **Answer (d)** is also incorrect. Treas. Reg. § 1.704–1(b)(2)(iv)(*h*)(*2*), the "headroom" regulation, requires a partnership to reserve a portion of its revaluation gain for the benefit of the option holder, so that it is available to allocate to her if and when the option is exercised. The function of this regulation is to minimize the role of corrective allocations—which is to say, to maximize the role section 704(c)—in this context. It is of no help to Jackie in this case, however, because the partnership did not revalue its book assets while Jackie's convertible debt was outstanding.

9.1.1   **The correct Answer is (c).** Partner S recognizes gain under section 731(a)(1) equal to the excess of the amount of money she receives ($15,000) over her outside basis immediately before the distribution ($10,000). Neither the value nor the basis of the receivable enters into this calculation, because the cash is deemed to be taken out first. This gain is capital gain under section 741. The partnership recognizes no gain or loss under section 731(b). **Answer (a)** is incorrect, because Partner S receives cash in excess of her outside basis and so must recognize gain. **Answer (b)** is incorrect, both because it misstates the character of Partner S's gain and because it reflects loss recognition by the partnership. **Answer (d)** is incorrect, because it takes the value of the distributed receivable into account in determining Partner S's gain.

9.1.2 **The correct Answer is (c).** On its face, the language of Section 732(b) provides that the basis of the receivable in this case is Partner S's $10,000 outside basis reduced by the $15,000 of money distributed to her, or ($5,000). This result as is surprising as it is wrong. It might be helpful if section 732(b) contained the same zero-basis limitation that is found in section 733 for current distributions, but it does not. Nevertheless, by recognizing $5,000 of gain Partner S has in effect added $5,000 of basis to her partnership interest, increasing it to $15,000, all of which is taken by the distributed cash. The amount left to allocate to the distributed receivable is $0. **Answer (a)** is incorrect, because it does not account for the distributed cash. **Answer (b)** gives Partner S the partnership's former basis in the receivable, which is incorrect for a liquidating distribution and would not even be correct in this case for a current distribution, which would be governed by the limitation of section 732(a)(2). **Answer (d)** is incorrect for the reason discussed above.

9.1.3 **The correct Answer is (c).** Under section 731(a)(2), Partner M claims a loss equal to the excess of her outside basis ($40,000) over the cash ($20,000) she receives in liquidation of her interest. The flush language at the end of section 731(a) tells us that this loss is considered a loss from Partner M's sale or exchange of her partnership interest, which section 741 characterizes as a capital loss. Section 731(b) confirms that LnL recognizes no gain or loss on this distribution. **Answer (a)** is incorrect, because this is one of the relatively few cases where a distributee-partner realizes loss. **Answers (b) and (d)** both miss the mark by requiring the partnership to recognize income or gain.

9.1.4 **The correct Answer is (a).** The key to answering this Question correctly is to recognize that the partnership has no section 751 assets. Under the facts, it has no inventory items. While it does have receivables, they are not "unrealized" because the partnership is an accrual taxpayer and has taken their full $5,000 value into income, thereby increasing their adjusted basis to $5,000. Accordingly, the special rule in section 731(a)(2), allowing loss recognition where the distribution consists of only cash and/or section 751 assets, has no application here. Instead this is a plain-vanilla distribution of cash and other property. Because the amount of cash distributed to Partner P ($10,000) does not exceed her outside basis immediately before the distribution ($30,000), she recognizes neither gain nor loss. As in the previous Question, the partnership recognizes no gain or loss under section 731(b). **Answers (b), (c) and (d)** all would allow Partner P to recognize loss and for that reason alone are all incorrect.

9.1.5   The correct Answer is (b). Under section 732(b), Partner P's tax basis in the distributed receivable equals her outside basis ($30,000) reduced by the amount of money distributed to her ($10,000). Notice that this allocation of basis gives her a built-in loss of $15,000 in the receivable, which she will recognize when she sells or collects it. Assuming that the receivable is a capital asset in Partner P's hands, this loss will be a capital loss. Section 735(a)(1) will not apply, because the receivable was not "unrealized." In determining whether her capital loss is long-term or short-term, Partner P will inherit the holding period of the partnership under section 735(b). **Answer (a)** neglects to reduce Partner P's outside basis by the amount of the cash distribution. **Answer (c)** would be correct if this were a current distribution, but it is not. **Answer (d)** would not be correct even then.

9.1.6   The correct Answer is (d). Here, because LnL is a cash-method taxpayer that has not yet taken the $5,000 amount of the receivable into income, the receivable is "unrealized" and loss recognition under section 731(a)(2) is possible. The amount of the loss may surprise you. It is very tempting to reason that Partner P has received $10,000 in cash and a $5,000 receivable in liquidation of a partnership interest in which she has a $30,000 basis, so her loss must be $15,000. This computation uses the value of the receivable and it is wrong.

The correct computation uses the basis of the receivable in Partner P's hands. Figuring out what this is under the statute is tricky. Section 732(b) starts with Partner P's outside basis ($30,000) and reduces it by the cash distributed ($10,000). This appears to give Partner P a basis of $20,000 in the receivable, just as in the previous Question. Section 732(c)(1)(A), however, forbids an allocation of basis to the receivable that is greater than its basis in the hands of the partnership—only "decreases," not "increases," can be allocated to section 751 assets. The partnership's basis in the receivable was $0. This leaves $20,000 outside basis left over, and there is no other distributed asset to which it can be allocated. Reason dictates that it must be allowable as a loss, which Treas. Reg. § 1.732–1(c)(3) confirms. The loss is capital loss under section 741.

When all is said and done, Partner P will actually recognize the $15,000 loss in the erroneous calculation we started with, but in two steps. She will have a $20,000 capital loss on the liquidation of her partnership interest. When she sells or collects the receivable, she will have $5,000 of ordinary income under section 735(a)(1). The basis system thus prevents LnL's ordinary income in the receivable from disappearing. The partnership itself recognizes no income, gain or loss on the distribution under section 731(b).

You may wonder why the facts state that the receivable reflects Partner P's share of the partnership's receivables. This prevents section 751(b) from applying to this distribution. *See* Topic 9.6.

Answer (a) is incorrect, because it fails to treat the distributed receivable as "unrealized." **Answers (b) and (c)** fall into the trap of computing Partner P's recognized loss by reference to the value, rather than the basis, of the distributed receivable.

9.1.7   The correct Answer is (c). Unlike any of the prior Questions, this one involves a current distribution. The distributee *never* recognizes a loss on a current distribution and recognizes a gain only if the amount of cash distributed exceeds her outside basis, which is not the case here. To determine Partner T's tax basis in the distributed receivable, you must reduce her outside basis ($40,000) by the amount of the cash distributed ($10,000), leaving $30,000. Under section 732(a), her basis in the receivable will be the lesser of that amount or the inside basis of the receivable, $5,000. Thus, Partner T recognizes no gain or loss on the distribution, takes a basis of $5,000 in the distributed receivable and has $25,000 remaining basis in her partnership interest. **Answer (a)** is incorrect. In a current distribution, the distributee's basis in distributed assets can never exceed their inside basis. **Answer (b)** is incorrect for the same reason. **Answer (d)** appears to apply section 732(a)(2) incorrectly, resulting in a zero limitation for the tax basis of the receivable.

9.1.8   The correct Answer is (b). Partner Q receives no cash here, so the issue is to spread her outside basis of $120,000 among the four properties she receives. Because the total inside basis of these properties was $250,000, it must somehow be decreased by $130,000 to match Partner Q's outside basis. Under section 732(c), she first divides the properties between section 751 assets and other assets. In the first category, she assigns the inside basis of $0 to the receivables distributed to her. She cannot reduce the basis of the receivables below that. Turning to the second category of assets, she assigns them tentative bases equal to their inside basis, then reduces the basis of any asset whose tentative basis is greater than its value down to such value. Finally, she allocates any remaining decrease among all of the assets in proportion to their tentative bases, as adjusted. The computations are as follows:

	(1) Initial Basis	(2) Decrease	(3) Adj. Basis	(4) Decrease	(5) Final Basis
Third St.	$ 90,000	$30,000	$ 60,000	$20,000	$ 40,000
Fifth St.	60,000	0	60,000	20,000	40,000
Ninth Ave.	100,000	40,000	60,000	20,000	40,000
TOTALS	$250,000	$70,000	$180,000	$60,000	$120,000

Answer (a) is the result of allocating $30,000 of basis to the receivables (their fair market value) in step one. **Answer (c)** allocates the decrease of $130,000 among the Third St., Fifth St. and Ninth Ave. properties in proportion to their inside bases—*i.e.*, skipping the decrease in column (2) above. **Answer (d)** makes two errors. Like **Answer (c)**, it skips the decrease in column (2). It also allocates the $130,000 decrease in proportion to the fair market values, rather than the bases, of the three properties.

9.1.9   The correct Answer is (b). Section 1245(b)(5) requires Partner W to assume responsibility for the amount of the recapture the partnership would have suffered if it had sold the washing machines for their fair market value on the date of the distribution. The facts of this Questions tell us that this amount is $8,000. Accordingly, if Partner W sells the distributed machines for $10,000 (their value at distribution), she will have ordinary (recapture) income of $8,000 and loss of $18,000, netting to $10,000.

Still, this distribution holds two possible tax advantages for Partner W. First, the basis allocation mechanism allows Partner W to shift her $20,000 basis in the partnership interest, a nondepreciable asset, to the washing machines, which are depreciable assets. She surely could not increase the basis of section 751 assets in that way, because that would allow her to understate ordinary income. With depreciation, however, she will get the same benefit, because the depreciation will offset ordinary income, albeit over time. Second, if Partner W decides to exit the laundry business, she can recover her remaining basis in the washing machines as a section 1231 loss, which may be ordinary under section 1231(a)(2). Treasury regulations proposed in 2014 would deny Partner W the second of these benefits, but not the first. Prop. Treas. Reg. § 1.732–1(c)(2)(iii).

Answer (a) is incorrect, because it does not acknowledge Partner W's obligation for recapture income. **Answers (c) and (d)** reflect possible responses to the depreciation issue discussed above. Both are interesting, but neither is the law.

9.2.1   The correct Answer is (d). In this liquidation, Austin receives a deemed distribution of $500,000 cash under section 752(b), reducing her outside basis to $400,000, and an actual distribution of $1 million cash, which causes her to recognize gain of $600,000 under section 731(a)(1). The partnership enjoys a $600,000 positive adjustment under section 734(b)(1)(A). **Answers (a) and (b)** are incorrect, because they neglect the $500,000 deemed distribution in computing Austin's gain. **Answer (a)** makes the further mistake of getting the sign wrong—when the distributee recognizes gain, the partnership has a positive adjustment. **Answer (c)** makes just the second mistake.

9.2.2   The correct Answer is (b). Under Treas. Reg. § 1.755–1(c)(1)(ii), an adjustment arising from the distributee's recognition of gain or loss on the distribution is allocated only to capital gain property. A positive adjustment is allocated, first, to capital gain property whose value exceeds its basis, in proportion to and to the extent of such appreciation. Here, Property 2, Property 3 and Property 4 are all appreciated properties. The allocation is as follows:

	(1) Initial Basis	(2) Appreciation	(3) Share of Appreciation	(4) Share of Adjustment	(5) Final Basis
Property 2	$ 600,000	$1,400,000	43.75%	$262,500	$ 862,500
Property 3	600,000	1,000,000	31.25%	187,500	787,500
Property 4	100,000	800,000	25.00%	150,000	250,000
TOTALS	$1,300,000	$3,200,000	100.00%	$600,000	$1,900,000

Each property takes a share of the $600,000 positive adjustment (column (4)) equal to its share of the total appreciation in all of the properties (column (3)). In this case, the positive adjustment is far less than the total appreciation. If it were greater, the next and final tranche of the allocation would be made in proportion to the properties' fair market values. Property 1, although not an appreciated property, would join in the allocation of this tranche. Treas. Reg. § 1.755–1(c)(2)(i).

Answer (a) allocates none of the $600,000 positive adjustment to Property 3, thus implicitly treating it as a depreciated property like Property 1, which it is not. **Answer (c)** would be obtained by allocating the $600,000 positive adjustment according to the relative fair market values of all of the partnership's properties, incorrectly skipping the allocation in the first tranche. **Answer (d)** allocates the $600,000 positive adjustment in accordance with the relative fair market values of only those properties that are appreciated. Closer, but still not right.

9.2.3   The correct Answer is (a). In this distribution, Austin receives a deemed cash distribution under section 752(b) equal to her share of the partnership's debt, $500,000, reducing her outside basis to $400,000, and an actual cash distribution of $100,000, reducing her outside basis to $300,000. This becomes her basis in distributed Property 4, producing a negative adjustment of $200,000 under section 734(b)(2)(B). **Answer (b)** gets the sign wrong—if outside basis is greater than the inside basis of the distributed property, the adjustment is negative, not positive. **Answers (c) and (d)** fail to take the section 752(b) deemed distribution into account, and thus compare the inside basis of the distributed property, $100,000, with an erroneous measure of outside basis, $800,000. Having made this error, **Answer (d)** compounds it by getting the sign wrong.

9.2.4   The correct Answer is (a). Under Treas. Reg. § 1.755–1(c)(2)(ii), a negative adjustment is allocated first to depreciated properties in proportion to their respective amounts of depreciation. Here, only Property 1 is depreciated, and the excess of its adjusted basis, $1,300,000, over its value, $500,000, is far larger than the negative adjustment of $200,000. Therefore, Property 1 soaks up the entire adjustment, and Property 3 gets nothing. **Answer (b)** is incorrect. It reflects the allocation of the negative $200,000 adjustment among all of the partnership's properties in proportion to their adjusted bases. **Answers (c) and (d)** are based on the mistaken assumption that the required adjustment is positive rather than negative. **Answer (c)** allocates this positive $200,000 adjustment correctly between Property 2 and Property 3 in proportion to their respective amounts of appreciation. **Answer (d)** allocates it incorrectly between Property 2 and Property 3 in proportion to their respective values.

9.2.5   The correct Answer is (c). A section 734(b) adjustment occurs in two circumstances: (1) if the partnership has made a section 754 election and (2) if the adjustment, if made, would produce a reduction in the partnership's basis in its assets in excess of $250,000. Section 734(d) defines the latter reduction as a "substantial basis reduction." Because the reduction in this case would be only $200,000, it is not a substantial basis reduction and no adjustment is required. **Answer (a)** is incorrect, because neither circumstance for a section 734(b) adjustment exists in this case. **Answer (b)** is incorrect, because it identifies only one of the two circumstances that can cause an adjustment. **Answer (d)** is incorrect, because the existence of a section 754 election is irrelevant for determining the distributee-partner's tax basis in distributed property.

9.2.6   The correct Answer is (b). In a current distribution of property, a section 734(b) adjustment can only occur if section 732(a)(2) applies. That is the case here. By virtue of the guarantee, Austin's share of the partnership's debt remains at $500,000. Her outside basis is $900,000, undiminished by any deemed distribution under section 752(b). This is less, however, than the partnership's $1,300,000 inside basis in Property 1, so Austin's tax basis is limited by section 732(a)(2) to $900,000. This $400,000 reduction in the tax basis in the distributed property produces a positive section 734(b) adjustment of like size. **Answer (a)** does not acknowledge this somewhat unusual section 734(b) adjustment. **Answers (c) and (d)** miscalculate it.

9.2.7   The correct Answer is (c). In this liquidating distribution, McKyra receives a deemed cash distribution under section 752(b) of $50,000 and an actual cash distribution of $15,000, bringing her outside basis down to $85,000. This is not, however, the tax basis she takes in the distributed receivables, because they are "unrealized receivables" as defined in section 751(c). Section 732(c)(1)(A)(i) assigns a tentative tax basis to the receivables equal to their inside basis, which is $0 in this case. There is no provision to increase the tentative tax basis in the case of section 751 assets such as these unrealized receivables. Thus, McKyra's tax basis in the receivables is $0. Under section 731(a)(2), she is entitled to claim a loss on the distribution equal to the excess of her outside basis ($150,000) over the sum of the cash actually and constructively distributed to her ($65,000) and her tax basis in the distributed receivables ($0). McKyra's loss is therefore $85,000. Under section 734(b)(2)(A), the partnership has a negative adjustment in this amount. This result checks out under the theory of section 734(b). Prior to the distribution, McKyra's share of inside basis was $150,000, which was the sum of her tax capital and her share of the partnership's debt. She only removed $65,000 of tax basis in the distribution, consisting entirely of the cash actually and constructively distributed to her. Because she took $85,000 less than her share of the partnership's inside basis, the partnership must reduce inside basis by this amount following the distribution.

Answer (a) is incorrect. It may seem as if there should be no section 734(b) adjustment in this case, because McKyra takes the receivables with the same basis as the partnership. A change in the basis of distributed property is not, however, the only way that a section 734(b) adjustment can be created. **Answer (b)** is incorrect. A loss on liquidation produces an adjustment for the partnership that is negative, not positive. **Answer (d)** neglects to take into account the deemed $50,000 cash distribution under section 752(b).

Section 751(b) does not apply to this distribution, because McKyra takes her share of the partnership's receivables. *See* Topic 9.6.

9.4.1 **The correct Answer is (a).** Because Raeburn contributed only money to the partnership, he does not have any precontribution gain or loss. Neither section 704(c)(1)(B) nor section 737 applies to him. Section 737, but not section 704(c)(1)(B), applies to Theo, because he is receiving a distribution of property within seven years after his contribution. The fact that this distribution does not seem to have been planned at the time of Theo's contribution is irrelevant. The gain Theo recognizes is the lesser of his excess distribution ("ED") and his net precontribution gain ("NPG"). The former is the fair market value of the property distributed to him ($120,000) over his outside basis ($30,000), or $90,000. Conceptually, this represents the gain Theo would recognize if the entire distribution consisted of cash. Theo's NPG is his remaining precontribution gain in Parcel T. This is the current difference between the book value of Parcel T ($80,000) and its adjusted basis ($30,000), or $50,000. Because this amount is less than Theo's ED, it is this amount he recognizes as gain under section 737(a). **Answers (b) and (d)** are incorrect, because they would have Raeburn recognize gain in this transaction. **Answer (c)** is incorrect, because it would have Theo recognize as gain the amount of his ED, thus interpreting section 737(a) to require gain recognition equal to the greater, rather than the lesser, of ED or NPG. There is another way you could have reached this incorrect answer. The $40,000 difference between the correct answer to this question and this incorrect answer represents the excess of the value of Parcel T over its book value. Including this amount in the gain that Theo must recognize would be equivalent to taxing him, not only on the precontribution gain in Parcel T, but on the full increase in its value after contribution. This is not the purpose or effect of section 704(c)(1)(B) or section 737.

9.4.2 **The correct Answer is (b).** Although neither section 704(c)(1)(B) nor section 737 requires the partnership to recognize gain, the necessary basis adjustments are best understood by assuming that it does. In this case, assume that the partnership recognizes $50,000 of gain with respect to Parcel T—the amount of gain that Theo must recognize under section 737(a). This increases its tax basis in Parcel T by $50,000 to $80,000. This gain is, in turn, allocated entirely to Theo pursuant to section 704(c)(1)(A). This increases Theo's outside basis by $50,000 to $80,000. This outside basis increase takes place prior to the distribution, so that it is taken into account under section 732(b) in determining Theo's tax basis in the properties distributed to him. Treas. Reg. § 1.737–3(b)(1). Thus, Theo takes New Properties A and B with an aggregate tax basis of $80,000 and has a built-in gain of $40,000 in those properties. **Answer (a)** is incorrect, because it does not take into account any basis adjustments. **Answers (c) and (d)** give the partnership a tax basis in Parcel T equal to its fair market value. That would be appropriate if the partnership's entire gain in Parcel T were recognized, but it is not—only the forward section 704(c) layer of $80,000 is recognized.

9.4.3 **The correct Answer is (b).** Here, both section 704(c)(1)(B) and section 737 apply. Section 737 applies to Theo, and the analysis is exactly the same as that in Question 9.4.1. Theo recognizes $50,000 gain. Because the partnership is distributing the property Osgood contributed, section 704(c)(1)(B) applies to Osgood. He recognizes his forward section 704(c) layer, which is $60,000, the excess of the book value of Parcel over its tax basis. **Answer (a)** is incorrect, because it fails to apply section 704(c)(1)(B) to Osgood. **Answers (c) and (d)** require Osgood to recognize, not his precontribution gain in Parcel O, but rather the full difference between the fair market value of Parcel O and its tax basis, and for this reason both are incorrect.

9.4.4 **The correct Answer is (b).** In this variation, section 704(c)(1)(B) applies to Theo. He recognizes his forward section 704(c) layer, which is $50,000. Neither section 704(c)(1)(B) nor section 737 apply to Raeburn, who contributed cash to the partnership. Raeburn recognizes no gain or loss under section 731(a). **Answer (a)** fails to apply section 704(c)(1)(B) to Theo. **Answers (c) and (d)** require Raeburn to recognize gain as though he had received a distribution of cash equal to the fair market value of Parcel T. Treating Raeburn in this manner would amount to repealing the nonrecognition rule of section 731(a). Although some have argued that this would be a good idea, it is not accomplished by the anti-mixing-bowl rules.

9.4.5 **The correct Answer is (d).** Theo and Raeburn both walk away with an $80,000 tax basis, but they take different paths. For Theo, it is once again useful to consider the basis adjustments that would occur if the partnership recognized $50,000 of gain with respect to Parcel T. Under section 704(c)(1)(A), it would allocate that gain entirely to Theo, who would enjoy an increase of $50,000 in his outside basis under section 705(a)(1)(A). Because section 704(c)(1)(B) does not actually require the partnership to recognize this $50,000 of gain, the basis adjustments do not actually occur in this manner. Nevertheless, these are the adjustments that are called for by section 704(c)(1)(B)(iii) and Treas. Reg. § 1.704–4(e)(1). For Raeburn, an $80,000 basis in the distributed Parcel T is called for by section 732(b). It is worth noting, however, that the partnership increases its basis in Parcel T by the $50,000 recognized gain immediately before the distribution. Treas. Reg. § 1.704–4(e)(2). Therefore, if this distribution had been a current distribution in which Raeburn's tax basis in Parcel T were determined under section 732(a)(1), this $50,000 increase would be reflected in his tax basis for the property and his remaining outside basis would be commensurately reduced. **Answer (a)** fails to adjust Theo's outside basis by the gain he recognizes and determines Raeburn's tax basis in Parcel T by reference to the partnership's inside basis without credit for the gain recognized. **Answer (b)** makes the same mistake as to Theo and **Answer (c)** repeats this mistake as to Raeburn.

9.4.6   **The correct Answer is (a).** The place to start with this Question is to figure out which statute applies to which partner. It works out like this:

	Section 704(c)(1)(B)	Section 737
Parcel T to Raeburn	Theo	
Parcel O to Theo	Osgood	Theo
New Properties to Osgood		Osgood

As previously stated, Raeburn is not subject to the anti-mixing-bowl statutes, because he contributed cash. Theo and Osgood, however, are each subject to both. In such case, section 704(c)(1)(B) comes first. Treas. Reg. § 1.737–1(c)(2)(iv). This simplifies the analysis. Under section 704(c)(1)(B), Theo and Osgood recognize their entire forward section 704(c) layers, $50,000 and $60,000 respectively, due to the distributions of Parcel T and Parcel O, respectively. Applying section 737 next, we see that their NPG has been eliminated by the prior application of section 704(c)(1)(B). Accordingly, they recognize no gain under section 737, which requires recognition of the *lesser* of ED or NPG. **Answer (b)** is incorrect, because it applies section 737 first, effectively requiring Theo and Osgood to recognize twice the amount of their NPG. **Answers (c) and (d)** are incorrect, because both require Raeburn to recognize gain. In addition, **Answer (d)** allows Theo to escape the application of the anti-mixing-bowl rules altogether.

9.4.7   **The correct Answer is (a).** Here, the application of these provisions is more nuanced. Starting with Theo, it is clear that only section 737 applies, because Parcel T remains in the partnership. Under section 737(a), Theo must recognize gain equal to the lesser of his ED or his NPG. The former is the excess of the value of the property distributed to him (one-third of $120,000 or $40,000) over his outside basis ($30,000) or $10,000. The latter is the amount of gain that he would recognize under section 704(c)(1)(B) if *all* of the property that he has contributed to the partnership within the past seven years were distributed to another partner—in other words, his full forward section 704(c) layer, which is $50,000. Accordingly, the gain that Theo recognizes under section 737(a) is $10,000, the lesser of these two amounts.

Section 704(c)(1)(B) surely applies to Osgood, but what about section 737? It would, but for the exception of section 737(d), which excludes from the coverage of that section a distribution of property that the distributee-partner contributed to the partnership. The thought here is that Osgood is taking back one-third of Parcel O with its built-in gain intact, so there is no reason to tax him on the distribution. Applying section 704(c)(1)(B), we see that it too excludes distributions of property contributed by the distributee. Section 704(c)(1)(B) (second parenthetical). Only two-thirds of Parcel O is distributed to partners other than Osgood, so he recognizes two-thirds of his forward section 704(c) layer, or $40,000.

Answer (b) is incorrect, because it makes two mistakes in applying section 737 to Theo. First, it requires Theo to recognize his NPG, rather than his ED, although his ED is smaller. Second, it miscalculates his NPG by taking into account only two-thirds of his forward layer in Parcel T. **Answer (c)** makes the same mistake as to Theo, and in addition requires Osgood to recognize his entire forward layer in Parcel O. One way to reach this incorrect answer would be to ignore the exception in section 737(d) for distributions of property to the contributing partner. **Answer (d)** makes the same mistake as **Answer (c)** for Osgood, and in addition requires Theo to recognize his entire forward layer in Parcel T. One way to reach this incorrect answer would be require Theo to recognize his NPG under section 737(a), even though his ED is smaller.

9.4.8   The correct Answer is (d). Theo is the easy one here. The partnership distributes Parcel T in its entirety to Osgood, so Theo recognizes gain of $50,000 (his entire forward layer) under section 704(c)(1)(B). Osgood is trickier. Begin with section 737. Osgood's ED is the excess of the value of the property, *other than money*, distributed to him ($150,000 less $30,000 money or $120,000) over his outside basis, reduced (but not below zero) by the money distributed ($20,000 less $30,000, limited to $0). Thus, Osgood's ED is $120,000. Osgood's NPG is, as always, $60,000, equal to his entire forward layer. Osgood therefore recognizes $60,000 of gain under section 737(a). The flush language at the end of that section warns, however, that we may not be done here. We have eliminated the cash distribution from both the minuend and the subtrahend in the ED computation, and we must now take the cash into account under section 731(a). Osgood's outside basis is $20,000, the cash distributed to him is $30,000 and his gain is $10,000. Adding this to the gain under section 737(a), Osgood recognizes total gain of $70,000 on this distribution.

Answers (a) and (b) fail to apply section 704(c)(1)(B) correctly (or at all) to Theo. **Answer (c)** gets Theo right, but misses the $10,000 gain to Osgood under section 731(a)(1).

9.5.1   The correct Answer is (b). Under section 731(c)(2)(A) marketable securities include financial instruments and foreign currencies which are "actively traded" within the meaning of section 1092(d)(1). A financial instrument includes stocks and other equity interests, evidences of indebtedness, options, forward contracts, futures contracts, notional principal contracts and other derivatives. Active trading is an expansive concept, which includes not only trading on national securities exchanges but also trading through an interdealer quotation system, an interbank market, an interdealer market or a debt market. While these are all terms of art, all connote systems for the dissemination of price quotes and market prices. **Answer (a)** is incorrect, because the London Stock Exchange is an established financial market. The fact that it is not in the United States is immaterial, as long as it satisfies regulatory requirements that are "analogous" to those in the United States. Treas. Reg. § 1.1092(d)–1(b)(1)(iv). While some emerging markets might not pass this test, the United Kingdom surely does.

Section 731(c)(2)(B) expands the definition of marketable securities further. Under section 731(c)(2)(B)(iv), the term includes gold and other precious metals, so **Answer (c)** is incorrect. **Answer (d)** is incorrect under section 731(c)(2)(B)(iii), which expands the term to include financial instruments that are not actively traded but are valued substantially by reference to marketable securities. This potentially very broad category includes many notional principal contracts entered into between dealers and their customers. Although these are private contracts that are unsuitable for trading, their notional amount is often determined by reference to publicly traded securities or indexes of such securities, such as the S&P 500 index.

9.5.2   The correct Answer is (c). Under Treas. Reg. § 1.1092(d)–1(b)(2)(ii) a "debt market" (which is one type of established financial market) exists for a debt instrument if price quotations for the instrument are readily available from brokers, dealers or traders. A safe harbor excludes a debt instrument that is part of an issue that does not exceed $25 million, presumably because price quotes would generally be hard to come by for an issue that small. **Answers (a) and (b)** run afoul of subsections (v) and (vi), respectively, of section 731(c)(2)(B). Under regulations, if 90% or more of an entity's gross assets by value constitute marketable securities, money or both, interests in that entity are deemed to be marketable securities in their entirety. If marketable securities and money make up at least 20% but less than 90% of the gross value of the assets of an entity, its interests are deemed to be marketable securities only to that extent. Treas. Reg. § 1.731–2(c)(3). **Answer (d)** is incorrect. Section 731(c)(2)(A) includes foreign currencies within the ambit of the term marketable securities, if they are actively traded.

9.5.3   The correct Answer is (a). Let's proceed by process of elimination. In order to be an investment partnership, a partnership cannot ever have been engaged in a trade or business. There is no five-year (or other) "cooling off" period that can cleanse a partnership's business history. Treasury regulations do, on the other hand, contain helpful exclusions from the trade or business concept that facilitate the efforts of venture and private equity funds to manage their portfolio companies. Treas. Reg. § 1.731(c)–2(e)(3). Megaron's activities are not of this nature, however, and **Answer (b)** is therefore incorrect. **Answer (c)** is incorrect. Although arising in an entirely private transaction, Megaron's demand note is treated as a marketable security. Because the holder of such a note can receive cash on demand, it is covered by section 731(c)(2)(B)(ii), which treats as a marketable security a financial instrument that is readily convertible into money or marketable securities. Finally, **Answer (d)** is incorrect, because the exception it invokes only applies to the distribution of a marketable security which was contributed to the partnership by the distributee-partner. Here, the distributee contributed a portfolio of publicly traded stocks and bonds and received a demand note convertible into cash.

9.5.4   The correct Answer is (d). Let's try process of elimination again. **Answer (b)** is incorrect. Megaron is not an investment partnership due to its business history, just as we concluded in the discussion of Question

9.5.3. **Answer (c)** is incorrect, because the shares of Megaron Inc. that Megaron LLC holds are of the same type as those the public holds (and trades). The fact that the particular shares owned by Megaron LLC have not been publicly traded is immaterial, as would be a trading restriction imposed on the partners for a designated period of time following the IPO. Treas. Reg. § 1.731–2(c)(2). **Answer (d)** refers to the exception provided by Treas. Reg. § 1.731–2(d)(1)(ii) for marketable securities acquired by the partnership in a nonrecognition transaction. This exception, which applies here, facilitates the incorporation and public offering of a going business. It is inapplicable if 20% or more by value of the incorporation transfer consists of money or marketable securities. Finally, **Answer (a)** is incorrect, because an exception applies.

    9.5.5   **The correct Answer is (d).** Section 731(c) applies here, no exception appearing applicable under the facts. The exception of section 731(c)(3)(B), which in many cases reduces the amount of the gain recognized by the distributee, does not apply, because the partnership has no gain in the newly acquired mutual fund shares. Section 731(c)(1) treats the $270,000 value of the mutual fund shares as money in applying section 731(a)(1) to this distribution. Beatrix recognizes gain equal to the excess of this amount over her outside basis ($120,000), or $150,000. Under section 731(c)(4), Beatrix' tax basis in the distributed shares equals her basis under section 732(b) ($120,000) plus her recognized gain ($150,000), or $270,000. **Answer (a)** is incorrect, because it fails to apply section 731(c) at all. The nearest possible exception appears to be that the mutual fund shares are not actively traded—there being nothing in the facts specifically bearing on this point. The assets of the mutual fund, however, likely consist entirely of marketable securities and money, so that its shares are marketable securities by virtue of section 731(c)(2)(B)(v). **Answer (b)** is incorrect, because it fails to include Beatrix' realized gain in her tax basis for the mutual fund shares. **Answer (c)** is incorrect, because it miscalculates Beatrix' gain.

    9.5.6   **The correct Answer is (a).** The first step is to compute Beatrix' recognized gain. This is harder than in the previous Question, because it involves the exception of section 731(c)(3)(B). Under that exception, the mutual fund shares distributed to Beatrix are not treated as marketable securities to the extent that her share of the partnership's gain in such shares immediately before the distribution exceeds her share of such gain immediately after the distribution. The former amount is one-third of $190,000, or $63,333. After the distribution, the gain in the partnership's remaining marketable securities is $95,000. The revaluation creates a reverse section 704(c) layer in this amount, and Beatrix is responsible for one-third, or $31,667 of this layer. The difference between Beatrix' pre- and post-distribution shares of the gain in the mutual fund shares is $31,667.

    Accordingly, under section 731(c)(3)(B), the value of the marketable securities distributed to Beatrix is reduced by $31,667 from $195,000 to $163,333. This amount, reduced by her outside basis of $150,000, measures the gain she recognizes on the distribution, which is $13,333.

Under section 731(a)(4), Beatrix takes a basis in the distributed shares equal to the basis she would have under section 732(a)(1), which is $100,000, plus her recognized gain of $13,333, or $113,333. Under section 731(c)(5), Beatrix' outside basis is reduced by $100,000 to $50,000.

Answers (b), (c) and (d) all neglect to apply the section 731(c)(3)(B) exception and are incorrect for this reason. In addition, **Answers (b) and (d)** reflect erroneous computations of outside basis.

9.5.7 The correct Answer is (a). Because Beatrix' tax basis in the distributed mutual fund shares is determined under section 732(a)(1), there is no section 734(b) adjustment in this case. Under section 731(c)(5), the gain that Beatrix recognizes under section 731(c) is ignored in applying section 734(b). A quick look at the partnership's balance sheet will show you why. The distribution of mutual fund shares to Beatrix reduced the tax basis of the partnership's assets by $100,000. It reduced the partners' aggregate tax capital by the same amount (the entire reduction going to Beatrix). Inside and outside were equal before the distribution and they are equal now. Any section 734(b) adjustment to the tax basis of the partnership's assets would upset that equality.

Answers (b), (c) and (d) make such an adjustment and they are therefore wrong, all in different ways. **Answers (b) and (c)** reflect a total positive adjustment of $13,333, which is the correct amount of Beatrix' gain. **Answer (b)** allocates that adjustment between the premises and the mutual fund shares, the partnership's two capital gain properties, which would be the correct approach if there were, in fact, an adjustment. **Answer (c)** allocates it entirely to the premises. **Answer (d)** takes as the section 734(b) adjustment an incorrect amount for Beatrix' gain, $45,000, and then allocates it entirely to the premises.

9.6.1 The correct Answer is (b). Taken separately, the inventory is "substantially appreciated," meaning that its aggregate value ($33,000) exceeds its aggregate adjusted basis ($21,000) by more than 20%. Under the 1956 regulations, however, this calculation must also include the accounts receivable which, although they are not unrealized receivables because their full value has been taken into income by this accrual partnership, are nonetheless inventory items under section 751(d)(2). Treas. Reg. §§ 1.751–1(d)(2)(ii), –1(g), example (2)(b). Thus, the correct calculation for substantial appreciation is to compare the aggregate value of the receivables and inventory ($60,000) with the aggregate adjusted basis of these assets ($48,000). Because the former is 125% of the latter, both the inventory and the receivables qualify as "inventory items which have substantially appreciated in value" under the 1956 regulations.

Answer (a) is incorrect, because it is incomplete. **Answers (c) and (d)** are incorrect, because they include recapture. There is no recapture on these facts, because (1) the value of the equipment is less than its basis and (2) section 1250 would not require recapture on the plant, which has been depreciated on a straight-line basis.

9.6.2   **The correct Answer is (a).** The best way to unearth the exchange deemed to have occurred under the 1956 regulations is to construct an "exchange table," which shows the distributee-partner's "interest" in each of the partnership's assets both before and after the distribution. In Bethany's case:

	Pre-Distribution "Interest"	Post-Distribution "Interest"	Surplus/(Deficit)
Cash	$25,000	$99,000	$74,000
Receivables	9,000	0	(9,000)
Inventory	11,000	0	(11,000)
Equipment	14,000	0	(14,000)
Plant	40,000	0	(40,000)
TOTAL	$99,000	$99,000	$ 0

Following the approach of the 1956 regulations, all of the entries in this table reflect the gross values of the assets, not their tax bases or appreciation amounts. The table reflects the easy (but in this simple case probably correct) assumption that Bethany's "interest" in each of the partnership's assets prior to the distribution equaled her overall interest in the partnership, which was one-third. In addition, it reflects the deemed cash distribution of $24,000 resulting under section 752(b) from Bethany's release from her one-third share of the partnership's debt.

Economically, Bethany has surrendered her "interest" in each of the partnership's non-cash assets for more cash. Section 751(b) is concerned, however, only with exchanges of section 751(b) assets for properties that are not section 751(b) assets. In the current case, it ignores Bethany's exchange of her "interest" in the partnership's equipment and plant for additional cash, thereby leaving in place for these assets the usual rules for partnership distributions. Following the approach of the statute, the 1956 regulations lump all section 751(b) assets together in the identification of the assets deemed exchanged. Treas. Reg. § 1.751–1(g), example (2)(c).

Answers (b) and (c) are incorrect, because they measure the amount of the partnership's section 751(b) assets by their basis and their appreciation, respectively, rather than by their value. **Answer (d)** is incorrect, because it includes all of the exchanges shown on the exchange table, rather than just those that are taken into account by section 751(b).

9.6.3   **The correct Answer is (b).** The deemed current distribution to Bethany consists of amounts of receivables and inventory that are proportional by value to the amounts of such assets owned by the partnership prior to the distribution. These amounts are $9,000 of receivables and $11,000 of inventory. Bethany takes the partnership's basis of $9,000 in the receivables and $7,000 in the inventory. When she exchanges these assets with the partnership for $20,000 additional cash, she recognizes $4,000 of ordinary income under Treas. Reg. § 1.751–1(b)(3)(iii). For its part, the partnership recognizes no income or gain on the deemed current distribution of receivables and inventory to Bethany. In the deemed exchange, it acquires these distributed assets for cash. From the partnership's perspective, this is simply a purchase, on which it recognizes no income or gain.

Answer (a) errs by giving Bethany a tax basis equal to fair market value in the distributed section 751(b) assets. This is incorrect: the deemed distribution is governed by the ordinary rules for current distributions, so that Bethany takes a basis in the distributed section 751(b) assets equal to the partnership's basis under section 732(a)(1), which is $16,000. **Answers (c) and (d)** are incorrect, because they show the partnership recognizing ordinary income.

    9.6.4   **The correct answer is (d).** The deemed exchange explored in the prior Question is only the first half of the story. The remainder of the cash distribution, after taking into account the $20,000 of cash paid to Bethany in the deemed exchange, is $79,000, which includes $24,000 under section 752(b). Bethany's remaining outside basis is $70,000. This is her initial outside basis ($86,000), reduced under section 733 by the basis of the receivables ($9,000) and the basis of the inventory ($7,000) distributed to Bethany in the deemed current distribution. Under section 731(a)(1), Bethany recognizes $9,000 of capital gain on the remaining cash distribution ($79,000 amount distributed less $70,000 remaining outside basis). Overall, Bethany recognizes $4,000 of ordinary income on the deemed exchange and $9,000 of capital gain on the remainder of the distribution.

To make sense of this result, have a look at the ABC Partnership's balance sheet. The $4,000 of ordinary income that Bethany recognizes equals one-third of the partnership's unrecognized gain in its section 751(b) assets. Adding $4,000 of ordinary income to the $9,000 capital gain Bethany recognizes on the remainder of the distribution yields a total gain of $13,000, which is the difference between her tax capital prior to the distribution ($62,000) and the total amount of cash ($75,000) that the partnership distributes to her.

The analysis for the partnership is easier. From Question 9.6.3, we know that the partnership recognizes no income or gain on the deemed current distribution and exchange. Under section 731(b), it recognizes no income or gain on its distribution of the remaining $79,000 of cash to Bethany in liquidation of her interest.

Answers (a) and (c) are incorrect, because they show the partnership recognizing ordinary income. Regarding Bethany's tax treatment, **Answer (a)** errs by giving Bethany a tax basis equal to fair market value in the distributed section 751(b) assets and by reducing her outside basis by the fair market value of those assets. This is incorrect: the deemed distribution is governed by the ordinary rules for current distributions, so that Bethany takes a basis in the distributed section 751(b) assets equal to the partnership's basis under section 732(a)(1), which is $16,000, and her outside basis is reduced by the same amount under section 733. Regarding Bethany's tax treatment, **Answer (c)** forgets about the remaining cash distribution that follows the deemed exchange. **Answer (b)** is incorrect, because it fails to reduce Bethany's initial outside basis to take into account the deemed current distribution in determining her gain on the remaining distribution.

9.6.5   The correct Answer is (d). Although the answer to this Question is not provided by the 1956 regulations or any other published authority, the agreement among the partners should not be given effect for federal income tax purposes. The effect of the agreement, if recognized, would be to shift Bethany's share of the partnership's unrealized ordinary income to the other partners. This is contrary to the purpose of section 751(b). Thus, the answer to this Question should be the same as the answer to Question 9.6.4.

Answer (a) is the result intended by the partners' agreement. If only receivables (value, $20,000, basis $20,000) were deemed to be distributed to Bethany in the current distribution, she would recognize no ordinary income on the sale of that asset back to the partnership. Her outside basis would be reduced by the basis of the receivables deemed distributed to her ($20,000) to $66,000. This would produce a capital gain on the remaining distribution of $79,000 less $66,000, or $13,000. **Answer (b)** is even worse from a policy perspective, because it would not only allow Bethany to shift her share of the partnership's ordinary income to the other partners, but also cause them to pay tax on the shifted amount immediately. **Answer (c)** gives effect to the partners' agreement, but miscalculates the gain on the remaining distribution.

9.6.6   The correct Answer is (d). The proposed regulations would reach the same answer as the 1956 regulations (at least in this case), but would do it in a manner that is different and more direct. Under the hypothetical-sale approach, the proposed regulations compare the amount of ordinary income that would be allocated to Bethany on the partnership's sale of all of its assets for fair market value immediately before the distribution ($4,000) with the amount of such allocation immediately after the distribution ($0), plus the amount of ordinary income to which Bethany is exposed by the ownership of the distributed assets ($0). Bethany therefore recognizes $4,000 of ordinary income using a reasonable method that is consistent with the purpose of section 751(b). Her outside basis is increased by the amount of the recognized income, from $86,000 to $90,000. On the cash distribution, she recognizes a capital gain of $9,000, which is the excess of the amount of the distribution ($75,000 actual cash plus $24,000 liability relief under section 752(b)) over Bethany's adjusted outside basis ($90,000). The partnership recognizes no income, gain or loss. **Answers (a), (b) and (c)** are incorrect, as they each reflect variations in the application of the deemed-exchange methodology under the 1956 regulations, which the proposed regulations would throw onto the scrap heap.

9.6.7   The correct Answer is (b). If the partnership actually distributes $20,000 worth of receivables to Bethany, section 751(b) does not apply at all under the 1956 regulations, because Bethany does not exchange an interest in section 751(b) assets for other property under the gross-value approach of those regulations. Under the usual distribution rules, Bethany first applies the cash distributed and deemed distributed, a total of $79,000, against her outside basis of $86,000, leaving $7,000. This becomes her basis in the distributed receivables. Neither Bethany nor the partnership recognizes income, gain or loss on the distribution.

Answer (a) is incorrect, because it applies Bethany's outside basis first to the distributed receivables and then to the distributed cash. This is not the correct order under section 731(a). **Answer (c)** is incorrect, because it reflects partnership income recognition. The partnership is simply distributing cash and property in this transaction. There is no deemed exchange under section 751(b). **Answer (d)** is incorrect. In effect, it ignores the actual property distribution made by the partnership, treating it as a distribution of only cash.

Notice what is missed by the gross-value approach. This distribution is a tax disaster for Bethany. She takes the distributed receivables with a tax basis of $7,000, meaning that she will recognize $13,000 of ordinary income if she collects or sells the receivables for $20,000. She has, in effect, converted the entire gain in her partnership interest into ordinary income. Because the partnership has not made a section 754 election, Albert's and Charlize's share of ordinary income is also increased by the distribution, from $4,000 each to $6,000 each. If, on the other hand, the partnership had made an election under section 754, its section 734(b) adjustment to the tax basis of the inventory would wipe out Albert's and Charlize's ordinary income entirely. The 1956 regulations would not notice. In a different case, the partnership could have distributed property other than cash to Bethany, with the result that she would take the receivables with a full $20,000 basis. In this case, Bethany would have no ordinary income after the transaction, and Albert and Charlize would inherit her share. The 1956 regulations would not notice that, either. Compare this casual indifference to the approach of the proposed regulations to similar issues in Question 9.6.11.

9.6.8 **The correct Answer is (d).** As before, construct Bethany's exchange table, using the values (not the adjusted basis or the appreciation) of each partnership asset:

	Pre-Distribution "Interest"	Post-Distribution "Interest"	Surplus/(Deficit)
Cash	$25,000	$39,000	$14,000
Receivables	9,000	27,000	18,000
Inventory	11,000	33,000	22,000
Equipment	14,000	0	(14,000)
Plant	40,000	0	(40,000)
TOTAL	**$99,000**	**$99,000**	**$ 0**

The 1956 regulations are concerned only with exchanges of section 751(b) assets for assets that are not section 751(b) assets. Thus, Bethany is treated as exchanging her "interest" in $40,000 of other assets for $40,000 more than her "interest" in section 751(b) assets.

Answer (a) is incorrect, because it describes the deemed exchange from the perspective of the partnership rather than Bethany. **Answer (b)** is incorrect, because it focuses on the entire gross value of the section 751(b) assets that Bethany receives, rather than the value in excess of her prior "interest" in such value as a partner in Partnership ABC. **Answer (c)** is incorrect, because it reflects Bethany's shares of the rights to ordinary income before and after the distribution, rather than the respective gross values.

9.6.9   The correct Answer is (b). The first step is to identify the properties that the partnership is deemed to have distributed to Bethany so that she can sell them back to the partnership in the exchange. Absent an agreement among the partners, the properties distributed are those identified as relinquished properties in the exchange table (*i.e.*, those with respect to which Bethany's "interest" has decreased by reason of the distribution). Here, the relinquished properties are the equipment and the plant. The partnership is deemed to distribute proportionate amounts by value of these two properties. Thus, of the $40,000 total distribution, $42,000/($42,000+$120,000) × $40,000, or $10,370 consists of land and $120,000/($42,000+$120,000) × $40,000, or $29,630 consists of plant.

The next step is to determine Bethany's basis in the equipment and land distributed to her. This equals the basis of the distributed properties in the hands of the partnership. For the equipment, this is $10,370/$42,000 × $45,000, or $11,111. For the plant, it is $29,630/$120,000 × $90,000, or $22,222.

In the next step, Bethany sells the equipment and the plant deemed distributed to her back to the partnership in exchange for more receivables and inventory. She recognizes section 1231 gain or loss on this exchange. With respect to the equipment, the amount is $10,370 less $11,111, or a loss of $741. With respect to the plant, the amount is $29,630 less $22,222 or a gain of $7,408. Bethany's net section 1231 gain so far is $6,667.

The final step (for Bethany) is to ascertain the tax consequences of the remaining distribution. In the exchange, Bethany has acquired $18,000 of receivables and $22,000 of inventory. The properties remaining to be distributed to her are cash in the amount of $39,000, receivables of $9,000 and inventory of $11,000. After taking into account the current distribution, Bethany's remaining outside basis is $86,000 less $33,333, or $52,667. Her outside basis is reduced further by the distribution of $39,000 in cash, to $13,667. The aggregate basis of the distributed receivables and inventory is only $12,000, so Bethany recognizes a capital loss on her partnership interest of $1,667 under section 731(a)(2). Her aggregate basis in the receivables and inventory is $12,000.

For its part, the partnership is deemed to distribute $10,370 of the equipment (with a tax basis of $11,111) and $29,630 of the plant (with a tax basis of $22,222) to Bethany. It then re-purchases this property in exchange for $40,000 of section 751(b) assets. The partnership should be deemed to exchange proportionate amounts by value of each of the receivables and the inventory. The value of the receivables exchanged is $27,000/$60,000 × $40,000 = $18,000. The value of the inventory exchanged is $33,000/$60,000 × $40,000 = $22,000. The exchanged amounts are two-thirds of the value of each of these assets. On this exchange, the partnership therefore recognizes two-thirds of the ordinary income in these assets, or $8,000.

How close did the 1956 regulations come to the "right" answer in this case? If it were an exam, I'd give it a B, but maybe I'm an easy grader. Bethany began with a gain in her partnership interest of $13,000 ($75,000 value net of debt versus $62,000 tax capital). She winds up with $6,667 of section 1231 gain on the deemed exchange and $1,667 capital loss on the remaining distribution and ordinary income built into the distributed receivables and inventory equal to $8,000 ($20,000 value less $12,000 tax basis). This nets out to $13,000, so her aggregate of income and gain comes out right. Her share of ordinary income, however, has increased from $4,000 before the distribution to $8,000 after. For this, she is taxed currently on $6,667 of net section 1231 gain and gets a $1,667 capital loss. It's hard to justify this tax treatment. It's also hard to justify the complexity of these computations, even in this relatively simple example. Okay, maybe a C+.

The 1956 regulations do better with Albert and Charlize. The distribution separates them from the partnership's section 751(b) assets entirely, and they each recognize $4,000 of ordinary income. This is the correct result.

Answer (a) is incorrect, because it neglects the partnership's side of the deemed exchange, and thereby allows Albert and Charlize to escape their $8,000 share of the partnership's ordinary income. It also improperly nets Bethany's net section 1231 gain and her capital loss. **Answer (c)** also neglects the partnership's side of the deemed exchange. In addition, it does not take into account the effect on Bethany of the remaining distribution, thereby missing her capital loss. **Answer (d)** is more a wish than the result of analysis. Bethany's recognition of zero capital or section 1231 gain or loss is a laudable result, but not the one reached in the deemed exchange under the 1956 regulations. The next Question explores whether there is a different exchange that could produce this answer.

9.6.10   The correct Answer is (b). The point of this agreement among the partners is to eliminate Bethany's recognition of capital or section 1231 gain or loss—a worthy goal. If the agreement is respected, Bethany will be treated as exchanging cash of $40,000 for an additional $40,000 worth of section 751(b) assets in the deemed exchange. From Bethany's perspective, this will make the exchange nothing more than a cash purchase, on which she will recognize no gain or loss. The partnership, of course, will recognize

$8,000 of ordinary income on its exchange (sale) of $8,000 worth of section 751(b) assets for cash.

There is no doubt that agreements of this general nature are permitted under the 1956 regulations. Treas. Reg. § 1.751–1(g), example (3)(c). This particular agreement, however, is probably offside. Bethany does not relinquish cash in this transaction. As shown in the exchange table in the discussion of Question 9.6.8, Bethany receives $14,000 more than her "interest" in the partnership's cash. The nature of the deemed exchange seems to require that the properties deemed distributed to Bethany and then sold back by her to the partnership must be those properties in which she is surrendering an "interest"—here, the equipment and/or the plant. So while the partners could agree that the only property deemed distributed to Bethany is $40,000 worth of the plant, or $40,000 worth of equipment, they probably cannot agree to a deemed distribution consisting solely (or even partly) of cash.

Assuming that the partners' agreement is not respected, the analysis of this Question is the same as that of Question 9.6.9.

9.6.11   The correct Answer is (d). At last, the promised land! Prior to the distribution, the share of each of the three partners in the partnership's rights to ordinary income is $4,000. Immediately following the distribution, Albert's and Charlize's shares are zero. Therefore, under the proposed regulations, Albert and Charlize must recognize $4,000 each of ordinary income using a reasonable method that is consistent with the purpose of section 751(b). Their outside bases in the partnership are increased to take account of this income recognition, and the partnership's basis in its inventory is increased by $8,000 to $29,000. In the distribution, Bethany's initial outside basis of $86,000 is reduced by the cash distribution of $39,000 ($15,000 actual cash distributed plus $24,000 deemed to be distributed under section 752(b)) to $47,000. Bethany takes the distributed receivables and inventory with this aggregate basis under section 732(b). She thus has $13,000 of inherent ordinary income ("net unrealized section 751(b) gain" in the parlance of the proposed regulations) following the distribution. Because this is more than the $4,000 she started with, she is required to recognize neither ordinary income nor capital gain.

Answers (a) and (c) are incorrect, partly because they do not reflect the recognition of ordinary income required of Albert and Charlize by the proposed regulations. **Answer (b)** is incorrect, because it reflects the deemed-exchange approach of the 1956 regulations.

The effect of this distribution is to convert all of Bethany's $13,000 built-in gain in her partnership interest into ordinary income. This is $1,000 more ordinary income than the partnership had to begin with, and Albert and Charlize have already recognized $8,000 of it. In a case like this, the proposed regulations would allow Bethany to elect to recognize $8,000 of capital gain (or perhaps $9,000) at the time of the distribution, which would increase her outside basis, and thus her basis in the distributed section

751(b) assets, by a like amount. Prop. Treas. Reg. §§ 1.751–1(b)(3)(ii)(B), – 1(g), example (7).

9.8.1   **The correct Answer is (d).** Under section 736, this liquidating distribution must be divided into the section 736(b) amount, which is paid with respect to Brody's interest in the partnership's assets, and the section 736(a) amount, which is the remainder of the distribution. In making this division, section 736(b)(2) requires that any amounts distributed with respect to Brody's interest in unrealized receivables and goodwill must be considered to be part of the section 736(a) amount. The only remaining components of the section 736(b) amount are the distributions with respect to Brody's interest in the partnership's cash (one-third of $27,000, or $9,000) and the partnership's equipment (one-third of $120,000, or $40,000). Thus, the section 736(b) amount in this case is $49,000 and the section 736(a) amount is the remainder of the distribution, $132,000.

Notice that ABC LLP is not subject to depreciation recapture under section 1245, because the fair market value of the equipment is less than its adjusted tax basis. Even if recapture were present, it would not be considered to be an unrealized receivable for purposes of section 736. *See* section 751(c) (flush language).

The answer to this Question would change if section 736(b)(3) caused section 736(b)(2) not to apply. **Answers (a) and (b)** suggest two ways this could happen. **Answer (a)** is not correct. According to the 1993 legislative history of section 736(b)(3), section 736(b)(2) is intended to continue to apply to law, accounting, consulting, medical and other partnerships where substantially all of the gross income of the partnership's business consists of fees, commissions and other compensation for personal services performed by individuals. A substantial capital investment in professional equipment or physical plant does not disqualify a partnership from this status, as long as the capital investment is incidental to the professional practice. H.R. REP. No. 103–111, 103d Cong., 1st Sess. 783 (1993).

Answer (b) is also incorrect. As a partner in a limited liability partnership, Brody plainly does not have the same personal liability for the partnership's debts as a general partner. The purpose of limiting the scope of section 736(b)(2) to distributions to "general partners" is not entirely clear, but likely it had nothing to do with their quantum of personal liability. The more likely purpose was to prevent limited partners who principally are investors (as opposed to service providers) from receiving deductible retirement payments. Although there is no precedent directly on point, in an analogous area, courts have consistently concluded that members of LLCs or LLPs are "general partners" for purposes of determining their material participation in passive activities. *See, e.g., Garnett v. Commissioner,* 132 T.C. 368 (2009).

Answer (c) is incorrect, because it applies section 736(a) only to the unrealized receivables. This, as we will see, mimics the result that would occur if section 751(b) applied to this distribution. Section 751(b) does not apply in this case, however, because it is supplanted by section 736(a). *See* section 751(b)(2)(B).

9.8.2   The correct Answer is (a). Whether or not the distributing partnership has liabilities, you must determine the section 736(b) amount (and by extension the section 736(a) amount) by reference to the gross value of the partnership's assets. Treas. Reg. § 1.736–1(b)(1). This is because section 752(b) requires that the partner's share of the partnership's liabilities be taken into account as an additional cash distribution. The liquidating distribution is therefore itself "gross." You divide the gross distribution between section 736(b) and section 736(a) by using gross asset values.

The gross distribution to Brody is $194,000 ($181,000 cash plus $13,000 deemed cash under section 752(b)). Her interest in the gross value of the section 736(b) property is $62,000 ($22,000 for the cash and $40,000 for the equipment). Thus, her section 736(b) amount is $62,000 and her section 736(a) amount is $132,000, which is the excess of the gross distribution ($194,000) over her section 736(b) amount. She recognizes a capital loss of $9,000, which equals the excess of her outside basis ($58,000 tax capital plus $13,000 liability share, or $71,000) over her section 736(b) amount. She recognizes ordinary income equal to her section 736(a) amount, $132,000. Her overall gain in the transaction is $123,000, which is the excess of the gross distribution of $194,000 over her outside basis of $71,000. Section 736 divides this overall gain into $132,000 of ordinary income and $9,000 of capital loss. Notice that Brody's capital loss equals her share of the partnership's loss in the equipment.

You will recall from the discussion in Topic 9.6 that it is sometimes difficult to determine a partner's "interest" in any particular partnership asset. Yet the section 736(b) payment is defined as that which is made "in exchange for the interest of the [withdrawing] partner in partnership property." That this is an aggregate determination, not property-by-property, does not eliminate the difficulty in making it. The Treasury regulations allow the partners to decide this by arms-length agreement. Treas. Reg. § 1.736–1(b)(1).

Answer (b) is incorrect, because it determines Brody's section 736(b) amount by subtracting her $13,000 liability share from her share of the values of the partnership's cash and equipment—in other words, it makes the mistake of using net, rather than gross, asset values. **Answer (c)** makes the interesting error of limiting the amount of Brody's ordinary income to her overall gain in the transaction. There is no such limitation on the section 736(a) amount, although if it exceeds the overall gain, it will be offset by a corresponding loss. **Answer (d)** is odd. It increases Brody's section 736(b) amount by her liability share and reduces her section 736(a) amount by her liability share. Why you would do that, I do not know.

9.8.3   The correct Answer is (b). In the two foregoing Questions, we had the advantage of knowing exactly the value of ABC LLP's goodwill, so that we knew exactly the amount to which section 736(b)(2)(B) applied. In fact, self-created goodwill does not appear on a balance sheet and its value may be difficult to ascertain in the absence of a sale of the whole business. Section 736(b)(2)(B) still applies—but it is difficult to know what it applies to.

Treas. Reg. § 1.736–1(b)(3) provides that the agreement of the partners as to the value of the partnership's goodwill will be respected if it is reasonable—a standard that generally will be met by an arms-length agreement among partners who are otherwise unrelated. That is the case here. Accordingly, the section 736(b) amount in this case includes Brody's share of the value of the cash ($22,000), the equipment ($40,000) and the goodwill ($50,000), a total of $112,000. The section 736(a) amount is the excess of the gross distribution ($194,000) over the section 736(b) amount, or $82,000. Brody recognizes ordinary income of $82,000 and capital gain of $41,000 (the excess of the section 736(b) amount of $112,000 over Brody's outside basis of $71,000).

Comparing this result to the result in Question 9.8.2, you will see that the partner's agreement as to the treatment and valuation of goodwill shifts $50,000 of this distribution away from section 736(a) into section 736(b). Accordingly, Brody recognizes $50,000 less ordinary income and $50,000 more capital gain.

Answer (a) is incorrect, because it does not take this shift into account. **Answer (c)**, like the misguided **Answer (d)** in Question 9.8.2, increases Brody's section 736(b) amount by her liability share and reduces her section 736(a) amount similarly. **Answer (d)** goes overboard, shifting not just the agreed $50,000 from section 736(a) to section 736(b), but the entire excess distribution, other than that attributable to Brody's share of the unrealized receivables.

9.8.4   The correct Answer is (a). The partnership is entitled to deduct the amount of Brody's guaranteed payment under section 162(a). Treas. Reg. § 1.736–1(a)(4). Absent an election under section 754, no adjustments to the basis of any partnership property are appropriate or allowed. **Answers (b), (c) and (d)** all provide for such adjustments and all are incorrect.

9.8.5   The correct Answer is (b). As in Question 9.8.4, the partnership has a $132,000 deduction. Section 734(b) may require an adjustment to the basis of one or more of the partnership's properties, due to the presence of a section 754 election. The size of this adjustment, if any, depends on the gain or loss Brody recognizes on the distribution. Here, the total distribution is $181,000, divided $132,000 to the section 732(a) amount and $49,000 to the section 736(b) amount. Brody recognizes a capital loss of $9,000 on the distribution, equal to the excess of her outside basis ($58,000) over her section 736(b) amount ($49,000). This, in turn, creates a negative $9,000 adjustment under section 734(b)(2)(A).

Treas. Reg. § 1.755–1(c)(1)(ii) requires the partnership to allocate this adjustment solely to capital gain property. Treas. Reg. § 1.755–1(c)(2)(ii) requires a negative adjustment to be allocated first to depreciated property to the extent of the depreciation. As a result, the entire $9,000 negative adjustment goes to the only capital gain property that is depreciated, the equipment.

Answer (a) is incorrect, because it provides for no adjustment to the basis of any partnership property. As a result, the net deduction/basis adjustment for the partnership is $132,000, which exceeds Brody's overall gain in the transaction by $9,000. This was the correct answer in Question 9.8.4, where the partnership did not make a section 754 election, but it is wrong here. **Answer (c)** provides for the correct $123,000 net deduction/basis adjustment, but it is allocated incorrectly between deduction and basis adjustment. The same is true of **Answer (d)**.

9.8.6   **The correct Answer is (d).** At least two new questions are raised by the presence of deferred payments. The first is the capacity in which a partner (like Brody) who has withdrawn from the partnership receives the payments made after the withdrawal. The answer, provided most clearly in Treas. Reg. § 1.736–1(a)(1)(ii), is that, although the withdrawing partner may cease to be a partner under local law, she remains a partner for tax purposes until her interest is completely liquidated—until, that is, the final payment has been made. The second question raised by deferred payments is the allocation of those payments between the section 736(a) amount and the section 736(b) amount. This is an issue whenever the section 736(b) amount exceeds the fixed amount, if any, paid to the partner upon her withdrawal. It is particularly nettlesome in a case, like this one, where the deferred payments are uncertain in amount, so there is no guarantee when, or even whether, the deferred payments will cover the deficit in the section 736(b) amount. Treas. Reg. § 1.736–1(b)(5)(ii) provides a simple solution, which applies unless the partners reach a contrary agreement: all deferred payments that are not fixed in amount are considered to be payments of the section 736(b) amount, until it is satisfied in full.

Brody's section 736(b) amount is, as before, $49,000. The fixed payment on June 30, 2016 falls $9,000 short. The first $9,000 of the payment on December 31, 2016 restores this deficit. Brody's recognized capital loss is $9,000, the excess of her outside basis ($58,000) over her section 736(b) amount ($49,000). The remainder of the December 31, 2016 payment ($16,000) is treated as a distributive share of partnership income under section 736(a)(1).

Answer (a) applies the reverse approach, treating 100% of the December 31, 2016 payment as distributive share and postponing the recovery of the remaining section 736(b) amount until the final payment. From a policy perspective, this would be a bad idea, because it would maximize the chance that the deficit would never be recovered. Under this approach, Brody would recognize no capital gain or loss in 2016, because the transaction would be still "open." **Answer (b)** applies the harsh and unnecessary rule that *only* the fixed payment of $40,000 can be treated as a section 736(b) amount. The transaction "closes" in 2016, resulting in a recognized $18,000 capital loss for Brody, and a distributive share of income equal to $25,000. **Answer (d)** is actually one considered by the drafters of section 736. *See* Jackson, Johnson, Surrey, Tenen & Warren, *The Internal Revenue Code of 1954: Partnerships*, 54 COLUM. L. REV. 1183, 1226 (1954). It divides the missing section 736(b) amount ($9,000) by the number of deferred, contingent payments (three), and allows $3,000 of each payment to be applied to the section 736(b) amount. It was recognized, however, that the approach ultimately adopted in the Treasury regulations was "probably more feasible." *Id.*

9.8.7   **The correct Answer is (c).** If capital is a material income-producing factor for the partnership, the application of section 736 is usually fleeting. Because section 736(b)(2) does not apply to a distribution made by such a partnership, the entire distribution is a section 736(b) amount, except to the extent that it demonstrably exceeds the interest of the withdrawing partner in the partnership's assets. That is not the case here, where the amount of Brody's distribution ($181,000) exactly equals her one-third share of the aggregate value of the partnership's assets. Section 736, thank you for playing.

Turning back to the ordinary rules that apply to liquidating distributions, you can see that Brody's interest in section 751(b) assets is $32,000 prior to the distribution and $0 after. Brody therefore recognizes $32,000 of ordinary income on this distribution, under either the existing or the proposed Treasury regulations under section 751(b). *See* Topic 9.6. The remainder of the distribution, $149,000, exceeds Brody's outside basis by $91,000, producing a capital gain in that amount.

Answer (a) is incorrect. It is the result reached by applying section 736(b)(2) to this distribution, which is prohibited in the case of a capital-intensive partnership by section 736(b)(3). **Answer (b)** is incorrect, because it attempts to apply section 736(b)(2), but does so incorrectly. **Answer (d)** is incorrect, because it fails to apply section 751(b).

9.8.8   **The correct Answer is (d).** The partnership can claim no deduction for a section 736(a) amount paid to Brody, because the entire liquidating distribution is governed by section 736(b). The partnership takes a $32,000 basis in the receivables that it is deemed to have purchased from Brody under section 751(b), giving the partnership a basis increase equal to the amount that Brody recognizes as ordinary income. Finally, the partnership is entitled to a positive basis adjustment under section 734(b)(1)(A) equal to the amount of capital gain that Brody recognizes on the distribution. This amount is $91,000, which under Treas. Reg. §§ 1.755–1(c)(1)(ii) and –1(c)(2)(i) is allocated entirely to the partnership's goodwill, because it is the only capital gain property having a value greater than its tax basis.

Answers (a), (b) and (c) all provide the partnership with some measure of deduction and all are incorrect for that reason alone. Notice that **Answer (a)** provides the partnership with a greater deduction than the total of income and gain Brody recognizes, which cannot be right for a partnership that has made a section 754 election. **Answers (b) and (c)** are closer, providing the partnership with a combination of deduction and basis increase that equals Brody's income and gain.

It is useful to compare this Question 9.8.8 to Question 9.8.5, in which the partnership also made a section 754 election. In each case, the total of deduction and basis adjustment to the partnership is $123,000. In Question 9.8.5, the application of section 736(a) delivers all of this net benefit to the partnership in the form of a deduction. In this Question 9.8.8, in contrast, the benefit is entirely in the form of a basis step-up.

9.8.9 **The correct Answer is (b).** It is tempting to conclude that section 736(a) never applies to a capital-intensive partnership. Never say never. If a partnership makes a distribution to a withdrawing partner that exceeds the value of her share of the partnership's assets, the excess is governed by section 736(a), whether or not capital is a material income-producing factor for the partnership. Be careful, though, to double-check that the payment is really a distribution, rather than something else, like a disguised sale, gift or payment for services. There is nothing in the facts to suggest any of these alternative characterizations here. In many real-world situations, the value of the partnership's goodwill may be difficult to determine with any degree of certainty, allowing the IRS to argue that the excess payment is not really excess at all. Here, that argument is explicitly negated in the statement of the facts. Accordingly, in addition to the $32,000 ordinary income determined under section 751(b), Brody recognizes $19,000 of ordinary income as a guaranteed payment under section 736(a)(2). Her capital gain remains the same as in Question 9.8.7.

Answer (a) is incorrect, being the result that would obtain if ABC LLP were a service partnership. **Answer (c)** is incorrect, because it treats the additional $19,000 distribution as a section 736(b) amount, rather than as a section 736(a) amount. **Answer (d)** ignores both section 736(a) and section 751(b).

10.1.1 **The correct Answer is (c).** The place to start answering this Question is Treas. Reg. § 1.708–1(b)(2), which identifies several common transactions that are not considered to be a "sale or exchange" for purposes of section 708(b)(1)(B). Included is a gift, bequest or inheritance, so **Answer (a)** is incorrect. This regulation also includes the following sentence: "The contribution of property to a partnership does not constitute such a sale of exchange." Treas. Reg. § 1.708–1(b)(2) (seventh sentence). This is a curious use of words. The sentence seems to be addressing whether there is a sale or exchange of the contributed property but, given the purpose of this regulation, that cannot be its intended meaning. The only sensible interpretation of this sentence is as a rule that the issuance of a partnership interest in exchange for contributed property is not a sale or exchange of the partnership interest. **Answer (b)** is therefore incorrect. **Answers (c) and (d)** are not directly addressed by Treas. Reg. § 1.708–1(b)(2), so you must rely on what you know about a sale or exchange in other contexts. Section 761(e) provides that a distribution of a partnership interest is treated as an exchange for purposes of several provisions of the Internal Revenue Code, including section 708. So **Answer (c)** is correct. Finally, **Answer (d)** is incorrect, because under general tax principles a pledge of property to a lender as security for a loan is not a sale or exchange. *Woodsam Associates, Inc. v. Commissioner*, 198 F.2d 357 (2d Cir. 1952).

10.1.2   The correct Answer is (d). First let's see which of the events identified in the facts are sales or exchanges for purposes of section 708(b)(1)(B). The February sale for cash is a sale or exchange, even though it is from one partner to another. The June resale of that same interest is also a sale or exchange, though it is subject to a special counting rule discussed below. The August liquidation is not a sale or exchange. Treas. Reg. § 1.708–1(b)(2) (third sentence). The increases in the interests of the remaining partners that occur by reason of the liquidation do not arise from sales or exchanges. Neither Boris' death in September, nor the passing of his interest to his son, is a sale or exchange, the former because it is not a sale or exchange under general tax principles and the latter because it is specifically excluded by Treas. Reg. § 1.708–1(b)(2) (third sentence). Finally, the January assignment is a sale or exchange under general tax principles. *Schultz v. Commissioner*, 59 T.C. 559 (1973).

Now, you need only add up the percentages. On the date of each sale or exchange of a partnership interest, look back 12 months and add together all of the sales or exchanges that have occurred during that period. The 12-month period may extend back into a different calendar year or tax year of the partnership. On February 1, the sum is 25%. No termination. The next sale or exchange is June 26, and it would seem to push the sum to 50%. The transfer of the same interest is, however, counted only once in each 12-month period. Treas. Reg. § 1.708–1(b)(2) (last sentence). So the sum is still 25%. The next sale of exchange occurs on January 27. On that date, the sum is 58%, and the partnership terminates.

10.1.3   The correct Answer is (b). This Question requires you to interpret the seventh sentence of Treas. Reg. § 1.708–1(b)(2). Based on the reading suggested above (*see* Question 10.1.1), this sentence protects the interest issued by Partnership AB from treatment as a sale or exchange. It does not, however, protect the interest in Partnership CD, which is exchanged by Cam for an interest in Partnership AB. The fact that this is a tax-free exchange does not prevent it from being counted as a sale or exchange for purposes of section 708(b)(1)(B).

10.1.4   The correct Answer is (c). This Question requires you to apply the fourth and fifth sentences of Treas. Reg. § 1.708–1(b)(2). Conceptually, there are two approaches, entity and aggregate. The entity approach is "all or nothing." Upon a sale or exchange of interests in Partnership ABC, either all of the interests in Partnership CD are deemed to be sold or exchanged, or none of them are, depending on whether Partnership ABC itself terminates. The aggregate approach, in contrast, considers interests in Partnership CD to be sold or exchanged only to the extent of Aaron's indirect interest in Partnership CD through his interest in Partnership ABC. The regulations adopt the entity approach. Accordingly, you must determine whether Partnership ABC terminates as a result of Aaron's sale. It does—the sale is clearly a sale or exchange, and Aaron owns 60% of Partnership ABC. Under the regulation, the termination of Partnership ABC causes its 62.5% interest in Partnership CD to be deemed sold or exchanged. This precipitates a termination of Partnership CD as well. **Answer (a)** is incorrect, although it would be the correct response under the aggregate approach, which would find a sale or exchange of only 37.5% (60% of 62.5%) of the interests in Partnership CD. **Answers (b) and (d)** are incomplete.

10.1.5   The correct Answer is (b). Under the third sentence of Treas. Reg. § 1.708–1(b)(2), the liquidation of a partnership interest is not a sale or exchange of that interest. Thus, **Answer (a)** is incorrect. On the other hand, when the property distributed in liquidation is itself a partnership interest, the distribution is a sale or exchange of the distributed interest under section 761(e)(1). This rule is analogous to the rules for contributions reviewed in Question 10.1.3. **Answer (c)** is over-inclusive and **Answer (d)** is under-inclusive.

10.1.6   The correct Answer is (d). There are two parts to this Question. The first is determining the classification of Duo-Tone for tax purposes. As a domestic limited liability company, it is an eligible entity under Treas. Reg. § 301.7701–3(a). Its default classification (that is, its classification if it files no contrary "check the box" election) is partnership, if it has two or more owners, and disregarded entity if it has only a single owner. *See* Topics 1.2 and 1.3. Thus, Duo-Tone is a partnership before A's sale of her interest to B and it is a disregarded entity thereafter. Duo-Tone terminates under section 708(b)(1)(A) in this transaction, because no part of its business is thereafter carried on by a partnership. B is the sole owner of Duo-Tone's assets. *See* Rev. Rul. 99–6, 1999–1 C.B. 432. Following the analysis of this ruling, and the earlier *McCauslen v. Commissioner*, 45 T.C. 588 (1966), A is treated as simply selling her Duo-Tone interest to B. B, on the other hand, is not treated as purchasing the Duo-Tone interest from A. Instead, B is deemed to have acquired Duo-Tone's assets through a deemed liquidation of Duo-Tone. In this liquidation, Duo-Tone distributes one-half of its assets to A and one-half to B. B purchases from A the assets deemed distributed to A. B's holding periods for the assets B receives in the deemed liquidation include Duo-Tone's holding periods under section 735(b). B's holding periods for the purchased assets begin the day after the purchase.

Answer (a) would be correct if Duo-Tone were treated as a corporation for tax purposes. **Answer (b)** treats Duo-Tone as a continuing entity, which would be the case if it were a corporation for tax purposes, but with a new holding period, which would be the case if all of its assets were treated as purchased by B. This hybrid analysis is inconsistent with both the corporate and the partnership tax regimes. **Answer (c)** would be correct if B were treated as acquiring A's interest in Duo-Tone immediately prior to the deemed liquidation, so that B would have holding periods determined under section 735(b) for all of the assets. While this approach would have the advantage of treating A and B consistently, it is not current law.

10.2.1 The correct Answer is (a). AB continues to own substantial assets and its existence as a limited partnership under state law and as an entity for tax purposes does not terminate. This disqualifies this transaction from treatment as a "merger" within the meaning of section 708(b)(2)(A). It is not sufficient that AB transfers all of the assets it uses in its active business. That said, none of the parties may care that this transaction is not a merger. As you will see in Topic 10.3, the steps of the transaction will be taxed under the ordinary rules governing partnership contributions and distributions, which are generally applicable whether the transaction is a merger or not. **Answer (b)** is incorrect, because assets-up is not the required, or even the preferred, form of a merger under Treas. Reg. § 1.708–1(c)(3). **Answers (c) and (d)** are not correct, because this is not a merger.

10.2.2 The correct Answer is (d). The difficulty in analyzing this Question is that A and B transfer AB interests to CD, in what might appear to be an interests-over form. The instant that CD acquires those interests, however, AB ceases to exist as a partnership, because it has only one owner, and becomes a disregarded entity. This is a "merger" within the meaning of section 708(b)(2)(A). All of the assets of two partnerships have been combined into a single partnership in a single transaction. **Answer (a)** is incorrect, because, although there are two legal entities at the conclusion of the transaction, there is only one tax entity, which is CD. For tax purposes, CD is the continuing partnership, because its partners own 65% of the resulting partnership, and AB terminates, because its partners own only 35%. **Answer (b)** is incorrect. A merger can be accomplished in interests-over form—it just cannot be taxed in that manner. Such a merger will be recharacterized as assets-over. **Answer (c)** is also incorrect, because AB is not the continuing partnership in this merger.

In Rev. Rul. 99–6, 199–1 C.B. 432 (Situation 2), the IRS analyzed a similar situation involving a taxable purchase of all of the interests in a limited liability company by a single, unrelated purchaser. It held that the transaction should be treated as interests-over from the perspective of the sellers and as assets-up from the perspective of the buyer. This creates some uncertainty regarding the proper characterization of the form of this transaction. It would probably be an assets-over transaction in which AB transfers all of its assets to CD in exchange for CD partnership interests which it distributes to A and B in liquidation. There is an argument, based on the analysis in Rev. Rul. 99–6, that this should be treated as either an assets-up or an interests-over transaction. As to the former, Treas. Reg. § 1.708–1(c)(3)(ii) explicitly requires A and B to take ownership of the AB assets for state-law purposes in order for the assets-up form to be respected. That did not happen in this case. Further, mergers accomplished in interests-over form are always recharacterized into the assets-over form. Thus it seems that the default assets-over characterization would apply, regardless of one's initial conception of this transaction.

10.2.3 The correct Answer is (d). In order for the resulting partnership to be treated as a continuation of a merging partnership, the partners of the merging partnership must own *more than* 50% of the total interests in the capital and profits of the resulting partnership. None of the three merging partnerships meet that standard here—although Partnership AB comes close, at exactly 50%. The other two are further out of the running.

10.2.4   The correct Answer is (d). All three of the merging partnerships terminate for tax purposes. Because this merger is "formless" under state law, the default assets-over characterization applies. All three terminated partnerships are deemed to transfer their assets to a new partnership in exchange for interests therein, which each distributes to its respective partners in liquidation. Treas. Reg. § 1.708–1(c)(1) (last sentence). **Answer (a)** is incorrect, because it treats the resulting partnership as a continuation of Partnership AB. **Answer (b)** is close, but complicates unnecessarily the operation of Treas. Reg. § 1.708–1(c). In a situation where no partnership survives the merger, all of the terminated partnerships are treated as transferring their assets directly to the new partnership. There are no asset transfers among terminated partnerships. **Answer (c)** makes two mistakes. First, it treats Partnership AB as the surviving partnership in this merger, which it is not. Second, it applies an assets-up form to this formless merger, rather than the assets-over form.

10.2.5   The correct Answer is (a). Under the facts of this Question, both Partnership AB and Partnership BCD are continuing partnerships, because the partners of the former own 76% of the resulting partnership and the partners of the latter own 64%. It seems that section 708(b)(2)(A) would be happy with this result, but Treas. Reg. § 1.708–1(c)(1) is not. Under this regulation, the resulting partnership in a merger can be treated as the continuation of, at most, one of the merging partnerships. The choice is made according to which of the combining partnerships brings the greatest net asset value to the resulting partnership. In this case, it is Partnership AB.

10.2.6   The correct Answer is (c). Unlike a "formless" merger under a state merger statute, this one has a form. Partnership AB, which we have determined to be the continuing partnership, transfers all of its assets to Partnership BCD, which we have determined to be the terminated partnership. This is not the assets-over form described in Treas. Reg. § 1.708–1(c)(3)(i), because assets are transferred by the wrong partnership, nor is it the assets-up form described in Treas. Reg. § 1.708–1(c)(3)(ii). Accordingly, the default characterization applies to this transaction. It will be treated as an assets-over transfer by Partnership BCD, the terminated partnership, to Partnership AB, the continuing partnership. Treas. Reg. § 1.708–1(c)(5), example (2). **Answer (a)** is incorrect, because the form in which this merger is consummated is neither of the two forms that are allowed by the regulations. **Answer (b)** is incorrect, because Partnership AB survives this merger and therefore it is not a transferor of assets. **Answer (d)** is incorrect, because assets-up is not the default form under the regulations.

10.2.7   The correct Answer is (a). Under these facts, the partnership resulting from this combination is treated as a continuation of Partnership AB, because it is the only partnership whose partners have a combined ownership of more than 50% of the capital and profits interests in the resulting partnership. Each of the pieces of this combination takes a form that is respected under Treas. Reg. § 1.708–1(c)(3). Partnership BCD, a terminated partnership, transfers its assets to Partnership AB in a permissible assets-over transaction, and Partnership EF, a terminated partnership, distributes its assets to its partners in a permissible assets-up transaction. Both should be taxed according to their form. **Answer (b)** assumes, incorrectly, that all parts of a combination must be consummated in the same form. **Answer (c)** is incorrect, because it misidentifies the continuing partnership as Partnership BCD. **Answer (d)** makes the same error.

10.3.1 **The correct Answer is (b).** As always, the first step in analyzing a partnership merger is to determine which of the merging partnerships is deemed to continue. Section 708(b)(2)(A) provides that the partnership resulting from a merger will be considered the continuation of any merging partnership whose partners own more than 50% of the capital and profits of the resulting partnership. Here, the facts tell us that ownership in the resulting entity is proportional to the net asset values (fair market value of gross assets less liabilities) contributed by each of the merging entities. The net asset value of AB LLC is $400,000 and that of CD LLC is $600,000. Thus, Ainslie and Briana will split the ownership of 40% of ABCD LLC and Colin and Dylan will split 60%. ABCD LLC will be treated as a continuation of CD LLC. **Answers (a) and (c)** are incorrect, because the members of AB LLC will own only 40% of ABCD LLC. **Answer (d)** is incorrect, because the members of CD LLC will own 60% of ABCD LLC, which is well above the 50% threshold established by section 708(b)(2)(A).

10.3.2 **The correct Answer is (a).** Because this merger undertaken under state law is "formless," the default, assets-over characterization of Treas. Reg. § 1.708–1(c)(3)(i) will apply. The terminated partnership (here, AB LLC) is deemed to be the transferor of assets. It transfers its assets to the continuing partnership (here, CD LLC) in exchange for interests therein, which it distributes to its partners in liquidation. **Answer (b)** is incorrect, because it treats AB LLC as the continuing partnership and CD LLC as the terminated partnership and transferor of assets. **Answers (c) and (d)** are incorrect, because Treas. Reg. § 1.708–1(c) never imposes an assets-up characterization on a formless merger.

10.3.3 **The correct Answer is (a).** For book purposes, AB LLC will realize all of the gain inherent in its assets when it transfers them to CD LLC in exchange for interests in CD LLC. AB LLC's total book gain will be $200,000, and Ainslie will be allocated one-half of that. Ainslie will recognize no tax gain or loss on this merger. Because Ainslie contributed Land 1 with built-in gain less than seven years prior to the merger date, the possible application of the anti-mixing-bowl rules must be considered. The fact that Ainslie receives a liquidating distribution from AB LLC that consists not of Land 1, but of a partnership interest, suggests, for example, that section 737 might apply to tax her on her net precontribution gain of $60,000. The application of either of the anti-mixing-bowl statutes to trigger current gain recognition in mergers is foreclosed, however, by regulation. Treas. Reg. §§ 1.704–4(c)(4), 1.737–2(b)(1). **Answer (b)** is incorrect, because it taxes Ainslie's net precontribution gain. **Answers (c) and (d)** measure Ainslie's book gain incorrectly, by looking at the appreciation over book value in the property she contributed, Land 1. Unlike built-in tax gain, book gain is shared by the partners in accordance with their agreement, here assumed to be a simple 50–50 arrangement. **Answer (d)** also mis-measures Ainslie's tax gain, as the entire excess of the value of Land 1 over its tax basis. This shows two misunderstandings of the anti-mixing-bowl rules. First, that they apply to create current recognition of tax gain in a merger. Second, that they apply to more than the forward section 704(c) layer in any contributed property. *See* Topic 9.4.

10.3.4 The correct Answer is (c). Prior to the merger, Ainslie was a 50% partner in AB LLC and her outside basis was $190,000, composed of her tax capital ($40,000) and her 50% share of AB LLC's $300,000 debt ($150,000). Ainslie's outside basis is adjusted by deemed contributions and distributions under section 752. After the merger, Ainslie is a 20% partner in ABCD LLC, and therefore has a liability share of $60,000 (20% of $300,000). Ainslie thus suffers a net distribution of $90,000 under section 752(b), reducing her outside basis from $190,000 to $100,000. **Answer (a)** forgets to include debt in the computation of Ainslie's outside basis. **Answer (b)** computes Ainslie's outside basis on the assumption that she has a one-sixth interest in ABCD LLC. This assumption is not as random as it may seem. It would be correct answer if the two partnerships had been combined based on net book values rather than net fair market values. **Answer (d)** forgets to adjust Ainslie's 50% debt share as a result of the merger.

10.3.5 The correct Answer is (d). CD LLC will likely revalue its book assets and book capital accounts immediately prior to the merger. In doing so, it will recognize $200,000 of book gain, one-half of which it will allocate to Colin. Colin will recognize no tax gain on the merger. Although he, like Ainslie, contributed property with built-in gain less than seven years before the merger date, neither he nor Dylan receives any sort of distribution in connection with the merger. Thus, no event occurs which might trigger current recognition of Colin's built-in gain. **Answer (a)** would be the correct answer if CD LLC did not undertake a revaluation. While this is possible, it is not likely. **Answer (b)** makes two errors. It allocates book gain to Colin equal to the appreciation of Land 3, the asset which Colin contributed, over its book value. Colin has no special claim to the book appreciation in that asset, however, and should be allocated one-half of the book gains from both Land 3 and Land 4. **Answer (b)** also taxes Colin on his precontribution gain in Land 3, although none of the assets of CD LLC are deemed to be distributed in this merger. **Answer (c)** makes only the second of these two errors.

10.3.6 The correct Answer is (c). Colin's outside basis in CD LLC was $60,000, which included no share of liabilities, because CD LLC had no liabilities. Following the merger, Colin is a 30% partner in ABCD LLC, and can include an additional $90,000 (30% of $300,000) in his outside basis, increasing it to $150,000. **Answer (a)** neglects this increase. **Answer (b)** includes a $75,000 liability share in Colin's outside basis, which would be correct if his interest in CD LLC were 25% (perhaps on the erroneous assumption that all four members in CD LLC have equal interests). **Answer (d)** includes a $100,000 liability share in Colin's outside basis, on the erroneous assumption that he has a one-third interest in CD LLC. This would be correct if the two LLCs had merged based on net book values.

Following the merger, the initial balance sheet of ABCD LLC (expanded to show asset values) looks like this:

Assets				Liabilities		
	Tax	**Book**	**FMV**		**Tax**	**Book**
Land 1	$ 40,000	$ 240,000	$ 240,000	Bank Debt	$300,000	$ 300,000
Land 2	400,000	460,000	460,000			
Land 3	60,000	250,000	250,000			
Land 4	200,000	350,000	350,000			
				Capital		
				Ainslie	40,000	200,000
				Briana	100,000	200,000
				Colin	60,000	300,000
				Dylan	200,000	300,000
Total Assets	$700,000	$1,300,000	$1,300,000	**Total Liabilities and Capital**	$700,000	$1,300,000

10.4.1 The correct Answer is (d). Under Treas. Reg. § 1.708–1(d)(4)(iv), a "resulting partnership" is a partnership resulting from a division that has at least two partners who were partners in the prior partnership. Under this standard, Utica Shale LLC is not a resulting partnership. It follows that this transaction is not a division, because a division must involve more than one partnership. **Answers (a) and (b)** are incorrect, because they recognize this transaction as a division. **Answer (c)** is incorrect, because the "assets up" form is not required in order for a transaction to be a division. Failing to qualify as a division may be just what the parties want, because the transaction will be taxed in accordance with its form. The contribution of property to Utica Shale LLC and the distribution of interests therein generally will be tax-free to Marcellus Drilling LP, Utica Shale LLC and Jack under sections 721 and 731, and if they are not (for example, due to the application of the anti-mixing-bowl rules), being characterized as a division will not help. *See* Topic 10.5.

10.4.2 The correct Answer is (c). Under section 708(b)(2)(B), every partnership that results from a division whose partners had an interest of more than 50% in the capital and profits of the prior partnership is a continuation of the prior partnership. Unlike the merger regulations, the division regulations do not disturb this result. The transaction described in the facts is a "spin-off," in which the same partners own 100% of both of the partnerships resulting from the division. **Answers (a) and (b)** are incomplete, and **Answer (d)** fails completely at applying the statutory rule.

10.4.3   The correct Answer is (d). The key to answering this Question is to identify correctly the divided partnership. The divided partnership is a continuing partnership that is treated as the transferor of assets. In a case where, as here, there is more than one continuing partnership, the divided partnership is the continuing partnership that actually made the asset transfer, if any. Here, that is Marcellus Drilling LP and the transaction actually executed is the same as the default assets-over form described in Treas. Reg. § 1.708–1(d)(3)(i)(A). Thus, this division will be taxed in accordance with its form. **Answers (a) and (b)** are incorrect, because both contemplate a distribution to the partners of Marcellus Drilling LP. The Treasury regulations never impose the assets-up form. **Answer (c)** is incorrect, because it fails to recognize that Marcellus (PA) Drilling LLC is a continuation of Marcellus Drilling LP.

10.4.4   The correct Answer is (b). We know from the facts that the partners of Marcellus (PA) Drilling LLC owned 75% of the interests in capital and profits of Marcellus Drilling LP and that the partners of what is now called Marcellus (Ohio) Drilling LP owned only 25%. Therefore, under section 708(b)(2)(B), only Marcellus (PA) Drilling LLC is a continuation of Marcellus Drilling LP. **Answers (a) and (c)** are incorrect, because they include as a continuing partnership one whose partners owned an interest of 50% or less in the capital and profits of Marcellus Drilling LP. This is contrary to the parenthetical language in section 708(b)(2)(B). **Answer (d)** is incorrect because it fails to recognize as a continuing partnership one whose partners owned more than 50% of the capital and profits of Marcellus Drilling LP.

10.4.5   The correct Answer is (d). Perhaps the hardest part of answering this Question is not to be confused by the names. For tax purposes, there is one continuing partnership, which is first named Marcellus Drilling LP and later is named Marcellus (PA) Drilling LLC. Because this entity is the only continuing partnership, it is the divided partnership and, therefore, the transferor of assets. The other entity is named Marcellus (Ohio) Drilling LP and it is a new partnership, born out of the division. It cannot be the transferor, so it must be a recipient. It receives the Ohio acreage, which is transferred to it by the continuing partnership.

When a division is not accomplished in accordance with the allowed assets-up form, it is recharacterized under the default, assets-over form described in Treas. Reg. § 1.708–1(d)(3)(i)(A). The current transaction does not follow the prescribed assets-up form, because the partnership making the distribution is not the divided partnership. How do you know that? The divided partnership is Marcellus Drilling LP/Marcellus (PA) Drilling LLC. It owns the Pennsylvania properties at the conclusion of the transaction, so it cannot possibly have distributed them. Accordingly, the transaction must be recharacterized in default form as a transfer of the Ohio acreage by the divided partnership to the new partnership, Marcellus (Ohio) Drilling LP. What name should we use for the continuing partnership? It does not matter for tax purposes. We could call it either Marcellus Drilling LP or Marcellus (PA) Drilling LLC, since they are both names for the same tax entity. *See* Treas. Reg. § 1.708–1(d)(5), example (6).

Answers (a) and (b) are incorrect, because they both entail distributions, which the Treasury regulations do not recognize unless they actually happen in the form prescribed by the regulations. **Answer (c)** is incorrect, because it misidentifies Marcellus (Ohio) Drilling LP as the divided partnership.

10.4.6 The correct Answer is (b). There is no continuing partnership in this example. Based upon the acreage owned, Marcellus (Ohio) Drilling LP owns 25% of the value of the prior partnership, Marcellus (NE PA) Drilling owns 40% and Marcellus (SW PA) Drilling LP owns 35%. There are no overlapping partners, which you can tell from the fact that all distributions made by Marcellus Drilling LP are liquidating distributions. So this division is a split-up. The assets-up form of the Ohio portion of the transaction is not be respected for tax purposes, because the distribution is not made by a continuing partnership (there being none). Treas. Reg. § 1.708–1(d)(3)(ii). Instead, the prior partnership (here, Marcellus Drilling LP) is treated as transferring its assets to three new partnerships in exchange for interests therein, which it then distributes in complete liquidation. Treas. Reg. § 1.708–1(d)(3)(i)(B). **Answer (a)** is incorrect, because it fails to recognize that Marcellus Drilling LP terminates in this transaction, and therefore it must be deemed to dispose of its own assets (the retained Southwestern Pennsylvania acreage), in addition to the assets that it transferred (the Northeastern Pennsylvania acreage) or distributed (the Ohio acreage). **Answer (c)** makes the same mistake, and errs also by respecting the form of the Ohio distribution. **Answer (d)** is the closest to right of the wrong answers, because it does recognize that Marcellus Drilling LP terminates. Its failing is to respect the form of the Ohio distribution.

10.5.1 The correct Answer is (a). Under Treas. Reg. § 1.708–1(d)(4)(i), the divided partnership must be a continuing partnership. The first step is therefore to see which of the two partnerships resulting from this division is treated as a continuation of the prior partnership. C and D collectively owned 60% of the prior partnership, so the resulting partnership in which they are partners is a continuing partnership. A and B, on the other hand, owned only 40% of the prior partnership, so the resulting partnership in which they are partners is not a continuing partnership. When, as here, there is only one continuing partnership, that partnership is the divided partnership. It is Duquesne Power Blinds LLC, continued under the same name after the division. Westside Properties LLC is a new partnership formed in the division.

10.5.2 The correct Answer is (a). The divided partnership is the transferor of assets in this division. The division is not executed in assets-up form as specified in Treas. Reg. § 1.708–1(d)(3)(ii). Accordingly, the divided partnership, Duquesne Power Blinds LLC, is treated as transferring assets to the recipient partnership, Westside Properties LLC, which in this case is a new partnership for tax purposes, in exchange for interests therein, which Duquesne Power Blinds LLC then distributes to Albany and Bryce in liquidation of their interests in Duquesne. Treas. Reg. § 1.708–1(d)(3)(i)(A). **Answer (b)** is incorrect, because it treats Westside as the divided partnership. **Answer (c)** is incorrect, because it adopts the characterization of the transaction that would be appropriate if there were no continuing partnership and, thus, no divided partnership. **Answer (d)** is incorrect, because it forces an assets-up characterization on a division that was not executed in that form.

10.5.3   The correct Answer is (d). The first step is to see if there are section 751(b) assets. *See* Topic 9.6. The receivables are not unrealized. There is no recapture in the equipment and no facts to indicate that there is recapture in the plant. But the inventory is appreciated, presenting the possibility that the inventory items of the partnership are "substantially appreciated" within the meaning of section 751(b)(3). In making this determination under current law, you must include the value and basis of all inventory items described in section 751(d), which include the inventory (section 751(d)(1)) and the receivables (section 751(d)(2)). The aggregate value of the inventory items ($1,300,000 plus $370,000) is 137% the amount of their adjusted basis ($850,000 plus $370,000). The partnership's inventory items are therefore substantially appreciated.

In principle, there is no reason that section 751(b) should not apply to a division, because a division, like a simple property distribution, can separate a partner from her share of the partnership's unrealized ordinary income. In the present case, the division will permanently eliminate any ownership interest that Albany and Bryce have in the partnership's section 751(b) assets. The value of each of their current interests in the section 751(b) assets is $334,000 (20% of $1,670,000). The basis of each of their interests is $244,000 (20% of $1,220,000). Thus, it stands to reason that each of them should recognize $90,000 of ordinary income under section 751(b). And they do. The 1956 regulations under section 751(b) are always full of surprises, however, and this time is no exception.

As we will see in later Questions, the anti-mixing-bowl statutes apply to this division. Where section 751(b) and the anti-mixing-bowl provisions both apply, section 751(b) goes first. Treas. Reg. § 1.737–1(a)(2). Under Treas. Reg. § 1.751–1(b)(3), the partnership is deemed to distribute $334,000 of section 751(b) assets to each of Albany and Bryce, which they exchange with the partnership for an aggregate $668,000 of "other property." This is a fully taxable exchange, to Albany and Byrce and to the partnership. Albany and Bryce each recognize $90,000 of gain on this exchange, treated as ordinary income under Treas. Reg. § 1.751–1(b)(3)(iii). Each has a tax basis in the "other property" received equal to its fair market value of $334,000.

What is this "other property"? It is probably an interest in Westside Properties LLC. If so, the application of section 751(b) changes the characterization of the division. Instead of distributing all of the interests in Westside to Albany and Bryce in liquidation, the partnership actually "sells" an initial interest worth $668,000 and then distributes the rest. Under Treas. Reg. § 1.751–1(b)(3)(ii), the gain on the partnership's sale is allocated to the partners remaining after the liquidating distribution—that is, to Chubb and Dumol. Prior to this deemed exchange, the value of the Westside interest is $5,600,000 (the aggregate value of Land A and Land D) and its basis to the partnership is $1,200,000 (the aggregate of the tax bases of Land A and Land D). In the exchange, the partnership disposes of 11.929% of Westside ($668,000/$5,600,000) and recognizes a gain of about $524,860. Under the cited regulation, this gain evidently is allocable to Chubb and Dumol in their post-distribution ownership percentages, 33.3% and 66.7%. Accordingly, Chubb recognizes capital gain of about $174,953 and Dumol recognizes about $349,907.

Answer (a) overlooks section 751(b) entirely and is incorrect. **Answer (b)** would be the correct response under the proposed section 751(b) regulations issued in 2014. Under the proposed regulations, the distributing partnership would not recognize capital gain. *See* Topic 9.6. **Answer (c)** allocates the gain on the partnership's sale of the Westside interest as though the partnership had sold Land A and Land C, for which the Westside interest is substituted section 704(c) property under Treas. Reg. § 1.704–3(a)(8). Using this approach, Albany and Chubb, who have forward layers in Land A and Land C, take this gain equally. One of the criticisms of the 1956 regulations is their failure to employ section 704(c) principles. **Answer (c)** is flatly contrary to the allocation required by Treas. Reg. § 1.751–1(b)(3)(ii).

10.5.4 **The correct Answer is (d).** Duquesne is entitled to revalue its book assets immediately before the division under Treas. Reg. § 1.704–1(b)(2)(iv)(*f*)(*5*)(*ii*). A revaluation in these circumstances allows the partnership to reset all of the partners' book capital accounts to current fair market values. The partnership's revaluation book gain is $7 million, allocated 20%, or $1.4 million, to each of Albany, Bryce and Chubb, and 40%, or $2.8 million, to Dumol. After allocation of these amounts, the capital accounts of each of Albany and Bryce are $2.8 million, which is the value of the property to be distributed to them. In this way, the revaluation facilitates distributions in liquidation that equal the capital account balances of the withdrawing partners. **Answer (a)** would be correct if the partnership did not revalue. **Answer (b)** is the book gain recognized by all of the partners other than Dumol. **Answer (c)** is the book gain in Land D. There is no indication in the facts that Dumol has any special right to the book gain in this particular asset, or that he does not have the right to share in the book gain of every other asset.

10.5.5 **The correct Answer should be (a), but there is a meaningful risk that it is (b) or even (c).** First, let's get section 751(b) out of the way. As we saw in Question 10.5.3, section 751(b) seems to require a "bifurcation" of the Westside interest that Albany receives. Under the 1956 regulations, Albany essentially "buys" 11.929 % of her Westside interest in exchange for section 751(b) assets, leaving about 88.071% of the Westside interest to be distributed to her in liquidation of her Duquesne interest. This has no impact on her possible exposure under the anti-mixing-bowl statutes. Her forward layer in Land A is $400,000, just as it has always been. (Query whether a section 754 election might help her, but Westside has not made one.)

On the question of how much of her $400,000 forward layer Albany should recognize on this distribution, plausible answers range from none of it to all of it. If you view the Westside interest as property that is fundamentally different from Land A, despite the fact that Westside will own all of Land A, then all $400,000 should be triggered. If, on the other hand, you believe that ownership of Land A creates an identity between Land A and the Westside interest, then none of the $400,000 should be triggered.

The "substitute property" rule provides that the Westside interest is treated as section 704(c) property with the same amount of built-in gain as Land A. Treas. Reg. §§ 1.704–3(a)(8), –4(d)(1) and 1.737–2(d)(3)(i). Read literally, this language suggests that Albany avoids gain recognition only if she receives 100% of the Westside interest. If she receives less than 100%, then by definition someone else (here, Bryce) has received a portion (here, 50%) of her section 704(c) property, and Albany should be taxed under section 704(c)(1)(B). Applying that analysis here would mean that Albany recognizes 50% of the $400,000 forward layer in Land A, or $200,000.

There is a real possibility that this is current law. In 2001, the preamble to the final section 708 regulations on mergers and divisions noted that, in an assets-over division, "the distribution of the partnership interests in the recipient partnership by the divided partnership generally will trigger section 704(c)(1)(B) where the interests in the recipient partnership are received by a partner of the divided partnership other than the partner who contributed the section 704(c) property to the divided partnership." The final regulations provide an exception from the application of section 737 that would apply to Albany in this case, but there is no parallel provision in the regulations under section 704(c)(1)(B). Treas. Reg. § 1.737–2(b)(2).

One wonders, however, why the language of the substitute property rule should be read quite so literally. In the present case, Westside owns 100% of Land A. Land A's forward layer of $400,000 is still intact. Albany is a partner in Westside. This partnership is obligated to allocate the forward layer of gain in Land A to Albany if it sells Land A, and to apply the anti-mixing-bowl rules. Nothing seems to have happened that would require imposition of current gain recognition. Questions like this have surrounded the taxation of divisions for years, and the IRS seems no closer to answering them now than it was in 2001.

Answer (a) reflects the enlightened view that Albany should not be currently taxed on this division. **Answer (b)** incorporates the suggestion that the Westside interest should be treated as "substitute property" to the extent of one-half, because one-half of its value is attributable to Land A. Although there is no support in the regulations for this approach, it seems logical enough. **Answer (c)** reflects full taxation of Albany's forward layer, which, though draconian, seems possible. **Answer (d)**, on the other hand, is not possible. It taxes Albany on more than her $400,000 forward layer in Land A, which is beyond the reach of the anti-mixing-bowl rules.

10.5.6   The correct Answer is (b). Bryce's initial outside basis in Duquesne is the sum of her tax capital ($1,050,000) and her share of the partnership's bank debt (20% of $3 million), or $1,650,000. The deemed section 751(b) transactions make two changes to Bryce's outside basis. The deemed distribution of section 751(b) assets reduces it by $244,000, which is Bryce's share of the partnership's basis in such assets. The deemed purchase of Westside interests in exchange for the distributed section 751(b) assets increases it by $334,000, which is the fair market value of the Westside interest that Bryce is deemed to acquire in the exchange. Netted together, these section 751(b) adjustments increase Bryce's outside basis by $90,000— which makes sense, because Bryce recognizes $90,000 of ordinary income. Finally, because Westside does not inherit any portion of Duquesne's bank debt, Bryce has a deemed distribution of her prior share of that debt, which is $600,000.

There are no further adjustments to Bryce's outside basis. On the distribution of the Westside interest in liquidation of her Duquesne interest, section 732(b) preserves her outside basis unchanged. Combining all adjustments, Bryce's initial outside basis in Westside is:

Outside basis in Duquesne		$1,650,000
plus section 751(b)	($244,000)	
	334,000	
		90,000
less section 752(b)		(600,000)
Outside basis in Westside		$1,140,000

Answer (a) neglects both the section 751(b) adjustments, and **Answer (c)** neglects one of them. **Answer (d)** forgets about section 752(b).

10.5.7   The correct Answer is (b). Unlike Albany's situation, Chubb's is pretty simple. The division permanently separates him from his forward layer in Land C, because it goes to Westside while he stays in Duquesne. His entire forward layer of $400,000 is triggered under section 704(c)(1)(B). **Answer (a)** is incorrect. There is really no argument that Chubb should not be currently taxed in this case. There is also no argument for taxing Chubb on the larger amounts shown in **Answer (c)**, which is the entire accrued gain in Chubb's partnership interest, and **Answer (d)**, which is the entire accrued gain in Land C, because section 704(c)(1)(B) reaches only the forward layer in Land C, which is $400,000.

10.5.8   The correct Answer is (b). Changing the form of this division would not help Chubb. At the end of the day, he is separated from

Land C, and this triggers his forward layer of $400,000. A change in form could help Albany, however, by eliminating the need to apply the uncertain "substitute property" rule. Duquesne could accomplish the desired end result by distributing Land A to Albany and Land C to Bryce. Albany would not recognize gain under either section 704(c)(1)(B) or section 737 on this distribution, because she would be receiving a distribution of the property she contributed to Duquesne. Treas. Reg. § 1.737–2(d)(1). She could then contribute Land A to Westside in a tax-free contribution. **Answers (a) and (c)** are incorrect, because both reflect a better deal for Chubb than he can get. **Answer (d)** is incorrect, because, with some good advice, Albany can do better than that.

PART 2
FINAL EXAMS

BASIC

FINAL EXAM 1

(Suggested time: 60 minutes)

1.1 Broadway Partners is a New York general partnership formed to buy, hold and sell the stock of publicly traded companies in entertainment and related businesses. It is an "investing partnership" within the meaning of Treas. Reg. § 1.761–2 that has validly elected to be excluded from all of Subchapter K. It has four individual partners, each of whom contributed $1 million in cash on formation of the partnership in 2003. Each of these individuals owns a 25% stake currently valued at $3.5 million. Robert Jungman, an industry insider, wants to join the club by making a cash contribution of $3.5 million in exchange for a 20% interest. If Robert makes this contribution:

a) The transaction will be tax-free to all parties under section 721.

b) All parties will recognize gain, because this is an "investment partnership" within the meaning of section 721(b).

c) The other partners will recognize gain, but not Robert.

d) Robert will receive a percentage interest in the partnership of lesser value than his contribution, creating a deemed gift or other transfer from Robert to the other partners, the tax effect of which will depend on the nature of his relationship to the other partners.

1.2 Alvin, Bill and Tom have decided it's time to take their garage band on the road. They form Jagged Edge Ltd, a limited partnership, of which Tom is the general partner and Alvin and Bill are the limited partners. Alvin contributes his drum sets, which are worth $10,000 and have an adjusted basis in his hands of $4,500. They are subject to a recourse debt of $6,000, which the partnership assumes on the contribution. What is the partnership's initial tax basis in the drum sets?

a) $0

b) $4,000

c) $4,500

d) $10,000

1.3 Mort Schwartz is a dealer in residential building lots. He is also a partner in Pharaoh Land Company, a partnership that holds real estate of all kinds for investment. In 2016, Pharaoh sells one of its holdings, a residential building lot, for $500,000. Pharaoh acquired this particular lot in a cash purchase for $700,000 in 2014. It allocates $20,000 of the loss on this sale to Mort as a 10% partner. How should Mort treat this loss on his federal income tax return for 2016?

a) $20,000 long-term capital loss under section 702

b) $20,000 disallowed loss under section 1091

c) $20,000 ordinary loss under section 724(b)

d) $20,000 ordinary loss under section 751(d)(3)

1.4 Derek is a partner in the Dunleavey Partnership, a general partnership. His tax capital is a negative $12,000. His share of the partnership's only liability, a recourse bank debt, is $12,000. Derek receives a liquidating distribution from the partnership consisting of $9,000 in cash. The partnership has no section 751 assets. How much gain or loss does Derek recognize on this distribution?

a) $3,000 capital loss

b) $9,000 capital gain

c) $12,000 capital gain

d) $21,000 capital gain

1.5 Rasheeda's 2016 Form K-1 shows her distributive shares of the partnership's tax items as follows:

Line	Partner's Distributive Share Items	Total Amount
2	Net rental real estate income (loss)	$ (6,000)
8	Net short-term capital gain (loss)	500
13A	Cash charitable contributions	100
13H	Investment interest expense	250
18A	Tax-exempt interest income	50

What is the net adjustment to Rasheeda's outside basis as a result of these items?

a)   ($5,850)

b)   ($5,800)

c)   ($5,700)

d)   ($5,500)

1.6 A, B, C and D have been equal partners in Partnership ABCD since its formation. On March 22, 2016, A sells her entire interest in the partnership to B. On June 28, 2016, the partnership liquidates C's interest with a distribution of property, on which C recognizes no gain or loss. On September 19, 2016, B sells her entire interest to E, who is thereupon admitted as a partner. When, if ever, does the partnership terminate for tax purposes under section 708(b)(1)(B)?

a)   March 22

b)   June 28

c)   September 19

d) The partnership does not terminate as a result of these transactions.

1.7 Judah is a partner in a partnership; both have tax years ending September 30. The partnership has no liabilities and no section 751(b) assets. As of September 30, 2016, Judah's outside basis is $120,000. On November 1, 2016, the partnership makes a current distribution to Judah of $130,000 cash and property worth $40,000 having an adjusted basis to the partnership of $15,000. Assume that Judah's share of the partnership's income is $3,000 per month both before and after this distribution. What gain, if any, does Judah recognize on the distribution?

a) $0

b) $10,000

c) $25,000

d) $50,000

1.8 Reynaldo pays Squarebox Ltd, a limited partnership, $25,000 for an option to acquire 1,000 limited partner units for a cash payment of $100,000 at any time over the following 18 months. What is the proper treatment of this option on Squarebox's balance sheet?

a) The option is a $25,000 asset of the partnership.

b) The option is a $25,000 liability of the partnership.

c) Issuance of the option creates an immediate $25,000 deduction for the partnership, which reduces partner capital.

d) Issuance of the option is treated as an open transaction, which has no current effect on the partnership's balance sheet.

1.9 MOP-Up Investments LP is an investment partnership in which Matthew, Oliver and Peter have equal interests. In lieu of making a cash contribution to the partnership, Peter, an auto dealer, contributes a car from his lot with the understanding that the partnership will sell the car to raise cash for investment. Peter paid $40,000 for the car, and at the time of his contribution, it is worth $55,000. Rather than selling the car, MOP-Up borrows the needed cash. Four years later, it sells the car, which has become something of an instant classic, for $67,000. What is the amount and character of the profit allocated to Oliver (*not* Peter) from this sale?

a) $15,000 ordinary income and $4,000 capital gain

b) $4,000 ordinary income

c) $19,000 ordinary income

d) $4,000 capital gain

1.10 Thad and Rad have always wanted to run a boat company. They approach their high school classmate Roderick to ask him to dip into his trust fund to invest in their dream. Thus is born Bareboat Charters LLC, a limited liability company taxed as a partnership. Rod owns 80% of the membership interests and Thad and Rad own 10% each. On the advice of his father's accountant, Rod insists on receiving an allocation of 99% of the tax losses from the first three years of operation, to be offset by an allocation of 99% of profits, when realized, up to the amount of losses previously allocated. All profit thereafter is to be split among the partners in accordance with their percentage interests. Thad's talent with customers proves to be a perfect complement to Rod's relationship with his dad, and the company prospers. By the end of the sixth year of operation, Rod's chargeback is complete and Bareboat sees nothing but smooth sailing ahead. Assume that all special allocations in the operating agreement have economic effect. If the IRS challenges these allocations, what will be the result?

a) The special allocations will be respected, because they do not violate any substantiality test.

b) The special allocations will be reversed due to the transitory presumption, which with the benefit of hindsight presumes that the actual results achieved by Bareboat Charters were strongly likely to be achieved.

c) The special allocations will be reversed, because the value-equals-basis presumption applies only to a chargeback of depreciation from gain on the sale of the depreciated asset, which is not the nature of the chargeback in this case.

d) The special allocations will be reversed, because the entire chargeback occurs within a three-year period, which violates the five-year presumption.

END OF EXAMINATION

FINAL EXAM 2

(Suggested time: 60 minutes)

2.1 What conclusion(s) can you reliably infer from the statement that a partner's tax capital and her basis in her interest in the partnership (outside basis) are equal immediately following a partnership's formation? (Circle all that apply.)

a) That the partnership has no liabilities

b) That the partnership's aggregate basis in its assets (inside basis) is greater than the partners' aggregate basis in their partnership interests (outside basis)

c) That the partner has a book-tax disparity, and therefore is responsible for a forward § 704(c) layer in at least one partnership asset

d) That the partner's share of the partnership's liabilities, if any, is $0

2.2 Avery owns an asset valued at $75,000, with an adjusted tax basis of $10,000, subject to a $50,000 nonrecourse liability incurred three years ago. She contributes the asset, subject to the liability, to an LLC in exchange for a 25% interest. The LLC operating agreement adopts the traditional method under section 704(c) and provides that excess nonrecourse liabilities will be shared in accordance with the partners' respective percentage interests in the LLC. Following this transaction, what is Avery's share of this liability for purposes of determining her tax basis in the LLC interest?

a) $0

b) $2,500

c) $12,500

d) $42,500

2.3 Naomi is a partner in a partnership; both have tax years ending December 31. Each year in January, the partnership makes a cash distribution to each of its partners equal to their respective shares of the partnership's taxable income for the prior year. Throughout the year, however, each partner is entitled to request cash payments from the partnership not exceeding 70% of the partner's share of the partnership's estimated taxable income to date. By agreement with its partners, the partnership reduces a partner's year-end distribution by the sum of these cash payments for the year. As of February 1, 2016, Naomi's outside basis in the partnership is $50,000. She takes a total of $120,000 in interim payments throughout the year, and her share of the partnership's taxable income for the year is $160,000. How much gain, if any, does Naomi recognize on the interim payments?

a) $0

b) $70,000

c) $120,000

d) $160,000

2.4 Buddy Bear Ltd, a limited partnership that owns and operates a regional chain of toy stores for young children, has total equity capital of $3.5 million. Management wants to lure Mary Harrison, a marketing executive, to the company, and to this end makes Mary an offer that includes a 10% interest in profits, subject to a vesting condition: if Mary leaves prior to her third work anniversary, she will forfeit her interest in the partnership. During the first three years, she will be treated as a partner and will receive a guaranteed payment of $200,000 per year, payable monthly, which she will be entitled to retain, to the extent paid, if she leaves prior to vesting. Mary accepts, the company prospers, and on her third work anniversary, a reasonable valuation of her partnership interest is $800,000. What are the tax consequences to Mary under current law on the grant and vesting of her partnership interest?

a) Mary recognizes no taxable income or gain on either the grant or the vesting of her partnership interest.

b) Mary recognizes no taxable income or gain on the grant, but recognizes $800,000 of ordinary compensation income on vesting.

c) Mary recognizes $350,000 of ordinary compensation income on the grant, assuming she uses the liquidation-value method. She recognizes no further income or gain on vesting.

d) Mary recognizes no taxable income or gain on the grant, and can avoid recognizing taxable compensation income on vesting by making a section 83(b) election.

2.5 Individuals A, B and C are forming a partnership to speculate in commodities. A will contribute commodity futures contracts with substantial built-in gains. B and C will contribute cash. You are representing B, an individual in a high tax bracket. In the course of negotiations over the partnership agreement, you are asked whether the partnership agreement should contain a choice as to the section 704(c) method and, if so, what it should be. You reply:

a) The agreement should be silent as to the section 704(c) method.

b) The agreement should specify the traditional method.

c) The agreement should specify the traditional method with curative allocations.

d) The agreement should specify the remedial method.

2.6 A is a partner in Partnership ABC. The partnership leased a building from A at an annual rent of $40,000 (its fair rental value). Partnership ABC is on the cash method of accounting, A is an accrual-method taxpayer, and A and the partnership are calendar-year taxpayers. The partnership did not make payment in Year 1 but waited until April of Year 2 to pay the annual rent to A. What is the result?

a) $40,000 income to A in Year 2 and an equal deduction to the partnership in Year 1

b) $40,000 income to A in Year 1 and an equal deduction to the partnership in Year 1

c) $40,000 income to A in Year 2 and an equal deduction to the partnership in Year 2

d) $40,000 income to A in Year 1 and an equal deduction to the partnership in Year 2

2.7 Each of A, B and C contributes cash of $10,000 to form a general partnership, which borrows $70,000 on a recourse basis and uses the proceeds of this loan plus the partners' capital to purchase a small commercial building for $100,000. Throughout its existence, the partnership desires to allocate the annual depreciation of $5,000 on this building, as well as all other partnership income, gains and losses, among its three partners in proportion to their capital-account balances. You are hired to draft the partnership agreement. The state law under which this partnership is organized obligates the partners to restore deficit capital accounts to the extent necessary to pay creditors and to return the positive capital accounts of other partners. What are the least restrictive provisions that you will have to include in the agreement to ensure that the desired allocations are given effect for federal income tax purposes? (Circle all that apply.)

a) Capital-account maintenance in accordance with Treas. Reg. § 1.704–1(b)(2)(iv) and liquidation in accordance with the capital accounts

b) A limited obligation of all partners to restore deficit balances not in excess of the positive capital account balances of the other partners

c) An unconditional obligation of all partners to restore deficit balances in their capital accounts

d) A qualified income offset

e) A minimum gain chargeback

f) None of the above

2.8 Same as Question 2.7 above, except that the partners desire to allocate 98% of the depreciation on the building to A, and 1% each to B and C. They wish to allocate all other income, gains, losses and deductions equally throughout the partnership's life. What are the least restrictive provisions that you will have to include in the partnership agreement to ensure that the desired allocations are given effect for federal income tax purposes? (Circle all that apply.)

a) Capital-account maintenance in accordance with Treas. Reg. § 1.704–1(b)(2)(iv) and liquidation in accordance with the capital accounts

b) A limited obligation of all partners to restore deficit balances not in excess of the positive capital account balances of the other partners

c) An unconditional obligation of all partners to restore deficit balances in their capital accounts

d) A qualified income offset

e) A minimum gain chargeback

f) None of the above

2.9 Partnership ABC is an equal partnership formed December 31, 2015 with a $90,000 cash contribution by each partner. Its tax year is the calendar year. The partnership spends 2016 setting up its production facility and producing inventory for sale the next year, and realizes no income. On January 1, 2017, its balance sheet, expanded to show the fair market values of its assets, is as follows:

Assets				**Liabilities**		
	Tax	**Book**	**FMV**		**Tax**	**Book**
Cash	$ 10,000	$ 10,000	$ 10,000	[None]	$ 0	$ 0
Inventory	60,000	60,000	30,000			
Plant (accumulated depreciation $3,000)	150,000	150,000	180,000			
Land	50,000	50,000	110,000	**Capital**		
				A	90,000	90,000
				B	90,000	90,000
				C	90,000	90,000
Total Assets	$270,000	$270,000	$330,000	**Total Liabilities and Capital**	$270,000	$270,000

The partnership computes depreciation on its plant on a straight-line basis, so no recapture under section 1250 would occur on its sale; gain equal to the depreciation taken would, however, be classified as "section capital 1250 gain." On January 1, 2017, A, who is a corporate lawyer, sells her partnership interest to D for $120,000 in cash. What is the amount and character of A's gain or loss?

a) Ordinary loss, $9,000; section 1250 capital gain, $0; capital gain, $39,000

b) Ordinary loss, $10,000; section 1250 capital gain, $1,000; capital gain, $39,000

c) Ordinary loss, $10,000; section 1250 capital gain, $1,000; capital gain, $29,000

d) Ordinary loss, $10,000; section 1250 capital gain, $10,000; capital gain, $30,000

2.10 On September 1, 2016, Partner A contributes Property A to Partnership ABCD. At the time of this contribution, the value of Property A is $420,000 and its adjusted basis in Partner A's hands is $260,000. On December 31, 2019, the partnership distributes Property A to Partner D in liquidation of her partnership interest, which she obtained at the same time as Partner A for a cash contribution of $420,000. At the time of this distribution, Property A has increased in value to $520,000 and Partner D's outside basis is still $420,000. What are the tax consequences of this distribution to Partner A and Partner D?

a) Partner A, $0 gain or loss; Partner D, $0 gain or loss

b) Partner A, $160,000 taxable gain; Partner D, $0 gain or loss

c) Partner A, $160,000 taxable gain; Partner D, $100,000 taxable gain

d) Partner A, $260,000 taxable gain; Partner D, $0 gain or loss

END OF EXAMINATION

FINAL EXAM 3

(Suggested time: 60 minutes)

3.1 On January 30, 2016, A, B and C make the following contributions of cash and capital assets to a newly formed general partnership in exchange for equal interests therein:

	Contribution	Value	Tax Basis	Date Acquired
A	Cash	$100,000	N/A	N/A
B	500 shares of Facebook common stock	$100,000	$ 50,000	9/30/2015
C	3,000 shares of Herbalife common stock	$100,000	$150,000	4/30/2015

Shortly after formation, the partnership uses its cash to purchase mutual fund shares. When does the holding period for each of the partners' partnership interests begin? You may assume B and C held the contributed shares of common stock as capital assets.

a) A, 1/31/2016; B, 9/30/2015; C, 4/30/2015

b) A, 1/31/2016; B, 9/30/2015; C, 1/31/2016

c) A, 1/31/2016; B, 1/31/2016; C, 4/30/2015

d) A, 1/31/2016; B, 1/31/2016; C, 1/31/2016

3.2 A revaluation of all of a partnership's property, resulting in increases or decreases in the book capital account balances of the partners, is:

a) Required whenever a new partner is admitted to the partnership or a partner's interest is liquidated

b) Required whenever a reverse section 704(c) allocation must be made

c) Required in certain circumstances in order to eliminate book-tax disparities in the partnership's assets

d) Not generally required under existing law, but failure to make a revaluation may have collateral federal income tax consequences

3.3 Partnership ABC, an equal general partnership, is a dealer in real estate which subdivides and sells building lots in a residential suburb. Its balance sheet and the fair market values of its assets are as follows:

Assets				Liabilities		
	Tax	Book	FMV		Tax	Book
Cash	$ 12,000	$ 12,000	$ 12,000	Recourse	$150,000	$150,000
Lot 1	50,000	50,000	50,000			
Lot 2	50,000	50,000	50,000	**Capital**		
Lot 3	73,000	73,000	88,000	A	40,000	40,000
Lot 4	85,000	85,000	100,000	B	40,000	40,000
				C	40,000	40,000
Total Assets	$270,000	$270,000	$300,000	**Total Liabilities and Capital**	$270,000	$270,000

On July 20, 2016, the partnership distributes Lot 1, which it purchased for cash on May 27, 2011, to C in liquidation of her partnership interest. The partnership files a section 754 election with its tax return for 2016. The building lots in the subdivision continue to appreciate in value, and on August 25, 2019, C, who holds Lot 1 as a capital asset, sells it for $65,000 to a family who wants to build a home there. What are the tax consequences of this sale to C?

a) $15,000 ordinary income

b) $25,000 ordinary income

c) $25,000 ordinary loss

d) $10,000 ordinary income and $15,000 capital gain

3.4 Partnership XYZ is an investment partnership that holds no section 751 assets and has no liabilities. The basis of Partner X's interest in Partnership XYZ is $100,000 and its fair market value is $300,000. Partner X receives a liquidating distribution of $20,000 cash and three capital assets: Property A, inside basis of $60,000 and fair market value of $70,000; Property B, inside basis of $40,000 and fair market value of $130,000; and Property C, inside basis of $100,000 and fair market value of $80,000. Following this distribution, what is Partner X's basis in Property A?

a) $20,000

b) $26,667

c) $30,000

d) $33,333

3.5 In exchange for services rendered and the payment of $1,000, Nell McHenry receives an interest in a partnership in the business of manufacturing and selling mobile homes. Nell will forfeit her interest if she ceases to be employed by the partnership at any time during the next three years. On your advice, Nell makes a timely election under section 83(b). Her best guess is that the interest is worth $5,000, and she reports the excess of this amount over her payment as ordinary income. Over the next two years, the partnership allocates profits to Nell in the aggregate amount of $20,000. Nell is paid a cash "salary" and receives no distributions with respect to her partnership interest. The next year, she gets a fantastic job offer from a competing manufacturer, quits her job and forfeits her interest in the partnership. Under current law (*i.e.*, without taking into account the effect of any proposed regulations), what is the loss that Nell can claim with respect to her forfeiture?

a) $1,000

b) $4,000

c) $24,000

d) $25,000

3.6 Individuals A, B and C each contribute cash of $10,000 to form Partnership ABC, a limited partnership of which C is the sole general partner. They agree to share profits and losses as follows:

Losses: 40% to each of A and B and 20% to C

Profits: 40% to each of A and B and 20% to C to the extent of previous losses; thereafter, 30% to each of A and B and 40% to C

The partnership agreement provides for the proper maintenance of capital accounts and for liquidating distributions to be made in accordance with the capital accounts, and all partners agree to an unlimited deficit-restoration obligation. Immediately following its formation and before any profits or losses are incurred, Partnership ABC borrows $60,000 on a recourse basis to finance the acquisition of a small industrial building. What is the initial outside basis of each of the partners?

a) A, $10,000; B, $10,000; C, $70,000

b) A, $26,000; B, $26,000; C, $8,000

c) A, $34,000; B, $34,000; C, $22,000

d) A, $36,000; B, $36,000; C, $18,000

3.7 Partnership PQR has a section 754 election in effect. Each partner has a basis of $30,000 for her one-third interest. The partnership has cash of $12,000 and two capital assets—Property X with a basis of $27,000 and a value of $27,000 and Property Y with a basis of $51,000 and a value of $42,000. Partner P receives Property X in liquidation of her interest. What is the basis adjustment, if any, to Property Y as a result of this distribution?

a) $0

b) Positive $3,000 adjustment

c) Negative $3,000 adjustment

d) Negative $9,000 adjustment

3.8 In 1996, Karen purchased land for $350,000 that is now worth $600,000. The land is subject to a recourse mortgage of $400,000, incurred in 2006. Karen forms a limited partnership with George. George, the general partner, contributes $600,000 in cash; Karen, the limited partner, contributes the land encumbered by the mortgage, which the mortgage lender permits the partnership to assume, releasing Karen. The partners agree to share all partnership profit and loss in accordance with their respective capital-account balances. Upon formation, what is Karen's tax basis in her partnership interest?

a) ($50,000)

b) $0

c) $50,000

d) $137,500

3.9 Aristide, Balthazar and Caspar have formed a production company, Ars Historia Ltd, a limited partnership, to make historical documentaries. They are equal partners. Aristide, the general partner, contributed production equipment with a value of $200,000 and an adjusted tax basis of $150,000. Balthazar and Caspar, the limited partners, contributed period costumes and cash, respectively, each worth $200,000. Balthazar's adjusted basis in the costumes at the time of contribution was $250,000. Reflecting the application of section 704(c)(1)(C), the opening balance sheet of the partnership looks like this:

Assets			Liabilities		
	Tax	Book		Tax	Book
Cash	$200,000	$200,000	[None]	$ 0	$ 0
Equipment	150,000	200,000			
Wardrobe	200,000	200,000	Capital		
			Aristide	150,000	200,000
			Balthazar	200,000	200,000
			Caspar	200,000	200,000
Total Assets	$550,000	$600,000	Total Liabilities and Capital	$550,000	$600,000

Shortly after formation, the production company changes its focus and needs to dispose of its equipment so that it can purchase new gear. The highest offer it can get on short notice is $185,000. If it sells all of its equipment for this price and elects to use the traditional method for purposes of section 704(c), how much tax gain or loss will it allocate to Caspar?

a) $0

b)   ($5,000)

c) $35,000

d) $50,000

3.10 Same facts as Question 3.9, except that the partnership sells its entire wardrobe for $215,000. Assuming that it still uses the traditional method, how much tax gain or loss will it allocate to Caspar?

a) $0

b) $5,000

c)   ($45,000)

d)   ($50,000)

END OF EXAMINATION

INTERMEDIATE

FINAL EXAM 4

(Suggested time: 75 minutes)

4.1 Corp X, a Delaware business corporation, owns all of the membership interest in Upper LLC, a Delaware limited liability company, and 60% of the membership interest in Lower LLC, also a Delaware limited liability company. The remaining 40% of the membership interest in Lower is owned by Upper. Lower sells an investment asset to Corp X for $400. The adjusted basis of this asset is $600. Assuming that all entities are taxed in accordance with the default rules, which of the following statements is true?

a) Lower LLC recognizes a loss of $200.

b) Lower LLC realizes a loss of $200, but no deduction is allowed for this loss. Upon any resale of the asset, Corp X may be entitled to relief under § 267(d).

c) Lower LLC realizes a loss of $200, but this loss is deferred. Corp X takes a basis of $600 in the asset for purposes of calculating its gain or loss on any subsequent resale.

d) Lower LLC realizes no loss on this sale.

4.2 Individuals A, B and C formed Partnership ABC by making equal contributions of cash. Each was an equal one-third partner. C later sold her partnership interest to D for $200,000 in an arms-length transaction. The partnership has not made a section 754 election. Its balance sheet (expanded to show the fair market values of assets) is as follows:

Assets				Liabilities		
	Tax	**Book**	**FMV**		**Tax**	**Book**
Cash	$180,000	$180,000	$180,000	Bank Debt	$300,000	$300,000
Receivables	0	0	90,000			
Land	300,000	300,000	630,000	**Capital**		
				A	60,000	60,000
				B	60,000	60,000
				D	60,000	60,000
				Total Liabilities		
Total Assets	$480,000	$480,000	$900,000	**and Capital**	$480,000	$480,000

The partnership liquidates D's interest by distributing to her $30,000 of receivables and $170,000 in cash. Assume that D's outside basis has not changed since the date of purchase. What are the tax consequences of this distribution to D?

a) No income, gain or loss; $30,000 basis in distributed receivables

b) Capital loss of $30,000; $0 basis in distributed receivables

c) Capital loss of $60,000; $30,000 basis in distributed receivables

d) Capital gain of $110,000; $0 basis in distributed receivables

4.3 Wise Crackers Ltd. is a Delaware limited liability company taxed as a partnership and engaged in the bakery business. Ted, a wealthy investor who has never rendered services to the company (or anyone else), procures an option to acquire a 20% interest in the company. The option premium is $10,000, which Ted pays by transferring to the company marketable stock with a value of $10,000 and a tax basis of $2,000. The option exercise price is $100,000, which Ted pays two years later by transferring to the company stock with a value of $100,000 and a tax basis of $22,000. How much gain does Ted recognize on these transactions?

a) $0

b) $8,000

c) $78,000

d) $86,000

4.4 Albany, Brooklyn and Charlotte are the members of Allstate Adventures LLC, a limited liability company that is treated as a partnership for federal income tax purposes. Allstate is contemplating taking a loan of $90,000 from a local Montana bank to finance acquisition of the newest generation of river rafts for use in its operation on the Middle Fork of the Flathead River. After careful review, Albany concludes that the loan agreement contains no provision limiting her personal exposure and demands that Brooklyn and Charlotte indemnify her from liability on the loan. Brooklyn, in turn, demands an indemnity from Charlotte with respect to any amount that she is required to pay to Albany (although not with respect to any amount she is required to pay to the bank). If the requested indemnities are given, what are the partners' respective shares of the bank loan under section 752?

a) Albany, $0; Brooklyn, $0; Charlotte, $0

b) Albany, $0; Brooklyn, $30,000; Charlotte, $60,000

c) Albany, $0; Brooklyn, $45,000; Charlotte, $45,000

d) Albany, $30,000; Brooklyn, $30,000; Charlotte, $30,000

4.5 A, B and C contribute $10,000 each to form a limited partnership, in which A is the general partner and B and C are limited partners. The partnership borrows $70,000 on a nonrecourse basis and uses the proceeds of this loan plus the partners' capital to purchase a small commercial building for $100,000. The partnership desires to allocate the depreciation on this building, as well as all other partnership income, gains, losses and deductions, to the partners in proportion to their capital-account balances. You are hired to draft the partnership agreement. The state law under which this partnership is organized obligates the general partner to restore a deficit capital account only to the extent necessary to pay creditors. Assuming satisfaction of the significant item consistency test, what are the least restrictive provisions that you will have to include in the agreement to ensure that the desired allocations are given effect for federal income tax purposes? (Circle all that apply.)

a) Capital-account maintenance in accordance with Treas. Reg. § 1.704–1(b)(2)(iv) and liquidation in accordance with the capital accounts

b) A limited obligation of the general partner to restore any deficit balance not in excess of the positive capital account balances of the limited partners

c) An unconditional obligation of all partners to restore deficit balances in their capital accounts

d) A qualified income offset

e) A minimum gain chargeback

f) None of the above

4.6 Same as Question 4.5 above, except that the partners desire to allocate 98% of the depreciation on the building to A, the general partner, and 1% each to B and C, the limited partners. They wish to allocate all other income, gains, losses and deductions equally throughout the partnership's life. Assuming satisfaction of the significant item consistency test, what are the least restrictive provisions that you will have to include in the agreement to ensure that the desired allocations are given effect for federal income tax purposes? (Circle all that apply.)

a) Capital-account maintenance in accordance with Treas. Reg. § 1.704–1(b)(2)(iv) and liquidation in accordance with the capital accounts

b) A limited obligation of the general partner to restore any deficit balance not in excess of the positive capital account balances of the limited partners

c) An unconditional obligation of all partners to restore deficit balances in their capital accounts

d) A qualified income offset

e) A minimum gain chargeback

f) None of the above

4.7 Bill and Wayne form a real estate partnership. Bill contributes Blackacre, which is worth $600,000 and in which he has a tax basis of $100,000, for an 80% interest in the partnership. Wayne contributes Whiteacre, which is worth $150,000 and in which he has a tax basis of

$125,000, for a 20% interest. Five years later, Blackacre is worth $750,000 and Whiteacre is worth $300,000 and there has been no change to either inside or outside basis. The partnership distributes Whiteacre to Bill and the interests of Bill and Wayne in the partnership are adjusted to 72% and 28%, respectively. The partnership has no liabilities. How much gain, if any, do Bill and Wayne recognize on this distribution?

a) Bill, $0; Wayne, $0

b) Bill, $650,000; Wayne, $175,000

c) Bill, $200,000; Wayne, $25,000

d) Bill, $500,000; Wayne, $25,000

4.8 Neil Anderson, an expert in cattle breeding, receives a 10% interest in the profits of the Dairy-Aire Partnership in exchange for services he has rendered and will render to the dairy-farming business of the partnership. Neil will forfeit his interest if he quits his job at any time during the next three years. Neil reports no income in the year of receipt and files no section 83(b) election. The partnership claims no deduction. Over the next three years, the partnership allocates profits to Neil in the aggregate amount of $70,000 and distributes $40,000 to him in cash. On the date of vesting, the value of Neil's interest could reasonably be estimated to be $180,000, including his $30,000 capital account on that date. Under current law (*i.e.*, without taking into account the effect of any proposed regulations), how much compensation income is Neil required to report as a result of the vesting of his profits interest?

a) $0

b) $30,000

c) $150,000

d) $180,000

4.9 Big Law LLP, a Delaware limited liability partnership, is a service partnership for which capital is not a material income-producing factor. The partnership and all of its partners use the cash method on the calendar year. The partnership does not revalue its book assets when partners retire, but does immediately distribute the full amount of the retiring partner's tax capital account. Following a decades-old practice, it distributes in ten equal, annual, cash payments the value of the retiring partner's share of the partnership's unrealized accounts receivable on the retirement date. These receivables are not included in the partner's tax capital accounts and the partnership has an adjusted basis of zero in them. Under current law, these annual payments are:

a) A distributive share of partnership income, taxable in the year of receipt

b) Guaranteed payments, taxable in the year of receipt

c) Guaranteed payments, taxable in the year of retirement

d) Payments in liquidation of the retiring partner's interest in the partnership, taxable as ordinary income in the year of retirement

4.10 Topco LLC owns 85% of the total interest in capital and profits of Subco LLC. The remaining 15% of Subco is owned by Ernest Lee, its chief executive. In exchange for a cash contribution to Topco of $4 million, AcquisitionCo LLC acquires a 60% interest in the total capital and profits of Topco. Mr. Lee owns 10% of AcquisitionCo; the remainder is owned by unrelated parties. Topco, Subco and AcquisitionCo have and will continue to have their default classifications for tax purposes. Which of the following statements reflects the most accurate analysis of this transaction under section 708(b)(1)(B)?

a) Topco terminates under section 708(b)(1)(B), as does Subco, because AcquisitionCo acquires indirectly 50% or more of the total interest in capital and profits of Topco.

b) Topco terminates under section 708(b)(1)(B), as does Subco, because Topco owns 50% or more of the total interest in capital and profits of Subco, which is deemed to be sold or exchanged on the termination of Topco.

c) Topco does not terminate, nor does Subco, because the contribution does not constitute a sale or exchange for purposes of section 708(b)(1)(B).

d) Topco terminates under section 708(b)(1)(B), but Subco does not, because the ultimate beneficial ownership of 50% or more of the total interest in capital and profits of Subco does not change, taking into account both the direct and indirect ownership of Mr. Lee.

END OF EXAMINATION

FINAL EXAM 5

(Suggested time: 75 minutes)

5.1 Partnership AB is an equal, accrual-method partnership with a calendar tax year. In December 2016, it agrees to pay Gimbel Bros. $10,000 for accounting services performed during the past year. It pays this amount in early January 2017. What is the effect, if any, of this agreement on the partnership's basis in its assets (inside basis) and the partners' aggregate basis in their partnership interests (outside basis) as of year-end 2016?

a) Inside basis is unaffected; outside basis is unaffected because the obligation to Gimbel Bros. is recognized as a $10,000 liability for tax purposes and offset by a $10,000 reduction in partners' tax capital arising from the current deduction of this amount.

b) Inside basis increases by $10,000; outside basis increases by $10,000 because the obligation to Gimbel Bros. is recognized as a $10,000 liability for tax purposes and this amount is not currently deductible by the partnership.

c) Inside basis is unaffected; outside basis is unaffected because the obligation to Gimbel Bros. is not currently recognized as a liability for tax purposes and is not currently deductible by the partnership.

d) Inside basis is unaffected; outside basis increases by $10,000 because the obligation to Gimbel Bros. is recognized as a $10,000 liability for tax purposes and this amount is not currently deductible by the partnership.

5.2 Jon contributes property with a basis in his hands of $75,000 to the JPS Limited Partnership in exchange for a one-third interest in the partnership. Jon is the sole general partner. The contributed property is worth $200,000 and it is subject to nonrecourse debt of $180,000, incurred five years ago. Jon's lender has the right to approve his transfer of the property and, as a condition of the transfer to the partnership, the lender requires that Paula, one of the limited partners, guarantee the repayment of $30,000 of the debt, which she does. The partnership has no other liabilities. The partnership agreement provides that the partnership uses the traditional method under § 704(c) and that excess nonrecourse debt is allocated in equal thirds to the three partners of JPS. How much gain does Jon recognize on this property contribution?

a) $0

b) $5,000

c) $55,000

d) $75,000

5.3 A and B want C to manage investment properties for them. Together, they form Partnership ABC, a general partnership. A contributes Property X, with a basis and value of $30,000, subject to a $12,000 nonrecourse mortgage, and B contributes Property Y, with a basis and value of $60,000, subject to a recourse debt of $42,000. Partnership ABC assumes this recourse debt and the lender releases B. In exchange for her agreement to perform services for Partnership ABC, C receives a one-third capital interest in Partnership ABC, the value of which is currently deductible by the partnership. The partnership agreement provides that all items of partnership income, gain, loss and deduction, and all excess nonrecourse liabilities, will be allocated equally among the partners. It adopts the traditional method under section 704(c). Assuming no disguised sale, what is the basis of each partner in her interest in Partnership ABC immediately following these formation transactions?

a)   A, $39,000; B, $39,000; C, $12,000

b)   A, $30,000; B, $30,000; C, $30,000

c)   A, $45,000; B, $45,000; C, $0

d)   A, $36,000; B, $36,000; C, $18,000

5.4 Same as Question 5.3, except that C must forfeit her partnership interest if she ceases to perform services for the partnership within three years. C chooses not to make an election under section 83(b). What is the basis of each partner in her partnership interest immediately following the formation transactions?

a)   A, $30,000; B, $60,000; C, $0

b)   A, $30,000; B, $30,000; C, $30,000

c)   A, $45,000; B, $45,000; C, $0

d)   A, $45,000; B, $45,000; C is not a partner

5.5 Tasty Bakery is an accrual-method, calendar-year partnership engaged in the business of manufacturing and selling sweet confections. Its assets are as follows:

	Adjusted Basis	**Fair Market Value**
Cash	$ 40,000	$ 40,000
Accounts receivable	90,000	75,000
Inventory	40,000	50,000
Equipment (recomputed basis $375,000)	275,000	285,000
Depreciable building	300,000	400,000
Land	120,000	180,000
TOTAL	$865,000	$1,030,000

The partnership has depreciated its building on a straight-line basis, so no recapture under section 1250 would occur on its sale; the resulting $10,000 gain would, however, be classified as "section 1250 capital gain" under section 1(h)(6). Tasty Bakery is considering a distribution of cash and possibly other assets to one of its partners in liquidation of her interest in the partnership. What is the *total fair market value* of Tasty Bakery's assets that must be taken into account under section 751(b)(1)(A)?

a) $10,000

b) $50,000

c) $60,000

d) $160,000

5.6 Law Firm is a general partnership that has elected an October 31 fiscal year for tax purposes. It has 75 individual partners, all of whom are calendar-year taxpayers and all of whom have equal financial interests in the partnership. Law Firm has recently admitted as a 20% partner a professional corporation that has a September 30 tax year. Law Firm desires to change its tax year to conform to that of its new principal partner, but does not believe that it can establish a business purpose for doing so. Absent such a showing, and assuming that it is willing to make any required payments under section 7519, Law Firm can change its tax year to years ending:

a) September 30, November 30 or December 31

b) November 30 or December 31

c) September 30

d) Law Firm cannot change its fiscal year without showing a business purpose.

5.7 A is the general partner of Partnership ABCD and B, C and D are limited partners. One of the assets of the partnership is a building with a fair market value of $150,000 and an adjusted basis of $110,000, encumbered by a nonrecourse liability of $90,000, which is the partnership's only liability. The partnership has no section 751 assets. Partner C, who has a 25% interest, receives a liquidating distribution consisting of $20,000 in cash and this building, subject to the foregoing liability. Immediately before this distribution (after taking into account C's share of the partnership's income or loss for the year of the distribution), C's basis in her partnership interest is $15,000. What is the gain or loss, if any, C realizes on this distribution and what is her basis in the distributed property?

a) Gain $0; tax basis $62,500

b) Gain $0; tax basis $85,000

c) Gain $5,000; tax basis $0

d) Gain $27,500; tax basis $0

5.8 Can o' Corn LLC produces and sells baseball gloves and other sports equipment. A seasonal business, it earns most of its profits during the summer months and has a tax year ending September 30. For its year ended September 30, 2016, the company has taxable income of $96,000. Bud Harrelson, an individual with a tax year ending on December 31, owns a 20% interest in Can o' Corn. On December 31, 2016, Bud sells one-half of his interest to a third party. Assume that the company will have the same taxable income for its year ending September 30, 2017 that it had in the previous year, and that it will earn $12,000 of such income in the three-month period ending December 31, 2016. The company is treated as a partnership for tax purposes and its operating agreement does not specify an allocation method under section 706(d). Ignoring any gain or loss from the sale of his interest, what amount of the company's taxable income does Bud include in his return for his taxable year ending December 31, 2016?

a) $2,400

b) $19,200

c) $20,400

d) $21,600

5.9 Individuals A, B and C are real estate investors. Following a slowdown in the housing market, they contact D, a homebuilder who is holding numerous single-family homes for sale to customers in the ordinary course of her business. In 2016, the four individuals form a partnership, in which each partner holds an equal 25% interest. Each of A, B and C contributes cash to the partnership and D contributes the unsold homes. During the year, the partnership uses its cash to purchase an adjacent shopping center to hold for investment. It plans to convert the homes to rental properties, which it will hold for the foreseeable future. Three of the homes, however, are located outside the area of the partnership's interest. In the aggregate, these homes have a book value of $900,000 and a tax basis of $720,000, unchanged in both cases from the corresponding values at the time that D contributed these properties to the partnership. What are the book and tax consequences to B if the partnership sells the three houses in 2016 for $1 million in the aggregate?

a) $25,000 book gain; $25,000 ordinary income

b) $25,000 book gain; $25,000 capital gain

c) $25,000 book gain; $205,000 ordinary income

d) $25,000 book gain; $45,000 ordinary income; $25,000 capital gain

5.10 The balance sheet of the XYZ Partnership (expanded to show asset values) is as follows:

Assets				Liabilities		
	Tax	**Book**	**FMV**		**Tax**	**Book**
Cash	$ 15,000	$ 15,000	$ 15,000	[None]	$ 0	$ 0
Inventory	60,000	60,000	20,000			
Capital Asset 1	0	0	60,000	**Capital**		
Capital Asset 2	210,000	210,000	170,000	X	195,000	195,000
Capital Asset 3	170,000	170,000	150,000	Y	195,000	195,000
Capital Asset 4	130,000	130,000	185,000	Z	195,000	195,000
Total Assets	$585,000	$585,000	$600,000	**Total Liabilities and Capital**	$585,000	$585,000

The partnership distributes its $15,000 in cash and Capital Asset 4 to Y in liquidation of her interest. If the partnership has made an election under section 754, what is its basis in Capital Asset 2 following this transaction?

a) $176,667

b) $190,000

c) $206,667

d) $210,000

END OF EXAMINATION

FINAL EXAM 6

(Suggested time: 75 minutes)

6.1 Luke was an early investor in CGI technology and now owns stock in Lightsource, Inc. that is worth ten times what he paid for it. Looking to diversify, Luke acquires an option to acquire a 10% interest in Skywalker LP, a film company, in exchange for $20 million in Lightsource shares. Luke acquires this option, which he may exercise at any time over the next three years, for a payment of $500,000, which he makes in Lightsource shares. Assuming no further change in the value of the Lightsource shares, how much gain, if any, will Luke recognize on the acquisition and exercise of this option?

    a) $0

    b) $450,000

    c) $18,000,000

    d) $18,450,000

6.2 After Luke acquires the option described in Question 6.1, but before he exercises it, how does Skywalker Partnership reflect the option on its balance sheet?

    a)   As an asset in the amount of $500,000

    b)   As a liability in the amount of $50,000

    c)   As a liability in the amount of $500,000

    d)   The option does not appear on Skywalker's balance sheet

6.3 George Stevens owns a small suburban office building which he acquired and remodeled extensively. His adjusted basis in the building is now $525,000, although it is worth only $300,000. Looking to raise cash to support his many habits, he sells the building, which is not encumbered by any debt, to his family partnership for $300,000 in cash. The partnership consists of George, with a 10% interest, and George's three adult children, each with a 30% interest, and it has elected the traditional method for purposes of section 704(c). If the partnership thereafter sells the building for $400,000, what tax gain or loss will George and each of the children recognize? (Assume no change in the building's adjusted tax basis during the period of the partnership's ownership.)

    a)   George, $0; children, $0

    b)   George, $10,000; children, $30,000 each

    c)   George, ($125,000); children, $0

    d)   George, ($215,000); children, $30,000 each

6.4 Thinkers Corner LP, a limited partnership, sells old, great books from a marble-clad storefront and has a small analytics business on the side, which it accounts for using the cash method. On March 31, 2016, Aristotle sells his entire interest as a general partner in Thinkers Corner for $120,000 in cash plus assumption of Aristotle's share of the partnership's liabilities. The sale is to Bentham, a limited partner in Thinkers Corner whose day job is subdividing and selling land. Pursuant to section 706(c)(2)(A), the partnership closes its books as to Aristotle's interest, resulting in the following balance sheet, expanded to show the fair market value of the partnership's assets:

Assets				Liabilities		
	Tax	**Book**	**FMV**		**Tax**	**Book**
Cash	$ 7,000	$ 7,000	$ 7,000	Recourse	$150,000	$150,000
Receivables	0	0	27,000			
Inventory	45,000	45,000	39,000			
Building (accumulated depreciation $33,000)	160,000	160,000	241,000			
Undeveloped land	190,000	190,000	160,000	**Capital**		
				Aristotle	84,000	84,000
				Bentham	84,000	84,000
				Cicero	84,000	84,000
Total Assets	$402,000	$402,000	$474,000	**Total Liabilities and Capital**	$402,000	$402,000

The partnership has depreciated its building and improvements on a straight-line basis, so no recapture under section 1250 would occur on its sale; gain equal to the depreciation taken would, however, be classified as "section 1250 capital gain." What is the amount and character of Aristotle's gain or loss on this sale?

a) Ordinary loss, $3,000; section 1250 capital gain, $0; capital gain $39,000

b) Ordinary loss, $3,000; section 1250 capital gain, $11,000; capital gain, $28,000

c) Ordinary income, $7,000; section 1250 capital gain, $0; capital gain, $29,000

d) Ordinary income, $7,000; section 1250 capital gain, $11,000; capital gain, $18,000

6.5 Fischer owns a piece of unimproved property (value $500,000, basis $150,000) that is ripe for development. He hires a lawyer to set up a limited partnership and to draft a private placement memorandum for offering limited partnership units to prospective investors. For these services, he pays the lawyer $50,000. The offering is successful and the partnership is organized with total capital of $4.5 million, $500,000 property received from Fischer as sole general partner and $4 million cash received from the investors as limited partners. Under the terms of the partnership agreement, profits and losses are allocated proportionately to the partners' capital accounts until all partners have received cash distributions equal to the amount of their initial investments plus a preferred return of 8%. Thereafter, profits and losses are allocated 50% to Fischer and 50% to the limited partners. Shortly after collecting the first capital call from the limited partners, the partnership reimburses Fischer for his $50,000 of expenses. All these transaction occur within the same tax year. What income or gain does Fischer recognize?

a) $0 compensation income; $0 gain on reimbursement

b) $500,000 compensation income; $0 gain on reimbursement

c) $0 compensation income; $35,000 gain on reimbursement

d) $0 compensation income; $50,000 gain on reimbursement

6.6 The balance sheet of Partnership ABCD (expanded to show asset values) is as follows:

Assets				Liabilities		
	Tax	Book	FMV		Tax	Book
Cash	$ 80,000	$ 80,000	$ 80,000	[None]	$ 0	$ 0
Receivables	0	0	60,000			
Inventory	40,000	40,000	60,000	Capital		
Cap. Asset 1	210,000	210,000	250,000	A	125,000	125,000
Cap. Asset 2	170,000	170,000	150,000	B	125,000	125,000
				C	125,000	125,000
				D	125,000	125,000
Total Assets	$500,000	$500,000	$600,000	Total Liabilities and Capital	$500,000	$500,000

Partnership ABCD is entitled to use the cash method, despite the fact that it holds an inventory of finished goods, on account of its relatively small size. C receives a distribution of $80,000 cash and inventory valued at $20,000 with a basis to the partnership of $13,333. This distribution reduces C's remaining interest in the partnership to 10%. Under current law (*i.e.*, not taking into account the effect of any proposed Treasury regulation) what are the tax consequences of this distribution to C?

a) C recognizes no income, gain or loss and takes a basis of $13,333 in the distributed inventory.

b) C recognizes no income, gain or loss and takes a basis of $20,000 in the distributed inventory.

c) C recognizes ordinary income of $10,000 and takes a basis of $23,333 in the distributed inventory.

d) C recognizes ordinary income of $8,333 and takes a basis of $21,667 in the distributed inventory.

6.7 The Main Street Investment Club is a general partnership with ten equal partners. For calendar year 2016, each of its partners is entitled to a 10% distributive share of interest income and qualified dividends. The Club proposes to allocate to Kim, a partner who pays tax at 25% on ordinary income and 15% on capital gains, $3,000 of interest income that would otherwise go to Li, a partner who pays tax at the maximum rate of 39.6% on ordinary income and 20% on capital gains. The Club proposes further to allocate to Li $3,000 of qualified dividends that would otherwise go to Kim. If the Club asks your advice on these special allocations, what will you say?

a) The special allocations are shifting allocations and therefore their economic effect is not substantial.

b) The special allocations violate the overall-tax-effect test, and therefore their economic effect is not substantial.

c) The special allocations are shifting allocations, but do not violate the overall-tax-effect test, and therefore their economic effect is substantial.

d) The special allocations are not shifting allocations and do not violate the overall-tax-effect test, and therefore their economic effect is substantial.

6.8 A and B want C to manage investment properties for them. Together, they form Partnership ABC LP, a limited partnership in which A and B are limited partners and C is the general partner. A contributes Property X, with a value of $50,000 and adjusted basis of $18,000, subject to a $32,000 nonrecourse mortgage. B contributes Property Y, with a basis and value of $60,000, subject to a recourse debt of $42,000. Partnership ABC LP assumes this recourse debt and the lender releases B. In exchange for her agreement to perform services for Partnership ABC LP, C receives a one-third interest in Partnership ABC LP, the value of which is currently deductible by the partnership. The partnership agreement meets the standards of the alternate test for economic effect and provides that all items of partnership income, gain, loss and deduction, and all excess nonrecourse liabilities, will be allocated equally among the partners. It adopts the traditional method under section 704(c). Assuming no disguised sale, what is the basis of each partner in her interest in Partnership ABC immediately following these formation transactions?

a) A, $0; B, $18,000; C, $60,000

b) A, $4,000; B, $36,000; C, $36,000

c) A, $6,000; B, $24,000; C, $48,000

d) A, $24,000; B, $42,000; C, $12,000

6.9 Partnership ABC holds two parcels of land for investment. It has the following balance sheet (expanded to show the values of its investment assets):

Assets			Liabilities		
	Tax	Book	FMV		Tax	Book
Parcel 1	$110,000	$110,000	$ 200,000	[None]	$ 0	$ 0
Parcel 2	820,000	820,000	1,000,000			
				Capital		
				A	310,000	310,000
				B	310,000	310,000
				D	310,000	310,000
Total Assets	$930,000	$930,000	$1,200,000	**Total Liabilities and Capital**	$930,000	$930,000

Partners A, B and C formed the partnership with cash contributions of $310,000 each. The partnership used this cash to acquire the two parcels, which it has held ever since, realizing no income, gain or loss. After the parcels had appreciated to the values shown in the balance sheet, C sold her interest to D for $400,000. The partnership made a section 754 election in connection with this sale. Time has passed, and the partnership now proposes to distribute Parcel 1 to D in redemption of one-half of her interest. Following this distribution, what will be D's basis in Parcel 1?

a) $110,000

b) $140,000

c) $155,000

d) $200,000

6.10 Partnership ABCDE is owned in the following proportions by its partners: A, 40%; B, 25%; C, 25%; D, 5% and E, 5%. Pursuant to state law, it divides into Partnership AB, Partnership BCD and Partnership CDE, each owned by the partners who appear in their respective names. Which, if any, of the resulting partnerships is treated as a continuation of Partnership ABCDE for tax purposes?

a) Partnership AB only

b) Partnership AB and Partnership BCD

c) Partnership AB, Partnership BCD and Partnership CDE

d) None of them

END OF EXAMINATION

ADVANCED

FINAL EXAM 7

(Suggested time: 90 minutes)

7.1 Arrington and Remington, who are brothers, each holds half of the membership interests in Wellington Street Properties LLC, a limited liability company treated as a partnership for tax purposes. Several years ago, Wellington purchased an apartment building for $3.5 million. It has claimed $1 million depreciation on the building, which it has allocated entirely to Arrington, who is in a higher tax bracket than Remington. The operating agreement provides that gain, if any, on the sale of the apartment building will be allocated first to Arrington to the extent of prior depreciation and then between the two brothers in accordance with their percentage interests. Wellington sells the building for its fair market value of $4.5 million, recognizing $1 million of section 1250 capital gain and $1 million of capital gain. The partnership allocates all of the capital gain to Arrington and splits the section 1250 capital gain equally between Arrington and Remington. If the IRS challenges this allocation, what will be the result?

a) The section 1250 gain will be reallocated to Arrington because, under the rule which is also applicable to section 1245 recapture income, it must be allocated to the partner to whom the corresponding depreciation was allocated.

b) The partnership's allocation of section 1250 gain will stand, because it is protected by the value-equals-basis presumption of substantiality.

c) The section 1250 gain will be reallocated at least in part to Arrington, because the partnership's allocation violates the shifting test for substantiality.

d) The partnership's allocation of section 1250 gain will stand, because it does not violate any substantiality test.

7.2 Stevie Rider owns cycling equipment valued at $90,000 with an adjusted tax basis of $24,000. She borrows $60,000 on a nonrecourse basis and 30 days later contributes the equipment, subject to the liability, to All Sports LLC, a limited liability company taxed as a partnership, in exchange for a 25% interest. The All Sports operating agreement adopts the traditional 704(c) method and allocates excess nonrecourse liabilities in accordance with the partners' percentage interests. What income or gain, if any, does Stevie recognize on this transaction?

a) $0

b) $13,200

c) $21,000

d) $33,000

7.3 K Street Investment Club is an entertaining, educational and sometimes profitable venture through which its 25 members invest a portion of their retirement funds. Partners' contributions are always made in cash. The partnership's balance sheet (expanded to show asset values) on June 30, 2016 is as follows:

	Adjusted Basis and Book Value	Fair Market Value
Assets		
Cash	$ 12,000	$ 12,000
Actively traded stock	464,000	678,000
Stock not actively traded	40,000	450,000
Stock in mutual funds (regulated investment companies)	1,440,000	1,520,000
Total Assets	$1,956,000	$2,660,000
Liabilities	$ 0	$ 0
Partners' Capital	$1,956,000	$2,660,000

On that day, the partnership distributes actively traded stock with a value of $106,400 and an adjusted tax basis to the partnership of $34,000 to Ron Lauren in complete liquidation of his interest. Ron's basis in his partnership interest immediately prior to the distribution is $78,240. What is his basis in the distributed stock?

a) $34,000

b) $72,400

c) $78,240

d) $106,400

7.4 Partnership ABC has had a taxable year ending September 30 since its formation. Its partners are A, who has a 75% interest in capital and profits and a taxable year ending September 30; B, who has a 15% interest and a taxable year ending June 30; and C, who has a 10% interest and a taxable year ending December 31. On December 31, 2016, A sells 60% of her partnership interest to D, who has a taxable year ending December 31. Following this sale, what is the required taxable year of the partnership and when is the partnership required to adopt this required taxable year?

a) Required year remains September 30

b) New required year ends December 31, effective for taxable year beginning January 1, 2017

c) New required year ends December 31, effective for taxable year beginning October 1, 2017

    d) New required year ends December 31, effective for taxable year beginning October 1, 2019

7.5 The balance sheet of Partnership ABC, an equal general partnership, is as follows:

Assets				Liabilities		
	Tax	**Book**	**FMV**		**Tax**	**Book**
Cash	$ 12,000	$ 12,000	$ 12,000	Recourse	$240,000	$240,000
Inventory	81,000	81,000	72,000			
Equipment (accumulated depreciation $18,000)	240,000	240,000	270,000			
Building (accumulated depreciation $27,000)	357,000	357,000	276,000			
Land	120,000	120,000	180,000	**Capital**		
				A	190,000	190,000
				B	190,000	190,000
				C	190,000	190,000
Total Assets	$810,000	$810,000	$810,000	**Total Liabilities and Capital**	$810,000	$810,000

    A and B were founders and made equal cash contributions. C purchased her interest from the third founder several years ago for a single cash payment of $245,000. The partnership has always had in effect an election under section 754, and C currently has a special basis adjustment of $35,000, taking into account depreciation since the date of C's purchase. C is now planning to sell this interest to D for $190,000. Will D have a special basis adjustment and, if so, how will it be allocated among the assets?

    a) D will have no special basis adjustment, because her share of the partnership's inside basis ($270,000) exactly equals her outside basis.

    b) D is entitled to retain C's special basis adjustment, so long as its allocation among the partnership's assets remains the same.

    c) D will have a special basis adjustment of zero, allocated ($3,000) to inventory, $6,000 to section 1245 recapture, $4,000 to equipment, ($27,000) to the building and $20,000 to land.

    d) D will have a special basis adjustment of $80,000, allocated as in (c), plus an allocation of $80,000 to an amortizable section 197 asset.

7.6 On January 1, 2016, A, B and C form Rentco LLC, a limited liability company taxed as a partnership, with cash contributions of $20,000 each. The LLC operating agreement provides for equal sharing of profits and losses among the three members, subject to any contrary allocations required by applicable tax law. Rentco incurs two nonrecourse loans of equal priority, each secured by a lien on all of Rentco's depreciable property. One of these loans is for $120,000 from an unrelated bank and the other is from C, also for $120,000. Rentco acquires depreciable property with an aggregate basis of $300,000, which produces an annual depreciation deduction of $30,000, beginning in 2016. Rentco has no other income, gains, losses or deductions and makes no distributions. What is the amount of the partner nonrecourse deductions for 2018, and to whom are they allocated?

a) $5,000 to each of A, B and C

b) $10,000 to each of A, B and C

c) $5,000 to each of A and B; $20,000 to C

d) $15,000 to C

7.7 The balance sheet of Partnership ABC (expanded to show asset values) is as follows:

Assets				Liabilities		
	Tax	Book	FMV		Tax	Book
Cash	$100,000	$100,000	$100,000	[None]	$ 0	$ 0
Inventory	20,000	20,000	20,000			
Equipment	40,000	40,000	30,000	Capital		
Land	20,000	20,000	150,000	Amelia	60,000	60,000
				Brody	60,000	60,000
				Corbett	60,000	60,000
Total Assets	$180,000	$180,000	$300,000	Total Liabilities and Capital	$180,000	$180,000

The partnership distributes $100,000 in cash to Brody in liquidation of her interest. The partnership has made an election under section 754. Following this distribution, what are the bases of the partnership's assets?

a) Inventory, $20,000; Equipment, $20,000; Land, $0

b) Inventory, $10,000; Equipment, $20,000; Land, $10,000

c) Inventory, $20,000; Equipment, $40,000; Land, $60,000

d) Inventory, $24,000; Equipment, $46,000; Land, $50,000

7.8 Following a nice run-up in the markets, A, B and C each contributes a diversified portfolio (Portfolios A, B and C, respectively) of publicly traded stocks to form the Broad Street Investment Partnership. On contribution, each portfolio has a value of $2 million, and their adjusted bases are: Portfolio A, $1 million; Portfolio B, $500,000; and Portfolio C, $1.5 million. A, B and C are equal, one-third partners in Broad Street, except that under the partnership agreement each partner retains the first $250,000 of book gain or loss from the sale of the stocks in the portfolio contributed by that partner. The partnership maintains proper capital accounts, which govern the distribution of liquidation proceeds, and has elected the remedial allocation method. What goes up must come down. If Broad Street now sells Portfolio B for $1 million, how much book and tax gain or loss will be allocated to B, including remedial allocations, if any?

    a)   Tax gain, $500,000; Book gain, $0

    b)   Tax gain, $1 million; Book loss, $500,000

    c)   Tax gain, $1.667 million; Book loss, $333,333

    d)   Tax gain, $666,667; Book gain, $0

7.9 In Notice 2006–14, the IRS acknowledged that the Treasury regulations promulgated over a half-century ago under section 751(b) have not exactly stood the test of time. The proposed regulations under that section are intended to remedy at least some of their defects. What problems have been identified with the existing regulations? (Mark all that apply.)

    a)   They can cause a distributee-partner who receives more than her share of the partnership's section 751(b) assets to recognize current capital gain.

    b)   They can cause basis to shift from section 751(b) assets to other property, thereby increasing the total amount of ordinary income recognized by the partners.

    c)   They do not tax a distributee-partner who receives her share of the gross value of the partnership's section 751(b) assets, even though the distributed assets have less than that partner's share of the partnership's unrealized ordinary income.

    d)   They do not take section 704(c) principles into account.

7.10 A and B each own 10%, and C and D each own 40%, of Partnership ABCD. In order to separate its two principal lines of business, the partnership distributes business assets to C and D in liquidation of their respective interests in the partnership. C and D immediately contribute all of the distributed assets to newly formed Newco LLC, a limited liability company taxed as a partnership. What is deemed to have happened for tax purposes?

    a)   The tax treatment follows the form adopted by the parties: the divided partnership distributes assets to C and D, who contribute such assets to a new partnership.

    b)   The transaction is recharacterized: the divided partnership distributes assets to A and B, who contribute such assets to a new partnership.

c) The transaction is recharacterized: the divided partnership transfers assets to a new partnership and distributes interests therein to C and D.

d) The transaction is recharacterized: the divided partnership transfers assets to a new partnership and distributes interests therein to A and B.

END OF EXAMINATION

FINAL EXAM 8

(Suggested time: 90 minutes)

8.1 American Electric, Inc. and National Electric, Inc. enter into an agreement entitled "Joint Power Supply Agreement" under which they agree to construct and own a power plant. Under the Agreement, the plant is owned by the two utility companies as tenants in common with undivided ownership interests of 50% each. Each of the utilities pays its equal share of all expenses of the operation, repair and maintenance of the plant. Half of the electricity produced by the plant is distributed to each of the utilities, which they sell to customers along with the power that each produces individually. None of the power produced by the plant is offered for sale jointly by the utilities or sold in the name of a joint venture. The Agreement specifically disclaims any intention for this arrangement to be treated as other than a co-tenancy. What is the best federal tax characterization of the arrangement created by the Agreement?

a) Because this is essentially a joint undertaking to share expenses, it is a not a partnership. The utilities should report separately their respective shares of the expenses of the arrangement and separately account for their sales of the electricity produced.

b) This is a mere co-ownership of property, without the level of activity necessary to constitute a partnership. The utilities should report separately their respective shares of the expenses of the arrangement and separately account for their sales of the electricity produced.

c) Because no power is sold, and therefore no revenue is earned, by the joint activity of the utilities, this arrangement has no joint profit motive and therefore cannot be a partnership. The utilities should report separately their respective shares of the expenses of the arrangement and separately account for their sales of the electricity produced.

d) This is a partnership, because it is a co-ownership through which the utilities realize profits from the distribution of power which each of them can sell.

8.2 The hypothetical sale at fair market value is used by some Treasury regulations to determine a partner's share of a partnership's attributes. Which of the following final or proposed Treasury regulations make use of this tool? (Circle all that apply.)

a) The determination of a partner's "previously taxed capital"

b) The determination of a partner's share of the partnership's recourse liabilities

c) The determination of a partner's share of the partnership's "hot assets" under section 751(b)

d)   The allocation of a partner's section 743(b) adjustment among the assets of the partnership

8.3 The balance sheet of equal Partnership OTR, expanded to show asset values, is as follows:

Assets				Liabilities		
	Tax	**Book**	**FMV**		**Tax**	**Book**
Land O	$ 20,000	$ 80,000	$120,000	[None]	$ 0	$ 0
Marketable Securities	30,000	80,000	120,000			
New Property A	50,000	50,000	80,000	**Capital**		
New Property B	30,000	30,000	40,000	Osgood	20,000	80,000
				Theo	30,000	80,000
				Raeburn	80,000	80,000
Total Assets	$130,000	$240,000	$360,000	**Total Liabilities and Capital**	$130,000	$240,000

On formation, Osgood contributed Land O, Theo contributed the marketable securities and Raeburn contributed cash which was later used to purchase New Property A and New Property B. The partnership is not an investment partnership described in section 721(b) due to its substantial land holdings. What are the tax consequences to Osgood and Theo if the partnership distributes all of its marketable securities to Osgood in liquidation of his interest?

a)   Theo, $0 gain; Osgood, $0 gain

b)   Theo, $50,000 gain; Osgood, $0 gain

c)   Theo, $50,000 gain; Osgood, $60,000 gain

d)   Theo, $50,000 gain; Osgood, $100,000 gain

8.4 Fred Blurton is a NASCAR driver who has an abiding interest in antique Duesenberg automobiles, one of America's earliest and best racing cars. A number of years ago, Fred found one in an old barn and bought it on the spot for $100,000, despite the fact that it needed a tremendous amount of work. That job fell to Randy Koons, the head of Fred's pit crew, who has never seen an automobile he could not fix. Randy has worked on the Duesey in his spare time for over a year. Fred has now learned of a racing circuit at which antique cars are run for prize money, and Randy says the Duesenberg is ready. To compensate Randy for his efforts, Fred offers Randy a 20% interest in a new partnership, Blurton Duesenberg Racing, which will own the car and enter it in races across the United States. Fred will own the remaining 80% of the partnership and will drive the Duesenberg, because he would not trust his baby (which is currently worth $750,000) to anyone else. Randy will maintain the car, for which the partnership will pay him in cash from its expected winnings. If Randy agrees to this deal, what are the tax consequences?

a) Fred and Randy have formed a business partnership and neither recognizes current income, gain or loss on formation.

b) Fred and Randy have formed a business partnership. Randy recognizes $150,000 of compensation income and the partnership is entitled to a corresponding deduction, which is allocated solely to Fred. The partnership recognizes no current gain or loss.

c) Whether or not Fred and Randy have formed a business partnership, Randy recognizes $150,000 of compensation income and Fred recognizes a current gain of $130,000.

d) Fred and Randy have not formed a business partnership, because their arrangement lacks a substantial profit motive. Randy recognizes no compensation income and therefore no deduction is available. Fred recognizes a current gain of $130,000.

8.5 The partnership agreement of the Zander law firm, a general partnership, provides that a retiring partner will receive a payment in the year she retires equal to the amount of her tax capital account. In each of the next three years, the partner receives one-third of the amount of her uncollected billings as of the date that she retired. Ruth Grant, a senior corporate partner of the firm, retires in 2016. Pursuant to the partnership agreement, she receives a lump-sum cash payment of $3,750,000 in 2016 and cash payments of $900,000 in each of 2017, 2018 and 2019 (the "runoff years"). The value of Ruth's share of Zander's goodwill is $1,500,000 on the date she retires, although such goodwill is not reflected on the firm's balance sheet. What are the tax consequences to Ruth of the receipt of these payments?

a) $3,750,000 capital gain in 2016; $900,000 ordinary income in each of the runoff years

b) $1,250,000 capital gain in 2016; $1,500,000 ordinary income in 2016; $900,000 ordinary income in each of the runoff years

c) $1,500,000 ordinary income in 2016; $900,000 ordinary income in each of the runoff years

d) No income or gain in 2016; $900,000 ordinary income in each of the runoff years

8.6 Equal Partnership ABC has elected the remedial method for section 704(c) allocations and has the following balance sheet:

Assets	Tax	Book	Liabilities	Tax	Book
Cash	$ 50,000	$ 50,000	Nonrecourse	$ 300,000	$ 300,000
Plant & Equipment	1,150,000	1,150,000			
Land	150,000	450,000			
			Capital		
			A	450,000	450,000
			B	450,000	450,000
			C	150,000	450,000
Total Assets	$1,350,000	$1,650,000	**Total Liabilities and Capital**	$1,350,000	$1,650,000

On formation of this partnership, C contributed the land, encumbered by the $300,000 nonrecourse liability, and the other partners contributed cash. What amount of the partnership's nonrecourse debt is allocated to C under the "second tier" of Treas. Reg. § 1.752–3(a)(2)?

a) $150,000

b) $250,000

c) $300,000

d)   The amount determined by any reasonable method, which might include any amount between $150,000 and $300,000.

8.7 Great Western Investments LP holds a diversified portfolio of high-quality bonds and, for purposes of this Question, it can be assumed to generate income and gain totaling $10,000 every month. The tax year of the partnership and all of its partners is the calendar year. The partnership agreement provides that all partners share the profits and losses of the partnership in proportion to the positive balances in their capital accounts. On June 30, 2016, George contributes $40,000 to the partnership, which increases his share of the partnership's total capital from 30% to 40%. The partners wish to recognize the timely nature of George's capital contribution and its great value to the partnership, and on March 1, 2017, they approach you for advice as to whether it is possible to amend the partnership agreement to allocate to George more of the partnership's income for 2016—perhaps up to $48,000, equivalent to a 40% share of the partnership's income for the year. Applying all applicable federal income tax rules, what do you say would be an acceptable allocation to George of the partnership's 2016 income?

a) $42,000

b) $45,000

c) $48,000

d) All of the above

8.8 Partnership AB has a net asset value of $60,000 and is owned by A and B. Partnership BC has a net asset value of $80,000 and is owned by B and C. In order to combine the businesses of these two partnerships, Partnership BC distributes all of its assets to its partners, who immediately contribute the distributed assets to Partnership AB in exchange for newly issued interests therein. Immediately following this transaction, A owns 20% of the capital and profits of the resulting partnership, B owns 45% and C owns 35%. What is deemed to have happened for federal income tax purposes?

a) The tax treatment follows the form adopted by the parties: Partnership BC distributes assets, which B and C contribute to Partnership AB.

b) The transaction is recharacterized: Partnership AB distributes assets, which A and B contribute to Partnership BC.

c) The transaction is recharacterized: Partnership BC transfers assets to Partnership AB in exchange for interests therein, which Partnership BC distributes in liquidation to B and C.

d) The transaction is recharacterized: Partnership AB transfers assets to Partnership BC in exchange for interests therein, which Partnership AB distributes in liquidation to A and B.

8.9 A, B and C are the partners in a modestly successful dressmaking business, which is conducted by the ABC Partnership. They have agreed to accept a capital contribution from D in exchange for a 25% interest in the partnership. The partnership revalues its book assets in accordance with Treas. Reg. § 1.704–1(b)(2)(iv)(*f*) and discovers that some of its assets are appreciated in value (value exceeds adjusted basis) and some are depreciated (adjusted basis exceeds value). The partnership elects to apply the traditional method under section 704(c) to the appreciated assets and the remedial method to the depreciated assets. If D is in a lower tax bracket than A, B, and C, the partnership's allocation method is:

a) Reasonable. An allocation method (or combination of methods) is not necessarily unreasonable merely because another method (or combination) would result in a higher aggregate tax liability.

b) Unreasonable. The partnership's choice of methods is calculated systematically to favor the higher-bracket partners, A, B and C.

c) Unreasonable. Following the enactment of section 704(c)(1)(C), section 704(c) allocations are not permitted to be made with respect to loss assets.

d) Reasonable. A partnership may choose to apply a different allocation method to each asset, and the combined effect of these choices is not taken into account in assessing reasonableness.

8.10 Several years ago, Ashley, Beatrice and Charlie each contributed $120,000 to a newly formed partnership. Ashley contributed cash, Beatrice contributed investment land with a tax basis of $30,000 and Charlie contributed investment stock with a tax basis of $40,000. The partnership uses the traditional method for applying section 704(c). The partnership has not yet found an appropriate investment for its cash, and its balance sheet today, expanded to show asset values, looks like this:

Assets				Liabilities		
	Tax	**Book**	**FMV**		**Tax**	**Book**
Cash	$120,000	$120,000	$120,000	[None]	$ 0	$ 0
Land	30,000	120,000	180,000			
Stock	40,000	120,000	90,000			
				Capital		
				Ashley	120,000	120,000
				Beatrice	30,000	120,000
				Charlie	40,000	120,000
Total Assets	$190,000	$360,000	$390,000	**Total Liabilities and Capital**	$190,000	$360,000

Daniel buys Charlie's partnership interest for $130,000 cash and in connection with this acquisition the partnership makes an election under section 754. What amount of Daniel's special basis adjustment is allocated to each of the partnership's assets?

a) Land, $20,000; Stock, $50,000

b) Land, $20,000; Stock, $50,000; Section 197 intangible, $20,000

c) Land, $30,000; Stock, $60,000

d) Land, $23,222; Stock, $46,667

END OF EXAMINATION

FINAL EXAM 9

(Suggested time: 90 minutes)

9.1 Major Electric Corporation, a public company that pays US tax at the highest corporate rate, enters into a partnership agreement with Robocop Bank NV, a foreign bank that does not pay US tax. Major Electric contributes equipment subject to pre-existing leases and Robocop contributes cash. Although Robocop contributes only 10% of the total capital of the enterprise, the partnership agreement provides that it will be allocated 90% of the income from the leasing business. These income allocations increase the capital account of Robocop, but it is prohibited from taking distributions in excess of the amount required to return its investment plus a 9% annual return, subject adjustment upward in the event of unexpectedly large partnership earnings. If the partnership is unable to make such distributions to Robocop, they are guaranteed by Major Electric. Later allocations of operating income and gains from sales of the leased equipment are to be made disproportionately to Major Electric to restore its capital account to proper balance. These special allocations are intended to reduce significantly the US tax liability of Major Electric without producing any US tax liability for Robocop. Is this arrangement a partnership for federal tax purposes?

a) No, because all of the leases were negotiated by Major Electric prior to contributing the equipment to the enterprise, it does not have sufficient activity to be considered a partnership for tax purposes.

b) Yes, although the substantiality of the special allocations should be closely scrutinized.

c) No, for tax purposes, Robocop should not be treated as a partner, because it does not participate meaningfully in either the upside or downside of the leasing business and therefore does not have a bona fide equity participation.

d) Yes, the expected stability of Robocop's return is not inconsistent with partner status. Robocop is receiving a guaranteed payment for capital under section 707(c).

9.2 GenX Labs LLC, a limited liability company treated as a partnership for tax purposes, is in the early stages of clinical trials for a new drug and it is running short of cash. Marci Owens acquires an interest in the partnership by contributing $10 million of the common stock of Gilead Sciences, Inc., which has an adjusted basis of $6 million in her hands. GenX pledges this stock as security for borrowing the needed funds. A year later, GenX raises $50 million fresh cash by selling interests to new investors, amid great publicly surrounding the progress of the trials. It uses a portion of this cash to make a $5 million distribution to Marci, which Marci negotiated with the partnership upon learning of the partnership's capital raise. This distribution returns half of Marci's capital and reduces her percentage interest by half. For federal income tax purposes, what is the best characterization of GenX's payment to Marci?

a) Proceeds of a disguised sale of one-half of Marci's Gilead stock to GenX

b) Current distribution

c) Distribution in partial liquidation

d) Proceeds of a disguised sale of one-half of Marci's partnership interest to the new investors

9.3 Charles and Chen form a limited liability company to operate their restaurant, Trottin' Charlie. Charles contributes the building where the restaurant is located, subject to a mortgage, and the restaurant equipment. Chen contributes cash for working capital and expansion. The company is treated as a partnership for tax purposes, in which Charles and Chen are 50:50 partners. On formation, the balance sheet is as follows:

Assets			**Liabilities**		
	Tax	**Book**		**Tax**	**Book**
Cash	$350,000	$ 350,000	Mortgage Debt	$400,000	$ 400,000
Equipment	60,000	200,000			
Building	450,000	550,000	**Capital**		
			Charles	110,000	350,000
			Chen	350,000	350,000
Total Assets	$860,000	$1,100,000	**Total Liabilities and Capital**	$860,000	$1,100,000

The equipment is depreciable on a straight-line basis over 10 years, with five years remaining at the time of contribution. Assume that the remaining economic life of the equipment is approximately 10 years at the time of its contribution. Assume further that the partnership is entitled to a full year's depreciation on the equipment during the first year. The partnership adopts the remedial method with respect to the equipment and makes a remedial allocation of $8,000 of ordinary income to Charles for the first year. The partnership's allocation method is:

a) Reasonable. It is the remedial allocation method.

d) Unreasonable. This allocation is not made over a reasonable period of time.

c) Unreasonable. This allocation is unreasonably large.

d) Reasonable. Although the partnership's method does not follow the remedial method, it eliminates Charlie's book-tax difference more quickly than such method, and therefore is consistent with the purpose of section 704(c).

9.4 Adelaide contributes unimproved land to Jersey Shore Realty LLC, a limited liability company treated as a partnership for tax purposes, on December 15, 2017. The land is worth $2.5 million and has an adjusted basis in her hands of $1 million. On March 31, 2019, the partnership distributes a different parcel of real property to Adelaide which is worth $1 million and in which the partnership has a basis of $500,000. The facts show that the partnership would not have made this distribution but for Adelaide's contribution and that the partnership's distribution is not dependent on the entrepreneurial risks of the partnership's operation. Ignoring imputed interest, what is the amount of gain, if any, recognized by the Adelaide and the partnership, and in what year?

a) Adelaide, $0; Jersey Shore, $0

b) Adelaide, $600,000 gain in 2017; Jersey Shore, $500,000 gain in 2017

c) Adelaide, $600,000 gain in 2017; Jersey Shore, $500,000 gain in 2019

d) Adelaide, $600,000 gain in 2019; Jersey Shore, $500,000 gain in 2019

9.5 Leapin' Lizards LLC is a limited liability company taxed as a partnership, in the business of hosting themed birthday parties for kids. It uses the cash method and its tax year is the calendar year. Its balance sheet, and the fair market values of its assets, are as follows at June 30, 2016:

Assets				Liabilities		
	Tax	**Book**	**FMV**		**Tax**	**Book**
Cash	$20,000	$20,000	$ 20,000	[None]	$ 0	$ 0
Receivables	0	0	80,000			
Equipment (accumulated depreciation $200,000)	40,000	40,000	180,000			
				Capital		
				Ken	30,000	30,000
				Alvin	15,000	15,000
				Erma	15,000	15,000
Total Assets	$60,000	$60,000	$280,000	**Total Liabilities and Capital**	$60,000	$60,000

On that date, Ken, a calendar-year taxpayer who owns 50% of the membership interests in Leapin' Lizards, sells one-half of his interests to Alvin for $100,000 in cash. The increase in price relative to the book value of the interests sold reflects the appreciation of the assets on the balance as well as the goodwill of the partnership, which is not shown on its balance sheet. The partnership earns $80,000 of book and taxable income for its 2016 year, $48,000 of which it earns on or before June 30. What are Ken's tax consequences on this sale? The LLC operating agreement is a simple document that has no provisions regarding this sort of transaction.

a) $20,000 ordinary income; $53,000 capital gain

b) $20,000 ordinary income; $65,000 capital gain

c) $55,000 ordinary income; $20,000 capital gain

d) $55,000 ordinary income; $30,000 capital gain

9.6   The Ivanhoe Company ("GP") is the general partner of Bazalon LP, a private equity fund (the "Fund") with 97 unrelated limited partners and a fiscal year ending December 31. An affiliated entity, Ivanhoe Management ("Management"), is the manager of the Fund, for which it is entitled to be paid 2% of the Fund's committed capital each year. As general partner, GP holds a 1% interest in the capital of the Fund and an additional 20% carried interest. On November 1, 2016, Management agrees with the Fund that it will waive its management fee for the coming year. In exchange, Management receives a profits interest (the "Additional Interest"), the value of which is expected to approximate the waived management fee. The Additional Interest entitles Management to receive an allocation of the first profits realized on the Fund's sales of portfolio companies, until the total amount allocated equals the waived management fee. Given the composition of the Fund's portfolio, it is highly likely that Management will receive the full profit allocation with respect to the Additional Interest within fiscal year 2017. Like the limited partners of the Fund, Management is entitled to withdraw the positive balance in its capital account, if any, at the end of each year on proper notice to the Fund. What are the tax consequences of this transaction to Management?

a)   Management is in constructive receipt of the amount of the waived fee upon receipt of the Additional Interest.

b)   The Additional Interest is a disguised payment for services and Management has ordinary income equal to the value of the Additional Interest (presumably, the amount of the waived fee) upon receipt.

c)   Rev. Proc. 93–27 controls the tax treatment of this transaction and mandates that the receipt of the Additional Interest is tax-free to Management.

d)   Management is not in constructive receipt of the waived fee and the Additional Interest is not a disguised payment for services. The receipt of the Additional interest is therefore tax-free to Management.

9.7   To form equal Partnership AB, A contributes land (Land A) worth $600,000 with an adjusted basis of $200,000 and B contributes $600,000 in cash. The land appreciates to a value of $1 million while the partnership is still holding the cash and considering its development plans. It is approached by C, who offers to contribute an adjoining property (Land C) worth $800,000 for a one-third interest in the partnership. C's adjusted basis in Land C is

$500,000. Partnership AB revalues its book assets and admits C. Time passes, and still the partnership does not commence development of its properties. The market weakens. The partnership receives an offer to purchase Land A for $850,000, which it accepts. Under proposed regulations, what is the tax gain allocated to B, assuming that the partnership uses the traditional method for section 704(c) allocations?

a) $125,000

b) $200,000

c) $525,000

d) The amount determined by any reasonable method, which might include $125,000 or $200,000

9.8 Reigeluth, Barnes & Noble LLP ("Reigeluth"), a law firm, is enduring a shake-up. Peter Barnes, a name partner and a principal source of the firm's billings, is leaving the firm to enter academia. Prior to his departure on June 15, 2016, Peter held 10% of the firm's units of ownership. The firm keeps its books using the cash method and the calendar year, and on that basis the firm's year-to-date earnings at May 31 and June 30 are $20 million and $24 million, respectively. Its earnings for the full year are $42 million. The management committee determines that Peter's share of the partnership's earnings for 2016 is $2.5 million, which is based on its estimate of the firm's year-to-date earnings as of the date of Peter's retirement. The firm has not elected a section 706(d) method or convention. For tax purposes, what is the allowable allocation to Peter of the firm's earnings for 2016?

a) $1.93 million, using the proration method and a calendar-day convention

b) $2.4 million, using the interim closing method and prorating with a calendar-day convention for the month of June

c) $2.5 million, using the determination of the partnership

d) The amount determined by any reasonable method, including **(a)**, **(b)** or **(c)**

9.9 Paul Rand is a 20% partner in Kind Rand, an Illinois general partnership. Both Paul and the partnership use the cash method and the calendar year. On January 1, 2016, Paul's adjusted basis in his partnership interest is $50,000 (including his share of the partnership's $60,000 recourse borrowing). On March 31, 2016, the partnership distributes $50,000 in cash to Paul, and Paul's partnership interest is reduced immediately from 20% to 10%. Paul's share of the partnership's income for the entire year 2016 is $20,000. Assume that Kind Rand has no section 751(b) assets. Does Paul recognize gain on the March 31 distribution?

a) Yes, because the total of the actual cash distribution and the deemed cash distribution under section 752(b) exceeds Paul's basis as of the distribution date.

b) No, because the section 752(b) deemed distribution is treated as an advance or drawing for this purpose, and Paul's share of the partnership's income for the year exceeds the amount of the section 752(b) deemed distribution.

c) No, because no section 752(b) deemed distribution arises from a current, as opposed to a liquidating, distribution.

d) Cannot answer this Question on the facts provided, because the taxability of the distribution to Paul will depend on the method chosen by the partnership to allocate Paul's share of the partnership's income between the period prior to the distribution and the period after it.

9.10 The balance sheet of Partnership ABC (expanded to show asset values) is as follows:

Assets				Liabilities		
	Tax	**Book**	**FMV**		**Tax**	**Book**
Cash	$ 75,000	$ 75,000	$ 75,000	Debt	$ 72,000	$ 72,000
Receivables	27,000	27,000	27,000			
Inventory	21,000	21,000	33,000	**Capital**		
Equipment	45,000	45,000	42,000	Albert	62,000	62,000
Plant	55,000	55,000	65,000	Bethany	62,000	62,000
Land	35,000	35,000	55,000	Charlize	62,000	62,000
Total Assets	$258,000	$258,000	$297,000	**Total Liabilities and Capital**	$258,000	$258,000

Partnership ABC is a general partnership which uses an accrual method and has made no section 754 election. Its plant is real property which it has depreciated on a straight-line basis. The partnership distributes to Bethany in liquidation of her interest the land and receivables valued at $20,000. How much ordinary income and capital gain or loss do Bethany and the partnership recognize on this distribution, applying the proposed regulations under section 751(b)?

a) Bethany, $0 income, $0 gain; ABC, $0 income

b) Bethany, $0 income, $0 gain; ABC, $4,000 income

c) Bethany, $4,000 income, $0 gain; ABC, $0 income

d) Bethany, $4,000 income, $9,000 gain; ABC, $0 income

END OF EXAMINATION

ANSWERS TO FINAL
EXAM QUESTIONS

QWIKCHECK

EXAM 1	
Question	Answer
1.1	C
1.2	C
1.3	A
1.4	D
1.5	B
1.6	C
1.7	B
1.8	B
1.9	B
1.10	A

EXAM 2	
Question	Answer
2.1	D
2.2	D
2.3	A
2.4	A
2.5	D
2.6	D
2.7	F
2.8	A
2.9	B
2.10	B

EXAM 3	
Question	Answer
3.1	C
3.2	D
3.3	B
3.4	B
3.5	A
3.6	D
3.7	C
3.8	B
3.9	A
3.10	B

EXAM 4	
Question	Answer
4.1	D
4.2	B
4.3	B
4.4	D
4.5	F
4.6	A,B,E
4.7	C
4.8	A
4.9	B
4.10	C

EXAM 5	
Question	Answer
5.1	A
5.2	B
5.3	B
5.4	D
5.5	A
5.6	B
5.7	A
5.8	B
5.9	A
5.10	A

EXAM 6	
Question	Answer
6.1	B
6.2	C
6.3	A
6.4	D
6.5	A
6.6	A
6.7	A
6.8	A
6.9	B
6.10	B

EXAM 7	
Question	Answer
7.1	C
7.2	D
7.3	C
7.4	C
7.5	C
7.6	D
7.7	C
7.8	B
7.9	A,C,D
7.10	D

EXAM 8	
Question	Answer
8.1	D
8.2	A,C,D
8.3	D
8.4	C
8.5	D
8.6	B
8.7	D
8.8	D
8.9	B
8.10	A

EXAM 9	
Question	Answer
9.1	C
9.2	B or D
9.3	C
9.4	D
9.5	D
9.6	B
9.7	D
9.8	D
9.9	B
9.10	C

COMPLETE EXPLANATIONS OF ANSWERS TO FINAL EXAM QUESTIONS

Final Exam 1

1.1 The correct Answer is (c). By electing to be excluded from all of Subchapter K, Broadway Partners loses the benefit of section 721(a). This is not a problem for Mr. Jungman, who is simply contributing cash. The other partners, however, all recognize gain. They have, in economic effect, sold 20% of their securities to Mr. Jungman for cash. **Answer (a)** is incorrect, because section 721(a) does not apply. **Answer (b)** is incorrect, because Mr. Jungman does not recognize gain. If he contributed appreciated securities rather than cash, he would recognize gain, but not because of the application of section 721(b), which, like the rest of Subchapter K, does not apply due to Broadway Partners' decision to elect out. **Answer (d)** is incorrect, because this appears to be a fairly valued transaction. Following Mr. Jungman's contribution, the value of Broadway Partners' assets will be $17.5 million. His interest will be 20%, which is $3.5 million/$17.5 million. *Reading Period: Topic 1.4.*

1.2 The correct Answer is (c). Under section 723, the partnership takes an initial tax basis in the drum sets equal to their basis in Alvin's hands at the time of the contribution. The fact that they are encumbered by debt that the partnership assumes in connection with the contribution does not change this result. The debt will appear as a liability of the partnership and Alvin's tax capital, which initially will equal his tax basis in the contributed property ($4,500), will be reduced by the entire $6,000 amount of the liability. Alvin's tax capital will then be a negative $1,500. As a limited partner, Alvin will have no share of the liability once it has been assumed by the partnership. He will therefore recognize $1,500 of gain and his outside basis will be zero. **Answer (a)** reflects this computation of Alvin's outside basis. **Answer (b)** is Alvin's opening book capital account. **Answer (d)** is the partnership's opening book value for the drum sets. None of these answers the question asked. *Reading Period: Topics 2.3 and 2.5.*

1.3 The correct Answer is (a). Under section 702(b), Pharaoh Land determines the character of its $200,000 loss on the sale of the residential lot by reference to its own relationship to that property. Because the partnership held the lot as a capital asset, the loss is capital. Under section 702(a)(2), Mort takes a distributive share of this capital loss, even though the loss would have been ordinary had he held and sold the lot directly. **Answer (b)** is incorrect, because there are no facts to indicate that the partnership has engaged in a wash sale. **Answer (c)** is incorrect, but instructive. If Mort had contributed to Pharaoh Land a residential lot that he held for sale to customers, section 724(b) would characterize as ordinary any gain or loss recognized by the partnership on a sale of the contributed lot within the next five years. This "safeguard" provision does not apply in the present case, however, because the partnership bought the lot for cash. **Answer (d)** is also incorrect. The residential lot is an "inventory item" described in section 751(d)(3). While this could cause Mort to recognize ordinary loss on a sale or liquidation of his partnership interest, it has no bearing on the character of

Mort's loss if the partnership sells the lot itself. ***Reading Period: Topics 4.1, 6.3 and 7.2.***

1.4 The correct Answer is (d). Derek's outside basis in the Dunleavey Partnership is zero, the sum of his negative $12,000 tax capital and his $12,000 share of the partnership's liabilities. His liquidating distribution consists of $9,000 in cash and a deemed distribution of $12,000 in cash under section 752(b), for a total of $21,000. Under section 731(a)(1), Derek recognizes gain equal to the excess of the actual and deemed cash distributions over his outside basis, or $21,000. **Answer (a)** would be correct if Derek's tax capital were positive $12,000, rather than negative $12,000. **Answer (b)** takes into account only the actual cash distribution of $9,000, neglecting the deemed cash distribution of $12,000 under section 752(b). **Answer (c)** makes the opposite mistake, neglecting the actual cash. ***Reading Period: Topics 2.5 and 9.1.***

1.5 The correct Answer is (b). Rasheeda's distributive share of all these items adjusts her outside basis under section 705(a). Leaving any of them out would cause her outside basis to diverge from her share of the aggregate inside basis of the partnership's assets, contrary to a basic goal of partnership taxation to keep these two amounts as nearly equal as possible. In the case of investment interest expense and charitable contributions, Rasheeda's outside basis decreases, even though she may be unable to claim a deduction for these amounts on her individual tax return, due to the limitations on deductions found in section 163(d) and section 170(d). Similarly, the passive-activity loss rules of section 469 may prevent Rasheeda from claiming a current tax benefit for her share of the partnership's loss from rental real estate. On the income side, capital gains, ordinary income and even tax-exempt income all adjust outside basis equally, although they certainly are not taxed equally. **Answers (a), (b) and (c)** exclude one or more of these items from the basis adjustment, and all are incorrect. ***Reading Period: Topic 5.2.***

1.6 The correct Answer is (c). Section 708(b)(1)(B) provides that a partnership terminates for tax purposes upon the sale or exchange of 50% or more of the total interest in capital and profits within a 12-month period. The sale of a 25% interest by A to B on March 22 is a sale or exchange for this purpose, even though it is between two existing partners, but it is not enough by itself to terminate the partnership. The liquidation of C's 25% interest on June 28 is not a sale or exchange, regardless whether C recognizes gain or loss on the distribution. Treas. Reg. § 1.708–1(b)(2) (third sentence). Upon this liquidation, the interests of B and D, the two remaining partners, increase to 66 2/3% and 33 1/3%, respectively. When B sells her interest to E on September 19, it is not counted as a sale of 66 2/3% of the entire interest in partnership capital and profits, because B's resale of the interest she acquired from A on March 22 is backed out of this number. Treas. Reg. § 1.708–1(b)(2) (last sentence). Nevertheless, when added to the March 22 sale, the September 19 sale is sufficient to terminate the partnership. **Answers (a) and (b)** are incorrect, because an insufficient interest has been sold or exchanged as of these two dates to terminate the partnership under section 708(b)(1)(B). **Answer (d)** is incorrect, because the partnership does, in fact, terminate on September 19. *Reading Period: Topic 10.1.*

1.7 The correct Answer is (b). Because this is a current distribution and does not appear to be an "advance" or "draw," Judah cannot take any portion of the partnership's income for the tax year of the distribution into account in determining outside basis. The cash distribution of $130,000 exceeds Judah's outside basis by $10,000, resulting in that amount of capital gain. Although not raised in this Question, Judah takes the distributed property with a tax basis of $0. **Answer (a)** seems to treat this cash distribution as an "advance" or "draw" within the meaning of Treas. Reg. § 1.731–1(a)(1)(ii), but there are no facts in the Question that support that characterization. **Answer (c)** includes in the taxable distribution not only the cash but the basis of the distributed property, which is not consistent with section 731(a)(1). **Answer (d)** includes the value of the distributed property in the taxable distribution. *Reading Period: Topics 6.2 and 9.1.*

1.8 The correct Answer is (b). Under Treas. Reg. § 1.752–1(a)(4), a partnership "liability" is an obligation of the partnership that (1) creates or increases the tax basis of the partnership's assets (including cash), (2) gives the partnership an immediate deduction or (3) is a nondeductible, noncapitalizable expense of the partnership. You can understand all three parts of this results-oriented definition by thinking about the effects on the partnership's balance sheet. Asset basis increases the aggregate amount on the left side of the balance sheet, and an offsetting entry (here, a liability) must increase the right side in order to satisfy the accounting identity. Similarly, a deduction or a nondeductible expense depletes capital without affecting assets, so an addition to liabilities is needing to rebalance the books. In the present case, the partnership receives $25,000 in cash on issuance of the option, increasing its aggregate assets by that amount. It therefore books the option as a $25,000 liability. **Answer (a)** describes the nature of the option to Reynaldo, not the partnership. **Answer (c)** is incorrect. The option will never produce a deduction for the partnership, although it will produce income of $25,000 if Reynaldo allows it to lapse without exercise. **Answer (d)** correctly explains why the partnership does not recognize current income on the receipt of Reynaldo's option premium payment. Its conclusion regarding the partnership's balance sheet is, however, incorrect. Treatment of the option as a liability is consistent with the open-transaction analysis. *Reading Period: Topics 2.4 and 2.8.*

1.9 The correct Answer is (b). The first step is to determine the amount of gain allocated to each partner. Regardless of the section 704(c) method chosen by MOP-Up, it allocates $15,000 of its tax gain to Peter, the contributing partner. The remaining $12,000 of tax gain is allocated equally to each of the three partners, $4,000 apiece. The second step is to determine the character of this gain. Ordinarily, section 702(b) would determine character by reference to the partnership's relationship to the car. It seems clear that the partnership holds the car as a capital asset, because it does not fall into any of the exceptions of section 1221(a). Section 724(b) applies to this case, however, because (1) the car was inventory in Peter's hands at the time he contributed it and (2) the partnership sold the car within five years after the date of its contribution. Under the simple-but-brutal rule of section 724(b), all of the gain recognized by MOP-Up on this sale is treated as ordinary income. Therefore, all of the $4,000 of gain the partnership allocates to Oliver is ordinary income. **Answer (a)** is incorrect for a couple of reasons. First, it seems to be focused on Peter, the contributor, rather than Oliver. Even then, it misapplies section 724(b) by recharacterizing only the built-in gain of $15,000 as ordinary income, rather than all of the gain recognized by the partnership on the sale. **Answer (c)** corrects this mistake, but still focuses on Peter, not Oliver. **Answer (d)** properly focuses on Oliver, but reaches the sensible but incorrect conclusion that Oliver is not tarred by Peter's dealer status. *Reading Period: Topics 7.2 and 8.2.*

1.10 The correct Answer is (a). It's great that things worked out so well for Bareboat Charters, but there was not a strong likelihood that it would happen. This is simply not the type of "pre-wired" tax deal that is the focus of the substantiality tests. **Answer (b)** is incorrect, because the transitory presumption may be rebutted by a showing of facts that prove otherwise. **Answer (c)** is incorrect, because the value-equals-basis presumption is not needed to defend the substantiality of this allocation. **Answer (d)** is incorrect, because it misapplies the five-year presumption. This presumption is pro-taxpayer, in the sense that it can shield from challenge an allocation scheme that might otherwise be found to be insubstantial. Failure to satisfy the five-year presumption does not provide independent grounds for challenging the substantiality of an allocation. *Reading Period: Topic 4.3.*

Final Exam 2

2.1 The correct Answer is (d). At formation, a partner's outside basis equals the sum of her tax capital, her section 704(c)(1)(C) basis adjustment, if any, and her share of the partnership's liabilities. If the partner's outside basis equals her tax capital, both her 704(c)(1)(C) basis adjustment and her share of the partnership's liabilities must be zero. (Neither can be a negative number.) This will be the case when the partnership has no liabilities, but it may also be the case when the partnership has liabilities, but none are allocated to the partner in question. **Answer (a)** is therefore incorrect. **Answer (b)** is incorrect, because at formation, inside basis (including any section 704(c)(1)(C) basis adjustment) equals outside basis. The foregoing relationships are all in the tax accounts, not the book accounts. It is entirely possible for a book-tax disparity to exist in this partnership, but its existence will not be signaled by the equality of a partner's tax capital and outside basis. Thus, **Answer (c)** is also incorrect. *Reading Period: Topic 2.4.*

2.2 The correct Answer is (d). The debt is a qualified liability under Treas. Reg. § 1.707–5(a)(6), so this transaction does not involve a disguised sale. The Question requires application of the allocation rules for nonrecourse debt found in Treas. Reg. § 1.752–3. There is no first-tier allocation to Avery (or any other partner) on contribution, because the book value of the contributed asset ($75,000) exceeds the amount of the debt ($50,000) so that there is no minimum gain. The second-tier allocation to Avery is made easier by the fact that the partnership uses the traditional method. If the contributed asset were sold for the amount of the debt and no other consideration, Avery would be allocated $40,000 of tax gain. This is the second-tier allocation. (Notice that this allocation by itself ensures that Avery recognizes no taxable gain on the contribution.) Finally, Avery's third-tier allocation is 25% of the remaining $10,000 of nonrecourse debt, or $2,500. Her total allocation is thus $40,000 + $2,500 = $42,500. **Answer (a)** would be correct if this were a recourse liability, none of which would be allocated to Avery, a limited partner. **Answer (b)** is the right answer to a different question than the one asked—namely, what is Avery's outside basis? It is $10,000 − $50,000 + $42,500 = $2,500. **Answer (c)** results from forgetting about the second-tier allocation, and allocating the entire $50,000 nonrecourse liability under the third tier. ***Reading Period: Topics 2.5, 2.7, 5.3 and 5.4.***

2.3 The correct Answer is (a). Ordinarily, the tax treatment of a cash distribution is determined by comparing the amount of the distribution with the distributee-partner's outside basis immediately before the distribution. The interim cash payments made by this partnership, however, do not appear to be distributions, but instead "advances or drawings of money" that are covered by the special rule of Treas. Reg. § 1.731–1(a)(1)(ii). This conclusion would be clearer—because the interim payments would more clearly be "advances"—if Naomi and the other partners had agreed to return to the partnership any excess of the interim payments over the distributions to which they are entitled at the end of the year. The fact that they cannot take interim payments in excess of 70% of monthly taxable income probably makes this provision unnecessary, however, because it is unlikely that a repayment provision, if one existed, would ever have to be enforced. Under the drawings rule, Naomi is entitled to treat all of the interim payments as current distributions occurring on December 31, 2016—*i.e.*, after adding her $160,000 distributive share of the partnership's 2016 income to her initial outside basis of $50,000. **Answer (b)** would be the correct answer if the interim payments were not protected by the drawings rule and thus were treated as current distributions on the dates actually paid to Naomi. **Answer (c)** would be correct if the drawings rule did not apply and Naomi's initial outside basis were $0. **Answer (d)** reflects Naomi's distributive share of the partnership's 2016 income, not its cash distributions to her. ***Reading Period: Topic 9.1.***

2.4 The correct Answer is (a). The facts in this example pose the issue resolved by Rev. Proc. 2001–43, 2001–2 C.B. 191. The partnership has offered Mary a profits interest, the issuance of which causes her to recognize no income or gain under Rev. Proc. 93–27, 1993–2 C.B. 343. But what if the profits interest is unvested when issued? This raises the possibility that Mary will recognize compensation income upon vesting, at least if she does not make a section 83(b) election on issuance. Rev. Proc. 2001–43 put that concern to rest. Mary recognizes no income or gain on issuance or vesting, as long as the partnership treats her as a partner from the date of issuance of the profits interest, the partnership claims no deduction with respect to issuance or vesting, and the profits interest is not such that it can be readily valued (discussed below). A section 83(b) election is not needed to attain this result. **Answer (b)** articulates the fear that Rev. Proc. 2001–43 laid to rest. **Answer (c)** is incorrect, if Mary's profits interest cannot be readily valued, which according to Rev. Proc. 93–27 is the case so long as (1) the partnership does not generate a substantially certain and predictable stream of income, (2) Mary does not dispose of her profits interest within two years of receipt and (3) Buddy Bear Ltd is not a publicly traded partnership. **Answer (d)** is incorrect, because under Rev. Proc. 2001–43, Mary need not make a section 83(b) election to attain these results (although she can make one if she wants). *Reading Period: Topics 3.1 and 3.4.*

2.5 The correct Answer is (d). As a cash contributor, B would prefer a section 704(c) method that minimizes the possibility that she will incur book losses without corresponding tax losses. This would occur if the ceiling rule applied to any allocations from the mark-to-market or sale of the futures contracts that A contributed with built-in gains. The most reliable way to avoid the ceiling rule is to elect the remedial method. **Answer (a)** is more an avoidance strategy than an answer. The partnership will have to make this decision sooner or later, and waiting is unlikely to change the parties' preferences—indeed, it is likely to make them stronger. The choice of section 704(c) method is a matter of economic significance and, like all such matters, is best decided upfront. **Answer (b)** is incorrect. The traditional method, which includes the ceiling rule, is A's preference, but not B's. **Answer (c)** is better than **Answer (b)**, but not as good as **Answer (d)**. The ability of the partnership to make curative allocations hinges on the partnership's recognizing other gains or losses. While this seems likely, it is not certain. *Reading Period: Topic 8.2.*

2.6 The correct Answer is (d). Your first thought may be that you cannot answer this Question because you do not know how much of the partnership A owns. That fact is, however, unnecessary: section 267(a)(2) can apply regardless of the size of A's interest. That said, section 267(a)(2) does not disturb the mismatch of income and deduction in this particular case, because A's income precedes the partnership's deduction. The statute, whose only power is to defer deductions, cannot cure this mismatch. **Answer (a)** is incorrect for two reasons. First, it "flips" the accounting methods of the two parties; second, it fails to apply section 267(a)(2) to these misunderstood facts. **Answer (b)** erroneously assumes that section 267(a)(2) can accelerate the partnership's deduction to match A's income. **Answer (c)** misapplies the accrual method to A's income. *Reading Period: Topic 7.3.*

2.7 The correct Answer is (f). The partners desire to have a partnership by shares, in which all allocations are proportionate to their capital accounts. Under section 704(b)(2), if the partnership does not provide for allocations meeting the rules for substantial economic effect, allocations will be in accordance with the partners' respective interests in the partnership. This is precisely what the partners want. **Answers (a)**

through (e) are incorrect, because they are all more than this particularly simple partnership agreement needs. *Reading Period: Topic 4.3.*

2.8 **The correct Answer is (a).** The special allocation of depreciation to A lowers her capital-account balance disproportionately with her capital contribution, so that all of the partnership's allocations—even the "equal" allocations of items other than depreciation—are special allocations. In order to assure that these allocations are respected for tax purposes, you need to include proper capital accounting in the partnership agreement, as set forth in **Answer (a)**. As described in the statement of the facts of this Question, state law provides an unlimited deficit-restoration obligation, and there is no indication that the partners have modified the effect of state law by agreement. Thus, there is no need for the partnership agreement to include the provisions described in **Answer (b)** or **Answer (c)**. At this point, this partnership meets the safe harbor for economic effect set forth in Treas. Reg. § 1.704–1(b)(2)(ii)(*b*). There is no indication that substantiality is an issue, so we are done. **Answer (d)** is incorrect, because a qualified income offset is unnecessary if every partner has an unlimited deficit-restoration obligation. **Answer (e)** is incorrect, because this partnership has no nonrecourse deductions. **Answer (f)** is inconsistent with the foregoing analysis. *Reading Period: Topic 4.3.*

2.9 **The correct Answer is (b).** A's overall gain on the sale is $30,000. This is a capital gain under section 741, except to the extent provided by section 751(a). The partnership holds one section 751 asset, its depreciated inventory, which would produce a $30,000 loss if sold for its fair market value. (Are they sure they want to be in this business?) A's share of this ordinary loss is $10,000, so A recognizes a $10,000 ordinary loss on her sale. Her capital gain is that number which, when added to the $10,000 ordinary loss, yields an overall gain of $30,000. This number is $40,000. This capital gain is divided between A's share of the partnership's section 1250 capital gain (one-third of $3,000, or $1,000) and residual capital gain of $39,000. **Answer (a)** is incorrect, because it nets together A's $10,000 ordinary loss and her $1,000 share of section 1250 capital gain. This netting is impermissible, because section 1250 capital gain is not a section 751 asset. **Answer (c)** is incorrect, because it determines A's overall gain as her share of the gain the partnership would realize if it sold all of its assets for fair market value. A's gain is $10,000 more than this amount, because A sold her partnership interest for $10,000 more than her share of the aggregate value of the partnership's assets, reflecting goodwill or some other off-balance-sheet asset. **Answer (d)** correctly computes A's overall gain, but misstates her section 1250 capital gain as $10,000, her share of the appreciation in the plant, rather than $1,000, her share of past depreciation. *Reading Period: Topic 6.3.*

2.10 **The correct Answer is (b).** As a contributor of property with built-in gain, Partner A is potentially subject to the so-called "anti-mixing-bowl" rules of section 704(c)(1)(B) and section 737. As a cash contributor, Partner D is not. This simplifies the analysis of this Question. On the distribution of Property A in 2019, section 704(c)(1)(B) requires Partner A to recognize the amount of her built-in gain, or $160,000. The ordinary rules for property distributions apply to Partner D, who recognizes no gain. **Answer (a)** is incorrect, because Partner A must recognize gain in this case. **Answer (c)** is incorrect, because Partner D does not. **Answer (d)** is almost right, but it requires Partner A to recognize the full amount of the gain present in Property A at the time of the distribution. The anti-mixing-bowl statutes reach only the forward layer of gain, which in this case is $160,000. *Reading Period: Topic 9.4.*

Final Exam 3

3.1 The correct Answer is (c). This Question is only partly about the holding-period rules found in section 1223. More fundamentally, it is about the tax treatment of the contributions. Under section 721(b), gain but not loss is recognized on transfers of property to a partnership that would be an investment company under section 351(e)(1) if it were incorporated. Applying the rules of that section and Treas. Reg. § 1.351–1(c), the Facebook and Herbalife common shares are listed assets. So is the cash, even taking into account the plans of the partnership to spend it, because it will be used to acquire a different sort of listed asset, the shares of a mutual fund. Accordingly, 100% of the assets of the partnership are listed and it is an investment partnership for purposes of section 721(b). Section 1223(1) provides that a partner may include ("tack") her holding period for the property contributed to her holding period for her partnership interest, provided that (1) she held the contributed property as a capital asset and (2) her basis in the partnership interest is determined, wholly or partly, by her basis in the contributed property. Here, both B and C meet the first test. But after applying section 721(b), only C meets the second test. So, both A's and B's holding periods for their partnership interests begin the day after acquisition. Rev. Rul. 66–7, 1966–1 C.B. 188. C, whose contribution is governed by section 721(a) not section 721(b), takes an exchanged basis and a tacked holding period for her partnership interest. **Answer (a)** is incorrect, because it assumes full nonrecognition under section 721(a). **Answer (b)** is incorrect, because it assumes recognition of loss by C but not of gain by B—a nifty answer, but unattainable. **Answer (d)** is incorrect, because it assumes full recognition of both gain and loss. *Reading Period: Topic 2.1.*

3.2 The correct Answer is (d). A revaluation of all the partnership's assets (a "general revaluation") is permitted only in the circumstances identified in Treas. Reg. § 1.704–1(b)(2)(iv)(*f*)(5). These include the admittance of a new partner or the liquidation of the interest of an existing partner. **Answer (a)** is incorrect, however, because general revaluations are not usually *required* in these cases. The revaluation generally creates book-tax disparities in the assets of the partnership and in the partners' capital accounts. These disparities are called "reverse section 704(c) layers" and are allocated according to the rules of section 704(c). **Answer (b)** is incorrect, because revaluations create the need to make reverse section 704(c) allocations, not the other way around. **Answer (c)** is incorrect for essentially the same reason: revaluations create book-tax disparities, they do not eliminate them. If a partnership fails to make a general revaluation in

circumstances where one is permitted, the IRS may look into whether value
is thereby shifted from one partner or group of partners to another and, if so,
whether this shift of value should be characterized as income. Treas. Reg.
§ 1.704–1(b)(2)(*f*) (flush language). ***Reading Period: Topic 2.6.***

3.3 The correct Answer is (b). Immediately before the liquidating
distribution, C's basis in her partnership interest is $90,000, consisting of her
tax capital ($40,000) and her share of the partnership's debt ($50,000). C
receives a deemed cash distribution of $50,000 under section 752(b), reducing
her basis to $40,000, which is the basis she takes in Lot 1 under section
732(b). Upon the sale of Lot 1, C therefore recognizes $25,000 of gain.

The character of this gain is governed by section 735(a)(2), which
provides that C's gain is ordinary if (1) the partnership held Lot 1 as an
"inventory item" within the meaning of section 751(d) and (2) C sold Lot 1
within five years of the date of the distribution. Both conditions are satisfied
here. (Although Lot 1, being real estate, is not properly classified as
inventory, it is property held for sale to customers in the ordinary course of
business, which is an inventory item within the meaning of section 751(d),
which controls here.) Therefore, C recognizes $25,000 of ordinary income on
the sale.

Answer (a) is incorrect, because it miscalculates C's gain by giving C an
adjusted basis in the distributed land of $50,000 (the partnership's former
inside basis) rather than $40,000 (C's former outside basis). **Answer (c)** also
miscalculates C's gain—in this case, by failing to reduce C's initial outside
basis by the deemed $50,000 cash distribution under section 752(b). **Answer
(d)** attempts to apply an approach that would split C's gain into an ordinary
component and a capital gain component. This is not permitted by section
735(b). ***Reading Period: Topics 7.2 and 9.1.***

3.4 The correct Answer is (b). Partner X has an initial outside basis
of $100,000, which is reduced by the $20,000 cash distribution to $80,000.
Under section 732(b), this becomes her tax basis in the distributed
properties. Following the methodology of section 732(c), you must first assign
a tentative basis to each of the distributed properties equal to their prior
basis in the hands of the partnership. The required "decrease" in tax basis is
equal to the excess of the sum of these tentative bases ($200,000) over
Partner X's outside basis ($80,000), or $120,000. It is allocated first to
Property C in an amount equal to its depreciation in value and then among
all of the properties in proportion to their adjusted bases, as follows:

	Initial Basis	Decrease	Adj. Basis	Decrease	Final Basis
Property A	$ 60,000		$ 60,000	$ 33,333	$26,667
Property B	40,000		40,000	22,222	17,778
Property C	100,000	$20,000	80,000	44,444	35,556
TOTALS	$200,000	$20,000	$180,000	$100,000	$80,000

Answer (a) is incorrect. It treats the allocation of the first $20,000 of
"decrease" to Property C as a reduction of the remaining outside basis of

Partner X from $80,000 to $60,000, which amount is then allocated among the three distributed properties in proportion to their adjusted bases. **Answer (c)** is incorrect. It allocates the required "decrease" in accordance with the relative fair market values of the three properties. **Answer (d)** is also incorrect. It fails to reduce Partner X's outside basis by the $20,000 of cash distributed before allocating the remaining basis among the distributed properties, resulting in a required "decrease" of $100,000 rather than $120,000.

It is possible, by the way, to get the correct answer to this Question by accident. If you first reduced the outside basis of Partner X by the $20,000 cash distribution to $80,000 and then divided that remaining basis equally among the three properties, your serendipitous calculation of the basis for Property X would yield $26,667. Of course, you would get the same basis for the other two properties, which would be incorrect. *Reading Period: Topic 9.1.*

3.5 The correct Answer is (a). The amount of Nell's loss is capped at $1,000, her cash investment, by section 83(b)(1) (last sentence) and Treas. Reg. § 1.83–2(a). (Treasury regulations proposed in 2005 would, if finalized, require the partnership to make a "forfeiture allocation" of gross deduction and loss to Nell in the amount of $20,000 (to the extent that such amount is available to the partnership), but forfeiture allocations are neither required nor permitted under current law. Prop. Treas. Reg. § 1.704–1(b)(4)(xii).) **Answer (b)** is incorrect, because it allows Nell to deduct the net amount she included in income on account of making the election, which is not allowed by current or proposed law. **Answer (c)** is worse, because it adds to the amount in **Answer (b)** the amount of the forfeiture allocation under the proposed regulations. **Answer (d)** is also incorrect; it adds to the amount in **Answer (c)** the $1,000 deduction that actually is available in this case. *Reading Period: Topic 3.4.*

3.6 The correct Answer is (d). Upon constructive liquidation, the partnership recognizes a loss of $90,000 on the sale of all of its assets for $0. It must allocate this loss among its partners. The partnership agreement meets all of the requirements for the safe harbor for economic effect and there are no facts to suggest that substantiality is an issue. Therefore, the $90,000 loss is allocated $36,000 (40%) to each of A and B and $18,000 (20%) to C. After this allocation, the balance sheet appears as follows:

Assets			Liabilities		
	Tax	**Book**		**Tax**	**Book**
Building	$0	$0	Recourse Debt	$ 60,000	$ 60,000
			Capital		
			A	(26,000)	(26,000)
			B	(26,000)	(26,000)
			C	(8,000)	(8,000)
Total Assets	$0	$0	**Total Liabilities and Capital**	$ 0	$ 0

The $60,000 recourse debt is shared in the proportions shown by these negative capital accounts. Adding the partners' initial capital contributions ($10,000 each) to these debt shares yields the partners' initial bases in their partnership interests. **Answer (a)** is incorrect, because it allocates 100% of the recourse liability to C, the general partner. This answer would be correct if the limited partners, A and B, did not have deficit-restoration obligations. **Answer (b)** neglects to include the partners' capital contributions in their outside bases. **Answer (c)** allocates the recourse debt by applying the loss-sharing ratio (40:40:20) directly to the $60,000 amount of the debt, rather than employing the constructive-liquidation analysis, which is necessary in this case because the loss-sharing ratio is not the same as the ratio of the capital contributions. *Reading Period: Topic 5.3.*

3.7 The correct Answer is (c). It appears that the total value of the partnership's assets is $81,000, so giving a one-third partner an asset with a value of $27,000 in liquidation of her interest makes economic sense. Under section 732(b), Partner P takes a basis in Property X equal to her outside basis, which is $30,000. This is $3,000 more than the partnership's basis, occasioning a $3,000 negative adjustment under section 734(b)(2)(B). **Answer (a)** is incorrect, because an adjustment is required by the presence of the section 754 election. **Answer (b)** is incorrect, because it has the wrong sign. When the basis of distributed property increases in the hands of the distributee-partner, the proper adjustment is negative, not positive. **Answer (d)** is incorrect, because it miscalculates the amount of the adjustment. A $9,000 negative adjustment would eliminate the loss in Property Y, which might seem like a good thing. Including the partnership's $12,000 of cash, however, this would cause inside basis to fall short of the remaining outside basis by $6,000, which would not be a good thing, because it would deprive

ANSWERS TO FINAL EXAM QUESTIONS

Partner Q and Partner R of their shares of the built-in loss in Property Y that existed before the distribution. ***Reading Period: Topics 9.1 and 9.2.***

3.8 The correct Answer is (b). The debt is a qualified liability under Treas. Reg. § 1.707–5(a)(6), so this transaction does not involve a disguised sale. The Question requires the determination of Karen's outside basis, which begins with her basis in the contributed land ($350,000). This is reduced by the net of (1) the deemed distribution to her under section 752(b) resulting from the partnership's assumption of her individual liability under the recourse mortgage loan and (2) the deemed contribution under section 752(a) resulting from her share of that loan as a partner. The former amount is $400,000. The latter amount is, regrettably, zero, because Karen is a limited partner and this is a recourse liability. Thus, her initial outside basis is $350,000 and must be reduced by a net deemed distribution of $400,000. So why isn't **Answer (a)** correct? Rather than creating a negative outside basis, this deemed distribution causes Karen to recognize $50,000 of gain, which increases her basis to zero. **Answer (c)** allocates to Karen her proportionate share (25%) of the mortgage liability. This would be correct if this were a general partnership, but it is not. **Answer (d)** recognizes that Karen is a limited partner, but allocates the liability under the rules applicable to nonrecourse debt, giving Karen $50,000 under the second tier and $87,500 under the third tier. ***Reading Period: Topics 2.5, 2.7, 5.3 and 5.4.***

3.9 The correct Answer is (a). On its sale of the equipment, the partnership recognizes a book loss of $15,000, which under the partnership agreement it allocates equally among its three partners. It recognizes a tax gain of $35,000, which under section 704(c) it allocates entirely to Aristide, the contributing partner for the equipment. Because the partnership uses the traditional method, it can do no more. It cannot allocate tax losses to Balthazar and Caspar, the noncontributing partners, equal to the book losses allocated to them, because of the ceiling rule. As a result, all partners have book-tax differences remaining in their capital accounts:

	Aristide		Balthazar		Caspar	
	Tax	**Book**	**Tax**	**Book**	**Tax**	**Book**
Initial	$150,000	$200,000	$200,000	$200,000	200,000	$200,000
Land sale	35,000	(5,000)	0	(5,000)	0	(5,000)
Ending	$185,000	$195,000	$200,000	$195,000	$200,000	$195,000

Answer (b) represents the remedial allocation that the partnership would make to Caspar (and Balthazar), if it had chosen to employ the remedial method. **Answer (c)** is the allocation of tax gain that the partnership makes to Aristide, not its allocation to Caspar. **Answer (d)** reflects the entire built-in gain on the equipment when it was contributed. It would not be appropriate for the partnership to allocate this amount of tax gain to anyone, even Aristide, because all partners, including Aristide, have suffered a $5,000 book loss. If the partnership used the remedial method, it would make a remedial allocation of $10,000 tax gain to Aristide, bringing his total allocation of gain to $45,000. ***Reading Period: Topics 8.1 and 8.2.***

3.10 The correct Answer is (b). On its contribution, the wardrobe of period costumes is a built-in loss property. This brings section 704(c)(1)(C) into play. Under proposed Treasury regulations, the partnership takes a tax basis in the wardrobe equal to its fair market value, and Balthazar, the contributing partner, has a $50,000 section 704(c)(1)(C) basis adjustment, which is equal to the amount of the built-in loss in the costumes at the time of the contribution and is personal to Balthazar alone. Thus, the partnership's tax basis in the costume wardrobe equals its book value of $200,000. When the partnership sells the wardrobe, it recognizes a book gain and tax gain of $15,000. It allocates $5,000 of book gain and $5,000 of tax gain to each of the three partners. In addition, Balthazar is entitled to write off his $50,000 section 704(c)(1)(C) basis adjustment, resulting in a net loss realized of $45,000 for Balthazar. **Answer (a)** would be the correct response if section 704(c)(1)(A) applied, as it did in Question 3.9, because the ceiling rule would prevent any allocation of tax gain to the noncontributing partners. **Answer (c)** is the net tax loss realized by Balthazar and **Answer (d)** is the loss occasioned by the use of Balthazar's section 704(c)(1)(C) basis adjustment. Neither of these has anything to do with Caspar. ***Reading Period: Topics 8.2 and 8.4.***

Final Exam 4

4.1 The correct Answer is (d). This Question encourages you to dive straightaway into the complex loss-deferral rules of section 267 and 707(b). Don't fall for it! Consider the ownership structure. Corp X owns all of Upper LLC, which together with Corp X owns all of Lower LLC. But because Upper LLC is a limited liability company, its default classification is disregarded entity. That means that Lower LLC has only one owner for tax purposes, Corp X, and thus Lower LLC is also a disregarded entity. Accordingly, when Lower LLC sells property to Corp X, for federal income tax purposes, Corp X is "selling" property to itself—a tax non-event. **Answers (a), (b) and (c)** are incorrect, because they treat Corp X and Lower LLC as separate tax entities. ***Reading Period: Topic 1.3.***

4.2 The correct Answer is (b). D's outside basis consists of her cash purchase price of $200,000 and her share of the partnership's debt which, depending on facts that are not stated in the Question, could be anywhere from $0 to $300,000. No matter—on liquidation, D receives a deemed cash distribution under section 752(b) in the same (unknown) amount, so you can safely ignore it in this case. The remainder of the liquidating distribution consists of $170,000 in cash and receivables with an inside basis of $0. This results in a loss under section 731(a)(2), which is a capital loss under section 741. Section 751(b) does not apply, because D receives exactly her share of the partnership's sole section 751(b) asset. **Answer (a)** is incorrect, because it allocates D's $30,000 remaining outside basis to the distributed receivables, which is not allowed by section 732(c)(1)(A). **Answer (c)** justifies giving D a $30,000 basis in the receivables by causing her to recognize an additional $30,000 capital loss. Here, as in grade school, two wrongs do not make a right. **Answer (d)** starts with the incorrect outside basis for D, using her tax capital of $60,000 rather than her purchase price of $200,000. *Reading Period: Topics 9.1 and 9.6.*

4.3 The correct Answer is (b). Section 721(a) applies to Ted's transfer of property to exercise this noncompensatory option, but not to his transfer of property to acquire the option. Treas. Reg. §§ 1.721–2(a), –2(b). **Answer (a)** is incorrect, because it applies nonrecognition treatment to both transfers. **Answer (c)** is incorrect, because it applies nonrecognition treatment to the wrong transfer. **Answer (d)** is incorrect, because it applies nonrecognition treatment to neither transfer. *Reading Period: Topic 2.8.*

4.4 The correct Answer is (d). This Question is substantially easier than it may look. Albany may be right that the loan agreement does not by its terms limit her personal liability, but as a member of a limited liability company she has that protection under state law, as do Brooklyn and Charlotte. The $90,000 loan is a nonrecourse loan for purposes of section 752, allocated equally to them under the third-tier allocation of Treas. Reg. § 1.752–3(a)(3). **Answer (a)** is incorrect. Although no partner has economic risk of loss, each is entitled to a share of the partnership's debt under the rules applicable to nonrecourse liabilities. **Answers (b) and (c)** are incorrect, because they give effect to one or both of the indemnifications. Because, however, no partner has any liability for the partnership's debt, the indemnifications will never be called upon. *Reading Period: Topic 5.5.*

4.5 The correct Answer is (f). The partners desire to have a partnership by shares, in which all allocations are proportionate to their capital accounts. Under section 704(b)(2), if the partnership does not provide for allocations meeting the rules for substantial economic effect, then the allocations will be in accordance with the partners' respective interests in the partnership. Further, if the partnership agreement fails to provide for allocations of nonrecourse deductions meeting the safe harbor of Treas. Reg. § 1.704–2(e), then the allocations of such deductions must be made in accordance with the partners' interests. In both cases, this is precisely what the partners want. **Answers (a) through (e)** are incorrect, because they are all more than required. *Reading Period: Topic 4.4.*

4.6 The correct Answers are (a), (b) and (e). Neither the allocations funded by partner capital nor those funded by nonrecourse debt will be in accordance with the partners' overall interests in the partnership in this case, so as the drafter you have no choice but to bring out the full dreadnought battleship of partnership allocation provisions. (You may decide instead to employ so-called "targeted allocations," but they do not provide the same level of assurance regarding the tax consequences as allocations meeting the safe-harbor requirements of the Treasury regulations.) Proper capital accounting (**Answer (a)**) is a must. A's capital account can be expected to reach zero before those of the other two partners. State law will impose a deficit-restoration obligation on A to the extent that the deficit balance in her capital account exceeds the aggregate positive balances in the capital accounts of the other partners. In order to qualify for the safe harbors, it is necessary to bridge this gap. The limited obligation described in **Answer (b)**, combined with state law, gives A in effect an unlimited deficit-restoration obligation. This qualifies the partnership's allocations under the safe harbor of Treas. Reg. § 1.704–1(b)(2)(ii)(*b*) (economic effect). The addition of a minimum gain chargeback (**Answer (e)**) qualifies the partnership's allocations under the safe harbor of Treas. Reg. § 1.704–2(e) (nonrecourse deductions). **Answer (c)** is incorrect, because state law creates an unlimited deficit-restoration obligation, as described above. **Answer (d)** is incorrect, because a qualified income offset is unnecessary if there is such an obligation. **Answer (f)** is inconsistent with the foregoing analysis. *Reading Period: Topic 4.4.*

4.7 The correct Answer is (c). Distributions of property (as opposed to distributions of money) are often tax-free. Watch out, however, whenever property has been contributed to the partnership within the seven years prior to the distribution, either by the distributee-partner or by someone else. In the present case, both Bill and Wayne recognize gain under the "anti-mixing-bowl" statutes, Bill under section 737(a) and Wayne under section 704(c)(1)(B). Upon the distribution of Whiteacre, Wayne, the partner who contributed that property, recognizes an amount of gain equal to his forward section 704(c) layer in Whiteacre. This amount is the excess of the book value of Whiteacre ($150,000) over its tax basis ($125,000), or $25,000.

Bill, the distributee-partner, recognizes gain under section 737(a) equal to the lesser of his "excess distribution" or his "net precontribution gain." Bill's excess distribution is the excess of the fair market value of Whiteacre on the date of distribution ($300,000) over Bill's outside basis ($100,000), or $200,000. *See* Treas. Reg. § 1.737–1(b). Bill's net precontribution gain is the amount of gain that he would have recognized under section 704(c)(1)(B) if the partnership had distributed Blackacre to a partner other than Bill ($500,000). *See* Treas. Reg. § 1.737–1(c). The lesser of these two is $200,000, which is the amount of gain Bill is required to recognize.

Answer (a) is incorrect. It applies the ordinary rules for property distributions, without taking the anti-mixing-bowl statutes into account. **Answer (b)** goes to the opposite extreme, requiring Bill and Wayne to recognize the full amount of the gains inherent in Blackacre and Whiteacre, respectively. **Answer (d)** requires Bill to take into account his net precontribution gain in Blackacre under section 737(a), rather than limiting the gain pick-up to his excess distribution. *Reading Period: Topic 9.4.*

4.8 The correct Answer is (a). Even though Neil does not actually file a section 83(b) election, both he and the partnership consistently behave as though he has, by treating Neil as the owner of the interest from the date of its grant and allocating to him his share of the partnership's profits. In these circumstances, Rev. Proc. 2001–43, 2001–2 C.B. 191, effectively deems such an election to have been made. In this case, the IRS will not require Neil to recognize compensation income on either the grant or the vesting of his interest in the partnership. **Answers (b), (c) and (d)** all treat the vesting of

Neil's interest as a taxable event, so all are incorrect. ***Reading Period: Topic 3.4.***

4.9 The correct Answer is (b). The place to start the analysis of a liquidating distribution to a partner in a service partnership (*i.e.*, one for which capital is not a material income-producing factor) is section 736. Like many tax statutes, this one is best read from the bottom up. Consider first whether this distribution is described in section 736(b)(3). The only question here is whether a distribution to a retiring partner from Big Law LLP should be considered to be a distribution to a "general partner" in light of the limitations on partner liability provided by the state statutes applicable to limited liability partnerships. Although not entirely free from doubt, the fact that the retiring partner would have provided primarily services, not capital, in exchange for her interest in the partnership should qualify her as a "general partner" within the meaning of section 736(b)(3). Thus, this distribution should be covered by the rules applicable to distributions from service partnerships to their general partners.

Next, divide the liquidating distribution between the amount paid for the retiring partner's interest in the partnership's assets (the section 736(b) amount) and the excess distribution (the section 736(a) amount). Because the exclusion under section 736(b)(3) does not apply, section 736(b)(2) does apply and provides that the amount the partnership pays with respect to the retiring partner's share of its unrealized receivables must be considered to be a section 736(a) amount. The annual post-retirement payments made by Big Law LLP are subject to this special rule. Because they are fixed in amount, they are treated by section 736(a)(2) as guaranteed payments. As such, they will be taxed as ordinary income to the recipient in the years that they are paid.

Answer (a) is incorrect, because the deferred payments described in this Question are fixed, not dependent on the partnership's income in any year. **Answer (c)** is incorrect, because the recipient of a guaranteed payment includes it in income for the tax year within or with which ends the tax year of the partnership in which it deducts the payment according to its method of tax accounting. Treas. Reg. § 1.707–1(c). As a cash-method taxpayer, Big Law LLP will deduct these guaranteed payments in the years the payments are made, and the retiring partner will include them as ordinary income in the same years. **Answer (d)** would be the correct answer if section 736(b)(3) applied in this case—that is, if Big Law LLP were a capital-intensive partnership or if its partners were not considered for this purpose to be general partners. ***Reading Period: Topics 3.5 and 9.8.***

4.10 The correct Answer is (c). The default classification of each of these three entities is partnership, because each is a domestic, eligible business entity which has more than one owner. This Question requires you to apply the rules of Treas. Reg. § 1.708–1(b)(2) to these tiered partnerships. The seventh sentence of that regulation provides that the partnership interest issued in exchange for a contribution of property is not considered to have been sold or exchanged for purposes of section 708(b)(1)(B). Thus,

AcquisitionCo's $4 million contribution does not result in the termination of Topco, even though AcquisitionCo acquires a 60% interest in Topco by making this contribution. Further, because Topco does not terminate, it is not treated as selling or exchanging any of its 85% interest in Subco, so the latter partnership does not terminate either. *See* Treas. Reg. § 1.708–1(b)(2) (fifth sentence). **Answer (a)** is incorrect, because it treats the contribution to Topco as a sale or exchange and also because it applies an "aggregate" rather than an "entity" approach in analyzing the extent to which an ownership change in an upper-tier partnership should be taken into account in determining the change in ownership of a lower-tier partnership. **Answer (b)** makes only the former error. It correctly applies an "entity" approach to the tiers question. **Answer (d)** also makes the mistake of treating the contribution to Topco as a sale or exchange of an interest in Topco. *Reading Period: Topics 1.2, 1.3 and 10.1.*

Final Exam 5

5.1 The correct Answer is (a). The accrual of the payable creates a $10,000 deduction for this partnership. For this reason, the payable is a "liability" under Treas. Reg. § 1.752–1(a)(4)(i)(B). The accrual does not affect the inside basis of the partnership's assets, but it has two offsetting effects on the aggregate outside basis of the partners, increasing it by $10,000 under section 752(a) and decreasing it by $10,000 under section 705(a)(2)(A). **Answer (b)** is incorrect, because the accrual of a liability does not increase the basis of the partnership's assets. **Answer (c)** is incorrect, because the lack of change in outside basis is actually due to two equal but opposite adjustments. **Answer (d)** is incorrect, because the partnership can deduct the amount of this payable as an accrual taxpayer. **Answer (d)** is "the worst" answer to this Question, because it is the only one that suggests unequal effects on aggregate inside basis, on the one hand, and aggregate outside basis, on the other—precisely the divergence that sections 705 and 752 seek to avoid. *Reading Period: Topics 5.2 and 5.3.*

5.2 The correct Answer is (b). The debt is a qualified liability under Treas. Reg. § 1.707–5(a)(6), so this transaction does not involve a disguised sale. Jon will recognize gain if the net liability assumed exceeds his basis in the property contributed. The liability must first be "bifurcated" into a $30,000 recourse debt, all of which is allocated to Paula on account of her guarantee, and a $150,000 nonrecourse debt. There is no need for Paula to waive subrogation on this guarantee, because the debt is nonrecourse, so she would have no right to proceed against the other partners in any event. Under section 752(a), Jon's continuing share of the $150,000 nonrecourse debt is $100,000, consisting of (1) zero in the first tier, (2) $75,000 in the second tier ($150,000—$75,000) and (3) $25,000 in the third tier (one-third of the remaining $75,000 of nonrecourse debt). Thus, the net liability assumed is $80,000 ($180,000—$100,000), which exceeds Jon's basis in the contributed property by $5,000. **Answer (a)** is incorrect, although it represents the result that one would usually expect when a partner contributes an asset encumbered by a nonrecourse liability. Ordinarily, the allocation in the second tier would completely shelter Jon from gain. It fails him here because of Paula's $30,000 guarantee, which reduces the amount of the debt allocated under the nonrecourse rules from $180,000 to $150,000. **Answer (c)** is what you get if you properly bifurcate the debt into recourse and nonrecourse pieces, but then ignore the second tier in allocating the nonrecourse portion. **Answer (d)** is the result if you allocate only the $30,000 recourse portion to Jon, although why you would do that is beyond me. *Reading Period: Topics 2.5, 2.7, 5.3 and 5.4.*

5.3 The correct Answer is (b). The tax capital of A following the contribution of Property X is $18,000, which is the adjusted basis of Property X less the $12,000 nonrecourse debt assumed by the partnership. The tax capital of B following the contribution of Property Y is also $18,000. The net value of the assets of the partnership is $36,000, so the one-third capital interest that C receives in exchange for services is worth $12,000. The facts tell us (unsurprisingly) that this amount is currently deductible by the partnership, which deduction should be allocated to A and B, not C. This creates a taxable capital shift of $12,000 to C, $6,000 from A and $6,000 from B. Consequently, the tax capital of all three partners is $12,000. There is no first-tier or second-tier allocation of the nonrecourse debt to which Property X is subject. The entire $54,000 of recourse and nonrecourse debt is split equally among the partners, $18,000 each. All have an outside basis equal to tax capital ($12,000) plus liability share ($18,000), or $30,000. **Answer (a)** is incorrect, because it does not allocate any of the debt to C. **Answer (c)** makes the same mistake and also gives C no tax capital. **Answer (d)** allocates the correct amount of debt to C, but does not shift any tax capital to her. *Reading Period: Topics 2.5, 3.1, 3.2, 5.3 and 5.4.*

5.4 The correct Answer is (d). C's interest in the partnership is subject to a substantial risk of forfeiture. She is not considered a partner until her interest is vested. Treas. Reg. § 1.83–1(a)(1) ("Until such property becomes substantially vested, the transferor shall be regarded as the owner of such property."). A's tax capital following the contribution of Property X is $18,000; B's tax capital following the contribution of Property Y is also $18,000. The outside basis of each includes their respective one-half shares of the partnership's total liabilities of $54,000. **Answer (a)** is incorrect, because it does not take into account any adjustments under section 752. **Answers (b) and (c)** are incorrect, because they treat C as a vested partner. *Reading Period: Topics 2.5, 3.1, 3.5, 5.3 and 5.4.*

5.5 The correct Answer is (a). Section 751(b) assets include unrealized receivables and substantially appreciated inventory items. Tasty Bakery's accounts receivable are not unrealized and in fact have an adjusted basis that is higher than their fair market value. The partnership does, however, have an unrealized receivable: the recapture on its equipment, which is treated for this purpose as a separate asset with a value of $10,000 and a tax basis of zero. Treas. Reg. §§ 1.751–1(c)(4)(iii), –1(c)(5). To determine whether Tasty Bakery's inventory items are substantially appreciated, you must aggregate the items described in sections 751(d)(1), (d)(2) and (d)(3). This includes the recapture, the accounts receivable and the inventory. The aggregate value of these items is $135,000 and their aggregate tax basis is

$130,000, so the inventory items are not substantially appreciated. Section 1250 capital gain, although similar in some respects to recapture, is not an unrealized receivable within the meaning of section 751(c) or otherwise captured by section 751. **Answers (b)** and **(c)** are incorrect, because Tasty Bakery's inventory items in the aggregate are not substantially appreciated. **Answer (d)** is incorrect for the additional reason that it includes section 1250 capital gain in the calculation. *Reading Period: Topic 9.6.*

5.6 The correct Answer is (b). Law Firm's majority interest taxable year is the calendar year, both before and after the admission of the new partner. In order to establish its existing October year-end, it must have made an election under section 444(b)(1). There is no reason that Law Firm cannot make a new election, but it will be governed by section 444(b)(2), which will limit the new year to one that entails no greater deferral than the existing year. Therefore, Law Firm's choices will be limited to taxable years ending November 31 or December 31. **Answer (a)** is incorrect, because it does not take into account this further limitation on the section 444 election. **Answer (c)** is incorrect for the same reason. September 30 is the taxable year of Law Firm's only "principal partner." Because Law Firm has a majority interest taxable year, however, the all-principal-partners rule of section 706(b)(1)(B)(ii) never comes into play. **Answer (d)** is incorrect, because section 444 allows the election of a taxable year other than the required taxable year without any showing of business purpose. *Reading Period: Topic 4.2.*

5.7 The correct Answer is (a). This liquidating distribution involves both a reduction in C's share of the partnership's liabilities, from $22,500 to $0, and an increase in C's individual liabilities by reason of the assumption of a partnership liability in the amount of $90,000. Under Treas. Reg. § 1.752–1(f), these two should be netted, resulting in a net deemed cash contribution and increase in outside basis equal to $67,500. Adding this to C's initial outside basis of $15,000 yields $82,500. Subtracting the cash distribution of $20,000 from that amount leaves a remaining outside basis of $62,500, which becomes C's basis in the distributed building under section 732(b). **Answer (b)** makes the all-too-easy mistake of forgetting the $22,500 deemed cash distribution under section 752(b). **Answer (c)** forgets about section 752 completely. **Answer (d)** remembers the section 752(b) deemed distribution, but neglects the section 752(a) deemed contribution. *Reading Period: Topics 2.4 and 9.1.*

5.8 The correct Answer is (b). This Question is far simpler than it may seem. It just requires triage. Note that Bud sells only one-half of his interest in Can o' Corn. Because he is selling less than his entire interest, the partnership's tax year does not close as to him on the date of the sale. Section 706(c)(2)(B). There is no pass-through of partnership income to him at that time. Instead, the income attributable to the transferred interest, for the period prior to the transfer, and the income attributable to the retained interest, for the entire year, passes through to Bud at the end of the partnership's regular tax year, which is September 30, 2017. The only income that passes through to Bud in his tax year ending December 31, 2016 is his share of the partnership's income for its tax year ending September 30, 2016. That amount is 20% of $96,000, or $19,200.

Answer (a) is incorrect for at least two reasons. It closes the partnership's tax year as to Bud on the date of the sale of one-half of his interest, contrary to section 706(c)(2)(B). It also forgets entirely about the partnership's income from its tax year ending September 30, 2016. **Answer (d)** makes only the first of these two errors. **Answer (c)** also closes the partnership's tax year on the date of sale, but only as to the 10% interest sold. Though an intriguing approach, this is not the law. ***Reading Period: Topics 4.2 and 6.2.***

5.9 The correct Answer is (a). This Question requires you to apply three provisions, section 704(b) and section 704(c)(1)(A), which govern the allocation of the partnership's gain on the sale of the three houses, and section 724(b), which determines its character. The partnership realizes $100,000 of book gain on the sale, which is allocated in accordance with the partnership agreement and section 704(b). The partnership agreement provides that this gain is to be allocated equally among the four partners and there is nothing in the facts to suggest that this allocation does not have substantial economic effect within the meaning of section 704(b). Accordingly, the partnership allocates $25,000 of the book gain to B. The partnership realizes $280,000 of tax gain on this sale. As one of the noncontributing partners (with respect to the houses sold), B should be allocated tax gain equal to book gain. Thus, the partnership allocates $25,000 of tax gain to B.

Prior to their sale, the partnership seems to have held the three houses as capital assets. They were not held for sale in the ordinary course of the partnership's business, nor were they held as rental properties. Under the general principle of section 702(b), one would therefore expect that the partnership's gain on sale would be capital gain, and gain of this character would be allocated to B. Section 724(b) changes this answer. Because D, the contributing partner, held the houses for sale in the ordinary course of business, and the partnership sold them within five years of contribution, section 724(b) requires that all of the gain realized by the partnership be treated as ordinary income. This is particularly unfortunate for B and the other noncontributing partners, because none of them is a dealer in this property.

Real estate is not "inventory" for federal tax purposes. *See Homes by Ayres v. Commissioner*, 48 T.C.M. (CCH) 1050 (1984), *aff'd*, 795 F.2d 832 (9th Cir. 1986). Therefore, one might wonder why section 724(b) applies in this case, because that section applies only to property that was an "inventory item" in the contributor's hands. The answer is found in section 724(d)(2), which defines this term to include any property which is an inventory item within the meaning of section 751(d). This includes any property which, on sale, would be considered property other than a capital asset or 1231 property. The houses, which D held for sale in the ordinary course of her business as a builder/dealer of single-family homes, fits this description.

Answer (b) applies section 704(b) and section 704(c) correctly, but fails to apply section 724(b). **Answer (c)** is the correct answer for D, not for B. **Answer (d)** fails to apply section 704(c)(1)(A) and simply divides the tax gain equally among the partners, giving capital treatment to the post-contribution appreciation. *Reading Period: Topics 7.2 and 8.1.*

5.10 The correct Answer is (a). Section 751(b) does not apply to this distribution because the partnership's inventory is not substantially appreciated. The distribution of $15,000 of cash to Y reduces her outside basis to $180,000, and this becomes her tax basis in Capital Asset 4 under section 732(b). Because this is $50,000 greater than the partnership's inside basis in Capital Asset 4, the partnership suffers a negative adjustment in that amount under section 734(b)(2)(B). Treas. Reg. § 1.755–1(c)(1)(i) requires that this adjustment be allocated only to assets of the same "class" as Capital Asset 4, meaning capital gain property. Treas. Reg. § 1.755–1(c)(2)(ii) requires that a negative adjustment be allocated, first, to properties in the appropriate class that are depreciated in value, up to the amount of their depreciation. Only two properties fit that description in this case, Capital Asset 2 and Capital Asset 3. The allocation is as follows:

	(1) Initial Basis	(2) Depreciation	(3) Share of Depreciation	(4) Share of Adjustment	(5) Final Basis
Capital Asset 2	$210,000	$40,000	66.67%	$33,333	$176,667
Capital Asset 3	170,000	20,000	33.33%	16,667	153,333
TOTALS		$60,000	100.00%	$50,000	

Because the total depreciation in capital gain properties in this case ($60,000) exceeds the required negative adjustment ($50,000), there is no need to proceed to the next tranche for the allocation of a negative adjustment, which is in accordance with the adjusted bases of all capital gain properties, regardless whether they are appreciated or depreciated. Treas. Reg. § 1.755–1(c)(2)(ii).

Answer (b) is incorrect, because it includes inventory among the depreciated properties to which the negative adjustment is allocated. Inventory is not in the same "class" of properties, and thus cannot be included in this allocation. Treas. Reg. § 1.755–1(c)(1)(i). **Answer (c)** mistakenly concludes that the section 734(b) adjustment to be allocated is a negative $5,000. **Answer (d)** is also incorrect. It shows no adjustment to the tax basis of Capital Asset 2, which would be the case if the required adjustment were zero or positive. *Reading Period: Topics 9.1, 9.2 and 9.6.*

Final Exam 6

6.1 The correct Answer is (b). Under Treas. Reg. § 1.721–2(b)(1), section 721 does not apply to a transfer of property to a partnership in payment of the premium to acquire a noncompensatory option, although under Treas. Reg. § 1.721(a)(1), section 721 does apply to the transfer of property to a partnership in payment of the exercise price of such an option.

Thus, even though Luke ultimately has transferred $20,500,000 worth of Lightsource shares in exchange for a 10% interest in the partnership, a portion of this transfer is taxable while the remainder is not. His taxable gain is the excess of the value of the shares paid as premium ($500,000) over his basis in these shares ($50,000). **Answer (a)** treats both transfers of shares as nontaxable, **Answer (d)** treats both transfers as taxable, and **Answer (c)** treats only the transfer of shares in payment of the exercise price as taxable. All are incorrect. *Reading Period: Topic 2.8.*

6.2 The correct Answer is (c). The answer to this Question is to be found in the basic accounting identity, Assets = Liabilities + Capital. The option is an "obligation" of the partnership within the meaning of Treas. Reg. § 1.752–1(a)(4)(ii). Incurring this obligation creates additional basis of $500,000 in the partnership's assets, because the partnership takes the Lightsource shares transferred by Luke in payment of the option premium with an adjusted basis of $500,000, their fair market value. Treas. Reg. § 1.721–2(h), example. In order for the accounting identity to remain satisfied, the partnership's balance sheet must reflect an option liability of $500,000. This result is confirmed by Treas. Reg. § 1.752–1(a)(4)(i)(A). **Answer (a)** is incorrect, because it refers to the Lightsource shares received by the partnership in payment of the option premium, not to the option itself. **Answer (b)** is incorrect, because it fails to take into account the basis step-up that the partnership receives in those shares. **Answer (d)** is incorrect, because the option meets the criteria of Treas. Reg. § 1.752–1(a)(4) to be treated as a partnership liability. *Reading Period: Topics 2.3 and 2.8.*

6.3 The correct Answer is (a). George realizes a loss of $225,000 on this sale, which section 707(b)(1) disallows. Although George personally owns only 10% of the family partnership, the ownership of his children is attributed to him by section 267(c)(2), made applicable by section 707(b)(3). The partnership takes a cost basis of $300,000 in the office building. When the partnership later resells the building for $400,000, it realizes a gain of $100,000, but this can be offset by George's disallowed loss under section 267(d), made applicable by the penultimate sentence of section 707(b)(1). Thus, neither George nor the kids recognize any gain.

The other answers are wrong in the sense that they are not the results reached under the statue, but they raise some interesting possibilities. **Answer (b)** can be dismissed quickly. It is the result of applying section 707(b)(1), but forgetting about section 267(d). **Answer (c)** results from treating George's sale as a nonrecognition transaction (*i.e.*, a contribution), in which the partnership takes George's basis of $525,000 in the office building. On the sale, the partnership recognizes a loss of $125,000 which, under the traditional method, would be allocated entirely to George. **Answer (c)** thus ignores the role of section 704(c)(1)(C) in a contribution of an asset with a built-in loss. Like **Answer (c)**, **Answer (d)** begins by treating the transaction as a contribution of the office building, but applies section 704(c)(1)(C) to give the partnership a basis of $300,000. George has a section 704(c)(1)(C) basis adjustment of $225,000. On the partnership's sale of the building, each of the children recognizes book and tax gain of $30,000. George recognizes a book and tax gain of $10,000, the latter offset by his $225,000 basis adjustment, bringing his net tax gain down to ($215,000). **Answer (d)** is arguably the "best" answer to this Question from the perspective of the policy of partnership taxation. The difference between it and the answer mandated by the statute is remarkable. ***Reading Period: Topic 7.3.***

6.4 The correct Answer is (d). Aristotle is the sole general partner of Thinkers Corner, so his share of the recourse debt is 100%. Including this debt share, his amount realized on the sale is $270,000, his outside basis (also including the debt share) is $234,000, and his gain is $36,000. Under section 741, this is capital gain, except to the extent required by section 751. The first step is to identify the partnership's section 751 assets, which are its receivables and inventory. The section 1250 capital gain is not a section 751 asset. Neither is the partnership's land, although it would be under section 751(d)(3) if Aristotle, rather than Bentham, were a land dealer. If the partnership were to sell all of its section 751 assets at fair market value in the hypothetical sale contemplated by Treas. Reg. § 1.751–1(a)(2), it would recognize $21,000 of gain, and Aristotle's share of that gain would be $7,000. Thus, Aristotle recognizes $7,000 of ordinary income and $29,000 of capital gain on the sale of his partnership interest, the latter amount further broken down into $11,000 of section 1250 capital gain and $18,000 of residual capital gain. **Answer (a)** is incorrect, because it includes in the category of ordinary income or loss Aristotle's $10,000 share of the loss on the hypothetical sale of the partnership's land and further omits his share of the section 1250 capital gain. **Answer (b)** makes only the first of these mistakes. **Answer (c)** computes Aristotle's ordinary income properly, but neglects to state separately his share of the section 1250 capital gain. ***Reading Period: Topic 6.3.***

6.5 The correct Answer is (a). Fischer receives a mere profits interest for his services. Although he has a disproportionately large "back end" allocation of profits, his initial book capital account of $500,000 is entirely attributable to his contribution of the unimproved property worth $500,000. Accordingly, under the liquidation-value methodology, Fischer recognizes no compensation income on the receipt of his partnership interest.

The second issue raised by this Question is whether the partnership's $50,000 payment to Fischer triggers a disguised sale of a portion of Fischer's property to the partnership under section 707(a)(2)(B) and Treas. Reg. § 1.707–3. If this amount were treated as the proceeds of a disguised sale, Fischer would be treated as selling 10% of his property ($50,000/$500,000) to the partnership, would recover 10%, or $15,000, of his basis, and would recognize $35,000 of gain. Fortunately for Fischer, Treas. Reg. § 1.707–4(d) contains an exception to disguised-sale treatment for the reimbursement of organizational and syndication costs incurred by a partner. He therefore recognizes no gain on the reimbursement.

Answer (b) is incorrect, because it overstates Fischer's compensation income by failing to take into account his property contribution. **Answer (c)** is incorrect, because it fails to take into account the special exception from disguised-sale treatment for expense reimbursements. **Answer (d)** is incorrect, because it treats the reimbursement as a distribution, which seems to be an incorrect characterization, and then does not allow Fischer to apply any portion of his $150,000 outside basis against the distribution, which is contrary to section 731(a). *Reading Period: Topics 2.7 and 3.3.*

6.6 The correct Answer is (a). The difficult issue in this Question is determining whether section 751(b), as interpreted by the 1956 regulations, requires C to recognize ordinary income because she does not take her "interest" in the section 751(b) assets of the partnership. These regulations make this determination solely based on the gross values of such assets, here $60,000 of unrealized receivables and $60,000 of substantially appreciated inventory. As a 25% partner, C's "interest" in such assets before the distribution is $30,000. After the distribution, C is a 10% partner who holds $20,000 of the section 751(b) assets directly and $10,000 indirectly through the partnership (10% of $100,000). This satisfies the 1956 regulations and section 751(b) does not apply to this distribution. Treas. Reg. § 1.751–1(b)(1)(i) ("[S]ection 751(b) applies only to the extent that a partner either receives section 751 property in exchange for relinquishing his interest in other property, or receives other property in exchange for his relinquishing any part of his interest in section 751 property."). C recognizes no gain, because the amount of the cash distributed to her does not exceed her outside basis. Under section 732(a)(1), she takes the inside basis in the distributed inventory, which is $13,333.

Answer (b) is incorrect, because it uses the value of the distributed inventory rather than its inside basis to determine C's basis. **Answers (c) and (d)** both fail to take into account C's indirect $10,000 ownership of section 751(b) assets following the distribution and conclude that C should have received $10,000 more of such assets in this distribution. In **Answer (c)**, the partnership distributes $10,000 more inventory to C, which she sells back to the partnership for cash, recognizing $6,667 ordinary income. **Answer (d)** is more refined, reasoning that the partnership should be treated as distributing $5,000 of unrealized receivables and $5,000 of inventory to C, the resale of which produces $8,333 of ordinary income.

How would the 2014 proposed regulations under section 751(b) handle this distribution? They too would take into account C's direct and indirect interests in section 751(b) assets. They would not measure that interest by gross values, but instead by C's shares of ordinary income on hypothetical sales of assets before and after the distribution. Before the distribution, C's share of the partnership's ordinary income is $20,000 (25% of $80,000). Assuming that the partnership revalues its book assets in connection with the distribution (which the proposed regulations would require it to do), C's share of ordinary income after the distribution would comprise three items: (1) $15,000 from the receivables held by the partnership (25% of the $60,000 reverse layer), (2) $3,333 from the inventory still held by the partnership (25% of the $13,333 reverse layer in the remaining inventory) and (3) $6,667 in the inventory that C holds directly ($20,000 value less $13,333 basis, taxed as ordinary income under section 735(a)(2)). The total is $25,000, which is

$5,000 more than C started with. This makes intuitive sense: C takes 100% of the ordinary income in the distributed inventory and is still responsible for his initial 25% share of all of the ordinary income remaining in the partnership after the distribution. The proposed regulations would therefore require the partnership (and through it, partners A, B and D) to recognize $5,000 of ordinary income on this distribution. ***Reading Period: Topics 9.1 and 9.6.***

6.7   The correct Answer is (a). Let's first investigate the tax effect of these special allocations on the two partners. Originally, Kim would have paid tax of $450 on $3,000 of qualified dividends (which under section 1(h)(11) are taxed at capital-gains rates) and Li would have paid tax of $1,188 on $3,000 of ordinary interest income. As revised by the special allocations, Kim pays $750 of tax on $3,000 of interest income and Li pays tax of $600 on $3,000 of qualified dividends. Their respective capital accounts are unaffected by this character switch and their aggregate tax liability is decreased by $288. This is all that is needed for a violation of the shifting test of substantiality. The overall-tax-effect test is not violated, because Kim is worse off on an after-tax basis. **Answer (b)** is incorrect, because the overall-tax-effect test is not violated under these facts. **Answer (c)** is incorrect, because the violation of any single substantiality test is enough to overturn an allocation. **Answer (d)** is incorrect, because these special allocations do in fact violate the shifting test. ***Reading Period: Topic 4.3.***

6.8   The correct Answer is (a). The tax capital of A following the contribution of Property X is a negative $14,000, which is the adjusted basis of Property X less the $32,000 nonrecourse debt assumed by the partnership. The tax capital of B following the contribution of Property Y is also $18,000. At this point, A's negative tax capital denotes gain recognition, unless it is "covered" by A's share of the partnership's debt. Happily, it is, courtesy of the allocation rules for nonrecourse debt. There is no first-tier allocation. The second-tier allocation is $14,000, all of which goes to A and solves her problem. There is $18,000 remaining to be allocated in the third tier, which for now is allocated $9,000 each to A and B. Taking this allocation into account, A's outside basis is $9,000 ($0 tax capital plus $9,000 nonrecourse debt share) and B's is $27,000 ($18,000 tax capital plus $9,000 debt share).

The net value of the assets of the partnership is $36,000, so the one-third capital interest that C receives in exchange for services is worth $12,000. The facts tell us that this amount is currently deductible by the partnership, which deduction should be allocated to A and B, not C. This creates a taxable capital shift of $12,000 to C, $6,000 from A and $6,000 from B. A's outside basis declines to $3,000, B's declines to $21,000, and C's starts at $12,000.

The final step is to adjust the debt shares. C is entitled to one-third of the third layer of the nonrecourse debt, $6,000. This allocation reduces the shares of A and B by $3,000 each, bringing A's outside basis down to zero and B's down to $18,000, and increasing C's outside basis to $18,000. The partnership allocates its $42,000 recourse debt entirely to C, as the sole general partner, increasing her outside basis to $60,000.

Answer (b) is incorrect, because it allocates all of the debt, recourse and nonrecourse, equally among the three partners. **Answer (c)** is incorrect, because it fails to take into account the capital shift required by C's taxable entry into the partnership. **Answer (d)** is also incorrect. There is no reason that a service partner cannot be allocated a share of the partnership's debt. *Reading Period: Topics 2.5, 3.1, 3.2, 5.3 and 5.4.*

6.9 The correct Answer is (b). The section 754 election is the key to this Question. As you saw in Topic 6.5, this election gives the transferee partner (here, D) a special basis adjustment equal, in total, to the excess of her outside basis (here, $400,000) over her share of inside basis (here, $310,000). This special adjustment is allocated among the partnership's assets in accordance with the gain that would be allocated to the transferee on the sale of each in a fully taxable transaction. Here, the allocation of D's special basis adjustment is $30,000 to Parcel 1 and $60,000 to Parcel 2. From D's perspective, inside basis now includes her special basis adjustment. Indeed, Treas. Reg. § 1.732–2(b) includes D's special basis adjustment in Parcel 1 as though it were part of inside basis in applying the rules of section 732. Thus, D will take a basis in Parcel 1 equal to its inside basis ($110,000), plus D's special basis adjustment therein ($30,000), which equals $140,000. D's outside basis will be reduced from $400,000 to $260,000 by this distribution. **Answer (a)** is incorrect, because it does not include D's special basis adjustment in these calculations. **Answer (c)** is incorrect, because it treats the distribution as a partial liquidation (a concept unknown in partnership tax law) and gives D a basis in Parcel 1 equal to one-half of D's tax capital in the partnership. **Answer (d)** is incorrect, because it gives D a basis in Parcel 1 equal to fair market value. *Reading Period: Topics 6.5 and 9.1.*

6.10 The correct Answer is (b). More than one of the partnerships resulting from a division can be treated as the continuation of the prior partnership. Under section 708(b)(2)(B), every resulting partnership whose partners owned more than 50% of the total interests in capital and profits of the prior partnership is deemed a continuation. In this case, B's overlapping ownership in Partnership AB and Partnership BCD allows both to claim the title. **Answers (a) and (d)** fail to include Partnership BCD and **Answer (c)** erroneously includes Partnership CDE. *Reading Period: Topic 10.4.*

Final Exam 7

7.1 The correct Answer is (c). Section 1250 capital gain is not recapture income and it is not governed by any of the rules that govern recapture income. There is currently no rule for section 1250 gain that parallels Treas. Reg. § 1.1245–1(e)(2) in prescribing how to allocate section 1250 gain among the partners. So we are left with the difficult question of determining what the baseline should be for applying the substantiality analysis. In keeping with the spirit of the substantiality rules, the baseline is not necessarily the "best" allocation from a policy perspective—which might well be the rule for allocating section 1245 recapture, discussed in Question 4.3.11. It should rather reflect the partners' respective interests in the section 1250 gain, ignoring any special allocations. There isn't much to go on here. Perhaps the best baseline is pro-rata allocation of character—that is, Arrington and Remington should each be allocated an amount of section 1250 gain that is proportional to the amount of gain that each is allocated. *See* Treas. Reg. § 1.704–1(b)(5), example (10)(ii) (baseline for allocating source of income is proportional to amounts of income). Under the operating agreement, Arrington is allocated $1.5 million (75%) of the total gain on sale and Remington is allocated $500,000 (25%). Therefore, it appears that Arrington should be allocated $750,000 (75%) of the section 1250 gain. **Answer (a)** is incorrect, because the rule applicable to section 1245 recapture does not apply to section 1250 capital gain. If it did, Arrington would be allocated $1 million of section 1250 gain. *See* Treas. Reg. § 1.1245–1(e)(2)(i). **Answer (b)** is incorrect. The value-equals-basis presumption protects the chargeback of gain to Arrington from challenge under all substantiality tests, but does not provide any protection from challenge on the grounds that the character of the gain is misallocated. **Answer (d)** is incorrect, because it appears that at least some section 1250 gain must be allocated to Arrington under the shifting test. ***Reading Period: Topic 4.3.***

7.2   The correct Answer is (d). Nothing in the facts indicates that the $60,000 nonrecourse debt is a "qualified liability" within the meaning of Treas. Reg. § 1.707–5(a)(6). Thus, Stevie has engaged in a disguised sale of a portion of the cycling equipment. The amount realized on this sale is the excess of the total amount of the nonqualified liability ($60,000) over Stevie's post-contribution share of it. The usual rules for allocating a nonrecourse liability do not apply here. Instead, Treas. Reg. § 1.707–5(a)(2)(ii) skips the first two tiers and goes straight to the third, for excess nonrecourse liabilities. Under the partnership agreement, Stevie's share of excess nonrecourse liabilities is 25%. For purposes of making disguised-sale calculations, then, her post-contribution share of the $60,000 nonrecourse liability is $15,000. Her amount realized on the disguised sale is $45,000 ($60,000–$15,000).

Because the amount realized is 50% of the value of the cycling equipment ($45,000/$90,000), Stevie uses 50% of her basis, or $12,000, in computing her gain on the disguised sale. Her gain on the sale is thus $45,000 less $12,000, or $33,000.

We might compare this result with the amount of gain produced by a calculation that used the usual rules for allocating nonrecourse debt. In that case, Stevie's share of the $60,000 nonrecourse liability would be composed of the first-tier allocation ($0), the second-tier allocation ($36,000) and the third-tier allocation ($6,000), for a total of $42,000. The amount realized on the disguised sale would be $18,000, or 20% of the equipment's value, so Stevie would be entitled to apply 20% of her basis, or $4,800. Her gain on the sale would be $18,000 less $4,800, or $13,200.

The significant reduction in the gain as calculated under the usual rules ($13,200 versus $33,000) may give you a hint as to why the IRS decided not to use them. Try one more variation. What would be Stevie's gain if her basis in the cycling equipment were zero? In that case, applying the usual rules for allocating nonrecourse debt, Stevie's share of the $60,000 nonrecourse liability would be composed of the first-tier allocation ($0), the second-tier allocation ($60,000) and the third-tier allocation ($0), for a total of $60,000. The amount realized on the disguised sale would be $0 and Stevie's gain would be $0. Under the special rule of Treas. Reg. § 1.707–5(a)(2)(ii), in contrast, Stevie's share of the $60,000 nonrecourse liability is still $15,000, the amount realized on the disguised sale is $45,000 and Stevie's gain is $45,000. The IRS adopted the special rule of Treas. Reg. § 1.707–5(a)(2)(ii) in order to avoid the "inverse relationship" between the amount of built-in gain and the amount of gain realized on the disguised sale that would exist if the usual rules for debt allocation were used for disguised sales.

Answer (a) is incorrect, because it ignores the disguised sale. As discussed above, **Answer (b)** reflects the gain you would calculate using the usual rules for allocating nonrecourse debt. **Answer (c)** properly computes the amount realized on the disguised sale, but then allows Stevie to apply her entire basis, rather than only 50% of it. *Reading Period: Topics 2.7 and 5.4.*

7.3 The correct Answer is (c). This Question is easier than it may appear. The description of the stock distributed to Ron as "actively traded" alerts you to the fact that it may be a marketable security subject to the special rules of section 731(c). The K Street Investment Club is, however, an "investment partnership" within the meaning of section 731(c)(3)(C)(i). It appears never to have been engaged in any trade or business and substantially all its assets appear always to have been the type of assets described in that subsection. It is of no concern that the partnership owns $450,000 worth of stock that is not actively traded, because stock in a corporation, whether or not actively traded, is a qualifying asset under section 731(c)(3)(C)(i)(II). Moreover, Ron is an "eligible partner" within the meaning of section 731(c)(3)(C)(iii), having contributed only money to the partnership.

Thus, the ordinary rules for partnership distributions apply here. Ron's tax basis in the distributed stock is determined under section 732(b) and equals his outside basis immediately before the distribution, $78,240. **Answer (a)** applies the basis rule of section 732(a)(1), which is incorrect for a liquidating distribution such as this. **Answer (b)**, which equals the partnership's built-in gain in the shares immediately before distribution, is not relevant for determining Ron's tax basis.

Answer (d) reflects an attempt to determine Ron's tax basis in the distributed shares under section 731(c)(4). This attempt is flawed in two respects. First, Ron's tax basis in the distributed shares is not determined under section 731(c)(4). Second, if it were, it would not be the amount shown in **Answer (d)**. It is so tempting to conclude that Ron would recognize

$28,160 of gain on this distribution, which is the excess of the value of the distributed stock ($106,400) over his outside basis ($78,240) and that Ron therefore takes the distributed stock with a basis of $106,400, which is the sum of his outside basis and the recognized gain. It seems to make so much sense that Ron would take the distributed stock with a tax basis equal to fair market value because, after all, section 731(c) treats marketable securities like cash. Resist this temptation! Always remember to consider the role of section 731(c)(3)(B), which in many cases reduces the gain that would otherwise be recognized by the distributee of marketable securities. This is one of those cases. The facts reveal that Ron's share of the gain in the partnership's marketable securities was $11,760 before the distribution. It is $0 thereafter, because this is a liquidating distribution. Therefore, if section 731(c) applied at all to this distribution, section 731(c)(3)(B) would reduce Ron's gain from $28,160 to $16,400, and he would take the distributed stock with a tax basis of $94,640 and a built-in gain of $11,760. **Reading Period: Topics 9.1 and 9.5.**

7.4 The correct Answer is (c). Prior to A's sale, Partnership ABC had a majority interest taxable year ending September 30. After the sale, its majority interest taxable year ends December 31, because 55% of the interests are owned by partners who have a calendar tax year. The remaining issue is to determine when the partnership must change to the new required taxable year. This date is the "testing day," defined by section 706(b)(4)(ii)(I) as the first day of the partnership's taxable year, determined without regard to the change. Thus, Partnership ABC may keep its existing taxable year until the expiration of the current year on September 30, 2017. On October 1, 2017, it will commence a short taxable year that ends on December 31, 2017. On January 1, 2018, it will commence its first full calendar tax year. *See* Treas. Reg. § 1.706–1(b)(3)(iv), example (5) (illustrating application of the least-aggregate-deferral method). **Answer (a)** is incorrect, because following A's sale, a total of 55% of partnership capital and profits is owned by partners with a December taxable year. **Answer (b)** is incorrect, because Partnership ABC is not required to change its taxable year until the end of the current year. **Answer (d)** is incorrect. Section 706(b)(4)(B) is inapplicable in this case, because it applies only where the majority-interest rule has forced a change in a partnership's taxable year within the past three years. According to the facts, Partnership ABC has had a September taxable year since formation. **Reading Period: Topic 4.2.**

7.5 The correct Answer is (c). Comparing the aggregate fair market value of the partnership's assets with their aggregate tax basis, it is clear that D would be allocated no gain on the hypothetical sale of the partnership's assets for fair market value. Accordingly, D's special basis adjustment is zero. (This conclusion can be double-checked by comparing D's outside basis, excluding her share of partnership liabilities, with her tax capital.) This zero amount must be allocated among the partnership's assets in accordance with the share of gain or loss that D would be allocated from the partnership's sale of each asset at fair market value. Recapture is a separate asset for this purpose. **Answer (c)** sets forth the proper allocation, which sums to zero.

Answer (a) is incorrect. The Treasury regulations are explicit that a special basis adjustment of zero cannot be ignored, but must be allocated among the assets. Treas. Reg. § 1.755–1(b)(1). There is good reason for this: even if there is no appreciation or depreciation in a partnership's assets in the aggregate, there can be sizable appreciation or depreciation in individual assets. **Answer (b)** is incorrect. Special basis adjustments under section 743(b) are personal to the partner. They do not travel with the partnership interest. Treas. Reg. § 1.743–1(f). **Answer (d)** incorrectly calculates the amount of D's special basis adjustment. The special basis adjustment is the excess of D's outside basis over D's share of inside basis. **Answer (d)** appears to have included D's $80,000 share of partnership liabilities in outside basis but not in inside basis in making this calculation. *Reading Period: Topic 6.5.*

7.6 The correct Answer is (d). C bears all of the risk of loss on the $120,000 loan she makes to Rentco, because if the company defaults she has no recourse to anyone else. This loan is therefore a partner nonrecourse debt. Increases in minimum gain attributable to C's debt are partner nonrecourse deductions, allocable solely to C. The bank loan is a nonrecourse debt. Increases in minimum gain attributable to the bank loan are nonrecourse deductions, allocable to all three of the partners. Because Rentco's two loans are of equal priority and equal size, the adjusted basis of the property securing them is allocated equally, $150,000 to each loan, for purposes of measuring minimum gain. Accordingly, by the beginning of 2018, the property encumbered by each of Rentco's loans has minimum gain equal to the amount of the loan ($120,000) less the allocated adjusted basis of the property ($150,000 less $30,000 accumulated depreciation, or $120,000), which is zero. For 2018, the increase in minimum gain attributable to each loan is $15,000, half of the company's $30,000 annual depreciation. Thus, C's partner nonrecourse deductions for that year equal $15,000. **Answer (a)** gives the allocable shares of nonrecourse deductions that are attributable to the bank loan in 2018, which is not the question asked. **Answer (b)** would be the allocable shares of nonrecourse deductions for 2018 if the entire $240,000 loan had been made by the bank. **Answer (c)** reflects the total nonrecourse deductions for 2018 attributable to both loans, again not the question asked. *Reading Period: Topic 4.4.*

7.7 The correct Answer is (c). Section 751(b) does not apply to this distribution because the partnership holds no section 751(b) assets. Its inventory is not substantially appreciated and no recapture would be required on a sale of the equipment at its current value. Brody recognizes $40,000 of gain on the distribution under section 731(a)(1) and this precipitates a $40,000 positive adjustment under section 734(b)(1)(A). Under Treas. Reg. § 1.755–1(c)(1)(ii), this adjustment can only be allocated to capital gain property. This category includes depreciable assets like the equipment as well as capital assets. No allocation is made to the equipment, however, because it is not appreciated, and the appreciation in the land is sufficient to absorb the entire positive adjustment under Treas. Reg. § 1.755–1(c)(2)(i). Therefore, the inside bases of the inventory and the equipment are unchanged, while the inside basis of the land is increased by $40,000 to $60,000. **Answer (d)** is incorrect, because it allocates the $40,000 positive adjustment according to the relative values of all of the partnership's properties, including inventory. This breaks two rules, by allocating both to an improper class (inventory) and according to the wrong principle (allocating positive adjustments according to relative values without first allocating among appreciated assets to the extent of their appreciation). **Answers (a) and (b)** are based on the incorrect conclusion that the adjustment is negative, not positive. ***Reading Period: Topics 9.1, 9.2 and 9.6.***

7.8 **The correct Answer is (b).** On its sale of Portfolio B, the partnership recognizes a book loss of $1 million and a tax gain of $500,000. In accordance with the partnership agreement, it allocates the first $250,000 of book loss to B and splits the remaining $750,000 equally among the partners. Under section 704(a)(1)(A), B must be allocated all $500,000 of the tax gain. The ceiling rule applies:

(in 000s)	A		B		C	
	Tax	**Book**	**Tax**	**Book**	**Tax**	**Book**
Initial	$1,000	$2,000	$ 500	$2,000	$1,500	$2,000
Sell Port. B	0	(250)	500	(500)	0	(250)
Subtotal	1,000	1,750	1,000	1,500	1,500	1,750
Remedial	(250)	0	500	0	(250)	0
Ending	$ 750	$1,750	$1,500	$1,500	$1,250	$1,750

Remedial allocations of $250,000 of tax loss to each of A and C, the noncontributing partners with respect to Portfolio B, give each a tax loss equal to book loss and thereby restore their book-tax differences to the initial level—which is the goal of allocations arising from the disposition of Portfolio B. A corresponding allocation of $500,000 of tax gain to B eliminates her book-tax difference entirely. The overall allocations to B, including both the allocation of the book and tax items from the sale of Portfolio B and the remedial allocation, are $1 million of tax gain and $500,000 of book loss. **Answer (a)** is incorrect, because it represents only the remedial allocation to B, not her overall allocation. **Answer (c)** is incorrect, because it forgets the allocation of the first $250,000 of book loss to B, instead allocating the entire $1 million book loss equally among the three partners. **Answer (d)** is incorrect. It makes the same error as **Answer (c)** and then reports only the remedial, rather than the overall, allocation to B. ***Reading Period: Topic 8.2.***

7.9 **The correct Answers are (a), (c) and (d). Answer (a)** identifies one possible side-effect of the "deemed exchange" approach of the 1956 regulations under section 751(b), which treat the distributee-partner in this case as exchanging her "interest" in property other than section 751(b) assets for additional section 751(b) assets. In this deemed exchange, the distributee may recognize capital gain on the disposition of such other property. **Answer (c)** illustrates one effect of the "gross value" approach of the 1956 regulations, which measures a partner's "interest" in the section 751(b) assets of the partnership by gross value, rather than by net gain. **Answer (d)** identifies an issue which causes section 751(b) to apply to distributions where no shifting of rights to ordinary income is taking place. Section 732(c)(1)(A) and section 731(a)(2) are set up to prevent the basis-shifting described in **Answer (b).** The 1956 regulations do not disturb the operation of these sections. *Reading Period: Topics 9.1 and 9.6.*

7.10 The correct Answer is (d). The first step in analyzing any division is to determine whether any of the partnerships resulting from the division is considered a continuation of the prior partnership. In this case, Newco LLC is a continuation of Partnership ABCD, because its partners, C and D, owned more than 50% of the interests in capital and profits of Partnership ABCD. This continuing partnership is the so-called divided partnership under Treas. Reg. § 1.708–1(d)(4)(i). The transaction in question was executed in assets-up form, but that form cannot be respected for tax purposes, because the divided partnership did not make it. How do you know it didn't? Because the divided partnership owns the distributed assets at the end of the day, so it cannot possibly have distributed them. Treas. Reg. § 1.708–1(d)(3)(ii). Accordingly, the transaction is recharacterized in the default, assets-over form under Treas. Reg. § 1.708–1(d)(3)(i)(A). The divided partnership (here, Partnership ABCD/Newco) transfers to a new partnership (here, Partnership ABCD as constituted after the division) the 20% of assets that it did not transfer in the actual transaction. It receives interests in the new partnership, which it distributes to A and B in liquidation of their interests. **Answer (a)** would be correct if Partnership ABCD as constituted after the division were the continuing partnership. **Answer (b)** is incorrect: the IRS will never recharacterize a division (or a merger) as an assets-up transaction. The only way to achieve an assets-up division (or merger) is to do it right in the first place. **Answer (c)** is almost right, but the new partnership is owned by A and B (20% aggregate ownership of Partnership ABCD), not C and D (80% aggregate ownership). *Reading Period: Topic 10.4.*

Final Exam 8

8.1 The correct Answer is (d). Let's proceed by process of elimination. **Answer (a)** is incorrect. One of the most oft-quoted examples in the Treasury regulations on this subject illustrates that a joint undertaking to share expenses is not a partnership: "For example, if two or more persons jointly construct a ditch merely to drain surface water from their properties, they have not created a separate entity for federal tax purposes." Treas. Reg. § 301.7701–1(a)(2). The undertaking between the utilities in this example is not a mere expense-sharing arrangement, however, because the utilities have joint ownership of the (very substantial) property devoted thereto. **Answer (b)** is a step in the right direction, but still incorrect. It acknowledges the joint ownership, but fails to pay due regard to the presumably enormous amount of joint activity that is required to build and operate a power plant.

Answer (c) is also incorrect, according to the Seventh Circuit Court of Appeals. It paraphrases the argument presented by the taxpayer when this issue was litigated in *Madison Gas & Electric Co. v. Commissioner*, 633 F.2d 512 (7th Cir. 1980). In the court's view, partnership characterization does not require that the joint undertaking accomplish all steps required to earn a profit. Here, the jointly owned plant does not itself sell the electricity it produces, but instead distributes it in kind to its owners, who can then sell it on their own. This establishes profit motivation. A similar analysis would apply, for example, to a joint extractive activity such as a mine. An election to be excluded from the application of Subchapter K is available to certain organizations availed of "for the joint production, extraction, or use of property, but not for the purpose of selling services or property produced or extracted." *Reading Period: Topics 1.1 and 1.4.*

8.2 The correct Answers are (a), (c) and (d). *See* Treas. Reg. § 1.743–1(d)(2) (previously taxed capital); Prop. Treas. Reg. §§ 1.751–1(b)(2)(ii), (iii) (net section 751 unrealized gain or loss before and after distribution); Treas. Reg. § 1.755–1(b)(1)(ii) (income, gain and loss recognized by transferee on sale immediately following transfer of partnership interest). **Answer (b)** is incorrect, because the "constructive liquidation" approach to determine a partner's share of the recourse liabilities of a partnership contemplates a hypothetical sale of all of the partnership's assets, not for fair market value, but instead for zero consideration. *See* Treas. Reg. § 1.752–2(b)(1). *Reading Period: Topics 5.3, 6.5 and 9.6.*

8.3 The correct Answer is (d). Section 731(c)(1) treats marketable securities as money for purposes of section 731(a)(1) and section 737. It does not affect the application of section 704(c)(1)(B). Under this section, Theo, who contributed the marketable securities to the partnership, must recognize an amount of gain upon their distribution equal to his forward section 704(c) layer in the marketable securities. This amount equals the excess of the book value of the securities ($80,000) over their adjusted basis ($30,000), or $50,000.

Because the marketable securities are treated as money for purposes of section 737, this section does not to apply to the distribution of the marketable securities to Osgood. Section 737 requires gain recognition equal to the lesser of Osgood's "excess distribution" or his "precontribution gain." Osgood's excess distribution is the excess of the value of property, *other than money*, distributed to him over his outside basis. In this case, however, Osgood's excess distribution is zero, because there is no property other than money distributed to Osgood after taking into account section 731(c). Osgood does not escape gain recognition. Under section 731(c), he reports gain equal to the excess of the value of the marketable securities ($120,000) over his outside basis ($20,000), or $100,000.

Answer (a) is incorrect, because it applies neither section 731(c) nor the anti-mixing-bowl rules. **Answer (b)** correctly applies section 704(c)(1)(B) to Theo, but makes the same mistake as **Answer (a)** with respect to Osgood. **Answer (c)** is once again correct as to Theo, but applies section 737(a), and not section 731(c), to Osgood, thereby taxing him on his net precontribution gain of $60,000. ***Reading Period: Topics 9.4 and 9.5.***

8.4 The correct Answer is (c). The key to answering this Question is paying attention to why Randy receives a 20% interest in Blurton Duesenberg Racing. It is not for services that he will be performing for the new partnership, for which he will be compensated in cash. It also does not seem that this is a gift. Although $150,000 is a lot of money, Randy's services appear to have turned a $100,000 antique car into one worth $750,000. So it is entirely plausible that Fred gave Randy the 20% interest for fixing up the Duesenberg. Accordingly, the analysis of *McDougal v Commissioner*, 62 T.C. 720 (1974), should apply here. Randy has compensation income equal to the value of his 20% interest, $150,000. Fred is deemed to have sold a 20% interest in the Duesenberg to Randy. His amount realized on this sale is 20% of the value of the car ($150,000) and he is entitled to recover 20% of his basis ($20,000), resulting in a gain of $130,000. Unlike Mr. McDougal, Fred probably cannot claim a current compensation deduction, but should instead increase his adjusted basis in the 80% interest he still owns to $230,000 ($80,000 + $150,000). Fred and Randy contribute their respective interests in the Duesenberg to the new partnership, which takes it with a basis of $380,000 ($230,000 contributed basis from Fred and $150,000 from Randy). **Answer (a)** could be correct if Fred's transfer to Randy were a gift, but it does not seem that it is. **Answer (b)** would be the correct analysis if Randy received his interest for services to be provided to the partnership, but this does not seem to be the case. **Answer (d)** is wrong for a couple of reasons. First, it is likely (though not certain) that Blurton Duesenberg Racing is more than a hobby, although to be sure we would need to know more about the prize money and the anticipated expenses. Even if the Duesenberg is just an expensive toy, however, Randy will not be able to avoid compensation income. ***Reading Period: Topic 3.1.***

8.5 The correct Answer is (d). Ruth's retirement payments together constitute a liquidating distribution made by a service partnership to one of its general partners. Under section 736, this distribution must be segregated into that portion which is paid with respect to the value of Ruth's interest in the partnership's assets, which is subject to section 736(b), and the excess amount, if any, which is subject to section 736(a). In making this division, section 736(b)(2)(A) requires that any payment made with respect to Ruth's interest in Zander's unrealized receivables must be treated as a section 736(a) amount.

Accordingly, Ruth's section 736(b) amount is $3.75 million, which is the distribution she receives with respect to her tax capital in the firm. This amount is taxed to her under the ordinary rules that apply to partnership liquidating distributions. She recognizes no gain or loss on this distribution, because it equals her outside basis. (If the partnership has liabilities, the additional deemed cash distribution under section 752(b) will be offset by additional outside basis equal to Ruth's share of such liabilities.) Ruth's section 736(a) amount is the sum of the payments in the runoff years. Under section 736(a)(2), these will be taxed to her as ordinary income in the years that they are paid.

Answers (a), (b) and (c) all reflect the correct analysis of the runoff payments, but each stumbles in a different way over the taxation of the distribution made in the year of Ruth's retirement. **Answer (a)** ignores Ruth's outside basis entirely. **Answer (b)** does the same and in addition taxes $1.5 million of the distribution as ordinary income. This amount of ordinary income equals Ruth's share of Zander's goodwill. Even if Ruth's outside basis were zero, this would not be the correct result. Her entire $3.75 million distribution can be traced to assets on the firm's balance sheet on the date of her retirement. Thus, there is no indication that Zander paid Ruth anything for her share of the partnership's goodwill. Section 736(b)(2)(B), which would require any such payment to be reclassified as a section 736(a) amount (unless the partnership agreement provided for payments with respect to goodwill), is inapplicable. **Answer (c)** repeats the error of **Answer (b)**. *Reading Period: Topic 9.8.*

8.6 The correct Answer is (b). A partner's second-tier allocation of a nonrecourse liability is the amount of gain that would be allocated to that partner if the partnership sold the property securing the nonrecourse liability for the amount of the liability and no other consideration. The decision of Partnership ABC to use the remedial method requires you to consider the possibility that such a hypothetical sale could trigger remedial allocations, which also must be considered in making the second-tier allocation. On a sale of the land securing the debt for the amount of the debt ($300,000), Partnership ABC would realize a tax gain of $150,000, which it would allocate entirely to C, the partner who contributed the land. The partnership would realize a book loss of $150,000, because the amount of the debt ($300,000) is $150,000 less than the book value of the land ($450,000). This book loss would be allocated equally among the partners, $50,000 each. A remedial allocation of $50,000 of tax loss would be made to each of A and B, with an offsetting remedial allocation of $100,000 of tax gain to C. Thus, C would be allocated a total gain of $250,000 on the hypothetical sale, and this is her second-tier allocation of the nonrecourse debt. Rev. Rul. 95–41, 1995–1 C.B. 132, a flawed and partially superseded ruling, discusses this issue (correctly) under the heading, "Second-Tier Allocations." **Answer (a)** would be the correct answer if Partnership ABC used the traditional method and thus made no remedial allocations. **Answer (c)** incorrectly allocates the entire nonrecourse debt to C in the second tier. **Answer (d)** is also incorrect, because there is no room for interpretation in this application of the allocation rules for nonrecourse debt. *Reading Period: Topic 5.4.*

8.7 The correct Answer is (d). This Question is easy to over-think. The first issue is whether any changes at all can be made to Great Western's partnership agreement, two months after the close of the taxable year. Section 761(c) says yes. The second issue may appear to be the varying interests rule of section 706(d). But is it really? You have the partners in your office, willing to execute an amendment to the partnership agreement to allocate George up to $48,000 of income for 2016. As long as they are willing to make such changes, if any, as may be necessary to ensure that special allocations will have substantial economic effect, they can surely accomplish their goal, regardless and even in spite of the varying interests rule.

Without any change to the partnership agreement, the varying interests rule would require an allocation to George of 30% of the income for the first half of the year ($18,000) and 40% of the income for the second half of the year ($24,000), or $42,000 in total. Suppose you suggest to the partners that George be allocated not 40%, but 45% of the income from the second half. His total allocation will increase from $42,000 to $45,000. If George is allocated 50% of the income from the second half, his total for the year increases to $48,000. Alternatively, you might suggest that George's allocation for the first half increase from 30% to 40%. Same result, $48,000. Any of these amendments can be made under section 761(c). *Reading Period: Topic 6.1.*

8.8 The correct Answer is (d). The first step in analyzing a partnership merger is to identify the continuing partnership, if any, and the terminated partnership(s). Under section 708(b)(2)(A), both Partnership AB and Partnership BC are continuing partnerships, because the partners of each own more than 50% of the capital and profits interests in the resulting partnership. Under Treas. Reg. § 1.708–1(c)(1), however, Partnership BC is the only continuing partnership, because it brings the higher net asset value to the resulting partnership. As to the characterization of the transaction, Treas. Reg. § 1.708–1(c)(3)(ii) allows for an assets-up transaction in which a terminated partnership distributes all of its assets to its partners in liquidation, and they immediately contribute all the assets they receive in this distribution to the resulting partnership in exchange for interests therein. That is not how this transaction was structured. Partnership CD, the continuing partnership, made the liquidating distributions. Because this transaction was not in the prescribed form for an assets-up merger, it will be recharacterized under the default assets-over form. **Answer (a)** is incorrect, because the form of this transaction will not be respected. **Answer (b)** is also incorrect. The regulations never create an assets-up transaction that did not actually happen. In **Answer (c)**, Partnership BC is the asset transferor. That is incorrect, because Partnership BC is not a terminated partnership. *Reading Period: Topic 10.2.*

8.9 The correct Answer is (b). The partnership's choice of section 704(c) methods allows the ceiling rule to apply to dispositions of those properties that are appreciated at the time of the revaluation ("Gain Properties") and prohibits the ceiling rule from applying to dispositions of those properties that are depreciated at the time of the revaluation ("Loss Properties"). There are two factors that lead to the conclusion that this combination of methods is unreasonable. First, it produces a net tax benefit for the existing partners (A, B and C). The partnership's choice of the remedial method for Loss Properties allows A, B and C to retain the full tax benefit of the losses existing at the time of the revaluation, even if the value of those properties increases in the future. The partnership's choice of the traditional method for Gain Properties will bring the ceiling rule into play if the value of those properties decreases in the future, thereby allowing A, B and C to escape taxation on at least a portion of the gains existing at the time of the revaluation.

The heads-I-win-tails-you-lose aspect of this combination of methods is highlighted by the second factor, which is that A, B and C are in a higher tax bracket than D. The combination of section 704(c) methods seems to have been selected "with a view" to reducing the aggregate tax liability of the partners, putting it within the anti-abuse rule of Treas. Reg. § 1.704–3(a)(10). Treas. Reg. § 1.704–3(a)(2) warns against this combination of methods ("It may be unreasonable to use one method for appreciated property and another method for depreciated property.") (fourth sentence).

Particularly given the difference in tax positions of the existing partners versus the new partner D, **Answer (a)** seems overly optimistic. **Answer (c)** is incorrect. For all its faults, at least section 704(c)(1)(C) does not apply to reverse section 704(c) layers, as we have here following the revaluation. Prop. Treas. Reg. § 1.704–3(f)(2)(i). **Answer (d)** would make for a kinder, gentler and certainly simpler world, but that is not the world we inhabit as tax lawyers. ***Reading Period: Topics 8.3 and 8.4.***

8.10 The correct Answer is (a). This Question requires, first, determination of the amount of Daniel's special basis adjustment under section 743(b) and, second, allocation of that adjustment under section 755. You need to use the hypothetical sale method of Treas. Reg. § 1.743–1(d) to determine the special basis adjustment in this case. The shortcut of comparing Daniel's purchase price to his (formerly Charlie's) tax capital will not work, because the ceiling rule limits the amount of gain that Daniel will recognize in the hypothetical sale.

Daniel's special basis adjustment is his outside basis less his share of previously taxed capital, there being no partnership liabilities. His previously taxed capital is the amount that he would receive on liquidation following the hypothetical sale, less the gain that he would recognize on the hypothetical sale. This gain is $70,000, which is $50,000 from the sale of the stock plus $20,000 from the sale of the land. (The first $90,000 of gain on the land goes to Beatrice and the remaining $60,000 is split equally among all three partners.) Therefore, Daniel's special basis adjustment is his outside basis ($130,000) less the amount of his revalued capital account ($130,000), plus the gain he would recognize on the hypothetical sale ($70,000), or $70,000.

The job of allocating Daniel's special basis adjustment among the partnership's assets is made easier by the fact that he purchased the partnership interest for exactly the amount of his revalued capital account, $130,000. In other words, Daniel's purchase price is exactly his share of the net value of the assets shown on the partnership's balance sheet. In this circumstance, the amount of the special allocation computed under section 743(b) equals the sum of the allocations computed under section 755. Under Treas. Reg. §§ 1.755–1(b)(2) and (3), these allocations are the amounts of gain that Daniel would be allocated from the hypothetical sale of each asset. Therefore, Daniel's special basis adjustment is allocated $50,000 to the stock and $20,000 to the land.

Answer (b) makes the mistake of determining Daniel's special basis adjustment by subtracting his tax capital from his outside basis. The resulting special basis adjustment, $90,000, exceeds the total amount of gain that Daniel would recognize in the hypothetical sale by $20,000. **Answer (b)** assigns this additional adjustment to a new section 197 intangible, following Treas. Reg. §§ 1.755–1(a)(4) and (5). **Answer (c)** makes the same mistake in determining the special basis adjustment and then allocates the adjustment in accordance with the relative fair market values of the stock and the land, following no regulation that I know of. **Answer (d)** computes the proper special basis adjustment, but then uses the same allocation method adopted in **Answer (c)**. *Reading Period: Topics 6.5 and 8.2.*

Final Exam 9

9.1 The correct Answer is (c). This Question is an adaptation and vast simplification of the justly famous *"Castle Harbour"* case. *TIFD III-E, Inc. v. United States*, 459 F. 3d 220 (2d Cir. 2006), *on remand*, 660 F. Supp. 2d 367 (D. Conn. 2009), *rev'd*, 666 F. 3d 836 (2d Cir. 2012). If you have not already read the first opinion of the Second Circuit Court of Appeals in this case, you really should. In this opinion, the court applied *Commissioner v. Culbertson*, 337 U.S. 733 (1949), to conclude that the foreign bank, lacking any significant economic upside or downside in the venture, did not hold a "bona fide equity participation" and therefore could not be considered to be a partner for federal income tax purposes. The D.C. Circuit Court of Appeals has disregarded tax-motivated partnerships in several other cases. *Boca Investerings Partnership v. Commissioner*, 314 F.3d 625 (D.C. Cir. 2003); *Saba Partnership v. Commissioner*, 273 F.3d 1135 (D.C. Cir. 2001); *ASA Investerings Partnership v. Commissioner*, 201 F.3d 505 (D.C. Cir), *cert. denied*, 531 U.S. 871 (2000).

Answer (a) is probably incorrect. A certain level of activity is necessary in order for an entity to exist for federal income tax purposes, as illustrated in Treas. Reg. § 301.7701–1(a)(2) ("[M]ere co-ownership of property that is maintained, kept in repair, and rented or leased does not constitute a separate entity for federal tax purposes."). However, the required level of activity is low: an investment partnership that only occasionally buys and sells stocks is nevertheless a tax entity. We do not know much about the equipment or the leases in the present case, so it is impossible to rule out that the quoted Treasury regulation might apply here. If, however, the items of equipment are numerous, the activities needed to keep the equipment in service, to replace damaged or destroyed items, to collect lease payments and to enter into replacement leases as necessary would surely justify entity status. **Answer (b)** is incorrect if this is not an entity for federal income tax purposes.

Answer (d) is incorrect and it is important to understand why. The owner of an entity may indeed have an equity interest that provides for a fixed return. Many partnerships, for example, have preferred interests with fixed returns. This is not, however, an accurate description of the foreign bank's interest in this case, for two reasons. First, the foreign bank's investment was subject to virtually no risk from the partnership's operations, particularly in light of the Major Electric guarantee. By itself, this might be sufficient to disqualify the bank's return as a guaranteed payment. *See* Topic 2.7.

Second, unlike the holder of a simple preferred return, the bank is intended to play a critical role in diverting the partnership's leasing income offshore, where it would not be subject to US tax. For a period of time, the bank receives an allocation of 90% of the income from the leasing business. The bank is not entitled, however, to withdraw this special allocation from the business in cash, except in very limited circumstances. Although this allocation is at the heart of the tax plan, it does not have a meaningful effect on the economic return of the foreign bank. The *Castle Harbour* court refused to allow the recipient of a fixed economic return to play this role in a tax-motivated transaction. ***Reading Period: Topics 1.1 and 2.7.***

9.2 The correct Answer is either (b) or (d). Following the withdrawal of proposed Treasury regulations on disguised sales of partnership interests in 2009, there is little detailed guidance on this subject. There is, however, the plain language of section 707(a)(2)(B), which tells us that the cash transfers in this Question should be treated as a transaction occurring between Marci and the new investors if the transfers to and by the partnership are "related" and the transfers when viewed together are "properly" characterized as a sale or exchange of a partnership interest. *See also* Treas. Reg. § 1.731–1(c)(3). Although it is hard to know for sure, this seems to be a pretty strong case to find a disguised sale of one-half of Marci's partnership interest to the new investors. There was essentially no risk that $5 million of the cash provided by the new investors would make its way to Marci. She negotiated a right to receive it prior to the capital raise and the partnership appears to have paid it through promptly. Nevertheless, there is no indication that Marci had any contact with the new investors at all. In light of that fact, it is difficult to conclude with certainty that she engaged in a disguised sale with them.

Answer (a) must be considered, because the partnership's cash distribution to Marci occurs just a year after her contribution, putting the two transfers well within the two-year presumption that this is a disguised sale of the Gilead stock. Treas. Reg. § 1.707–3(c). This presumption can be rebutted by facts that "clearly establish" that the two transfers do not constitute a sale. Given the inherent riskiness of the development process for new drugs and the fact that GenX had no apparent resources to make a $5 million distribution, or any distribution, to Marci at the time of her contribution, this seems a perfect situation for rebutting the presumption. **Answer (c)** is incorrect, because Subchapter K contains no concept of a distribution in partial liquidation of a partnership interest. *Cf.* section 302(b)(4). **Answer (d)** is incorrect if you believe that the lack of direct communication between Marci and the new investors is fatal to the finding that they engaged in a disguised purchase and sale of one-half of her partnership interest. ***Reading Period: Topics 2.7 and 6.7.***

9.3 The correct Answer is (c). For purposes of computing book depreciation on the contributed equipment under the remedial method, its book value is separated into two components, one equal to its adjusted tax basis ($60,000) and the other equal to the excess of the book value over that amount ($140,000). The first component is depreciated on a straight-line basis over five years, using the tax depreciation method and recovery period, and the second is depreciated on a straight-line basis over 10 years, like newly purchased property of this type. The book depreciation is the sum of these two components, ($60,000/5) + ($140,000/10) = $26,000 for the first year. A reasonable remedial allocation to Charles is $1,000 of ordinary income. The determination of this amount is shown in the following computation, which ignores depreciation on the building, because it is not ceiling-limited:

	Charlie		Chen	
	Tax	**Book**	**Tax**	**Book**
Initial	$110,000	$350,000	$350,000	$350,000
First year's depreciation	0	(13,000)	(12,000)	(13,000)
Subtotal	110,000	337,000	338,000	337,000
Remedial allocation	1,000	0	(1,000)	0
End of first year	$111,000	$337,000	$337,000	$337,000

Answer (a) is incorrect, because the partnership overstated its remedial allocations. It did so by failing to apply the special computation for book depreciation under the remedial method. Book depreciation equals tax depreciation under the traditional method (including the traditional method with curative allocations), but not under the remedial method. **Answer (b)** is incorrect. It is unclear whether the IRS would ever assert that properly computed remedial allocations are taken over an unreasonable period. Such a challenge seems very unlikely in this case, because the book depreciation will be claimed over a period that equals the remaining economic life of the contributed equipment (10 years). **Answer (d)** is incorrect. In the case of depreciation, the goal of section 704(c) is to take built-in gain into account ratably over the remaining economic life of the contributed property, not faster. *Reading Period: Topic 8.3.*

9.4 The correct Answer may be (d). Generally speaking, it should be harder than usual to conclude that this is a disguised sale, because this is a nonsimultaneous exchange. In such cases, the Treasury regulations pose two questions: (1) would the partnership's distribution have been made but for the partner's contribution, and (2) was the partnership's distribution dependent on the entrepreneurial risks of the partnership's operation? Treas. Reg. § 1.707–3(b)(1). Both of these questions are answered in the negative in the given facts, so we have a disguised sale. This forecloses the application of section 737, because the partnership transfers property to Adelaide in payment of the purchase price for the disguised sale, not as a distribution.

From here, we are Alice descending into the Wonderland that is the tax treatment of nonsimultaneous disguised sales. The deemed transaction in this case is an exchange of one parcel of land for a different parcel of land—really two exchanges, one by Adelaide and the other by the partnership. Although the Treasury regulations call this a disguised "sale," they are quick to point out that the term "sale," as used in this particular context, encompasses an exchange. This characterization applies for all purposes of the Internal Revenue Code, including section 1031, which applies to like-kind exchanges. Treas. Reg. § 1.707–3(a)(2). **Answer (a)** treats the disguised sale as a like-kind exchange from the perspective of both Adelaide and the partnership. It is incorrect not in concept, but because there is no indication that either Adelaide or the partnership has taken the procedural steps required to qualify these exchanges for like-kind treatment. *See* section 1031(a)(3) (requirement to identify replacement property within 45 days and close within 180 days). In practice, many non-simultaneous disguised sales that might otherwise qualify as like-kind exchanges will be disqualified for this reason, because the characterization as a disguised sale applies retroactively, after it is too late to meet these procedural requirements.

Answer (b) jumps to the opposite extreme, treating the disguised sale as fully taxable to both Adelaide and the partnership in 2017, the year of the first transfer (the contribution). Adelaide sells 40% of the contributed property ($1 million/$2.5 million), recognizing a gain of $600,000 ($1 million proceeds less $400,000 adjusted basis). The partnership sells 100% of the distributed property, recognizing its full gain of $500,000. These amounts are correct, but the timing is not. One problem is that the partnership does not transfer any property until 2019, so it should not recognize gain until that time, and this should be treated as an "open transaction" for the partnership until that time. Thus, **Answer (b)** is incorrect, but **Answer (c)** might be right. The remaining issue is whether Adelaide's disguised sale qualifies for reporting under the installment method, which would defer her recognition of gain until the year she receives payment in the form of the distribution of the partnership's property. Treas. Reg. § 15a.453–1(a)(3)(i) states that "payment" may be received in "cash or other property," suggesting that the installment method does apply here, deferring Adelaide's gain recognition until 2019. This is **Answer (d)**. If Adelaide reports her gain on the installment method, she and the partnership will have to deal with imputed interest on her "contingent installment sale"—a complexity that the Question asked you to assume away. *See* Treas. Reg. § 1.483–4(b), example (2).

If, however, you believe that the installment method does not apply, so that **Answer (c)** rather than **Answer (d)** is the correct response to this Question, you are in very good company. *See* B. BITTKER & L. LOKKEN, FEDERAL TAXATION OF INCOME, ESTATES AND GIFTS ¶ 108.3.3 (3d ed. 2000) (suggesting that installment reporting is limited to cases where the property received is fungible, like wheat or foreign currency: "[I]f *T* transfers stock of *X* Corp. to *B* in exchange for *B*'s promise to deliver Whiteacre to *T* in two years, the transaction is probably a taxable exchange of the stock for a future interest in Whiteacre, on which *T* must recognize her gain or loss fully at the time of the exchange.") ***Reading Period: Topics 2.7 and 9.4.***

9.5 The correct Answer is (d). The first step is to calculate the amount of Ken's gain. Because he is selling only one-half of his interest in the partnership and not all of it, the partnership's tax year does not close as to him. Section 706(c)(2)(B). Accordingly, there is no pass-through of partnership income to him at that time and no adjustment to his outside basis. Ken must equitably apportion his outside basis of $30,000 between the interest sold and the interest retained. This is simple, because the two are equal. Ken's gain on the sale is thus $100,000 amount realized less $15,000 basis, which equals $85,000.

The next step is to identify the section 751 assets held by the partnership. These are the unrealized receivables and the recapture, an unrealized receivable under section 751(c). To determine the amount of Ken's gain that is characterized as ordinary income, Treas. Reg. § 1.751–1(a)(2) requires a determination of the amount of gain from the sale of section 751 assets that would be allocated to Ken, with respect to the one-half interest he is selling, if the partnership sold all of its assets for their fair market value in a fully taxable transaction immediately before Ken's sale. One-quarter (one-half of Ken's one-half interest) of the collection gain on the receivables is $20,000 and one-quarter of the recapture is $35,000, for a total of $55,000. Thus, Ken realizes $55,000 of ordinary income and $30,000 of capital gain on the sale.

Answer (a) miscalculates both the ordinary income and the overall gain on the sale. The former error results from not treating the recapture as a section 751 asset. The latter error results from increasing Ken's outside basis by $12,000, the amount of partnership income attributable to the one-half interest he sold. **Answer (b)** makes just the first of these two errors. **Answer (c)** makes only the second error, although it mistakenly uses the proration method under section 706(d) (unavailable to a partnership that has not elected it) to determine a $10,000 income amount and basis adjustment. ***Reading Period: Topics 6.1, 6.2 and 6.3.***

9.6 The correct Answer is (b). The management fee waiver illustrated in simplified form in this Question is the proximate cause for the issuance of the proposed regulations on disguised payments for services under section 707(a)(2)(A). The idea behind a fee waiver is to convert the ordinary income represented by the management fee into capital gain in the form of an interest in the profits of a partnership generating all or mostly capital gain. The waiver described here would surely fail under the proposed regulations, which identify certain facts and circumstances that create a presumption that an arrangement lacks significant entrepreneurial risk and will be treated as a disguised payment for services unless other facts and circumstances establish the presence of significant entrepreneurial risk by clear and convincing evidence. One of the enumerated facts and circumstances is:

An allocation (under a formula or otherwise) that is predominately fixed in amount, is reasonably determinable under all the facts and circumstances, or is designed to assure that sufficient net profits are highly likely to be available to make the allocation to the service provider (*e.g.*, if the partnership agreement provides for an allocation of net profits from specific transactions or accounting periods and this allocation does not depend on the long-term future success of the enterprise).

Prop. Treas. Reg. § 1.707–2(c)(1)(iv). Although the proposed regulations are not in force as of this writing, the facts of this Question seem close to those identified as troublesome in the legislative history of section 707(a)(2)(A), particularly "allocations for a fixed number of years under which the income that will go to the partner is reasonably certain." **Answer (a)** is incorrect. Despite its other infirmities, this arrangement does not seem to involve constructive receipt of the management fee, which is waived before the start of the year in which it was to be earned. **Answer (c)** is incorrect. One might quibble that Rev. Proc. 93–27, 1993–2 C.B. 343, does not apply by its terms to this arrangement, because it excludes a "profits interest [that] relates to a substantially certain and predictable stream of income from partnership assets." Whether you buy that argument or not, it is clear that the revenue procedure must bow to the application of a contrary statute. The preamble to the proposed regulations under section 707(a)(2)(A) indicate that Rev. Proc. 93–27 will be amended to include this carve-out. **Answer (d)** is incorrect, because the Additional Interest is, in fact, a disguised payment for services. *Reading Period: Topic 3.5.*

9.7 The correct Answer is (d). In the revaluation prior to C's admission, Partnership AB realizes a book gain of $400,000 on Land A, which it allocates equally to A and B. On the sale of Land A for $850,000, the partnership realizes a $150,000 book loss, which is the excess of the book value established in the revaluation ($1,000,000) over the selling price ($850,000). It allocates this book loss equally among the three partners. The partnership's tax gain on the sale of Land A is $650,000, the excess of the sale price ($850,000) over the adjusted basis of Land A ($200,000). Because the ceiling rule applies, the partnership is unable to allocate any tax loss to match the book loss allocated to the partners.

The partnership now must spread its $650,000 tax gain over two section 704(c) layers, a forward gain layer of $400,000 and a reverse gain layer of $400,000. Under Prop. Treas. Reg. § 1.704–3(a)(6)(ii), it may choose any reasonable method for doing so. If it chooses to allocate its tax items first to the oldest section 704(c) layer, it will allocate $400,000 to A and then $125,000 each to A and B:

(in 000s)	A		B		C	
	Tax	**Book**	**Tax**	**Book**	**Tax**	**Book**
Initial	$200	$600	$600	$600		
Revaluation	0	200	0	200		
Subtotal	200	800	600	800	$500	$800
Sell		(50)		(50)		(50)
Forward gain layer	400		0		0	
Reverse gain layer	125		125		0	
"Book layer"	0		0		0	
Ending	$725	$750	$725	$750	$500	$750

If it chooses to allocate its tax items first to the newest section 704(c) layer, it will allocate $200,000 each to A and B and then $250,000 to A:

(in 000s)	A		B		C	
	Tax	**Book**	**Tax**	**Book**	**Tax**	**Book**
Initial	$200	$600	$600	$600		
Revaluation	0	200	0	200		
Subtotal	200	800	600	800	$500	$800
Sell		(50)		(50)		(50)
"Book layer"	0		0		0	
Reverse gain layer	200		200		0	
Forward gain layer	250		0		0	
Ending	$650	$750	$800	$750	$500	$750

If it chooses to allocate its tax items pro rata among the layers based on the size of each, it will allocate its $650,000 tax gain between A and B in the ratio of $600,000:$200,000, or 3:1. None of these approaches will eliminate all book-tax differences, but all appear to be reasonable. **Answers (a) and (b)** are incorrect because they are incomplete. **Answer (c)** is incorrect because it is a reasonable allocation of tax gain to A, not to B. ***Reading Period: Topic 8.5.***

9.8 The correct Answer is (d). Treas. Reg. § 1.706–4(b)(2) provides that partnerships for which capital is not a material income-producing factor may use any reasonable method for applying the varying interests rule to determine allocations to partners in a year during which interests change. The preamble to this regulation states that such partnerships "do not raise concerns that may be present in allocations among partners in capital-intensive partnerships." Under this rule, it should be unnecessary for partnerships in service industries to elect methods or conventions under section 706(d), and the management committee's good-faith estimate of Reigeluth's income up to the date of Peter's departure, set forth in **Answer (c)**, should be respected without need for a formal interim closing. This is not to say that other approaches, resembling if not matching the methods prescribed by the section 706 regulations, would not also be acceptable. **Answer (a)** seems to match the proration method exactly and should certainly be reasonable, despite the fact that Reigeluth did not explicitly adopt the proration method, a requirement for capital-intensive partnerships that wish to avoid the interim closing method. **Answer (b)**, while not exactly the interim closing method (which would require either an interim closing on June 15 or the adoption of the semi-monthly or monthly convention), should also be okay. *Reading Period: Topic 6.1.*

9.9 The correct Answer is (b). This is the holding of Rev. Rul. 94–4, 1994–1 C.B. 195. **Answer (a)** would be the correct analysis in the absence of this ruling. Under section 706(c)(2)(B), the partnership year does not close as to Paul, and he cannot include any portion of the partnership's income for the year in his outside basis, by reason of this current distribution. Accordingly, his outside basis remains at $50,000 for purposes of analyzing the current distribution under section 731. The amount of the actual cash distribution ($50,000) plus the deemed cash distribution under section 752(b) ($6,000) would exceed his outside basis by $6,000, and Paul would recognize capital gain in that amount. Rev. Rul. 94–4 permits Paul to treat the section 752(b) deemed cash distribution as a current distribution on the last day of the partnership's tax year—*i.e.*, after Paul has included his share of the partnership's income for the year in outside basis. Because the income share ($20,000) exceeds the deemed distribution ($6,000), Paul recognizes gain on neither the $50,000 cash distribution on March 31 nor the $6,000 deemed distribution on December 31. **Answer (c)** is incorrect. Current distributions can produce section 752(b) deemed distributions whenever they change a partner's interest in the partnership. **Answer (d)** is also incorrect. Section 706(c)(2)(B) prohibits a distributee-partner from adjusting her outside basis as a result of a current distribution. *Reading Period: Topic 9.1.*

9.10 The correct Answer is (c). Following the hypothetical-sale approach of the proposed regulations under section 751(b), you must determine each partner's "net unrealized section 751(b) gain" both before and after this distribution. The partnership's section 751(b) assets under the proposed regulations are the receivables and the inventory. There is no recapture inherent in the equipment, because its value is less than its basis, or in the plant, which has been depreciated on a straight-line basis and therefore is not subject to recapture under section 1250. Albert's and Charlize's net unrealized section 751(b) gain before the distribution is $4,000 each, being one-third of the partnership's $12,000 unrealized gain in its inventory. After the distribution, these amounts increase to $6,000, because the partnership distributed none of its inventory to Bethany. Bethany's predistribution amount is also $4,000. To determine Bethany's post-distribution amount, you must investigate the effect on her of the distribution. Applying the usual rules for distributions, her outside basis of $86,000 is reduced first by the deemed cash distribution of $24,000 under section 752(b) and is then applied to the distributed receivables in an amount equal to the partnership's basis prior to the distribution, $20,000. Bethany's remaining outside basis of $42,000 becomes her basis in the land. Upon the hypothetical sale of all of the distributed assets immediately after the distribution, Bethany would recognize no net income from section 751(b) assets. Because the distribution reduces her net unrealized section 751(b) gain by $4,000, the proposed regulations would require her to recognize that amount of ordinary income on the distribution using a reasonable method consistent with the purpose of section 751(b). The partnership would increase its basis in the inventory by $4,000 to reflect the recognized ordinary income, and Bethany would increase her outside basis by an equal amount, thereby increasing her basis in the land upon distribution to $46,000. Prop. Treas. Reg. §§ 1.751–1(b)(3)(iii), –1(g), example (3)(v).

Answer (a) is incorrect, although it is the answer reached by current law. **Answer (b)** imposes current ordinary income on the wrong parties. **Answer (d)** is incorrect, because it requires Bethany to realize her entire income and gain currently, treating the distribution of the land as if it were a distribution of cash. ***Reading Period: Topic 9.6.***